On the Road around the South of France

THOMAS COOK

On 5 July 1841 Thomas Cook, a 32-year-old printer from Market Harborough, in Leicestershire, England, led a party of some 500 temperance enthusiasts on a railway outing from Leicester to Loughborough which he had arranged down to the last detail. This proved to be the birth of the modern tourist industry. In the course of expanding his business, Thomas Cook and his son, John, invented many of the features of organised travel which we now take for granted. Over the next 150 years the name Thomas Cook became synonymous with world travel.

Today the Thomas Cook Group employs over 14,000 people across the globe and its Worldwide Network provides services to customers at more than 3000 locations in over 100 countries. Its activities include travel retailing, tour operating and financial services – Thomas Cook is a world leader in traveller's cheques and foreign money services.

Thomas Cook believed in the value of the printed word as an accompaniment to travel. His publication *The Excursionist* was the equivalent of both a holiday brochure and a travel magazine. Today Thomas Cook Publishing continues to issue one of the world's oldest travel books, the *Thomas Cook European Timetable,* which has been in existence since 1873. Updated every month, it remains the only definitive compendium of European railway schedules.

The *Thomas Cook Touring Handbook* series, to which this volume belongs, is a range of comprehensive guides for travellers touring regions of the world by train, car and ship. Other titles include:

Touring by train

On the Rails around France (1995)
On the Rails around Britain and Ireland (1995)
On the Rails around Europe (Second Edition 1995)
On the Rails around the Alps (1996)
On the Rails around Eastern Europe (1996)

Touring by car

On the Road around California (Second Edition 1997)
On the Road around Florida (1995)
On the Road around Normandy, Brittany and the Loire Valley (1996)
On the Road around the Capital Region USA (1997)
On the Road around the Pacific Northwest (1997)

Touring by ship

Greek Island Hopping (Published annually in March)

For more details of these and other Thomas Cook publications, write to Passport Books at the address on the back of the title page.

ON THE ROAD AROUND THE

South of France

Touring by car in
Provence,
the Côte d'Azur,
coastal Languedoc,
the Rhône valley,
and the Auvergne

Edited by
Melissa Shales

A THOMAS COOK TOURING HANDBOOK

Published by Passport Books,
a division of NTC Publishing Group
4255 West Touhy Avenue,
Lincolnwood (Chicago),
Illinois 60646-1975 USA.

ISBN 0-8442-4954-8
Library of Congress Catalog Card
Number: 96-72599
Published by Passport Books in conjunction with The Thomas Cook Group Ltd.

Managing Editor: Stephen York
House Editor: Kate Hopgood
Map Editor: Bernard Horton

Cover illustration by Adam Green
Text design by Darwell Holland
Text typeset in Bembo and Gill Sans using QuarkXPress
Maps and diagrams created using Macromedia Freehand and GSP Designworks
Text imagesetting by Goodfellow & Egan Ltd, Peterborough
Printed in Great Britain by Fisherprint Ltd, Peterborough

This edition written and researched by
Nick Hanna
Melissa Shales
Gillian Thomas and John Harrison

Book and Series Editor: **Melissa Shales**

ABOUT THE AUTHORS

Melissa Shales is Series Editor of the *Thomas Cook Touring Handbooks* and editor of, and contributor to, this volume. Former Editor of *Traveller* magazine, she is the author of eight guides on destinations as far apart as India, Zimbabwe and France, and editor of *On the Rails around Europe* and *On the Rails around the Alps* in this series.

Nick Hanna is a freelance writer and photographer who has published eight guidebooks and contributed to numerous newspapers and magazines. He has also written extensively on tourism and environment issues and scuba-diving, and is series consultant on the new *Dives of the World* guidebooks. When not travelling and writing, he lives in England on a small farm in Sussex with his wife and two sons.

Gillian Thomas and John Harrison are married and have three children. Both are freelance travel writers, and are contributors to *On the Rails around the Alps* in this series.John has spent many years with the BBC. Gillian worked for its News Office in Paris before she became a freelance journalist.

PHOTOGRAPHS

The publishers are grateful to the individuals and organisations who provided the photographs for this book (all photographs copyright the named contributors):

AA Photo Library: St Tropez, Lourmarin, Clermont-Ferrand, Pont du Gard, Nice, Eze. Nick Hanna: Arlempdes, Girl in traditional costume, Camargue avenue, Camargue flamingoes, Séguret, Cassis, Var Vineyard, Lac d'Allos, Port Grimaud, Bormes-les-Mimosas, Toulon market. Deborah Parker: Arles amphitheatre, Avignon. Melissa Shales: Gorges du Tarn, Arles Place de la République, Camargue horses, Cévennes, Marseille, Nîmes. Gillian Thomas and John Harrison: Pont-en-Royans. Stephen York: Lubéron, Bonnieux, Gordes, Rousillon, Salon-de-Provence, back cover picture.

ACKNOWLEDGEMENTS

The authors have had an enormous amount of assistance in the preparation of this book and would like to thank the many people who have given freely of their time and expertise. In the UK, particular thanks go to Peter Mills and Christine Lagardère of SNCF French Railways; Marie-Therèse Smith and Elizabeth Powell of the French Tourist Office; Alison Cryer, Anne-Marie Muller and all at Representation Plus; John Ette at Bed and Breakfast France; Allyson Andrews and the Eurotunnel Group; and Susi Golding of the Rhône-Alpes Tourist Board.

In France, thanks to Nicolas Geoffroy and all at Provence International; Logis en Liberté hotels; Jean-Marie Carret and Charléric Gensollen of Cuisine en Provence; Sylvie Schmitt of the CDT du Var; and Pascale Mandon in Grand Lyon. Above all, we acknowledge the invaluable assistance of the many individual hotel-keepers who provided us with accommodation, and the vast army of regional and local tourist officials, who paved ways, organised itineraries and provided sack-loads of irreplaceable information.

On a more personal note, Melissa Shales would like to thank her parents, David and Jennifer Shales, for their assistance in researching the Auvergne, and in-house editors, Kate Hopgood and Debbie Parker, who ventured out from behind their desks to drive her around southern Provence. Nick Hanna would like to thank Nicole Padula in Le Beausset for her warm hospitality and his wife Paula for enduring his long absences.

CONTENTS

Authors and Acknowledgements 5
Route Map 8
Introduction 10
How to Use This Book 11
Travel Essentials 15
Driving in France 28
Getting to the South of France 35
Background 41
Touring Itineraries 55

ROUTES AND CITIES

In alphabetical order. Routes are listed in both directions – the reverse route is shown in italics. See also the Route Map, pp. 8–9, for a diagrammatic presentaion of all the routes in the book. To look up towns and other places not listed here, see the Index, pp. 348–350

AIX-EN-PROVENCE 60
Aix-en-Provence to Castellane 66
Aix-en-Provence to Cavaillon 70
Aix-en-Provence to Fréjus 75
ARLES 80
Arles to Montpellier 86
Arles to Avignon 98
Arles to Marseille 237
AVIGNON 92
Avignon to Arles 98
Avignon to Aubenas 107
Avignon to Digne 112
Avignon to Nîmes 115
Avignon to Lyon 209
AUBENAS 196
Aubenas to Avignon 107
Aubenas to St Étienne 325
BARCELONNETTE 118
Barcelonnette to Gap 118
Barcelonnette to Menton 253
Barcelonnette to Nice 288
CANNES 121
Cannes to Grenoble 125
Cannes to Nice 131
Cannes to Fréjus 178
CARPENTRAS 141
Carpentras to Sisteron 136
Carpentras to Vaucluse Loop 141
CASTELLANE 126
Castellane to Aix 66
CAVAILLON 73
Cavaillon to Aix 70
CÉVENNES 149
CHORGES 173
Chorges to Digne 170
CLERMONT-FERRAND AND VICHY 155
Clermont-Ferrand to Le Puy 163
Clemont-Ferrand to St Étienne 167
DIGNE-LES-BAINS 171
Digne to Chorges 170
Digne to Avignon 112
FRÉJUS AND ST RAPHAËL 174
Fréjus to Cannes 178
Fréjus to Aix-en-Provence 75
Fréjus to Toulon 336

GAP 128
Gap to Barcelonnette *118*
GRASSE 297
Grasse to Nice *293*
GRENOBLE 181
Grenoble to Sisteron 185
Grenoble to Cannes *125*
Grenoble to Lyon *219*
LE PUY-EN-VELAY 189
Le Puy to Montélimar 194
Le Puy to Valence 198
Le Puy to Clermont-Ferrand *163*
Le Puy to Montpellier *272*
Le Puy to St Étienne *330*
LYON 201
Lyon to Avignon 209
Lyon to Grenoble 219
Lyon to St Étienne 224
MARSEILLE 228
Marseille to Arles 237
Marseille to Toulon 243
MENDE 275
Mende to Montpellier 247
MENTON 304
Menton to Barcelonnette 253
Menton to Nice *299*
MONACO 261
MONTÉLIMAR 214
Montelimar to Le Puy *194*
MONTPELLIER 267
Montpellier to Le Puy 272
Montpellier to Perpignan 276
Montpellier to Arles *86*
Montpellier to Mende *247*
NICE 281
Nice to Barcelonnette 288
Nice to Grasse 293
Nice to Menton 299
Nice to Cannes *131*
NÎMES 306
Nîmes to Avignon *115*
ORANGE 311
Orange to Sisteron 315
PERPIGNAN 318
Perpignan to Montpellier *276*
ST ÉTIENNE 322
St Étienne to Aubenas 325
St Étienne to Le Puy 330
St Étienne to Clermont-Ferrand *167*
SISTERON 126
Sisteron to Carpentras *136*
Sisteron to Grenoble *185*
Sisteron to Orange *315*
TOULON 333
Toulon to Fréjus 336

REFERENCE SECTION

Language 343
Driving Distances and Times 345
Hotel Codes and Central Booking Numbers 346
Conversion Tables 347
Index 348
Reader Survey 351
Colour Planning Maps *Facing back cover*

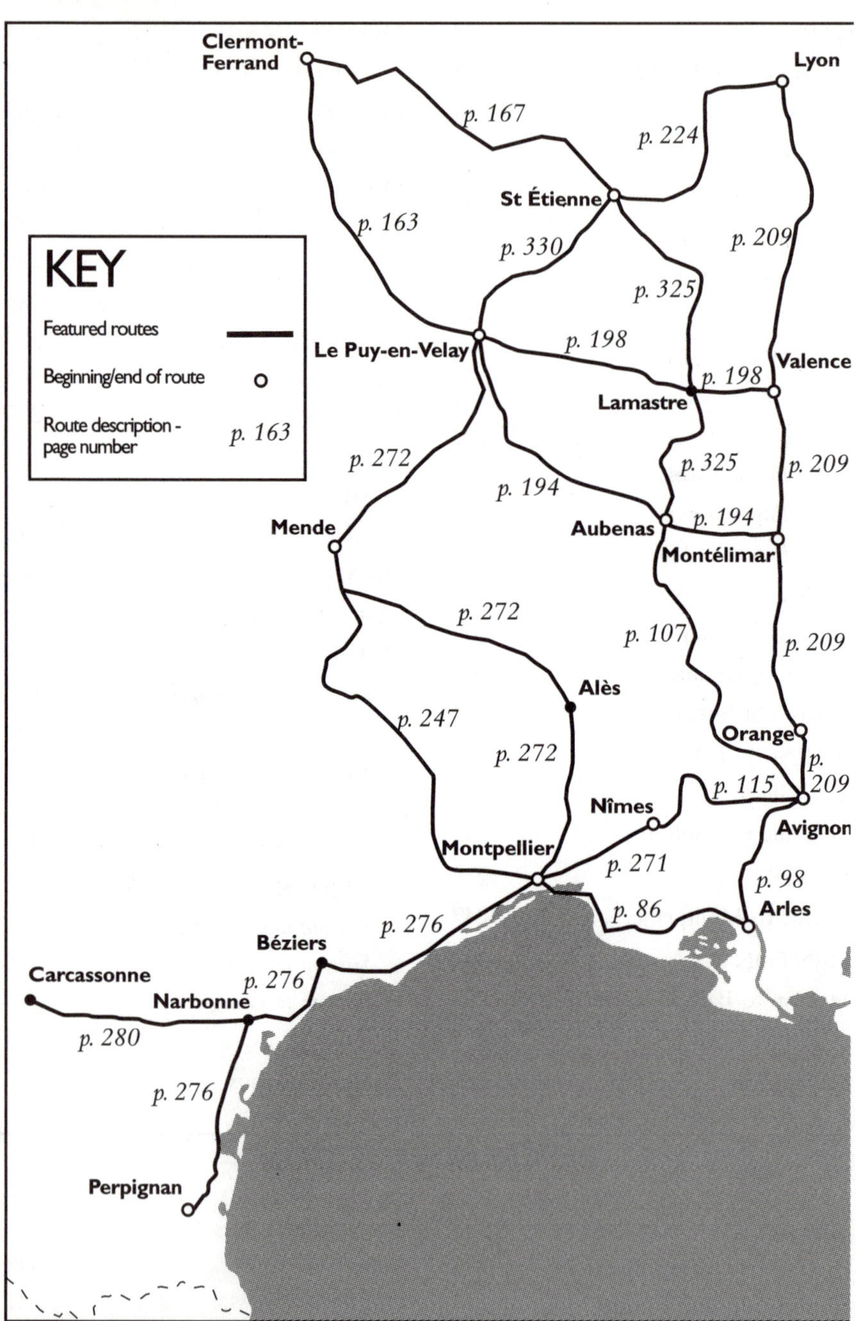
KEY
Featured routes
Beginning/end of route
Route description - page number
p. 163
Clermont-Ferrand
Lyon
p. 167
p. 224
St Étienne
p. 163
p. 330
p. 209
p. 325
Le Puy-en-Velay
p. 198
Valence
p. 198
Lamastre
p. 272
p. 325
p. 209
p. 194
Mende
Aubenas
p. 194
Montélimar
p. 272
p. 107
p. 209
Alès
p. 247
p. 272
Orange
p.
209
p. 115
Nîmes
Avignon
Montpellier
p. 271
p. 98
p. 86
Arles
p. 276
Béziers
Carcassonne
p. 276
Narbonne
p. 280
p. 276
Perpignan

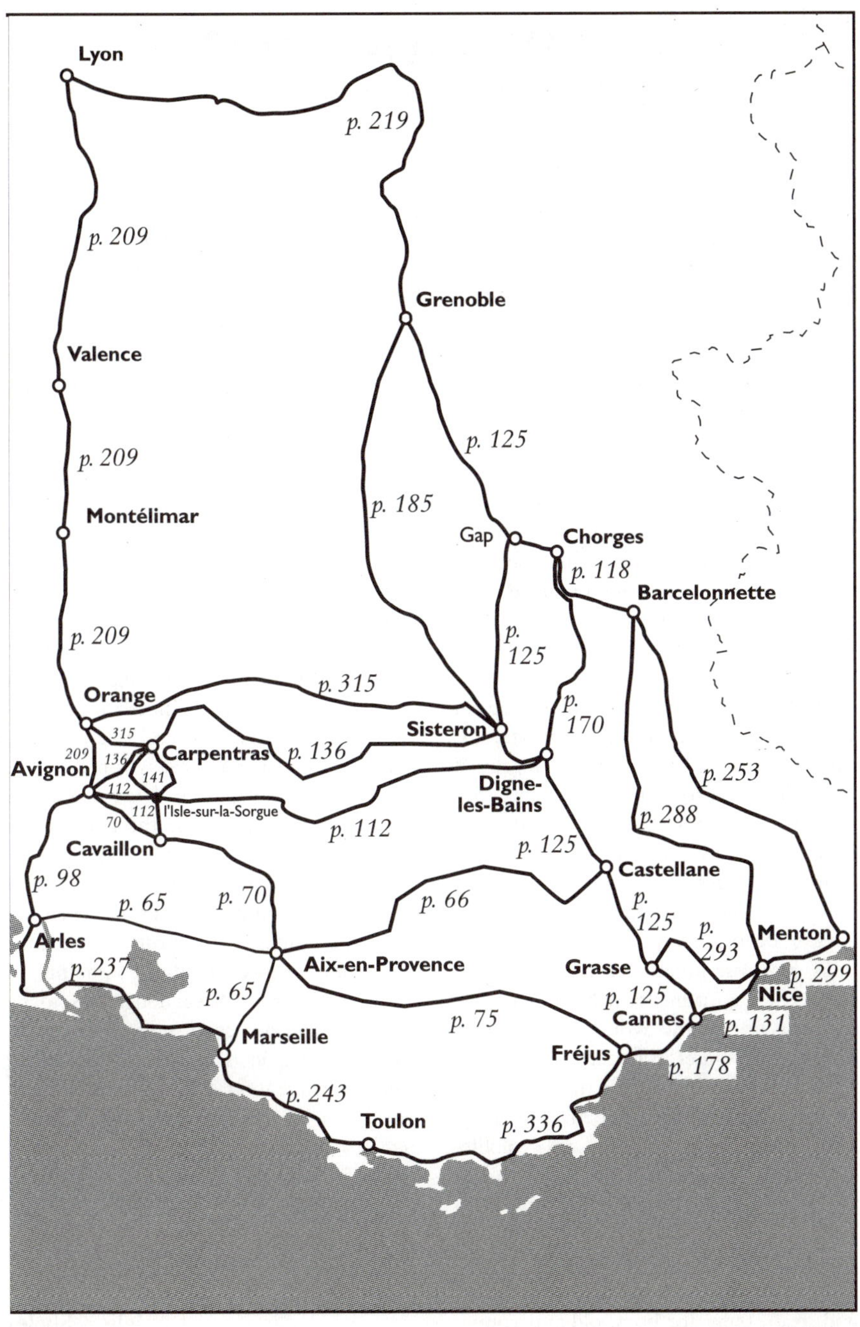

Lyon
p. 219
p. 209
Grenoble
Valence
p. 209
p. 125
p. 185
Montélimar
Gap
Chorges
p. 118
Barcelonnette
p. 209
p. 125
p. 315
Orange
p. 170
Sisteron
315
209
136
Carpentras
p. 136
Avignon
141
p. 253
112
Digne-les-Bains
112
l'Isle-sur-la-Sorgue
70
p. 112
p. 288
Cavaillon
p. 125
Castellane
p. 98
p. 65
p. 70
p. 66
p. 125
Arles
p. 293
Menton
Aix-en-Provence
Grasse
p. 237
p. 299
p. 65
p. 125
Nice
p. 75
Cannes
p. 131
Marseille
Fréjus
p. 178
p. 243
Toulon
p. 336

9

INTRODUCTION

The French call this huge sweep of land 'le Grand Sud' (the Great South). It is simply big, but the area is also truly great in many other ways. It includes two of France's largest cities – Lyon and Marseille – together with many of its oldest and most romantic, from Cannes and St Tropez to ancient Arles and Avignon. The twisting cliffs and beaches of the Côte d'Azur with its millionaires' villas and jet-set marinas give way to the marshy, wind-swept isolation of the Camargue. The volcanic cones of the Auvergne lead into the remote forests of the Cévennes, which in turn look across the winelands of the Rhône valley and the rolling lavender and sunflower fields of Provence to the snow-capped crags of the southern Alps.

The South of France conjures up an instant image of sunshine and relaxation. It smells of tomato, basil and garlic, is painted in sunflower yellow and cobalt blue, specialises in good food, good wine and warm hospitality, and has charmed everyone from Julius Caesar to Vincent Van Gogh. It is much busier and more built-up these days, with motorways and high-speed rail links, high-rise hotels and shopping malls, but it is still a magnet which draws people in from around the world, inspiring the poet or the painter in us all.

This is probably one of the best places in the world to have a perfect holiday, with magnificent scenery and wildlife, space to let off steam if you want to run away, sophisticated highlife for those who need to be seen, discos and clubs for the trendy, opera in ancient amphitheatres for more romantic souls, beaches for children, and steam trains for boys, old and young, all of it bathed in 3000 years of history. And the perfect way to see it all is by car. The roads are good, although you must nerve yourself for mountain driving on corkscrew bends with dramatic drops; the landscape is superb; and a hilltop village, hidden Romanesque chapel or picnic in a chestnut forest adds immeasurably to your experience.

All families with schoolchildren, and most other continental Europeans, take their holidays in July and August. Southern France becomes a zoo, as prices double, hotels and campsites sell out, every attraction has a permanent queue, and temperatures soar. It is much better, if possible, to travel in June or September. Most sights run more limited opening hours, but they are open, as are the hotels and restaurants. The roads are also relatively empty, the prices cheaper and the weather cooler.

We have carried out detailed research and tried to give you all the information you will need for an idyllic touring holiday, from suggested routes to hotel and restaurant recommendations and even the opening times of various attractions. Inevitably, however, the constraints of space and format have obliged us to be selective and not every sight or village in this busy region is included. Also, many things change too fast for us to catch them all. Please forgive any errors which might creep in over the life of this edition and write in with any comments, suggestions or additions. With your help, we can make the next edition even better. Meantime, *bon voyage* and *bon appetit.*

Melissa Shales

How to Use This Book

ROUTES AND CITIES

On the Road around the South of France provides you with an expert selection of 30 recommended routes between key cities, towns and attractions of Southern France (including Provence, the Côte d'Azur, coastal Languedoc and the Auvergne), each in its own chapter. Smaller cities, towns, attractions and points of interest along each route are described in the order in which you will encounter them. Additional chapters are devoted to the major places of interest which begin and end these routes. These route and city chapters form the core of the book, from page 60 to page 342.

The routes have been chosen to take in as many places of interest as possible. Where applicable, an alternative route which is more direct is also provided at the beginning of each recommended route chapter. This will enable you to drive more quickly between the cities and towns at the beginning and end of the route, if you do not intend to stop at any of the intermediate places. To save space, each route is described in only one direction, but of course you can follow it in the reverse direction, too.

The arrangement of the text consists of a chapter describing a city or large town first, followed by chapters devoted to routes leading from that place to other major destinations; e.g. the city of Lyon is described in one chapter (pp. 201–208), followed by routes from Lyon to Avignon (pp. 209–218), Lyon to Grenoble (pp. 219–223), and Lyon to St Étienne (pp. 224–227). The key towns and city chapters are ordered alphabetically, followed by routes leading out from that starting point. Thus the first city is Aix-en-Provence (pp. 60–65) followed by the routes from Aix-en-Provence to Castellane (pp. 66–69), Cavaillon (pp. 70–74) and Fréjus (pp. 75–79), followed by Arles and a route from Arles, and so on. To find the page number of any route or city chapter quickly, use either the alphabetical list on the **Contents** pages, pp. 6–7, or the master **Route Map** on pp. 8–9. The routes are designed to be used as a kind of menu from which you can plan an itinerary, combining a number of routes which take you to the places you most want to visit.

WITHIN EACH ROUTE

Each route chapter begins with a short introduction to the route, followed by driving directions from the beginning of the route to the end, and a sketch map of the route and all the places along it which are described in the chapter. This map, not drawn to scale, intended to be used in conjunction with the driving directions, summarises the route and shows the main roads and road numbers; for a key to the symbols used, see p. 13.

Direct Route

This will be the fastest, most direct, and sometimes, predictably, least interesting drive between the beginning and end of the route, usually along autoroutes and N roads.

Scenic Route

This is the itinerary which takes in the most places of interest, usually using secondary and minor roads. Road directions are specific; always be prepared for detours due to road construction, etc. The driving directions are followed by sub-sections describing the main attractions and places of interest along the way. You can stop at them all or miss out the ones which do not appeal to you.

Always ask at the local Tourist Office (Office du Tourisme) or tourist information centre (usually Syndicat d'Initiative) for more information on sights, guided tours, accommodation and places at which to eat.

SIDE TRACK

This heading is occasionally used to indicate departures from the main route, or out-of-town trips from a city, which detour to worthwhile sights, described in full or highlighted in a paragraph or two. The grey side lines indicate the extent of the side track description.

CITY DESCRIPTIONS

Whether a place is given a half-page description within a route chapter or merits an entire chapter to itself, we have concentrated on practical details: local sources of information; getting around in city centres (by car, by public transport or on foot as appropriate); accommodation and dining; communications; entertainment and shopping opportunities; and sightseeing, history and background interest. The largest cities have all this detail; in smaller places some categories of information are less relevant and have been omitted or summarised. Where there is a story to tell which would interrupt the flow of the main description, we have placed **feature boxes** on subjects as diverse as 'Camague Wildlife', 'Marcel Pagnol' and 'Avignon Popes'.

Although we mention good independently owned lodgings in many places, we always also list the hotel chains which have a property in the area, by means of code letters to save space. Many travellers prefer to stick to one or two chains with which they are familiar and which give a consistent standard of accommodation. The codes are explained on p. 346, and central booking numbers for the chains are also given there.

MAPS

In addition to the sketch map which accompanies each route, we provide maps of major city centres as well as smaller towns. At the end of the book is a section of **colour road maps** covering the whole area described in this book, which is detailed enough to be used for trip planning. The **key to symbols** used on all the types of map in the book is on the facing page.

THE REST OF THE BOOK

Travel Essentials is an alphabetically arranged chapter of general advice for the tourist new to France, covering a wide range of subjects from accommodation and currency to facilities for disabled travellers and telephones. **Driving in France** concentrates on advice for drivers on the law, rules of the road, and so on. **Getting to the South of France** describes the ways of arriving at your touring starting point. **Background** gives a concise briefing on the history and geography of the three diverse regions covered in this book. **Touring Itineraries** provides ideas and suggestions for putting together an itinerary of your own using the selection of routes in this book. At the end of the book, **Driving**

Distances is a tabulation of distances between main places, to help in trip planning. The **Hotel Codes and Central Booking Numbers** page has already been described. To assist those with little knowledge of French, the **Language** section provides a number of useful phrases, together with phonetic spellings for ease of pronunciation. The **Conversion Tables** decode weights, measures and sizes for those outside continental Europe. Finally the **Index** is the quick way to look up any place or general subject. And please help us by completing and returning the **Reader Survey** at the very end of the text; we are grateful for both your views on the book and new information from your travels.

KEY TO PRICE DESCRIPTIONS

It is impossible to keep up to date with specific tariffs for lodging and accommodation or restaurants, although we have given some general advice under 'Accommodation' in the Travel Essentials chapter on pp. 15–17. Wherever possible, we have given the admission price to the sights mentioned under 'Sightseeing' in any city or place description, or the cost of any tours, boat-trips etc., but do remember that these are liable to change. The price quoted is usually the price per adult; if there is a price in brackets after the full price, then that is the cost per child.

KEY TO MAP SYMBOLS

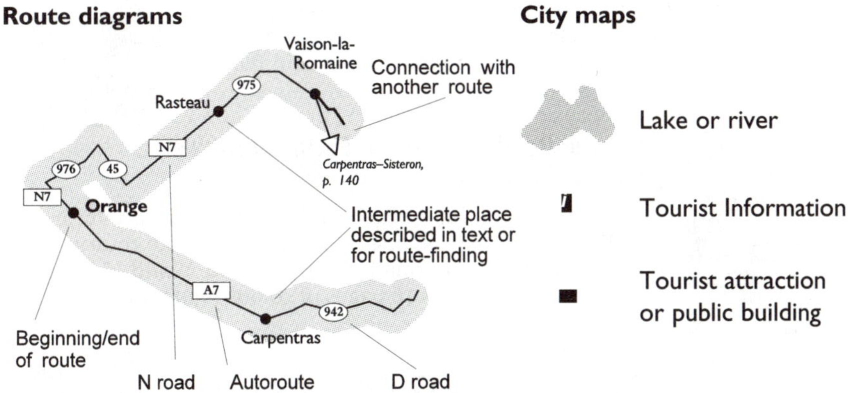

ABBREVIATIONS USED IN THE BOOK

(For hotel chains, see p. 346)

av.	avenue	pl.	place
blvd	boulevard	r.	rue
FFr.	French Franc	rte	route
hr(s)	hours	sq.	square
km	kilometres	tel:	telephone number
m	metres	Jan, Feb are January, February, etc.	
min(s)	minute(s)	Sun, Mon are Sunday, Monday etc.	

THOMAS COOK TOURING HANDBOOKS

The perfect companions for your holiday

These route-based guides are crammed with practical information and maps. From advice on road laws to ideas for accommodation and sightseeing, they contain all the information you need to explore the USA by car.

On the Road around New England
Price: £10.95

40 routes with side-trips and scenic drives throughout this varied region. The area covered stretches from New York up to northern Maine, with side trips into Canada to visit Montreal and Quebec.

On the Road around Florida
Price: £10.95

With clear city and regional maps and honest sightseeing advice, this book will help you to get the most out of your visit to Florida. Over 30 routes combine famous and more unusual sights.

On the Road around the Pacific Northwest
Price: £12.95 Published March 1997

Covers Washington, Oregon and the Canadian province of British Columbia as one touring region. 40 routes are accompanied by information on the cultural and historical background. Includes 16 pages of colour photographs.

On the Road around the Capital Region USA
Price: £12.95 Published March 1997

The historic heartland of the USA boasts dramatic scenery and major cultural sites. Washington, DC as well as Virginia, Maryland and parts of Pennsylvania and Delaware are covered. Includes 16 pages of colour photographs.

Also available: **On The Road Around California, 2nd edition. £12.95**

These publications are available from bookshops and Thomas Cook UK retail shops, or direct by post from Thomas Cook Publishing, Dept (OWN), PO Box 227, Thorpe Wood, Peterborough, PE3 6PU, UK. (Extra for postage and packing.) Tel: 01733 503571/2.
Published in the USA by Passport Books

TRAVEL ESSENTIALS

This alphabetical list of topics provides advice and information on the main practical considerations when holidaying in the south of france.

ACCOMMODATION

Southern France has a wide variety of excellent accommodation, from spartan youth hostels to unabashed five-star luxury hotels. Inevitably, small towns offer considerably less choice and hotels everywhere are heaving in July and Aug, but you shouldn't have too many problems through the rest of the year. It's always wise to book ahead, however some resort hotels close for the winter.

Local Tourist Offices all provide free listings of hotels and other accommodation. **Accueils de France** (see p. 26) will also help with reservations, for a fee of about FFr.10. Specify your price limits when asking. French tourist boards in your home country will also provide accommodation lists, but do charge for them. Bookings can usually be arranged by Thomas Cook or another good travel agent, or through one of the marketing organisations or chains listed below.

Room rates vary considerably from town to country, according to region and season. The price quoted is usually for a double room, with no discount for single occupancy. A small supplement may be charged if several people share a family room. Breakfast *(petit déjeuner)* is generally extra (FFr.25–40). Hotels may also offer half board *(demi-pension)* and full board *(pension)* and prices will rise according to the facilities, e.g. a room with private shower and toilet will cost more than one with a shower alone. Be warned that 'private facilities' in many cheaper hotels means a private shower but shared toilets.

By law, the room rate must be displayed at reception and in the rooms. As a guide, at time of going to press (autumn 1996) expect to pay FFr.260–400 for a comfortable two- or three-star double room. Rates are higher for comparable accommodation along the Riviera and you may have to pay a little more for reasonable quality in the major cities. In this book, all hotels are listed as budget, moderate or expensive. There are no hard-and-fast price bands, but as a rough guide, budget is below FFr.350; moderate between FFr.350 and FFr.550; and expensive above FFr.550. There will also be a government tourist tax on your bill.

The five-grade local authorities scale can be a useful guide (e.g. 3-star establishments usually have a lift), but it is based solely on facilities and takes no account of atmosphere. A good 2-star establishment may be infinitely more charming, and just as pricey, as some 3-stars. Those '*sans étoile*' – unstarred – may still be good value and the best advice is to look at a room before taking it. If a hotel is listed as 'IC' – *Instance de classement* – it means that it is waiting for its grade to be awarded.

For reasons of space, hotels belonging to one of the major branded chains have usually been listed in the text using two letter codes. For instance, the initials *BW, Hd, Nv* mean that the city has a Best Western, Holiday Inn and Novotel. A full list of the codes with the chains' central reservation numbers is listed on p. 346.

Two letter codes have also been assigned to several associations set up to market smaller, independent establishments. **Relais et Châteaux (RC)**, *15 r. Galvani, 75017 Paris; tel: 01 45 72 96 50*, is a group of luxurious manors and châteaux, which pride themselves on their cuisine. A French-English directory is available free from **Relais et Châteaux**, *7 Cork Street, London W1X 2AB; tel: 0171 287 0987*, or £5 by post.

Châteaux et Hôtels Independents (CS), *Galerie du Carrousel du Louvre, 99 r. Rivoli, 75001 Paris; tel: 01 47 57 23 67;* **USA**, *tel: (800) 553 50 90*, is a similar organisation marketing comfortable to gorgeous hotels, restaurants and châteaux guesthouses, moderate–expensive.

Logis de France (LF), *83 av. d'Italie, 75013 Paris; tel: 01 45 84 70 00, fax: 01 44 24 08 74*, are family-run one- to three-star hotels offering good standards and excellent-value. Over 4000 are listed in their guide, available from bookshops (£12.95) or by post (£13.95) from the French Government Tourist Office in the UK (see Useful Addresses, p. 26). The distinctive yellow *cheminée* (fireplace) logo symbolises warmth and atmosphere; saucepans mark the best places to eat, often featuring regional specialities. The **Logis en Liberté** scheme involves up to 500 hotels in the Logis chain, which have standardised prices and facilities. You can order vouchers for bed and breakfast or half-board or book ahead through central reservations; *tel: 01 45 84 83 84; fax: 01 44 24 08 74.*

Self-catering and Bed & Breakfast

Provence is littered with delightful self-catering country cottages, converted barns or farmhouses available for renting, usually by the week. For the many British companies letting holiday homes in the region, look in the British Sunday papers. The **Fédération National des Gîtes Ruraux (GF)**, *35 r. Godot de Mauroy, 75009 Paris; tel: 01 49 70 75 75*, controls standards in French-owned properties. **Agence Avignon Provence**, *BP 67, 24 r. Grande Fusterie, 84005 Avignon Cédex; tel: 04 90 85 90 95*, handles 600 properties in western Provence. *Gîtes d'Etapes* are not cottages, but basic dormitory-style accommodation at rock-bottom prices, designed for hikers. In mountain areas, a chain of refuge huts is run by **Club Alpin Français**, *24 av. de Laumière, 75019 Paris; tel: 01 53 72 87 00.*

Chambres d'Hôte (Bed and Breakfast) is also becoming increasingly popular in the region. Prices range from about FFr.180–500 per person. Properties vary from farmhouses to châteaux, and many also provide excellent family dinners if booked in advance. If you want a chance to polish your French, meet locals and get a real flavour of life, this is the way to do it. The British firm, **Bed & Breakfast France (BF)**, *International Reservations Centre, PO Box 66, Henley-on-Thames, Oxon RG9 1XS; tel: 01491 578803; fax: 01491-410806*, publishes an annual guide (£5.50) and runs a booking agency. Gîtes de France also publish *'French Country Welcome'* with details of around 14,000 Bed and Breakfast establishments; £11.50 from Gîtes de France (by post £2.35 extra). Local Tourist Offices supply lists.

Camping and Caravanning

The French love camping and wherever you find a pretty river or lake, you will also find a range of campsites, with facilities ranging from basic (clean toilets and showers) to luxury sites with dining rooms and swimming pools. Near the coast, there are even vast complexes of permanent tents aimed at package tourists. All sites are classified from one to four stars, according to facilities; the best value are usually *Camping Municipal*, run by the local commune. Farm campsites *(camping à la ferme)* are a more rustic alternative, restricted by law to a maximum of six plots (20 people). French Government Tourist Offices can provide listings, while Michelin and the Fédération Française de Camping et Caravanning (see below) produce nationwide site guides. Book ahead or avoid popular areas in July and Aug, when the French flock to the coast and country. Alternatively, make sure you always arrive in a new town with plenty of daylight to spare and ask at the local Tourist Office when you get there.

Don't camp on private land without obtaining permission, or you may be liable to prosecution for trespassing.

The national camping organisation is the **Fédération Française de Camping et Caravanning**, *78 r. de Rivoli, 75004 Paris; tel: 01 42 72 84 08.* **Camping Qualité France**, *105 r. Lafayette, 75010 Paris; tel: 01 48 78 13 77*, operates 200 sites throughout France and **Étapes André Trigano**, *111 r. de Reuilly, 75012 Paris; tel: 01 44 68 17 17*, runs 150 three- and four-star sites. In the UK, the **Caravan Club (CC)**, *East Grinstead House, East Grinstead, West Sussex RH19 1UA; tel: 01342 326944,* publishes an annual directory of caravan sites throughout Europe.

Youth Hostels

Youth hostels *(Auberges de Jeunesse)* are open to people of all ages and offer a good budget, no-frills option. Membership of your national **Hostelling International (HI)** association will entitle you to use over 5000 HI member association hostels in more than 60 different countries, including any of the 200-plus hostels in France run by the **Fédération Unie des Auberges de Jeunesse**, *27 r. Pajol, 75018 Paris; tel: 01 44 89 87 27.* For information, to join, and to book accommodation in advance, see Useful Addresses, p. 26. If you are not a member of an association and a hostel has a vacancy you can usually buy a Hostelling International Card on the spot. Members of Hostelling International can book in advance by letter or fax or using the IBN (International Booking Network; details from local associations). Booking ahead is advisable for popular destinations and in peak periods. You are usually allowed to stay in a hostel for as long as you require but if you have not already booked to stay more than three days, you may be asked to move out and make way for newcomers. In winter (except around Christmas) bookings can be slow, so ask about special price deals. A directory, *Hostelling International Europe*, available on joining or from bookshops, lists addresses, contact numbers, locations and facilities of all HI member associations in Europe.

Hostels are graded according to their standard of comfort and facilities. Some, especially those in larger cities, are open 24 hours daily, while others have lock-out times. Usual opening hours are 0700–1000 and 1700–2200 (later in summer). Sleeping arrangements are usually in dormitories, though some hostels also have smaller one- and two-bedded rooms. Many also have excellent-value dining, cooking and, in some cases, laundry facilities. Details of some hostels are given in the accommodation section of main tourist towns.

The **Ligue Française pour les Auberges de la Jeunesse**, *38 blvd Raspail, 75007 Paris; tel: 01 45 48 69 84*, is another membership organisation which runs more than 90 hostels in France.

Bicycles

The French are passionate about bicycles. Throughout the summer, every hill has a steady stream of puffing cyclists, all red faces and steaming lycra, slowly pumping their way to the top. Bikes can usually be taken on the train free of charge, but there may be restrictions or a supplement to pay on some busy services and inter-city trains. SNCF publishes a leaflet, *Guide du Train et du Vélo*, which gives details. Cycles can be hired in most towns and villages, and in many SNCF stations. The types of bikes available are basic, 'Rover' 10-speed bikes (FFr.44 a day with a deposit of FFr.1000), and mountain bikes (FFr.55 a day and a FFr.1500 deposit). For more information on cycling in France contact the **Fédération Française de Cyclo-tourisme**, *8 r. J-M.Jégo 75013 Paris; tel: 01 45 80 30 21.*

Children

France is an excellent destination for family holidays, with good hygiene and food, plentiful supplies of baby food and nappies, excellent health care, and entertainment for all ages. Along the coast are many large hotels and resorts catering specifically for families, while cheaper chain hotels, such as *Campanîle*, provide family rooms or add cots to a normal double. Always check before booking, however, as many smaller hotels ban children under 12, while others are sufficiently discouraging about noise to make life a misery. The sensible and more cost-effective solution may well be to hire a *gîte* with a private pool, garden and space to let off steam.

Baby-sitters are not that hard to find if you ask around – try the local hotel reception, Tourist Office or church. Most restaurants open early enough for evening meals and will provide a simple menu on demand. There are also numerous coffee shops, snack bars or fast-food places with children's menus or the ubiquitous hamburger and fries. Many sights, hotels and forms of transport will accept babies for free, and those under 12 for half-price.

Watch out for the weather. The sun is ferocious in summer and children need hats and heavy duty sunblock. Also make sure they wear shoes; there are a number of biting insects and other creepy-crawlies which may lead to tears or worse.

Climate

The climate in Southern France varies widely according to region. The coastal strip is dry, with less than 800mm of rain a year, usually produced in short sharp bursts. The temperature is hot in summer, averaging 28–30°C at midday. Winters are mild, at about 12°C. Severe winds such as the Mistral (see p. 314) blow for up to 75 days a year, dropping the temperature by up to 10°C. Further north, the mountain systems produce far more complicated and extreme weather with sufficient snow for skiing in many areas. Temperatures on the Puy de Dome rarely rise above 15°C and are below zero in midwinter.

The weather forecast service, **Metéo Consult,** runs an 8-day regional weather information service in English. For the south, *tel: 36 70 12 34,* press #, touch *1* then *4*; for maritime forecasts, *tel: 36 70 12 34*, press #, then *2*.

Clothing

Most tourist spots in France are informal these days and, you'll rarely need formal clothes. Do take some smart casual clothes (not jeans and trainers) for evening wear. People wearing shorts or sleeveless tops may be excluded from some churches, the most traditional of which still expect women to cover their head, so pack a long-sleeved shirt or blouse and a shawl or large scarf. You can encounter rain or cool weather everywhere, and many of the inland areas are at high altitude. Take at least one sweater or jacket and some sort of rainwear, even in high summer.

Currency

The French Franc (FFr.) is divided into 100 centimes. There are 5, 10, 20 and 50 centime coins, and FFr. 1, 2, 5, 10 and 20 coins. Notes come in FFr. 20, 50, 100, 200 and 500 denominations. There is a comma between the francs and the centimes, instead of a decimal point.

European Union countries place no limit on the import/export of currency between member states (though you may be asked to declare anything over FFr. 50,000 at French Customs). That said, it is never advisable to carry more cash than necessary, and it is sensible to take most of your money as Eurocheques, traveller's cheques and/or credit cards.

You can cash **traveller's cheques** at most major banks and hotels (the bank Société Générale does not charge commission on Franc-denominated cheques). **Eurocheques** are not popular amongst traders, but are easily cashed at most banks. You will need your passport/ID as well as your bank card. The best option is to use your Eurocheque card in the ATM machines outside most main banks, so remember your PIN number.

The Thomas Cook offices listed in this book will cash any type of Eurocheque/travellers' cheque (commission-free if they are Thomas Cook Travellers Cheques).

Credit cards are accepted at most hotels, shops and restaurants, although some smaller establishments may not take them. Carte Bleue/Visa, Eurocard/Mastercard, Diners Club and American Express are all widely accepted. French credit cards have a chip or '*puce*' which contains ID information, so cards with information on magnetic strips are not always easily read by French card machines. If you have a problem you will need to persuade the shop assistant/hotelier to confirm its validity with their '*centre de traitement*'. To report lost or stolen cards phone the following numbers: **VISA/Carte Bleue**, *tel: 01 42 77 11 90* (Paris) or *02 54 42 12 12* (Provinces); **American Express**, *tel: 01 47 77 72 00*; **MasterCard/Eurocard**, *tel: 01 45 67 53 53;* **Diners Club**, *tel: 01 47 62 75 50.* To report lost or stolen **Thomas Cook Travellers Cheques**, *tel: 0800-90 83 30* (toll-free 24-hr line).

Customs

As usual, the importation of offensive weapons, pornography, narcotics and animals is prohibited. If you are taking prescribed drugs, carry a doctor's letter of authority. For up-to-date regulations, contact your nearest French consulate.

Customs allowances in the EU

For those travelling between EU member countries, there are few restrictions on goods bought in ordinary shops and intended for personal use. However, you may be questioned if you have excessive amounts. The indicative limits (which apply to anyone aged 17 or over) for tobacco and alcohol are:

800 cigarettes, 200 cigars, 400 cigarillos and 1 kg tobacco
+ 90 litres wine (max. 60 litres sparkling)
+ 10 litres alcohol over 22% volume (e.g. most spirits)
+ 20 litres alcohol under 22% volume (e.g. port and sherry)
+ 110 litres beer.

These allowances also apply when re-entering the UK or another EU country.

Allowances for those returning home

Allowances for those returning home to other parts of the world are as follows:

Australia: goods to the value of A$400 (half for those under 18) plus 250 cigarettes or 250g tobacco and 1 litre alcohol.

Canada: goods to the value of C$300, provided you have been away for over a week and have not already used up part of your allowance for that year. Also 50 cigars plus 200 cigarettes and 1kg tobacco (if over 16) and 40oz/1 litre alcohol.

New Zealand: goods to the value of NZ$700. Anyone over 17 may also take 200 cigarettes or 250g tobacco or 50 cigars or a combination of tobacco products not exceeding 250g in all, plus 4 litres of beer or wine and 1.125 litres spirits.

South Africa: 400 cigarettes, 250 g tobacco, 50 cigars; 1 litre spirits, 2 litres wine; 50ml perfume and 250ml toilet water.

USA: goods to the value of US$400 as long as you have been out of the country for at least 48hrs and only use your allowance once every 30 days. Anyone over 21 is allowed 1 litre alcohol plus 100 (non-Cuban) cigars and 100 cigarettes.

Disabled Travellers

France, in theory, provides more facilities for the disabled traveller than most other countries. In practice, the facilities still fall short of real needs, and there are few people to provide muscle-power as an alternative. Travel is feasible, but it will be more expensive, as few small hotels have wheelchair access. You also need to plan well ahead to make sure you have access to the necessary lifts and side-entrances. All taxis accept wheelchairs and guide dogs.

Some concessions are made to cars displaying symbols such as the UK Orange Badge but these vary from place to place. There are no countrywide parking concessions, but police are reasonably sympathetic to those with limited mobility – providing that you park sensibly.

Touristes Quand-Même is a guide providing general information on facilities and access for disabled travellers in France, available from *28 blvd Raspail, 75007 Paris; tel: 01 45 48 90 13.*

People who are registered blind can take a companion free of charge on SNCF journeys with a full fare return ticket (an official certificate is provided when you buy the ticket). Further advice can be obtained from:

UK: **RADAR** (Royal Society for Disability and Rehabilitation), *Unit 12, City Forum, 250 City Road, London EC1V 8AF, tel: 0171-250 3222*, publishes a useful annual guide called *Holidays and Travel Abroad* (£5 including p&p) detailing facilities for the disabled in various countries.

Other useful books include: *The AA Guide for the Disabled Traveller* (AA Publishing, £3.95 – free to AA members); Alison Walsh, *Nothing Ventured: A Rough Guide Special* (Penguin, £7.99).

USA: **SATH** (Society for the Advancement of Travel for the Handicapped), *347 5th Avenue, Suite 610, New York NY 10016; tel: 212-447 7284.* Equivalent national organisations for disabled people in other countries will be able to offer advice and information.

Discounts

Reductions are available on public transport and on entrance fees for senior citizens, students and the young. Some proof of your eligibility is usually required. Students should obtain an International Student Identity Card (ISIC) from their union, as this is universally recognised and offers a wider range of discounts than a national union card.

Eating and Drinking

Eating out is one of the great pleasures of France. In recent years a little complacency – and a touch of Euro-standardisation – has crept in; if you are unlucky, you will wonder what all the fuss was about. On the other hand, France is still obsessed with food and can offer unparalleled eating experiences. If you avoid the obvious tourist traps, you can eat extremely well for surprisingly few francs.

Breakfast normally consists of coffee, tea or hot chocolate and croissants or bread with butter and jam. Eggs, cold meats etc. can often be ordered as extras and may come as part of a buffet.

Lunch is served from midday until around 1400. Set-price meals often offer better value than their evening equivalent. Light lunches, such as salads or crêpes, are proportionately pricey. For a cheap option, look at the dish of the day *(plat du jour)*. Sunday lunch is very busy for most restaurants, so book ahead. If you want to save money, buy a baguette, a bit of cheese and some fruit, for a picnic.

France has its own well-established **fast-food** tradition – baguette sandwiches at cafés, *crêpes* (pancakes) and *frites* (french fries) at roadside stalls; the Quick chain is a French answer to McDonalds and Burger King, though these ubiquitous multinationals have a firm foothold in major cities.

Dinner is served from about 1900–2100. Few restaurants outside the tourist areas will take orders any later than this. The three to four course set menus *(menu du jour)* are infinitely better value than the à la carte selection. A few restaurants offer only the more expensive set-price menus if you sit outside. By law, prices displayed outside restaurants should include all charges, including service (usually 15%). Customers can leave tips if they are especially pleased with the service, but are under no obligation to do so. Brasseries tend to be more flexible than restaurants, but offer a more limited and less exciting choice of food.

For most foreigners, the essence of France lies in a lazy cup of coffee or pastis under the stripy awning of a pavement café on a warm summer evening. It is a dream for which you pay dearly. With a cup of coffee starting at around FFr.15, and a glass of beer at FFr.20, a round of drinks or cooling ice-creams can be the stuff of bankruptcy. Cafés usually charge less to eat or drink while standing at the counter *(comptoir)* than to sit at a table *(salle)* or outside *(terrasse)*.

Under recent legislation, all cafés and restaurants are meant to provide no-smoking areas, but don't bank on them doing so. Restaurants in this book are listed as cheap (under FFr.150); moderate (FFr.150–200); and expensive (above FFr.200), based on a set 3-course menu. For more on regional food and drink, see p. 47.

Electricity

The French system is 220V, using Continental two-pin round plugs. If you are taking any sort of electrical gadget, you will need a travel adaptor (these are inexpensive and widely available). You are unlikely to face power cuts, but a small torch (flashlight) is a useful back-up and essential if camping. French sockets are always live, so do not leave anything (eg the iron) plugged in.

Health

There are no compulsory vaccination requirements, but it is advisable to keep your tetanus and polio protection up to date. You must be able to produce a certificate against yellow fever if you have been in a yellow fever endemic zone in the six days before entering Europe. Have a dental check-up before leaving home.

There are relatively few risks. French tap water is safe to drink. AIDS is as prevalent in France as anywhere else. Rabies still exists here and, while the risk is very small, you should be wary of stray and wild animals. There are a few poisonous insects, snakes and underwater creatures, so if stung or bitten, get it checked. The weather is probably the greatest risk, from the ferocious sun to the sudden onset of mountain fog, with attendant hypothermia.

Tourist Offices have lists of doctors, dentists and pharmacists (and can tell you which ones speak English). French pharmacists are qualified dispensers, sell a wide range of drugs without prescription, and provide advice about minor health problems. The emergency rota – *Pharmacie de grade* – is usually displayed on the door of every pharmacy, in local newspapers and in the police station.

If you need medication regularly take an up-to-date prescription with details of the trade name and pharmaceutical name of the drug(s) you require, the name of the manufacturer and details of the precise dosage (it may be useful to get a French translation of the prescription as well). If you wear prescription glasses, take a spare pair and/or a copy of your prescription.

Insurance

Your existing private medical insurance may cover you while in France; if not, you may be able to extend the cover for an additional premium. EU residents are entitled to reduced cost health care under reciprocal arrangements between member states. To claim this, get form E111 from the social security authorities before travelling.

You will have to pay then reclaim the money before you leave France. Get an authorised form from the doctor to present to the local sickness insurance office *(Caisse Primaries d'Assurance Malade)*.

In spite of these options, you are strongly advised to take out full travel insurance, covering your health as well as your belongings, cancellation and emergency flights home if something goes really wrong. You will probably have to pay an additional premium if you plan to ride a moped or indulge in any adventure sports. The Thomas Cook Independent Traveller Insurance Package, which includes comprehensive medical insurance, is available from all Thomas Cook retail travel shops in the UK. For car insurance, see pp. 28 and 33.

Language

The official language of the whole country is French. The south has its own distinct dialect, based on the medieval language of Occitan (as in *Langue d'oc*). This is very rarely spoken now, but the Provençal accent is very different from the Parisian standard usually taught in schools and can be difficult to understand.

Many people speak or understand a little English, but they appreciate even the most fumbled attempts to speak French as a courtesy and are scornful of those who make no effort, so don't be too self-conscious. Carry a pocket phrase book and dictionary and keep pen and paper handy, so that you can ask people to write down figures such as times and prices.

Maps

The **Institut Géographique National** (IGN) is the official cartographic body in France; the IGN Map 901, a general map of France (scale 1 cm = 10 km) is useful for planning countrywide routes. Specialist maps include Map 902 (1 cm = 10 km) showing major historic sites; Map 903 (1 cm = 10 km) tracing the national long distance footpaths; and Map 906 (1 cm = 1 km) designed for cyclists. Various Outdoor Activities maps (1 cm = 1 km) cover national parks and tourist areas. In the UK, IGN mapping is the basis of the *AA Big Road Atlas of France* (see offer on p. 59).

The most useful regional maps are the *Série Verte* (Green Series), covering mainland France in 74 sheets (1 cm = 1 km). For walkers and cyclists, the *Série Bleue* (Blue Series) has 2000 sheets (4 cm = 1 km). Local maps and guides can usually be bought at Tourist Offices, which also provide free town plans.

Road maps are also published by some motoring clubs and by Michelin, who produce national and regional maps as well as a series of sectional 'close-up' maps and a motoring atlas scale 1:200,000.

Opening Hours

Banks: Mon–Fri or Tues–Sat 0900–1200 and 1400–1600. Banks usually close early on the day before a public holiday. Bureaux de change usually remain open from 0830–1800, Mon–Fri, with a half-day on Sat. **Post Offices**: see below.

Museums: Generally 0900–1700/1800 in July and Aug. Most national museums close on Tues; municipal museums tend to close on Mon. On Sun, entrance is often free or reduced. Most museums close on major public holidays and many attractions close altogether in winter, only opening for part-time in spring and autumn.

Shops: Mon–Sat 0900–1200/1230 and 1400/1430–1900; food shops tend to open earlier and on Sun mornings. Large supermarkets and shopping complexes will stay open all day. The small grocery chain, *Huit à 8*, stays open over lunchtime, useful for emergency picnic supplies.

Please note that the times given are only intended as a rough guide. There is enormous local and seasonal variation. Sightseeing tours must be planned carefully to avoid frustration. Wherever possible we have detailed opening times, but we have also given phone numbers for on-the-spot checking.

Passports and Visas

For stays of less than three months, British and Irish visitors need a full valid passport; other EU Nationals do not need passports, but must carry their national identity cards. For longer visits, a residence permit *(carte de séjour)* is required, either from your local French consulate or from the *Service des Étrangers* at local *préfectures de police* in France. Visas are not needed by nationals of Canada, New Zealand or the USA for stays of under 90 days. Australians and South Africans do need visas. Other nationalities should check with their nearest French Consulate before departure.

Post Offices

Opening hours: Mon–Fri 0800–1200 and 1430–2000, Sat 0800–1200. Offices in city centres usually remain open during lunchtime. Both offices and the small metal post boxes are easily recognised by their yellow signs with *La Poste* in blue.

There can be long queues at post office counters, but many now have self-service franking machines which weigh letters and packages and print franked stickers (there are usually English-language instructions available). There are also coin-operated stamp machines and you can buy stamps from shops and cafés showing the red diamond-shaped Tabac sign. A postcard or letter (up to 20 g) costs FFr.2.80 to EU countries, FFr.4.30 overseas.

Mail sent *c/o Poste Restante, Poste Centrale* will be held for up to a month. To collect it, you have to show proof of identity – usually a passport or driver's licence

– and pay a small fee. Post information; *tel: 0800-05 02 02*.

Public Holidays

France has 11 official public holidays, most of which mark religious occasions, though some celebrate historical events.

New Year 1 Jan; **Easter Mon** late Mar or early Apr; **Labour Day** 1 May; **VE Day** 8 May; **Ascension Day** five weeks after Easter Day; **Whit Mon** late May; **Bastille Day** 14 July; **Assumption** 15 Aug; **All Saints** 1 Nov; **Armistice Day** 11 Nov; and **Christmas Day** 25 Dec. When they fall on Tues or Thur, the French like to '*faire le pont*' – extend the holiday by including the preceding Mon or following Fri.

Public Transport

Coaches and buses: Most long-distance coaches are international services in transit through France. Bus and coach lines tend to provide local and regional transport, supplementing rail services. Information and timetables are available locally from tourist information offices and bus stations *(gares routières)*. Train and bus stations are usually close together. Bus services shown as *Autocar* are run by SNCF and accept rail passes/tickets. Regional transport authorities and SNCF produce a free regional service guide, *Guide Regional des Transports*, with information about train and bus services between major towns. Bus services within towns are good during the day, but infrequent after around 2030 and on Sun. Public transport in rural areas is sparse.

Taxis: Licensed taxis are metered, with white roof-lights if available, orange ones if they are not. You can pick them up at ranks (*stations de taxi*, marked 'T'), but they rarely stop if you hail them in the street. There are surcharges for luggage, extra passengers and animals and you may be charged for the round-trip, not just the time you are actually in the car. Avoid unlicensed taxis, and always keep an eye on the charges. The final fare has a nasty habit of swelling to twice the original size. If your journey will take you out of town, check the price with the driver before starting. The usual tip is 10–15%.

Trains: The national rail company, **Société Nationale des Chemins de Fer Français (SNCF)**, operates nationwide (premium-rate) numbers for information and bookings; *tel: 36 35 35 35* (French; 0700–2200); *36 67 68 69* (French; 24 hrs); *36 35 35 39* (English). The network of local lines is not very extensive, but there are good connections through the Rhône Delta and right along the coast. French trains are fast, reliable and comfortable, though not always frequent. The TGV (*Train à Grande-Vitesse*) is one of the fastest in the world, with speeds of up to 300kph. Most long-distance trains have a buffet or trolley service.

All tickets must be date-stamped before you board, by using the orange machines (*composteurs*) at the platform entrance. France has two fare periods on most routes (more on some); basically, blue is for quiet periods and white for peak. SNCF issues a (free) calendar detailing the periods. Reservations, for a small supplement, are compulsory for sleeping-cars and the TGV. They are recommended for international travel and during white periods. See also Getting to the South of France, p.35 and Driving in France, p.28.

Sales Tax

Hefty TVA, Value Added Tax (VAT in the UK) is automatically added to most goods in France. Non-EU residents may claim the tax back on expensive items, although an impenetrable bureaucracy provides a strong deterrent. If you spend more than FFr.2000 in one shop, ask for a TVA reclaim form which must be completed and stamped by the sales person (not all shops operate this service). When you leave France you will need to present the form(s) at Customs for verification before claiming any refund.

Security

The best way to avoid becoming a victim of theft is to give the impression you are not worth robbing (do not flash expensive jewellery or rolls of banknotes). Use a hidden money-belt for valuables, travel documents and spare cash. Never carry a wallet in your back pocket or leave your handbag open, and use a bag with a shoulder strap slung diagonally. Wind camera or bag straps around your chair in cafés and never leave luggage unattended; even if it isn't stolen, France is very terrorist-conscious, and it may be reported as a possible bomb.

Mugging is a problem in some areas, so don't wander alone into deserted, dubious or poorly lit areas, especially after dark. You should be safe in the city centres, although pickpockets are a risk there. If you are attacked, it is safer to let go of your bag or hand over the small amount of obvious money – you are more likely to be attacked physically if the thief meets with resistance. If anything is stolen, report it to the police (either Gendarmeries Nationales or Police Nationale) immediately – this is often a requirement of insurance policies. Police have a right to stop anyone at any time to request and inspect identity documents. Always carry a small amount of money or you could be arrested as a vagrant, and always keep your driver's licence and the car's papers with you when driving. Take a friend with you whenever dealing with the police. If you get into real trouble, contact your nearest embassy or consulate.

Finally, take half a dozen passport photos and photocopy the important pages and any visa stamps in your passport. Store these safely, together with a note of the numbers of your traveller's cheques, credit cards and insurance documents (away from the items themselves). If you are unfortunate enough to be robbed, you will at least have some identification, and replacing the documents will be much easier.

Telephones

The French telephone system is considered one of the best in the world. The plentiful public phone boxes are free-standing clear-glass cabins with *Téléphone* signs or the *France Telecom* logo (a digital dialling pad in an oval surround) on the handle.

In city centres and major tourist centres, phones have instructions in English and French. There are still a few coin-operated boxes but most now take only phone cards *(télécartes)*, sold at post offices and newsagents *(tabacs)*, or credit cards. A 50-unit card costs FFr.40.60, a 120-unit card FFr.97.50. Many post offices have metered phones where you pay when you have finished.

In Oct 1996, all telephone numbers in France were changed to ten digits. There are now five telephone regions within France: all numbers in Paris and the Île de France now start with *01*; those in the south-east (including the whole area of this book) start with *04*. Simply add *04* to the front of the old 8-digit numbers. There are four billing periods during the day; the cheapest is 2230–0600 daily; next cheapest is Mon–Fri 0600–0800, 2130–2230, Sat 1330–2230 and Sun 0600–2230. For the operator, *tel: 13*; for directory enquiries, *tel: 12*.

To phone abroad, *tel: 00* and wait for the dialling tone, then dial the country code (*44* for the UK, *353* for Ireland, *1* for USA or Canada, *61* for Australia, *64* for New Zealand, *27* for South Africa), the area code (excluding any initial *0*) and number. For an international operator, *tel: 00*, wait for the dialling tone and then dial *33 12* and the country code. For reverse charge/collect calls, ask for *'PCV'*. A free French/English France Telecom brochure, *Guide du Téléphone International*, (from most Tourist Offices) fully explains the telephone system. You can also bill calls to your home phone using BT, AT&T and other calling cards. It is much cheaper to phone from a call box than from a hotel.

To phone France, dial your own international code, e.g. *00* from the UK, then *33*, then the number, dropping the first *0*.

Emergency calls are free. **Police**, *tel: 17*; **Fire** service *(Pompiers)*, *tel: 18*; **Ambulance** and emergency medical care *(SAMU)*, *tel: 15*; **Coast Guard** *(Gendarmerie maritime)*, *tel: 04 94 27 27 11*. For loss or theft of traveller's cheques or credit cards, see the numbers listed under 'Currency' on p. 19.

Time

French time is GMT (Greenwich Mean Time) + 1 hr in winter, GMT + 2 hrs in summer (last Sun in Mar to last Sun in Sept).

Toilets

Toilets are usually single-sex (Men – *Messieurs*, Women – *Dames*), but often share a common entrance and washing facilities. Basic holes-in-the-ground are still common, while unisex, automatic coin-operated cabins are an increasingly familiar feature in streets and parks.

Tourist Offices

There is a wide network of local Tourist Offices known as *Syndicats d'Initiatives* or *Offices de Tourisme*; offices in larger centres are called *Acceuil de France*. The symbol to look for is a large white '**i**'. Staff may speak English and are usually helpful. There are always copious numbers of free town plans and brochures (some in several languages) while larger offices may help with hotel bookings and sightseeing tours. Tourist Offices are listed throughout the book.

Useful Addresses

Australia: **Embassy,** *6 Perth Ave, Yarralumla, Canberra, ACT 2600; tel: (06) 270 5111*. **Consulate**, *St Martin's Tower, 31 Market St, Level 26, Sydney NSW 2000; tel: (02) 261 5779*. **Tourist Office**, *BNP House, 12 Castlereagh St, Sydney NSW 2000; tel: (02) 231 5244*. **HI**: *Level 3, 10 Mallett St, Camperdown, NSW 2050; tel: (02) 565 1699*.

Canada: **Embassy**, *42 Promenade Sussex, Ottawa, Ontario K1M 2C9 or Q1M 2C9; tel: (613) 789 1795*. **Consulate**: *1 pl. Villa-Marie, bureau 2601, Montréal; tel: (514) 878 4381* (also in Edmonton, Moncton, Québec, Toronto and Vancouver). **Tourist Office**, *1981 av. McGill College, Bureau 490, Montréal, Québec H3A 2W9; tel: (514) 288 4264* and *30 St Patrick St (Suite 700), Toronto, Ont M5T 3A3; tel: (416) 593 6427*. **HI**: *400-205 Catherine St, Ottawa, Ontario K2P 1C3; tel: (613) 237 7884*.

Republic of Ireland: **Embassy**, *36 Ailesbury Rd, Ballsbridge, Dublin 4; tel: (01) 260 1666*. **Tourist Office**, *35 Lower Abbey St, Dublin 1; tel: (01) 703 4046*. **HI**: *6 Mountjoy St, Dublin 7; tel: (01) 830 4555*.

New Zealand: **Embassy**, *Robert Jones House, 1–3 Willeston St, Wellington; tel: (04) 472 0200*. **HI**: *cnr Gloucester and Manchester Sts, Christchurch; tel: (03) 379 9970*.

South Africa: **Embassy**, *807 George*

Ave, Arcadia, Pretoria 0083; tel: (012) 435 564 and *1009 Main Tower, Cape Town Centre, Heerengracht, Cape Town; tel: (021) 212 050.* **Consulate**, *35th Floor, Carlton Centre, Commissioner Street, Johannesburg 2000; tel: (011) 331 3460.* **Tourist Office**, *1st Flr, Oxford Manor, 196 Oxford Road, Illovo, Johannesburg 2196; tel (011) 880 8062.* **HI**: *101 Boston House, Strand St, Cape Town 8001; tel: (021) 419 1853.*

UK: **Embassy**, *58 Knightsbridge, London SW1X 7JT; tel: 0171 201 1000.* **Consulate General**, *21 Cromwell Rd, London SW7 2DQ; tel: 0171 838 2001.* **Maison de la France (Tourist Office)**, *178 Piccadilly, London W1V 0AL; tel: 0891-244 123* (calls cost 39p per minute cheap rate and 49p per minute at other times). **French Railways (SNCF) and Rail Shop**, *179 Piccadilly, London W1V 0BA; tel: 0990 300003.* **HI**: *Trevelyan House, 8 St Stephen's Hill, St Albans, Herts AL1 2DY; tel: 01727 855215.*

USA: **Embassy**, *4101 Reservoir Road NW, Washington DC 20007; tel: (202) 944 6000.* **Consulate**, *934 Fifth Ave, New York, NY 10021; tel: (212) 606 3689; 10990 Wilshire Blvd, Ste 300, Los Angeles, CA 90024; tel: (310) 479 4426.* **Tourist Office**, *444 Madison Ave (16th Flr), New York, NY 10020-2452; tel: (212) 838 7800* and *9454 Wilshire Blvd, Los Angeles, CA 90912-2967; tel: (310) 271 6665.*

HI: *733 15th St NW, Ste 840, Washington DC 20005; tel: (202) 783 6161* or toll-free *(800) 444 6111.*

Provence Travel Reservations Service, *275 Madison Ave, Ste 1819, New York, NY 10016; tel: (0800) 292 0219; fax: (212) 986 3720.*

Useful Reading

Most guidebook series contain titles on Provence, but relatively few include Languedoc and the Auvergne. For good illustrated guides, try the *Thomas Cook Travellers Guide to Provence* (pub. AA/ Thomas Cook; Passport in USA/Canada) and *Explorer Provence* (AA; Fodor in USA and Canada), for detailed coverage of cultural, historical and architectural sights, buy the *Michelin Green Guides* or the *Blue Guide to France* (A&C Black).

There are many books, fiction and non-fiction, on the region. Amongst the more famous are: Peter Mayle, *A Year in Provence* and *Toujours Provence*; F. Scott Fitzgerald, *Tender is the Night*; Marcel Pagnol, *Le Château de ma Mère, La Gloire de mon Père, Jean de Florette, Manon des Sources* (and many others); Alphonse Daudet, *Lettres de Mon Moulin* and *Tartarin de Tarascon*; Vincent van Gogh, *Letters from Provence*; Robert Louis Stevenson, *Travels with a Donkey*.

What to Take

The great dilemma if you are driving your own car across the Channel is that a large boot and the necessity to be ready for all contingencies conflict with the desire to leave space for heavy-duty hypermarket shopping on the way home. How you strike the balance is a matter of personal choice, but avoid carrying so much on the way back that the entire back of the car is so full of belongings that the driver's rear vision is obscured. Do remember that many of your belongings will be left in the car all day, calling longingly to local thieves and that if you have a flight at the end of your trip, you could face a hefty bill for excess baggage.

You can, of course, buy anything you need, but France is not cheap. Really useful items include: a picnic coolbag (with a couple of freezer packs, a good-sized thermos/water bottle, and plates and cutlery); wetwipes; bottle opener; sunglasses, hat and sunblock; and an electrical adaptor.

DRIVING IN FRANCE

This chapter provides practical advice for those taking to the road in France.

BASICS

Most visitors, apart from the British and some other Commonwealth residents, will be used to **driving on the right**. Those who are not should keep reminding themselves, even on small roads. You also give way to the right, go round roundabouts (traffic circles) anti-clockwise and overtake on the left (see p. 31). It can be difficult to see out from a right-hand drive car, so if in doubt, use an extension mirror.

Speeds on major roads may be higher than many, especially North Americans, are accustomed to (see p. 31). Also be prepared for drivers coming up very close behind, especially if they are hoping to overtake. Though dangerous, it seems to be a national habit.

Signposting can be confusing, with some roads signed from one direction only, other notices on the far side of a crossroads, often lurking behind a tree. Most confusing of all, there is no straight arrow marking the road ahead. Instead, the arrow seemingly points sideways (ie the road to the left of the sign), which can easily be confused with a left turn.

Cars with a red 'A' plate (for *apprentice)* indicate that the driver has passed their test in the last two years. 'CA' denotes a *conduiseur accompagné* (a learner driver).

To drive in France you must carry a full and valid **driver's licence** (or an international licence if planning to stay more than 6 months), **insurance certificate** and, if you take your own car, a **vehicle registration document**. If the car is not registered in your name, you will need a letter of authorisation from the owner. You must have these documents with you whenever you are in the car. By law, you may not hire a car in France if you have held a full licence for less than 1 year.

If driving your own car, you no longer need an **International Insurance Certificate** (green card) by law, but it is still highly advisable to get one. They can be obtained from your insurers, the AA or RAC, are issued for periods of 8, 15 or 30 days, and provide immediate proof of insurance in case of an accident. You must also display a nationality sticker.

You must have **headlamp converters** to deflect the beams on left-hand drive cars, but yellow-tinted headlights are not compulsory for tourist vehicles. It is strongly advisable to carry a **warning triangle** (compulsory for cars towing a caravan or trailer) and a complete **spare-bulb** set, as it is illegal to drive with faulty lights. It is also sensible to carry a few other **spares** as standard, including a spare wheel and jack, fanbelt, fire extinguisher and first-aid kit.

CAR HIRE

Booking a car in advance can be cheaper than hiring on the spot, especially as part of a fly-drive or train-car package, best organised through travel agents in your home country. Most international car-hire companies, such as *Budget, Avis, Hertz* and *Europcar*, have offices in all the major French cities, at airports, ferry ports and large railway terminals. It is also possible to hire from French national, regional and local companies – details are usually available from French Government Tourist Offices. French car hire firms with several city branches include *Citer, Dergi Cie Location* and *Mattei.* On the whole, the smaller the company, the more restricted the service. For example, you may have to return the car to the same office; and during holidays and peak travel times, there may be few or even no cars available. If you can live with the drawbacks, the smaller companies may well prove cheaper than the large international organisations. Prices can vary considerably, so shop around.

To hire a vehicle in France you have to be over 21 (25 with some hire companies) and in possession of a valid driving licence with a minimum of one or two years' driving experience. Credit cards are preferred for most bookings (otherwise the company will demand a substantial cash deposit). Some firms impose a maximum age ranging between 69 and 75.

Fee options vary and can include a per-day, per-kilometre charge (often with a free allowance of up to 300km each day); or flat rates on a daily, weekly or monthly basis. Collision damage waiver (for damage to your vehicle) adds considerably to the price, so it is worth checking whether your own insurance covers this option (though most major hire companies include the waiver charge automatically). Personal accident insurance is only necessary for those not already covered by a general policy.

Make sure your hired car is equipped with a spare tyre and jack, and preferably with a first-aid kit, torch, warning triangle and petrol container.

ROADS

France has an excellent system of motorways and major roads, and even the minor roads in most areas are well maintained. They are classified by letter and number: A roads *(Autoroutes)* are motorways (freeways); other main roads carry the prefix N (for *route nationale*). Other roads are designated by D (for *départementale*) i.e. maintained by local government; hence the number may change abruptly as you cross into a new *département.*

In recent years there has been a flurry of road-building and upgrading throughout France and there have also been several changes to the numbering system, changing some N roads into D ones (sometimes retaining the same number, sometimes being given a new one). As part of the Europe-wide network, some motorways also have E numbers (for trans-European routes) as well as A numbers. Recent maps should give a clear idea of the current system, but events may have overtaken even the latest edition. Get the most up-to-date map possible and keep it handy. Many direction signs include only place names, without road numbers, so you always need to know the name of the next place you are heading for. For details of motorway routes into the region, see p. 38.

AUTOROUTES

Except for limited stretches of road approaching cities and large towns, most autoroutes are toll roads. This ensures that the autoroutes are fairly empty and they are generally considered to be safer than other roads, as well as faster. They can be pricy, however. **Tolls** vary according to the type of vehicle: motorcycles pay less and cars with caravans more than single cars. Between Calais and Nice (avoiding Paris) you will have to pay about FFr.400 in a car, FFr.550 with a caravan and FFr.250 on a motorcyle; to Marseille the charges are respectively about FFr.350, FFr.450 and FFr.200.

Toll booths (*péages*) may be situated at motorway exits, at the point where a free stretch of road begins, or where one network meets another. Some credit cards are accepted for sums over Fr.50. As you enter the toll road, collect a ticket (you may need to press a button first) from a machine on the left hand side; hand this in at the booth at the exit. The attendant will tell you the sum due, if you have not already worked it out from the ticket, and you can usually also read it on an electronic display. On some networks, smaller sums are paid at automatic, change-giving machines or maybe thrown (exact money only) into large nets.

There are comparatively few full-service rest areas, but you can find a reasonable range of facilities along or just off the motorways. Many toll stations have picnic areas with toilets and phones. Every 10 km or so along the motorways, you come to *aires*, or rest places, most of which have picnic areas, public toilets and a small children's playground. Many have phones, operated with phonecards, while some even have exercise circuits and sports facilities, nappy-changing and feeding caravans, and snack bars (open only during the peak summer months). Other relatively sparsely sited kiosks and restaurants provide service ranging from basic to semi-luxurious. All-year snack bars open at least 14 hours a day, while some stay open all night; and there is a chain of drive-in cafés. You will find snack areas in a few petrol stations including some offering cooked meals. Self-service restaurants (*caféterias*) tend to open 16-17 hours a day; some are open 24 hours. Restaurants (*grilles*) are rather more formal, with table service, set and *à la carte* menus, and are more expensive than the self-service variety. They usually open for 3-4 hours in the middle of the day and for 3 hours in the evening.

Road Signs

Standard international European road signs are used throughout France, except for the odd corners of remote regions where older versions still display local place-names in wood or stone. International signs indicate their meaning by their shape: triangular for hazard warnings; circular for instructions and rectangular for general information.

To reach a town or city centre, follow the *Centre Ville* sign. To leave a town, follow *Toutes Directions* or *Autres Directions* until you see a sign for your destination, or, more probably the first town of any size on the right road. Avoid roads marked with signs reading *seulement riverains* (residents only) or *sauf riverains* (except for residents): these indicate private roads and are mainly found in smaller towns and villages. Market towns also have signs to specify market days and you should certainly avoid parking on the square overnight as the stalls will be set up very early in the morning.

Motorway and main N road signs often appear next to each other, so remember that motorway signs are blue and N-road signs are green. If an N-road sign has a small blue motorway square in one corner, it means that the road also leads to a motorway. *'Bis'* on a direction sign indicates the main alternative route. On the outskirts of major towns, you may occasionally get two blue alternatives, one leading to an N road which has been upgraded into a dual-carriageway; the other with the word *péage* added, indicating the toll-road.

A sign showing a car in a blue square denotes no stopping.

Rules of the Road

The minimum age for driving in France is 18. Seat-belts must be worn by the driver and front-seat passenger, and also, if fitted,

Common Road Signs

absence de marquage no road markings
aire (de repos) rest area
bis alternative route (to avoid traffic jams on major roads)
boue mud
carrefour dangereux dangerous-crossroads
cédez le passage give way (yield)
chantier/travaux road works
chausée déformée uneven surface
chausée glissante slippery road
dépassement interdit no overtaking
déviation diversion (detour)
gravillons loose chippings
lacet hairpin bend
péage toll
périphérique ring road (around a city)
priorité à droite give way to the right
priorité aux piétons pedestrians have right of way
prochaine sortie next exit
ralentir/ralentissez slow down
rappel remember – a reminder of restrictions applying to your route, such as speed limits
renseignements information
restez sur votre file stay in your lane
route barrée road closed
sens unique one-way street
sens interdit no entry
servez la droite/gauche keep to your right/left
sortie d'usine factory exit
stationnement interdit no parking
toutes directions through-traffic route
virages dangereux dangerous road edges
voie de détresse escape road
voie rétrécie road narrows
vous n'avez pas la priorité you do not have the right of way

by anyone in the rear. Children under 10 years old and/or 1.5 metres in height are not generally permitted to travel in the front of a vehicle unless using an approved restraint system facing backwards.

Driving is on the right. Priority is usually given to traffic approaching from the right *(priorité à droite)*, but a yellow diamond and the words *passage protégé* (right of way) means that the main road has priority over secondary roads coming in from the right. If a black line runs through the diamond, the main road has no priority *(vous n'avez pas la priorité)* and traffic approaching from the right has precedence. At most roundabouts (traffic circles/rotaries), a sign shows a circle of arrows and the words *cédez le passage* (give way). Priority is given to cars already on the roundabout rather than those waiting to enter. If a driver flashes his headlights in France, he is usually indicating that *he* has priority and that you should give way..

When overtaking a car, return immediately to the right-hand lane. Overtaking on a solid single centre line is heavily penalised. Never overtake on the inside.

Distances and Speeds

France uses the metric system. Distances and speeds are always quoted in kilometres (km) and kilometres per hour (kph) and these units are used throughout this book. A kilometre is 0.6 of a mile; a mile is 1.6 km. For further conversions, see the table on p. 347.

Speed limits

Unless otherwise stated and on dry roads: **130 kph** on toll motorways (110 kph on wet roads). There is a minimum speed requirement of 80 kph in clear weather in the outside (left-hand) lane of motorways. **110 kph** on non-toll motorways and dual carriageways (divided highways) (100 kph on wet roads).**90 kph** on other roads (80 kph on wet roads).**50 kph** in towns (the town name starts the limit, a bar through the town name is the derestriction sign). There is a **50 kph** limit on motorways in foggy conditions when visibility is less than 50m.

Visiting drivers who have held a licence for less than two years are restricted to 80 kph outside built-up areas, 100 kph on duel carriageways and 110 kph on motorways.

Police and Security

Heavy on-the-spot fines can be imposed by French police for driving violations. Those without the ready cash to pay can sometimes offer vouchers if they have insurance cover. Drivers who wish to argue their innocence can choose to pay a deposit (an *amende forfaitaire)* and take a receipt in exchange. Anyone arrested by the police has the right to contact their consulate (for addresses and phone numbers, see p. 26). Police operate infrequent random breath tests but drink-driving laws are strictly enforced if you are caught. The limit is 80mg per 100ml of blood. Failure can lead to a large fine or a ban from driving in France. Fines can also be handed out for speeding, not wearing a seat belt and failing to stop at a red light. Gross violations may result in the immediate roadside suspension of your licence.

In towns and cities, the police are eagle-eyed and thorough when it comes to illegal parking. Again they have the power to deliver on-the-spot fines or to have the offending car towed away or clamped.

The biggest security problem for motorists is theft from cars; those carrying foreign number plates are particularly vulnerable. Never leave luggage or other valuables within sight in the car; if your tape deck or radio is detachable, always lock it in the boot before leaving your vehicle. If anything is stolen from your car, telephone 17 for the police: you must report the theft in person and sign a written statement at the nearest *gendarmerie* (police station). Contact your insurance office at the first opportunity.

There have been occasional outbreaks of violent crime against motorists. Don't pick up hitchhikers or stop to assist someone in trouble. Drive on to the nearest phone and ask the authorities to help them.

Accidents and Breakdowns

If you are unlucky enough to break down, move your car off the road onto the hard shoulder or roadside. All motorists should carry a red warning triangle; place this 30–50m behind the car and flash your hazard warning lights. On major roads, there should be no problem finding an emergency phone: orange *postes d'appel d'urgence* are placed every 4 km on main routes and every 2 km on the motorways where some are equipped with flashing lights to warn of approaching hazards. On minor routes, there are often emergency phones at the top of mountain passes. To operate the phone, press the button and wait until you hear a reply before speaking. If your

---

Colour section:

(i) Driving through the Gorges du Tarn (p. 248); Insets: Arlempdes (p. 195); The beach at St Tropez (p. 340).

(ii) Arles (p. 80). Place de la République; l'Arlésienne – traditional Provençal costume is still worn on festive occasions by young and old; the Arènes.

(iii) The valley of the Lubéron (p. 73); Lourmarin (p. 72); Bonnieux (p. 72).

(iv) Sights of the Camargue (p. 87).

50

Architecte

French is up to it, give exact details of your location, your car model and, if possible, the cause or nature of the problem. If not, use the Driving Vocabulary on p.34. From a motorway phone, you can only call the police or the official breakdown service, not your own assistance company. Local garages are open for breakdown services every day of the week, including holidays, 24 hours a day. Their charges for towing and repairs are set by the state and specified on the emergency phones and in the garages themselves. There are three hourly rates - T1, T2 and T3 - depending on the complexity of the repairs. Both you and the garage should sign an *Ordre de Réparation* specifying the work to be done, its cost and how long it will take. Expect to pay an extra 25% for night-time, week-end and holiday repairs.

In the event of a breakdown on a remote country road, open the bonnet of the car and tie something white to the door handle or the radio aerial.

If you are involved in an accident, you have to inform the police: dial the emergency number, 17, to reach them and the ambulance service. You will need to provide a signed statement of events (a *constat á l'aimable* – you may need a translator for this), and to swap your insurance details with any other motorist involved. Make sure you keep copies of any documentation to present as evidence to your insurance company.

Thomas Cook (in the UK) and some motoring associations such as the AA and RAC offer breakdown assistance abroad. Most schemes provide roadside help, alternative travel and accommodation arrangements, and some can meet the cost of transporting the car back home. The AA operates an English-speaking emergency centre in Lyon, open 24 hours a day, every day of the year.

Information

Members of motoring associations - the AA in the UK, AAA in the USA and their international equivalents – can obtain a fairly wide range of information and advice before starting out. In the UK, call the AA on premium-line 0336-401 869 (39p per minute cheap rate, 49p at other times). They will help you draw up pre-planned travel itineraries designed to avoid the most congested and busy routes and will also book accommodation and provide a route map. Members may also ring an information line for recorded details of the traffic conditions abroad.

Information points are stationed at the first and last toll booths of each motorway network. Most provide free motorway maps showing the *Bison Futé* fast routes, avoiding areas prone to traffic hold-ups, as well as information centres, restaurants, garages and hotels. Maps can also be obtained from garages showing the *Bison Futé* sign, from tourist offices and from **Autoroutes Information**, *3 rue Edmond Valentin, 75007 Paris; tel: 01 47 05 90 01.* Telephone information about roadworks is available (in French): *tel. 01 48 94 33 33.* Electronic displays placed a couple of kilometres before some motorway exits give the latest news about traffic conditions on the next section.

The routes in this book often use a maze of minor roads and although the driving instructions and route diagrams provide the basic information, and the maps at the end of the book give an overview of the road system, good road maps will be essential (see p. 22).

Parking

Peak-season parking can be a nightmare in larger towns and cities. Usually the easiest option is to head for an underground or covered car park, indicated with a blue 'P' sign. However short-stay parking on the street *(stationnement payant)* is usually less expensive. Parking meters and ticket machines take coins, so equip yourself with plenty of small change. On-street parking is invariably free between 1200 and 1400 and overnight, usually 1800 to 0900. Free parking may be restricted in some areas to one side of the road, every other day so check local signs. The zones are indicated with signs reading *côté du stationnement jours pairs/impairs* (even/odd-numbered dates). Parking is forbidden on roads where the kerb is marked with yellow paint. Cars found illegally parked are clamped or towed away to *fourrières* (pounds) and not released until the driver has paid a hefty fee, as well as the parking fine which may be anything between FFr.20 and FFr.250. Suggested parking places are listed in all key cities.

Fuel

Petrol (gas), or *essence*, is supplied in three basic types: *gazole* (diesel), *essence* (95 octane leaded) and *sans plomb* (95 octane unleaded, from a green pump). *Super* in either leaded or unleaded indicates 98 octane. Minimum filling is 5 litres. Large supermarkets generally sell petrol at considerably lower prices than other stations. Motorway garages *(stations d'essence)* are usually open 24 hours a day and may have other facilities but are usually fairly expensive. Costs may be lower in provincial towns and in the countryside, but stations here can be thin on the ground and tend to shut on Sundays and public holidays.

Driving Vocabulary

Unleaded (lead-free)/Standard/Premium Sans plomb/normal/super *Sahng plong/normall/sewpehr*

Fill the tank please. Le plein s'il vous plaît. *Ler plahng seelvooplay.*

How do I reach the motorway/main road? Pour aller jusqu'à l'autoroute/la route principale? *Poor ahleh zhewskah lowtohroot/lah root prahngsipahl?*

I've had a breakdown at . . . Je suis tombé(e) en panne à . . . *Zher sewee tombay ahng pan ah . . .*

I'm lost. Je suis perdu. *Zher swee pairdoo.*

I am on the road from . . . to . . . Je suis sur la route de . . . à . . . *Zher sewee sewr lah root der . . . ah . . .*

I have a flat tyre. J'ai un pneu crevé. *Zhai ang punerr krervay.*

The windscreen (windshield) has smashed/cracked. Le pare-brise est cassé/fendu. *Ler pahrbreez ay kahseh/fahngdew.*

There is something wrong with the engine/brakes/lights/steering/gearbox/clutch/exhaust. Il y a un problème avec le moteur/les freins/les feux/la direction/la boîte à vitesses/l'embrayage /le pot d'échappement. *Eeleeyah ang problairm ahvek ler mowturr/leh frahng/leh fur/lah deerehk-seeawng/lah bwahtahveetess/lahngbrayyazh/ler poh dehshahpmahng.*

It won't start. La voiture ne démarre pas. *Lah vwahtewr ner dehmahr pah.*

Will it take long to fix? La réparation prendra longtemps? *Lah rehpahrasseeawng prahngdrah lohngtahng?*

Can you help me? There has been an accident. Vous pouvez m'aider? Il y a eu un accident. *Voo poovay mayday? Eelyaew ang akseedahng.*

Please call the police/an ambulance. Appelez la police/une ambulance s'il vous plaît. *Ahperlay lah poleess/ewn ahngbewlahngss seelvooplay.*

GETTING TO THE SOUTH OF FRANCE

The South of France is the most easily accessible region in the country after Paris itself, as it is served by international airports at Nice and Lyon, a network of fast autoroutes and frequent high-speed TGV train services. The many visitors travelling by car from the United Kingdom now have the convenience of using the Channel Tunnel in addition to a choice of ferry routes. On arrival in France, motorists who prefer not to face the 1000 km drive south can travel in comfort all the way to the Mediterranean by putting their car on a Motorail train from Calais or Lille.

BY AIR

The main international airports in the South of France are Lyon, Nice, Marseille and Montpellier. Perpignan also has some flights from the UK. Toulouse is worth considering for access to the western part of the area. Grenoble is served by domestic flights, particularly from Paris. During the ski season, Chambéry is used for charter flights by UK tour operators. All have car-hire facilities.

Useful Airline Addresses in the UK

Air France, *Colet House, 100 Hammersmith Rd, London W6 7JP; tel: 0181-742 6600; fax: 0181-750 4488.*
Bluebird Express, *Vanguard House, 277 London Rd, Burgess Hill FH15 9QU; tel: 01444-235678; fax: 01444 235789.*
British Airways, *156 Regent St, London W1R 5TA; tel: 0181-897 4000; fax: 0161-247 5707; reservations: tel: 0345 222111.*
British Midland, *Donnington Hall, Castle Donnington, Derby DE74 2SB; tel: 0345 554554; fax: 01332 845238.*
EasyJet Airline Company, *London Luton Airport, Bedfordshire LU2 9LS; tel: 0990-292929; fax: 01582 443355.*

International Airports

Chambéry–Aix-les-Bains, *Le Vivier du Lac,* 8km from the town centre; *tel: 04 79 54 49 54.* Facilities include car-hire (advance booking only), shop (open Sat). 35

Served from the United Kingdom by charter flights from Gatwick during the winter season (mainly for skiers).

Aéroport de Grenoble–Saint-Geoirs: 40km from town centre; *tel: 04 76 65 48 48.* Facilities include car-hire, cafe and shop.

Served from the United Kingdom by charter flights from Gatwick during the winter season (mainly for skiers).

Aéroport Lyon-Satolas: 32km east of city centre; *tel: 04 72 22 72 21.* Facilities include car hire, restaurants, bureau de change and tourist information.

A bus service runs every 20 mins (30 mins on Sun) between 0600 and 2300 to and from *Perrache* rail station (via *Part-Dieu* rail station); fare FFr.50. Taxis: about FFr.300 to the city centre.

Served from the United Kingdom by British Airways from Heathrow, Gatwick and Birmingham; and Air France from

Heathrow and regional airports via Paris.

Aéroport Marseille-Provence: at Marignane, 22km north-west of the city centre; *tel: 04 42 89 09 74*. Terminal 1 handles international flights; Terminal 2 domestic. Facilities include car hire, restaurants, shops, bureaux de change and tourist information. There are several airport hotels in the immediate vicinity.

A shuttle bus, *tel: 04 42 89 03 65*, runs between the airport and Gare St-Charles every 20 mins from 0620 to 2250 (last bus out to airport 2150), taking 25 mins (FFr.42). Taxis to the centre cost about FFr.240 (FFr.300 on Sun and at night).

Direct flights to over 80 cities in 34 countries, with over 20 flights a day to Paris. Served from the United Kingdom by British Airways from Gatwick and Heathrow; also from Cork in the Irish Republic.

Aéroport Montpellier Mediterranée: 8km east of town centre; *tel: 04 67 20 85 00*. Facilities include car-hire, hotel reservations, hotel (*tel: 04 67 20 07 08*), restaurants, nursery, local products shop ('*Pais d'Oc*') and bureau de change (open for international flights).

A shuttle bus to the town centre and bus station runs every 30–50 mins (depending on time and day); information *tel: 04 67 20 85 00*; journey time 15 mins; fare FFr.25.

Served from the United Kingdom by British Airways, out of Gatwick.

Nice Côte d'Azur: 7km from the city centre; *tel: 04 93 21 30 12*. Terminal One handles international, Air Littoral and TAT flights. Terminal Two handles other domestic flights. Facilities include car-hire, bureau de change, meeting rooms, restaurants and tourist information.

The no. 23 bus runs along the *promenade des Anglais* to the SNCF railway station every half-hour; the 20-min journey costs FFr.8. There is also an airport coach to *pl. Masséna* (FFr.24), as well as coach services to Antibes, Beaulieu, Cannes, Cap d'Agde, Cap Martin, Cros-de-Cagnes, Eze-sur-Mer, Golfe-Juan, Juan-les-Pins, Menton, Monte Carlo, Roquebrune and Villefranche. Taxis to the centre cost about FFr.200.

Héli Inter, *tel: 04 93 21 46 46* offers helicopter transits every 20 mins to **Monte Carlo** (15 mins) and seven flights a day during summer to **St Tropez**.

From the United Kingdom, British Airways has flights from Heathrow, Gatwick, Birmingham, Edinburgh, Glasgow and Manchester; also from Cork in the Irish Republic. Air France has flights via Paris from Heathrow and regional aiports. British Midlands has flights from Heathrow. Bluebird Express has low-cost charter and scheduled flights from Gatwick, Birmingham and Manchester. EasyJet has low-cost flights from Luton.

Aéroport Perpignan-Rivesaltes: *av. Maurice Bellonte,* 7km north-east of town centre; *tel: 04 68 52 60 70*. Facilities include car-hire, restaurant, shop.

Shuttle bus to SNCF station connects with flights; 15-min journey; fare FFr.27.

Served from the United Kingdom by British Airways, out of Gatwick.

Toulouse-Blagnac: 10km from city centre; *tel: 04 61 42 44 00*. Facilities include car-hire, restaurants, shops and bureau de change.

Bus to the centre every 20-mins (40-mins at weekends); FFr.25.

Served from the United Kingdom by British Airways from Gatwick and Air France from Heathrow.

By Ferry

From the south-east of England, the many links between Kent and the French ports of Boulogne, Calais and Dunkerque offer fast, frequent crossings, with excellent links straight onto the motorway network to the South of France. There are also increasingly frequent services through the Channel Tunnel, where the exit from the Calais terminal leads directly onto the motorway.

If you are starting from the north or west of the UK, however, it is probably worth considering one of the longer western crossings to Dieppe, Le Havre or Caen, which are little more expensive and do cut out quite a bit of driving. As these leave from Portsmouth and Poole, many drivers will be able to avoid going anywhere near London. Ferry operators are:

Dover–Calais

Hoverspeed, *Western Docks, Dover CT17 9TG; tel: 01304-240 241, fax: 01304-240 088*. Nine sailings each way daily by catamaran; 35 mins.

P&O-Stena Line, *Channel House, Channel View Rd, Dover CT17 9TJ; tel: 0990-980 980, fax: 01304-223 464*. Up to 50 crossings daily in each direction; 1 hr 15 mins.

Sea France, *106 East Camber Building, Eastern Docks, Dover CT 16 1JA; tel: 01304-212 696; fax: 01304-212 726*. 15 sailings daily each way; 1 hr 30 mins.

Folkestone–Boulogne

Hoverspeed *(as above)*. Five crossings daily in each direction by Sea Cat; 55 mins.

Newhaven–Dieppe

P&O-Stena Line *(as above)*. 2 ferries (4 hrs) and 2 fast craft (2 hrs) sailings daily each way.

Portsmouth–Caen

Brittany Ferries, *The Brittany Centre, Wharf Rd, Portsmouth PO2 8RU; tel: 0990-360 360*. Three sailings daily each way; 2 on Wed; 6 hrs.

Portsmouth–Le Havre

P&O *(as above)*. Three crossings daily each way; 5 hrs 30 mins.

Ramsgate–Dunkirk

Sally Line, *York St, Ramsgate, Kent CT11 9DS; tel: 0990-595 522; fax: 01843-589 329*. Five crossings daily each way; 2 hrs 30 mins.

By Le Shuttle

The vehicle-carrier known as Le Shuttle operates between the two terminals at Cheriton (near Folkestone) and Coquelles (near Calais), both situated on their respective countries' motorway networks. Using the world's largest passenger-carrying rail vehicles (each train can carry 180 cars in carriages 5.6m high), Le Shuttle runs 24 hrs a day, 365 days a year, with up to four departures every hour taking 35 mins from platform to platform. Motorists simply drive onto the train at one terminal and off at the other, staying with their vehicles in the air-conditioned carriages throughout. The carriages have toilet facilities but no refreshments. With border formalities all completed at the boarding terminal, motorists can drive straight off the train and onto the motorway on completion of the crossing. The aim is to offer a service with a total journey time, inclusive of waiting, loading and unloading, of no more than 1 hr. Travellers must curently book in advance ('turn up and go' service suspended at time of going to press).

Both terminals have restaurants and duty-free shops. A special package known as Le Swap, which includes return Le Shuttle tickets, allows motorists to hire a right-hand drive car from Hertz in the UK

The Channel Tunnel

The tunnel has been a long time coming. Napoleon approved plans for a tunnel in 1802, and the British began digging one in 1880 only to abandon work for fear of a military invasion. The idea was revived after World War II, but it was not until July 1987 that work began on Europe's most ambitious construction project of the century: a 50 km tunnel, one of the longest undersea tunnels in the world, between France and Britain. On 6 May 1994, the tunnel was officially opened, a ceremony that marked the linking of Britain to Continental Europe for the first time since the Ice Age.

The undersea link is not, in fact, one tunnel but three – two for rail tracks and one service tunnel for maintenance work – side by side 25–45 km below the sea bed.

(or take their own), swap the car on arrival in Calais for a left-hand drive model without any further paperwork, and swap it back on the return journey.

For Le Shuttle details and reservations *tel: 0990 353535.*

By Rail

France is known for its **TGV**s *(Trains à Grande Vitesse)* which purr across the countryside like supersonic snakes, at 300 kph. At the vanguard of the new generation is the **Eurostar**, which connects London with Paris and Brussels via the Channel Tunnel. Its journey times of little over 3hrs are due to fall even further when the British and Belgian segments of the high-speed link are eventually completed around the turn of the century.

Two classes of accommodation are provided aboard the quarter-mile-long trains. First class passengers are served a meal at their seats, while two buffet-bars and a refreshment trolley are available to all.

Eurostar trains leave from London Waterloo International. Most stop at Ashford, Kent, and, after 2 hours, at Lille-Europe, where a custom-built terminus connects with SNCF's TGV trains to many destinations, including Lyon, Avignon, Marseille, Montpellier and Nice. Remember to date-stamp all French rail tickets in the small orange machines at the entrance to the platforms before travelling or your ticket will not be valid.

Meantime, as the international network expands and the number of services each day rises rapidly, prices are falling in a cut-throat war of attrition between ferry and rail operators. Reservations are essential on both Eurostar and TGV services anyway, and you can make even greater savings by booking at least 2 weeks ahead. **Eurostar** information: *tel: 0345 303030;* reservations, *tel: 0345 881881.* Eurostar and **SNCF** services: French Railways' **Rail Shop**, *179 Piccadilly, London W1V OBA; tel: 0990 300003.* In France, most railway information is now on a single nationwide number; *tel: 08 36 35 35 35* (premium rate: FFr.2.23 per min.)

By Road

New roads are providing fast links between the Channel Tunnel and Paris but sadly, there are still few sensible ways to bypass the city completely and both the outer and inner ring roads around the capital are always very busy.

From Paris, the A6 (*Autoroute du Soleil*), via Lyon and the Rhône Valley, is the main route south, but it is to be avoided at all costs just before and after public holidays and around Assumption Day (15 August) when Parisians take to it in vast numbers, turning it into the most dangerous road in France.

A slightly longer alternative is to take

MOTORAIL

39

the A5 from south-east Paris which links with the A6 south of Dijon and after Lyon becomes the A7. This runs due south down the east bank of the Rhone in parallel with the often quieter N86 on the other side. Just north of Avignon, the A7 turns eastwards for Marseille or Nice and the Italian border while the A9 runs west to Montpellier and the Spanish border.

As a third option, leave Paris on the A10 followed by the A71, and from Clermont-Ferrand, take the A75 (the *Autoroute Meridionnelle)* to Montpellier. This has the major advantage of being the only toll-free motorway in France (in an attempt to attract tourism into the under-developed regions of the Auvergne and Cevennes), although a few southern stretches are not yet at motorway standard. A leaflet distributed at motorway offices lists the most congested days and routes. The government's *Bison Futé* – 'cunning bison' – scheme (see p. 32) is designed to divert tourist traffic from the roads most prone to congestion onto speedier through-routes.

Distances from Calais by fast road are Clermont-Ferrand 713km, Lyon 765km, Grenoble 873km, Marseille 1077km, Montpellier 1082km, Perpignan 1150km and Nice 1234km. As most motorways are toll-roads, expect to pay the following: Calais–Nice (avoiding Paris) – about FFr.400 in a car, FFr.550 with a caravan and FFr.250 on a motorcyle; Calais–Marseille – the charges are respectively about FFr.350 for a car, FFr.450 for car and caravan and FFr.200 for a motorbike.

By Motorail

If you want to travel south across France with your own car, the fastest and least stressful way of dong so is on one of SNCF's overnight Motorail services from Calais. The terminal, which has a small restaurant and sells take-aways, is down a short road opposite the town hall; 15 mins drive from the Channel Tunnel or 10 mins from the ferries.

You have to book sleeping accommodation, either couchettes (6 bunks per compartment or 4 in 1st-class) or a sleeping compartment with wash-basin (3 bunks or 1 or 2 in 1st-class). It is very comforting to look out of the window and see your car trundling along at the rear on one of the vehicle-carrying wagons, knowing that you have avoided wear and tear on the car itself, driver and passengers, and saved the cost of petrol, motorway tolls and stops for sleep or meals on the way.

You should get a reasonable night's sleep (many carriages are air-conditioned) and can usually buy refreshments, though most people find it more fun to take a picnic. Continental breakfast is served at the end of the journey either on the train or while your car is being unloaded.

Services run from Calais to various destinations, such as Nice for the eastern part of the area, Avignon for the centre and Narbonne for the west. Calais–Nice (about 14 hrs 30 mins) operates daily July–Aug and usually three times per week Sept–June. Calais–Avignon (12 hrs 30 mins) and Calais–Narbonne (14 hrs) operate at least weekly Apr–Sept with up to 5 per week July–Aug. Other Motorail services run from Paris and Lille daily throughout the year for Avignon (7 hrs 30 mins), Marseille (8hrs 30mins), Toulon (10hrs), Fréjus (11hrs) and Nice (12hrs) and daily June–Sept (less frequently Oct–May) to Narbonne (10 hours). Also Lille–Avignon, weekly Mar–May and up to four per week June–Sept.

Bookable through **French Railways**, *179 Piccadilly, London W1V OBA; tel: 0171-203 7000.*

BACKGROUND

Embracing nearly a quarter of the largest country in western Europe, the South of France is a huge area of enormous variety. The only guarantee is that each new day will bring a new experience, from rolling pastures to forests thick with legends or plunging gorges twisting through cliffs of sheer rock. The flashy resorts of the Riviera stand alongside the ancient cities of the Rhône Valley, or the hill-top villages of medieval Provence, while even the food ranges from sturdy pots of vegetable stew in the mountains of the Auvergne, to summery basil and tomatoes in Provence. Generations of artists, writers and celebrities have been drawn to a region which many feel encapsulates all that is best about France.

THE LAND

It is not easy to define the South of France. Even its boundaries are fluid, defined as much by individual perception as by political fiat. It covers a hugely diverse area, with as many different types of landscape, vegetation, and geology as you might expect to find in an entire country.

At its westernmost extension, the region embraces parts of that vast chunk of mountains, rivers, plateaux and lakes known as the **Massif Central**. This is geologically one of the oldest parts of France and its traditions, too, are deeply rooted in the past. The volcanic **Auvergne**, its landscape pocked by ancient craters, lava flows and thermal springs, is one of the least developed regions in France. Still predominantly rural (apart from cities such as Clermont-Ferrand and Le Puy), much of it lies above 1000m and many villages are still often isolated and snowbound in winter. In summer, the extensive pasturelands are grazed by cattle and sheep. To the south, the **Cévennes** form the southern border of the Massif in a wild, untamed part of the country, where windswept limestone plateaux are bisected by magnificent, rocky gorges.

Delineating the eastern boundaries of the Massif, the **Rhône Valley** cuts a swathe down from the great industrial and gastronomic metropolis of Lyon. On the flanks of the Rhône-Alpes region are the two *départements* of the Ardèche and the Loire, both harbouring scenic gorges carved out by the rivers after which they are named. On the Rhône's eastern banks the *départements* of the Drôme and Isère lead up to the invigorating Alpine foothills, with the thriving city of Grenoble straddling the Isère and Drac rivers.

The Rhône Valley has been one of France's great thoroughfares since Roman times. Although today the *Autoroute du Soleil* and the TGV railway line snake down alongside the powerful river, barges still ply its waters, carrying cargo for the industries which have mushroomed along the valley. Further south, the river curls through and around the great cities to which it has given birth – Valence, Montélimar, Orange, Avignon and Arles – before disgorging into the massive delta of the Camargue.

To the south-west of the Rhône Valley lies **Languedoc**, now covering a mere fraction of the territory where the *langue d'oc*, the ancient tongue of Occitan, was once spoken. What used to be the heartland of Occitan is now known as the Bas Languedoc, which stretches from Nîmes to Carcassonne and features long tracts of empty sand on the coast backed by dry, stony hills in the hinterland. Leading south toward the Pyrenees, **Roussillon** also has its own particular identity, defined more by its proximity to Catalunya over the border in Spain than by association with France. Around the lively capital of Perpignan the broad plains feature innumerable vineyards, whilst further south still is the Côte Vermeille ('Vermillion Coast') where the red clay and crystalline rocks mark the transition into the Pyrenees.

Leaving the marshy Camargue, the *département* of the **Bouches-du-Rhône** sweeps east to join the Var and north towards the Durance. Although mostly low-lying, it encompasses the highest cliffs in France at Cap Canaille as well as the magnificent, fjord-like inlets of the Calanques. The oldest city in Provence, Marseille, shelters beneath the peaks of the Chaîne de l'Etoile, on the other side of which lies Aix, dominated by the limestone ridges of the Massif de St Baume.

To the north of the broad sweep of the Durance, the **Vaucluse** is one of the smallest *départements* in France and yet boasts a wide variety of attractions, including Roman antiquities, well-preserved *villages perchés* (hilltop villages), the dramatic spring of Fontaine-de-Vaucluse, the heights of the Lubéron chain, and the red ochre cliffs of Roussillon. At its northernmost limit rises mighty Mont Ventoux, the highest peak between the Alps and the Pyrenees and the traditional boundary marker of Provence.

To the east of Mont Ventoux are the Montagnes de Lure and the *département* of the **Alpes de Haute-Provence**, a land of windswept passes, deep ravines, foaming torrents and captivating Alpine landscapes. The most sparsely populated region in Provence, it also includes major towns such as Barcelonnette, Digne and Sisteron. There are over 140 mountain lakes (including the lovely Lac d'Allos), vast fields of fragrant lavender (principally on the Plateau de Valensole) and, of course, the great natural wonder of the Grand Cañon de Verdon.

To the south of the Grand Cañon, the **Haut Var**, a remote region renowned for truffles, honey and olives, rolls down towards Draguignan. Covering around 6000 sq km, the **Var** features numerous historic sights as well as a wonderful coastline, over 400 km long and peppered with tranquil bays and charming resorts. The Massif de l'Esterel and the Massif des Maures are both still outstandingly beautiful areas despite the forest fires which have ravaged their slopes, and are easily accessible from the coast.

The more easterly resorts in the Var (such as St Tropez) mark the beginnings of the **Riviera**, which continues on through historic resorts such as Cannes and Nice to the tiny principality of Monaco. This is the most well-known and glitziest corner of the South of France – and the most overcrowded, particularly at the height of the summer season. Thankfully, it is easy to escape into the hinterland and the cooler climes of the **Alpes-Maritimes**, where twisting mountain roads lead up to spectacular *villages perchés*. On the higher ground, the Parc National du Mercantour encompasses a vast wilderness area, home to ibex and chamois, and the setting for the prehistoric marvels of the Vallée des Merveilles.

History

The earliest traces of human habitation in the South of France, dating from the Cro-Magnon period 40,000 years ago, come from the mouth of the Vallée de Paillon in Nice. Paleolithic remains have also been found in Menton, and spectacular cave paintings, thought to date back around 20,000 years, have recently been discovered in the Cosquer caves near Marseille.

During the succeeding centuries nomadic peoples, including the Celts from the north and the Ligurians from the east, roamed the region. The early Ligurians left behind dolmens (huge standing stones), and elaborate rock carvings in the Vallée des Merveilles. Within the last millenium BC, both groups, their identities by now confused and intermingled, established small fortified villages (known as *oppidi*), and started trading with seafaring peoples such as the Phocaeans and Etruscans.

The Classical Years

In the 6th century BC, the Greeks arrived and established their first trading colonies – notably Massalia (Marseille), with outposts at Hyères, Nice, Antibes and elsewhere along the coast, as well as inland towns such as Arles. They introduced the cultivation of vines, olives, figs, cherries and walnuts and thrived for the next 500 years.

After the Roman Empire expanded into Spain following the Second Punic War, the conquest of Gaul was the next logical step. In 125BC the Roman legions helped the Greeks defend Marseille from a Celtic raid, and from then on their progress was unstoppable. They founded their first major settlement around the springs of *Aquae Sextiae* (now Aix-en-Provence), and then the capital at Narbonne; the new province became known as *Gallia Narbonensis*. In the Auvergne, Julius Caesar had to contend with a troublesome local chief, Vercingétorix, before he was able to establish the new capital of Augustonementum (now Clermont-Ferrand).

Within a hundred years the Romans had created a thriving, prosperous province. Pockets of resistance remained, but the last of the Alpine tribes were finally subjugated in 14BC, an event marked by the creation of the *Trophée des Alpes* at La Turbie. The Rhône became an important trading route once Caesar had completed the conquest of the rest of Gaul, and significant towns, complete with amphitheatres, baths, temples and aquaducts, were built in Arles and Nîmes. Glanum (St Rémy-de-Provence), Fréjus, Riez, Carpentras and Vaison-la-Romaine were also important colonies.

Christianity is thought to have arrived first in about 40AD when, according to legend, the boat bearing Lazarus and the four Marys landed on the shores of the Camargue (see p. 89). By the late 3rd century St Trophimus had become bishop of Arles and in 314AD, Emperor Constantine boosted Christian influence by sponsoring the first Christian council in the city. By the end of the 4th century, evangelists were establishing the church throughout the Auvergne, just ahead of the barbarian invasions.

The Dark Ages

As the Roman empire declined in the 5th century, the province was left vulnerable and subject to numerous raids. The following centuries saw control of the region pass between a succession of invaders such as the Visigoths, Ostrogoths, Islamic Saracens (Arabs), Franks, and Normans.

The Saracens were finally expelled from Provence by Guillaume le Libérateur (William the Liberator) in 1032 and the region began to emerge from the Dark

Ages as monasteries were established, trade routes opened up once more, and new cities (such as Montpellier) were founded. The feudal system remained intact, with local *seigneurs* (lords) controlling their own fiefdoms and the growing cities becoming increasingly independent. In 1125AD overall control of Occitania (as most of southern France was then called) was divided between the Counts of Barcelona (who held sway over most of the territory south of the Durance) and the Counts of Toulouse. Meanwhile, in 927AD, control of the Auvergne passed from the Duchy of Aquitaine (formed in 614AD) to the Counts of Poitiers but the pattern was similar to that elsewhere in the south, with robber barons constantly feuding for territory.

Popes and Heretics

During the 11th and 12th centuries, with the church wielding the real power over peasant and monarch alike, numerous religious sects flourished unhindered. In the end however, the success of just one of these sects was to cause the downfall of Occitania and lead to its eventual loss of sovereignty to France. The Cathars (or Albigensians) of Languedoc believed in the Manichean doctrine of the duality of Good and Evil and advocated leading a virtuous, simple life; their faith attracted converts amongst town folk, peasants and nobility alike, but it was too popular for the Papacy's liking.

Rome forged an alliance with the French crown to put down this heresy and in 1209 a crusade under Simon de Montfort pillaged the south, sacking Béziers, Carcassone and numerous other towns. Count Raymond of Toulouse and his allies were finally defeated at the Battle of Muret in 1213, and the inevitable annexation of the south by France had begun. Count Raymond Bérenger of Barcelona managed to form an alliance with the French crown, marrying his daughter Beatrice to Charles of Anjou, and upon his death Charles became the Count of Provence, ushering in nearly 200 years of Angevin rule.

As part of the pay-off to Rome for its support in the Albigensian crusade, France handed over territories north of Avignon (known as the Comtat Venaissin) to the papacy in 1247. In 1309 this became a convenient bolt-hole for French Pope Clement V, who was fleeing war-torn Italy. His arrival heralded more than a century of papal rule from Provence. Clement V's successor, Pope John XXII, moved the papal seat from Carpentras to Avignon, which he purchased in 1348. The papal court became a prosperous centre for the arts and learning, and its influence spread widely in the region.

The 14th century saw South sufferering from the Black Death (1348) and political feuding under the rule of Queen Jeanne (1343–82). The papacy returned to Rome in 1377, and stability returned under Good King René, under whose patronage Aix became a flourishing centre for arts and culture. Following René's death in 1434, Provence was annexed by the French crown, and gradually lost its independent powers. A similar fate befell the Auvergne, which was subject to repeated raids (notably in 1465, 1471, and 1476) by the French military.

In the 16th century, Protestantism gained a strong foothold in the region, not only as a protest against the Catholic church but also as a sign of rebellion against French control. Fifty years of bloodshed and massacre followed, with the end result being an even greater weakening of regional autonomy in the 1630s. This process was further hastened under the powerful Cardinal Richelieu, who ordered the destruction of fortresses throughout the Auvergne and Provence. Religious dissent lingered on in the Auvergne during the beginning of the 18th century, when the revolt of the Camisards led to further massacres.

Revolution

Coastal ports (particularly Marseille) prospered thanks to their trading links with the Near East from the 18th century onwards, although this also led to a devastating outbreak of the plague in 1720, during which over 100,000 died (50,000 in Marseille alone). Ship-building flourished in Toulon, La Ciotat and Marseille, and grand *hôtels particuliers* (private mansions) were built in Avignon, Aix and elsewhere. But economic hardship prevailed in the countryside, and peasants pillaged the châteaux and monasteries at the outbreak of the Revolution in 1789. In the Auvergne, by contrast, the Revolution met with a lukewarm response. The royalists (with the help of an English fleet) took Toulon in 1793, but they were swiftly defeated thanks to the brilliant campaign of a junior officer, Napoleon Bonaparte, who first made his name here.

Tourists and Trade

During the 19th century, the South began to change rapidly. Only 16 years after Napoleon landed at Golfe-Juan from Elba and marched north on Paris, the first tourists were beginning to arrive on the coast; the opening of the railway line along the coast in the 1860s, linking coastal resorts with Italy, Marseille and Paris, marked the real beginnings of the winter season. Grand hotels, casinos and exotic gardens were built to pander to the needs of visiting nobility and royalty, while artists and writers flocked south, drawn by the luminous landscapes and Mediterranean climate.

In the Auvergne the railways also had a dramatic impact, but of a different sort: many Auvergnats left the area, mostly to seek work in Paris. But the period also saw the foundation of one of France's great industrial empires when two brothers, Édouard and André Michelin, began the manufacture of rubber tyres in their Clermont-Ferrand factories to exploit the advent of the motor car.

The opening of the Suez Canal in 1869 led to Marseille becoming France's premier port, but the development of light industries led to the decline of many traditional rural activities. The migration from rural villages to the cities began, a demographic trend which was accelerated over the following decades, creating an ever-widening gap between the prosperous coastal areas and the impoverished rural hinterland. World War I further depleted the manpower of rural villages.

After the war, tourism once again boomed; the season switched from winter to summer after Coco Chanel made suntans fashionable in the 1920s, and a whole new wave of artists and writers descended on the by-now-glamorous Côte d'Azur. World War II put a stop the party, and the South found itself under the Vichy government in 1940. After the start of the Allied counter-offensive in 1942 the Germans occupied the region, forcing the scuttling of the French fleet in Toulon harbour to prevent it falling into their hands. The Resistance became active in harassing the Germans in the Massif Central and Provence, preparing the way for the Allied invasion in August 1944 and the subsequent liberation of the South.

The Last Fifty Years

The South took more than a decade to

recover from the damage to its infrastructure caused by the war: Nice opened its airport in 1946, but the first tourists only returned in 1948 once the beaches had been cleared of German mines. The 1960s saw massive immigration from North Africa (particularly to Marseille), the development of heavy petro-chemical industries in the Étang-de-Berre and at Fos, and the building of hydroelectric schemes and the Canal de Provence to boost the agricultural economy. By 1970 the *Autoroute du Soleil* was completed, and France's first technology park, at Sophia-Antipolis (near Antibes) had opened.

During the 1970s mass tourism transformed whole sections of the coastline, with concrete monstrosities disfiguring the Mediterranean landscapes; the first purpose-built ski resort, Isola 2000, was also opened. In 1981, the TGV link to Paris was completed. Today, the region receives around 24 million annual visitors, with eight million of those visiting the Côte d'Azur alone. In the Massif Central and the Auvergne, tourism has not had such a dramatic impact, but it is now on the increase as more and more visitors (particularly the French themselves) enjoy the benefits of *tourisme verte* – 'green tourism' – in the region's wide open spaces.

The Year in Provence

Given the huge area and the different environments it covers, it is not surprising to discover that the South of France is a region of climactic extremes, from the blistering heat of the coast at the height of summer to the snow-bound mountain valleys in the depths of winter. Overall, of course, it has a temperate Mediterranean climate but this is subject to considerable local variation and the ever-present threat of the Mistral (see p. 314) whooshing down the Rhône Valley and bringing misery in its wake.

Throughout the year, the region has an enviable line-up of festivals, many of them deeply rooted in tradition and revolving around the natural calendar of tending and harvesting the produce upon which many people still depend for their livelihood. There is also a vast range of cultural, artistic and music festivals ranging from the big international arts festivals (such as those in Avignon and Orange) to more specialist events devoted to film, jazz, dance, books, and much more besides.

Spring is one of the most pleasant times to visit, with wild flowers carpeting the hillsides and the first *primeurs* (early fruit and vegetables) finding their way to the markets. The weather is warm enough to eat outside (if not to swim), and most resorts are delightfully uncrowded.

From June onwards temperatures begin to rise, rarely dropping below 20°C until the end of summer on the coast; mountain areas also start to open up for outdoor activities such as walking, and the sea becomes tolerable for swimming.

July and August are the peak season, with temperatures often soaring during heatwaves and tempers becoming increasingly frayed as *tout le monde* descends for their holidays. Drought-stricken forests in the far south may be closed off during this time because of the risk of fire.

Many towns and villages hold a summer festival, often in honour of a saint's day, and sometimes coinciding with the arrival of a touring fun fair. The older generation may attend a church service during the day, but for the young people it is a chance to meet people of their own age from neighbouring villages and let their hair down. Some of the more popular saints' days (falling between mid June and early September) are those of St Eloi, St John, and St Roch, and usually these will feature a procession (often with the menfolk riding horses and the women and children in horse-drawn carts), with villagers dressed in traditional costume. In larger towns, the parade may take the form of a medieval pageant. Add to these the national events such as the Feux de St Jean on Midsummer's Eve, and Bastille Day fireworks on July 14th.

Autumn is the time of the harvest; most visitors go home by mid September (when the school term starts) and continuing good weather is an added bonus. As opening hours shorten and lunches get longer, a whole new round of local festivals starts. Almost every area has a celebration at the end of the *vendange* (the grape harvest). In certain places there will also be festivals of lavender, rice, lemons, apples, olives, chestnuts or mushrooms and all the other bounteous products of this generous land.

The first snow starts to settle on the peaks of the Alps and the Auvergne during October, but coastal resorts may still experience mild, sunny days. November is traditionally the month with the highest rainfall, often causing flooding, and many tourist attractions, hotels and restaurants will start to close down for the winter season. By December the skiing season is in full swing, lasting through to March/April.

Whatever your tastes and whenever you travel, there is bound to be something of interest taking place somewhere in the region: Provence alone boasts an annual programme of around 500 festivals embracing over 4000 separate performances or events. *Bonne fête!*

Food and Drink

Food in the South of France covers a vast array of different types of regional cuisine, ranging from the hefty peasant dishes of the Auvergne to the sumptuous seafoods found in coastal resorts. Throughout most of the region the Mediterranean influence prevails, with liberal use of olive oil, garlic, herbs (principally thyme, rosemary and basil) and tomatoes. These are the classic ingredients of dishes often described as *à la Provençale* and of the well-known *ratatouille*, which combines the above with courgettes, onions, aubergines and peppers to provide a filling vegetable stew. Plump, flavourful tomatoes appear in many guises - sliced with onions and dressed lightly with olive oil and basil in an appetising *salade de tomates,* or as *tomates farcies*, stuffed with rice, breadcrumbs, garlic and parsley before being baked in the oven. Cut into chunks and accompanied by lettuce, olives, beans, hard-boiled eggs and anchovies they are an essential ingredient in *salade niçoise*, which appears in many guises throughout the region.

The most prevalent local meat is lamb, with one of the best varieties being the tender *agneau de Sisteron*, raised on mountain pastures. Beef often features as a *daube*, where it is slowly braised with red wine, black olives, herbs and vegetables; in the Camargue the local variation is *boeuf à la gardianne*. Rabbit and hare are also simmered in wine and herbs in a similar fashion in inland areas.

Along the coast, seafood menus proliferate, although prices can often seem astronomic for tempting items such as a platter of *fruits de mer* (literally, fruits of the sea) which usually includes mussels, scallops, *gambas* (giant prawns), *oursins* (sea urchins) and *langouste* (crayfish). *Loup de mer* (sea bass) is often grilled with fennel, and then flamed with *pastis* before being served. Grilled fresh sardines, *merlan* (hake), and *rouget* (red mullet) are also perennial favourites. Up in the hills the trout (*truite*) may well have been hauled out of a mountain stream a very short while before making its appearance on your table. The region is also noted for its fish stews such as the famous *bouillabaisse* of Marseille, a less pricey version of which is the excellent *bourride*, made with white fish and accompanied by *aïoli*.

A classic of the region is *aïoli*, a thick mayonnaise made with lashings of garlic and olive oil which is known as 'the butter of Provence'. It can be served alongside raw vegetables *(crudités)* as an hors d'oeuvre, or as a main course in *aïoli garni*, when it is accompanied by salt cod, vegetables, hard-boiled eggs or snails.

In Languedoc-Roussillon you will also find variations on the Provençal classics, with the addition of hearty stews such as the popular *cassoulet*, made from beans, pork, and sausage. In the countryside traditional local ingredients such as *cèpes* (wild mushrooms) are used in dishes with rabbit, duck, game or pigeon. Raised in coastal lagoons, mussels and oysters are found in seaside restaurants, and a speciality of Nîmes well worth trying is the strongly-flavoured *brandade*, a cod purée with garlic. *Escargots* (snails) are widely available, as are the piquant *anchoïade*, a paste of anchovies, oil, garlic and basil, and *tapenade*, a similar paste of olives, both of which are served as an apéritif spread on toast.

All this changes in the mountains of the Massif Central and the Auvergne. The most well-known specialities of the region, since exported worldwide, are *coq-au-vin*, a chicken casserole which is at its best when made with the light red wines of Auvergne, and Vichysoisse, a creamy leek and potato soup, served either chilled or hot. Local *charcuterie* (home-cured hams, pâtés, saucisson and the like) is also excellent, with wild boar another regional speciality worth trying. The real cuisine of the mountains is found in the sort of copious, hearty dishes intended to fortify the farmer who has worked a hard day outdoors in all weathers. Dishes include the hefty *potée Auvergnate*, based on salt pork and home-made *saucisson* cooked as a stew with thick cut vegetables; *pounti*, a heavy meat and prune loaf; cabbage soup (more appetising than the name suggests, it may also contain chicken, pork, or veal); heaps of the soft green lentils of Le Puy, traditionally served with salted ham; *truffade* and *aligot*, both of which involve a great deal of potato and cheese. Cheese is the real local delicacy, with famous names including *St Nectaire* and *Fourme d'Ambert*.

The gastronomic delights of Lyon almost require a separate chapter of their own, given that the joys of the table occupy such a prominent place in the city's reputation and that it has the largest number of famous chefs and starred restaurants outside Paris. Here, the cuisine of the north (based on butter) meets the olive-oil inspired dishes of the south, accompanied by famous wines from the Côtes du Rhône, Beaujolais, Burgundy, and Mâcon.

Amongst the many Lyonnais specialities are classic recipes such as *quenelles au brochet et aux morilles* (dumplings flavoured with pike and morel mushrooms), *sole au vin blanc* (sole in white wine), shallot-flavoured vinaigrettes, crispy macaroni cheese, and full-flavoured *saucisson*.

In the Mediterranean climate a vast range of fruit flourishes, from mouth-watering melons to strawberries, figs, peaches, apricots, nectarines, cherries, and of course table grapes. In any market you will also find a fantastic selection of cheeses, particularly local goat's cheese, which comes in many variations from mild (creamy and fresh) to stronger-tasting and herb-flavoured versions. Desserts (always served after the cheese) include a tempting array of fruit tarts, pastries and flans; one of the lightest is the tangy *tarte au citron*, a flan filled with creamy lemon custard. The ice-creams and sorbets may be less traditional but are, without doubt, some of the finest in the world.

If you're putting together a picnic the large, colourful markets are the best place to start; held daily in cities and once or twice weekly in smaller towns and villages, they usually finish around noon. The *boulangeries* (bakeries), essential for bread, are also good for home-made pizzas (including the local version, *pissaladière*, made with anchovies, onion pureé and olives) while *traiteurs* (delicatessens) and *charcuteries* also stock a range of pre-prepared foods. Mobile vans also sell a range of snacks such as the hugely-filling *pan bagnat* (a crusty roll stuffed with tuna, salad, and olives), *croque-monsieurs* (toasted ham and cheese sandwiches) *crêpes (pancakes)*, *frites (chips)*, and pizza slices.

No other region in the country can compare to the South of France in terms of the enormous variety of different types of wine produced. From the robust reds of the Côtes-du-Rhône to the aromatic whites of Cassis, the sweet muscats of Beaumes-de-Venise or the dry rosés of Bandol, the range encompasses wines to suit all occasions.

The most well-known label is that of the Côtes-du-Rhône, which embraces those vineyards which flank the river all the way from Lyon down to Avignon. The best known wines are the reds from Châteauneuf-du-Pape but there are many others, such as the excellent rosés from Tavel and Lirac, full-bodied reds from Gigondas, and sweet Muscat wines from Beaumes-de-Venise. West of the Rhône, the Auvergne is known for its light red wines, such as Châteaugay and St Pourçain, and the vast vineyards of the Languedoc-Roussillon, until recently renowned for low-grade plonk, have now made great improvements in quality (two of the best known labels are Minervois and Corbières).

To the east of the Rhône lie the vineyards of the Côtes de Ventoux, Côtes du Lubéron, Côteaux d'Aix-en-Provence and the Côteaux Varois, all of which produce perfectly acceptable table wines. Along the coast, the vineyards around the port of Cassis are renowned for their production of light, dry whites, whilst the Bandol area excels in soft, dark reds. Further east, the enormous area covered by the Côtes-de-Provence label ranks sixth by volume production in the country, with the majority of the 100 million bottles sold annually being their trademark dry, fruit rosés.

Apart from wines, all the usual beverages (spirits, beers, soft drinks, mineral waters and so on) are available in bars and restaurants. There is one alcoholic liquor which stands out, however, both for the high rate of consumption amongst locals and its effortless association with the warmth and generosity of the Mediterranean climate: this is *pastis*, an aniseed-based spirit which comes under various brand names (including Ricard, Pernod and Pastis 51). The clear spirit turns milky when diluted and served with ice, and once visitors have acquired the taste they may well find themselves also acquiring a large hangover the following morning. Usually over 50 degrees proof, *pastis* packs a potent punch. The same warning, incidentally, applies to some Provençal wines, whose alcoholic content is often far higher than the standard 10 or 12 degrees.

Art and Artists

The earliest known artworks in the South of France are the extraordinary paintings of the Grottes Henri Cosquer and rock engravings in the Vallée des Merveilles (see pp. 256–257). The legacy of the Celto-Ligurian period is numerous items of ironwork and jewellery, many of which can be seen in the region's museums. A few artefacts from Marseille are the only remnants from the Greek period, whereas of course the Romans left behind substantial buildings, as well as mosaics and statues.

From the early Christian period numerous sarcophagi survive, the biggest collection being in the Musée de l'Arles Antique. The Auvergne, at one end of the pilgrim route to Santiago de Compostela (see p.193) has a magnificent collection of Romanesque churches lavishly decorated with carved capitals and frescos dating back to the 11th and 12th centuries.

During the later Middle Ages the region was home to the flourishing Schools of Avignon and Nice. The former owes its origins to the patronage of the papal court at Avignon, developing a distinctive style in the early 15th century, best exemplified by the works of Nicolas Froment and Enguerrand Quarton. During the same period the School of Nice (led by the prolific Ludovic Brea) created dozens of altarpieces for churches in the hinterland.

In the 17th century the region produced one of France's greatest baroque artists, the sculptor and architect Pierre Puget, who was born in Toulon. As a youth he earned his living painting elaborate decorations on warships in the harbour, later turning his talents to altarpieces and then the sculptures for which he is most famous. One of his few surviving buildings is the unusual hospice complex, Notre-Dame-de-la-Charité, in Marseille. Meanwhile, the era's most celebrated painter was Jean-Honoré Fragonard, whose rococo fantasies are awash with flowers and Romantic imagery.

Drawn to the Light

The pivotal role the region was to play in modern art began in the 1880s, when a young Dutch painter decreed that 'the future of modern art lies in the south of France'. This prophetic statement was uttered by none other than Vincent Van Gogh, whose innovative works took on a whole new dimension – suffused with intense colour and light – when he moved to Arles in 1888. Paul Cézanne spent a brief period in Paris (where he met Monet, Renoir, Sisley and other early Impressionists) but he soon retreated to his native Aix, where his work gained a new richness as he captured the surrounding landscapes.

Inspired by Van Gogh and Cézanne, a growing number of avant-garde artists started painting in Provence from the 1890s onwards. Monet visited Antibes, and Auguste Renoir moved permanently to Cagnes. Félix Ziem had already popularised Martigues, and he was followed by Augustus John and the Dadaist Picabia. Paul Signac bought a house in St Tropez which soon became an important focal point for the emerging Fauvist movement, including Matisse, Vlaminck, Raoul Dufy and Kees Von Dongen. Dufy and Georges Braque painted in L'Estaque, where Braque developed what came to be called Cubism.

After World War I, it was the turn of the hill villages rather than the coast, with places such as Mougins and St Paul-de-Vence attracting visiting artists like Pablo Picasso, Fernand Léger, Jean Cocteau and Marc Chagall. This trend continued after World War II, although surrealists such as Max Ernst, André Breton and Jacques Hérold preferred Marseille. Picasso moved permanently to the region from 1945 onwards, first staying in Antibes, then Vallauris and Cannes, before retreating to a remote castle below the Montagne St Victoire and, finally, Mougins, where he died in 1973. Other great artists followed his example, with Max Ernst living in Seillans and Chagall in Vence.

During the 1960s Nice became the focus of new talent in the so-called 'Second School of Nice', with iconoclasts such as César, Arman, Yves Klein and Ben creating unusual multi-media works. The Lubéron was settled by abstract artists such as Nichola de Staël and André Lhote, as well as the Hungarian 'op-artist' Victor Vasarély.

Architecture

From the grandeur of Roman buildings to the futuristic constructions of 20th century architects, the South of France features a wonderful array of different architectural styles spanning the centuries.

From the prehistoric era a few dolmens and menhirs survive, as do some of the ancient, dry-stone huts with corbel roofs known as *bories* – the best-known examples, at Gordes (see p.145), in fact date from a later period.

Remains of the *oppidi* or fortified strongholds of the Celtic period can be seen in places such as la Garde-Freinet in the Massif des Maures.

The brief contact with the Greeks has bequeathed few remains of substance, apart from the harbour walls and jetties in the old port of Marseille. By contrast, the Roman legacy is extraordinarily rich – indeed the number of intact and semi-intact Roman monuments in the region is unmatched anywhere else in Europe outside Italy itself. Arles and Nîmes still have many fine monuments, including temples, theatres and amphitheatres, as well as numerous other artefacts on display in museums. Many other garrison settlements were developed along classic Roman lines, complete with a forum, public baths, temples, and small amphitheatres; settlements such as Orange, Fréjus, Glanum (outside St Rémy-de-Provence) and Vaison-la-Romaine all feature extant Roman architecture. Other notable constructions include the magnificent aquaduct of the Pont du Gard (near Uzès), the Pont Julien (near Apt) and the truncated *Trophée des Alpes* at La Turbie high above the Riviera coast.

During the Dark Ages and Early Christian Era the most significant buildings were churches, with outstanding examples of 5th and 6th century octagonal baptistries still surviving in Aix, Fréjus, Riez and Six-Fours-les-Plages. Most buildings of the early Christian period where razed during the Saracen invasions.

The region's second great wave of building came during the 11th and 12th centuries. This was the great era of Romanesque architecture in churches, inspired by the Roman style but with the addition of more free-flowing and elaborate ornamentation. Elegance, symmetry and simplicity were otherwise the key characteristics, although there are differences between the Romanesque styles of Provence, the Languedoc and the Auvergne. In Provence, churches were often of squat proportions with simple floor plans, minimal decoration, and few windows in the solid masonry. This sombre, austere style is best exemplified in the so-called 'Three Sisters', the Cistercian monasteries of Le Thoronet, Sénanque and Silvacane, all of which display the Romanesque at its most rigorous and unornamented. Further north, the Auvergne developed a distinctive style of narrow, towering buildings with octagonal arcaded towers, the local sombre volcanic rocks often used to create stripes and patterns in the stonework wherever they could not carve or paint the walls.

Moving west towards the Rhône valley and into the Languedoc, church architecture becomes more classically decorative and ornate, resulting in the marvellous façades of churches such as St Gilles du Gard, and St Trophime in Arles. Defence also became an important consideration during the latter half of this troubled period, resulting in the fortified church of Stes-Maries-de-la-Mer and the crenelated monasteries of St Honorat on the Iles des Lérins and St Victor in Marseille, as well as secular forts such as the walled town of Aigues-Mortes (built by Louis IX in the 13th century).

The Romanesque style lingered longer in the south than it did elsewhere in France, and even when architecture finally succumbed to Gothic influences few religious buildings of importance were produced. The Gothic style did, however, gain a major foothold in the papal seat at Avignon during the 14th century, as witnessed by the flamboyant Palais des Papes and many convents and chapels in the city.

The Renaissance largely by-passed the South of France, although its influence is evident in carvings in churches at Fréjus, Bar-sur-Loup and Vence and in the exquisite façade of the Maison des Chevaliers in Viviers. From the Classical period (17th and 18th centuries) there are numerous *châteaux* and palaces (such as those in Barbentane, Aix and Montpellier, to name but a few) with the trademark formal gardens of the era. Graceful squares and boulevards with fountains and statuary were also created in many town centres (for instance Aix, Barjols, and Pernes-les-Fontaines). The forts and defensive walls of Louis XIV's military adviser Maréchal Sébastian Vauban, remain as notable landmarks from this era throughout the region.

The late 18th–mid 19th century was marked by the devastation of many old buildings rather than the creation of new ones, a trend which was only ameliorated by the efforts of the architect Viollet-le-Duc, who restored the archbishop's palace in Narbonne and the walls of Avignon

The builder-emperor Napoleon III and his henchman Baron Haussman redeveloped huge swathes of Marseille in the 1860s. Their efforts became the forerunner of a frenzy of building all along the coast in the opulent Belle Epoque style, which borrowed freely from Moorish and other exotic influences. Many of these extravagant follies were later sadly demolished, although a handful survive in key resorts such as Nice, Cannes, Menton and Monaco and inland spas such as Vichy.

Post-war reconstruction and the arrival of mass tourism witnessed a less edifying rush to build apartment blocks (although Le Corbusier's Cité Radieuse, built in 1952, is one of the most influential buildings of the era) and, later, monstrous resorts such as La Grande Motte in the Languedoc.

Contemporary architecture has had a dramatic impact in the last decade or so, most notably in the creation of modern art galleries such as the superb Fondation Maeght in St Paul-de-Vence and the Musée d'Art Contemporain in Nice. Some of the most adventurous buildings have been designed by British architects, notably Norman Foster's Carré d'Art in Nîmes and Will Alsop's controversial Hôtel du Département in Marseille.

Language and Culture

The birth of Provençal culture dates from the beginnings of the second millennium, a period of growing prosperity and relative peace in the Occitania region. This was the age of the troubadours, poets who sang or recited their works to the feudal courts, travelling from castle to castle around the countryside. Troubadour poetry was, in effect, the forerunner of all Western lyric verse, and although its influences came from both Arabic and Latin cultures in Occitania it developed its own particular style. The golden age of the troubadours was in the latter half of the 12th century, when poets such as Guirault de Borneth, Arnaut Daniel, Folquet of Marseille and Peire Vidal were much in demand; one of the few female troubadours was the Countess of Die, one of the four great women poets of the Middle Ages..

During the 14th century the verses of the troubadours were an enormous influence on Petrarch, Europe's greatest lyric poet of the Renaissance period. Born in Italy in 1304, he was exiled with his family to Provence in 1312 and until 1353 was mainly based in Avignon. In 1327 he fell in love outside a church in Avignon with Laura de Noves, who inspired his *Canzonière* poems and became his life-long muse; in true troubadour tradition, it remained a love which was entirely unrequited. The Vaucluse was Petrach's adopted homeland.

The troubadour tradition was one of the guiding influences on the revival of Provençal culture under Frédéric Mistral and the Félibrige in the mid 19th century. Mistral founded the Félibrige along with six other poets (Roumanille, Brunet, Giera, Aubenal, Tavan and Mathieu) in 1854, with the aim of reviving interest in the Provençal language. In 1855 they launched the annual *Armanan Provençau*, the first journal written in Provençal, and soon afterwards Mistral began work on his monumental *Trésor du Félibrige*, an encyclopedia of Provençal culture. In the 1890s the Félibrige established the Museon Arletan in Arles and launched a more popular journal, called *L'Aïoli*.

The greatest failure of the Félibrige was their lack of involvement in politics, thus allowing the central state to eclipse forever the notion of Occitania. But they did generate a revival of Provençal culture and traditions which continues to this day. These traditions are most evident in the numerous festivals, for which locals may well dress up in traditional costumes and perform dances such as the *farandole*, accompanied by the *tambourin* (a small drum) and *gaboulet* (flute). The folk art of making *santons* (see p. 76) is a Provençal tradition dating from the 17th century which is still flourishing – with quite a bit of help from the tourists.

Writers and Celebrities

The South of France – and in particular the Côte d'Azur – has been a magnet for writers, artists and celebrities since the early 19th century. Many French authors have also used it as a backdrop for their fiction: one of the earliest was Alexander Dumas, who used the Château d'If, off Marseille, as the backdrop for the *Count of Monte Cristo*. Another was Victor Hugo, who set the first part of *Les Misérables* in Digne-les-Bains. In 1869 Alphonse Daudet published his *Lettres de Mon Moulin (Letters from my Windmill)*, set in what is now known as 'Daudet's Windmill' near Fontvieille. Robert Louis Stevenson took to his feet in 1878 when he published *Travels with a Donkey*, based on a walk through the Cévennes. Emile Zola set his novel *Germinal* (1885) in the countryside surrounding Aix and in 1892 Friedrich Nietzsche brought out the last part of *Thus Spake Zarathustra*, which he had been inspired to write whilst walking down an old mule track from Eze to Eze-sur-Mer –

now named the Sentier Frédéric-Nietzsche in his honour.

But the region also had many home-grown authors such as Jean Giono who was born in Manosque in 1895 and devoted most of his life to evocative poems and stories about the surrounding countryside. One of the best known is Marcel Pagnol, himself a film-maker, thanks to the international success of recent films of works such as *Jean de Florette* and *Manon des Sources*.

The earliest tourists to the Riviera were mainly Russian and English nobility, escaping winter in the mild coastal climate. The pace began to change when the casino opened in Monte Carlo in 1878, and stories of *fin-de-siècle* decadence were legion.

After World War I a new influx of celebrities, writers and musicians (many of them American) discovered the Riviera. Colette bought a house in St Tropez, which then featured in some of her short stories; Ernest Hemingway stayed in La Napoule, where he set *The Garden of Eden*; Somerset Maugham wrote *Cakes and Ale* from the seclusion of his villa on Cap Ferrat; Katherine Mansfield retreated to Menton to recover from consumption, and Aldous Huxley settled for Sanary, where he wrote both *Brave New World* and *Eyeless in Gaza*. The era was perhaps best encapsulated by the American author F. Scott Fitzgerald, whose book *Tender is the Night* was based on his high-living friends, Sara and Gerald Murphy, who owned a villa near Juan-les-Pins.

In the post-war years other authors who descended on the south included Françoise Sagan (her novel *Bonjour Tristesse* was set on the Esterel coast) and Albert Camus, who retired to a house in Lourmarin to write his autobiography. But the newly emerging focus was on the glamorous world of the movies, and after the inauguration of the Cannes Film Festival in 1947, the coast became a regular haunt for screen idols such as Errol Flynn, Clark Gable, Kirk Douglas and Lana Turner. In 1957 St Tropez came under the spotlight when Roger Vadim's film *Et Dieu Créa la Femme (And God Created Woman)* was released, establishing the young Brigitte Bardot as an icon of the swinging resort. St Tropez is still a hotspot for visiting celebrities, with everyone from supermodels such as Naomi Campbell and ageing rockers such as Mick Jagger and Elton John passing through in the summer months.

In recent decades the South of France has continued to exert its pull on British novelists, including actor-turned-author Dirk Bogarde, Anthony Burgess (who wrote his final work, *Dead Man in Deptford*, in Monaco, where he died in 1993), and Grahame Greene (who lived in Antibes until his death in 1991). In 1989 copywriter-turned-novelist Peter Mayle published his first book, *A Year in Provence*, a whimsical account of life in the Lubéron which generated enormous interest in the area, despite criticism of its patronising attitudes to local people.

Meanwhile, royalty and politicians continue to migrate to Europe's playground for their summer holidays, although nowadays they are more likely to be staying in heavily-guarded private *châteaux* or low-key villas; the latest trend (following the example of Princess Caroline of Monaco) is to rent a traditional *mas* (farmhouse) in the area around St Rémy-de-Provence, in the Bouches-du-Rhône.

TOURING ITINERARIES

Half the fun of a journey lies in the planning and plotting, in the endless hours of daydreaming before you set out. By dividing the region into recommended routes, this book is intended to make it easy and pleasurable for you to plan your ideal tour. Many of the routes we suggest are so full of treasures, that it would be easy to spin one of them out into a week-long idyll. However many people on a touring holiday prefer to cram in as much as possible.

For those who like a little help in making up their minds, we have put together a few sample itineraries, each based on a different area.Each of the itineraries forms a loop starting and finishing at a city with an international airport. All are action-packed and allow little time for doing nothing. You will need to build in extra time for sunbathing or if you wish to drive to Provence (2 days each way from the UK).

Planning Your Itinerary

There are a few golden rules to remember when planning a trip:

1 Always prebook your first and last nights' accommodation, particularly if you are arriving in the evening or have an early morning flight out. This takes the pressure off and leaves you free to sort yourselves out at leisure.

2 Unless you have accommodation prebooked, plan to arrive at your overnight stop in plenty of time to find lodgings (usually by about 4pm). Make the tourist information office your first call. Always prebook in high summer (Jul-Aug) or if there is a festival.

3 Don't move towns or hotels every night. You get tired and also run out of clean clothes. Laundry breaks are essential on a touring holiday.

4 Keep a good, up-to-date road map in the car (see p. 22 for suggestions). France has embarked on a major programme of road-building and upgrading and you may well find that roads have appeared from nowhere or numbers have been changed. Think of it as a treasure-hunt.

5 When deciding on your daily schedule, check the opening times of any 'must see' sights. There is nothing worse that travelling hundreds of miles to see a château only to find that it is closed. Make sure you are in a suitable place over any public holidays. Remember that the sights may be quite a distance apart, and build in enough time to get there, as well as for meal breaks, such as the often irritatingly long French lunchhour. Try to build in plenty of free attractions, such as views or churches. Too many entrance fees can be crippling to your holiday budget and bad for the stress levels.

6 Don't try to be too ambitious or too organised. If you try and cram absolutely everything in to a split second timetable, you will end up frazzled and fractious and unable to enjoy anything. Rather, allow for a leisurely meander, with time to smell the flowers and sip the coffee. If you miss a few sights, or have to cover a smaller area, does it really matter? If it does, you can come back next year.

1. Riviera Days

14 days

NB: This route would work equally well starting in Nice.

Day 1: arrive **Marseille** (p. 228); Day 2: in **Marseille**; Day 3: **Marseille–Toulon** (p. 243); Day 4: in **Toulon** (p. 333); Days 5/6: **Toulon–Fréjus-St-Raphaèl** (p. 336); Day 7: **Fréjus–Cannes** (p. 178); Day 8: in **Cannes** (p. 121); Day 9: **Cannes–Nice** (p. 131); Days 10/11: in **Nice** (p. 281); Day 12: **Nice–Menton** (p. 299), via **Monaco** (p. 261); returning to Nice; Day 13/14: **Nice–Marseille**, via autoroute A8 and sections of the **Fréjus–Aix-en-Provence** route (p. 75).

2. Rhône Delta Highlights

14 days

Day 1: arrive **Marseille**; Day 2: **Marseille–Arles** (p. 237); Day 3: in **Arles** (p. 80); Day 4: **Arles–Montpellier** via the **Camargue** (p. 86); Day 5: **Montpellier** (p. 267); Day 6: **Montpellier–Nîmes, with Nîmes sightseeing** (p. 306); Day 7: **Nimes–Avignon** (p. 115); Day 8: **in Avignon** (p. 92); Day 9: **Avignon–Arles, via St-Rémy** and **Les-Baux** (p. 98); Days 10/11/12: **Arles–Marseille via Salon-de-Provence** (p. 238) and **Aix-en-Provence** (p. 60); Days 13/14: **in Marseille** (p. 228).

3. Village Provence

14 days

Day 1: arrive **Marseille** (p. 228); Day 2: in Marseille; Day 3: **Marseille–Aix-en-Provence**, via the Calanques, Cassis and Aubagne (see Marseille–Toulon, p. 243); Day 4: in **Aix-en-Provence** (p. 60); Days 5/6: **Aix–Castellane** (p. 66); Day 7: **Castellane–Sisteron** (see Cannes–Grenoble route, p. 125); Days 8/9: **Sisteron–Carpentras** (p. 136); Days 10/11: **Carpentras–Vaucluse Loop** (p. 141); Day 12: **Carpentras–Cavaillon**, via Avignon (p. 92); Days 13/14: **Cavaillon–Aix-en-Provence** (p. 70), and return to Marseille.

4. The Wild West

21 days

Day 1: arrive **Lyon;** Day 2: in Lyon (p. 201); Days 3/4: **Lyon–Clermont-Ferrand**, via Lyon–St Étienne (p. 224) and St-Etienne–Clermont-Ferrand (p. 167); Days 5/6: **Clermont–Ferrand**, including side-tracks to Puy de Dome, Mont-Dore and Vichy (pp. 160–162); Days 7/8: **Clermont-Ferrand–Le Puy-en-Velay** (p. 163); Day 9: in **Le Puy** (p. 189); Days 10/11: **Le Puy–Cévennes** via Le Puy–Montpellier (p. 272); Days 12/14: **Mende–Montpellier** (p. 247); Day 15: in **Montpellier** (p. 267); Day 16: **Montpellier–Avignon**, via Nîmes (p. 306) and the Pont du Gard (p. 115); Day 17: in **Avignon** (p. 92); Days 18/21: **Avignon–Lyon**, along the Rhône Valley (p. 209).

5. Mountains and Mediterranean

14 days

Day 1: arrive **Nice**; Day 2: in Nice (p. 281); Day 3: **Nice–Grasse** (p. 293) or **Nice–Cannes** (p. 131); Days 4/5: **Grasse–Gap** or **Cannes–Gap** (see Cannes–Grenoble; p. 125); Day 6: **Gap–Barcelonnette** (p. 118); Days 7/8/9: **Barcelonnette–Menton** (p. 253); Days 10/11: **Menton–Nice** (p. 299), via Monaco (p. 261); Days 12/13/14: in Nice, with side-tracks to Cannes or Grasse (dependent on which you did earlier) and to the Gorges de la Vésubie and Utelle (see Nice–Barcelonnette, p. 288).

Themes

If you like to shape a holiday by following a particular theme, here is a selection of 'must-see' places categorised by special interest.

Art and Artists

Aix-en-Provence, Atelier Cézanne and the Fondation Vasarely (p. 65). **Antibes**, the Musée Picasso (p. 134). **Arles**, the Picasso drawings in the Musée Réattu, and Van Gogh associations (p. 80). **Avignon**, the Petit Palais (p. 92). **Biot**, the Ferdinand Léger Museum (p. 135). **Collioure**, for connections with Matisse (p. 321). **Clermont-Ferrand**, the Musée des Beaux-Arts (p. 155). **Graveson**, the Musée Chabaud (p. 99). **Grenoble**, the Musée de Grenoble (p. 181). **Les-Baux-de-Provence**, the Musée Yves Brayer and the Chapelle des Penitents Blancs (p. 101). **Lyon**, the Musée des Beaux-Arts (p. 201). **Marseille**, the Musée des Beaux-Arts and the Musée d'Art Contemporain (p. 228). **Martigues**, the Musée Ziem (p. 241). **Menton**, the Musée Jean Cocteau (p. 304). **Montpellier**, the Musée Fabre (p. 267). **Nice**, the Musée Matisse, Musée Chagall and the Musée d'Art Moderne (p. 281). **Nîmes**, the Carrée d'Art (p. 306). **St Étienne**, the Musée d'Art Moderne (p. 322). **St-Paul-de-Vence**, the Fondation Maeght (p. 294). **St-Rémy-de-Provence**, the Centre d'Art Presence Van Gogh (p. 100). **St Tropez**, the Musée de l'Annonciade (p. 340). **Vallauris**, for its pottery and the Picasso and Magnelli museums (p. 132). **Vence**, Matisse's Chapelle du Rosaire (p. 295). **Villefranche-sur-Mer**, Cocteau's Chapelle St-Pierre and the Musée Volti (p. 299).

Castles and Palaces

Aigues-Mortes (p. 90). **Aix-Cavaillon** La Tour d'Aigues, the Château d'Ansouis, Château de Lourmarin and Entrecasteaux (p. 70). **Avignon**, the Palais des Papes (p. 82). **Barbentane**, the Château de Barbentane (p. 104). **Beaucaire** (p. 106). **Les-Baux-de-Provence** (p. 101). **Cagnes**, the Château Grimaldi (p. 203). **Carcassone** (p. 280). **Chambéry**, the Palais des Ducs de Savoie (p. 220). **Colmars**, the Fort de Savoie (p. 291). **Entrevaux**, the Citadel (p. 290). **Monistrol-sur-Loire**, the Château Episcopal (p. 331). **Monaco**, the Palais Royal (p. 261). **Montpellier–Perpignan**, the Château de Quéribus, Grau de Maury (p. 276). **Perpignan**, the Château des Rois de Majorque (p. 318). **Roquebrune** (p. 303). **Tarascon**, the Château du Roi René (p. 105). **Salon-de-Provence**, the Château de l'Emperi (p. 238). **Uzès**, the Duché d'Uzès (p. 116). **Viviers**, the Citadel (p. 215).

Gorgeous Gorges

Digne–Chorges, the Clues de Barles and Clues de Verbaches (p. 170). **Gorges de l'Allier** (p. 166). **Gorges de l'Ardèche** (p. 110). **Gorges de l'Hérault** (p.252). **Gorges de la Nesque** (p. 139). **Gorges de la Vésubie** (p. 289). **Gorges du Loup** (p. 296). **Gorges du Tarn** (p. 248). **Grand Cañon du Verdon** (p. 69). **Grenoble–Sisteron**, the Gorges de la Borne, the Grand Goulets and the Barrangues de Verains (p. 185). **Menton–Barcelonnette**, the Roya Valley, the Gorges de Daluis, and the Gorges de Bachelard (p. 253).

Body . . .

One of the main reasons for holidaying in France is for sybaritic indulgence in wonderful food and wine.

Aix-en-Provence, for calissons (p. 60). **Apt**, for crystallised fruit (p. 112). The Auvergne, for cheese; including **Ambert** (p. 169) and **St Nectaire** (p. 161). **Avignon–Arles**, the heart of olive country (p. 98). **Beaumes-de-Venise**, for Muscat (p. 137). **Carpentras**, for berlingots (p. 141). **Cassis**, for white wine and seafood (p. 244). **Cavaillon**, for melons (p. 73). **Lyon**, for classic gourmet cuisine (p. 201). **Lyon–Avignon** (p. 209), the great vineyards of the Côte du Rhône, such as Châteauneuf du Pape (p. 217). **Marseille**, for unsurpassed *bouillabaise* and other seafood (p. 228). **Montélimar**, for nougat (p. 214).

. . . and Soul

Magnificent churches, large and small, dating from the 4th to the 20th centuries. .

Abbaye de la Chaise-Dieu (p. 169). **Abbaye de Montmajour** (p. 104). **Abbaye de St-Michel-de-Frigolet** (p. 105). **Abbaye du Thoronet** (p. 77). **Abbaye de Silvacane** (p. 71). **Abbaye de Sénanque** (p. 145). **Arles**, the Cathédrale et Cloître St-Trophime (p. 80). **Brioude**, the Basilique St-Julien (p. 165). **Clermont-Ferrand**, the Cathédrale de Notre-Dame de l'Assomption and the Basilique du Notre-Dame du Port (p. 155). **Corps**, the Sanctuaire de la Salette (p. 128). **Fréjus**, the Cathédrale de St Léonce et Cloître (p. 174). **Issoire**, the Église de St-Austremoine (p. 164). **La Brigue**, the Chapel of Notre-Dame-des-Fontaines (p. 256). **Le Puy-en-Velay**, the Cathedral and the Church of St-Michel d'Aiguile Dyke (p. 189). **Lyon–Grenoble**, the Correrie de la Grande Chartreuse, the Abbaye d'Hautecombe, and the Église St Hugues de Chartreuse (p. 219). **Mane**, the Prieuré de Notre-Dame-de-Salagon (p. 113). **Marseille**, the Abbaye de St-Victor and the Basilique de Notre-Dame-de-la-Garde (p. 228). **Martigues**, the Chapelle de l'Annonciade (p. 241). **Narbonne**, the Cathédrale de St-Just et St-Pasteur (p. 279). **Nice**, the Russian Orthodox Cathedral of St Nicholas (p. 281). **Palavas-les-Flôts**, the Cathédrale de Maguelone (p. 91). **Perpignan**, the Cathédrale de St-Jean and the Campo Santo (p. 318). **St-Gilles**, the Church of St-Gilles (p. 87). **St-Maximin-la-Ste-Baume**, the Basilica of Ste-Marie-Madeleine (p. 75). **St-Nectaire**, the Église de St-Nectaire (p. 161). **St-Saturnin**, the Église de St-Saturnin (p. 164).

The Ancients

Apt, the Pont Julien (p. 112). **Arles**, the Arènes and many other Roman remains (p. 80). **Beaulieu-sur-Mer**, the Villa Kerylos (p. 301). **Gordes**, the Village des Bories (p. 144). **La Turbie**, the Trophée des Alpes (p. 302). **Lyon**, the remains of Roman Lugdunum and the Musée de la Civilisation Gallo-Romain (p. 201). **Marseille**, the many remains and museums around the Vieux-Port (p. 228). **Narbonne**, the L'Horreum (p. 279). **Nîmes**, the Arènes, the Maison Carrée and the Jardins de la Fontaine (p. 306). **Orange**, the Théâtre Antique and the Arc de Triomphe (p. 311). **Pont du Gard** (p. 115). **St-Mitre-les-Remparts**, the Oppidum St-Blaise (p. 242). **St-Rémy-de-Provence**, for Glanum and Les Antiques (p. 100). **Vaison-la-Romaine** (p. 316). **Vienne**, the Temple of Augustus and Livia, St-Romain-en-Gal and other Roman monuments (p. 210).

Museums Great and Small

Aix-en-Provence, the Musée des Tapisseries, the Musée Granet and others (p. 60). **Ambert**, the Moulin Richard-de-

Bas, the Musée de la Fourme and other traditional craft museums (p. 169). **Arles**, the Musée Arlaten, the Musée de l'Arles Antique and others (p. 80). **Biot**, the Galerie Internationale du Verre (p. 135). **Brignoles**, the Musée du Pays Brignolais (p. 65). **Cagnes**, the Château Grimaldi (p. 293). **Chazelles-sur-Lyon**, the Musée du Chapeau (p. 226). **Draguignan**, the Musée des Arts et Traditions Populaire de Moyenne Provence (p. 79). **Fontaine de Vaucluse**, the Musée de la Résistance (p. 146). **Grasse**, the Musée Internationale de la Parfumerie (p. 297). **Graveson**, the Musée des Aromes et du Parfum (p. 99). **Grenoble**, the Musée de Ski in the Musée Dauphinois (p. 181). **La Brigue**, the Musée des Merveilles (p. 256). **Marseille**, the Musée d'Histoire Marseille, the Musée de Faïence and many other compelling collections (p. 228). **Ménerbes**, the Musée du Tire-Bouchon (p. 73). **Le Mont-Dore**, the Musée de la Toinette (p. 160). **Monaco**, the Musée Océanographique and the Musée National Automates et Poupées d'Autrefois (p. 261). **Montélimar**, the Musée de la Miniature (p. 214). **Perpignan**, the Musée de Tautavel (p. 318). **Salon-de-Provence**, the Musée de l'Art et l'Histoire Militaire, the Maison de Nostradamus and the Musée de Coca Cola (p. 238). **St Pierreville**, the Maison du Châtaignier (p. 328). **Thiers**, the Musée de la Coutellerie (p. 168). **La Voulte-sur-Rhône**, the Musée de Paléontologie (p. 214). **Uzès**, the Musée International de la Confiserie Haribo and the Musée du Train et du Jouet (p. 116). **Vizille**, the Musée de la Révolution Française (p. 130).

AIX-EN-PROVENCE

Originally founded by the Romans as Aquae Sextiae on the site of a thermal spring, Aix rose to become the capital of Provence under Good King René in the 15th century. It was here that the treaty joining Provence to France was signed in 1487, and it was here that the first Parliament of France was called in 1501. During the 17th and 18th centuries the city enjoyed a period of great prosperity, when grand mansions and the cours Mirabeau were built, but it lost out as a regional capital when power was transferred to Marseille in 1880. Today it is an elegant, lively town with a large student population, famed for its numerous graceful fountains and busy cultural calendar.

TOURIST INFORMATION

Tourist Office: *2 pl. Gén. de Gaulle, tel: 04 42 161 161.* Open Mon–Sat 0830–2000, Sun 1000–1300, 1400–1800 (Apr–Sept), (July–Aug until 2200); Mon–Sat 0830–1900, Sun 1000–1300, 1400–1800 (Oct–Mar). The office is remarkably helpful, with English-speaking staff, and will make room reservations. Festival tickets on sale.

ARRIVING AND DEPARTING

By Air

Airport: Aix is 30km from Marseille-Provence International Airport. Buses leave hourly for the 30-min journey (FFr.45) from the bus station.

By Bus

Bus Station: **Gare Routière**, *r. Lapierre, tel: 04 42 27 17 91.* Five-mins walk west of the rail station. Local bus services to the surrounding Provençal countryside are often erratic but highly entertaining.

By Train

Train Station: *av. V. Hugo, tel: 36 35 35 35*; hourly connections to Marseille. For the town centre walk (north) up *av. V. Hugo* to *La Rotonde* on *pl. Gén. de Gaulle* at the end of *Cours Mirabeau.*

By Road

Aix is well connected by road. The *Autoroute du Soleil* (A8) passes the southern fringes of the city, whilst the A51 (Marseille–Sisteron) autoroute passes to the west. Aix is also at the junction of the N7, N96, and N8. Getting into the city centre is easy, and hotels are very well signposted.

Parking: parking on the street can be difficult, but there are numerous underground car parks including the centrally-located **Semeva Parking Bellegrade**, *pl. Bellegrade; tel: 04 42 21 02 88;* **Parking Carnot,** *pl. Carnot; tel: 04 42 21 51 71;* **Parking Gare Routière**, *r. Lapierre; tel: 04 42 26 07 02;* and **Parking Signoret**, *r. Signoret; tel: 04 42 21 02 88.*

Be warned that thefts from foreign or hire cars stopped at traffic lights are becoming common, with motorbike pillion passengers opening rear car doors to snatch cameras, bags and so on (so-called *vol à l'italien*, said to be perpetrated by gangs from the northern suburbs of Marseille).

Getting Around

Aix is entirely accessible by foot and most of the central area is pedestrianised. Guided tours of Aix in English leave from the Tourist Office at 0930 daily, July–Sept (2 hrs; FFr.45). Guided tours in French visit different areas on different days (ask for the leaflet, *Visites Commentées*). The tourist office also houses a shop and a desk for **Aix-en-Bus**, *tel: 04 42 26 37 28* (open Mon–Fri 1000–1800, Sat 1000–1230) for ticket sales and information.

Bronze markers in the pavement mark the route of a walking tour *In the Footsteps of Cézanne* (a brochure with trilingual text from the Tourist Office also contains details of a 40 km round trip through many of the local landscapes immortalised by Cézanne in his paintings). Regular excursion to relevant locations (including his birthplace, Jas de Bouffan, and landscapes he painted) are run by the **Compagnie des Autocars en Provence** (CAP). Their leaflet, *Balades en Provence*, is also available from the tourist office.

Taxis: Cours Mirabeau, *tel: 04 42 26 29 29 30*; Station SNCF, *tel: 04 42 27 62 12*; Gare Routière, *tel: 04 42 27 20 92*; Radio taxis, *tel: 09 32 24 63* or *07 56 89 71*.

Staying in Aix

Accommodation

Aix has a good selection of hotels, from luxury down to basic student hostels. Chains represented include *Ca, Ct, Hd, Ib, Mc, Nv* and *Rc*. Cheaper accommodation tends to be found hugging the ring road, *blvd Carnot*. Many picturesque old buildings have been converted into luxury hotels. Right in the heart of the city, the **Hôtel des Augustins**, *3 r. de la Masse; tel: 04 42 27 28 59; fax: 04 42 26 74 87* (expensive) is a superb conversion of a 12th-century priory, with vaulted ceilings and stained glass enhancing the ambience of discreet and attentive service. The spacious rooms all have their own jacuzzis. A similar level of comfort and service is found at the **Hôtel Le Pigonnet**, *5 av. du Pigonnet; tel: 04 42 59 02 90; fax: 04 42 59 47 77* (expensive), which is five mins' walk from the centre and set in 1 hectare of lovely gardens (Cézanne painted the Mt Ste Victoire from the grounds, a view which is still visible). Run by the same family since 1924, the hotel has been much enlarged from the original Provençal *mas* (farmhouse) over the years and has 51 quiet rooms, many recently renovated, all with large marble bathrooms. Pool, gastronomic restaurant (Le Riviera). Also in a peaceful location, although further from the centre, is the **Hôtel Le Prieuré**, *rte des Alpes (RN96; direction: Sisteron); tel: 04 42 21 05 23* (cheap/moderate), which has 23 large, comfortable rooms in a converted 17th-century priory overlooking the adjoining formal gardens. Housed in an 18th-century mansion, the **Hôtel Cardinal**, *24 r. Cardinal; tel: 04 42 38 32 30; fax: 04 42 26 39 05,* (cheap/moderate) has 30 large rooms furnished with antiques, good value considering the quality of the hotel. The **Hôtel de France**, *63 r. Esparait, tel: 04 42 27 90 15; fax: 04 42 26 11 47,* (cheap/moderate) is also good value and centrally located. The **Hôtel des Quatre Dauphins**, *54 r. Roux-Alpheran; tel: 04 42 38 16 39; fax: 04 42 38 60 19* (cheap/moderate) is charming little hotel, although rooms are on the small side. A good budget choice is the **Hôtel Paul**, *10 av. Pasteur; tel: 04 42 23 23 89; fax: 04 42 63 17 80* (cheap), with 24 basic but well-kept rooms.

HI: **Auberge de Jeunesse**, *3 av. M.*

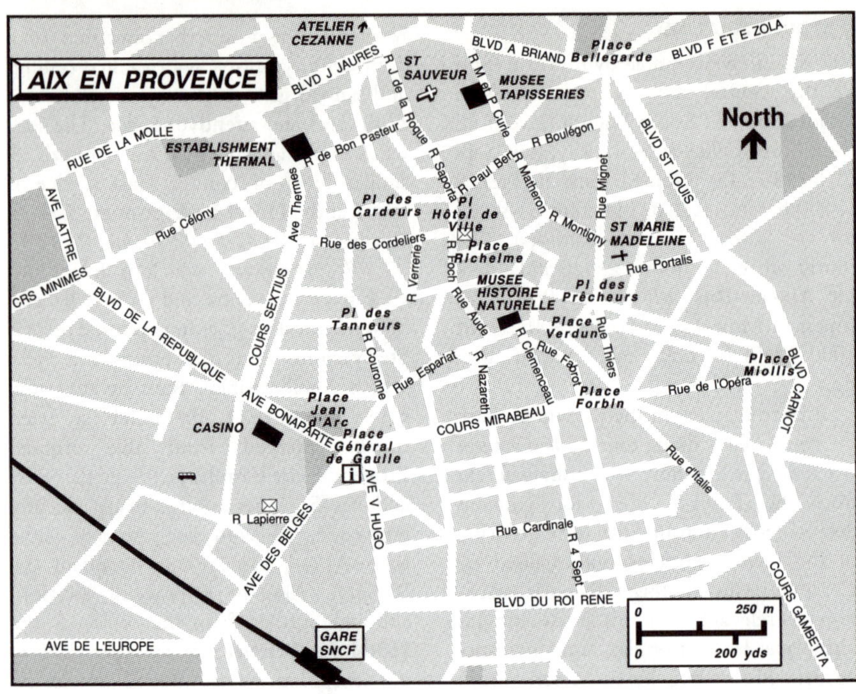

Pagnol, quartier Jas de Bouffan, tel: 04 42 20 15 99. Two km west of the centre, garden, tennis. **Campsites: Airotel Camping Chantecler**, *Val-St-André, rte de Nice; tel: 04 42 26 12 98* (caravans; open year round); **Arc en Ciel**, *Pont des Trois-Sautets, rte de Nice; tel: 04 42 26 14 28* (open Mar–Oct).

Eating and Drinking

Aix has a huge range of restaurants, cafés, brasseries, and bistros across all price ranges while a thriving university crowd supports numerous ethnic restaurants (the range is surprisingly large and covers Armenian, Belgian, Egyptian, Korean, Spanish, Greek, Indian, Japanese, Lebanese, Moroccan, Pakistani, Thai, Tunisian, Turkish and even an English restaurant). Many of the *restauration rapide* (fast food) and ethnic restaurants are found in the back streets of the old town between *pl. des Augustins* and *pl. des Cardeurs*.

Aix also has a wide range of traditional and gastronomic restaurants. **Les Frères Lani**, *22 r. Victor Leydet; tel: 04 42 27 76 16* (moderate/expensive), is a modern restaurant with an inventive menu, presided over by the Lani brothers. The *menu du marché* features unusual fish dishes while the gourmet menu offers *foie gras*, duck and home-made desserts. **Le Clos de la Violette**, *10 r. de la Violette; tel: 04 42 23 30 71* (moderate–expensive) is also another of Aix's top restaurants, with a choice of gastronomic menus. Provençal cuisine can be found at **Chez Gu et Fils**, *3 r. F. Mistral; tel: 04 42 26 75 12* (moderate–expensive), which has become rather more costly since it featured in Peter Mayle's *A Year in Provence*; but it still serves a good *gigot d'agneau* and excellent desserts.

La Brocherie, *5 r. Fernand-Dol; tel; 04 42 38 33 21* (cheap/moderate) has a rustic ambience and a Renassiance fireplace where game is spit-roasted on the original spit; fish specialities include *loup grillé au feu du bois* and *lotte a la Provençal.* **L'Hacienda**, *7 r. Mérindol; tel: 04 42 27 00 35* (cheap), is good value and very popular at lunchtimes; specialities include lamb and seafood.

Another enjoyable spot for lunch is the **Trattoria Chez Antoine**, *3 r. Clemenceau; tel: 04 42 38 27 10* (cheap/moderate), with Italian and Provençal specialities and some interesting pasta dishes.

There is only one place in Aix to drink during the day, *cours Mirabeau*, the most pretentious and stylish strip of cafés outside Paris. Those wanting a less studied ambience should try the *pl. de l'Hôtel de Ville* and *Forum des Cardeurs*. Students keep Aix lively at night: *cours Sextius* and its back streets host numerous bars.

Communications

Main Post Office: **Poste Principale PTT**, *2 r. Lapierre; tel: 04 42 16 01 50.* Open Mon–Fri 0830–1900, Sat 0830–1200. Poste restante, currency exchange, telephones and photocopying.

Money

Most of the major French banks are represented on either *cours Mirabeau* or *cours Sextius*, and have automatic cash dispensers. Several *bureaux de change* open longer hours, including **L'Agence**, *15 cours Mirabeau; tel: 04 42 26 84 77* (open Mon–Sat 0900–2100, Sun 1000–1300, 1600–1900 July–Aug; Mon–Fri 0900–1900, Sat 0930–1730, Sun 1000–1300, 1600–1900 Sept–June); and **CRAMP**, *7 r. Nazareth,* just off cours Mirabeau; *tel: 04 42 38 28 28* (open Mon–Sat July–Aug 0900–1230, 1330–1900, Sun 0900–1700 only).

Entertainment

Aix is the region's cultural centre and nightlife hotspot. A free information sheet, *Le Mois à Aix*, available from the Tourist Office, gives details of concerts, theatre, cinema and other performances. Key venues include the **Casino Municipale**, *2 av. Napoléon Bonaparte; tel: 04 42 26 30 33*, and 10 theatres and café-theatres, such as the **Théâtre du Jeu de Paume**, *r. de l'Opéra; tel: 04 42 38 07 39;* the **Théâtre de la Fonderie**, *14 cours St Louis; tel: 04 42 63 10 11;* the **Théâtre 108**, *37 blvd Aristide Briand; tel: 04 42 21 06 70;* the **Théâtre J. Prevert**, *24 blvd de le République; tel: 04 42 26 36 50;* and the **Théâtre des Ateliers**, *29 pl. Miollis; tel: 04 42 38 10 45.* There are also several large multiplex cinemas, numerous piano-bars and pubs, and 13 discos. The numerous churches house classical music concerts throughout the year.

Throughout the year students keep Aix happening with numerous jazz and rock bars, not to mention dance clubs. Jazz bars include **Hot Brass**, *chemin de la Plaine-des-Verguetiers, tel: 04 42 21 05 57*; the slightly less expensive **Scat Club**, *r. de la Verrerie, tel: 04 42 23 00 23*; and the **Blue Note**, *10 r. de la Fonderie, tel: 04 42 38 06 23*, which also features country music. There is a jazz brunch on Sundays (1000–1500) at the **Holiday Inn Garden Court**, *5-7 rte de Galice, tel: 04 42 20 22 22.* On Fri and Sat there are Latin American nights at **La Cascada**, *29 r. Fermée, tel: 04 42 38 66 91.*

Events

Summers sees a series of festivals: July is the busiest month, with the **International Dance Festival**, **International Music**

Festival, the **Provençal Festival of Aix and the Pays d'Aix**, and the **Festival des Vins**. Other festivals include a **Winter Music Festival** (Jan–Mar), and the **Theatre and Book Festivals** (Oct). Information on Aix's festivals from the **Comité Officiel des Fêtes**, *Complexe Forbin, cours Gambetta; tel: 04 42 63 06 75.*

Shopping

Aix is a shopper's paradise, with a dazzling array of speciality food shops and designer boutiques. The central area has many luxury bakers, butchers and grocers, not to mention fashion outlets such as Chanel, Hermes, Gap and more. Aix's markets are a delight: **flower markets** are held in *pl. des Prêcheurs* (Sun, Mon, Wed, Fri), and *pl. de la Mairie* (Tues, Thurs, Sat); there are **general markets** in *pl. Richelme* (daily), *pl. des Prêcheurs* (Tues, Thurs, Sat), and *pl. de la Madeleine* (Tues, Thurs, Sat). An **antiques/flea market** is held in *pl. de Verdun* (Tues, Thurs, Sat). One of Aix's specialities are delicious sweets know as *calissons*, made from almonds and crystallised fruits. First made here for the wedding of Good King René in 1473, the tradition is still alive, with some 20 manufacturers in the vicinity; around a dozen shops in the city centre make and sell *calissons* (the tourist office can provide a list).

Sightseeing

Aix is a town of culture and charm, housing one of France's premier universities, founded in 1409. Little remains of the city's imperial past, but wander at will through the honey-coloured streets and you'll meet elegant façades, haughty statues and gracious fountains. The tree-lined **Cours Mirabeau**, built in the 17th-century along the old line of the city wall and named after a revolutionary, is flanked by some of the city's finest mansions. This is Aix's strolling ground. When you've done the promenade up to the magnificent iron **Fontaine de la Rotonde** (1860), turn back to relax, sip coffee and people-watch (the 18th-century café, **Les Deux Garçons**, is the most famous on the cours, with an attitude to rival any Parisian establishment).

Aix's museums are on the whole fairly uninspiring. A combined ticket covering five museums costs FFr.60 (available from the Tourist Office or any one of the museums). One of the best is the **Musée des Tapisseries**, *Palais de l'Archevêché, 28 pl. des Martyrs de la Résistance; tel: 04 42 23 09 91* (open Wed–Mon 1000–1200, 1400–1745; FFr.15) with beautiful textiles, 18th-century Beauvais tapestries and opera costumes and set designs. Other museums include the **Musée d'Histoire Naturelle**, *6 r. Espariat; tel: 04 42 26 23 67* (open daily 1000–1200, 1400–1800, FFr.16) in the 17th-century Hôtel Boyer d'Eguilles, designed by Pierre Puget, with a few prehistoric remains, including dinosaur eggs; and the **Musée du Vieil Aix**, *17 r. Gaston de Saporta; tel: 04 42 21 43 55* (open Tues–Sun 1000–1200, 1400–1800 Apr–Sept; 1000-1200, 1400-1700 Oct–Mar; FFr.15) in a magnificent building housing antiques, paintings, santons, marionettes and masks.

Aix was the birthplace of painter Paul Cézanne. He despised his home town, and, during his life, the townsfolk ridiculed him and his art. Nonetheless, the town has capitalised on his former presence and today his studio is carefully preserved, as it was on his death here in 1906. Walk up *av. Pasteur* from the Cathedral (500m) to **L'Atelier Cézanne**, *9 av. Paul Cézanne; tel: 04 42 21 06 53* (open Wed–Mon 1000–1200, 1400–1800 June–Sept; 1000–1200 and 1400–1700 Oct–May; FFr.16). Several of Cézanne's paint-

Cézanne in Aix

Born in Aix on 19 Jan 1839, Paul Cézanne attended a classical school where he became friends with Émile Zola, and then enrolled in art school, but his father insisted he study law. Cézanne went to work in his father's bank but a year later, at the urging of Zola, left to live in Paris, where he exhibited in 1863. During the 1870s he took part in several of the early Impressionist exhibitions, and in 1882 his work was accepted for the first (and only) time at the Paris Salon. But he began to spend more and more time in Aix, renting a hut in the Bibemus Quarry and painting the landscapes of the Mont Ste Victoire. In 1901 he bought a plot of land and built his studio at Chemin des Lauves, on a hill above the cathedral, where he painted all morning before venturing out in the afternoons into the surrounding countryside. In 1906, aged 67, he caught pnuemonia in a rainstorm whilst out painting, and died on 23 October.

ings are also held in the **Musée Granet**, *pl. St-Jean-de-Malte; tel: 04 42 38 14 70* (open Wed–Mon 1000–1200, 1400–1800; FFr.18), in the 17th-century priory of the Knights of St John. Along with a number of French, Italian and Flemish paintings, the museum also has a fascinating section in the basement, on archaeological finds from the local Iron Age hillfort, the Oppidum d'Entremont, including Celto-Ligurian sculptures (said to be the oldest in France) and ritual masks.

Within the old town, you will also find the **Cathédrale St-Sauveur**, *r. Gaston Saporta*, which was completed in the 15th century and includes a 12th-century Romanesque door. As you enter, on the right, there is a baptistry dating from the 4th–5th centuries. This incorporates Roman columns which were once part of the temple to Apollo that previously stood on this site. There is also an 7th–8th century cloister and, in the Gothic nave, a famous triptych by Nicolas Froment, the *Buisson Ardent* (1476).

To the west of *cours Sextius* is the **Pavillon de Vendôme**, *32 r. Célony; tel: 04 42 21 05 78* (open daily; 1000–1200, 1400–1800 May–Sept; earlier closing in other months; FFr.15). Built by Louis de Mercœur, the Duke of Vendôme, in the 17th century (although enlarged in the 18th), this beautiful house sits in a typically formal French park and houses a collection of fine 17th–18th century furniture, paintings and sculpture.

In the *Quartier Marazin*, south of *cours Mirabeau*, the **Musée Arbaud**, *2a r. du Quatre Septembre; tel: 04 42 38 38 95* (open Mon–Sat 1400–1700; FFr.15) is the former home of collector and bibliophile Paul Arbaud. It contains an extensive library on Provence with items dating back to the 14th century, as well as an important collection of *faïence*, paintings and sculptures.

On the outskirts of Aix is the **Fondation Vasarely**, *av. M. Pagnol, Jas de Bouffan; tel: 04 42 20 01 09* (open daily 1000–1300, 1400–1900; closed Jan–Mar; FFr. 35; take bus no. 8 or 12, stop: *Fondation Vasarely*). Donated and designed by the artist himself, this striking building is the principal showcase for the unusual works of the Hungarian architect/artist Victor Vasarely.

⟷ Connections from Aix-en-Provence

To reach **Marseille** quickly from Aix, take the A5 and then the A7,or the N8 to avoid tolls; 27 km. To **Arles**, take the A8, bypassing Salon to join the N113; 63 km.

AIX-EN-PROVENCE–CASTELLANE

This route passes the massif of Mont Ste-Victoire and traverses the plains of the Haut Var before arriving at the historic towns of Gréoux-les-Bains, Riez and Moustiers-Ste-Marie. It then passes through one of the great natural wonders of Provence, the Grand Cañon de Verdon. Allow: 1–2 days.

DIRECT ROUTE: 142 KM

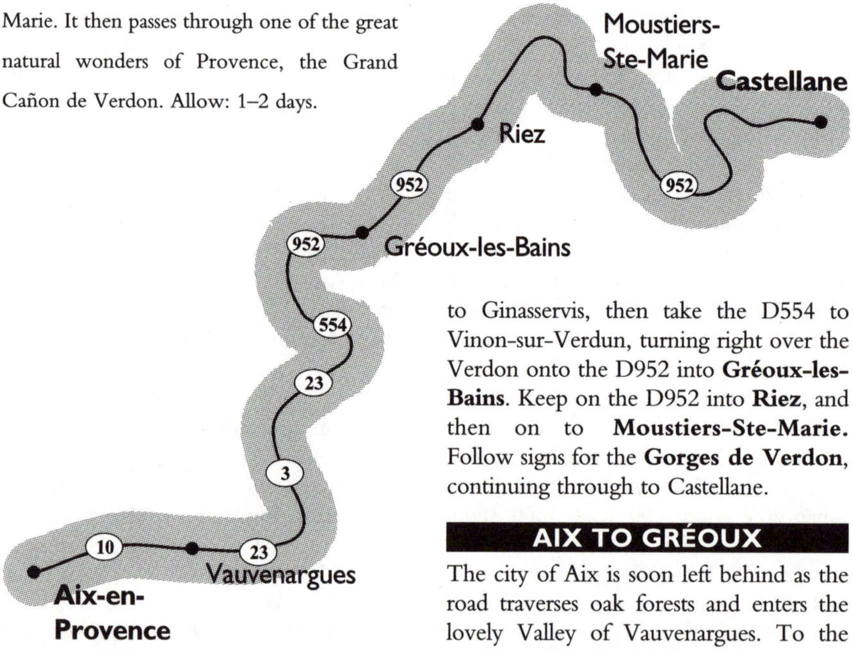

ROUTE

There is no more direct route than the one detailed below.

Leave Aix by the D10 (clearly sign-posted as the Route de Vauvenargues to the right off *blvd Carnot*), following it through **Vauvenargues**. From here, turn left onto the D23, which then becomes the D3 into Rians. Continue on the D23 to Ginasservis, then take the D554 to Vinon-sur-Verdun, turning right over the Verdon onto the D952 into **Gréoux-les-Bains**. Keep on the D952 into **Riez**, and then on to **Moustiers-Ste-Marie.** Follow signs for the **Gorges de Verdon**, continuing through to Castellane.

AIX TO GRÉOUX

The city of Aix is soon left behind as the road traverses oak forests and enters the lovely Valley of Vauvenargues. To the right are the wooded limestones ravines which form the backbone of Mt Ste Victoire. Just past St Marc-Jaumegarde, take a right turn towards the **Barrage de Bimont**. This dam, which forms part of the Canal de Verdon irrigation system, blockades the Infernet River, creating a superb lake which stretches back up the valley. Return to the D10 and continue on into **Vauvenargues**. To the right of the village is the prominent **Château de**

Vauvenargues, the last home of Pablo Picasso until his death in 1973; his tomb lies within the park surrounding the château, but there is little point in stopping since it cannot even be glimpsed from the gates. The château is private; a notice proclaims 'No visits – please do not insist', adding helpfully that the Musée Picasso is in Paris!

Beyond Vauvenargues, the road starts to climb gently towards the **Col des Portes** (631 m), and as you top the small pass a panorama of Alpine foothills opens up to the east. Through Rians and Ginasservis the route crosses typical Haut Var landscapes, with *garrigue* (scrubland) interspersed with fields of cereal crops, corn, and sunflowers. Four km before Vinon-sur-Verdon, you cross the **Canal de Provence,** and at Vinon, you meet the wide, fast-flowing **Verdon River** itself, following it upstream towards Gréoux-les-Bains.

GRÉOUX-LES-BAINS

Tourist Office: *5 av. des Marronniers; tel: 04 92 78 01 08*. Open Mon–Sat 0900–1200, 1400–1800.

Accommodation and Food

Although Gréoux does not have quite so many hotels as it does doctors and health clinics (at least two dozen), there is a good choice of high quality lodgings, many of them with health centres and all the other add-ons such as hairdressing salons which one would expect to find in a spa town. Foremost amongst them is the **Hôtel Villa Borghese** *(RS), av. des Thermes; tel: 04 92 78 00 91; fax: 04 92 78 09 55* (moderate/expensive) which has vine trellises draped over its balconies and peaceful, well-furnished rooms; the restaurant features a gastronomic menu as well as more health-conscious dishes. Another well-established hotel is **La Crémaillère**, *rte de Riez, tel: 04 92 74 22 29; fax: 04 92 74 27 38* (moderate–expensive), whose rooms have all been recently renovated. Near the centre of the village the **Grand Hôtel des Colonnes** *(LF), av. des Marronniers; tel: 04 92 78 00 04* (cheap–moderate) has characterful rooms and a shady garden. **Campsite**: **Camping-Caravanning Les Cygnes**, *Domaine de la Padulette; tel: 04 92 78 08 08*, is just on the other side of the Verdon with a pool and a nice riverbank location.

Gréoux has a good selection of restaurants, most of them lining *Grand Rue,* off the *pl. de l'Hôtel de Ville*, as well as several pizzerias and café-bars. It makes a convenient stopping point for lunch, and if you want to have a picnic there are some excellent *traiteurs*, *boulangeries* and the like on *Grand Rue* and *av. des Marronniers*, with a pleasant picnic area by the riverside (follow the road down past the Établissement Thermale).

Sightseeing

The healing properties of Gréoux's thermal springs were first discovered by the Romans, although the spa fell into disuse for many centuries before being re-opened in the 17th century. Today the **Établissement Thermale**, *tel: 04 92 74 22 22*, is a modern complex which pumps out some four million litres a day of the curative waters (rich in thoron and radon; good for rheumatism and respiratory complaints), which emerge at a constant temperature of 37°C.

The town is dominated by the imposing ruins of a **Château** (no visits) built by the Knights Templar, which is used for various events including the annual Theatre Festival (Aug). Within the town you can visit the **Maison de Pauline**, *av. des Marronniers* (open 1500-1700 mid

Apr–mid Oct; FFr.10) which features a reconstructed 9th-century Provençal home as well as displays on local traditions, and the **Musée du Vitrail et de la Mosaique**, *3, 6 and 7 Grand Rue; tel: 04 92 74 27 85* (open Sun–Fri 1000–1200, 1500–1900 Mar–Dec; FFr.30). As well as an audio-visual presentation on the making of stained glass there are displays of contemporary stained glass and mosaic work.

RIEZ

Tourist Office: *4 allée L. Gardiol; tel: 04 92 77 82 80.* Open Tues–Sat 0800–1200, 1400–1900 June–Aug; 0900–1200, 1400–1700 Sept–May. Guided visits of the old town (1hr) on demand (minimum 2 persons) during opening hours (FFr.25). The Tourist Office also houses a small **Musée d'Histoire Naturelle en Provence** (same hours; FFr.20) with fossils and displays on local flora and fauna.

Several fine Renaissance mansions adorn Riez, which has a long history as a market town, on the crossroads of the mountain trade routes between Aix and the coast. It was an important Roman colony with numerous villas – recent excavations have also revealed a monumental portico which may have been part of a forum. The most visible evidence of the colony is four granite **Corinthian columns**, possibly part of a temple to Apollo, which sit in a field on the left of *av. F. Mistral*, leading into town. There is also a 5th-century Merovingian **Baptistry**, on the other side of the river (open daily 0930–1230, 1500–1800 June–Sept; Oct–May by appointment; FFr.25) which now houses a lapidary museum. Just outside the town (800m along the D953 to Digne) is the **Maison de l'Abeille**, *tel: 04 92 77 84 15* (open daily 1000–1200, 1430-1900; free) which has displays on bees and honey production as well as a shop selling their products.

MOUSTIERS-STE-MARIE

Tourist Office: *Mairie; tel: 04 92 74 67 84.* Open July–Augdaily 1030–1230, 1400-1900; Mon–Sat 1030–1200, Sept–Dec, Apr–June 1400–1730; Jan–Mar Mon–Sat 1330–1700 only .

ACCOMMODATION AND FOOD

Moustiers has numerous creperies, pizzerias and cafés providing *restauration rapide* (fast food), but for something a little more elevated you could try the recently-opened **Bastide de Moustiers**, *la Grisolière; tel: 04 92 74 62 40; fax: 04 92 74 62 41* (expensive), 1km south of the village. The restaurant is the latest creation of young chef Alain Ducasse, who has already made a name for himself (and earned three Michelin stars) in Monte Carlo's Louis XV restaurant. The old farmhouse also has seven fully-equipped rooms, and a swimming pool.

SIGHTSEEING

Moustiers is a busy tourist town at the western entrance of the Grand Cañon du Verdon, famous for its scenic setting as well as the tin-glazed ceramics *(faïences)* which have been produced here since the 17th century. It's well worth visiting the small **Musée de la Faïence**, *pl. du Presbytère,* adjoining the Mairie; *tel: 04 92 74 61 64* (open Wed–Mon 0900–1200, 1400–1800 Apr–Oct (July–Aug 1900); FFr.10). Here you can see some of the classic designs before looking around the dozen or so workshops and more than 20 shops which cram every street in the village with *faïence* displays, many of the modern products still following traditional designs. Moustiers was originally settled in the 5th century AD by monks from the

Îles des Lérins, who lived in caves carved out of the cliffs which tower above the present-day village. Perched high up in the breach between the cliffs is the **Chapelle de Notre-Dame de Beauvoir**, which was started in the 14th century and enlarged in the 16th. A path lined with oratories leads up to the chapel, from where there are superb views of the gorges and the Lac du Saint-Croix. Suspended between the cliffs above the chapel is a massive chain, 227m long, with a five-pointed gold star hanging from the centre: the present star dates from 1957, but the original was placed here in the 12th century by Baron Blacas as an offering to Notre Dame de Beauvais after being released from captivity during the Crusades.

MOUSTIERS TO CASTELLANE

Accommodation and Food

If you're thinking of stopping for the night or a meal, try the excellent **Hôtel des Gorges de Verdon** (*LF*), *La Palud; tel: 04 92 77 38 26; fax: 92 77 35 00* (moderate). In a fabulous setting on a small hill to the south of the village with a panorama of the whole valley, it has 30 modest but adequate rooms, a pool, and a very good restaurant serving Provençal specialities.

Sightseeing

From Moustiers it takes but a few mins to reach the start of one of the classic tourist routes of Provence, the road through the **Grand Cañon de Verdon**. The Verdon, a tributary of the Durance River, has carved a dramatic gash up to 700m deep through the rock, which was only fully explored in 1905 by Isadore Blanc. There are numerous view-points and stopping places on this road, but be warned that in peak season, traffic in both directions can be considerable. From Moustiers the road climbs up through forested slopes before arriving at the **Belvédère de Galetas**, with a view reaching backwards to the impressive canyon mouth, from where the river pours out into the **Lac de Ste-Croix**. The road continues to climb upwards. The next major stopping point is at the **Mayreste Belvédère**, where a 10-min scramble over the rocks brings you to the first view of the river and canyon upstream. The road then crosses the **Col d'Ayen** (1032m) before descending into a broad valley with **La Palud-sur-Verdon** at its centre. This small town has become a busy activities base for climbing, hiking, canoeing and mountain-biking in and around the canyon. The old **château** (currently being restored) houses a **Syndicat d'Initiative** (open Mon–Sat 1000–1200, 1630–1830, Sun 1000–1200 July–Aug only).

Just after La Palud a right fork in the road leads around the **Route de Crêtes**, one of the most scenic stretches of the north bank road. This 23km loop encompasses several stunning viewpoints of the canyon, notably **Imbut Belvédère**, **Tilleul Belvédère**, and **Escales Belvédère**. Returning to La Palud, continue along the D952 until you reach **Pointe Sublime**, where a track from the carpark leads up to a clifftop with a fabulous view of the meeting point of the Baou and Verdon rivers 180m below, with the opening of the western end of the Grand Canyon rearing up dramatically ahead. Beyond here the road winds its way downhill through several tunnels, eventually reaching the river itself, which it follows until reaching Castellane.

CASTELLANE

See p. 126.

AIX-EN-PROVENCE–CAVAILLON

This route encompasses three fine châteaux, of varying styles, in the South Lubéron, before crossing the massif to meander around the picturesque *villages perchés* on the northern flanks of the Petit Lubéron, overlooking the Coulon Valley and the Vaucluse plateau.

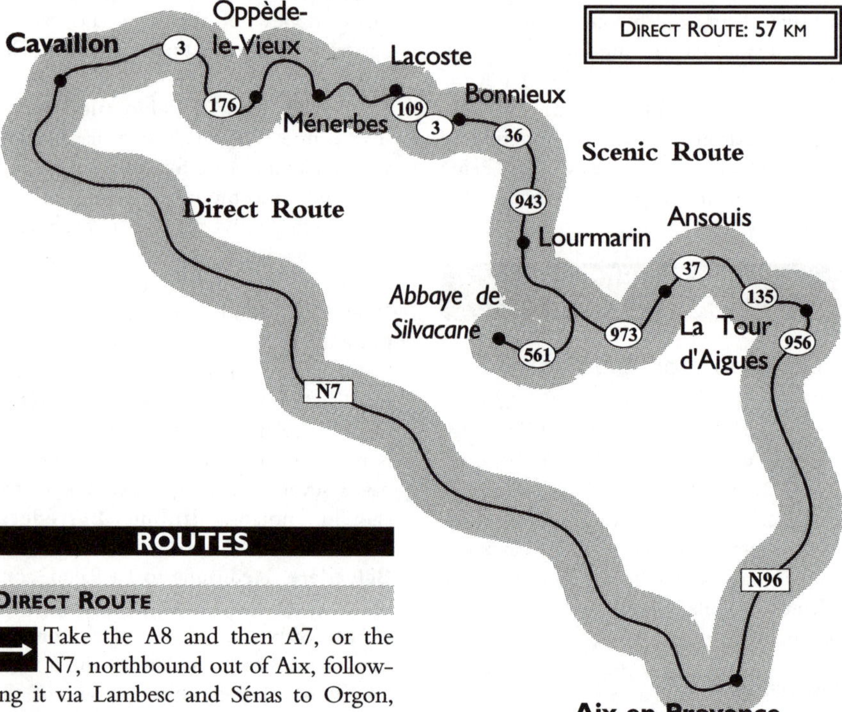

ROUTES

DIRECT ROUTE

Take the A8 and then A7, or the N7, northbound out of Aix, following it via Lambesc and Sénas to Orgon, turning right onto the D26 and right again onto the D99 to reach Cavaillon. Distance: 57 km; allow: 1–1½ hrs.(You can continue another 25 km on the autoroute or N7 to reach **Avignon**.)

SCENIC ROUTE

Take the N96 north from Aix, branching left onto the D556 to cross the Durance on the Pont de Pertuis to Pertuis; from here follow the D956 to **La Tour d'Aigues**. Leave on the D135, turning left on the D37 to **Ansouis**. Continue on the D37, then turn right to Cadanet. Detour back across the Durance on the D943, then turn right onto the D561 to the **Abbaye de Silvacane**. Return to Cadanet and follow the D943 to **Lourmarin**. Keep on the D943 through the Combe de Lourmarin, turning left on the D36 to **Bonnieux**. From Bonnieux take the D3, then the D109 to **Lacoste**. From Lacoste, follow the D109, then the D3A to **Ménerbes**, from where the D3 descends to the valley. Turn left onto the D29 through Les Poulivets, take the D178 to **Oppède-le-Vieux**, then the D176 back down to the D3, turning left towards the D2 and then left again towards **Cavaillon.** Distance: 120.5 km; allow: 1-2 days.

LA TOUR D'AIGUES

Tourist Office: *Château de la Tour d'Aigues; tel: 04 90 07 50 33.* Open July–Aug daily 1000–1200, 1530–1930; daily Apr–June, Sept 0930–1130, 1500–1800, closed Tues pm, Sat/Sun am; daily Oct–Mar 0930–1130, 1400–1700, closed Tues pm, Sat/Sun am. Tastings of Lubéron wines throughout July and Aug.

The **Château** (open the same hours as the Tourist Office; FFr.25) is the main focal point of this village.It was one of the most unusual Renaissance ruins in Provence, designed by an Italian architect and built on the foundations of a medieval castle but unfortunately it was damaged by fire in 1780 and finally sacked during the Revolution in 1792. The ruins are, nonetheless, highly dramatic, comprising a richly decorated entrance gateway, and a chapel and restored keep inside the old walls. The cellars now house various exhibitions, including a displays of ceramics, an audio-visual show about the South Lubéron, and a museum of rural life. The latest attraction is a musical promenade which plays different tunes as you walk over the paving stones in the courtyard. The château is the setting for the **Festival du Sud Lubéron** (theatre, dance and music) in July and Aug each year.

ANSOUIS

Tourist Office: *Mairie; tel: 04 90 09 86 98.* Open daily 1000–1200, 1400–1800. 1-hr guided visits of the village, Sun 1600; FFr.20.

The village clusters around the southern slopes of a rocky hill, dominated by the ancient **Château d'Ansouis**, *tel: 04 90 09 82 70* (open daily 1430–1830; closed Tues in winter; FFr.30). As you approach from the north, this resembles a formidable fortress (as indeed it once was). The southern side reveals a more elegant 18th-century façade, surrounded by terraced gardens and chestnut trees. Inside, it is again part-fortress (with magnificent displays of medieval armour) and part-mansion (with superb tapestries and Renaissance furniture); the old Provençal kitchen is particularly fascinating, and still in use.

Elsewhere in the village, the picturesque streets shelter various craft workshops and one or two café-restaurants. At the bottom of the hill, children will enjoy the **Musée Extraordinaire de Georges Mazoyer**, *tel: 04 90 09 82 64* (open daily 1400–1800 (1900 in summer); FFr.20) which is one man's collection of oddities (fossils, shells etc.) and artistic creations (paintings of underwater life, ceramics, and a walk-through 'blue coral grotto').

ABBAYE DE SILVACANE

Set in a rural landscape on the south bank of the Durance is the **Abbaye de Silvacane**, *Roque d'Anthéron; tel: 04 42 50 41 69* (open Apr–Sept daily 0900–1900; Oct–Mar Wed–Mon 0900–1200, 1400–1700; FFr.28). As with the other two 'Cistercian sisters' (Sénanque and Le Thoronet; see pp .

145 and 77), the pure architecture of Silvacane reflects the austere principles of the order, with a simple, bare church and high vaulted transept. The adjoining cloisters date from the late 13th century; the abbey itself was founded in the 12th century. It went into decline in the 14th century, was badly damaged during the Revolution and later became a farm. It is still under restoration.

LOURMARIN

Tourist Office: *17 av. Philippe de Girard; tel: 04 90 68 10 77*. Open Easter–Oct Mon–Sat 1030–1230, 1600–1800.

Accommodation and Food

This attractive village makes an appropriate stopping point for lunch, with several good cafés and restaurants. Foremost amongst them is the **Moulin de Lourmarin**, *r. Temple; tel: 04 04 90 68 06 69; fax: 04 90 68 31 76* (moderate–expensive). The millstones are still intact in this converted olive mill and the food is prepared with as much care as has gone into the décor. The Moulin also has 22 rooms (expensive) in the same exquisite taste. Other options include **le Bistrot**, *2 av. Philippe de Girard; tel: 04 90 68 29 74* (cheap–moderate), and **L'Oustalet**, *opposite the château, tel: 04 90 68 07 33* (cheap–moderate) with Provençal specialities.

Sightseeing

Lourmarin is amongst *Les Plus Beaux Villages de France*, and as well as simply enjoying wandering around the well-kept streets you can also visit the tomb of the philosopher and writer, Albert Camus (1913–60), one of many intellectuals and artists who have made Lourmarin their home. On the edge of the village is the imposing **Château de Lourmarin**, *tel: 04 90 68 15 23* (45-min guided visits every half-hour, daily July–Aug 0930–1130, 1500–1800; Sept–June 1000, 1100, 1430, 1530, 1630; FFr.30). The oldest part of the château was built in the 15th century, whilst the 'new' section dates from the Renaissance. Restored in the 1920s, the château was later bequeathed to the Academy of Arts in Aix and now houses an art foundation. The Renaissance section contains some lovely old chimneypieces and a grand staircase, as well as Provençal and Spanish furniture.

LOURMARIN TO CAVAILLON

From Lourmarin the road winds up through the lovely **Combe de Lourmarin,** which separates the Grand and Petit Lubéron, before arriving at the hilltop village of **Bonnieux**. This large, sprawling village has excellent views across the Calavon Valley to Mt Ventoux from the terrace below the **Église Vieille**. In the lower half of the village is the **Tourist Office**, *7 pl. Carnot, tel: 04 90 75 91 90* (open mid June–Sept Tues–Sat 1030–1230, 1430–1830; Oct–mid June 1400–1800). Half way down the main street is the **Musée de la Boulangerie**, *12 r. de la République; tel: 04 90 75 88 34* (open Wed–Mon 1000–1200, 1500–1830; FFr.10) which covers the history of breadmaking down the ages.

The road snakes down the flank of the Lubéron to another characterful *village perché*, **Lacoste**. The cobbled streets lead upwards through the village to the partially-restored ruins of the **Château** (no visits), whose main claim to fame is that it was once the residence of the notorious Marquis de Sade, who lived here for around 30 years between serving numerous prison sentences for his debaucheries.

From Lacoste the route traverses vine-

The Lubéron

The limestone range of the Lubéron runs east-west 65 km from Cavaillon towards Manosque, much of it belonging to the *Parc Naturel Régional du Lubéron* whose headquarters are in Apt (see p. 112). The massif offers a striking contrast between the fertile slopes leading down towards the Durance on the southern side and the rocky ravines and lovely wooded areas on its northern flanks. The range is divided in two by the Combe de Lourmarin, with the Grand Lubéron to the east reaching its peak at the Mourre Nègre (1125m) and the Petit Lubéron to the west rarely rising above 700m. The whole area is dotted with numerous charming *villages perchés*. Perhaps the most famous village in the Lubéron is Ménerbes, whose inhabitants achieved celebrity through Peter Mayle's account of *A Year in Provence* and its sequel, *Toujours Provence*. Having unleashed bus-loads of tourists on the village, Mayle himself decamped to California in the early 1990s (he couldn't stand the sightseers), only to return to buy another house near Bonnieux in 1996.

yards and woods to reach **Ménerbes**, perched on a promontory with lovely views of the valley. Walk up through the village, past the Mairie, to reach a 17th-century bell-tower, beyond which are a 14th-century church and the remains of a 13th-century citadelle. Looking northwards, the panorama encompasses the villages of Roussillon and Gordes, with the Vaucluse plateau and Mt Ventoux beyond. As well as the village bar-tabac there are a couple of bistros, amongst them the charming **Le Galoubet**, *104 r. M. Poncet, tel: 04 90 72 36 08* (cheap), housed in a 16th-century vaulted room and specialising in traditional Provençal cuisine.

Descending from Ménerbes into the valley, you come to the **Musée du Tire-Bouchon**, *Domaine de la Citadelle; tel: 04 90 72 41* 58 (open Apr–Sept daily 1000–1200, 1400–1800 (until 1900 July–Aug); Oct–Mar Mon–Fri 1000–1200, 1400–1800, Sat 0900–1200; FFr.20). This collection is an eye-opener, with some fascinating examples (including the oldest known corkscrew in the world) amongst the thousand or so corkscrews which have been assembled here. Entrance to the museum also includes a tour of the cellars and winery; there are also wine tastings and sales and a wine bookshop.

The next perched village is **Oppède-le-Vieux**. From the car park (compulsory, FFr.10) overgrown paths lead up through the ruined upper half of the village to a 16th-century Gothic church and the ruins of a château (beware of steep drops to the south of the ruins). The delight of Oppède is to wander along the rubble-strewn pathways on the hillside between the ivy-covered walls, courtyards and other tumbledown ruins, discovering a Renaissance window, a Romanesque doorway, or the remains of a Gothic arch. This upper part of the village was abandoned at the beginning of the century. Around the central square there are a couple of souvenir shops, a café, and a pleasant restaurant, **L'Oppidum**, *pl. de la Croix, tel: 04 90 76 84 15* (cheap), with good value *plats du jour.*

From Oppède-le-Vieux the road leads down through Maubec and Robion towards the Coulon, which it then follows into Cavaillon.

CAVAILLON

Tourist Office: *pl. F. Tourel; tel: 04 90 71 32 01.* Open June–Aug Mon–Sat 0900–1300, 1400–1900, Sun 0900–1300;

June–Aug Mon–Sat 0900–1230, 1330–1830 Sept–May.

Accommodation and Food

Cavaillon has a good selection of hotels (including an *Ib.*) and restaurants. In a peaceful location just to the south of town (follow *av. de Verdon*) is the **Hôtel-Restaurant Le Christel**, *quartier Boscodomini; tel: 04 90 71 07 79; fax: 04 90 78 27 94* (moderate), a modern hotel with comfortable rooms set in gardens with a pool. Just opposite the Roman arch and the Tourist Office is the traditional style **Hôtel du Parc**, *183 pl. F. Tourel; tel: 04 90 71 57 78; fax: 04 90 76 10 35* (cheap–moderate), an old mansion with adequate rooms (the quieter ones face the park) and a pleasant sunny courtyard. Another good quality hotel is **Le Toppin**, *70 cours Gambetta, tel: 04 90 71 30 42; fax: 04 90 71 91 94* (cheap), with 32 rooms, right in the town centre. **Campsite**: **Camping de la Durance**, *Digue des Grands Jardins; tel: 04 90 71 11 78* (caravans) on the banks of the Durance.

Top chef Jean-Jacques Prévot presides over **Prévot**, *353 av. de Verdon; tel: 04 90 71 32 43* (expensive), where gourmet dishes are served in a regal atmosphere of chandeliers and gilt mirrors. Another atmospheric restaurant is the **Fin de Siècle**, *46 pl. du Clos; tel: 04 90 71 12 27* (cheap/moderate), which has good food at very reasonable prices. The **Restaurant Pantagruel**, *5 pl. P. de Cabassole; tel: 04 90 76 11 30* (cheap–moderate) is a lively restaurant inside a huge vaulted room with a spit roast - good value. Cavaillon also has numerous crêperies, pizzerias, cafés, *traiteurs*, and *charcuterie* shops. A huge market occupies *pl. du Clos* and surrounding streets on Mon. Cavaillon's name is synonymous with the fragrant, rose-pink melons grown in the market gardens surrounding the town; they start to appear in shops, markets and restaurants from May onwards.

Sightseeing

Cavaillon was originally a Celto-Ligurian settlement which later became a prosperous Roman colony. The Celto-Ligurian oppidum was at the top of the **Colline St Jacques** (a path leads upwards just to the right of the Tourist Office, behind the *pl. F.Tourel*, 45 mins rtn), from where there are good views of the town, the Durance, the Lubéron, and Mt Ventoux.

On *pl. du Clos* is a 1st century **Roman arch**, which was moved here from its former position near the cathedral in 1880. Finds from Celto-Ligurian and Roman Cavaillon are displayed in the **Musée de l'Hôtel Dieu**, *Porte d'Avignon, tel: 04 90 76 00 34* (open daily Apr–Sept 0930–1200, 1400–1830 Oct–Mar Wed–Mon 1000–1200, 1400–1700; FFr.20 for joint ticket with the Musée Juif Comtadin). Housed inside a former hospital and its chapel, the museum also contains mementos of the hospital itself, such as 18th-century *faïence*.

In the heart of the town, the **Ancienne Cathédrale Notre-Dame-et-St-Véran** is an elegant building with a fine apse and a lovely Romanesque **cloister** (open Apr–Sept Mon 1500–1800, Tues–Sat 1000–1200, 1500–1800; Oct–Mar Mon 1400–1800, Tues–Sat 1000–1200, 1400–1600). The town also has a small **synagogue**, dating from the 17th century, adjoining which is the **Musée Juif Comtadin**, *r. Hébraïque; tel: 04 90 76 00 34* (open Apr–Sept Wed–Mon 0930–1200, 1400–1830; Oct–Mar 1000–1200, 1400–1700; FFr.20 for joint ticket with the Musée de l'Hôtel Dieu). The museum charts the history of the Jewish community in the region.

AIX-EN-PROVENCE–FRÉJUS

Much of this route runs through the heartland of the Var, encompassing typical Provençal landscapes and market towns as well as important Gothic and Romanesque monuments and a series of unusual and interesting little villages.

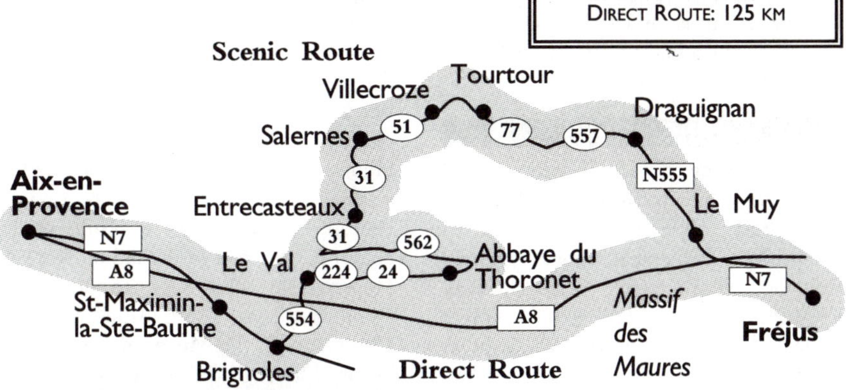

ROUTES

DIRECT ROUTE

Leave Aix on the A8 autoroute, which swings around behind the Massif des Maures to reach the coast at Fréjus. Distance: 125km; allow: 2 hrs.

SCENIC ROUTE

Leave Aix on the N7, which skirts Mont St Victoire, to **St Maximin-la-Ste-Baume**. Continue along the N7 to **Brignoles.** From here, head north on the D554 for 5 km to **Le Val**, then take the D224 to Vins-sur-Carami and the D24, D19 and D10 to the **Abbaye du Thoronet**. Continue on towards the village of Thoronet, turning left on the D84, left again on the D562, and right on the D31 to reach **Entrecasteaux**. From there follow the D31 to **Salernes**, then take the D51 to **Villecroze** and **Tourtour**. From Tourtour, take the D77 down towards the D557, turning left to reach **Draguignan**. Take the N555 towards Le Muy to rejoin the N7 for the last stretch into Fréjus. Distance: 188km; allow: 2 days.

ST MAXIMIN-LA-STE-BAUME

Tourist Office: *Hôtel de Ville, tel: 04 94 78 00 09.* Open daily 0930–1215, 1400–1715.

Set in the centre of a small basin with wooded hills to the north and vineyards leading south to the Massif de la Ste-Baume, the town is dominated by the monumental **Basilica Ste-Marie-Madeleine** (open daily 0830–1200, 1400–1800; 1900 in summer). One of Provence's finest Gothic buildings, the basilica stands on the spot where, according to legend, Mary Magdalene and, later on, St Maximin were buried. The saints' remains were hidden from the Saracens in the 8th century and rediscovered in 1279 by Charles of Anjou, who began building the basilica and monastery. It wasn't completed until 1532, and was spared during the Revolution because Lucien Bonaparte, younger brother to Napoleon, commandeered it for use as a food store. The interior contains one of the finest 18th century organs in France, with some 3000 pipes; the crypt contains several 4th-century sarcophagi and a 19th-century gilt reliquary containing what is said to be the skull of Mary Magdalene.

BRIGNOLES

Tourist Office: *pl. des Augustins, tel: 04 94 69 01 78.* Open Mon–Fri 0900–1200, 1400–1800 (1500–1900 in summer), Sat 0900–1200. The pedestrianised streets of Brignoles' old town have several excellent *rotisseries, traiteurs* and *boulangeries* if you're stopping for picnic supplies, but the other main reason to visit the town is the eclectic and entertaining **Musée du Pays Brignolais**, *pl. des Comtes de Provence; tel: 04 94 69 45 18* (open Apr–Sept Mon–Sat 0900–1200, 1430–1800, Sun 0900–1200, 1500–1800; Oct–March Mon–Sat 1000–1200, 1420–1700, Sun 1000–1200, 1500–1700; FFr.20). Housed in a château which was once a summer retreat for the Counts of Provence, it contains a diverse collection of oddments ranging from 7th-century ex-votos to a reconstruction of the bauxite mines upon which Brignoles built its fortunes, and a Provençal farm kitchen. Pride of place, however, goes to a tomb, the *Sarcophage de Gayole,* which dates from the 2nd century AD and is said to be the earliest Christian tomb ever discovered. The images carved on its sides clearly illustrate the transition from pagan to Christian iconography. In the same hall is an equally surprising exhibit – the world's first reinforced concrete boat. It was built in 1849 by a local man, Joseph Lambot, the inventor of reinforced concrete.

LE VAL

Tourist Office: *4 pl. de 4 Septembre; tel: 04 94 86 34 69.* Open Mon–Fri 0900–1200, 1400–1800, Sat 0930–1200, 1400–1830, Sun 1000–1200, 1400–1830. Housed in an old vaulted room at the centre of the village, they also sell crafts and wines, and have a workshop where you can watch santons being made.

Le Val is an interesting village to wander around with many curiosities including a 12th-century vaulted alleyway, an old olive mill (currently in use for art exhibitions), and a very unusual *lavoir* (public washing place) with the water running beneath a graceful set of 16th-century columns, once part of the old market hall. Housed inside what was once the village's communal bread oven (dating from the 12th century), the **Musée du Santon**, *2 rue des Fours, tel: 04 94 86 48 78* (open Mon–Fri 0900–1200, 1400–1800, Sat 0930–1200, 1400–1830, Sun 1000–1200, 1400–1830; FFr.10) includes santons from all over the world. The best tableau of *santons,* however, is found in an adjoining annexe, where a miniature period realisa-

Santons

Although the tradition of making the small figurines known as *santons* ('little saints' in Provençal) dates back to the 17th century, they first became widely popular after the Revolution when churches were closed, since it allowed every family to have their own Christmas crib. Later, the nativity scene came to include typical Provençal figures (the innkeeper, baker, and so on) and was transposed to a Provençal village scene. Today the craft is thriving, with a wide range of characters, usually brightly painted and dressed in traditional costumes.

tion of the village has been crafted in astonishing detail (you may have to plead to see it, since only groups are normally admitted).

Next door to the Tourist Office, the **Église de Notre-Dame** has a lovely vaulted Romanesque ceiling – common enough in Provence – but, more surprisingly, a chancel with a fresco painted in 1989 by Marcel Le Couedic, a pupil of Salvador Dali's, who now lives in the village. It is a colourful mélange of the classic and surreal, with symbolic butterflies and doves blurring the dimensional boundaries in the imagery. More of Le Couedic's work is visible in the adjoining chapel (ask for the key in the Tourist Office) and in the **Musée de Art Sacré**, *pl. des Penitents* (same hours as tourist office; ask for key), which also contains a painting of *The Visitation* by Pierre Puget.

LE VAL TO SALERNES

From Le Val, the D224 skirts Vins-sur-Carami (note the façade of a fine 16th-century château, currently under restoration, on your left), and then touches the southern edge of the scenic Lac de Carces before meandering through woodland to arrive at the **Abbaye du Thoronet**, *Le Thoronet; tel: 04 94 60 43 90* (open Apr–Sept Mon–Sat 0900–1900, Sun 0900–1200, 1400–1900; Oct–Mar daily 0930–1230; 1400–1700; FFr.28). In a typically remote setting, this is one of the three 'Cistercian sisters' of Provence (the other two being the Romanesque abbeys of Sénanque and Silvacane (see pp. 145 and 71).

Founded in 1146 and completed in 1190, it was the first of the three to be built and displays the precise and harmonious Cistercian architectural principles of simplicity, strength and sobriety in their purest form, generating an impression today of stark beauty. The heavy walls, stone barrel-vaults, transverse arches and pillars combine to create a vision of austere majesty, particularly in the huge inner space of the church itself. Surrounding it are a cloister, chapter house, dormitory, parlour, and *armarium* (library). The monastery was in decline by the 15th century and was on the verge of total dilapidation until it was discovered and saved by Prosper Mérimée, Napoleon III's Inspector of Historic Monuments, who instigated a restoration programme which still continues to this day.

From Le Thoronet the route crosses the River Argens and winds its way towards **Entrecasteaux**, a small village with a rather intriguing **château**, *tel: 04 94 04 43 95* (open Apr–Sept daily 1000–1900; Oct–March Thur–Tues 1100–1800; FFr.30). Built in the 17th century, the castle was bought in 1974 by an eccentric Scottish painter, Ian McGarvie-Munn, and is now filled with his peculiar paintings alongside period furnishings. Below the château is a small public garden, designed by Le Nôtre. Just behind the château is a good restaurant, **La Fourchette**, *2 r. de l'Église, tel: 94 04 42 78* (cheap/moderate), which has a welcoming ambience and an imaginative menu.

SALERNES

Tourist Office: *r. Victor Hugo; tel: 04 94 70 69 02*. Open July–Aug daily 0830–1200, 1400–1900; Sept–June Tues–Fri 0930–1200, 1430–1700, Sat 0900–1200.

This large village, best known for tile manufacturing *(carrelage)*, has a good selection of food shops, cafés and bars. The Tourist Office stands at one end of the main square; above it is a small **Exposition Archaéologique** (open same hours; FFr.5). Although dull in its presentation, it does reveal some astonishing facts about life in the locality during the Stone Age. Based on discoveries made in the nearby cave of Fontbregoua, north-west of the village, it has photographs and skulls showing evidence (rare in Europe) of mesolithic cannibalism (altogether twelve people were dissected with flint knives in order to be cooked and eaten). It also has intriguing evidence of prehistoric trepanning, whereby huge circular holes were cut in peoples' skulls (possibly to remove pieces of fractured cranium) as a medical remedy.

After this, Salernes' little **Romanesque bridge** is a bit of an anti-climax (it is not signposted: take *r. J-J.Rousseau* west from the tourist office and turn left down a small road between buildings, marked 'Pierre Basset – Carrelage 200m'; the bridge is just past the tile factory).

VILLECROZE

The next village north from Salernes, Villecroze has a rambling medieval quarter with arcaded streets. Behind the town a series of cave dwellings are set in cliffs down which a waterfall, framed by palm trees and cycads, plummets to a public garden (open daily 0830–2000). It is like the Garden of Eden redesigned by a municipal committee, with rose beds and flower borders alongside venerable chestnuts, magnolias, and the palm trees.

The **Grottes Troglodytes** (open July–mid Sept daily 1000–1200, 1430–1900; May–June daily 1400–1900; mid Sept–mid Oct Sat–Sun 1400–1800; FFr.10), on several levels, were turned into dwellings by the local lords in the 16th century.

TOURTOUR

Tourist Office: *tel: 04 94 70 54 36*, in Tourtour's attractive, shaded square. Open June–Sept daily 1000–1300, 1500–2000.

Accommodation and Food

On the edge of the village (500 m) is the superb **Bastide de Tourtour (*RC*)**, *tel: 04 94 70 57 30; fax: 04 94 70 54 90* (expensive). Set in a 4 hectare park, the bastide has 25 rooms (modern and comfortable), a pool, tennis, and gastronomic restaurant. Other options include the **Hostellerie Les Lavandes**, *quartier de Verdaine; tel: 04 94 70 57 11; fax: 04 94 70 59 75* (moderate), which is in a very peaceful location, with 12 rooms, a pool, and a restaurant specialising in *cuisine traditionnelle*, or **Le Mas des Collines** (*LF*), *tel: 04 94 70 59 30; fax: 04 94 70 57 62* (expensive), which has 7 rooms and a stunning view. There are several *crêperies, salons de thé,* restaurants and bars surrounding the main square.

Sightseeing

Tourtour is a beautiful little village perched 635m up in the Haut Var which styles itself 'the village in the sky'. From the **orientation table** in front of the **Église St-Denis** there is an astonishing panorama which sweeps from the Gulf of St-Raphael to the east to Mt Ventoux in the north-west, encompassing the massifs of the Maures, Sainte-Baume, l'Étoile, Ste-Victoire and the Lubéron in between. The Tourist Office provides a series of sheets in English with information on the village's history, the local olive oil mill (visits take place in Jan when the olives are being processed), and a list of historic houses to look at in the town.

From Tourtour the road sweeps downhill, with the views still unfolding some 80 km toward the sea, then cuts through woodlands and small valleys to reach Draguignan.

DRAGUIGNAN

Tourist Office: *9 blvd Clemenceau; tel: 04 94 68 63 30.* Open summer Mon–Sat 0900–1300, 1400–1900, Sun 0900–1300; winter Mon–Sat 0830–1230, 1400–1800, Sun 1000–1200. Guided visits of the old town mid June–mid Sept Wed, Sat 1030, 1630; FFr.20.

Accommodation and Food

Draguignan's top hotels are **Les Étoiles de l'Ange**, *rte de Lorgues, 1308 av. de Tuttlingen; tel: 04 94 68 23 01; fax: 04 94 68 13 30* (cheap–moderate), on the outskirts, and **Le Victoria** (*BW*), *52–54 blvd Carnot; tel: 04 94 47 224 12; fax: 04 94 68 31 69* (moderate–expensive), which is close to the town centre. A good budget choice is the old-fashioned **Dracénois**, *14 r. du Cros; tel: 04 94 68 14 57* (cheap), a stone's throw from the market square. Most of Draguignan's restaurants and cafés are clustered around the old town's central *square Ar. Briand.*

Events

Draguignan's lively programme of year-round events includes a traditional Pentecost festival, the **Corso Fleuri de la Ste-Hermentaire**, with floats decorated with carnations (May), a ten-day **Olive Festival** (July), a street festival with comedians, rock, jazz and much more, known as the **Draguifolies** (July–Aug) and a jazz festival (Oct). Market days are Wed and Sat in the *pl. du Marché.*

Sightseeing

Former capital of the Var département, Draguignan is a busy market town ringed by unattractive industrial suburbs, but it has an attractive *vielle ville*, mostly pedestrianised. The old town is dominated by the 17th-century **Tour de l'Horloge**, 24m high and surmounted by a wrought-iron campanile. Adjoining it is the tiny **Chapelle de St-Sauveur**, built in the latter half of the 12th century by the Knights of St John (currently undergoing restoration, the interior can only be visited on Heritage Days, usually in Sept). In front of the tower and chapel, overlooking the rooftops of the town, is a lovely **Théâtre de Verdure** (open-air theatre) set amidst olive trees and rocks.

In the heart of the old town is one of the best ethnographic museums in Provence, the **Musée des Arts et Traditions Populaire de Moyenne Provence**, *15 r. Romanille, tel: 04 94 47 05 72* (open Tues–Sat 0900–1200, 1400–1800, Sun 1400–1800; FFr.20). Housed inside a 17th-century mansion, it features a series of lively and imaginative displays on the region's cultural and agricultural heritage which encompasses silkworm breeding, tanning, spinning, cork-making, bee-keeping, and olive-oil processing, as well as Provençal costumes, santons, and musical instruments.

There is also a surprisingly good **Musée Municipal**, *9 r. de la République, tel: 04 94 47 28 80* (open Tues–Sat 0900–1200, 1400–1800, Mon 1400–1800; free). The paintings include a Rembrandt and a Renoir; it also features sculpture, ceramics, furniture, and contemporary art displays. Draguignan is also a military base, which is reflected in the **Musée du Canon et des Artilleurs**, *quartier Bonaparte; tel: 04 94 60 23 85* (open by arrangement only) which covers the development of artillery, with ancient and modern pieces.

Just outside the town (1km north along the D995, signposted off to the left) is the **Pierre de la Fée** ('fairy stone'). Thought to have been a communal sepulchre, it is the only true prehistoric dolmen in Provence; the top slab weighs over 20 tons.

Arles

Van Gogh and Gauguin found this little city sufficiently congenial to spend over a year painting its narrow streets and rolling fields. It is easy to see why – Arles, considered by many to be the spiritual heart of Provence, is totally delightful, a maze of narrow gold-grey alleys with doors and windows ready-framed by elaborate architraves and shutters and surely, more restaurants and cafés per plaza than any other town in the world.

There are sights aplenty for the most avid tourist, charming strolls and gift shops for those less enamoured of history, fine food, and a friendly welcome. In high season, people throng here in huge numbers, so always book ahead.

Tourist Information

Tourist Office, *Esplanade Charles de Gaulle, off blvd des Lices; tel: 04 90 18 41 20*. Open Oct–Mar, Mon–Sat 0900–1800, Sun 1000–1200; Apr–Sept, Mon–Sat 0900–1900, Sun 0900–1300. Hotel bookings, currency exchange, and transport tickets as well as heaps of useful information.

Branch: at the station; *tel: 04 90 49 36 90*. Open Apr–Sept Mon–Sat 0900–1300, 1400–1800; Oct–Mar Mon–Sat 0900–1300, 1330–1700.

Arriving and Departing

Airport

Nîmes, Arles and the Camargue share a small airport, 25km south-west, near St Gilles; *tel: 04 66 70 70 70*.

By Car

There are excellent road connections with all the other towns in the Bouche du Rhône, and easy access to the motorways north, east and west. There is limited parking at most hotels, with open-air car parks (metered) along the river in *pl. Constantin* and *pl. A Peyron*, behind the Arena near *pl. de la Redoute* and *r. JJ Rousseau*, and an underground car park on the *blvd des Lices*; *tel: 04 90 96 68 58* (open Mon–Sat 0800–2000). It is sensible to avoid driving through the town centre, especially in a motorhome or with a caravan. The streets are very narrow, and most are filled with tourists, dogs, racks of souvenirs and café tables.

By Bus

The bus station is opposite the rail station; *tel: 04 90 49 38 01*. **Cars de Camargue**, *tel: 04 90 96 36 25*, run regular buses to the Camargue.

By Train

Station: *av. Talabot* (closed 0100–0430). Information 0900–1800 (closed for lunch during winter) *tel: 04 90 99 35 03*. For the town centre, walk down *av. Talabot*, through the walls at *pl. Lamartine*, and along *r. Laclavière*. For the Tourist Office, take bus no. 4 to *blvd des Lices*. Regular services from Marseille and Nîmes and direct TGV services from Paris and Lille.

By Boat

The Rhône is navigable here, with a

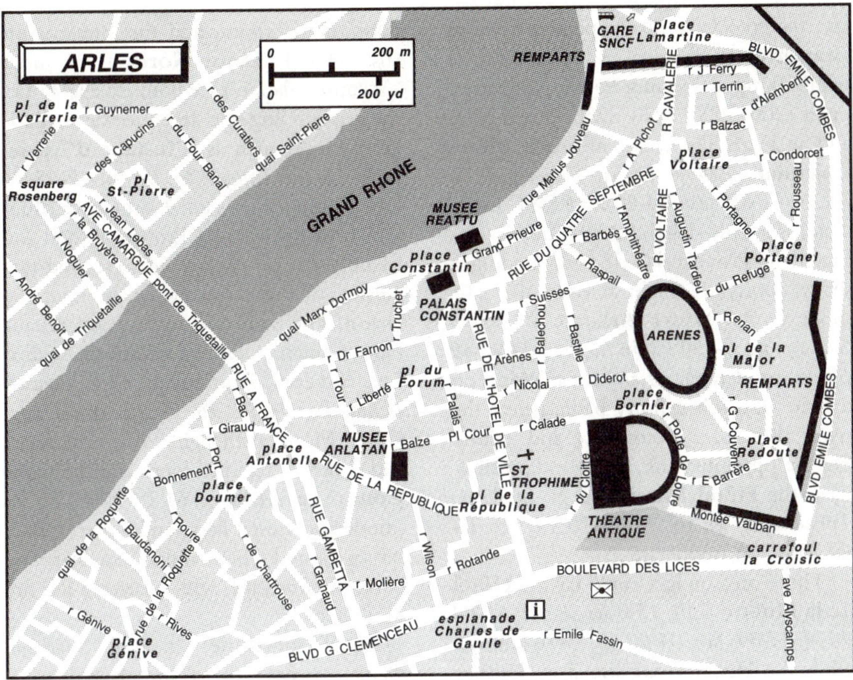

mooring point at **Arles-Trinquetaille**, *quai St Pierre*, on the west bank.

Getting Around

It takes little more than 15 mins to walk from one side of Arles to another, although there are also regular buses for the footsore and weary.

A **Petit Train** *tel: 04 09 34 54 04* runs regular sightseeing tours of the town between Easter and Oct (Mon–Fri 1000–1200, 1400–1900, Sat 1000–1200, from the Tourist Office and the Arena; 35 mins; FFr. 25*)*.

Ask the Tourist Office about **guided walking tours,** *tel: 04 90 18 41 22.* **Taxis**: *blvd des Lices; tel: 04 90 96 90 03.* **Bike Hire**: at the station *tel: 04 90 96 43 94*, or **DallOppio**, *10 r. Portagnel tel: 04 90 96 46 83* (inside the walls then left from the station).

Staying in Arles

Accommodation

Arles is immensely popular and probably slightly less expensive than its more grandiose neighbours, so it can be difficult to get a room in high summer. Advance booking is essential. Chains include *Ba, BW, Ch, CS, Hf, Ib, IH, Ne, Pl* and *RC*.

For the rich at heart, the **Jules César**, *5 blvd des Lices; tel: 04 90 93 43 20, fax: 04 90 93 33 47* (expensive; closed early Nov–23 Dec) is one of the most elegant hotels in town, in a 17th-century Carmelite convent, with the renowned gastronomic **Restaurant Lou Marques**, (expensive; open 1200–1330, 1930–2130). Much smaller, but more famous still, used by the top matadors and numerous celebrities, is the **Grand Hôtel Nord-Pinus**, *pl. du Forum; tel: 04 90 93 44 44,* *fax: 04 90 93 34 00,* (expensive) whose **Brasserie**, serves delicious Provençal food overlooking a bustling square (moderat; open 1200–1500, 1930–2230; closed Mon and all Feb). The more affordable **Hôtel Calendal**, *22 pl. du Docteur Pomme; tel: 04 90 96 11 89; fax: 04 90 96 05 84* (moderate) is a truly delightful little hotel, decorated in Provençal style, surrounding a shady courtyard. Light meals only. The more formal **Hôtel Arlatan**, *26 r. du Sauvage; tel: 04 90 93 56 66; fax: 04 90 49 68 45* (moderate), an ancient mansion on the site of a 4th-century basilica near the river, also oozes atmosphere and charm. On the opposite bank, one good possibility is the **Hôtel Mireille**, *2 pl. St Pierre, Trinquetaille; tel: 04 90 93 70 74; fax: 04 90 93 87 28* (moderate).

Those on a budget could try the **Hôtel de la Muette** *(LF), 15 r. des Suisses; tel: 04 90 96 15 39; fax: 04 90 49 73 16* (cheap), while the **Hôtel Gauguin**, *5 pl. Voltaire; tel: 04 90 96 14 35; fax: 04 90 18 98 87,* (cheap) is one of the better budget places around the slightly shabby *pl Voltaire.*

Campsites: **City Camping** (2-star), *67 rte de Crau, tel: 04 90 93 08 06* (caravans; open Mar–Sept); **Bienheureuse** (2-star), *Raphèle-Les-Arles, rte Nationale 453, tel: 04 90 98 35 64* (caravans; open all year round, 7km from town). **HI**: *20 av. Foch; tel: 04 90 96 18 25,* 1.8km south-east of town (bus no.8: *Fournier*).

Eating and Drinking

Numerous small but good quality restaurants grace Arles. The *pl. du Forum* is lively and attractive, but most of its restaurants are uninspiring and overpriced, although the **Bistro Arlésien**, *tel: 04 90 93 28 05* (cheap) offers good plain food in vast quantities. The **Vaccarès**, *r. Favarin; tel: 04 90 96 06 77* (expensive; closed Mon), which overlooks the square from its first floor dining room, and the Brasserie **of the Hôtel Pinus-Nord** (see under 'Accommodation') are both excellent. Try the surrounding side streets for better budget options, such as **L'Instant d'Après**, *22 r. Docteur Fanton; tel: 04 90 49 95 96* (cheap–moderate; closed Sun and Mon) which offers delicious Provençal food and friendly service. *Pl. Voltaire* is a second-rate version of the *pl. du Forum*, without the charm, but there are some good restaurants in the surrounding sidestreets, such as **Les Saveurs Provençal**, *65 r. Amédée Pichot; tel: 04 90 96 13 32,* (moderate; closed Mon), with light Provençal décor and delicious regional food, and the **Côté Cour** *r. Amédée Pichot; tel: 04 90 49 77 76,* (moderate; closed Mon and Tues), which serves classic French cuisine in a charming covered courtyard, with a roaring log fire in winter.

Local specialities include *Saucisson d'Arles*, a type of salami created by a descendant of Saracen slaves in 1655; a simple beef-in-red-wine casserole, *Daube Provençale*; and *Brouffado*, slices of beef stuffed and cooked with garlic and onion, capers and anchovies.

Communications

Post Office: *5 blvd des Lices; tel: 04 90 96 07 80.* Open Mon–Fri 0830–1900, Sat 0830–1200.

Money

There are numerous banks with exchange facilities, with clusters on *blvd des Lices, r. de la République*, and *av. Stalingrad.* **Société Générale** has three branches at: *31 r. de la République; tel: 04 90 18 48 48; 21 r. de la Verrerie; tel: 04 90 96 73 56;* and *19 av. Stalingrad; tel: 04 90 96 25 84.*

Entertainment and Events

There are three cinemas, but for much of

the year, Arles is a quiet country town whose inhabitants have to travel for action. Major **feria** at Easter and during the **Rice Festival** in Sept, fill the Arena with afficionados of the bullring. The 1st May sees the **Fête des Gardians**, a celebration of the Camargue 'cowboys'. The annual **Rencontres du Sud**, *tel: 04 90 96 06 27,* in mid July, combines the finest in music, theatre, cinema, art and dance to celebrate the culture of the Mediterranean lands, with performances in both the Roman theatre and Arena. July also sees the **Rencontres Internationales de la Photo**, a prestigious international gathering of photographers, with exhibitions.

Shopping

There are souvenir shops everywhere – this is probablyone of the best places to do your serious present shopping. For Provençal material, try **Les Olivades**, *2 r. J Jaurès*.For santons, visit **Santons Chave**, *14 rond point des Arènes, tel: 04 90 96 15 22*, which also does factory visits. **Actes Sud**, *quai M Dormay*, and **Forum Books**, *r. du Président Wilson*, are both good bookshops with a wide variety of guides and some English books. There is a large **market** every Sat morning in the *blvd des Lices* and *blvd Clémenceau*, and on Wed morning in *blvd E Combes*. A Santon-makers' Fair is held in Dec–mid Jan.

Sightseeing

To visit all the monuments and museums more cheaply, buy a *Visite Générale* pass from participating attractions or the Tourist Office (FFr.60).

The **Arènes**, *r. des Arènes, tel: 04 90 96 03 70* (open daily Apr–Sept 0900–1900; Oct–Mar 1000–1630; guided tours Mon–Sat 1100; FFr.15) is a mini-Colosseum built in about 80AD, one of the world's finest surviving amphitheatres, measuring 136m by 107m. Originally, it had 34 rows of seats, with a capacity of 20–22,000 – considerably more than the entire population of the town.

Today, with the top rows demolished, it can seat around 12,000. Used for gladiators and animal combat by the Romans, it became a fortress during the barbarian invasions and grew into a thriving village, with watchtowers added to the highest levels by the 12th century. It was returned to its original purpose as a stadium in the mid 19th century, when 212 houses and two churches were destroyed and over 1000 people were moved out.

It is still used for bullfights, with Spanish-style *feria* at Easter and Sept, and

History

Perched on the banks of the Grand Rhône, a few kilometres downstream from where the river splits at the start of its massive delta, Arles was first colonised by Greek traders in around 600BC, although only a few fragmentary pots and wall foundations still testify to their long and successful life as an unwilling satellite of Marseille. The site was chosen because of its height, a towering 25m above the flat, fever-laden marshes.

'Modern' Arles dates from 46BC. Three years earlier, the townsfolk had supported Julius Caesar in his quest for power – chiefly because arch-enemy Marseille was supporting Pompey. With Caesar's victory, they became favoured children of the Roman Empire, receiving colonial status and a great deal of subject land, while the town was decked out with all the trappings of wealth, such as a theatre, amphitheatre, circus, baths, and forum, most far larger than the population demanded. Many of these still survive, albeit in ruinous form.

Bring on the Bulls

Small, black and muscled, weighing about 200kg, with sideways curving horns, all Camargue cattle are called bulls, no matter what their gender. Bred especially for the bullring, they are also considered a speciality at the table.

Bullfighting is increasingly popular throughout Mediterranean France, and close to an obsession in the Bouche du Rhône. During the Provençal *cours Camarguais*, local lads attempt to snatch a cockade from between the bull's horns without being gored. The bull is named, remains alive, is able to win and sometimes gains its own fame and following.

The major *feria*, however, are all Spanish-style fights, with professional matadors, and much larger Spanish bulls (up to 400kg, with straight horns), which are always slaughtered. This is officially illegal in France, but the government turns a very blind eye.

cours Camarguais at other times.

The **Théâtre Antique**, *r. du Cloître; tel: 04 90 96 93 30* (open daily Apr–Sept 0900–1900; Oct–Mar 1000–1630; FFr.15) was built in 20–10BC, with space for around 10,000 people. It was closed with advent of Christianity and was used as the local quarry for centuries. It could be rebuilt – all its stones are still in town, but to do so, you would need to demolish a third of the houses in Arles and remove two-thirds of the pillars in the neighbouring cloisters. It is still used for concerts and dance, although, with its back wall destroyed, the acoustics sadly no longer support straight theatre.

At the heart of the town is the *pl. de la République*, surrounded by several magnificent buildings, including the 17th-century **Archbishops' Palace**, now part of the University and the **Hôtel de Ville**, topped by Mars, the God of War, facing belligerently westwards across the border to Languedoc – Arles was the eastern frontier of the County of Provence.

The town's traditional emblem, inherited from the VI legion, is the lion – there are 49 in the square alone. At the centre is an **obelisk** of Turkish granite brought here from the old Roman Circus and erected on a 17th-century base. Pride of place however goes to the superb **Cathédrale de St Trophime**, *pl. de la République*, completed in the 12th century, and named after the first bishop of Arles (late 3rd-century AD), with a superb Romanesque façade depicting key scenes from the Bible. Recently restored (a task lasting some 10 years), many of the sculptures have been returned to their pristine medieval condition. Inside are some fine Aubusson tapestries and the **Musée Nécropole** (Cemetery Museum), with a rich selection of Roman artefacts.

The **Cloître St Trophime**, *pl. de la République* (open daily 0900–1845; FFr.15) is accessed through the courtyard of the old library next door. This is another wonderful Romanesque building, surrounded by imaginative capitals, two-thirds of them topping off Roman pillars. Side-galleries house more splendid Aubusson tapestries and you can also access the roof-level balconies.

The **Musée Arlaten**, *29 r. de la République; tel: 04 90 96 08 23* (open Nov–Mar Tues–Sun, 0900–1200, 1400–1700; Apr, May until 1800; June until 1830; July, Aug daily until 1900; Sept daily until 1800; Oct, until 1730; FFr.15), was founded by Provençal poet, Frédéric Mistral (see p.97). The original medieval mansion was expanded as an 18th-century Jesuit college, while the remains of the

Roman basilica in the courtyard were discovered during its conversion in the early 20th century. Inside are a series of fascinating and wide-ranging exhibits demonstrating different aspects of Provençal history and traditions, from lace to plough-shares, all donated by locals.

Nearby, a series of underground tunnels, the **Cryptoportiques du Forum**, *r. Balze* (open daily Apr–Sept 0900–1900; Oct–Mar 1000–1630; FFr.12) make three sides of a rectangle (89m by 59m). Built in 30–20 BC, they are part of the substructure of the Roman forum.

The **Espace Van Gogh**, *r. Dulau,* (open access) is a 16th–19th century hospital, closed in 1975 and turned into a cultural centre. Van Gogh became a patient here after he famously lopped off his ear (actually only the earlobe). During his year in Arles (Feb 1888–Apr 1889), he painted some 200 paintings and between 150–200 drawings, but sent them all to his brother when he moved to St Rémy (see pp. 100–101). Even his house was flattened by a bombardment on 25th June, 1944. Today, Arles has not a single work by its most famous visitor and has to content itself with signboards and Van Gogh tours.

The **Musée Réattu**, *r. du Grand Prieuré; tel: 04 90 49 37 58* (open daily Apr–Sept 0900–1200, 1400–1900; Oct–Mar 1000–1200, 1400–1630; FFr.15) on the waterfront, houses the city's imaginative fine art collection, in the 12th–17th-century Priory of St Gilles, built by the military Knights of St John. In pride of place is a large, compelling set of Picasso drawings donated by the artist himself after his horrified discovery that the city had no works by Van Gogh. The museum does however have some of Van Gogh's letters and a collection of works by the florid 18th-century artist, Jacques Réattu, after whom the gallery was named. Nearby are the **Thermes de Constantin** (open daily Apr–Sept 0900–1200, 1400–1900; Oct–Mar 1000–1200, 1400–1630; FFr.12), a set of largely ruinous, but still impressive 4th-century AD Roman baths with a formidable hypocaust (under-floor central heating) system.

On the other side of town, the monumental tombs of **Les Alyscamp** (open daily Apr–Sept 0900–1900; Oct–Mar 1000–1630; FFr.12) form a sombre but beautiful avenue, whose name means Elysian Fields (an earlier variation of the more famous Champs-Elysées). The cemetery was first laid out in the 1st century AD outside the city walls, but remained in use until the 12th century when Benedictine monks built the little Church of St Honorat.

Across the river, only a few foundations remain of the **Roman Circus**, a magnificent horse-racing track (450m by 101m), built in 150AD, with space for 20,000 spectators. At one end is the **Musée de l'Arles Antique**, *Presqu'île du Cirque Romain; tel: 04 90 18 88 88;* information, *tel: 04 90 18 88 89* (open Apr–Sept 0900–1900; Oct–Mar 1000–1800; closed Tues. Guided tours: Wed and Fri 1400–1600; a free shuttle bus connects the museum with the old town centre; FFr.35). Inside the ultra-modern building designed by Henri Ciriani, is a wonderful museum offering real insight into the prehistory of the region and life in Roman Arles, until the 6th century AD, with scale models of the town and all its major monuments. The collection also includes exhibits from the old Musée Lapidaire.

⟷ Connections from Arles

To reach **Aix-en-Provence** quickly, take the N113 east, bypassing Salon to join the A8 south; 63 km.

ARLES–MONTPELLIER

It would be hard to find greater contrasts than exist on this route across the flat, marshy Bouches du Rhône, between the modern development of La Grande-Motte and the untouched medieval splendour of Aigues-Mortes, or between the narrow lanes and peaceful grasslands of the *Parc Régional de la Camargue* and the busy holiday resorts pressing in on its boundaries.

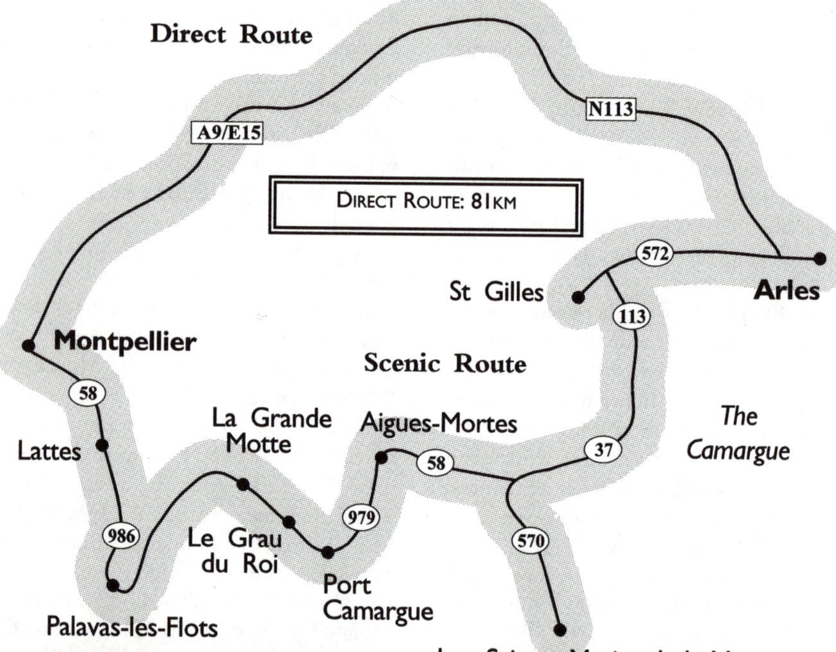

ROUTES

DIRECT ROUTE

Leave Arles on the N113, signposted to **Nîmes** (see p.311). About 27km on, bypass the city and pick up the A9/E15 motorway heading south to **Montpellier**, a further 54km.

If you wish to avoid paying motorway tolls, the N113 runs parallel the whole way, but it is significantly slower, with roundabouts breaking the flow of traffic every few kilometres. Much of the scenic route is also on good roads and is probably a viable alternative, even for those in a hurry. Allow 1hr 30 mins.

SCENIC ROUTE

Leave Arles on the N113, signposted to Nîmes. At Fourques, turn left onto the D572 to **St Gilles**. Backtrack across the Petit Rhône and along the D113 for 3km to the hamlet of Saliers, then turn right (south) onto the D37 to Tour l'Albaron. Head straight across the main crossroads to the **Etang de Vaccarès** and the heartland of the **Camargue.** Alternatively, turn right onto the D570 to **Les-Saintes-Maries-de-la-Mer**. From here, follow the signs back up to the D58 and turn left (west) to **Aigues-Mortes**. Take the D979 south to **Port Camargue**, **Le Grau-du-Roi** and **La Grande-Motte**. Follow the coast road around to **Palavas-les-Flots**, turn inland on the D586, then turn right on the D172 to **Lattes**. From here, take the D58 north to **Montpellier**. Allow 1 day with normal sightseeing stops; 2 days if you wish to go walking, pony-trekking or bird-watching in the Camargue.

ST GILLES

Tourist Office: *1 pl. F. Mistral; tel: 04 66 87 33 75.* Tourist Office and all monuments are open June and Sept, Mon–Sat 0900–1200, 1400–1800; July–Aug Mon–Sat 0900–1200, 1500–1900; Oct–May Mon–Sat 0900–1200, 1400–1700; FFr.15 for a joint ticket.

An ancient settlement, inhabited by the Greeks, then Romans, 2–3000 years ago, St Gilles grew up again in the 11th century around the hermitage of an obscure 8th-century martyr, became a convenient stop on the pilgrim route to Santiago de Compostela (see p.193). The result of its commercial success was the huge 12th-century **Abbey Church**, with its superb Romanesque façade, all three arches crammed with biblical figures. Astonishingly, this survived the Wars of Religion, although the rest of the church did not; this was largely rebuilt in the 17th century. Nearby are the 12–13th century **Maison Romane**, *tel: 04 66 87 40 42,* birthplace of Pope Clement IV (1265–68) and now a small museumof local crafts and traditions,, an ancient staircase and several abbey ruins.

THE CAMARGUE

Until about 4 million years ago, the sea stretched north as far as Lyon. When it retreated, it left salt deposits in the earth. Between the twin arms of the Grand and Petit Rhône, there is today a 85,000 sq km triangular marshland of brackish lagoons and coarse grass, roamed by white horses and black bulls, while flamingos perch on stilts in the shallow water. This is the Camargue, one of the last remaining wild wetlands in Europe. Much of the northern section is agricultural, with apple orchards, wheatfields, but above all, rice paddies, which are used by local farmers as a way of filtering the salt from the fields. The central district is used for herding hardy black long-horn cattle (see p. 84) and the famed white horses, thought to have been introduced by the Arabs about 1000 years ago. None are actually wild, and all have an owner, but they do live out all year round. They are born dark and only turn white with maturity. The south, around the salty lakes, is a regional park and haven for hundreds of species of birds.

Tourist Information

Centre d'Information: *Parc Naturel Régional du Camargue, Pont de Gau; tel: 04 90 97 58 58.* Open Apr–Sept daily 0900–1800; Oct–Mar Sat–Thur 0930–1700.

Accommodation and Food

In the Camargue, the best hotels are in the country, surrounded by nature. The lagoonside **Mas de la Fouque**, *rte du Petit Rhône*, 4km north-west of Stes Maries-de-la-Mer; *tel: 04 90 97 81 02; fax: 04 90 97*

96 84 (expensive), is peaceful, smart and very exclusive. **Le Boumian**, *rte d'Arles, 13400 Stes Maries-de-la-Mer; tel: 04 90 97 81 15; fax: 04 90 97 89 94* (moderate), offers accommodation in cabins or terraced rooms; Provençale cuisine; horses and bicycles for hire; and 4x4 safaris. For cheaper options, try the **Hostellerie du Pont de Gau** *(LF), rte d'Arles, Stes Maries-de-la-Mer, tel: 04 90 97 81 53; fax: 04 90 97 98 54* or **Le Mas de Layalle** *(LF), rte d'Arles* (D570), *Stes Maries-de-la-Mer; tel: 04 90 97 94 81; fax: 04 90 97 70 16.* **HI**: **Hameau de Pioch Badet**; *tel: 04 90 97 51 72*, 10km from Stes Maries-de-la-Mer (take the bus towards Arles and get off at Pioch Badet).

Campsites: **Clos du Rhône** (4-star), *rte d'Aigues Mortes, Stes Maries-de-la-Mer; tel: 04 90 97 85 99* (caravans); **Brise** (3-star), *r. M Carrière, Stes Maries-de-la-Mer; tel: 04 90 97 84 67* (caravans); **Crin Blanc** (3-star), **Hameau de Saliers**, *Albaron; tel: 04 66 87 48 78* (caravans).

Sightseeing

The Camargue has long been romanticised by writers and artists alike with the result that it is noticeably more built-up and fenced in than many visitors expect. There is also more grass and less of obvious interest when driving through. The only way to experience the true nature of the area is slowly, preferably on foot, bicycle or horseback (bike hire in Arles or Stes Maries-de-la-Mer, horse hire from about 30 farms throughout the area; ask the Tourist Office for a list, or contact the **Association Camarguaise de Tourisme Équestre**, *Centre de Gines, Pont de Gau, Stes Maries-de-la-Mer; tel: 04 90 97 86 32*).

There are also numerous sightseeing excursions including trips by Landrover (**Camargue Aventure**, *12 r. du Levant, Le Grau du Roi; tel: 04 66 51 90 90* or *91 r. F Mistral, La Grande Motte; tel: 04 67 56 66 01*) or boat (**Bateau Soleil**, *tel: 04 90 97 85 89*; Apr–June, Sept 1045, 1430, 1615; July–Aug 0915, 1100, 1430, 1615, 1800; **Les Quatres Maries**, *tel: 04 90 97 70 10*; departures 1030, 1430, 1615, and 1800 (July–Aug only); both leave from the *Port Gardian, Stes Maries-de-la-Mer*).

Most of the sights in the Camargue are simply those surrounding you; the breeze playing on the steely water, a flamingo balancing on one leg while fishing, a snowy horse up to its fetlocks in the reeds. The **Parc Ornithologique de Pont de Gau**, *rte d'Arles, Stes Maries-de-la-Mer* (next to the Information Centre); *tel: 04 90 97 82 62* (open 0900–sunset daily) offers a short-cut to birdwatching, with large aviaries and 12 hectares of marshland with well-signed trails. Just to the north is a small museum of gypsy life, the **Panorama des Voyages,** *Pioch Badet, rte de Cacharel; tel: 04 90 97 52 85* (open daily 100–1800; until 2000 in summer, FFr. 18). **The Musée de Cire,** *on D570, just outside Les Sites Maries, tel: 04 90 97 82 65* (open daily Apr–Oct 1000–1200, 1400`–1900) uses wax models to create traditional Camarguais scenes. It has a farm museum and collection of over 200 local birds. The **Musée Camarguais**, *Mas du Pont de Rousty, Albaron* (on the Arles to Stes Maries-de-la-Mer road); *tel: 04 90 97 10 82* (open Oct–Mar Wed–Mon 1000–1645; Apr–Sept daily 0915–1745, until 1845 in July–Aug; FFr.25) is a small museum, housed in an old sheepshed, which gives a vivid portrait of the traditional local lifestyle. The **Château d'Avignon**, on the D38, near the Petit Rhône; *tel: 04 90 97 58 58* (open Apr–Oct, guided tours only at 1000, 1100, 1200, 1330, 1430, 1530, 1630, FFr.20) is a grandiose 19th-century hunting lodge filled with Aubusson and Gobelin tapestries and fine furniture, and surrounded by magnificent gardens.

At the centre of the park, the largest of the local lakes, the **Étang de Vaccarès,** has numerous small paths leading to viewing points and hides for birdwatching. On its eastern shore, the **Centre d'Information Nature**, *La Capelière; tel: 04 90 97 00 97* (open Mon–Sat 0900–1200, 1400–1700; free) has exhibitions on local wildlife.

As an extraordinary hangover from its Roman grants, the municipality of Arles actually stretches some 45km to the coast, where it has its own beaches. Halfway between the two, the little town of **Le Sambuc** is a green resort, offering a range of outdoor activities and the **Musée du Riz** (open 1000–1200, 1400–1800; FFr.25). Nearby **Salin-de-Giraud** (tourist information, *tel: 04 42 86 80 87*; open July–Aug, Mon–Fri 0900–1200, 1400–1800, Sat 0900–1200; Sept–June Mon–Fri 0900–1200, 1330–1600) marks the south-eastern corner of the delta. About 10km south of the town, the étang meets the open sea at the **Plage de Piémançon**, one of the longest stretches of fine sandy beach on the Mediterranean Coast. Also nearby, the **Îlot du Fangassier** offers a protected breeding ground to some 30,000 flamingos who spend their summers in the delta.

LES SAINTES-MARIES-DE-LA-MER

Tourist Office: *5 av. Van-Gogh; tel: 04 90 97 82 55.* Open daily, Oct–Mar, 0900–1800; Apr, May, June, Sept 0900–1900; July–Aug 0900–2000.

Until recently, this was a small, overlooked village without even a harbour. Fishermen simply pulled their boats up onto the beach and the only visitors were pilgrims. Once a year in May, thousands of gypsies arrived for a major festival. Today, it is a thriving little resort town, with fine beaches and watersports. It has also become the main tourist centre for the Camargue. The small **Musée Baroncelli,** *r. Victor Hugo; tel: 04 90 97 87 60* (open Wed–Mon, 0930–1200, 1400–1800, FFr.11) displays Camargue tradition, flora and fauna.

The main attraction is the beautiful **Church of Notre Dame de la Mer** (open daily 0800–1200, 1400–1900 FFr.11 for the crypt) built originally in the 12th century, but extended and fortified in the 15th century by King René of

The Four Marys

Shortly after the Crucifixion, many of Christ's disciples were run out of Palestine. According to legend, one group, including Lazarus, his sister Mary Martha, Mary Magdalene, Maria Jacobe and Maria Salome, was put out to sea in an open boat with no sail and no oars. God guided them safely across the Mediterranean to Provence. On arrival, Martha went north to Tarascon; Mary Magdalene and Lazarus went east towards Marseille; the other two remained in the Camargue, where they built a small church and eventually died. Their graves were lost after locals hid them from pirates so well that they forgot where they had put them.

With them lived their servant, Sara. Some say she was an Egyptian who came with the group; most believe that she was a local gypsy who helped them on their arrival and remained with them to the end. Whichever is true, she has been adopted as the patron saint of all gypsies and a huge gypsy fair is held in Les-Saintes-Maries towards the end of May each year.

Provence, after a vision showed him where to find the relics of the Saintes Maries. Above the door is the symbol of the Camargue with a cross of faith, a heart for charity and an anchor for hope (a sign of safety amongst seafarers). The relics are kept in a tower chapel above the main altar and are only brought down for the festival procession. In the crypt are a magnificently robed statue of Sara and a modern statue presented by Silesian coal miners.

AIGUES-MORTES

Tourist Office: *Porte de la Gardette; tel: 04 66 53 73 00.* Open daily Jun–Sept 0900–2000, Oct–Mar 0900–1200, 1400– 1800.

Accommodation and Food

There are several excellent hotels and restaurants in this very touristy town. The **Hôtel Les Templiers**, *23 r. de la République; tel: 04 66 53 66 56; fax: 04 66 53 69 61* (moderate–expensive) and **Le Saint Louis**, *10 r. Amiral Courbet; tel: 04 66 53 72 68; fax: 04 66 53 75 92* (moderate) are both delightfully decorated old houses within the walled city. **The Hôtel des Croisades**, *2 r. du Port; tel: 04 66 53 67 85; fax: 04 66 53 72 95* (cheap) is an small, simple hotel outside the old town, with views of the ramparts. **Les Arcades**, *23 blvd Gambetta; tel: 04 66 53 81 13; fax: 04 66 53 75 46* (cheap) is a charming old restaurant with a small number of individually decorated bedrooms.

La Camargue, *19 r. de la République; tel: 04 66 53 86 88* (moderate) is another fine restaurant, where gypsy musicians play flamenco in the garden (this is the homeland of the Gypsy Kings). The local centre of café society is *pl. Saint Louis*. **Campsites**: **La Petite Carmargue** (4-star), on the D62; *tel: 04 66 53 84 77. CC* and *Hf* are also represented here.

Sightseeing

In 1241, King Louis IX of France needed a point of embarkation for the 7th Crusade. This small, swampy strip was France's only Mediterranean coast, squeezed between the lands of Aragon and the Counts of Provence. The result was this custom-designed harbour-fort, whose name means 'Dead Water'. It flourished for a century, but by 1350 the sea had retreated, leaving a little backwater town whose powerful walls rise foursquare like a mirage. A **Petit Train**, *tel: 04 66 53 63 40*, offers 20-min tours from the **Porte de la Gardette**, but it is better to park outside the walls and wander at will through the tight grid of narrow streets crammed with small houses, shops and restaurants. At the centre, *pl. Saint Louis* has both a 19th-century statue of the king and the small early Gothic **Chapel of Notre-Dame des Sablons,** where Louis kept vigil the night before sailing, now restored with bright modern windows. There are two other interesting chapels, dedicated to the **Penitents Blancs**, *r. de la République*, and the **Pénitents Gris**, *r. P. Bert*, both built in the 17th century. Access to the ramparts is via the **Tour de Constance,** *pl. Anatole France; tel: 04 66 53 61 55* (open daily 0930–1930; FFr.28), built as a watchtower and the King's residence but later converted into a prison for the Templars, then Huguenots.

Near the station, the **Cinema 3-D Relief**, *pl. de Verdun; tel: 04 66 88 40 91*, shows giant three-dimensional films about the flora, fauna and traditional life of the Camargue. The **Pescalune**, *tel: 04 66 53 79 47* (1000 and 1500 daily) and the **Isles de Stel**, *2 pl. St Louis; tel: 04 66 53 60 70* (1030, 1500, and 1800) offer boat trips round the nearby canals, departing from near the *Tour de Constance.* There is a medieval **Festival of St Louis** at the end of Aug and a local festival in early Oct, with bullfighting.

PORT CAMARGUE TO MONTPELLIER

Tourist Office: *Le-Grau-du-Roi, 30 r. Michel Rédarès; tel: 04 66 51 67 70*; **La Grande-Motte**, *Palais des Congrès, av. Jean Bene; tel: 04 67 56 40 50.*

The last stretch of the journey takes you abruptly into the holiday zone. The strip through Le-Grau-du-Roi, Port Camargue, La Grande-Motte and Palavas-les-Flôts is an almost continuous ribbon of highway, shopping centres, high-rise hotels, beachfront cafés, souvenir shops, overcrowded beaches, watersports centres and marinas. This may be a good area for children to let off steam, but for those acclimatised to the serenity of ancient Provence, it comes as a severe shock.

Between le Grau-du-Roi and Port Camargue, the **Palais de la Mer** is home to **Babyland**, with fairground rides for small children, the **Seaquarium**, *tel: 04 66 51 57 57* (open Jan–Apr, Oct–Dec 1000–1800; May, June and Sept 1000–2000; July–Aug 1000–2200), with some 200 species of fish and other aquatic life and the **Musée de la Mer**.

A little further along, **L'Aquarium Panoramique**, port of La Grande-Motte; *tel: 04 67 56 85 23* (open daily Easter–mid June 1000–1200, 1400–1800; mid June–mid Sept 1000–1230, 1430–1930, and 2045–2200; Nov–Easter Tues–Sun 1400–1800, closed Jan) has over 100 species of Mediterranean sealife. **L'Espace Grand Bleu**, *195 r. Saint Louis, La Grande-Motte; tel: 04 67 56 28 23* (open mid June–mid Sept daily 1000–2000, 1900 on Sat–Sun; FFr.59 a day) is a massive water park, with pools and giant waterslides. The town also has three golf courses, 32 tennis courts and a large watersports centre.

La Grande-Motte is probably the most famous of these coastal developments because of what was, in the 1960s, daringly innovative modern architecture. The whole resort was designed by Jean Balladur, with buildings shaped like pyramids and zigurats. From close to, it is impossible to see the grand plan and the buildings simply look like faded inner city housing estates. From a distance, however, the skyline becomes suitably dramatic.

Palavas-les Flôts is a far gentler town, with over 9km of excellent beaches. The **Musée Albert Dubout**, *r. Abbé de Brocardi; tel: 04 67 68 56 41* (open July–Aug, daily 1600–2400; Nov–Mar Sat–Sun and school holidays (except Mon) 1400–1800; Apr–June, Sept–Oct, Tues–Sun 1400–1900) exhibits works by Albert Dubout in an 18th-century watchtower. Four km west, on a tiny island, reached by a narrow strip between the lagoons and the open sea, stands the remote, ancient **Cathédrale de Maguelone** (open daily 1000–1800; free; ignore the No Entry sign to reach the cathedral).

The first church here was built in the 6th century and it remained the seat of the bishopric for over 1000 years. The existing huge and magnificent Romanesque building was consecrated in 1085 and is one of the most sacred sights in Languedoc. The surrounding area is run as a working community for adults with mental disabilities.

Inland, along the D986 towards Montpellier, **Lattes** was once a port on a river mouth protected by lagoons. The **Musée Archéologique Henri Prades**, *390 rte de Pérols; tel: 04 67 65 31 55* (open Wed–Mon 1000–1200, 1400–1730; FFr. 15) covers some 12 hectares of the ancient town, detailing its history from the 6th century BC to 3rd century AD.

AVIGNON

City of Popes, Petrarch (1304–74) and popular dissent, Avignon is a wonderful mix of history and high culture on the banks of the Rhone. Beginning life as a pre-Roman Celtic settlement, it really appeared on the world map in 1303 when the papal powers decided to move from the anarchic violence of Rome to the peaceful pastures of Provence. Wealth followed the Popes and remained after they moved back to Rome 70 years later.

Today, it is a charming, bustling town with a population of about 90,000 inhabitants and several times that number of tourists in high season.

TOURIST INFORMATION

Tourist Office: *41 cours J Jaurès; tel: 04 90 82 65 11.* Open Mon–Fri 0900–1300 and 1400–1800, Sat 0900–1300 and 1400–1700 (all year); plus Sun 0900–1300, 1400–1700 (Apr–Aug). **Branch**: at the station, *tel: 04 90 82 05 81.* Open Mon–Sat, Apr–Aug 0900–2000; Sept–Mar 0900–1800; at the *Pont d'Avignon*, Mar–Oct, daily 0900–1830; Nov–Feb, Tues–Sun 0900–1700.

ARRIVING AND DEPARTING

Airport

Avignon-Caumont Airport, *tel: 04 90 81 51 15.* Avignon is also within easy reach of Marseille-Provence airport (see p. 60).

By Car

Avignon is very close to both the A7 and A9 motorways, with excellent road connections to other delta towns, Marseille and the rest of France. A ring road runs round the city walls, but there are only seven gates. Whichever one you use, keep going as straight as possible and you will eventually find yourself near the Palais des Papes. **Parking**: There are several large 24-hr underground car parks, including the **Parking Palais des Papes**, *pl du Palais, tel: 04 90 27 50 39*, **Parking des Gares**, *7 av. Monclar, tel: 04 90 82 90 02*, near the station; and the **Parking de l'Oratoire**, *allées de l'Oulle; tel: 04 90 86 97 09*, near the river. Don't leave belongings in the car overnight.

By Train

Station: *porte de la République; tel: 36 35 35 35.* Information open 0900–1830. Station closed 0100–0430. For the town centre, head through *porte de la République* and straight up (north) *cours J Jaurès*.

By Bus

Bus Station: *blvd St Roch, tel: 04 90 82 07 35*, just to the right of the railway station. Regular buses run to Fontaine-de-Vaucluse, Vaison-la-Romaine and the Lubéron.

By Boat

The Rhône is navigable in both directions. For the **Halte Nautique**, *tel: 04 90 85 65 54.*

GETTING AROUND

Tourist Avignon is entirely accessible on

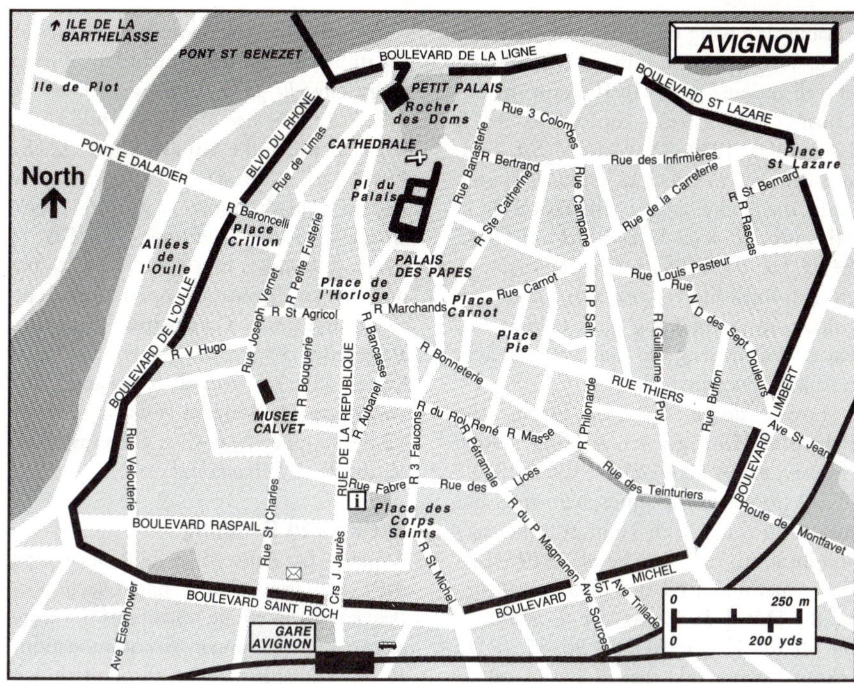

foot. Distances are small and free walking tour maps are supplied by the tourist office. For **guided walking tours**, *tel: 04 90 82 15 98.*

A **Petit Train**, *tel: 04 90 82 64 44*, offers guided tours of the old town (every 30 mins, Easter–Oct), departures from the tourist office and the *pl. des Papes*. The **Mireio** (FFr.250) offers boat tours along the Rhône to Arles, the Camargue and Roquemaure amongst various itineraries, while the **Bateau-Bus** runs round-trips to Villeneuve-les-Avignons (1000, 1115, 1230, 1500, 1615, 1730, 1845; FFr.35). Both depart from *allée de l'Oulle*, near *Pont Daladier; tel: 04 90 85 62 25.*

Taxis: *tel: 04 90 82 20 20.* **Bike Hire**: *Masson Richard, pl. Pie; tel: 04 90 82 32 19*; **Velomania**, *1 r. de l'Amelier; tel: 04 90 82 06 98* and **Depot Sport**, *15 av. de l'Orme fourchu; tel: 04 90 89 77 77.*

Staying in Avignon

Accommodation

Avignon is a tourist honeypot in high season (July–Aug) and reservations are essential. Hotel chains include *Ba, BW, Ch, Ct, CS, F1, Ib, IH, LF, Mc, MO, Nv, Pl* and *RC*, RS.

To tread in the footsteps of the famous, look no further than 16th-century **Hôtel d'Europe**, *12 pl. Grillon; tel: 04 90 82 66 92 ; fax: 04 90 85 43 66* (expensive) where Napoleon was the first of many – it's still the height of comfort and atmosphere, while its **Restaurant de la Vieille Fontaine** offers fine dining in an elegant setting (expensive), closed all day Sun and Mon lunch; Sun brunch served 1130–1500. The 4-star **Hôtel Cloître Saint Louis**, *20 r. du Portail Boquier; tel: 04 90 27 55 55; fax: 04 90 82 24 01,* inhabits one wing of a 17th-century Jesuit monastery and is still imbued with a sense of well-ordered peace. Its **Restaurant St-Louis** (expensive), open Mon–Fri 1200–1400, 1930–2200; closed Sat, Sun, and Feb, serves delicious regional cuisine under the cloister arches. The **Hôtel de la Mirande**, *pl. de la Mirande; tel: 04 90 85 93 93; fax: 04 90 86 26 85* (expensive), an elegant, small and very exclusive hotel in a golden stone building just behind the Palais des Papes, also has an excellent restaurant (expensive).

Lower down the price scale, the **Primotel Horloge**, *1 r. F David, 84000 Avignon; tel: 04 90 86 88 61; fax: 04 90 82 17 32* (moderate) is atmosphere-free, but makes up for it with comfort, efficiency and location, right on the *pl. de l'Horloge*. For something a bit out of the ordinary, try the **Hôtel de Mons**, *5 r. de Mons; tel: 04 90 82 57 16; fax: 04 90 85 19 15* (cheap) whose odd-shaped rooms reflect its origins as a 13th-century chapel. Other good, cheap options include the **Hôtel Provençal**, *13 r. Joseph Vernet; tel: 04 90 85 25 24; fax: 04 90 82 75 81* and the **Mediéval**, *15 r. Petite Saunerie; tel: 04 90 84 11 06; fax: 04 90 82 08 64*, which has some self-catering and family rooms. There are several others in the *r. J Vernet* and *r. Perdiguier*, both off cours *J Jaurès*.

Just outside Avignon, the **Auberge de Cassagne**, *450 allée de Cassagne, 84130 Le Pontet, tel: 04 90 31 04 18; fax: 04 90 32 25 09* (expensive) is a comfortable country hotel with an outstanding restaurant, serving haute cuisine based on traditional Provençal dishes. The **Hostellerie Les Frênes**, *645 av. Les Vertes Rives, 84140 Avignon Montfavet; tel: 04 90 31 17 93; fax: 04 90 23 95 03* (expensive) is an elegant manor, set in its own park, decorated with antiques, and again has a fine traditional restaurant.

Youth Hostels: there is no HI hostel. Unaffiliated hostels include: **Foyer Bagatelle**, *Île de la Barthelasse; tel: 04 90 86 30 39* (bus no. 10; in the midst of a large campsite); the **Squash Club**, *32 blvd Limbert; tel: 04 90 85 27 78* (bus no. 1 to *Hôpital*; squash courts with 16 rooms attached); and the **Foyer YMCA**, *7 chemin de la Justice; tel: 04 90 25 90 20* (bus no. 10 to Monteau; open Apr–Sept; swimming pool). **Campsites**: **Camping Bagatelle** (3-star); *tel: 04 90 86 30 39* (open all year round; caravans), and **Camping St. Bénézet** (4-star), *tel: 04 90 82 63 50* (open Mar–Oct; caravans), both on the *Île de la Barthelasse*.

Eating and Drinking

Avignon has enjoyed its food since papal days, and still offers a fine selection of Provençal and ethnic restaurants (for hotel restaurants, see under Accommodation). *R. des Teinturiers* has several good choices while fast food abounds on *cours J Jaurès*. The *pl. de l'Horloge* by the Palais des Papes is filled with cheerful-looking outdoor restaurants and cafés, but most serve over-priced, poorly presented food.

For a real gastronomic treat, try **Christian Étienne**, *10 r. de Mons; tel: 04 96 86 12 50* (expensive), closed Sat lunch and Sun, an award-winning restaurant in a 12th-century residence beside the Palais des Papes. Nearby, **L'Épicerie**, *10 pl. St Pierre; tel: 04 90 82 74 22* (moderate) is small, informal, friendly and serves delicious Provençal food. Regional specialities are also available at the **Vernet**, *58 r. J Vernet; tel: 04 90 86 64 53* (moderate) and the **Jardin de la Tour**, *9 r. de la Tour; tel: 04 90 85 66 50* (moderate), closed Mon. For really cheap and cheerful food, try **Le Grand Café**, *4 r. Escalier Ste Anne; tel: 04 90 86 86 77* (cheap), a popular student hangout, or an Australian-run tea room,

Woolloomoolloo, 16 bis *r. des Teinturiers; tel: 04 90 85 28 44* (cheap), closed Sun–Mon.

Communications

Post Office: *cours Kennedy; tel: 04 90 86 78 00*, just inside the walls, near the rail station. Currency exchange. Poste restante upstairs.

Money

Several large banks have branches along *r. de la République*. **Chaix Conseil**, *43 cours J Jaurès; tel: 04 90 27 27 89*, has a huge bureau de change (Apr–Oct).

Entertainment

Avignon is proud of its role as one of the main cultural centres of Provence. The tourist office publishes a calendar of events, *Rendez-vous*, every fortnight. From Jan–Mar, **Musique Spirituelles du Soir** runs a series of classical concerts; *tel: 04 90 82 37 92*. The last week in Feb sees the annual **Hivernales de la Danse**, featuring dance from classical ballet to rap and tango; *tel: 04 90 82 33 12*. From Apr–mid May comes the **Festival Arts Baroques en Provence**, with baroque art, music and theatre; *tel: 04 90 27 11 11*. Nov sees the **Automnales de l'Orgues**, a series of organ recitals in many city churches; *tel: 04 90 82 37 92* and the **Baptême des Côtes du Rhône Primeurs**, *tel: 04 90 27 24 16*, when winemakers celebrate the vintage with processions, music, fireworks and liberal tastings.

Above all, Avignon is famous for its summer festival, held each July–Aug. Begun in 1946 by theatre director Jean Vilar, this now ranks as one of the world's great theatrical gatherings, pulling in crowds of up to 500,000; the French equivalent of the Edinburgh festival. For further details and bookings, contact **Bureau du Festival d'Avignon**, *8 bis r. de Mons; tel: 04 90 82 67 08*. There is also an active fringe programme; *tel: 04 48 05 20 97*, and a simultaneous festival of Provençal music and theatre; *tel: 04 90 80 80 88*.

Shopping

There is a flea market every Sat and Sun morning, at the Remparts St Michel, a major craft market, *allées de l'Oulle*, throughout July, and a book fair on *cours J Jaurès* on the first Sat of every month. The narrow alleys to the east of the *r. de la République* are a treasure trove of small boutiques and gift shops.

Sightseeing

Avignon is dominated by the gargantuan **Palais des Papes** (Popes' Palaces), *pl. du Palais; tel: 04 90 27 50 74* (open Nov–Mar 0900–1245, 1400–1800; Apr–Oct 0900–1900 (until 2100 during the Festival; guided visits in English 1130 and 1645; FFr.48). The heavily fortified palace was founded in 1309 when Pope Clement V moved to Avignon, although the earliest surviving tower dates to 1335. Its size is staggering, from the great staircase to the 45 m-long banqueting hall, the *Grand Tinel*. Most rooms are empty, but there are still some superb tiled floors and magnificent frescos, the finest of them, in the *Tinel Chapel* and the Pope's private apartments, by the 14th-century Italian artist, Matteo Giovannetti.

Next door, the **Cathédrale de Notre-Dame-de-Doms** stands at the top of a monumental staircase, on the site of a 4th-century basilica. The current building dates back to 1111, although it was much altered during the reign of John XXII, one of several popes buried in the side chapels, in the 1670s; and the early 19th century, after its use as a Revolutionary prison.

Used by the popes during the Avignon papacy, it saw several coronations and canonisations including that of St Thomas Aquinas. The papal throne stands to the left of the altar. Beyond the cathedral, a path leads up to the gardens of **Rocher-des-Doms**, from where there are wonderful views.

Opposite the palace, the **Conservatoire de Musique** inhabits a glorious Renaissance palace, built in 1619 as a papal mint. At the far end of the vast square, the Renaissance **Petit Palais**, *pl. du Palais des Papes, tel: 04 90 86 44 58* (open Wed–Sun, Sept–Jun 0930–1200, 1400–1800; July–Aug, 1030–1800; free Oct–Mar) was built in the early 14th century by Bérenger Frédol and Arnaud de Via and later became the residence of the Archbishops of Avignon. It is now home to a superb collection of over 300 paintings, including works by Botticelli, Carpaccio and Giovanni di Paolo, showing the progression of art from the symbolic formality of the middle ages to the flowing passion of the High Renaissance.

Elsewhere in the city centre are several other museums. **Musée Calvet**, *r. Joseph Vernet; tel: 04 90 86 33 84* (open Wed–Mon, 1000–1200, 1400–1800; FFr.20) has something for everyone, with an eclectic mixture of Impressionist and romantic art, Egyptian mummies and other artistic curios. Nearby, **Musée Requien**, *67 r. J. Vernet; tel: 04 90 82 43 51* (open Tues–Sat 0900–1200, 1400– 1800; free) is dedicated to natural history, while **Musée Louis Vouland**, *17 r. Victor Hugo; tel: 04 90 86 03 79* (open Tues–Sat, June–Sept 1000–1200, 1400–1800; Oct–May 1400–1800; FFr.20) exhibits 18th-century furniture and objets d'art. The **Musée Lapidaire**, *27 r. de la République; tel: 04 90 85 75 38* (open Wed–Mon, 1000–1200,

The Avignon Popes

In 1305, a massive quarrel between King Philip the Fair of France and the Pope led to the election of the first in a long line of French popes, Clement V (1305–14). Life became increasingly uncomfortable due to serious unrest in Rome and he moved to Avignon, although he always considered the move temporary. His successor, Jean XXII (1316–34) continued to live in Avignon, away from trouble. Benedict XII (1334–42) gave up the pretence that the move was temporary and began the rebuilding of Avignon on a grand scale, with the simple, powerful monastic **Angel Tower**. Clement VI (1342–52) required more pomp and luxury, bought the town in 1348 and began work on a second adjoining palace. Work continued under Innocent VI (1352–62), Urban V (1362–70) and Gregory XI (1370–78). Gregory finally achieved a semblance of peace and took the papacy back to Rome, but his death led to new disasters. Determined to keep the papacy in Italy, the curia elected Urban VI, who proved a cruel and ruthless leader. Many cardinals met to annul the vote and elect Clement VII in his place. Clement (1378–94) returned to Avignon and set up a rival court, where he was followed by Benedict XIII (1394–1423). The city was abandoned in 1403, after a 5 year siege, and the Council of Pisa began work in 1409 to try and heal the breach – which it did by dismissing both popes and electing a third contendor. It was 1417 before the Great Schism was finally healed when all three were sacked and all the different factions agreed to the election of Martin V. The papacy never returned to Avignon, but the city remained Vatican land until 1791 when it was reunited with France during the Revolution.

1400–1800; FFr.6) is the local archaeology museum, in a fine baroque chapel; exhibits include numerous Roman inscriptions.

The **Musée Théodore Aubanel**, *7 pl. St Pierre; tel: 04 90 82 95 54* (open by appointment; free) covers the history of printing and Provençal literature; the **Palais de Roure**, *3 r. Collège du Roure; tel: 04 90 80 80 88* (open Mon–Fri 0900–1200, 1400–1730; free) covers Provençal tradition, popular art and history; and the **Maison Jean Vilar**, *8 r. de Mons; tel: 04 90 86 59 64* (open Tues–Fri 0900–1200, 1400–1800; Sat 1000–1700; free) houses exhibitions and information about the Avignon Festival.

The existing city walls, erected with the palace in the 14th century, are some 5-km long, with 39 towers and seven gates. Jutting from the north-eastern section along the river is the **Pont St-Bénézet**, *r. Ferruce; tel: 04 90 85 60 16* (open Nov–Feb Tues–Sun 0900–1300, 1400–1700; Oct, Mar, daily 0900–1300, 1400–1700; Apr–Sept, daily 0900–1830; FFr.10). Better known, from the famous song, as the Pont d'Avignon, it had 22 arches when built in 1177 by St Bénézet, who was inspired by a vision. The little Chapel of St Nicholas, patron saint of bargemen, was added in the 16th century. Its toll-collecting brought sizeable riches to the town, but the bridge required rebuilding several times before they finally gave up in the 17th century. Today, only four arches tumble into the Rhône. You still have to pay to walk to the end and dance back. In fact, you should sing *sous le pont*, as the dancing took place on a small island, now vanished, under the bridge. Next door, the **Musée en Images**, *r. Ferruce; tel: 04 90 82 56 96* (open Mar–Sept 0900–1900; Oct–Feb Tues–Sun 0900–1700; closed Jan–mid Feb and mid Nov–mid Dec; FFr.24) has 1000 panoramic photos of Avignon.

The **Île de Barthelasse**, in the middle of the Rhône, has been long been Avignon's playground. During the Papacy this was home to prostitutes and thieves, whilst in the 19th century Provençal poets, the *Félibres* led by Frédéric Mistral, would recite verses beneath the weeping willows. Today it is a favourite picnic spot with a large summer swimming pool and several campsites.

Local Hero

Frédéric Mistral (1830–1914) lived in Maillane, studied law in Avignon, but went on to become a poet, journalist and philosopher. As founder of the Félibres group of writers, he also became the champion of the Provençal language and culture. In the late 19th century the Parisian authorities decided that all education should be in French and the regional languages came close to extinction. Mistral took a stand, writing all his works, from poetry to articles, in Provençal, always adding a translation, so that others could understand. In 1904, he won the Nobel Prize for Literature and used the money to found the Arlaten Museum (see p. 84) in an effort to preserve other aspects of traditional Provençal life. A statue of him stands in the *pl. du Forum*, Arles.

AVIGNON–ARLES

It is only a short hop between these two great Rhône cities and it would be easy to whisk between them in a matter of minutes, but to do so would be almost criminal in an area positively bulging with fascinating sights. The first of our two scenic routes, in particular, is one of the finest in the book Allow 1–2 days for Route 1, one day for Route 2.

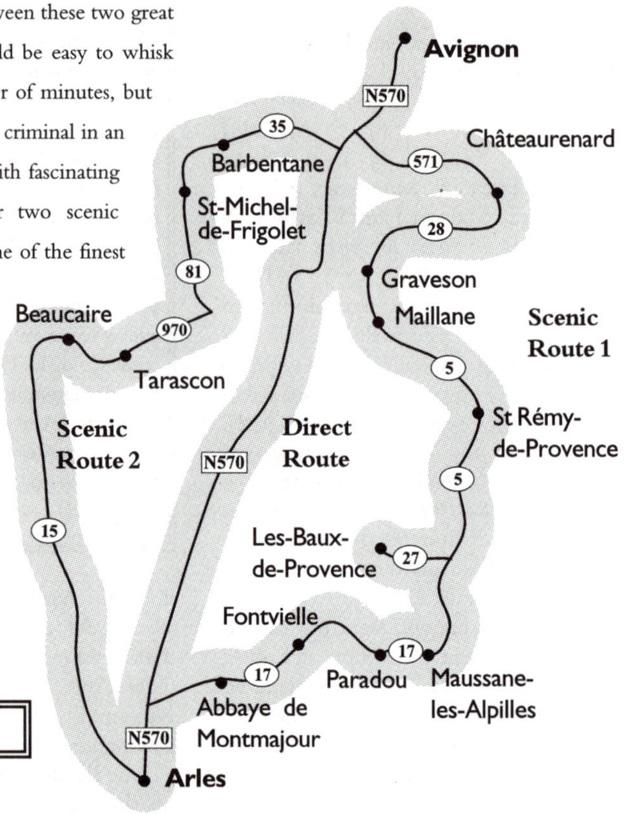

DIRECT ROUTE: 35 KM

ROUTES

DIRECT ROUTE

Leave Avignon on the N570 which crosses the Durance river and continues down to Arles. Allow up to 40 mins to do the 35 km.

SCENIC ROUTE I

Leave Avignon on the N570, signposted to Arles. Cross the bridge and turn left immediately onto the D571, then left again onto the D28 to **Châteaurenard**. Leave here on the D28 and follow it south-west to **Graveson**, then turn south onto the D5 through **Maillane** to **St-Rémy-de-Provence**. Keep going south on the D5 and then turn right onto the D27 for **Les Baux-de-Provence**. Retrace your route back laong the D27 to the D5. turn right and continue south until you reach **Maussane-les-Alpilles**, then turn right onto the D17, which continues through **Paradou**,

Fontvieille, and past the **Abbaye de Montmajour** to link up with the N570 for the last small stretch into Arles.

Scenic Route 2

Leave Avignon on the N570, signed Arles, cross the bridge, and at Rognonas, turn right onto the D35. After about 6km, a small slip road leads to **Barbentane**. Rejoin the D35, then turn left onto the D81, which leads over the hills to **St-Michel-de-Frigolet**. Continue on the D81 to the main crossroads then turn right onto the D970 for **Tarascon**. Cross the bridge into **Beaucaire** then head south on the D15 which follows the line of the river through the reedbeds and apricot orchards to Fourque, where another bridge leads across to Arles.

CHÂTEAURENARD

Tourist Office: *Tour de Griffon; tel: 04 90 94 23 27*. Open Tues–Sat 0845–1200, 1500–1900, Sun 1000–1200 July–Sept; Tues–Sat 0845–1200, 1400–1800 Oct–June. Accommodation includes **Les Glycines** *(LF), 14 av. V. Hugo; tel: 04 90 94 10 66; fax: 04 90 94 78 10* (cheap). **Campsite**: **Camping Châteaurenard**, *746 av. Jean Mermoz; tel: 04 90 94 46 81* (2-star; caravans).

This is an attractive hillside town surrounded by market gardens. The Tourist Office is housed in the town's main attraction, the **Tour de Griffon** (opening hours as above; FFr.15), one of two medieval towers which are all that remain of a 12th–15th century fort.

Châteaurenard is the ideal place to shop for your picnic with several speciality shops as well as a vast wholesale produce market. The **Moulin Christian Rossi**, *quartier St Eloi; tel: 04 90 94 02 00* (open Mon–Fri 0800–1200, 1330–1800) is an olive mill, open for visits and shopping. You can also visit the **Distillerie Frigolet**, *26 r. Voltaire; tel: 04 90 94 11 08* (open business hours) for a tasting of the famous liqueur which supports the local monastery and the **Fromagerie Kilgus**, *684 chemin du Maire; tel: 04 90 94 56 88*, where goats' cheeses are handmade on the premises.

GRAVESON

Tourist Information: *Mairie; tel: 04 90 95 71 05*. Open Mon–Fri 0830–1200, 1400–1800. For accommodation, try **Le Mas des Amandiers** *(LF), rte d'Avignon; tel: 04 90 95 81 76* (cheap).

Like many of the local villages, Graveson seems to thrive on equal parts of tourism and fruit. The **Musée des Aromes et du Parfum**, *La Chevèche, Petite Rte du Grès; tel: 04 90 95 81 72* (open daily 1000–1800 Apr–Sept; 1000–1200, 1400–1800 Oct–Mar; FFr.20) offers a delightful tour of the perfume business, from copper stills to a 19th-century laboratory, an experimental garden filled with aromatic plants and a fine collection of Lalique perfume bottles. There are occasional aromatherapy courses (dates on request).

The **Musée de Peinture Auguste Chabaud**, *cours National; tel: 04 90 90 53 02* (open daily 1000–1200, 1500–1900 June–Sept; 1330–1830 Oct–May) is dedicated to the Fauvist artist, Auguste Chabaud, who was born in Nîmes in 1882, but spent most of his life in Graveson, where he died in 1955. Every Fri 1600–2000 mid May–Oct, there is a **Marché Paysan**, selling local crafts.

MAILLANE

Tourist Information: *Mairie; tel: 04 90 95 74 06*. Open Mon–Fri 0800–1200, 1400–1800, Sat 0800–1200. For a good regional meal, try **L'Oustaler Maïanen**,

16 r. Lamartine; tel: 04 90 95 74 60 (moderate).

Maillane is a pleasant, but uneventful little town filled with typically Provençal houses. The real reason to stop here is to visit the **Museon Mistral**, *11 r. Lamartine; tel: 04 90 95 74 06* (open Apr–Sept 0930–1130, 1430–1830 Tues–Sun; 1000–1130, 1400–1630 Oct–Mar; FFr.20), home of Frédéric Mistral, champion of Provençal language and culture (see p. 52), from 1876–1914. At the **Fabrique des Santons**, *av. des Meuilles; tel: 04 90 95 80 27* (open Mon–Sat 0900–1200, 1400–1800, Sun 1500–1800) you can watch the tiny pottery figures being produced.

ST-RÉMY-DE-PROVENCE

Tourist Office: *pl. J.Jaurès; tel: 04 90 92 05 22.* Open June–Sept Mon–Sat 0900–1200, 1400–1900, Sun 0900–1200; Oct–May Mon–Sat 0900–1200, 1400–1800.

Accommodation and Food

Near the town centre, the **Château de Roussan**, *rte de Tarascon; tel: 04 90 92 11 63; fax: 04 90 92 37 32* (expensive) is a small 18th-century château set in magnificent grounds, built by a descendant of Nostradamus. Small hotels worth inspecting include **Le Chalet Fleuri** (*LF*), *15 r. F. Mistral; tel: 04 90 92 03 62; fax: 04 90 92 60 28* (cheap); the **Ville Vert**, *pl. de la République; tel: 04 90 92 06 14; fax: 04 90 92 56 54* (cheap) and the **Hôtel des Arts**, *30 blvd Victor-Hugo; tel: 04 90 92 08 50; fax: 04 90 92 55 09* (cheap).

Just out of town are a couple of elegant 4-star hotels, which also serve wonderful haute cuisine in their formal restaurants. The 19th-century **Château des Alpilles**, D31 (near Glanum)*; tel: 04 90 92 03 33; fax: 04 90 92 45 17* (expensive; closed 14 Nov–19 Dec, 7 Jan–19 Mar) is a magnificently furnished historic home which has, in the past, played host to many famous names, including Châteaubriand, Lamartine and Thiers. The **Domain de Valmouriane**, *Pte Rte des Baux* (D27)*; tel: 04 90 92 44 62; fax: 04 90 92 37 32*, (expensive) is a restored *mas* (stone Provençal farmhouse) with 14 bedrooms. **Campsites: Camping Municipal Mas de Nicholas**, *av. T. Aubanel, tel: 04 90 92 27 05* (4-star); **Camping Pegomas**, *rte de Noves, tel: 04 90 92 01 21* (3-star; caravans); **Camping Mon Plaisir**, *chemin Mon Plaisir, tel: 04 90 92 22 70* (2-star; caravans).

For a good Provençal meal without accommodation, try **Alain Assaud**, *13 blvd Marceau; tel: 04 90 92 37 11* or **La Maison Jaune**, *15 r. Carnot; tel: 04 90 92 56 14* (both moderate).

Sightseeing

This attractive small town has more than its fair share of interesting museums. In 1748, Marquis Joseph de Pistoye built a magnificent stone mansion, the *Hôtel Estrine*, which became the home of their official representative of the Princes of Monaco (overlords of St-Rémy). It now houses the **Centre d'Art Presence Van Gogh**, *8 r. Estrine; tel: 04 90 92 34 72* (open Tues–Sun 1000–1200, 1500–1900, closed Jan–Mar; FFr.8). The ground floor is devoted to the life and times of Van Gogh, who lived in St Rémy from 1889–90; the upper floors have a series of constantly changing exhibitions of contemporary art. The Tourist Office also organises Van Gogh walks around the sites of various paintings *(tel: 04 90 92 05 22).* The **Musée Archéologique**, *Hôtel de Sade, pl. Favier; tel: 04 90 92 13 07* (open daily 1000–1800; FFr. 14) is home to the many finds from archaeological digs at Roman Glanum, with a fascinating collection of architectural details and everyday objects while the **Musée des Alpilles**, *Hôtel Mistral de Mondragon, pl. Flavier; tel: 04 90 92 08 10* (open daily 1000–1200, 1500–2000 July–Aug; 1000–1200, 1400–1800 Sept–Oct, Jan–June; 1000–1200, 1400–1700 Nov–Dec; FFr.14) covers local geology, archaeology, ethnology and history. Even the little **Chapelle de Notre-Dame de Pitié**, *av. Durand-Maillane; tel: 04 90 92 35 13* (open daily 1030–1230, 1500–1930 July–Aug, 1430–1830 Apr–June, Sept–Oct; Nov–Mar by appointment; FFr.15) is now home to the **Donation Mario Prassinos**, holding regular temporary exhibitions. While in town, also visit the mainly 18th-century **Collegiate Church of St-Martin**, *off blvd Marceau*, which has a Gothic bell-tower, one of the largest and most magnificent organs in France (free concerts, Sat 1730, July–Sept) and several fine paintings and sculptures; and the **Parfumerie Artisanale Sommerard**, *34 cours Mirabeau; tel: 04 90 92 48 70* (open Mon–Fri 0900–1200, 1400–1800; Sat–Sun 1000–1200, 1500– 1800), to see the production of perfumes and the vegetable-based *Savon de Marseille* (soap).

As you leave town, heading south towards Les Baux, you reach the remains of the ancient town of **Glanum**, *av. Van Gogh* (D5); *tel: 04 90 92 23 79* (open 0900–1900 Apr–Sept; 0900–1200, 1400–1700 Oct–Mar; FFr.32), founded by Phocaean traders in the 3rd century BC. It reached its zenith under the Caesars when it was a major stop on the Via Domitia, the major road between Italy and Spain, but it continued to flourish until destroyed by a barbarian invasion in 370 AD. Unusually, the later town moved to a different site, leaving many of the streets, squares and even sewers remarkably intact. Within the former Roman quarries, an old farmhouse, the **Mas de la Pyramide**, *tel: 04 90 92 00 81* (open daily 0900–1200, 1400–1700; FFr.15) houses a small rural life museum. Just behind the Roman town is the **Cloître St-Paul de Mausole**, *quartier St Paul; tel: 04 90 92 05 22* (open daily 0900–1200, 1400–1800; free), a former monastery, later converted into a nursing home where Van Gogh lived during one of the unhappiest, but most prolific years of his life. You can still visit the fine 12th-century Romanesque church and cloister.

On the opposite side of the main road are **Les Antiques**, two of the finest Roman monuments in Provence; a Triumphal Arch, dating to about 6BC, which celebrates Caesar's victory over the Gauls and the memorial monument (known incorrectly as the Mausoleum), built in about 30 AD by the Julii family in honour, probably, of Caius and Lucius, the grandsons of Augustus Caesar.

LES ALPILLES

South of St Rémy, the road crosses the **Alpilles**, a small mountain range some 25 km long and up to 8km wide. The hills are fairly low, at only 300–400m high, but the 'little Alps' were given their name with good reason. From a distance, their jagged limestone crests appear uncannily like the towering peaks of their big brothers. There are numerous birds, wildflowers and ruined châteaux to be seen on the many walks in the vicinity, while the lower slopes are quarried or provide shelter for vineyards and olive groves.

LES BAUX-DE-PROVENCE

Drive carefully on the approach road to Les Baux. This is one of the most popular tourist attractions in France, and the small, winding mountain road is hair-raisingly crammed with a caterpillar trail of coaches. Set on a table-flat mountain (425m) surrounded by sheer walls of rock, the village has been inhabited on and off since the Neolithic era, but reached the height of its prosperity in the 10th–12th centuries under ambitious and unruly local warlords who claimed descent from the Magi and again after 1483 when Louis XI pulled down the castle and brought the area under the mantle of the French crown. A further flush of money has been injected since the 19th century both by tourism and by the discovery of a local mineral, to which the town gave its name – bauxite.

Given the difficult access to the summit, it is hard to imagine why anyone felt the need for further fortification, but they did and the crest is entirely surrounded by solid defensive walls. Inside, half the area is given over to a village of golden-stone houses and narrow streets, now dedicated entirely to tourism, with wall-to-wall souvenir shops and crêperies; the other half is a splendid, if ruinous citadel.

Tourist Information

Tourist Office: *Impasse du Château; tel: 04 90 54 34 39.* Open 0900–1200, 1400–1700 Apr–Oct; daily 0900–1830 Nov–Mar.

Accommodation and Food

There are plenty of small cafés and restaurants within the walls, but most of the best hotels are at the foot of the mountain. For a truly luxurious experience, with gastronomic food, try the **Oustau de Baumanière**, *Val d'Enfer* (D27); *tel: 04 90 54 33 07; fax: 04 90 54 40 46* (expensive; restaurant closed Wed and Thur lunch; from mid Nov–mid Dec). The **Auberge de la Benvengudo**, *Vallon de l'Arcoule; tel: 04 54 32 54; fax: 04 90 54 42 58* (expensive) offers an ivy-clad, country-house style comfort. The **Mas d'Aigret**, *tel: 04 90 54 33 54; fax: 04 90 54 41 37* (moderate–expensive) is a rambling old farmhouse designed for life outdoors, with plentiful terraces and balconies and delicious food. Surrounded by olive groves, the **Mas de L'Oulivie**, *tel: 04 90 54 35 78; fax: 04 90 54 44 31* (moderate) is a small, comfortable country hotel (light lunches by arrangement, no dinners). For something more affordable, try the **Hostellerie de la Reine Jeanne**, *Village des Baux; tel: 04 90 54 32 06; fax: 04 90 54 32 33* (cheap), at the entrance to the village itself.

Sightseeing

The best way to tackle the sights is to climb right through the village to the citadel, then work your way back downhill. The largely ruinous but intensely atmospheric **Citadel**, *Grande Rue; tel: 04 90 54 55 56* (open 0830–2030 Apr–Sept; 0900–1700 Oct–Mar; FFr.33 for a *Passeport Musée* ticket, valid for 1 day, which also covers entry to the Santons, Paintings, History and Olive-tree museums) covers a 5-hectare site, much of it taken up with a vast empty spur of rock, once used for military training and parades, now adorned with several faithfully reconstructed **siege machines** and a huge **monument** to the poet, Charles Rieu (1846–1924). There are also spectacular views. Near the citadel entrance, the **Musée de l'Histoire des Baux**, *Hôtel de la Tour de Brau; tel: 04 90 54 37 37* (open daily Apr–Sept 0830–2000; Nov–Feb 0900–1700) tells the history of the settlement with models and illustrations from prehistoric times right up to World War II. Next door, the little **Musée d'Olivier** (open daily Apr–Sept 0830–2000; Nov–Feb 0900–1700) in the 12th-century Romanesque **Chapel of St-Blaise** pays homage to the olive tree with an audio-visual presentation of paintings by Van

Gogh, Gauguin and Cézanne. Nearby are the parish **Church of St Vincent**, built in the 13th century as part of a local priory, and the tiny 17th-century **Chapelle des Penitents Blancs** is lavishly decorated with frescos of the Nativity by modern artist, Yves Brayer.

Within the village are many fine Renaissance houses. The 15th-century *Hôtel Jean de Brion* is home to the **Fondation Louis Jou**, *Grand Rue Frédéric Mistral; tel: 04 90 54 34 17* (open daily 1000–1300, 1400–1900 Apr–Sept; FFr. 15), a small museum of medieval books, with works by the local master printer, Louis Jou, and engravings by Dürer, Rembrandt and Goya, amongst others. The 15th-century *Hôtel de Manville* houses a **Musée d'Art Contemporain**, *Grand Rue; tel: 04 90 54 34 03* (open daily 0900–2000 Apr–Sept; 0900–1200, 1400–1700 Oct–Mar) with engravings and paintings by François Hérain, prints by Louis Jou and changing exhibitions of modern art. The 16th-century *Hôtel des Porcelets* is home to the **Musée Yves Brayer**; *tel: 04 90 54 36 99* (open daily 1000–1200, 1400–1830 Apr–Oct; 1000–1200, 1400–1730 Nov–Dec, mid Feb–Mar; FFr.20) with a retrospective of Brayer's paintings, drawing and prints. The 16th-century *Hôtel de Ville* has a small **Musée des Santons**, *r. de l'Ancienne-Mairie; tel: 04 90 54 34 17* (open summer daily 0930–1800; winter Mon–Fri 0900–1200, 1400–1700; free) with a large collection of 17th- and 18th-century santons and a superb Christmas crib.

At the bottom of the hill, the **Cathédrale d'Images**, *Val d'Enfer, rte de Maillane* (D27); *tel: 04 90 54 38 65* (open daily, 1000–1900 mid Mar–mid Nov; FFr.40; shows last 30 mins) is a vast stone hall, cut into old quarries in a spur of Les Alpilles. With 38 white stone screens, and powerful sound track, each season offers a new, dazzling audio-visual presentation, with up to 2500 photographs, with subjects covering anything from the underwater world to the Sistine Chapel. The quarries remain at a constant temperature of 15°C. Nearby, **La Petite Provence du Paradou**, *75 av. de la Vallée des Baux; tel: 04 90 54 35 75* (open daily 1100–2000 June–Oct; 1400–1900 Nov–May) is a lovingly handmade Provençal village in miniature, with 32 buildings and 300 santon figurines.

MAUSSANNE-LES-ALPILLES

Tourist Office: *pl. de Laugier de Monblan; tel: 04 90 54 52 04.* Open Mon–Sat 1000–1200, 1500–1800.

Accommodation and Food

In the centre of the village, **L'Oustalon**, *pl. de l'Eglise; tel: 04 90 54 32 19; fax: 04 90 54 45 57* (cheap–moderate) offers simple antique-clad rooms and honest solid regional cusine. **Les Magnanarelles** *(LF), 104 av. de la Vallée des Baux; tel: 04 90 54 30 25; fax: 04 90 54 40 04* (cheap–moderate) is a pleasant small hotel with attached restaurant. **Ou Ravi Provençau**, *34 av. de la Vallée des Baux; tel: 04 90 54 31 11* (expensive) serves delicious Provençal food. **Campsite: Camping Romarain**, *rte de St Rémy; tel: 04 9054 33 60* (4-star).

Sightseeing

Maussane has relatively little of its own to offer, but is still within the magic tourist circle of Les Baux. The olives of the Alpilles are renowned for their quality and rich golden oil. Visit the **Cooperative des Baux**, *Maitre Cornille; tel: 04 90 54 32 37*, for a look at a working mill, and, most importantly, to buy. For your wine, try the **Mas de la Dame**, *rte de St Rémy* (D5);

tel: 04 90 54 32 24 (open daily 0800–1800 for sales; by apointment for tours; FFr.10). Nearby, the **Musée des Santons Animés**, *rte de St Rémy; tel: 04 90 54 39 00* (open daily 1000–1400; Oct–Mar 1330–1900 Apr–Sept; FFr.20) has numerous tableaux of local scenes decorated by the little pottery figurines, with a special Christmas exhibition (see p. 76).

FONTVIEILLE

Tourist Office: *5 r. Marcel Honorat; tel: 04 90 54 67 49.* Open daily 0900–1200, 1400–1830 July–Sept only.

Accommodation and Food

The **Auberge de la Regalido** *(RC), r. Frédéric Mistral; tel: 04 90 54 60 22; fax: 04 90 54 64 29* (expensive) is a lovingly restored oil mill with 15 bedrooms and a small restaurant serving *haute cuisine* with a Provençal twist (open Mon–Sat, 1200–1330, 1930–2130 Oct–June; closed Mon, Tues lunchtime July–Sept only). Those on a smaller budget should try the **Hostellerie de la Tour** *(LF), 3 r. des Plumelets; tel: 04 54 72 21* (cheap), **La Ripaille**, *rte des Baux; tel: 04 90 54 73 15; fax: 04 90 54 60 69* (cheap–moderate); or **La Peiriero**, *av. des Baux; tel: 04 90 54 76 10; fax: 04 90 54 62 60* (cheap–moderate). **Campsite: Camping Pins**, *r. Michelet; tel: 04 90 54 78 69* (3-star).

Sightseeing

The famous 19th-century Alphonse Daudet catapulted Fontvieille to fame when he published a book, *Lettres de Mon Moulin*, set in the local area. The mill itself is still there and open to the public, now housing a small museum dedicated to the life and works of Daudet; the **Moulin Daudet**; *tel: 04 90 54 67 49* (open 0900–1230, 1400–1800 Apr–Sept; 1000–1200, 1400–1700; FFr.10). Between Apr and Sept, there are guided tours of Daudet-country; contact **Parcours Daudet**, *5 r. M. Honorat; tel: 04 90 54 67 49.* Nearby is a working olive oil mill, the **Moulin Bédarrides**; *tel: 04 90 54 70 04* (open Mon–Sat 0800–1200, 1400–1800; Sun by appointment). Also nearby are the 19th-century **Château de Montauban**, where Daudet was a frequent guest, and, at **Barbegal**, a complex system of Roman aqueducts and watermills. In the town centre is a fine 17th-century church.

Just beyond the village is the **Abbaye de Montmajour**, *rte de Fontvieille; tel: 04 90 54 64 17* (open daily 0900–1900 Apr–Sept; 0900–1200, 1400–1700 Oct–Mar; FFr.28). Built on three small hills which rose out of the swamps, it towers up into the sky, a landmark for miles around, one of the largest monasteries of medieval France. Founded in the 10th century, by the late 13th century it was a formidably rich and powerful motherhouse with a network of 56 priories. Later years were less kind, but a religious community remained here until the Revolution. There is still a huge complex, with some magnificent buildings and fine architectural details.

BARBENTANE

Tourist Information: *Mairie, Le Cours; tel: 04 90 95 50 39.* Open Mon–Thur 0800–1200, 1330–1730, Fri 0800–1200, 1330–1630.

Barbentane is an attractive small town surrounded by market gardens, overlooking the Rhône. Behind high walls within the village, the **Château de Barbentane**, *tel: 04 90 95 51 07* (open daily 1000–1200, 1400–1800 July–Aug; Thur–Tues 1000–1200, 1400–1800 Apr–June, Sept–Oct; open Sun 1000–1200, 1400–1800 Nov–Mar; FFr.30) is a delightful 17th–18th-century building, both interior and exterior modelled on the great châteaux of northern France. The interior is filled with Louis XV and XVI furniture; the lavish gardens include formal Italianate terraces. The **Moulins à Huile du Mogadore**, *9 av. Bertherigues; tel: 04 90 95 57 90* (open Apr–Sept daily 1000–1200; Oct–Mar by appointment; free) has oil presses from the 16th and 17th centuries. On the slopes above the town, there are excellent views from the terrace beside the formidable **Tour Anglica** (not open), the ruined keep of a 14th-century castle built by Cardinal Anglic de Grimoard, brother of Pope Urbain V.

The **Parc Floral Tropical**, *Terre-Fort, rte de la Gare; tel: 04 90 95 50 72* (open daily 0930–1200, 1430–1800 mid July–Aug; Fri–Mon, Wed 1000–1200, 1430–1700 Sept–mid Oct, mid Feb–mid July; Sat–Mon 1400–1700 mid Oct–mid Feb) is a huge and lavishly luxuriant park with a banana plantation, spice and exotic fruit gardens, orchid houses and a global collection of butterflies and insects. The best time to see the orchids is in winter, but in summer (June–Sept) tropical butterflies fly freely through the greenhouses.

ABBAYE DE ST-MICHEL-DE-FRIGOLET

Still a working abbey, St Michel, *tel: 04 90 95 70 07* (open daily year round; guided tours on request) was founded in the 10th century for monks recouperating from fevers caught in the unhealthy marches around Montmajour (see above). It has had a colourful history, owned by several different monastic orders. It was closed during the Revolution, besieged in 1880, and served as a concentration camp in World War I, but today, all is calm. The highlight of the visit is the **Chapel of Notre-Dame-du-Bon-Remède**, filled with fine 17th-century gilded woodwork donated by Anne of Austria, after a pilgrimage led to her one and only pregnancy (the child later became Louis XIV) and the sumptuously decorated 19th-century **Abbey Church of St Michel**. There are also 12th-century cloisters and a 17th-century Chapter House, a small museum and even little hotel.

TARASCON

Tourist Office: *59 r. des Halles; tel: 04 90 91 03 52.* Open Mon–Sat 0900–2000, 1400–1800.

Accommodation and Food

Several friendly, inexpensive hotels hug the square by the station. Chain hotels include *F1.* **Le Saint Jean** *(LF), 24 blvd V. Hugo, tel: 04 90 91 13 87; fax: 04 90 91 32 42*, is cheap and cheerful. For something a little further up the scale, try the **Mazets des Roches**, *rte de Fontvieille* (D33); *tel: 04 90 91 34 89; fax: 04 90 43 53 29* (moderate). **Campsites: Camping St Gabriel**, *Mas Ginoux, quartier St Gabriel, tel: 04 90 91 19 83* (2-star); **Camping Tartarin**, *rte de Vallabrègues, tel: 04 90 91 01 46* (2-star). **HI**: *31 blvd Gambetta; tel: 04 90 91 04 08* (500m from the station). There are a few reasonable restaurants in the small streets between the castle and Tourist Office.

Sightseeing

This rather drab town, which suffered heavy bombing during World War II, is named after the last of the legendary dragons in France. The *tarasque* was a fearsome beast which terrorised the region until it was defeated by St Martha (see also p. 89), who used her crucifix to banish it to the depths of the river in about 48AD. A festival in honour of her victory was instituted in 1474 by Good King René and she is still honoured twice a year on the

Monday of Pentecost, with a bullfight, and the 29th July with a procession. The **Maison de Tartarin**, *55 bis blvd Itam; tel: 04 90 91 05 08* (open Mon–Sat 1000–1200, 1400–1900 Apr–Sept; 1000–1200, 1400–1700 Oct–Mar; FFr.8), named after Alphonse Daudet's fictional character, contains a model of the dragon amongst its exhibits. The **Musée Charles Demery-Tissus Souleïado**, *39 r. Proudhon, 13150 Tarascon; tel: 04 90 91 08 80* (open Mon–Fri 0900–1200, 1330–1800; FFr.30), belongs to one of the foremost exponents of Provençal materials, with 40,000 print screens, costumes, cloth and ceramics. The **Cloître des Cordeliers**, *pl. F. Mistral* (open Wed–Mon, 1000–1200, 1430–1730 summer; Wed–Mon 1000–1200 winter) is a beautiful Renaissance cloister, dating to about 1550. In pride of place, towering over the town and Rhône is the monumental **Château du Roi René**, *blvd du Roi René; tel: 04 90 91 01 93* (open daily0900–1900 Apr–Sept; 0900–1200, 1400–1700 Oct–Mar; FFr.28), built on the site of a Roman legionary camp and 9th-century fort. Work on the present edifice began in 1401 under Louis II of Anjou and was completed by his son, 'Good King René'. Abandoned after the integration of Provence into France in 1481, it later became a prison, until 1926. The architecture and views remain impressive, and there are some fine tapestries, but there are few other furnishings.

BEAUCAIRE

Tourist Office: *24 cours Gambetta; tel: 04 66 59 26 57.* Accommodation can be found at **L'Oliveraie** *(LF), rte de Nîmes; tel: 04 66 59 16 87; fax: 04 66 59 08 91* (cheap); the **Hôtel Robinson** *(LF), rte de Remoulin; tel: 04 66 59 21 32; fax: 04 66 59 21 32* (cheap). **Campsite**: **Camping Le Rhodanien**, *Champ de Foire; tel: 04 66 59 25 50* (3-star; open Mar–Oct).

Sightseeing

Directly opposite Tarascon, Beaucaire is much smaller but rather prettier, with parks right along the river which make excellent picnic sites. From 1217 until the arrival of the railway in the mid 19th century, this was the site of a massive annual fair (late July) which would attract anything up to 300,000 people. Just behind the fairground is an imposing, 11th–13th century **castle** dismantled by Richelieu in in the 17th century and still largely ruinous. It comes to life each summer when used for a dramatic show of birds of prey in free flight: **Les Aigles de Beaucaire**, *tel: 04 66 59 26 72* (performances daily 1500, 1600, 1700, 1800 July–Aug; Thur–Tues 1400, 1500, 1600, 1700 25th Mar–1st Nov). The **Musée Auguste Jacquet**, *Montée du Château; tel: 04 66 59 47 61* (open Wed–Mon) has displays on the history of the Beaucaire Fair, local archaeology, history and traditions.

Out of Town

The **Mas des Tourelles**, *rte de Bellegarde; tel: 04 66 59 19 72* (open Apr–Oct daily 1400–1900; Nov–Mar Sat 1400–1800) is a Roman wine cellar, reconstructed on an archaeological site; visits come complete with tastings of 'Roman' wines. **Le Vieux Mas**, *rte de Fourques; tel: 04 66 59 60 13* (open daily 1000–1900, closed Jan; FFr.25) is a working farm with animals, a petting section for small children and demonstrations of traditional crafts and tools. The **Abbaye de St-Roman**, 5 km north on the D999, followed by a short walk through the woods, began life in the 12th century, was transformed into a castle in the 16th and demolished in 1850. There are still excellent views, a small chapel and abbey ruins.

AVIGNON–AUBENAS

This stunningly scenic alternative to the busy Rhône Valley route north crosses the vineyards and scattered hill villages of the Côtes du Rhône before soaring along the rim of the magnificent Gorges de l'Ardèche, and dropping to meander through a series of charming old stone villages.

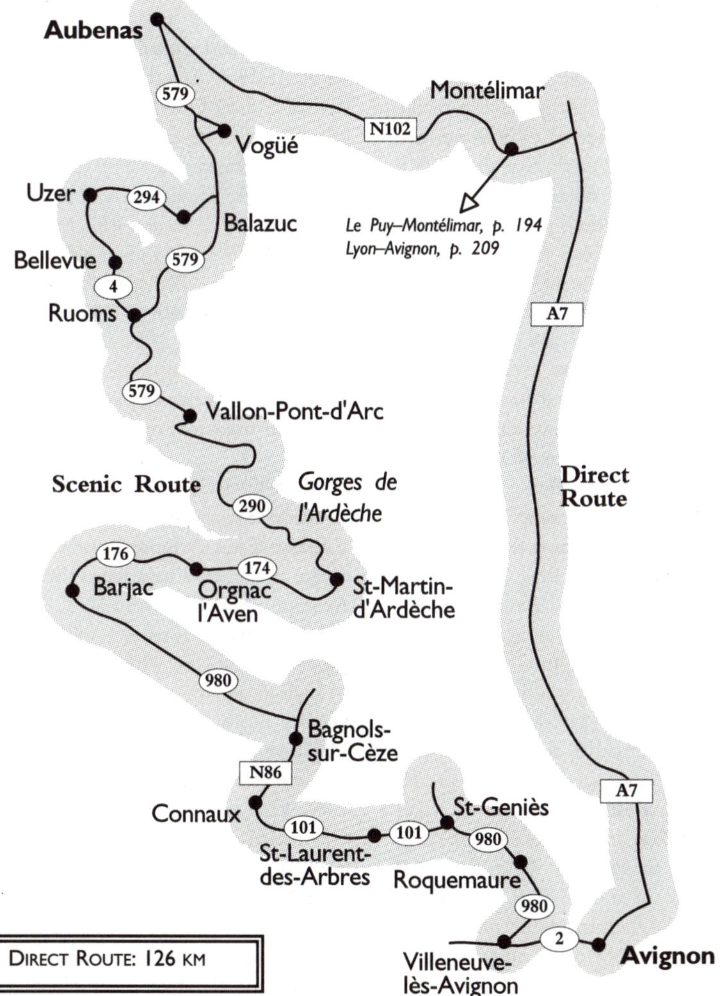

DIRECT ROUTE: 126 KM

ROUTES

DIRECT ROUTE

Leave Avignon, heading north and follow signs to Orange. Pick up the A7 autoroute and keep going north, up the Rhône Valley to Montélimar. From here, take the N102 west to Aubenas. Allow 2–3 hrs.

SCENIC ROUTE

Leave Avignon heading west on the N100 signed towards Nîmes. Cross the river on the Pont de l'Europe and immediately turn right on the D2 to **Villeneuve-lès-Avignon**. Leave town on the D980, which heads north along the Rhône to **Roquemaure** before turning inland towards Bagnols-sur-Cèze. At St-Geniès-de-Comolas, turn left onto the D101 through **St-Laurent-des-Arbres** and St-Paul-les-Fonts to Connaux, then turn right onto the N86 to **Bagnols-sur-Cèze**. Continue north on the N86, but just out of town, turn left onto the D980, and left again onto the D901 to **Barjac**. From here, the small D176 winds steeply up the hill, becoming the D317, D217 and D174 as it makes its way to **Orgnac l'Aven** and across the plateau to meet the entrance to the **Gorges de l'Ardèche** at **St-Martin d'Ardèche**. Turn left up the D290 which wriggles its way along the gorges to **Vallon-Pont-d'Arc**, where you turn left onto the D579 through **Ruoms** to join the D104 just south of Aubenas. An alternative, more picturesque route north of Ruoms crosses the river and loops round to **Bellevue** on the D4, takes the D104 to **Uzer**, then turns onto the tiny D294 through **St Maurice d'Ardèche** and **Balazuc**, to rejoin the D579. A little further on, the small D1 turns right to **Vogüé**, rejoining the D579 before turning onto the D104 at St-Etienne de Fontbellon for the last stretch into Aubenas.

VILLENEUVE-LÈS-AVIGNON

Tourist Office: *1 pl. Charles David; tel: 04 90 25 61 33*. Open Sept–June Mon–Sat, 0845–1230, 1400–1800; July–Aug daily 0845–1230, 1430-1830. Sells *Passeport* tickets to 5 monuments for FFr.45 (valid for 1 year).

ACCOMMODATION AND FOOD

Villeneuve-lès-Avignon makes a good alternative base to Avignon itself, with a number of fine hotels and restaurants. The **Hostellerie le Prieuré**, *7 pl. du Chapître, tel: 04 90 25 18 20, fax: 04 90 25 45 39* (expensive; closed 15 Oct–15 Mar) is a luxurious, hotel in a 14th-century priory, with a gourmet restaurant and lush garden (expensive). More affordable is the **Hôtel de l'Atelier**, *5 r. de la Foire; tel: 04 90 25 01 84; fax: 04 90 25 80 06* , in an old stone townhouse with a shady courtyard, or the **Résidence Les Cedres** *(LF), 39 av. Pasteur Bellevue; tel: 04 90 25 52 29; fax: 04 90 25 68 90* (both cheap-moderate). **Campsite**: **Camping l'Ile des Papes**; *tel: 04 90 15 15 90* (4-star; caravans; open Mar–Oct).

SIGHTSEEING

Unjustly overshadowed by its neighbour, Villeneuve-les-Avignon is well worth exploring (for boat trips across the river from Avignon, see p. 92). From 1271, this was the border between France (Villeneuve) and Provence and the Holy Roman Empire (Avignon) and the town was founded as a frontier fortification surrounding the **Tour Philippe le Bel**, *av. Gabriel Péri; tel: 04 90 27 49 68* (open Tues–Sun Apr–Sept 1000–1230, 1500–1900 (daily June–Sept); Oct–Mar 1000–1200, 1400– 1730; FFr.10), built in 1293–1307 at the approach to the Pont St-Bénézét (see p. 97). Even before this, the great 10th-century Benedictine **Abbaye de St-André** occupied pride of place beside the river. The abbey is now ruinous, but still has magnificent formal terraced gardens. In the 1360s, the massively secure **Fort St André**, *chemin Bourg St André; tel: 04 90 25 45 35* (open daily Jul–Aug 0930–1930; Apr–Sept 1000– 1230, 1400–1800; Oct–Mar 1000–1200, 1400–1700; FFr.22) was built around the abbey. The view from the towers across the water to the Palais des Papes is incomparable.

From the 14th century, the town became an outlying suburb of papal Avignon, with many cardinals clustering into the area to build fine mansions. The **Chartreuse du Val de Bénédiction**, *chemin des Chartreux; tel: 04 90 25 05 46* (open daily Apr–Sept 0900–1830; Oct–Mar 0930–1730; FFr.32) was founded by Pope Innocent VI, who is buried in the church, and became the most important Carthusian monastery in France. You can still visit the grandly austere buildings, with their magnificent 14th-century frescoes by Matteo Giovannetti. Within the town, the **Collégiale Notre-Dame**, *pl. St Marc*, has a number of fine sculptures and paintings and beautiful late 14th-century cloisters (open Tues–Sun Apr–Sept 1000–1230, 1500–1900 (daily June–Sept); Oct–Mar 1000–1200, 1400–1730; FFr.7). The **Musée Pierre de Luxembourg**, *r. de la République; tel: 04 90 27 49 66* (open Tues–Sun Apr–Sept 1000–1230, 1500–1900 (daily June–Sept); Oct–Mar 1000–1200, 1400–1730; FFr.20), housed in a 14th-century *livrée* (cardinal's palace), has a collection of medieval and Renaissance French art. There is a flea market every Sat morning.

VILLENEUVE TO THE GORGES DE L'ARDÈCHE

Tourist Offices: **St-Laurent-des-Arbres:** *Tour Ribas; tel: 04 66 50 10 10;* **Bagnols-sur-Cèze:** *Espace St-Gilles; tel: 04 66 89 54 61;* **Barjac:** *tel: 04 66 24 53 44* .

ACCOMMODATION AND FOOD

In this remote rural area, good hotels are relatively few, but those there are prove worth a stop. The **Hôtel Galinette**, *pl. de l'Arbre, St-Laurent-des-Arbres; tel: 04 66 50 14 14; fax: 04 66 50 46 30* (moderate) is a delightful old hotel in a charming old village. The **Château de Montcaud** *(RC)* , *Bagnols-sur-Cèze; tel: 04 66 89 60 60; fax: 04 66 89 45 04* (expensive) stands in its own park with a gastronomic restaurant, pool, tennis courts and other luxuries. Lower down the luxury scale, but still comfortable, is the **Hôtel de l'Aven** *(LF), Orgnac l'Aven; tel: 04 75 38 61 80; fax: 04 75 38 66 39* (cheap). **Campsites**: **Camping Les Genets d'Or**, *rte de Carmignan, Bagnols-sur-Cèze; tel: 04 66 89 58 67* (3-star; caravans; open Apr–Sept); **Camping La Buissière**, *rte d'Orgnac; tel: 04 66 24 54 52* (3-star; caravans; open Apr–Sept); **Camping Municipal**, *Orgnac L'Aven; tel: 04 75 38 63 68* (3-star; caravans; open Jun–Aug).

SIGHTSEEING

Follow the river north through **Roquemaure**, a pretty old town whose ruined castle, the **Château de Hers**, glares across the river at the Château de Roquemaure. As the road turns away from the river, the landscape opens up into rolling vineyards and sunflower fields, following the line of the Côte du Rhône wine trail. Leaflets available locally provide lists of the many vineyards and *caves* open for tastings and sales. Dotted across the skyline are several tiny villages, clustered onto hills and each topped by a church. Of them all, **St-Laurent-des-Arbres**, once the property of the bishops of Avignon, is one of the prettiest. There is little specific to see, other than a heavily fortified church, but it is a joy to wander round.

Bagnols-sur-Cèze is one of the largest towns in the area, marked chiefly by the huge **Marcoule Nuclear Power Station** just outside town. Those interested in it can visit the **Centre d'Information du**

Belvedère, *Cogema; tel: 04 66 79 51 55* (open daily Jul–Aug and school holidays; Wed, Sat, Sun pm at other times). More traditional attractions include the **Musée Albert André**, *Hôtel de Ville, pl. Mallet; tel: 04 66 50 50 56* (open Jul–Aug daily 1000–1200, 1500–1900; Sept–Jan, Mar–Jun Wed–Mon 1000–1200, 1400– 1800; free), an imposing collection of 19th and 20th century art founded by a friend of Renoir's and housed in a 17th-century mansion.

The next stretch of the road follows the pretty Cèze River valley, passing several charming old villages, including **La Roque-sur-Cèze,** a delightful, almost vertical village with a Romanesque church. The views of it and from it are both spectacular and a gentle walking trail from the car park at the bottom of the hill leads along the river to a pretty waterfall, the **Cascade du Sautadet**.

Barjac, further upstream, is the main market centre for the river valley. Canoes and kayaks are available for trips on the Cèze River, with or without a guide, from **Bâteaux Nouche**, *pl. du 8 Mai; tel: 04 75 37 10 70*. From here, the road climbs onto the Orgnac plateau, where several dolmens are well-hidden in the undergrowth just off the road. A huge car park heralds your arrival at the **Aven d'Orgnac**, *tel: 04 75 38 62 51* (open daily 1st Mar–15th Nov 0930–1200, 1400–1800; FFr.38 for the cave; FFr.49 for the cave and museum), a vast limestone cave system first explored in 1935. The tour lasts about 1 hr and involves 788 steps, but the enormous chambers and dramatic formations make the trip well worth while. For the more adventurous, there are guided rope descents and underground hikes. The complex is also home to the **Musée Régional de Préhistoire**, *tel: 04 75 38 65 10* (open daily 1st Mar–15th Nov 1000–1300, 1400–1800; FFr.28 for the museum; FFr.49 for the cave and museum), with a fascinating collection covering 350,000 years (until 6000BC).

THE GORGES DE L'ARDÈCHE

There are 37 km of gorges along the Ardèche River. A stone's throw from the Rhône Valley, they are a popular tourist destination, with all the facilities to match. In high summer, there can even be traffic jams along the dramatic clifftop road.

Accommodation and Food

L'Escarbille *(LF), r. Andronne, St-Martin-d'Ardèche; tel: 04 75 04 64 37; fax: 04 75 98 71 13* (cheap) is a pleasant small village hotel-restaurant. At the far end of the gorge, **Le Manoir du Paveyron** *(LF), r. du Raveyron, Vallon Pont-d'Arc; tel: 04 75 88 03 59; 04 75 37 11 12* (cheap) is a charming, modest stone-built hotel with a shady garden and restaurant as popular with locals as tourists. Five km from the village (1300m from the Pont d'Arc), **Le Belvedère** *(LF), rte des Gorges, Vallon Pont-d'Arc; tel: 04 75 88 00 02; fax: 04 75 88 12 22* (moderate) provides an excellent alternative. **Campsites**: there are numerous campsites at both ends of the gorges, including **Camping Municipal Le Moulin**, *St-Martin-d'Ardèche; tel: 04 75 04 66 20* (3-star; caravans; open Apr–Sept); **Le Provençal**, *Vallon-Pont-d'Arc; tel: 04 75 88 00 48* (4-star; caravans; open Apr–Sept) and **Le Mondial**, *Vallon-Pont-d'Arc; tel: 04 75 88 00 44* (4-star; caravans; open Mar–Oct).

Sightseeing

The charming little riverside village of **St-Martin-d'Ardèche** marks the official entrance to the gorges, a series of deep, thickly wooded canyons. The best and virtually only way to see them properly, from the bottom, is by one of the hundreds of canoes which make the descent each day, creating a brightly coloured caterpillar trail along the muddy yellow line of the water. Pick a hire company from the many clustered at either end of the gorges. The road, for the most part, winds along the clifftop, with regular spectacular viewing points up to 300 m above the river. En route there are two sets of spectacular caves, both offering 1-hr underground tours of caverns and stalactite formations and son et lumière performances They are the **Grottes de St Marcel d'Ardèche**, *tel: 04 75 04 66 11* (open mid-Mar–mid-Nov daily 1000–1800) and the **Grotte de la Madeleine**, *tel: 04 75 04 22 20* (open Apr–Oct daily 1000–1800; FFr.37), where you can also find a free exhibition about the natural history of the gorges. At the far end of the gorges, the river swirls into a natural pool under the magnificent **Pont d'Arc**, a natural rock bridge 34m high and 66m wide. This is a hive of activity, home to most of the local canoe operators, amongst them **Rivière et Nature**, *tel: 04 75 88 03 30;* **Viking-Bâteaux**, *tel: 04 75 88 08 87* and the **Base Nautique du Pont d'Arc**, *tel: 04 75 88 00 69.* The village of **Vallon-Pont d'Arc**, a short way further on, is the area's major resort, with a ruined castle, a couple more caves for exploration and *caves* for *dégustation*. **La Magnanerie**, *rte de Ruoms; tel: 04 75 88 01 27* (open mid-Apr–Sept Mon–Sat) is a silk farm.

RUOMS TO AUBENAS

Tourist Office: Ruoms: *r. Alfonse Daudet; tel: 04 75 93 91 91.* Open; Mon–Sat 0900–1200 (not Mon a.m. or Sat p.m.).

Accommodation and Food

For accommodation, try the cosy family-run **La Chapoulière** *(LF), quartier la Chapoulière, Ruoms; tel: 04 75 39 65 43; fax: 04 75 39 75 82* (cheap-moderate; closed mid Nov–mid Mar), whose shady terrace restaurant specialises in seafood. For a light meal, **Le Vieux Ruoms**, *1 r. Clemenceau Ruoms; tel: 04 75 39 61 39* (moderate) serves healthy salads and sinful desserts in a charming small terraced café tucked into the medieval town walls. Further north, the **Village Vacances Vogüé**, facing Vogüé across the river, *tel: 04 75 37 71 32; fax: 04 75 37 01 29* (cheap-moderate) provides modern accommodation with built-in activities from canoeing to mini-golf, while the more traditional **Hôtel-Restaurant Des Voyageurs**, *rte de Ruoms; tel: 04 75 37 71 13; fax: 04 75 37 01 25* (cheap-moderate), a farmhouse-style building with pleasant gardens and pool. **Campsites**: **Camping Le Retourtier**, *Balazuc; tel: 04 75 37 77 67* (2-star; open Apr–Sept); **La Chapoulière**, *Ruoms; tel: 04 75 93 90 72* (3-star; caravans; open Apr–Sept); **Les Roches**, *Vogüé; tel: 04 75 37 70 45* (3-star; caravans; Apr–Sept).

Sightseeing

This stretch of road may pale scenically after the gorges, but it is full of delightful little grey-stone villages, perfect for leisurely wandering. One of the most charming is **Ruoms**, whose walled medieval town hides within a mass of modern development. Beyond here, a dramatic road leads through the **défilés de Ruoms**, a series of tunnels overlooking the Ardèche River to **Uzer,** a pretty village surrounding a riverside castle. Beyond this, **Balazuc** is even more enchanting, a tumbling village precariously balanced on the side of a cliff overlooking the churning river. The best view is from the opposite bank. Squeezed in between the twisting river and a stern, grey cliff, **Vogüé** huddles around a splendid 12th-16th century **castle**. In summer, **Le Train Touristique de l'Ardèche Méridionale,** *Gare de Montfleury, St Germain; tel: 04 75 94 76 76* (Easter-Sept, Sat–Sun; also Thurs, Jul-Aug) runs between Vogûé and St-Germain. Both Balazuc and Vogüé are classified amongst the most beautiful villages in France.

AUBENAS

See p. 196.

AVIGNON–DIGNE

This route traverses the entire length of the Lubéron Valley, with views of the mountains and hilltop villages on either side, before crossing over into Haute Provence and descending into the Durance Valley and the approaches to the Alps.

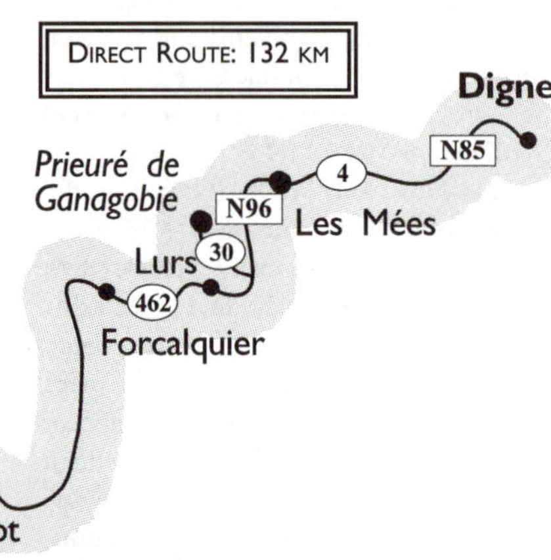

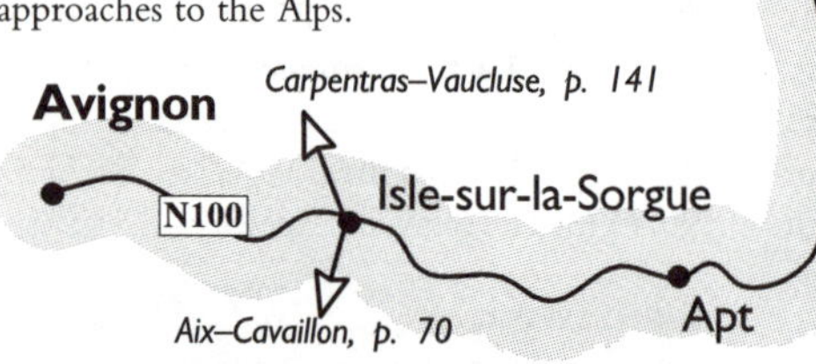

ROUTE

From Avignon take the N100 eastbound towards **Isle-sur-la-Sorgue**. (From here you can join the Carpentras–Vaucluse Loop, p. 41, or take the N98 south for 10 km to Cavaillon to join the Aix–Cavaillon route.) Stay on the same road all the way through the Lubéron Valley (see p. 73) through **Apt**, **Mane** and **Forcalquier**, turning left 8.5 km beyond Forcalquier onto the D462 to **Lurs**. Follow the road out of the other side of the village, descending to the Durance Valley and the N96; just before reaching the main road, a sharp left turn leads onto the D30, which winds steeply up to the **Prieuré de Ganagobie**. Take the same road back down, turning left on the N96 and then right across the Durance to **Les Mées**. From Les Mées take the D4 then the N85 into **Digne** (see p. 171). Allow 3–4 hrs without stopping; 1-1½ days with sightseeing.

ISLE-SUR-LA-SORGUE

See p.147.

APT

Tourist Office: *4 av. P. de Gerard; tel: 04 90 74 03 18.* Open July–Aug Mon–Sat 0900–1300, 1500–1700, Sun 0900–1200; Sept–June Mon–Sat 0900–1200, 1400–1800.

ACCOMMODATION AND FOOD

There are several hotels in Apt, although none are exceptional. The **Auberge du Lubéron**, *17 quai L. Sagy; tel: 04 90 74 12 50* (cheap–moderate) is conveniently placed on the river bank, with well-kept rooms. Another option is the **Hôtel-Restaurant Le Palais**, *24 pl. G. Péri; tel: 04 90 04 89 32* (cheap) which also has a restaurant serving traditional cuisine (cheap).

EVENTS

During the **Fête de Ste-Anne** (last Sun in July) grapes are offered to the town's patron saint in a traditional pilgrimage. The **Festival Trétaux de Nuits** is a music and arts festival (late July–Aug).

SIGHTSEEING

Just before Apt look out for signs on the right hand side of the road for the **Pont Julien**, a graceful triple-arched Roman bridge which spans the Calavon and formed part of the ancient Via Domitia between Italy and Spain.

A busy market town in the Calavon valley, Apt is known for its crystallised fruits), truffles and lavender essence. It has an attractive old town centre, with squares shaded by plane trees, lively on Sat when a huge market takes up almost every corner and byway. Apt is at the extremity of the **Parc Naturel Régional du Lubéron** and home to the **Maison du Parc**, *1 pl. J. Jaurès; tel: 04 90 74 36 60* (open mid Apr–mid Sept Mon–Sat 0830–1200, 1330–1900; mid-Sept–mid Apr Mon–Fri 0830–1200, 1330–1800, Sat 0830–1200. This information centre houses displays on the natural and human environment of the Lubéron and has a wide range of leaflets and books for sale. Downstairs there is a small **Musée de Paléontologie** (open as above) with animated models of dinosaurs and displays of fossils.

Apt's most significant monument is the **Cathédrale Ste-Anne**, *r. Ste-Anne; tel: 04 90 74 36 60* (open Tues–Sun 0900–1200, 1530–1800) which has been remodelled many times since its initial construction in the 11th century. According to legend, the veil of Ste-Anne was brought back from Palestine in the 3rd century and hidden here by Apt's first bishop; the shroud now lies in the **treasury** (15-min guided tours July–Sept Mon–Sat 1100, 1700, Sun 1100) along with other medieval reliquaries.

Nearby, housed in an 18th-century mansion, is the **Musée Archéologique**, *4 r. de l'Amphithéâtre; tel: 04 90 74 00 34* (open June–Sept Sun–Fri 1000–1200, 1400–1700, Sat 1430–1730; Oct–June Mon, Wed, Thur, Fri 1400–1700, Sat 1430–1730; FFr.10). It features various carvings, mosaics and jewellery from the Gallo-Roman period as well as prehistoric implements and 19th-century ceramics.

APT TO FORCALQUIER

From Apt the road follows the Cavalon upstream, with views of the Grand Lubéron and the peak of Mourre Nègre (1125m) off to the right. As the valley narrows, the road climbs gradually, leaving the Lubéron behind and entering the Pays du Forcalquier in Haute-Provence, where lavender scents the roadsides during summer. Approaching the village of **Mane**, a sign on the left indicates a short detour (500m) to the **Prieuré de Notre-Dame de Salagon**, *tel: 04 92 75 19 93* (open July–Sept daily 1000–1200, 1400–1900; daily Apr–June 1400–1800; Oct–mid Nov Sat–Sun 1400–1800; mid Nov–May Sun 1400–1800; FFr.25). This Benedictine priory dates mainly from the 15th century but it also has a superb 12th-century Romanesque chapel, which re-opened in 1996 after extensive restorations). Salagon is home to the *Conservatoire du Patrimoine Ethnologique de Haute Provence* (Conservatory of the Ethnic Heritage of Haute Provence), which carries out research, runs an extensive bookshop on the premises, and mounts various high-quality exhibitions on topics such as ancient crafts and lavender production. In the priory grounds you can also wander around medieval, medicinal herb and scented gardens.

FORCALQUIER

Tourist Office: *blvd des Martyrs, tel: 04 92 75 10 02.* Open June–Sept Mon–Sat 0930–1230, 1400–1900, Sun 1000–1300; Mon–Sat 0900–1200, 1400–1800, Oct–May Sun 1000–1300. Guided tours (2 hrs) of the old town, Apr–Oct Wed, Sat 1000

(FFr.15); self-guided tours with CD Walkman in English (FFr.30).

Accommodation and Food

Forcalquier's oldest hotel is the **Hostellerie des Deux Lions**, *11 pl. du Bourget; tel: 04 92 75 25 30; fax: 04 92 75 06 41* (moderate),17th-century. Rooms are spacious, and there is also an excellent restaurant (cheap/moderate) with a range of menus. Just nearby is the **Grand Hôtel**, *10 blvd Latourette; tel: 04 92 75 00 35; fax: 04 92 75 06 32* (cheap) with good-sized rooms and a garden with panoramic views. Forcalquier also has many cafés, a pizzeria, crêperie and Vietnamese restaurant.

Sightseeing

This was once an important citadel from which the Counts of Forcalquier held sway over an independent state which included the territories of Apt, Sisteron and Gap until the 15th century, when Louis XI sent an army to bombard it into submission. Little remains of the Counts' **citadel** above the town, but it is well worth the steep walk to the top for the views across the Pays de Forcalquier, the Montagne du Lure, the Plateau de Valensole and the Lubéron. The old town features several 13th- and 15th-century mansions, whilst at its base are the spacious *pl. du Bourguet* and the **Cathedral**, with a Gothic nave and choir. The one remaining medieval gateway is the **Porte des Cordeliers**, to the west of the square, and nearby is the **Couvent des Cordeliers**, *blvd des Martyrs; tel: 04 92 75 02 38* (open July–mid Sept Thur–Tues for guided tours 1100, 1430, 1530, 1630 and 1730; May–Jun, mid Sept–Oct Sun 1430, 1600 only; FFr.15). Founded in 1236, this is one of the oldest Franciscan monasteries in France. The library, cloisters, scriptorium and refectory have all been restored.

FORCALQUIER TO DIGNE

From Forcalquier, the road leads towards the Durance valley, with the tiny village of **Lurs** perched on the edge of the valley high above the river. The village fell into earlier this century but was saved from decrepitude by a group of artists and printers (led by the typographer Maxmilien Vox) who moved here after World War II, and today plays host to the annual Rencontres Internationale d'Art Graphiques (last week in Aug). The **Syndicat D'Initiative**, *tel: 04 92 79 10 20* (open mid May–mid Sept Tues–Sat 0900–1200, 1400-1800) provides a leaflet detailing historic buildings within the village, which also offers superb views.

Side Track from Lurs

Just to the north of Lurs, also in a remarkable position with sweeping views in all directions, is the **Prieuré de Ganagobie**, *tel: 04 92 68 00 04* (open Tues–Sun 1500–1700). Founded in the 10th century, it features a remarkable set of carefully restored 12th-century mosaics, outlined in red, black and white.

Heading down onto the broad expanses of the **Durance Valley** and across the river itself, the **Penitents des Mées** loom up behind the village of Mées on the opposite bank. This unusual rock formation comprises a serried row of rock columns some 100m high and extending for 2km beyond the village to the north. According to legend, these rocks are monks who were turned to stone by St Donat, a local hermit, as a punishment for lusting after Moorish slave girls captured during the Saracen invasions.

From Les Mées, the route follows the valley of the Bléon up towards Digne.

AVIGNON–NÎMES

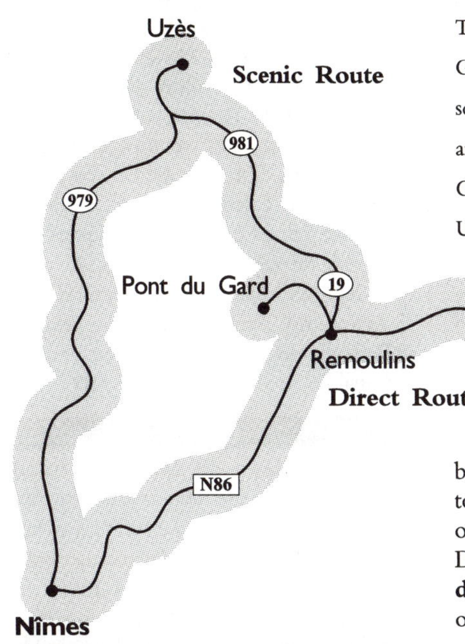

This short route crosses the pretty limestone Garrigue plateau, through rolling fields, scented scrub, and picture-book hill villages, and visits the magnificent Roman Pont du Gard and the delightful medieval town of Uzès.

DIRECT ROUTE: 44 KM

ROUTES

DIRECT ROUTE

Leave Avignon on the N580, signposted to Nîmes and Bagnols-sur-Cèze. After 5km, branch left onto the N100 and follow it to Remoulins. From there take the N86 to Nîmes. Allow about 1 hr.

SCENIC ROUTE

From Remoulins take the N86 towards Nîmes. After 3km, a turning on the right leads to the Right Bank of the **Pont-du-Gard**. Return to the main road and turn onto the D19 to Uzès to cross the river; if you wish, turn off again at La Bégude, to see the bridge from the left bank. Return to the main road, which becomes the D981 and follow it through to **Uzès**. Leaving Uzès, retrace your route on the D981, then turn right onto the D979 and follow it through the **Gorges du Gardon** to Nîmes. Allow half a day, or a lazy full day.

PONT DU GARD

Tourist Office: *beside the bridge (Rive Droite); tel: 04 66 37 00 02* and *r. du Moulin d'Aure, Remoulins; tel: 04 66 37 22 34* . The bridge itself is free; parking is not. To walk out along the bridge, go to the right bank, which also gives access to the river and swimming beaches (parking FFr.15); the left bank offers a superb view, but no access (parking FFr.22).

ACCOMMODATION AND FOOD

On the right bank is a small hotel-restaurant, **Le Colombier** *(LF), tel: 04 66 37 05 28; fax: 04 66 37 35 75* (cheap). On the left bank, an old flour mill, **Le Vieux Moulin**, *tel: 04 66 3714 35; fax: 04 66 37 26 48* (moderate) has been converted into a charming hotel-restaurant, right on the river, with superb views of the bridge. About 3km away, the **Hostellerie Le Castellas**, *Grande Rue, Collias; tel: 04 66 22 88 88; fax: 04 66 22 84 28* (moderate) is a charming small country-style hotel with restaurant and pool, while the **Auberge du Gardon** *(LF), Collias; tel: 04 66 22 80 54; fax: 04 66 22 88 98* (cheap) is a true country inn, buried deep in the Gorges du Gardon. **Campsites**: **Camping International des Gorges du Gardon**, *chemin de Barque Vieille, Vers-Pont-du-Gard; tel: 04 66 22 81 81* (2-star; open Mar–Oct; caravans); **La Soubeyrane**, *rte de Beaucaire, Remoulins; tel: 04 66 37 03 21* (4-star; open May–Sept; caravans); **Camping Municipal La Sousta**, *av. du Pont du Gard, Remoulins; tel: 04 66 37 12 80* (3-star; open all year).

Sightseeing

By the mid 1st century AD, during the reign of Claudius, Nîmes had become such a boomtown that it was running short of water. Work began on a series of canals, tunnels, ditches and aqueducts, to bring in water from the source of the Eure River, some 50km away. Amongst the obstacles to be crossed was a deep crevice carved out by the Gardon River. The result was this towering spectacular bridge (48.77m high), built using stone from nearby Vers-Pont-du-Gard. It consists of three tiers; the lowest has 6 arches (142m wide); the middle one has 11 arches (242 m across); and the top has 35 smaller arches (275m wide). Abandoned between the 5th and 7th centuries, it became the local quarry before gaining a new lease of life as a toll bridge in 1295. In 1747, the new bridge alongside it was built, allowing traffic to cross without further damage to the ancient structure. There have been several restorations over the years; the latest is still ongoing.

Side Tracks from Pont du Gard

It is possible to do descents of the Gardon River by canoe from nearby Collias; contact **Kayak Vert**, *Collias; tel: 04 66 22 84 83*. The enchanting old hill village of **Castillon-du-Gard** has several small Romanesque chapels, including the 12th-century **Chapelle St Caprais**. The beautiful 4-star hotel **Le Vieux Castillon** (*RC*), *r. Turion Sabatier, tel: 04 66 37 28 17* (expensive) spreads through several houses. As well as delightful medieval architecture, fine views and terraces, the gastronomic **Restaurant Le Fumoir** offers exceptional local cuisine and wine.

UZÈS

Tourist Office: *av. de la Libération; tel: 04 66 22 68 88*. Open Mon–Fri 0900–1900, Sat 1000–1200, 1500–1700 June–Sept (also Sun 1000–1700, July–Aug only); Mon–Fri 0900–1200, 1330–1800, Sat 1000–1200 Oct–May. **Parking**: a ring of car parks surrounds the peripheral boulevards. The old town is completely pedestrianised.

Accommodation and Food

For a little gracious living, try the **Château d'Arpaillargues**, *Arpaillagues; tel: 04 66 22 14 48; fax: 04 66 22 56 10* (moderate), 4km out of town. The **Hôtel d'Entraigues**, *8 r. de la Calade; tel: 04 66 22 32 68; fax: 04 66 22 57 01* (moderate) and **Hôtel du Champ de Mars** *(LF), 1087 rte de Nîmes; tel: 04 66 22 36 55* (cheap) are both central. There are numerous small restaurants in the old town.

Campsites: **La Paillote**, *Mas Fran Val, quartier de Grezac; tel: 04 66 22 38 55* (3-star; open Mar–Oct); **Camping Municipal Val de l'Eure**, *rte de Bagnols-sur-Cèze; tel: 04 66 22 11 79* (2-star; open

June–Sept); **Camping du Mas de Rey**, *Arpaillargues; tel: 04 66 22 18 27* (4km out of town; 3-star; open Apr–Oct; caravans).

Events

There is a **market** every Sat morning. The annual **Modern Dance Festival** takes place in mid June. During the last week in July, Uzès is home to a major festival of classical music, **Les Nuits Musicales**; *tel: 04 66 22 68 88.*

Sightseeing

Built round a series of small arcaded squares, the mellow stone streets of the pedestrianised medieval town are filled with delightful cafés, shops and market stalls. Uzès began life as the Roman town of Ucetia, and the Lords of Uzès are one of the oldest lines of nobility in France.

The formidable **Duché d'Uzès**, *pl. du Duché; tel: 04 66 22 18 96* (guided tours daily 1000–1830 June–Sept; 1000–1200, 1400–1800 Oct–May; FFr.48) has been owned by the same family for nearly 1000 years. The Tour Bermond, the massive square keep, was built for strength in the 11th century, although its splendid battlements and turrets were rebuilt in 1839. The Tour de la Vicomté, with the octagonal turret, dates from 1328. The lower, but infinitely more elegant Renaissance palace was designed in about 1550, by Philibert Delorme. Inside, there are magnificent furnishings and waxwork scenes of past inhabitants.

Virtually opposite, the **Crypt** is an 4th century church carved from the bedrock, with a bas-relief sculpture of St John the Baptist. Behind the duke's castle, glaring across *r. Entre Les Tours*, are two other towers, the **Tour du Roi**, built in the 12th century by King Guillaume VIII, and the **Tour de l'Horloge**, now a clock tower, but originally the 13th-century creation of the local bishops.

The **Cathedral of St Théodorit**, *pl. de l'Éveché* (open daily 0830–1830) began life in 1090, although most of the present edifice dates from about 1652, and the neo-Romanesque façade was added in 1873. Next to it, the Italianate **Tour Fenestrelle** is the only surviving remnant of the Romanesque cathedral. On the far side, the old Bishops's Palace is now home to the **Musée Municipal Georges Borias**, *tel: 04 66 22 40 23* (open Tues–Sun 1500–1800 Feb–Oct; 1400–1700 Nov–Dec; FFr.10) has a fine collection of local ceramics, traditional crafts and a hall dedicated to the writer André Gide, who spend his boyhood holidays here.

On the edge of town, the **Musée International de la Confiserie Haribo**, *Pont des Charrettes; tel: 04 66 22 54 99* (open Tues–Sun 1000–1800; FFr.25) is every child's fantasy, a museum dedicated entirely to sweets, with tastings and a shop.

Side Tracks from Uzès

At **Arpaillargues**, 3km from Uzès off the D982, the **Musée du Train et du Jouet** has one of the world's finest model railways (built in 1923), with some 400m of track, a number of 1950s toys and a large collection of butterflies. Next door, the **Musée 1900** has a fascinating collection of early 20th-century technology, from cars to cameras and mechanical pianos. **Both sites**: *le Moulin de Chalier; tel: 04 66 22 58 64* (open daily 0900–1900 July–Aug; 0900–1200, 1400–1900 Sept–June; FFr.30; FFr.55 for both).

The **Haras National d'Uzès**, *Mas de Tailles; tel: 04 66 22 33 11* (open Tues, Fri 1500 July–Aug; FFr.15) is the French National Stud, home to some of the world's finest stallions.

BARCELONNETTE–GAP

The busy little town of Barcelonnette, with its unexpected Mexican connections, provides a lively beginning to this short route which leads around Europe's largest reservoir, the Lac de Serre-Ponçon, an easily accessible blue oasis in the mountainous landscape.

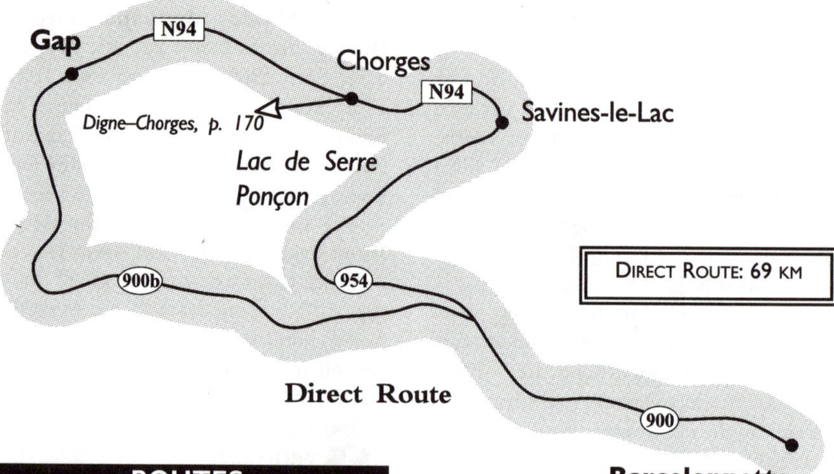

ROUTES

Direct Route

Head west out of **Barcelonnette** on the D900 towards **Lac de Serre-Ponçon**. Near St Vincent-les-Forts, the road divides. One branch, the D900, heads south to Digne-les-Bains while the other, the D900B, continues round the southern side of the lake. Follow this past the massive dam (*Barrage de Serre-Ponçon*), across the River Durance and, after a sharp turn north, all the way to **Gap**. The journey takes about 1 hour 15 min.

Scenic route

Leave **Barcelonnette** the same way, on the D900, but, after 21km, fork right onto the D954 to twist up and down along the east bank of **Lac de Serre-Ponçon**. At **Savines-le-Lac**, turn left onto the N94 to cross the lake and continue on along the north shore and through the **Parc National des Ecrins** to **Gap**. Distance 74km; allow 3 hours to enjoy the views.

BARCELONNETTE

Tourist Office: *pl. F. Mistral; tel: 04 92 81 04 71.* Open daily 0900-2000 July–Aug; 0900–1200, 1400–1800 Oct–Nov (closed Sun afternoon). The **Bureau des Guides**, at the Tourist Office, organises walking, climbing and canyoning activities.

Accommodation and Food

In a converted haçienda-style villa built by one of Barcelonnette's returning Mexicans (see below), the **Hotel Azteca**, *3 r. F. Arnaud; tel: 04 92 81 64 36; fax: 04 92 81 43 92* (cheap) is near the town centre, with 27 rooms and a garden. **Le Grand Hotel**, *pl. Manuel; tel: 04 92 81 03 14* (cheap) is on the bustling town square. **Campsites**: **Du Plan**, *52 av. E. Aubert; tel: 04 92 81 08 11* (3-star; open June–Sept); **Le Tampico**, *70 av. E. Aubert, tel: 04 92 81 02 55* (2-star; open mid Dec–Sept; caravans). Among the restaurants which capitalise on the town's American connections is **Adelita**, *19 r. E. Donnadieu; tel: 04 92 81 16 12*, serving Mexican specialities.

Sightseeing

Sheltered by a ridge of snowy peaks in the broad Ubaye Valley, Barcelonnette is the most northerly town in Provence. Named after its founder in 1231, Count of Barcelona and Provence, it centres on an attractive cobbled square, *pl. Manuel*, which is traffic-free and surrounded by terrace restaurants and shops.

The most surprising thing about Barcelonnette is its close connections with Mexico. For centuries, all along the Ubaye Valley, tradition dictated that the farmers, who had little work during the winter months when the ground was covered in snow, would take to the roads as travelling salesmen, to sell the locally-made woollens and silk thread. In 1814, 18-year old Joseph-Antoine Couttolenc decided to try his luck further afield and set off for Mexico. He was followed seven years later by the Arnaud brothers who set up a fabric business there and later invited former employees to join them. Fifty years later, two of the original families returned to Barcelonnette, sharing some of their wealth with those who had stayed behind. They built grand Mexican-style mansions, colour-washed with elaborate stucco decoration. Ties between the two places remain strong. Indeed the town gets a constant stream of visitors from Mexico who come over on holiday to trace their roots. Their legacy is not only the mansions, some of which have become hotels, but also in several restaurants which specialise in Mexican food and shops selling items from Mexico. There is even a small exhibition on Mexico, the **Maison de Mexique**, *av. de la Libération; tel: 04 92 81 45 78* (open July–Aug) and an **Honorary Consul**, Pierre Audibert, *7 av. Portfirio Diaz, tel: 04 92 81 00 27*. In Aug there is a **Festival of Mexican Folklore**

The reasons why the farmers emigrated, and their lifestyle and achievements in the Americas, are the subject of the **Musée de la Vallée**, *av. de la Libération, tel: 04 92 81 27 15.*

LAC DE SERRE-PONÇON

As far back as 1895 there were plans to dam the River Durance and make a reservoir, but the technology was not sufficiently advanced to allow the project to get under way until 1955. The work, which took six years, necessitated the flooding of the villages of Savines and Ubaye at the bottom of the valley. Now Europe's largest dam, into which flow both the Durance and the smaller River Ubaye, holds back 1270 million cubic metres of water, creating Europe's largest man-made lake, a beautiful L-shaped oasis surrounded by wooded hillsides. Stretching 19km up the Durance Valley and 9km up the Ubaye Valley, it generates one million kilowatts of electricity an hour as well as providing a much-used amenity for watersports with six beaches and a *plan d'eau* (swimming area).

The route hugs the northern bank of the Ubaye arm, climbing up to the village of **Le Sauze** where there are splendid views from an observation terrace high above the lake. You look down on the shimmering blue water, dotted with little craft and surrounded by woods with mountain ridges in the distance. Then the road swings north-east to go all round the longer Durance arm, soon passing **Les Demoiselles Coiffées** (Girls with Hats), curious rock formations, surrounded by woods, which look like a group of thin armless people wearing round flat hats. They were formed by erosion of the softer outside rock which left the round-topped pillars behind.

SAVINES-LE-LAC

Tourist Office: *av. de la Combe d'Or; tel: 04 92 44 31 00.* Open Mon–Sat 0900–1230, 1500–1900, Sun 0900–1230 July–Aug; Mon–Sat 0930–1200, 1430–1800 Sept–June. It houses a permanent exhibition on the creation of the lake and its effects on the local community.

Accommodation and Food

Several small hotels are situated on the main lakeside road, including **Les Sources**, *r. des Chaumettes, tel: 04 92 44 20 52.* **Campsite: Camping Muncipal Les Eygoires**, *tel: 04 92 44 20 48.* **HI: Les Chaumettes**, *tel: 04 92 44 29 52.*

Sightseeing

This little resort, consisting almost entirely of a long straight street bordered by shops and apartments leading down to the water, was built in 1962 to replace Savines which was flooded when the reservoir was created. It has a remarkable modern church, triangular in shape inside with brightly-coloured stained-glass windows.

Boasting 300 days of sun a year, this is very much a holiday centre for those who enjoy watersports or walking in the mountains. Indeed its population of 800 doubles in summer.

A reminder of the past is provided at the small **Musée d'Ancienne École**, *Pontis; tel: 04 92 81 27 15* (open daily 1500–1900 July–Aug; FFr.6). Its single classroom still has its old desks and inkwells.

CHORGES

See p. 173.

PARC NATIONAL DES ECRINS

Park Information Office: Chateau de Charance, Gap; tel: 04 92 40 20 10. Open Mon–Fri 0800–1200, 1400–1800; also July–Aug Sat–Sun 0800–1200, 1400–1800.

Between Chorges and Gap the route skirts an area of spectacular mountains which was designated as the **Parc National des Ecrins** in 1973. It stretches north to Bourg d'Oisans and across to Briançon to the east. With time to spare, it is well worth taking one of the small roads from the village of **la Batie-Neuve** and twist up to mountain villages like **La Rochette** and **Les Borels**.

The Park is remarkable in that the scenery is Alpine, with more than 100 peaks over 3000m and always dusted with snow, yet much of the vegetation is Mediterranean. Indeed lavender is as much at home as edelweiss. A thousand km of footpaths enable visitors to make the most of the Park. In winter, several areas including **Orcières-Merlette, Serre Chevalier** and **Les Deux-Alpes** offer downhill and cross-country skiing.

GAP

See p. 128.

Cannes

First the aristocracy, then movie stars, catapulted Cannes from an obscure seaside fishing village, to the brightest showcase of the world's film industry. By chance England's Lord Brougham, on his way to Italian sunshine in 1834 with his sick daughter, stayed at the village's only *auberge*. He liked the place and its mild climate so much that he bought a large plot of land, built a mansion and set a trend. The first Film Festival in 1946 heralded its star-studded future, boosted by holidaymakers who like gloss with their sunshine.

Tourist Information

Tourist Office: *Palais des Festivals, esplanade G Pompidou; tel: 04 93 39 24 53.* Open July–Aug daily 0900–2000; Sept–June, Mon–Sat 0900–1830. **Branches**: at the station: *tel: 04 93 99 19* 77, open Mon–Fri 0830–1830, and at the Town Hall annexe, *Cannes la Bocca; tel: 04 93 47 04 12*, open mid June–mid Sept, Mon–Sat 1000–1300, 1600–2000.

Arriving and Departing

By Car

Driving around the town is not a pleasure, owing to the narrow streets and heavy traffic, so head for one of the 18 car-parks. The one under the **Palais des Festivals** on the seafront has nearly 1000 places. For short stays, leave your car at a meter or pay-and-display, but places can be hard to find and expensive, except inland, north of the railway line.

By Bus

Long distance buses: *5 sq. Mérinée; tel: 04 93 39 79 40;* **Local buses**: *pl. Hôtel de Ville; tel: 04 93 39 18 71.*

By Train

Station: *r. J. Jaurès;* 250m from the sea and Tourist Office, straight down *r. des Serbes*. For information *tel: 08 36 35 35 35,* (open 0800–2100; station closed 0100–0500).

Getting Around

Orientation is easy. The wide palm-lined seafront road, **blvd de la Croisette**, runs right round the bay from the harbour – **Vieux Port** – and marina in the west to the two marinas on **Pointe Croisette** in the east. The town stretches back from here, with the sea providing a constant reference point. Everything is within walking distance though there are few specific sights. This is a place to stroll and soak up glamour.

Buses: **Bus Azur**, *tel: 04 93 90 67 50,* runs an excellent network around the town centre and suburbs. Tickets cost FFr.6.80 from the driver, or FFr.47.50 for a carnet of 10, from shops or the train station. A one-week pass costs FFr.50.

Taxis: **Allo Taxi**, *tel: 04 92 99 27 27.*

Bicycle Hire: **Cycles Daniel**, *2 r. du Pont Romain; tel: 04 93 99 00 30.*

Staying in Cannes

Accommodation

Cannes' seafront hotels are amongst the most luxurious in the world. Made famous by publicity-hungry visitors during the

Film Festival, these seaside palaces survive mainly on a diet of conferences for the rest of the year. Inexpensive hotels exist too, though inevitably away from the sea. Try *r. Mar Joffre, pl. du 18 Juin, r. Fortville*, and the surrounding side-streets. The Film Festival (May) is the busiest time of all – book a year in advance – but the town is packed all summer, so reservations are imperative. Off-season (Oct–Apr), many hotels offer cheaper winter tariffs. Chain hotels include *Ba, BW, Ch, Cn, Ct, Cs, Mo, Hn, Ib, IC, IH, Mc, Nv, Sf* and *Tp*.

Most palatial of all is the **Carlton**, *58 la Croisette; tel: 04 93 68 91 68, fax: 04 93 06 40 25* (expensive), a white wedding-cake extravaganza built in 1911. Its two black cupolas are said to be formed after the breasts of a notorious flamenco dancer who had befriended the architect. Also high in the luxury class are the **Majestic**, *14 la Croisette; tel: 04 92 98 77 00, fax: 04 93 38 97 90* (expensive), built in 1926 and the modern **Noga Hilton**, *50 la Croisette; tel: 04 92 99 70 00, fax: 04 92 99 70 11* (expensive). Lower down the price scale, try the adequate **Hôtel Bourgogne**, *13 r. de 24 aoû;, tel: 04 93 38 36 73, fax: 04 92 99 28 41* (cheap), or **Hôtel Touring**, *11 r. Hoche; tel: 04 93 38 34 40; fax: 04 93 38 73 34* (moderate).

HI: **Auberge de la Jeunesse**, *35 av. de Vallauris, tel: 04 93 99 26 79.* **Campsite: Le Grand Saule**; *24 blvd J Moulin; tel: 04 93 90 55 10* (caravans; bus no. 9 from the Hôtel de Ville, direction Grasse, to Ranguin; open Apr–Oct).

Eating and Drinking

Good food abounds in Cannes, especially seafood and bouillabaisse (see p. 233). For those really splashing out, the posh restaurants in la Croisette's grandest hotels offer some of the finest cuisine in the South of France – at top prices – like the Michelin star-loaded **La Palme d'Or** in the **Hôtel Martinez**, *73 la Croisette; tel: 04 92 98 74 14* (expensive). The restaurants down on the beach, just below the promenade, many owned by the big hotels across the road, provide an experience no visitor should miss. If funds are low, confine yourself to an omelette. The tourist traps along the other side of *la Croisette* are best avoided. Instead try *r. F Faure*, parallel to the sea by the port, where there are several good eateries such as *Pierrot 1er, 51 r. F Faure, tel: 04 93 39 03 95* (cheap), which specialises in fish, and **Le Pistou**, *53 r. F Faure, tel: 04 93 39 20 88* (cheap). Really low budgeters should head for pizza places on the west side of the port on *quai St Pierre*.

Communications

Post Office: *22 Bivouac Napoléon; tel: 04 93 39 14 11.* Open Mon–Fri, 0800–1900; Sat 0800–1200. Telephones, poste restante facilities.

Money

Croisette Change, *1 la Croisette; tel: 04 92 99 18 20* (open July–Aug daily 0900–2300; Sept–June Mon–Sat 0930–1200, 1400–1800); **Thomas Cook bureau de change**: *8 r. d'Antibes; tel: 04 93 39 41 45.* Open daily 1015–1220, 1400–1900.

Entertainment

Cannes proudly upholds the Riviera's reputation as an overpriced overcrowded fleshpot. Entertainment here consists of looking good, spending money and sleeping little. The bars and clubs are expensive, while the casinos attract some of Europe's most upmarket gamblers.

Barely a day goes by without some conference or festival, usually centred on the glossy Palais des Festivals which has made the town France's no. 2 conference

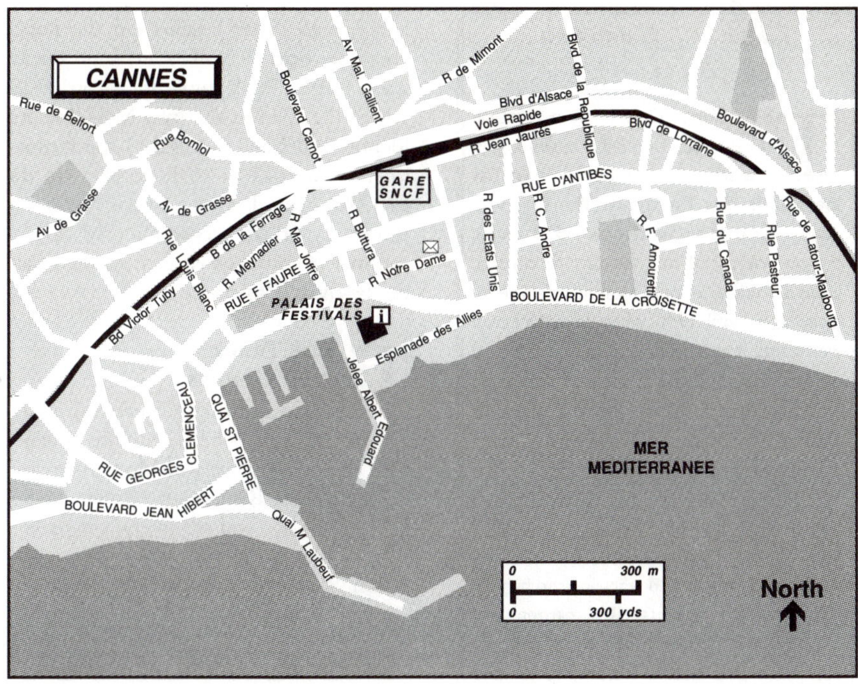

venue after Paris. Nightlife can be fun and the casinos are always busy. Visitors with less money and more sense should head for *r. Macé* and *r. F Faure* where bars are reasonably priced. Otherwise, promenade up and down *la Croisette* enjoying the free entertainment of watching the world go by.

Events

Jan: **MIDEM** – International music and records market; Feb: **Classical Music Festival**; Apr: **MIP** – International TV programme market; May: **Film Festival**; July: **Jazz Festival**; Sept: **MIPCOM** – International TV and video programme market; Oct: **Puppet Festival**; Nov: **International Dance Festival**.

Shopping

Exclusive little shops selling expensive clothes, jewellery and leatherware line *r. d'Antibes*, which runs parallel to *la Croisette*. **Monoprix** opposite the railway station is worth checking for stylish fashions at chain-store prices. A colourful flower market is held each morning on *allée de la Liberté* beside the old port; also an antique market on Sat.

Small food shops and fashion boutiques line the narrow *r. Meynardier* which leads to the appetising aromas of the town's market hall, **Marché Forville** (open daily).

Sightseeing

Begin at the **Palais des Festivals**, built in 1982 and christened 'the bunker'. Look out for your favourite filmstars' handprint cast in the cement on the *allée des Stars*. Climb *r. St Antoine* to the hill of **Le Suquet**, the oldest quarter, where you get

Lights, Camera, Action!

The 13-day Cannes Film Festival takes place annually, beginning in the second week in May, based at the **Palais des Festivals**. The first was due to be held in September 1939 under the presidency of the inventor of cinema, Louis Lumière. World War II intervened, delaying it until 1946 when Jean Cocteau welcomed it as 'a living comet, an apolitical no-man's-land'. Now it attracts everyone who is anyone in the film industry together with a multitude of hangers-on, many young and shapely.

Public tickets for films outside the main competition are sold daily from the office next to the Tourist Office. Competition among the moguls and stars for the biggest hotel suites is intense. Red carpets are unrolled and gleaming stretch limos glide up, disgorging world-famous faces and many that seem vaguely or not-at-all familiar, as the world of cinema pats itself on the back. Glimpses of stars can be frequent (practise climbing lamp posts). Hype is everything, publicity craved and good films all too rare, but the town's hoteliers and restaurateurs love it.

a splendid view east over the town and bay. The château is home to the **Musée de la Castre**, *tel: 04 93 38 55 26* (open daily 1000–1200, 1400–1700), with antiquities and a history of the town. Otherwise there are few specific sights, though you may want to pay homage to Lord Brougham's statue on *allée de la Liberté*.

If the glitz begins to pall, the perfect antidote is available 4km off-shore – the **Îles de Lérins** are two pine-clad islands offering small beaches and extensive woodlands. **Île de Ste Marguerite** is the larger, with better beaches. At the north end, the **Fort Royal** is an impressively stark fortress built by Vauban in 1712 where the Man in the Iron Mask (whose identity is debated to this day) was imprisoned from 1687 to 1698. Smaller **Île de St Honorat** houses a small working monastery. Boats depart hourly during summer from the quays next to the Palais des Festivals' **Casino**; *tel: 04 93 39 11 82.*

Side Track from Cannes

Climb 5km north of Cannes (up *blvd Carnot*, then branch left onto the N285) for the hilltop village of Mougins – *the* place on the Riviera for dinner. Grab the first space you see in the car-parks below the traffic-free medieval streets, then walk up through the fortified Saracen Gate.

MOUGINS

Tourist Office: *av. C Mallet; tel: 04 93 75 87 67.* Open July–Aug daily 0930–1900; Sept–June, Tues–Sat 0900–1200, 1400–1800.

Small restaurants grace the ground floors of over 50 of the village's old red-roofed houses, most with tables spilling picturesquely onto the tiny squares and narrow streets which form near-perfect circles within the village's 15th-century ramparts. However it does not necessarily cost a fortune to eat there. Try **Au Rendez-Vous de Mougins**, *pl. du Village; tel: 04 93 75 87 47* (cheap), or **Relais à Mougins**, *pl. du Village; tel: 04 93 90 03 47* (moderate).

Mougins is also a smart address. Picasso spent his last years at Les Muscadins opposite the Chapelle de Notre-Dame-de-Vie, and has been followed by royalty, film stars, couturiers and just the very rich.

CANNES–GRENOBLE

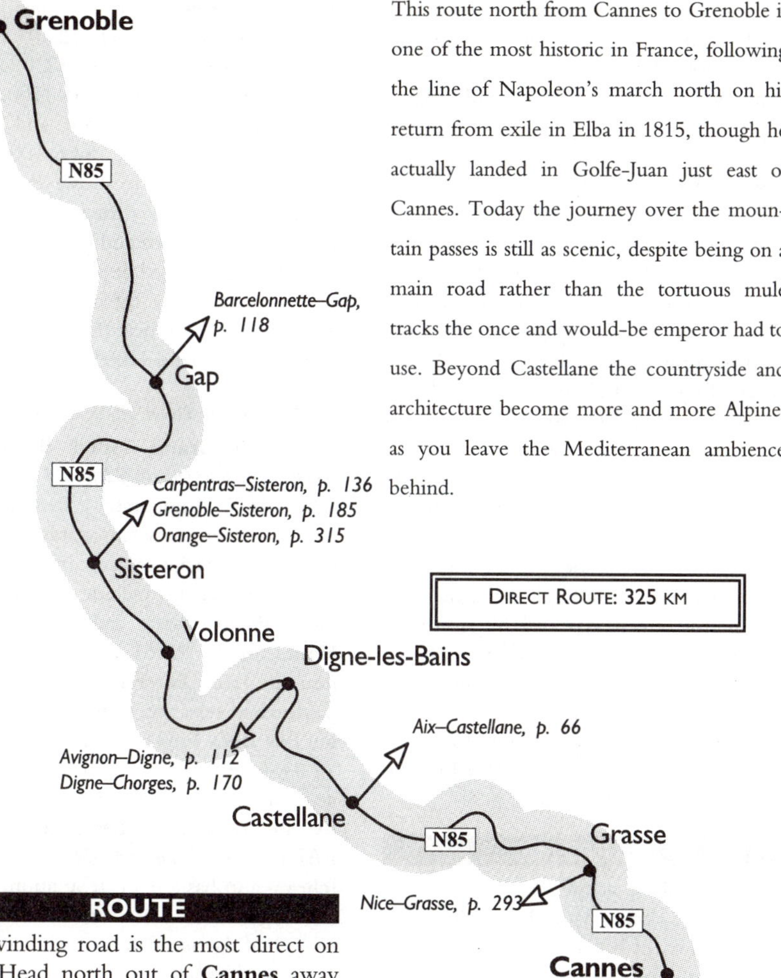

This route north from Cannes to Grenoble is one of the most historic in France, following the line of Napoleon's march north on his return from exile in Elba in 1815, though he actually landed in Golfe-Juan just east of Cannes. Today the journey over the mountain passes is still as scenic, despite being on a main road rather than the tortuous mule tracks the once and would-be emperor had to use. Beyond Castellane the countryside and architecture become more and more Alpine, as you leave the Mediterranean ambience behind.

DIRECT ROUTE: 325 KM

ROUTE

This winding road is the most direct on offer. Head north out of **Cannes** away from the sea on *blvd Carnot*, initially following signs for the A8 or **Le Cannet**. **Mougins** and **Grasse** are then signposted, taking you over the A8 motorway onto the N85 which skirts round Mougins before wriggling its way north-west to **Castellane** and **Digne-les-Bains**. Here it turns left over the **River Bléone** to **Volonne**, **Sisteron**, **Gap** and finally **Grenoble**. Driving time about 5 hours. Allow 2–3 days with sightseeing.

GRASSE

See p. 297.

CASTELLANE

Tourist Office: *r. Nationale; tel: 04 92 83 61 14.* Open Apr–Sept, Mon–Sat 0900–1215, 1400–1830, Sun 1000–1230; Oct–Mar, Mon–Fri 0830–1200 and 1330–1700.

Sightseeing

Although the route climbs steadfastly away from the coast into the mountains over the 1054-m high **Col de Luens**, Castellane still has a thoroughly Mediterranean feel. This little town nestles at the foot of a 184-m limestone crag with a small chapel, **Notre-Dame-du-Roc**, built in 1703, standing guard at the top. A 20-min walk up, following the remains of the walls which encircled the town in the 14th century, is rewarded by a magnificent panorama over the dramatic countryside all around (to go inside, get the key from the **Église Paroissiale**, *pl. de l'Église*).

On the third day of his journey, Napoleon made a fleeting stop at Castellane to have lunch at the *Sous-Préfecture*. For today's visitors the town often serves as a starting-off point for a tour to the west of the **Gorges de Verdun** (see Aix-en-Provence–Castellane, p. 66).

BARRÊME

Tourist Office: at the Mairie, *tel: 04 92 34 20 04.* Open Mon–Fri 0900–1130. Napoleon spent his third night, in one of the houses, now marked by a small plaque, in this quiet village.

More recently it was a centre for the Maquis, the French Resistance against the Nazi occupation forces during World War II. A large map in the square, records their brave exploits between Digne-les-Bains and Castellane.

DIGNE-LES-BAINS

See p. 171.

SISTERON

Tourist Office: *Hôtel de Ville, 04202 Sisteron; tel: 04 92 61 12 03.* Open July–Aug Mon–Sat 0900–1230, 1330–1930; Sun 1000–1200, 1400–1700; Sept–June, Mon–Sat 0900–1200 and 1400–1900 (1700 Nov–Jan), Sun 1000–1200 and 1400–1700. Slide shows during the summer season; also free guided tours around the old town and cathedral.

Parking: Pay and display on the streets is supplemented by three car parks. Free parking is available near the Tourist Office opposite the Grand Hôtel du Cours.

Accommodation and Food

The 3-star **Grand Hôtel du Cours**, *04200 Sisteron; tel: 04 92 61 04 51, fax: 04 92 61 41 73,* (moderate) is centrally-situated and surprisingly reasonably-priced for its location, facilities and graceful ambience. Hotel chains include *Ib*. **Camping**: the municipal 4-star campsite **Les Prés Hauts**, *tel: 04 92 61 19 69,* (caravans) is near the river. For eating out, *r. Saunerie* has the best selection of restaurants including **Les Becs Fins** at *no. 16, tel: 04 92 61 12 04,* (cheap) where you can enjoy *magret de Canard* (sliced duck) and a local speciality, lamb roasted with herbs. **Lou Pebre e l'Aiet**, *r. St Ursule, tel: 04 92 61 25 79* (cheap) also has a good reputation. At the boulangeries, look out for another speciality, a loaf flavoured with anchovies called *fougasse à l'anchois*.

Events

The citadel provides the romantic setting for **Nuits de la Citadelle**, the annual music, drama and dance festival from mid July to mid Aug. For reservations, *tel: 04 92 61 06 00*, from July, Mon–Sat 0900–

The Train Des Pignes

One of the most scenic railway routes in France, the privately-run metre-gauge Chemins de Fer de la Provence line runs between Digne and Nice, a distance of 151km. The Train des Pignes (pine cones), as it is popularly known, winds through the quiet foothills of the Southern Alps, gradually dropping down to the wide valley of the River Var.

Four trains a day make the 3¼-hr journey each way, most consisting of single 50-seater railcars which lurch and jolt around the deep gorges, pine forests and hillside villages. The track passes through 25 tunnels – the longest (at La Colle-St.Michel) is 3457m – and crosses 31 bridges and viaducts. The highest point, 1022m, is near Thorame-Haute station. The first section of the track, from Digne to Mézek, opened in 1891 but the full line took 20 more years to complete. Steam trains run on Sun during summer between Puget-Théniers and Annot and on some Sats between Nice and Puget. From Nice there are also various day-trips.

During a freak storm in Nov 1994, the line was badly damaged by flooding in several places, including a viaduct over the Var which was completely swept away. The cost of repairs, FFr.80 million, was so high that permanent closure seemed likely. However the public outcry was so fierce – not least because the line serves 30 isolated communities and also forms part of Nice's suburban network – that funding was found from local, regional and government sources.

Single fare Digne–Nice is FFr.103. The end stations are Nice *(4 bis, r. A.Binet)* and Gare de Digne-les-Bains where SNCF buses provide connections with trains at St Auban. Information, *tel: 04 93 82 10 17.*

1200 and 1500–1900. Tickets cost FFr.100–250.

Sightseeing

The town's setting is dramatic, beside the River Durance at the foot of a rocky outcrop, first fortified with a citadel in the 13th century. This towers over the Durance which is joined there by the River Buèch and then narrows to squeeze past the Rocher de la Baume, another massive rock on the far side. For centuries these features have made the town a natural stronghold but as a result it suffered heavy bombing during World War II.

Vauban, Louis XIV's famous military architect, conceived a grand plan for the **Citadelle** and the town in 1692 following the invasion of the upper Durance valley by the Duke of Savoy, but it was never fully completed. However, much work was done in the 1840s to improve the defences; the citadel's dungeon, chapel and ramparts can still be visited; *tel: 04 92 61 27 57* (open Mar–mid Nov daily, 0900–1800; FFr. 18). It also contains a museum with a section devoted to Napoleon's return from Elba and an exhibition of horse-drawn vehicles.

Three cylindrical stone towers, once part of the ramparts, still stand in the town centre near the **Cathedral of Notre-Dame des Pommiers** (the name means the space between town and rampart). Built in typical Provençal Romanesque style, it is particularly worth visiting for its paintings and carvings. In the oldest quarter beside the river, arches *(andrônes)* span the alleys between the tall buildings.

The atmospheric conditions around Sisteron make the area the best place in Europe for **gliding**. Courses and initiation flights are available at the **Aero-Club Sisteron**, 12km north of the town, *04200 Vaumeilh, tel: 04 92 62 17 45.*

GAP

Tourist Office: *12 r. Faure du Serre; tel: 04 92 52 56 56.* Open July–Aug, Mon–Sat 0900–1900, Sun 0930–1230; Sept–June, Mon–Sat 0900–1230, 1400–1830. **Parking**: Meter parking in the town centre, plus 20 large car-parks, some free. **Post Office**: *18 r. Carnot; tel: 04 92 52 38 11.*

Accommodation and Food

As the capital of the Southern Alps, Gap is an important commercial centre and so has a wide selection of accommodation and restaurants, including modern business hotels and more traditional establishments. The larger hotels tend to be on the edge of the town. Chains include *F1* and *Ib*. The small modern 2-star **Le Michelet**, *pl. de la Gare, tel/fax: 04 92 51 27 86* (cheap) is centrally situated. **Camping**: 2-star **Camping Napoléon** (caravans), *05000 Gap, tel: 04 92 52 12 41* on RN 85 in the direction of Grenoble. The most interesting restaurants are around the old town.

Sightseeing

Sheltered by high rocky ridges, Gap is a warm sunny town, well placed for visitors to make the most of the glorious mountains all around. In winter, there are ten ski resorts within easy driving distance. But it is a working town too and more visitors come on business or to shop rather than just to sightsee.

The pedestrianised old town is attractive with interesting little shops crowded along the narrow streets. The 600-year old clock tower of the **Hôtel de Ville** is the only part that survived when the Duke of Savoy's army burned down the town hall in 1692; rebuilding was completed in 1743. The mock-Gothic **Cathédrale de Notre-Dame**, built in a variety of local stone including pink marble from Chorges, was only completed in 1895.

Napoleon spent the night of 5 Mar 1815 at the inn at *19 r. de France* where he left his flag to thank Gap for the welcome he received. It is now on show in the **Musée Departemental de Gap**, *6 av. Mar Foch, tel: 04 92 51 01 58* (open July–mid Sept, daily 1000–1200, 1430–1830; mid Sept–June, Wed–Mon 1400–1700), together with other local history exhibits, a fine archaeological collection and paintings, sculpture and china. He also gave the local *Département des Hautes-Alpes* a grant for the construction of a series of mountain refuges, most of which still exist today.

Four km north of the town in the Ecrins National Park is the **Domaine de Charance**, *tel: 04 92 51 21 79* (open Mon–Fri 0800–1200, 1400–1800 (1900 mid June–mid Oct). Guided tours daily July–Aug at 1500 and 1700; FFr.25), an 18th-century mansion surrounded by gardens which display one of France's five national botanic collections. The International Folk Festival is in mid July. Leaving Gap the N85 quicly leads back into the open countryside, climbing through the mountains with wide panoramas on both sides.

CORPS

Tourist Office: in the town centre, *38970 Corps; tel: 04 76 30 03 85.* Open mid June–mid Sept, Mon–Sat 0930–1230, 1500–1900; mid Sept–mid June, Thur

Colour section: (i) Avignon (p. 92). Pont St-Bénézet; the Palais des Papes.
(ii) Pont de Montvert in the Cévennes (p. 154); old Clermont-Ferrand (p. 155); the Pont du Gard (p. 115).
(iii) Séguret (p. 137).
(iv) Gordes (p. 144); the ochre quarries of Roussillon (p. 143).

OPTICIA
petit bateau

0900–1200, Sat 1500–1800.

Accommodation and Food

Hotels and restaurants line the long main street of Corps which is a busy little holiday resort in summer.

It has four 2-star **LF** including the **Hôtel de la Poste**, *rte Napoléon, 38970 Isère; tel: 04 76 30 00 03, fax: 04 76 30 02 73* (cheap) which has 17 rooms and a restaurant (cheap).

Sightseeing

Tucked into the edge of the mountainous Ecrins National Park at the junction of three beautiful valleys, Corps attracts visitors who want to go walking, mountain biking and paragliding or sailing and canoeing on the nearby **Lac du Sautet**.

It also attracts pilgrims who come in their thousands to the **Sanctuary de la Salette**, a 2km drive from the village up into the mountains. It was built at the place where, on 19 Sept 1846, a 'beautiful woman' appeared to an 11-year old boy and 14-year old girl from Corps while they were looking after sheep. She was in tears and spoke to them at length, finally ascending in a cloud of light radiating from the crucifix she wore. Five years later, after thoroughly examining their story, the Bishop of Grenoble declared that the children had witnessed an appearance of the Virgin Mary. The huge **basilica** has become a place of pilgrimage (with room for 650 people to stay), a missionary centre and convent, **Les Soeurs de la Salette**. Three services a day are held in summer and at 1045 on Sun and 1800 on Sat in winter; *tel: 04 76 30 00 11.*

LA MURE

Tourist Office: *43 rte du Breuil, 38350 La Mure, Isère; tel: 04 76 81 05 71.* Open July–Aug, Mon–Sat 0900–1200, 1500–1800; Sept–Oct, Mon–Fri 0900–1200, 1400–1700. This small industrial town, which has held a market on Mon mornings for nearly seven centuries, has been put on the tourist map thanks to its metre-gauge railway, the **Chemin de Fer de la Mure**. It closed in 1988 to regular passenger and goods traffic, mostly coal from La Mure, after exactly 100 years but now operates special services Apr–Oct using carriages and locomotives dating from between 1915 and 1932. In 1903 it was the first line in the world to be electrified, using high voltage DC power, earning itself a special place in railway history.

Reputed to be the most spectacular stretch of railway in France, it twists and climbs for 20 miles from La Mure to St-Georges-de-Commiers, (10 miles south of Grenoble on the line to Veynes), providing breathtaking Alpine views. The route passes the Lac de Monteynard, runs beneath the dramatic cliffs of the Vercors and clings to the sides of the River Drac gorge.

Trains make brief stops, usually on top of some of the 12 viaducts. There are also 18 tunnels. Leaving La Mure, sit on the left side for the best views. One to four trains a day run between Apr and mid Oct; daily June–Aug, otherwise weekends only; *tel: 04 76 72 57 11.* Return fare FFr.95.

LAFFREY

Tourist Office: *38220 Laffrey; tel: 04 76 73 16 36.* Open mid June–mid Sept, Mon–Fri 1330–1900, Sat–Sun 0930–1500.

Sightseeing

The section of the Route Napoléon across the Matheysine Plateau between la Mure and Vizelle is one of its most famous stretches. At the heart of the Dauphiné region, the road runs past the four attractive Laffrey lakes. It was just south of Laffrey on 7 March 1815 that Napoleon's army found itself face to face with the royalist troops under Maréchal Ney who had been sent by Louis XVIII to bar his way.

Several campsites border the lakes and there are five hotels in Laffrey.

VIZILLE

Tourist Office: *pl. du Château; tel: 04 76 68 15 16.* Open July–Sept daily 1030–1230, 1400–1800.

SIGHTSEEING

The town's impressive 17th-century château, built in typically French style with steep tiled roofs and turrets, overlooks the main square. It is surrounded by formal gardens with a lake and waterside paths which are open Apr–Oct, Wed–Mon 0900–1900 (until 2000 Jun–Aug); Nov–Mar, Wed–Mon 1000–1700; free. Inside, the **Museum of the French Revolution**, *tel: 04 76 68 07 35* (open Apr–Sept, Wed–Mon 0930–1200, 1400–1800; Oct–Mar, Wed–Sun 1000–1200, 1400–1700; admission FFr.15) displays documents, paintings, sculptures and artefacts depicting the events which led up to the French Revolution and France's subsequent history up to the Third Republic. The museum was created at the castle because it was the venue in 1788 of the assembly of the Trois Ordres du Dauphiné whose demands for reforms were the trigger for the French Revolution a year later.

Napoleon's Return

It's hard to believe that Napoleon took only a week to travel from Golfe-Juan (see Cannes–Nice, p.131) near Cannes to Grenoble, after landing there on his return from Elba on 1 March 1815. In his bid to regain power, he made the 325-km journey through the Southern Alps with 1000 soldiers along rough roads and mule-tracks over mountain passes.

He knew the main route north along the Rhône Valley lay through an area which would be hostile to his ambitions, so chose the more difficult way through Grasse instead. This also enabled him to spend the second night in the village of Séranon at the country house of one of his supporters, the Marquess of Gourdon, and the third one with another supporter, Judge Tartanson, at Barrème.

The royalist town of Sisteron presented him with a major challenge because of its strategic position, but it was not as heavily guarded as he had feared, and his march into it was triumphant. Beyond it, his progress became easier as he followed the coaching road to Gap.

One week into the journey at Laffrey, he came face to face with Louis XVIII's troops who had been sent to bar the way. Alone, Napoleon advanced and proclaimed 'Soldiers, if any of you wishes to kill his Emperor, here I am'. The soldiers immediately rallied to his side. The field where they met, now known as the **Prairie de la Rencontre**, has became the most famous place on the route and is marked with a bold statue of the Emperor on horseback. From there on, it was cheers all the way until he reached Grenoble where he spent the night at the Hôtel des Trois Dauphins (which no longer exists).

The Route Napoléon was inaugurated as a tourist itinerary in 1932 with plaques bearing an eagle to mark the points along it. As Napoleon said, 'The eagle will fly from steeple to steeple as far as the towers of Notre-Dame'. But his return proved brief. In June he was defeated at Waterloo and finally banished to St Helena, where he died in 1821.

CANNES–NICE

Millionaires' mini-chateaux are secluded in near-botanical gardens on the Cap d'Antibes headland where Riviera tourism began to flourish in the 1920s with an influx of wealthy fun-seeking Americans. Now it has spilled out all along this classy stretch of coast which is sandy as far as the Cap and then turns to pebbles.

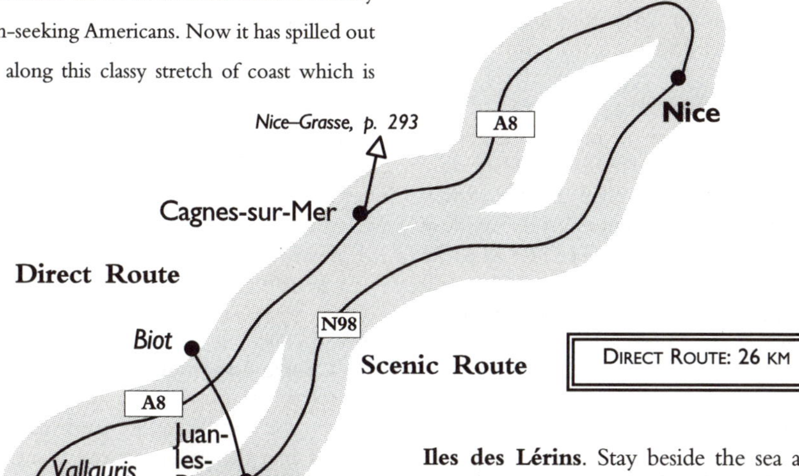

DIRECT ROUTE: 26 KM

ROUTES

DIRECT ROUTE

Leave **Cannes** heading north up *blvd Carnot*, then take the N285, following signs onto A8, which leads straight to **Nice**. Distance 26 km; allow 30 mins, or longer at peak times.

SCENIC ROUTE

Drive east along the seafront to the far end of **Cannes** bay at the **Pointe de la Croisette** headland opposite the **Iles des Lérins**. Stay beside the sea and join the N7 coast road, but fork off right at **Golfe-Juan** onto the N98, which skirts the shore of the next bay. At **Juan-les-Pins**, join the D2559 which goes right round the **Cap d'Antibes** headland before entering **Antibes**. From there, pick up the N98 along the coast past Nice airport and enter **Nice** on the *promenade des Anglais*. Distance 34km; allow at least half a day, depending on time spent on Side Tracks, admiring the sea views and ogling villas and yachts.

GOLFE-JUAN

Tourist Office: *av. de la Liberté* (opposite *sq. Nabonnand); tel: 04 93 63 18 38*. Open daily 0900–1800 July–Aug; Mon–Sat 0900–1200, 1400–1800 Sept–June. **Parking**: free beside the **Plages du Midi** at the eastern end of the town; there are meters and a pay car park on the sea front in the centre.

Station: *pl. de la Gare*. Information: *tel: 36 35 35 35*. On the scenic line along the coast with frequent trains to **Cannes** (10 min) and **Nice** (30 min) – a simple way to avoid their parking problems.

Boat excursions to the **Iles des Lérins** (see Cannes, p. 121) and Monaco (see Monaco, p. 261) from *quai St-Pierre; tel: 04 93 63 45 94*.

Accommodation

Surprisingly there is no line of hotels enjoying sea views. Instead they are scattered around the edge of the town. However, **Le Provence**, *15–17 av. de la Gare; tel: 04 93 63 35 40; fax: 04 93 63 35 53*, (cheap,) is right in the centre and wonderfully French. Watch the locals shopping over breakfast, then join them for their first tot of the day in the bar. Terrace restaurants along the seafront, *blvd des Frères Roustan*, are pleasant for leisurely dining at night. **Tétou**, *tel: 04 93 63 71 16*, (expensive) and **Nounou**, *tel: 04 93 63 71 73*, (moderate) both have a good reputation for *bouillabaisse* and other fresh fish.

Events

July: **Fishermen's festival**; Aug: **St-Sauveur country festival** with procession celebrating local products – jasmine, oranges, olives and roses; 1st–2nd Mar: **Re-enactment of Napoleon's landing** and review of his 1200 troops in 1815.

Sightseeing

A memorial plaque on the seafront, opposite the main street, *av. de la Gare*, proudly commemorates Napoleon's landing at 5 pm on 1 March 1815 from Elba and the start of his historic march north from exile (see p. 130). Though this unassuming seaside town is overshadowed by its ritzier neighbours, Juan-les-Pins and Antibes, its moment in history has not been forgotten. And if you prefer your Riviera less sophisticated, Golfe-Juan is definitely worth considering.

Don't be put off by the railway running through the centre of town. The north end of the main street, *av. de la Gare*, is like a busy village as it runs down to the station. Separate pedestrian and vehicle underpasses make it easy to cross the line and reach the seafront. With two fine stretches of sandy **beach**, *plages du Soleil* and *plages du Midi*, on either side of the old harbour (where freshly caught fish is sold every morning) and a new **marina**, fully of glossy white craft, it is a pleasant place to stay, particularly with children. Scuba-diving is especially good in the bay and several clubs offer diving courses, including **Centre International de Plongeé**; *tel: 04 93 63 00 04*. The promenade is perfect for gentle strolls, particularly at night when the pavement restaurants are in full swing and crafts people set up their stalls.

Side Track from Golfe-Juan

VALLAURIS

Tourist Office: *sq. du 8 May 1945; tel: 04 93 63 82 58*. Open daily 0900–1800 July–Aug; Mon–Sat 0900–1200, 1400–1800 Sept–June.

A 2-km climb inland from Golfe-Juan, the little hillside town is the pottery capital of the Riviera. In the early 1500s several Italian potters settled there, boosting a tradition which dated back to Roman times. Picasso's arrival in the area in 1946 put new artistic life into the industry. Leading potters continue to work there. Appropriately, huge flowerpots form an attractive guard of honour down both sides of the main street. Many small craft studios sell interesting modern items. Pottery exhibitions and workshops are staged at various venues (June–Sept).

The splendid Renaissance **castle**, *pl. de la Libération, tel: 04 93 64 16 05* (open Wed–Mon 1000–1200, 1400–1800; FFr.13) houses three museums. The **Musée National Picasso** in the chapel displays his two-panel fresco, *War and Peace*; the **Musée Magnelli** has a collection of works by the Italian abstract painter, Alberto Magnelli; and the **Musée Municipale** features ceramics and modern art.

JUAN-LES-PINS

Tourist Office: *51 blvd Guillaumont; tel: 04 92 90 53 05.* Open Mon–Sat 0900–2000, Sun 1000–1300 July–Aug; Mon–Fri 0900–1200, 1400–1830, Sat 0900–1230, 1400–1800 Sept–June (also Sun 1000–1200 Easter–June and Sept)

Boat excursions to the **Iles des Lérins**, *quai Courbet, tel: 04 92 93 02 36.*

Accommodation and Food

One block back from the sea front, *r. Bricka* has a selection of small reasonably-priced hotels including the **Gallia** *(no. 30); tel: 04 93 61 26 78* (cheap), and **Colbert** *(no. 12); tel: 04 93 61 20 08, fax: 04 93 67 33 98* (cheap). For a really special meal, there are plenty of top-class restaurants like **Bijou Plage**, *blvd Charles Guillaumont, tel: 04 93 61 39 07* (expensive) which specialises in *bouillabaisse*, but you can eat more cheaply. **Le Chantilly**, *27 av. de l'Esterel; tel: 04 932 61 98 90* (cheap) is noted for its pizzas.

Entertainment

No excuse for going to bed early here, even if you only stay up to shop, stroll and stare. Night owls pour in from miles around and midnight passes unnoticed. The lively *blvd de la Pinède* has discos like **Voom-Voom**, *tel: 04 93 61 18 71*, and **Whisky à Gogo**, *tel: 04 93 61 26 40.* Or try your luck just around the corner at the glittering **Eden Casino**, *blvd Baudoin; tel: 04 92 93 71 71*, beside the beach. For quieter music, **Le New Orleans** in the **Hôtel Garden Beach**, *blvd Baudoin; tel: 04 93 67 25 25*, is one of several piano bars.

Events

Mar: **New Orleans-les-Pins Jazz Festival** with four days of marching bands, concerts and Cajun-style dining; July: **Jazz à Juan** attracts performers and afficionados from all over the world. Tickets from the Tourist Office.

Sightseeing

This busy resort is a newer playground than Antibes, on the opposite side of the Cap d'Antibes headland, though the two now merge across the Cap's neck. It sprang into fashion only in the 1920s but now hotels, piano bars, restaurants, discos and a casino provide all the requisites for the smart and young on holiday. These thin out as the route climbs into the pine groves above the Cap's secluded rocky coves. Some of the most sumptuous mini-châteaux in France lurk amongst the trees, guarded by high wrought-iron gates and security cameras. Uninvited guests glimpse little more than the occasional rooftop above the lush gardens. The drive round the Cap is superb all the way with views over Cannes and the Iles des Lérins to the west and the Baie des Angles to the east. A footpath leads along the tip of the headland, nicknamed the **Baie de Milliardaires** (Millionaires' Bay).

ANTIBES

Tourist Office: *11 pl. du Gén. de Gaulle; tel: 04 92 90 53 00.* Open Mon–Sat 0900–2000, Sun 1000–1300 July–Aug; Mon–Fri 0900–1200, 1400–1830, Sat 0900–1230, 1400–1800 Sept–June (also Sun 1000–1200 Easter–June, Sept). **Branch**: in the **Old Town**, *32 blvd d'Aguillon; tel: 04 93 34 65 65.* Open Mon–Sat 0830–1930, Sun 1000–1300 July–Aug; Mon–Sat 0900–1200, 1400–1800 Sept–June. **Parking**: free on the *pré des Pêcheurs* opposite **Port Vauban**, just outside the old town walls, plus a paying car park opposite *av. de Verdun.*

Station: *av. Robert Soleau; tel: 04 93 99 50 50.*

Bus Station: Local coastal buses from *pl. Gén. de Gaulle; tel: 04 93 85 61 81;* others from the **Gare Routière**, *r. de la République; tel: 04 93 34 37 60.*

Accommodation and Food

One of the world's most luxurious hotels, **Hôtel du Cap Eden Roc**, *blvd Kennedy; tel: 04 93 61 39 01; fax: 04 93 67 76 04* (very expensive; open May–Oct) secludes itself on the tip of **Cap d'Antibes**. This white château, built in 1870 and surrounded by formal gardens, provided the inspiration for F. Scott Fitzgerald's *Tender is the Night*, and Charlie Chaplin and Ernest Hemingway often stayed there. It now has 130 rooms and guests frequently include Hollywood stars.

The town has eight other 4-star hotels, including the exclusive **Hôtel La Baie Dorée**, *579 blvd de la Garoupe; tel: 04 93 67 30 67; fax: 04 92 93 76 39* (expensive), whose 17 rooms all have balconies overlooking the sea. However there are also plenty of less exhalted (and less expensive) places to lay your head. Try those around the bus station, such as the **Nouvel Hôtel**, *1 av. du 24 Août; tel: 04 93 34 44 07, fax: 04 93 34 06 66* (cheap) or **Hôtel National**, *7 pl. Amiral Barnaud; tel: 04 93 34 31 84* (cheap).

HI: *blvd de la Garoupe; tel: 04 93 61 34 40,* under pines by the sea on Cap d'Antibes (bus from *pl. Gén. de Gaulle).* No surprise that it gets booked up early in summer. **Campsites**: the many campsites near the river at **La Brague** to the north, include **Rossignol**, *2074 av. Jean Michard Pellisier; tel: 04 93 33 56 98* (caravans) which has a pool.

For restaurants, *pl. Nationale* and the surrounding side streets, two blocks inland from the Picasso museum, offer several inexpensive places like **La Cascade**, *25–27 r. de Sade; tel: 04 93 34 12 82* (cheap), which has a large terrace. *R. Aubernon*, just up from the port, has several cheerful bistros frequented by yachting types. Try **Le Café des Chineurs**, *28 r. Aubernon; tel: 04 93 34 57 58* (cheap), or, if you want to splash out, dine on a terrace above the sea and perhaps spot a celebrity or two, the **Restaurant de Bacon**, *blvd de Bacon; tel: 04 93 61 65 19* (expensive) which is renowned for *bouillabaise* and fresh fish.

Sightseeing

Mixing chic and tackiness, Antibes is a pleasure port, not for Anglophobes, with a long history and relaxed atmosphere. Take a walk along the harbour, **Port Vauban**, where some of the biggest boats in the Med are moored.

At one end the formidable **Fort Carré** is part of the fortifications erected by Louis XIV's military architect, Vauban, in the 17th century.

The old town is a charming maze of narrow streets centred on *cours Massena*, famous for its **Provençal market** (Tues–Sun mornings June–Aug) and craft stalls (Fri and Sun afternoons; also Tues

Tourism comes to Cap d'Antibes

Although the Duke of Albany, son of Queen Victoria, discovered the beaches and pine forests of Juan-les-Pins in 1881, it was Frank J. Gould, the American railway baron, who set the place alight in the 1920s. He opened a summer casino and built himself a mock castle on Cap d'Antibes, La Vigie, now owned by a racing car millionaire. The Scott Fitzgeralds and Hemingways followed, launching a craze for sea bathing – and swimsuits that were daringly brief for the time – on the Garoupe beaches near the end of the Cap. A string of Hollywood stars soon followed, as ever-more-palatial villas were built. In 1938 the Duke and Duchess of Windsor took a ten-year lease on one of them, La Croe. Lesser mortals have settled for the hotels, apartments and campsites along the bays on either side of the Cap.

and Thur afternoons, Easter–Sept). From here, a narrow alley leads up to a headland on which stands the **Musée Picasso,** *pl. Mariejol, tel: 04 93 34 91 91* (open Tues–Sun 1000–1200, 1400–1800 Dec–Oct; closed 1200–1400 Oct–May; FFr.30) in the **Château Grimaldi** which the artist was given to use as his studio when he moved to the town with Françoise Gilot in 1946. This excellent museum displays some of his most entertaining pottery as well as drawings, paintings and prints.

At the southern end of the sea wall in the **Bastion St-André Further**, the **Musée Archéologique**, *tel: 04 93 34 48 01* (open Dec–Oct Tues–Sun 1000–1200, 1400–1800; closed 1200–1400 Oct–May; FFr.25) contains traces of the port's Greek and Roman past.

BIOT

Tourist Office: *6 pl. de la Chapelle; tel: 04 93 65 05 85.* Open Mon–Fri 1000–1200, 1430–1900, Sat–Sun 1000–1200 July–Sept; Mon–Fri 0900–1200, 1400–1800 Oct–June.

Three km inland, high above the **River Brague**, this is one of the oldest and most charming perched villages on the Riviera, having been occupied originally by the Knights Templar in 1209. Less overwhelmed by tourists than many other local towns, it has quaint arched alleys, arcades and carved façades. Today many artists and craft workers have studios and galleries there.

Once a pottery town, it is now renowned for its bubble-flecked glass. On the road up to the village is the **Verrerie de Biot**, *chemin des Combes; tel: 04 93 65 03 00,* (open Mon–Sat 0900–1830 (2000 July–Aug) Sun 1000–1300, 1430–1900; free) where visitors can watch glass-blowers at work. The **Galerie International du Verre** (open Mon–Sat 1030–1830 (2000 July–Aug) Sun 1030–1300 and 1430–1900) displays and sells glass by 32 leading artists.

Just outside the town, the **Musée Fernand Léger**, *chemin du Val-de-Rome; tel: 04 92 91 50 30* (open Wed–Mon 1000–1230, 1400–1730; FFr.28) is a remarkable modern building decorated outside with huge colourful Ll Léger mosaics. It was specially designed to house 400 of his bold post-Cubist paintings.

CAGNES-SUR-MER

See p. 293.

CARPENTRAS–SISTERON

This route skirts the Dentelles of Montmirail passing through famous and picturesque wine villages on its way to Vaison-la-Romaine. Then there is the breathtaking ascent and descent of Mt Ventoux, 'the Provençal giant', before climbing up through the scenic Gorges de la Nesque towards the Pays de Sault. From this renowned lavender-growing area, the route traverses the Gorges de la Méouge to arrive in the Durance valley.

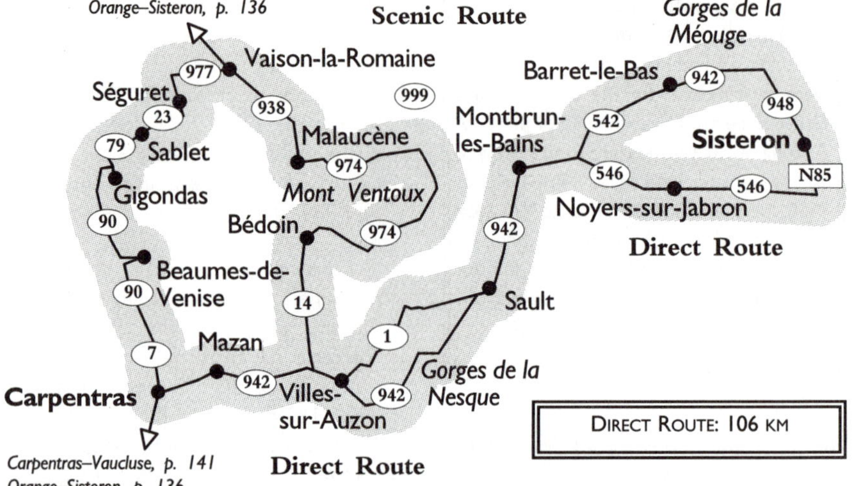

DIRECT ROUTE: 106 KM

ROUTES

DIRECT ROUTE

From Carpentras, take the D942 to Mazan and Villes-sur-Auzon, then the D1 to Sault. From Sault, follow the D942 to Montbrun-les-Bains, then the D542 and D546 through Noyers-sur-Jabron to the N85, turning left to Sisteron. Distance: 106 km; allow: 4–5 hrs. You can begin this route in **Avignon**, taking the N7 south and turning on to the D942; about 25 km.

SCENIC ROUTE

From Carpentras, take the D7 to Aubignan where you branch off along the D90 to **Beaumes-de-Venise.** Follow the D81 out of the other side of town to rejoin the D90, turning right 2 km out of Vacqueyras on the D7 towards **Gigondas**. From Gigondas follow the D79 to **Sablet**, then take the D23 to **Séguret**. Leave Séguret on the D88 and turn right onto the D977 into **Vaison-la-Romaine**. Leave Vaison on the D938 to **Malaucène**, taking the D974 up the north face of **Mont Ventoux** to the summit. Descend the other side to Bédoin. From here, take the D974, then the D14 to Mormoiron, turning left on the D942 outside the village towards Villes-sur-Auzon. Turn right to follow the D942 through the **Gorges de la Nesque**, joining the D1 into **Sault**. From Sault, take the D942 to **Montbrun-les-Bains** from where you follow the D542 through Barret-sur-Lioure and Séderon. It becomes the D942 as it passes through Barret-les-Bas and the **Gorges de la Méouge**. At the end of the gorges, turn right onto the D948 to Sisteron. Distance: 217 km; allow: 2–2½ days.

CARPENTRAS TO VAISON-LA-ROMAINE

Tourist Offices: Beaumes-de-Venise: *cours J. Jaurès; tel: 04 90 62 94 39* (open Mon 1430–1800, Tues–Sat 0900–1200, 1430–1800); **Gigondas**: *pl. du Portail; tel: 04 90 65 85 46* (open daily 1000–1200, 1400–1800; **Sablet**: *r. de Levant; tel: 04 90 46 82 46* (open Mon–Sat 0900–1200, 1400–1800); **Séguret**, *tel: 04 90 46 92 94* (open daily July–Aug 0900–1900; Apr–Oct 1000–1800).

This section of the route skirts around the fringes of the Dentelles de Montmirail, a series of jagged limestone peaks (named after their likeness to a row of ragged teeth) which form the westernmost foothills of Mont Ventoux. With their upper slopes clad in pine and oak plantations and extensive vineyards, they shelter numerous important wine-producing villages on the edge of the Rhône Valley, the first of which is **Beaumes-de-Venise**, best known for the delicious fortified white wines which bear its name. There are numerous *caves* both in and around the town where they can be sampled and bought (full list available from the tourist office). The village is surmounted by a ruined castle (no visits), with numerous limestone caves, once inhabited, dotting the hillside beneath it. These ancient dwellings gave the village its name (*baume* is Provençal for grotto; 'de Venise' refers to the fact that it was one part of the Comtat Venaison).

At the junction with the main road on leaving Beaumes-de-Venise, a small side road leads to the **Chapelle de Notre-Dame-d'Aubune**, whose 9th-century bell-tower, oranamented by pilasters, is a jewel of the Romanesque period.

The next village along is **Gigondas**, named Jocunditas (or 'joy') by the Romans, no doubt because of the quality of the now world famous red Gigondas wines (made from the Grenache grape). On the main square, next to the tourist office, you can sample the products of nearly 50 local producers in the **Caveau de Gigondas**, *pl. de la Mairie; tel: 04 90 65 82 29* (open daily 1000–1230, 1400–1900; 1830 mid Oct–mid March).

Behind Gigondas a road leads up to a car park at the foot of the Dentelles, from where you can walk up to the **Col de Cayron** (396m) at the centre of the Dentelles' peaks. A track from here leads up to a **Saracen Tower** (1 hr rtn) from where there are superb views across the Rhône plain and the Vaucluse plateau.

Continuing along the route, the village of **Sablet**, not as attractive as some of its neighbours, but its Syndicat d'Initiative (see above for details) also acts as a tasting and sales point for the robust Sablet wines.

The last of the Dentelles' villages is **Séguret**, a picturesque and lovingly restored medieval village built into the side of the hill. Under the first archway a souvenir shops serves an an Information Centre (see above). A covered passageway leads through into a network of cobbled streets, with a 15th-century fountain and a 14th-century belfry. Next to the **Église St-Denis** at the top of the village there is an **orientation table** from where there are sweeping views along the length of the Dentelles and the Comtat Venaissin. The streets are lined with numerous shops selling santons (see p. 76) and traditional crafts, as well as numerous *caves* where you can buy Séguret wines.

VAISON-LA-ROMAINE

See p. 316.

MALAUCÈNE

Tourist Office: *pl. de la Mairie, tel: 04 90 65 22 59.* Open Mon–Fri 0900–1200, 1500–1700, Sat 0900–1200. It has a wide variety of leaflets on walks and cycle routes in the vicinity and on Mt Ventoux. In July–Aug every Fri, night-time ascents of Mt Ventoux can be made, arriving at the summit at dawn (FFr.25).

Accommodation and Food

There are half-a-dozen or more hotels to choose between in the town itself and the surrounding area, including the **Hostellerie La Chevalerie** (*LF*), *r. des Remparts; tel: 04 90 65 11 19; fax: 04 90 12 69 22* (cheap–moderate) which is central, comfortable and has a restaurant (cheap–moderate) with local specialities. Also central is the **Hôtel de Venaissin**, *cours des Isnards; tel: 04 90 65 20 31; fax: 04 90 65 18 03*, which has 12 rooms (cheap) and a restaurant (cheap) serving Provençal dishes such as *bourride à l'aïoli*. There are several brasseries and cafés along the main *cours*.

Sightseeing

A large Provençal town surrounded by a boulevard of plane trees, Malaucène styles itself 'the capital of Mt Ventoux' and is a major base for hiking, cycling and other activities on the mountain. The old town, entered by one of four fortified gates, features many attractive old houses, fountains, and narrow streets; following *r. St Étienne* and *r. du Château* leads you up past a crumbling old bell tower to a belvedere (created in the ruins of a château) from where there are views of Mt Ventoux and the Drôme mountains. At the western edge of the old town is Malaucène's **Église**, rebuilt in the 14th-century, which blends the Romanesque and Gothic and has a remarkable 17th-century gilded organ.

MONT VENTOUX

Just outside Malaucène on the way to Mt Ventoux you can see the **Chapelle de Notre-Dame du Groseau** (no access) on the right hand side of the road, all that remains of a 12th-century Benedictine abbey. Immediately afterwards is the **Source Vauclusienne de Groseau**, which wells up from fissures in the rock beneath the trees on the left of the road; the Romans channeled this source via an aquaduct to Vaison-la-Romaine.

As the road climbs slowly up the north face of the mountain, the Vaucluse Plateau opens up below, and, as it passes Mt Serein (1445 m), a panorama of the Ouvèze valley and the Massif des Baronnies is revealed. Finally, the vegetation thins out and only rocks remain as the summit of **Mont Ventoux** (1909 m) is reached. Bristling with military and television antennae, it has two viewing platforms, a café and souvenir shop. On a clear day, there is an extraordinary panorama extending north to the Alps, west to the Alpilles, the Rhône Valley and the Cévennes, and south to the Mediterranean (at night, the sweeping lights of the coastal lighthouses can be spotted). The top is sometimes shrouded in mist, but this is often blown away by the piercing winds of the Mistral (see p. 314), which have reached record speeds of 230 kph up here. They can make it hard to stand up straight and it comes as no surprise to learn that 'ventoux' means 'windy'.

The mountain's slopes, once heavily wooded, were largely denuded (partly for building warships at Toulon) by the beginning of the 19th century. A massive re-forestation programme – mainly on the southern slopes – later that century led to the extensive plantations of pines and cedars which cover it today. These provide a home for creatures such as deer, wild boar and over 100 species of bird, including rare eagles and owls. The mountain habitat also shelters some 950 species of Alpine and Mediterranean plants, and in recognition of this a large portion of Mt Ventoux was designated a UNESCO Biosphere Reserve in 1990.

Descending the south face, the road passes the **Col des Tempêtes** (1829m) which, as the name suggests, is renowned for its stormy weather. Altogether the road winds down 22 km through a series of hairpin bends to Bédoin. This was the first road to be built up the mountain in 1885, to serve the observatory at the summit. It was often used for early car rallies and is still frequently included as a gruelling stage in the Tour de France cycle race. British cyclist Tommy Simpson died of heart failure on this section in 1967.

GORGES DE LA NESQUE

From the southern flanks of Mt Ventoux the road gradually rises up from the plain of the Comtat Venaissin and ascends through typical Provençal *garrigue* (scrubland) into the low-lying hills on either side of the river's exit from the gorges. The road follows through hunting reserves and reforested areas, with the abandoned village of **Fayol** above to the left, almost hidden beneath vegetation. As the gorge begins to deepen, there is a belvedere followed by a series of tunnels through the rock until it emerges at the most dramatic belevedere on a bend in the gorges. The view across the gorges to the massive **Rocher du Cire** (872 m) is spectacular, with the Nesque murmuring over its bed in a deep cleft some 754 m below. The road then climbs up past the village of **Monnieux**, towards the plateau and the town of Sault.

SAULT

Tourist Office: *av. de la Promenade; tel: 04 90 64 01 21.* Open Apr–Sept daily 0900–1230, 1400–1830; Oct–March Mon–Sat 0930–1230, 1430-1630, Sun 1000–1200. A wide range of books, videos and leaflets on local walks and bike routes are for sale.

ACCOMMODATION AND FOOD

Sault has a handful of café-bars and the **Hôtel-Restaurant Signoret**, *av. de l'Oratoire; tel: 04 90 64 11 44; fax: 04 90 64 12 47* (moderate), with 25 rooms and a restaurant specialising in regional dishes. On the outskirts is **le Lavandin** (*LF*), *rte d'Apt, 84390 St Christol; tel: 04 90 75 08 41; fax: 04 90 75 08 40* (moderate), with modern, comfortable rooms and a pool.

SIGHTSEEING

Sault is at the centre of one of Provence's most important lavender growing regions, as well as being known for its nougat, honey, a flavoursome local sauasage, and mushrooms and truffles from the surrounding oak forests (*saltus*), which gave the village its name. There are plenty of shops selling lavender essences, soaps, perfumes and other local products along the main *r. de la République*, amongst them the Coopérative Agricole's *Maison des Producteurs*, *Le Jardin des Lavandes*, and the nougat shop (founded in 1887) of *André Boyer.* A good day to visit is Wednesday, when local producers flock in for the market (which has been going since 1515).

Opposite the tourist office there is a terrace with superb views of Mt Ventoux, the Vaucluse plateau and the entrance to the Gorges de la Nesque. A short distance away the **Église St-Sauveur**, which dates from the 12th century, has a remarkable nave with broken barrel vaulting and a Gothic chancel lined with 17th-century panelling. Behind the main market square is the **Maison de la Chasse et de l'Environment**, *r. de l'Oratoire; tel: 04 90 64 13 96* (open Tues, Thur–Sun, July–Aug 1000–1200, 1500-1900; Sept–June 1000–1200, 1400-1800; FFr.12) which features a series of changing exhibits on the themes of the forest, hunting, water, flora and fauna and the exploitation of natural resources covering the Pays de Sault, Mt Ventoux, and surrounding areas.

SAULT TO SISTERON

From Sault the road traverses the topmost part of the Plateau d'Albion, with views across to the eastern flanks of Mt Ventoux, before arriving in **Montbrun-les-Bains** in the Toulourenc Valley midway between Mt Ventoux and the Montagne de Lure. This picturesque village, topped by the ruins of a château, has a pleasant old quarter with vaulted alleyways, fountains, small squares, and an 18th-century bell-tower.

From Montbrun, the road winds around behind the Montagne d'Albion to reach Séderon, and then follows the Méouge River downstream through a scenic valley with the Montagne de Chabre on its northside, before entering the **Gorges de la Méouge**. Although not as big as the Gorges de la Nesque, the gorges are flanked by pines, oaks, and beech woods (particular lovely in the autumn), and provide a pleasant drive down to the mouth of the gorge, where the road and river emerge onto the fertile plains of the Durance, passing through vast orchards, with stunning views back towards the Alps, to arrive at Sisteron.

Lavender

The unmistakable scent of lavender is as characteristic of Provence as pastis and *pétanque*, and almost every souvenir shop has a stock of lavender sachets, soaps and essential oils. The main growing area is the the 'mauve triangle' between Banon, Sault and Séderon, where, from July to September the fields are a sea of mauve stalks. Harvesting takes place throughout this period, and although much of it is now mechanised some hard-to-reach fields are still harvested by hand. The first distilleries were built in the 1880s to supply essence to the apothecaries of Carpentras and Apt, but systematic production only took after after World War I, to meet the demands of the *parfumeurs* of Grasse. Provence currently accounts for 80 per cent of world production of lavender, with around 8500 hectares under cultivation. Most of the products sold in shops are in fact made from lavandin, a hybrid which grows at lower altitudes and in the valleys. Lavandin is less highly scented than lavender but more productive, and costs far less. Both lavender and lavandin are dried for 2–3 days before being processed in the distilleries. Tourist offices in the region can supply a brochure on *Les Routes de la Lavande*, detailing distilleries and local producers to visit and the most scenic routes through the lavender fields. Lavender festivals take place in Sault, Valensole, Digne, Valréas and other locations, usually in late July–mid Aug.

CARPENTRAS–VAUCLUSE LOOP

This route starts and finishes in the lively market town of Carpentras, circling the eastern edge of the Vaucluse plateau and several picturesque *villages perchés* (hilltop villages), as well as the famous source of the Sorgue at Fontaine de Vaucluse and the delightful towns of Isle-sur-la-Sorgue and Pernes-les-Fontaines.

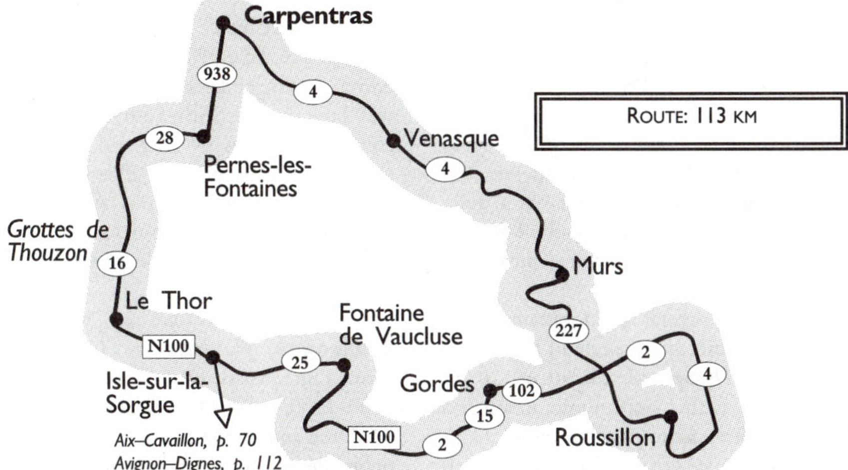

ROUTE: 113 KM

ROUTE

Leave **Carpentras** by the D4 (signposted St-Didier), following it across the D1 as it climbs up towards **Venasque**. From here, continue on the D4 to Murs, then cross the valley, turning right onto the D227 to **Roussillon**. Leave Roussillon on the Apt road (D199), then turn left on the D4 back to the crossroads, turning left again onto the D2, then taking the D102 towards **Gordes**. From Gordes, take the D15 downhill towards the **Village des Bories**, and then follow the D2, D148, N100 and D100A to **Fontaine de Vaucluse**. Leave here on the D25 to **Isle-sur-la-Sorgue**, from where you take the N100 to **Le Thor** and follow the D16 north to the **Grottes de Thouzon**. Continue along the D16, turning right on the D28 into **Pernes-les-Fontaines**. Take the D938 from Pernes to Carpentras. Distance: 113 km; allow: 2 days.

CARPENTRAS

Tourist Office: *170 allée J. Jaurès; tel: 04 90 63 57 88.* (Open July–Aug daily 0900–1900; Sept–June Mon–Fri 0900–1230, 1400–1830, Sat 0900–1200, 1400–1800. There is a rotating programme of guided visits to most major sights at fixed hours July–mid Sept (FFr.25).

Accommodation and Food

Central Carpentras is not over-endowed with good hotels but there are a few reasonable choices, amongst them **Le Fiacre**, *153 r. Vigne; tel: 04 90 63 03 15; fax: 04 90 60 49 73* (cheap–moderate), which occupies a converted 18th-century mansion in a quiet street, with 19 individually-decorated rooms and a pleasant courtyard. The **Coq Hardi**, *36 pl. de la Marotte; tel: 04 90 63 00 35; fax: 04 90 60 40 76* (cheap–moderate) is also well situated and reasonably-priced. A good budget option is the unpretentious and friendly **Le Théâtre**, *7 blvd A. Durand; tel: 04 90 63 02 90* (cheap). The town's best hotel is the **Safari**, *av. J. H. Fabre; tel: 04 90 63 35 35; fax: 04 90 60 49 49* (cheap–moderate), on the outskirts of town, which has a quiet position, modern, well-appointed rooms, a swimming pool, and an excellent restaurant.

There are several good restaurants in the town centre, amongst them **L'Atelier**, *30 pl. de l'Horloge; tel; 04 90 60 20 15* (moderate), with a gastronomic menu and fish specialities; **Lou Cacalas**, *av. N. D. de Santé, tel: 04 90 60 54 32* (cheap), which offers traditional Provençal cuisine; and **Restaurant Marijo**, *73 r. Raspail; tel: 04 90 60 42 65* (cheap), which has a nice atmosphere and is very good quality for the price. There are also pizzerias, and crêperies.

Events

An enormous **market** occupies much of the town centre on Fri, with a **truffle market**, *pl. A. Briand,* in season (Dec–Apr, Fri 0800–1100). On the **Journée Comtadine** (late July), the town hosts a major festival with street performances, craft and food stalls, dances and other events. There is also a major festival of music, dance and theatre in July.

Sightseeing

Carpentras has been an important market centre since the 5th century BC and became a prosperous town under the Romans. Little remains of the Roman occupation except for a small **Arc de Triomphe**, hidden away on the north side of the cathedral; built at the same time as the arch in Orange, although unfortunately only a third of it is still intact. However, it has some excellent bas-reliefs on the east face. The **Cathédrale St-Siffrein**, *pl. Gén. de Gaulle; tel: 04 90 63 08 33* (open daily 0900–1700; free) which dominates the pedestrianised town centre, was built in the 15th–16th centuries. Is contains paintings by Mignard, Duplessis and Parrocel, as well as gilded wooden sculptures by Jacques Bernus. Amongst its relics is the supposedly miraculous Holy Bit, said to have been made from two nails used in the crucifix.

Carpentras also has an important **Synagogue**, *pl. Hôtel de Ville* (open Mon–Thurs 1000–1200, 1500–1700, Fri 1000–1200, 1500–1600; free), built in 1367 and among the oldest in France. The richly decorated interior is testament to the importance of the large Jewish community which once existed here.

The town has some lovely old mansions from the 17th and 18th centuries. Inside the **Hôtel-Dieu**, *pl. A. Briand, tel: 04 90 63 80 00* (open Mon, Wed, Thurs 0900–1130; FFr.8) is a superbly preserved 18th-century **Pharmacie** – complete with pestles, mortars, and all the other tools of the apothecary's trade, alongside an extensive collection of *faïence.* The room itself is decorated with panels painted by Duplessis. On the other side of town, the impressive, 27 m high **Porte d'Orange** is the last remaining gateway of 32 built around the town in the 14th century. There are also four small municipal

museums, covering folklore, art, archaeology and period furniture, which fade into insignificance behind many other regional collections.

Carpentras is known for the manufacture of *berlingots* (mint-flavoured caramels), and several factories can be visited (free) on fixed days in July-Aug. Enquire at the Tourist Office for details.

VENASQUE

Tourist Office: *Grand Rue; tel: 04 90 66 11 66.* Open daily July–mid Sept 1000–1230, 1500–1900; Mar–June, Oct 1000–1230, 1400–1800. Information, book sales, and a small exhibition space with local pottery, weavings, sculptures and paintings.

Accommodation and Food

One of the best places for lunch is the charming and cheerfully decorated glassed-in terrace (with views over the gorges to the south of Venasque), at the **Hôtel Les Ramparts** *(LF), r. Haute; tel: 04 90 66 02 79* (cheap–moderate), with three menus featuring tempting local specialities; the hotel also has reasonably-priced rooms. A delightful place to stay is the **Auberge La Fontaine**, *pl. de la Fontaine; tel: 04 90 66 02 96; fax: 04 90 66 13 14* (expensive) which has just five exquisite and fully-equipped suites, with a small bistro below.

Sightseeing

This ancient citadel, perched on a rocky outcrop, dominates the only mountain route between Apt and Carpentras, effectively controlling two valleys. Today it is a charming village, classified since 1992 amongst *Les Plus Beaux Villages de France.* It also possesses one of the oldest religious buildings in the country, the **Baptistère** (Baptistry), *Grand Rue; tel: 04 90 66 11 41* (open 1000–1200, 1500–1900; Oct 1400–1800; closed Wed, Sun am; FFr.10). Probably dating from the Merovingian period (6th century) and remodelled in the 11th century, it is designed on the Greek cross plan with an octagonal font set in the floor. Just next door, the 12th-century **Église** (open daily 0900–1900) features a 15th-century crucifixion tableau from the Avignon School. At the other end of the village, there is a massive pair of fortified towers known as the **Tours Sarrazines** which were built to defend the weakest part of the village from Saracen attack.

Venasque has a superb view over the Comtat Venaissin and Mont Ventoux; as you leave the village this view is gradually obscured as the route winds through the attractive oak thickets of the **Forêt de Venasque**. The road climbs through 400 m before peaking at the **Col de Murs** pass (627 m), after which it descends towards the Apt basin with views across Roussillon and the Lubéron massif beyond.

ROUSSILLON

Tourist Office: *pl. de la Poste; tel: 04 90 05 60 25.* Open mid April–mid Nov Mon–Sat 1000–1200, 1430-1900, Sun 1400–1800; mid Nov–mid Apr Mon–Sat 1000–1200, 1400-1800, Sun 1400–1800.

Accommodation and Food

As befits such a well-established stop on the tourist route, Roussillon has numerous restaurants and several good hotels nearby. Down on the main road (D2), the **Mas de Garrigon** *(RS), tel: 04 90 05 63 22; fax: 04 90 05 70 01* (expensive), has just nine rooms, all with their own balconies, a pool, and a restaurant (moderate–expensive). Also on the outskirts of the village (D104) the **Tie Break**, *Bois de la Cour; tel: 04 90 05 65 46* (cheap–moderate), is in a quiet position with a tennis court and 7 rooms. Within the village the **Hôtel des**

Ocres, *rte de Gordes; tel: 04 90 05 60 50; fax: 04 90 05 73 06* (moderate) is well-positioned, peaceful, and has 16 rooms with terraces.

Places to eat include the **Restaurant David**, *pl. de la Poste; tel: 04 90 05 60 13* (cheap–moderate) which has a superb terrace with views over the ochre cliffs and a variety of menus. **La Treille**, *r. du Four; tel: 04 90 05 64 47* (cheap–moderate), in the heart of the village, serves a variety of Mediterranean dishes, while **La Val des Fées**, *r. R. Casteau; tel: 04 90 05 64 99* (cheap–moderate) serves Provençal cuisine on a terrace with a panoramic views.

Sightseeing

Roussillon is a highly picturesque village which owes its appeal to the nearby quarries which (in the past) produced up to 17 different shades of red and yellow ochre pigments, many of which have been used to decorate the village houses. The overall effect is of a whole village painted in a palette of rich, warm colours. The village is not very large, and it doesn't take long to wander up through the pretty streets to the **Castrum**, which has an **orientation table** and superb views northwards across to the Vaucluse plateau and Mt Ventoux. On the other side of the village the view encompasses the **Val des Fées** (Valley of the Fairies), with dramatic vertical clefts in the blood-red cliffs. To the east of the village, the **Chausée des Géants** (Giant's Causeway) leads to the **Sentier des Ocres** (open daily 1000–1230, 1330-1830; FFr.10) where a trail (45 mins on foot) leads down through the former ochre quarries with signboards explaining how they were worked. For a more detailed insight into the creation of pigments a new exhibition centre has recently opened up in a former ochre factory 500 m from the village (on the D104 to Apt); this is the **Conservatoire des Ocres et Pigments Appliqués**, *Usine Mathieu; tel: 04 90 05 66 69* (guided tours July–Sept daily 1100, 1400, 1500, 1600, 1700; Oct–Nov Sat–Sun only; FFr.15). They also run workshops for artists interested in creating their own pigments.

GORDES

Tourist Office: *Salle des Gardes du Château; tel: 04 90 72 02 75.* Open

Villages Perchés

One of the most distinctive features of Provence is the presence of numerous *villages perchés* ('perched' villages), dotted across the countryside on small conical hills, or clinging precariously to the edge of cliffs. Most were built to protect the villagers from marauding bands during the Middle Ages and had strong, thick ramparts and narrow gateways. Inside the ramparts, houses cluster together in narrow, winding streets and alleys, some with arcades or archways which bolstered the buildings on either side and provided shelter from the elements. Small squares often have fountains, sometimes elaborately decorated, which were the main source of water for washing and drinking. At the highest vantage point, there is usually a castle keep (often with the village church alongside).

During the 19th century, many *villages perchés* fell into ruin as peasants deserted the countryside for urban centres, and it wasn't until the post-war years that artists, writers and craftworkers began to repopulate them, restoring old houses and breathing life back into the village economy.

Mon–Fri 0900–1200, 1400–1830, Sat–Sun 0900–1200, 1400–1800.

On the edge of the Vaucluse Plateau, Gordes is a picturesque *village perché* with houses spilling down in terraces towards the Imergue Valley. It has an attractive old quarter with *calades* (narrow, cobblestoned alleyways) leading through vaulted passageways and between the old village houses. A popular and very busy tourist spot, with boutiques, craft shops, galleries, restaurants, and cafés. The village's popularity with artists dates back to the arrival of the Cubist painter André Llhote in the 1930s. In the 1970s, the Op Art painter Victor Vasarely bought and restored the enormous **Château** which dominates the village centre. Vasarely's works were displayed here until recently (the entire collection is now housed in the Fondation Victor Vasarely in Aix, see p. 65). The top floor of the château now houses the **Musée Pol Mara**, *tel: 04 90 72 02 89* (open daily 1000–1200, 1400–1800; FFr.25), dedicated to the contemporary Flemish painter Pol Mara (b. 1921), with displays of modern art. The château has a fine Renaissance doorway but the best part is a beautiful Renaissance fireplace, in a grand hall on the first floor which is now part of the *Mairie* (open Mon–Sat 0800–1200, 1400–1800; free).

Side Tracks From Gordes

The **Abbaye de Sénanque**, *tel: 04 90 75 05 72* (open Mar–Oct Mon–Sat 1000–1200, 1400–1800, Sun 1400–1800; Nov–Feb Mon–Sat 1400–1700, Sun 1400–1800; FFr.20) is 4 km north on the D177. One of Provence's three Cistercian sisters (see also Silvacane, p. 71 and Thoronet, p. 77), the Abbaye de Sénanque is set in a superb position amidst lavender fields and oaks in a small hollow of the Vaucluse plateau. Founded in the 12th century, the abbey was at its peak in the 13th century when it owned numerous outlying farms but the increased wealth, which was at odds with the Cistercian ideals, soon led to corruption and decline; by the 17th century only two monks remained. Now it has been fully restored and is once again occupied by monks. The buildings of the abbey – the church, dormitory, cloisters, and chapterhouse – are fine examples of the pure, harmonious principles of Cistercian architecture.

Four km south of Gordes (signposted off the D15) is the **Village des Bories**, *tel: 04 90 72 03 48* (open daily 0900–dusk; FFr.30). This collection of *bories* (dry-stone huts) has been turned into a museum of rural life, illustrating how the inhabitants of the *bories* may have lived in times past: the *bories* themselves were built using an ingenious technique of overlapping *lauzes* (limestone slabs) some 200 to 500 years ago, and are grouped around a communal bread oven with various smaller *bories* (for housing livestock or storing goods) alongside. The building technique dates back to the Iron Age.

Also to the south (5 km, continue down the D103 and then turn left onto the D148) is the **Musée du Vitrail and du Histoire du Verre**, *rte de St-Pantaléon; tel: 04 90 72 22 11* (open Wed–Mon 1000–1200, 1400–1800; winter 1000–1200, 1400–1800; closed Nov–Feb; FFr.20, or FFr.30 including the Moulin des Bouillons, see below). This modern museum traces the history of glass-making from prehistoric times, with displays of stained glass from the Renaissance through to the contemporary works of Frédérique Duran. In the same park is the **Moulin des Bouillons**, an old *bastide* (farmhouse) with displays on the history of oil lighting. The centrepiece is an enormous olive press made from the trunk of an oak tree which weighs 7 tonnes.

FONTAINE DE VAUCLUSE

Tourist Office: *chemin de la Fontaine; tel: 04 33 90 20 32 22.* Open Mon–Sat July–Aug 0900–2000; Sept–June 1000–1900. Compulsory car parking charge: FFr.13 for the whole village.

One of the natural wonders of Provence, the **Fontaine de Vaucluse** is one of the most powerful resurgent springs in the world: drawing on underground sources which drain the Vaucluse Plateau over an area of 2000 sq km, the spring pours out to feed the Sorgue River at a rate of between 100 and 200 cubic metres a second during peak months. The poet Petrarch lived here from 1337 to 1353, seeking solace from his unrequited love for Laura in this tranquil valley. The source itself is at the head of a narrow valley which the Romans named *Vallis Clausa*, 'the enclosed valley'; this in turn gave its name to the *département* of the Vaucluse. A pedestrianised road, the *chemin de la Fontaine*, leads up from the village square along the Sorgue to the source (2 km, 45 mins), although in the summer you may only find a disappointingly stagnant pool at the base of the cliffs. The stream itself only emerges from beneath a pile of rocks further down, except during winter and spring floods.

The **Chemin de la Fontaine** has become one of the great tourist honeytraps of Provence, a circus of garish souvenir stalls and over-priced cafés, with a peculiar collection of museums and exhibitions. One of the best is **le Monde Souterrain de Norbert Casteret**, *tel: 04 90 20 34 13* (open Wed–Sun May–Aug 1000–1200, 1400–1800 (July–Aug 1830); Feb–Apr, Sept–Nov 1000–1200, 1400-1700; FFr.29). This 'underground world' covers the history of caving, with specimens collected by one of the country's most renowned speleologists, together with displays on the numerous attempts by divers and remote-control submarines to explore the mysterious source itself. Another excellent exhibition is the **Musée de la Résistance**, *tel: 04 90 24 00* (open Mon, Wed–Fri 1000–1800, Sat–Sun 1000–1230, 1330-1800; FFr. 10) which is an evocative portrayal of the history of the French resistance from 1870 to 1940. One of the most bizarre museums is the **Musée Historique de la Justice et des Châtiments** (Museum of Justice and Punishment), *tel: 04 90 20 24 58* (open daily 1000–1900; FFr. 20), run by one of France's last official executioners, featuring a wide range of instruments of torture and execution, including a real guillotine.

Running alongside the river is a vast concrete bunker, the **Galerie Vallis Clausa**, which houses craft, jewellery and paper shops as well as the **Moulin à Papier** (free) which explains how the Sorgue was used to power water wheels to make paper; **La Provence en Relief**, *tel: 04 90 20 29 06* (open July–Sept daily 1030–1900; April–June daily 1400–1830; Oct–Mar Sat–Sun 1400–1830; FFr.10) which offers a three-dimensional projection of various Provençal scenes; and the **Musée du Santon**, *tel: 04 90 20 20 83* (open daily 1030–1300, 1400-1900; FFr.20) which features over 1500 santons. On the other side of the bridge which crosses the Sorgue from the village square, it comes as something of a relief from this unrelenting commercialism to visit the little **Musée Pétrarque**, *Rive Gauche, tel: 04 90 20 37 20* (open Wed–Mon

1030–1230, 1330–1800; FFr.10), housed in the poet's former home.

ISLE-SUR-LA-SORGUE

Tourist Office: *pl. de l'Église; tel: 04 90 38 04 78.* Open June–Sept Tues–Sat 0900–1900, Sun–Mon 0930–1300, 1500–1900; Oct–May Tues–Sat 0900–1230, 1430–1800, Sun 1000–1230.

Accommodation and Food

Isle-sur-la-Sorgue has some very attractive hotels and restaurants, particularly those on the banks of the Sorgue at the outskirts of town. Foremost amongst them is the **Hôtel Araxe**, *rte d'Apt; tel: 04 90 38 40 00; fax: 04 90 20 84 74* (moderate–expensive), which is a modern property with well-appointed accommodation (ranging from standard rooms to bungalows or duplex apartments), a gourmet restaurant, two swimming pools, and lawns and gardens reaching down to the riverbank. Nearby and also on the river is **Le Pescador**, *le Partage des Eaux; tel: 04 90 38 09 69; fax: 04 90 38 27 80* (cheap) with just 8 simple, clean rooms at reasonable prices. On the other side of the road, the **Mas des Gres**, *rte d'Apt; tel: 04 90 20 32 85; fax: 04 90 20 21 45* (expensive) has character, its own gardens and a pool. Near the town centre, **La Gueulardière**, *1 ave J. Charmasson; tel: 04 90 38 10 52; fax: 04 90 20 83 70* (moderate) is another charming old hotel, set in a small park with a pleasant terrace and restaurant. Good budget options in the centre include the friendly **Le Vieux Isle**, *15 r. Damon; tel: 04 90 38 00 46* (cheap) and the very reasonable **La Saladelle**, *r. Carnot; tel: 04 90 20 68 59* (cheap), which is run by a young family.

The town has a number of good restaurants (due, no doubt, to the large number of affluent antique buyers who visit), amongst them **Le Vivier de la Sorgue**, *cours F.Peyre; tel: 04 90 38 52 80* (expensive) which specialises in seafood (particularly lobster); **Le Prêvoté**, *4 r. J.J.Rousseau; tel: 04 90 38 57 29* (expensive), and **Bernard Auzet**, *quartier Camphoux; tel: 04 90 38 09 74* (expensive), which is in a lovely old building in the backstreets and has a good reputation for regional cooking. Budget options include **La Saladelle**, see above (cheap), and **Le Basilic**, *9 quai Rouget de Lisle; tel: 04 90 38 39 84* (cheap), which is an adorable, quirky little restaurant where salads and pasta alike come smothered in basil and garlic.

Sightseeing

Isle-sur-la-Sorgue is a charming town whose older quarter straddles an island between two branches of the River Sorgue. Its early fortunes were built on fishing for crayfish, but in later years a series of waterwheels were built to power oil, grain and paper mills, tanneries, and textile and silk works. Only a handful of the 64 waterwheels still remain, but several of these still turn at a leisurely pace, dipping their moss-covered paddles in the fast-flowing waters (they can be seen on *quai des Lices, quai Bertholet, r. Jean-Theophile* and *r. J.Roux*). The wealth which industry (and the waterwheels) brought to the town is evident in the rich Baroque decoration adorning the **Église**, *pl. de l'Église* (open summer Tue–Sat 1000–1200, 1500–1800 (July–Aug only Sun–Mon 1500–1800); winter Tues–Sat 1000–1200, 1500-1700). Originally dating from the 12th century, it was partially rebuilt in the 16th and 17th centuries but most of the interior décor dates from the end of the 18th; the paintings and sculptures represent one the most important baroque collections in Provence. Not far from the church is the **Hôtel Dondaeï de Campredon**, *r. du Dr Talelt; tel: 04 90 38 17 41* (open Tues–Sun summer 1000–1300, 1500-1900; winter 0930–1200, 1400–1730; FFr.25), a beautiful 18th-century mansion which has been fully restored and now hosts prestigious art exhibitions. There are at least a dozen art galleries and exhibition spaces in the town (a full list from the tourist office).

Apart from the pleasure of simply wandering the backstreets and admiring the waterwheels and plant-filled balconies overlooking the river, the other main reason to visit Isle-sur-la-Sorgue is for **antiques**: one of the largest antique centres in the South of France, the town has five different 'antique villages' grouped inside old warehouses and other buildings, with nearly 200 stalls and shops. There is also a large antiques market on Sun (*av. des Quatre Otages*) and massive antiques fairs at Easter and in mid Aug.

LE THOR AND GROTTES DE THOUZON

An attractive market town in the Sorgue Valley, **Le Thor** was once the main growing centre in France for the Chasselas white dessert grape. Within the old town walls is the **Église de Notre Dame du Lac**, an impressive church rising up alongside a pretty bridge over the Sorgue. Completed in the early 13th century, the church is an important landmark in the transition from the Romanesque to the Gothic style, the latter being most evident in its vaulted nave, which is one of the earliest of its kind in the region. The unfinished bell tower and massive buttresses rising up from the banks of the river had a profound effect on Camus, who compared it to a bull at bay – 'the church at Le Thor moves no more, by the force of stone'.

Just to the north (1.5 km on the D16) are the **Grottes de Thouzon**, *tel 04 90 33 93 65* (open July-Aug daily 0930–1900; Apr–June, Sept–Oct daily 1000–1200, 1400–1800; Nov, March Sun 1400–1800 only; FFr.34). Leading into a hillside crowned by a ruined château, the cave system was discovered in 1902 whilst a quarry was being excavated in the hillside. Following the path of an old underground river, its 230 m-long gallery is mainly horizontal and therefore easy to visit: the cave roof (rising to 22 m in places) is adorned with fistulous stalactites and many other delicate and beautiful concretions.

PERNES-LES-FONTAINES

Tourist Office: *pl. du Comtat Venaissin; tel: 04 90 61 31 04* (open mid June–mid Sept Mon–Sat 0900–1200, 1430-1830, Sun 1000–1200; mid Sept–mid June Mon–Sat 1000–1200, 1500–1700.

Pernes owes its name to the 30 fountains which decorate its numerous squares and open spaces. Most were built in the 18th century, although some (such as the **Fontaine Reboul**) date back even further. The most famous is the **Fontaine du Cormoran**, *quai des Lices*, which is topped off by a swooping cormorant. Pernes also has several other sights worth seeing, in particular the **Tour Ferrande** (viewing on request at the tourist office; FFr.15) which is a 13th-century crenellated tower. The frescos on the third floor date from around 1285 and are thought to be the oldest religious frescos in France. They depict the Virgin and Child, St Christopher, and the adventures of Charles of Anjou in southern Italy. There is a lovely cameo view of the town's elegant **Tour de l'Horloge**, topped by a wrought-iron bell cage, from beside the **Pont Notre-Dame** over the Nesque, whilst the bridge itself has a small chapel, **Notre-Dame des Graces**, built onto one of its piles.

CÉVENNES

The Parc National des Cévennes is enormous, covering an area of nearly 900 sq km of sharp mountain ridges and plunging, heavily forested river valleys in some of the wildest and most remote scenery still to be found in France. Nonetheless, even this is still inhabited by some 600 farmers, who work under strict ecological guidelines. For tourists, it is a magnificent but little-known haven of rare flowers and birds, heatherclad moorland, forests of chestnut and oak, and babbling brooks which will grow into mighty rivers – the Lot and Tarn, the Gardon, Cèze and Hérault, to name but a few. It has an astonishing 45 species of mammal, 150 species of bird, 23 types of reptile, 13 species of fish and 1656 species of plant. The air is clear and fresh and the scenery superb. There are also limitless possibilities for outdoor activities: skiing (in winter), hiking, riding, climbing or whitewater rafting, or even a gentle game of pétanque or golf.

Tourist Information

Park Headquarters and Information: **Château de Florac**, *Florac; tel: 04 66 49 53 01* (open July–Aug daily 0900–1900; May–June, Sept–mid Nov Mon–Fri 0900–1200, 1400–1800, Sat–Sun 1000–1300, 1400–1800; mid Nov–Apr Mon–Fri 0900–1200, 1400–1800; information free; exhibitions FFr.10). As well as local tourism and park information, regular exhibitions, lectures, walking tours and photographic safaris on local flora, fauna, history and crafts are held throughout the park. Ask here for details.

Local Tourist Offices: **Anduze:** *Plan de Brie; tel: 04 66 61 98 17;* **Génolhac:** *Maison de Pays; tel: 04 66 61 18 32;* **Le Pont-de-Montvert:** *tel: 04 66 45 81 94;* **St-Hippolyte-du-Fort**: *Les Casernes; tel: 04 66 77 91 65;* **St-Jean-du-Gard**: *pl. Rabaud St Étienne; tel: 04 66 85 32 11;* **Villefort**: *r. de l'Église; tel: 04 66 46 87 30.*

Accommodation and Food

Most hotels in the area are small, cheap, family-run hotels or bed and breakfasts, but there are also many campsites. Almost all restaurants are attached to hotels.

Southern Cévennes

Les Demeures du Ranquet *(CS), rte de St-Hippolyte; tel: 04 66 77 51 63; fax: 04 66 77 55 62* (expensive), 6 km from Anduze, is a traditional Cévenol farmhouse converted into a luxurious small hotel with a gastronomic restaurant. Lower down the scale, there is a selection of pleasant logis, including the **Auberge du Peras** *(LF), rte de Nîmes, St-Jean-du-Gard; tel: 04 66 85 35 94; fax: 04 66 52 30 32* (cheap); **La Regalière** *(LF), rte de St-Jean du Gard, Anduze; tel: 04 66 61 81 93; fax: 66 61 85 94* (cheap); the **Porte des Cévennes** *(LF), 2300 rte du St-Jean du Gard, Anduze; tel: 04 66 61 99 44; fax: 04 66 61 73 65* (cheap); and the **Auberge Cigaloise** *(LF), rte de Nîmes, St Hippolyte du Fort; tel: 04 66 77 64 59; fax: 04 66 77 25 08* (cheap).

To experience the wilderness, try one

of the remote rural B&Bs. The **Château de Cauvel** *(BF), just off the D13, between St Germain de Calberte and St Martin de Lanuscle; tel: 04 66 45 92 75; fax:: 04 66 45 94 76* (cheap) is a small, delightfully rustic 17th-century slate-built château, tucked into the mountainside, the outbuildings converted into 15 rooms. Further south, **Le Ranc des Avelacs** *(BF), north of St Etienne Vallée Française; tel: 04 66 45 71 80; fax:: 04 66 45 75 58* (cheap) is hidden deep in the forest, up a hair-raising dirt road, in a lovingly converted, slate-built silk farm.

Campsites: Most of the campsites are strung along the more easily accessible river valley, between *St-Jean-du-Gard* and *Anduze*. Amongst them are the **Camping La Foret**, *Falguières, St-Jean-du-Gard; tel: 04 66 85 37 00* (3-star; open Easter–Sept); **Camping Mas de la Cam**, *rte de St-André de Valborgne, St-Jean-du-Gard; tel: 04 66 85 12 02* (3-star; open Apr–Sept; caravans); **Camping Le Malhiver**, *rte de Nîmes, Aunduze; tel: 04 66 61 76 04* (4-star; open May–Sept; caravans); **Camping de l'Arche**, *quartier Labahou, Anduze; tel: 04 66 61 74 08* (3-star; open Apr–Sept; caravans).

Northern Cévennes

The **Hôtel Les Cévennes**, *Le-Pont-de-Montvert; tel: 04 66 45 80 01* (cheap) is a small, simple but charming hotel, serving plain but hearty local food. Opposite, **Aux Sources du Tarn** *(LF), Le Pont-du-Montvert; tel: 04 66 45 80 25; fax: 04 66 45 85 73* (cheap) provides more comfort but less atmosphere in a purpose-built modern hotel.

Down the road, the **Hôtel-Restaurant Balme** *(LF), pl. du Portalet, Villefort; tel: 04 66 46 80 14; fax: 04 66 46 85 26* (cheap) has character, charm and good food. For a good local B&B, try **Le Merlet**, *5 km from Pont-de-Montvert on the D998 towards Vialas; tel: 04 66 45 82 92; fax: 04 66 45 80 78* (cheap).

Campsites: Again there are numerous sites in the area, including **Camping La Châtaignerie**, *Génolhac; tel: 04 66 61 44 29* (2-star; caravans; open Apr–Sept) and **Camping La Palhere**, *rte du Mas de la Barque, Villefort; tel: 04 66 46 80 63* (2-star; caravans).

Shopping

There are relatively few places for serious souvenir hunting. The best places to try include **La Vitrine Cévenole**, *La Poterie, Anduze; tel: 04 66 61 87 28;* **Terroirs Cévennes**, *rte d'Anduze, St-Jean-du-Gard; tel: 04 66 85 15 26;* and **Entre thym et châtaigne**, *r. Sabatier, St-Hippolyte-du-Fort; tel: 04 66 77 95 20*, all of which have a wide selection of good quality local produce. St-Jean-du-Gard has a market on Tues while St-Hippolyte-du-Fort has one on Tues and Fri.

Sightseeing

The main road (N106) from Alès to Mende (see p. 247, Mende–Montpellier route) splits the park neatly into northern and southern sections.

The southern section, encompassing the Cévennes ranges and the three Gardon River valleys (they join at Anduze to form the Gard), is busy and touristy, an excellent place for children. Those who wish to escape the crowds can do so easily by turning off onto the tiny side roads which wind up through thick forest to the high, knife-edge mountain ridges.

The northern section revolves around the vast, bleak, windswept bulk of Mont Lozère, an area of granite and gorse ringed by a series of small, almost Alpine villages. For the Gorges du Tarn and Mont Aigoual in the west, see pp 248–250.

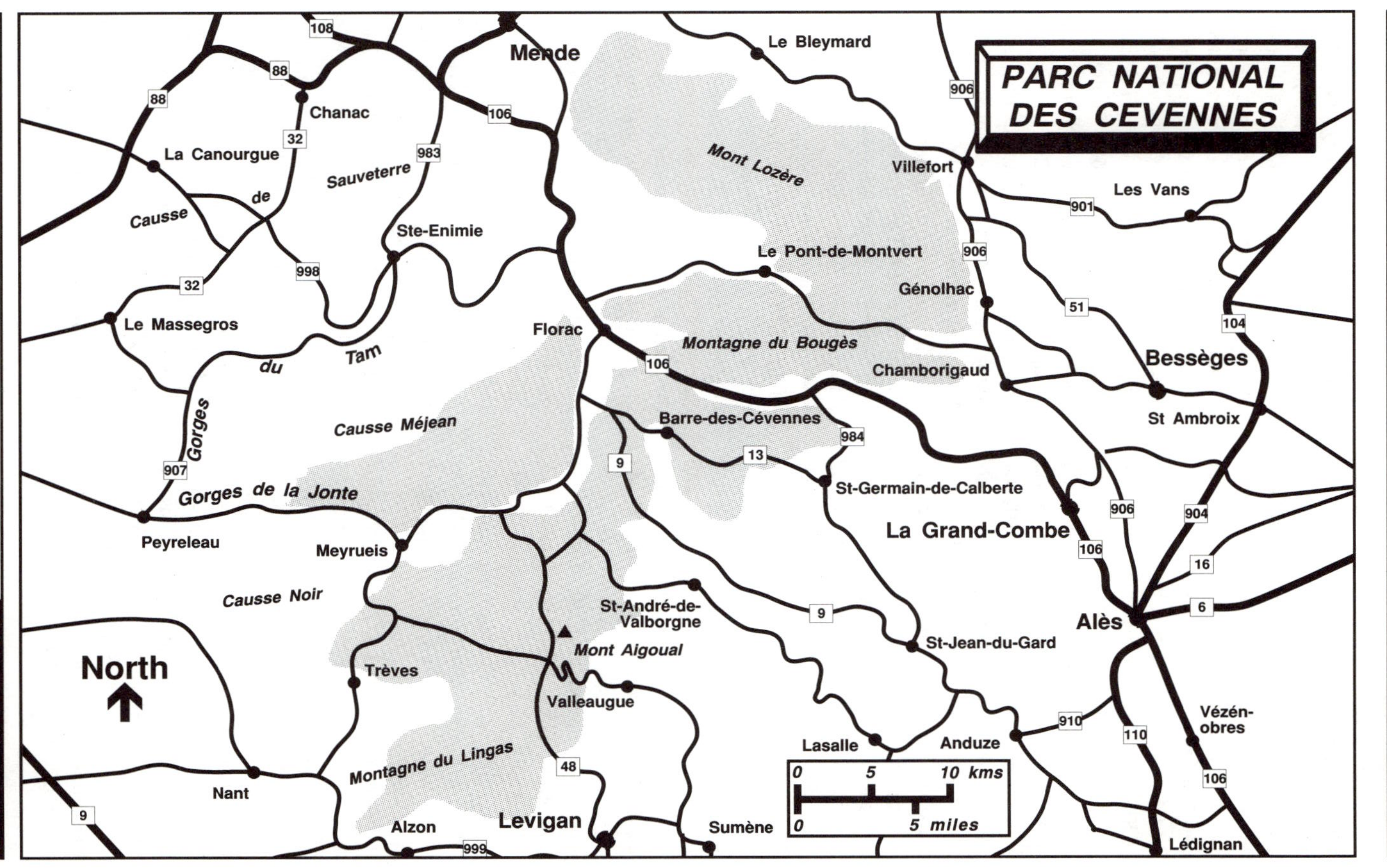
PARC NATIONAL
DES CEVENNES
Mende
Le Bleymard
Chanac
La Canourgue
Sauveterre
Causse
de
Mont Lozère
Villefort
Les Vans
Ste-Enimie
Le Pont-de-Montvert
Génolhac
Le Massegros
Florac
Montagne du Bougès
Chamborigaud
Bessèges
du
Tarn
Gorges
St Ambroix
Causse Méjean
Barre-des-Cévennes
St-Germain-de-Calberte
Gorges de la Jonte
La Grand-Combe
Peyreleau
Meyrueis
Causse Noir
St-André-de-
Valborgne
Alès
Mont Aigoual
St-Jean-du-Gard
North
Trèves
Valleaugue
Vézén-
obres
Lasalle
Anduze
Montagne du Lingas
Nant
0
5
10 kms
0
5 miles
Alzon
Levigan
Sumène
Lédignan
108
88
32
983
106
906
901
998
51
104
984
13
9
907
904
16
6
910
110
48
999

Southern Cévennes

The largest and busiest town in the Gardon Valleys is **St-Jean-du-Gard**, which offers a whole raft of opportunities, for adults and children alike. The **Musée des Vallées Cévenoles**, *95 Grand-Rue; tel: 04 66 85 10 48* (open July–Aug daily 1030-1900; May–Jun, Sept Tues–Sat, Sun pm 1030–1230, 1400–1900; Oct–Apr, Sun 1400–1800, Tues and Thurs for groups, by prior arrangement; FFr.16) is a 17th-century inn dedicated to the art, traditions, culture and history of the Cévenol people, from the crucial role of the chestnut tree to the importance of silk-worms in the local economy.

Near the station, **L'Atlantide Parc**, *av. de la Résistance; tel: 04 66 85 32 32* (open daily all year, 0930–1900 in winter, 0930–2000 in summer; FFr.46) is a large and unexpected aquarium, with 52 tanks, designed on an ancient theme, housing fish from the tropical oceans, Asian and South American rivers. **Magic Voyage**, *4 av. de la Résistance; tel: 04 66 85 30 44* (open Jun–Aug daily 1000–1900; Apr–June Tues–Sun 1000–1230, 1400–1830; Sept Tues, Thur, Sat–Sun 1000–1230, 1400–1830; Oct–Nov Sat–Sun 1000–1230, 1400–1830; FFr.30) is an extraordinary seaside-style attraction where you can have your photo taken with the transport or comedy scene of your choice.

From the station, **Le Train à Vapeur des Cévennes**, *Gare du TVC; tel: 04 66 85 13 17* (mid June–Aug daily; Apr–June Tues–Sun; Sept Tues, Thur, Sat–Sun; Oct Sat–Sun; departs St-Jean: 1030, 1400, 1600, 1800; departs Anduze: 0930, 1130, 1500, 1700; return FFr.56, one-way FFr.45) is a steam train which runs for 13km along the Gardon Valley to Anduze, stopping at **La Bambouseraie de Prafrance**, *Générargue, 2km from Anduze on the D129; tel: 04 66 61 70 47* (open Mar–Oct daily 0930–1900; Nov–Dec Wed–Sun 1000–1700; FFr.30). This extraordinary garden is filled with over 150 species of towering bamboos, planted in 1850, around 30 species of exotic trees, greenhouses filled with flowering plants, a water-garden and Asian village. Nearby, the **Musée du Santon**, *pl. du Village, Générargues; tel: 04 66 61 66 74* (open mid June–mid Sept daily; mid–Sept–mid June Wed, Sat–Sun pm; FFr.20) has an animated panorama of traditional life, using santon figurines and *son et lumière*. From Nov–Easter, there is a traditional crib.

A little way north of here, in **Mialet**, the **Musée du Désert en Cévennes**, *Mas Soubeyran, Mialet; tel: 04 66 85 02 72* (open July–Aug daily 0930–1830; Mar–June, Sept–Nov daily 0930–1200, 1430–1800; guided tours last 45 mins; FFr.20) is a fascinating museum of Huguenot history, set in the birthplace of camisard Chief Rolland, concentrating on the 'desert' period between the repeal of the Edict of Nantes in 1685 and the Edict of Tolerance in 1787, the Camisard Wars, persecution and resistance, and everyday clandestine life, with audio-visual presentations and 15 rooms of paintings, objects and documents.

Next door, the **Grottes de Trabuc**, *Mialet; tel: 04 66 85 03 28* (open July–mid Sept daily 0930–1830; mid Mar–June, mid Sept–mid Oct daily 0930–1200, 1400–1800; mid Oct–Nov Sun 1400–1800, or by appointment; FFr.40) has over 1 km of magnificent galleries hung with giant stalactites, leading past waterfalls to an underground lake.

The other major town in the region is **Anduze**, set in an open green valley, surrounded by grey cliffs. This is also a popular tourist halt, with an excellent **Musée de la Musique**, *Faubourg du Pont, rte d'Alès; tel: 00 66 61 86 60* (open Jul–Aug daily 1000–1300, 1500–1900; June, Sept and school holidays Sun 1400–1800; FFr.25), housing over 1000 musical instruments from around the world, with demonstrations, concerts and workshops.

Beyond the Gardon Valleys, a number of other attractions are widely scattered through the park. To the north, the **Maison de la Châtaigneraie et du Châtaignier**, *Mas de Manières; St-Martin-de-Boubaux; tel: 04 67 59 13 13* (open Oct–Nov by appointment) is a living exhibition dedicated to the cultivation of chestnuts, for centuries the staple food of central France.

The **Corniche des Cévennes** is the 'high road' (D9) which runs spectacularly along the mountain ridge, offering superb views to north and south. Along the corniche, the **Musée du Cévenol**, *Pont-Ravagers, near St-Croix-Vallée-Française; tel: 04 66 44 71 02* (open July–Aug daily 0800–2000; June, Sept by appointment) describes human life and its impact on the Cévennes over the last 5000 years. Further west, **St-Laurent-de-Trève** is a tiny mountain village distinguished by two things – a spectacular view and a series of dinosaur footprints fused into some local rocks. The village church is now home to a small **museum of prehistory**; *tel: 04 66 45 07 53* (open July–Aug daily 1000–1900; mid May–Jun, Sept–Oct Wed–Mon 1000–1200, 1400–1800; mid Apr–mid-May, Oct–mid Nov daily 1400–1800; FFr.20) showing audio-visual presentations of the age of dinosaurs. Nearby, **Barre-des-Cévennes** is a truly beautiful medieval village which has long guarded one of the key routes through the mountains. Both the church and the château date originally to the 12th century, but have been much altered since. They are still amongst the finest of many delightful old buildings which make a walk through the narrow streets worthwhile.

In the far south of the park, **St-Hippolyte-du-Fort** is another small market town, now home to the **Maison de la Soie**, *Les Casernes, pl. du 8 Mai; tel: 04 66 77 66 47* (open Apr–Nov daily 1000–1230, 1400–1830; until 1900 July–Aug; Dec–Mar by appointment; FFr.10) describes the process, from breeding silkworms to weaving, in fascinating detail. Silk production in the Cévennes began in the 1296, but grew in importance with the new techniques of spinning and weaving in the 18th and 19th centuries, when the area produced over half of all the

Ardèche Chestnuts

Sweet chestnut forests have provided a livelihood for the inhabitants of the Massif Central for the last five centuries - hence their local designation as *l'arbre à pain* ('bread tree'). Every part of the tree was used extensively: dried chestnuts provided food throughout the year for humans and animals; the leaf litter was used as bedding for animals, and the timber was used for making everything from furniture to farm tools. In the 18th century grafting produced a local variety of sweet chestnut, the *comballe*, which still forms the main harvest in the Ardèche and provides the basis for many regional chestnut products (such as *marrons glacés*, *crême de marrons* and so on). In recent decades the trees have been struck by a disease which threatened entire forests, but it is now being brought under control with biological treatment: each infected branch is treated individually, which explains the strange phenomenon visible along the roadside on this route, whereby otherwise healthy trees sport huge, lifeless branches.

silk in France – 26,000 tons in 1853 alone. It is still an important local industry. Nearby, the **Exposition de Préhistoire**, *r. Blanquerie; tel: 04 66 77 91 65* (open July–Aug daily 0800–2000; Sept–June by appointment; FFr.10) has a collection of local prehistoric finds.

Northern Cévennes

At 1700m, the vast granite bulk of **Mont Lozère** is one of the highest points of the entire Massif Central. It is a bleak but compellingly beautiful place, with poor soil, sparse moorland vegetation, bright with gorse and broom, and craggy bare peaks. In winter, it offers both downhill and cross-country skiing, focused on the resort of **Le Bleymard**; ski-line *tel: 04 66 48 66 48.*, where there is also a charming old village with a 13th-century Benedictine priory. There are also more limited ski possibilities from Le Pont-de-Montvert; ski-line *tel: 04 66 45 80 36*, to the south of the mountain. Both are designed primarily for the local market, with few glamorous options for *après-ski*. A ring road circles the foot of the mountain joining the few small towns and villages, and making an excellent daytrip.

Le Pont-de-Montvert, the largest town on the ring, is a delightful little place with rickety roofs and rocky walls. Through the centre, the fledgling River Tarn babbles comfortingly over the rocks, under a 17th-century bridge complete with its little combination toll-booth and clock tower. Pope Urban V was born here in 1309, in spite of which the town became a hotbed of Protestantism during the Wars of Religion. Just above the town is the fascinating **Ecomusée du Mont Lozère**; *tel: 04 66 45 80 73* (open Apr–Sept daily 1030–1230, 1430–1830; FFr.20) which has a number of permanent and temporary exhibitions on the geology, flora and traditional life of Mont Lozère. Satellite attractions scattered across the mountain include a couple of working traditional farms, reached via hiking trails.

Going clockwise, you reach the small spa town of **Bagnols-les-Bains**, dominated by a massive **Établissement Thermal**; *tel: 04 66 47 60 02*, said to be particularly beneficial to rheumatism, arthritis and respitory complaints. Just out of town, the **Vallon du Villaret**; tel: 04 66 47 63 76 (open Easter–mid Sept daily 1000–1900; last entry 1700; mid Sept–Oct 1000–1800; last entry 1600; FFr.42) is a magical two km playground of games and obstacles for children and adults alike, strung out along the river valley; allow about 3 hrs. A few kilometres west of here, the village of **Lanuéjols** hosts a fine **Roman mausoleum** (late 3rd century AD), a 16th-century **fountain** and the pretty 12th-century Romanesque **Église de St Pierre**, amidst of a welter of atmospheric old-stone cottages.

Continuing east around the ring, **Villefort** is a pretty village with a number of attractive 14th and 17th century buildings (particularly on the *r. de l'Église)* which thrives as the centre of a range of outdoor activities. A delightful Alpine-style lake, 1.5 km from the centre, created originally to produce hydro-electric power is now a powerhouse of water-sports. At the far end stands the squarely-built Renaissance **Château de Castenet**, tel: 04 66 46 81 11 (open guided visits only Jul–Aug and school holidays at 1030, 1400, 1530, 1700 and 1830; May–Jun, Oct Sat–Sun, same hours; FFr.30).

Beyond this, the village of **Concoules** has a pretty Romanesque church, while the old fortified town of **Genolhac** has a few interesting medieval facades, but survives primarily for the neighbouring ski station of **La Maz de la Barque.**

Clermont-Ferrand

Once upon a time, there were two towns. Clermont began life in as a Celtic settlement in the 4th century BC, was occupied and built up by the Romans under the name of Augustonemetum, and became the episcopal see of the Auvergne after St Austremoine arrived in the late 4th century AD. The early Middle Ages were marked by a continuous struggle for supremacy between the bishops and the Counts of Auvergne. Eventually, in the 12th century, the Counts broke away to form the new small town of Montferrand a short way to the north-east. In 1630, the two were combined in name by the Edict of Troyes, but it took another 200 years and the construction of the giant Michelin factory between them for the reality to follow. Even today, with the bustling city centred on old Clermont, the gridlike streets of the *bastide* of Montferrand form a distinct quarter both in geography and atmosphere, Together the twin towns have a population of 136,000, plus around 30,000 students, while a further 254,000 live in outlying communities, such as the now suburban spa towns of Royat and Chamalières.

Tourist Information

Tourist Office: *69 blvd Gergovia; tel: 04 73 93 30 20.* Open June–Sept Mon–Sat 0830–1900, Sun 0900–1200, 1400–1800; Oct–May Mon–Fri 0845–1830, Sat 0900–1200, 1400–1800. Free maps and leaflets and regional information. **Branch**: *Gare SNCF; tel: 04 73 91 87 89.* Open June–Sept Mon–Sat 0915–1130, 1215–1700; Oct–May Mon–Fri 0915–1130, 1215–1700. During high season, there is also an office in the *pl. de la Victoire* and a kiosk in the *pl. de Jaude*. The main Tourist Office is scheduled to move to the *pl. de la Victoire*, next to the Cathedral, sometime in 1997.

Comité Régional du Tourisme d'Auvergne, *43 av. Julien; tel: 04 73 93 04 03.* Open Mon–Fri 0800–1830. **Conseil General du Puy-de-Dôme**, *24 r. St Esprit; tel: 04 73 42 20 20.* Open mid July–Oct Mon–Sat 1000–1800. **Espace Info Jeunes**, *5 r. St Genès; tel: 04 73 92 30 50.* Open Mon–Fri 1000–1800, Sat 1000–1300, 1400–1800. Information, and discount services for 16–25 year olds.

Arriving and Departing

By Air

Clermont-Aulnat Airport, *tel: 04 73 62 71 00*, 7 km east of the city, handles a variety of domestic and international flights, aimed at the business trade and priced accordingly. The nearest major airports are Lyon–Satolas and Paris Charles-de-Gaulle.

By Car

There are excellent road connections with motorway links to Paris, Lyon and Montpellier. The city centre is surrounded by a peripheral ring of 18th boulevards, following the line of the old city walls. To find the town centre, follow signs to the *pl. de Jaude*. **Parking**: street parking can be difficult, and most is metered, for a maximum of 2 hrs. Convenient underground car parks include the **Centre Jaude**, *pl. de Jaude; tel: 04 73 34 46 56* (24 hr); and **Parking St Pierre**, *pl. Gaillard; tel: 04 73 31 24 03* (open 0700–0100).

By Train

Station: Gare SNCF, *av. de l'Union Soviétique: tel: 36 35 35 35*. There are good rail connections with most parts of France, including Paris, Lyon and Marseille.

By Bus

Bus Station: **Gare Routière**, *blvd F. Mitterand; tel: 04 73 93 13 61* (open Mon–Sat 0830–1830).

Getting Around

Clermont-Ferrand is a large city. Most sights of interest are clustered into the tiny old hill towns of Clermont and Montferrand and are easily accessible on foot. You will probably need transport to get to or between these centres. The T2C buses mainly follow the circle of thoroughfares around Clermont and all, except bus no. 17, stop at *pl. de Jaude*, where the **T2C Boutique**, *tel: 04 73 26 44 90* (open Mon–Sat 0830–1830) sells books of 10 tickets (FFr.47; also available at selected news-agents), and one-day tickets (FFr.22). Closed Sun and holidays.

The Tourist Office has created three **self-guiding walks** of old Clermont with explanation boards in French (ask for the route map and English-language brochures) and a *Circuit des Fontaines*. In July–Aug, there are **guided walking tours** of old Clermont (Mon, Wed, Fri at 1500 from the *Musée du Ranquet*; Tue, Thurs at 2030 from the tourism kiosk at *pl. de Jaude*) and Montferrand (Tues, Thurs, Sat at 1500 from the *Musée des Beaux-Arts;* FFr.25).

There are **taxi** ranks are outside the *rail station* and at the *pl. de la Victoire*. For 24 hr radio taxis, *tel: 04 73 19 53 53*.

Staying in Clermont-Ferrand

Accommodation

There are no luxury hotels but a wide choice of moderate hotels mainly in two areas – the streets spreading out from the rail station and around *pl. de Jaude*. There are also possibilities near the airport, in old Montferrand and in Royat (see p. 160). Hotel chains include *Ca, Co, Ib, IH, Mc,* and *Nv*. Good central hotels include the **Frantour Auvergne**, *16 pl. Delille; tel: 04 73 91 92 06; fax: 04 73 91 60 25* (3-star; moderate), the **Hôtel de Bordeaux**, *39 av. Franklin Roosevelt; tel: 04 73 37 32 32; fax: 04 73 31 40 56* (cheap), the **Dav'Hôtel**, *10 r. des Minimes; tel: 04 73 93 31 49; fax: 04 73 34 38 16* (cheap), and the **Ravel**, *8 r. de Maringues; tel: 04 73 91 51 33; fax: 04 73 92 28 48* (cheap).

About 4 km south of town, on the D978, the **Hostellerie Saint Martin**, *Pérignat-les-Sarliève; tel: 04 73 79 81 00; fax: 04 73 79 81 01* (moderate) is a charming country hotel set in its own park, with a fine restaurant, tennis court, swimming pool and sauna.

HI: *55 av. de l'Union Soviétique; tel: 04 73 92 26 39* (open Mar–end of Oct; a couple of minutes' walk from the rail station). **Foyer International des Jeunes**, *Home Dôme, 12 pl. Regensburg; tel: 04 73 93 07 82*.

Eating and Drinking

From Canadian to Vietnamese, Clermont's many restaurants reflect international cuisine as well as traditional Auvergnat dishes. The many cheap bistros,

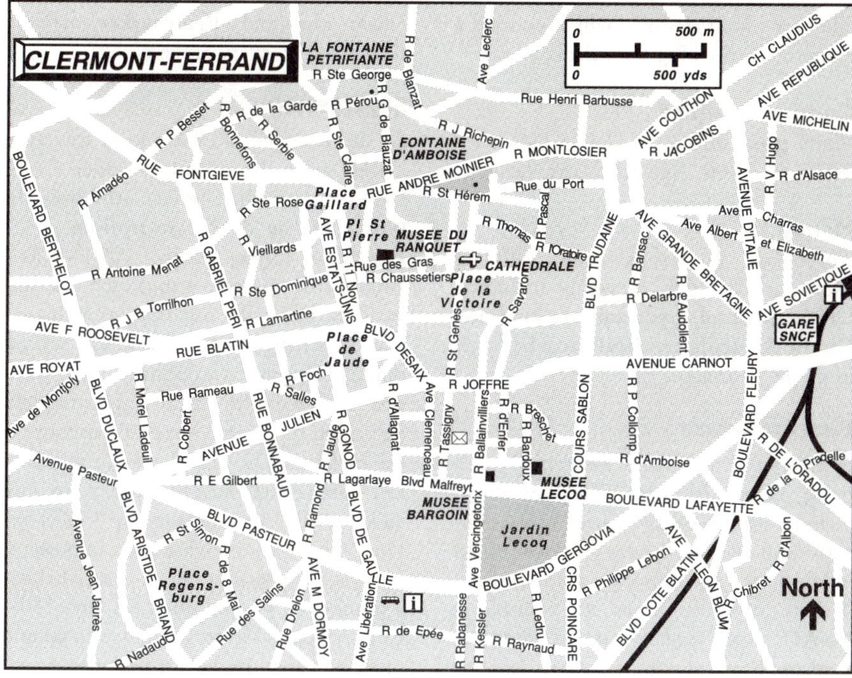

delicatessens, pizzerias and snack bars all thrive thanks to the large number of students around.

In Michelin's hometown, there are three restaurants with a Michelin rosette. **Jean-Yves Bath**, *pl. du Marché-St Pierre; tel: 04 73 31 23 22* (expensive) has a glamorous restaurant upstairs and a more affordable brasserie on the ground floor. **Le Radio**, *43 av. Pierre-Curies, Chamalières; tel: 04 73 30 87 83* (expensive) is the dining room of a chic art deco hotel, built at the height of the spa's popularity. The third is **Bernard Andrieux**, *rte de la Baraque, Durtol; tel: 04 73 37 00 26* (expensive).

For Auvergnat specialities, try **Les Caves**, *corner of r. Philippe Marcombes and Tour-la-Monnaie; tel: 04 73 19 01 50* (cheap; closed Sun, Mon evenings), a lively, cheerful cellar restaurant in the Renaissance Hôtel Savaron; **Aux Délice de la Treille**, *33 r. de la Treille; tel: 04 73 91 26 90* (cheap) – small, intimate and charming, with a vaulted roof; or **Le Bougnat**, *29 r. des Chaussetiers; tel: 04 73 36 36 98* (cheap) with cooking over a wood stove and a determinedly rustic ambience. **Le 1513**, *3 r. des Chaussetiers; tel: 04 73 92 37 46* (cheap) is a popular crêperie, with live music on Wed–Sat evenings and a delightful summer courtyard. Hardened carnivores should head to **Le Gril'Ville**, *2 r. Lamartine; tel: 04 73 93 71 11* (cheap). For an international mix of karaoke, paëlla and sauerkraut, as well as an excellent selection of wines, try **Les Caves de Vermont**, *16 r. Massillon; tel: 04 73 90 18 28* (cheap).

The produce market at *pl. St Pierre* is open daily except Sun and holidays. For picnics, head for the benches in the leafy avenues of the well-landscaped **Jardin Lecoq**, a popular background for wedding day photo sessions, which also has a cafeteria overlooking a small lake.

Communications

Main post office: *r. Maurice-Busset; tel: 04 73 30 63 00. Poste restante* available.

Money

There are numerous banks offering exchange facilities. Several, including **Crédit Mutuel**, **Lyonnais de Banque**, **Crédit Agricole** and **BNP** have branches in the *pl. de Jaude.*

Entertainment

A quarterly magazine, *Demain* (French only; FFr.6; free at Tourist Offices) includes listings of the many events, concerts, film seasons, theatre productions, art exhibitions and sports competitions. Tickets for most events are available at **FNAC**, *Centre Jaude; tel: 04 73 93 44 86.*

Piano bars and pubs with rock, jazz and blues nights are popular. Hotels, restaurants, discos and clubs are listed in a brochure, *L'étape du bon vivre*, free from the Tourist Office. There are several **cinemas**, with 12 screens in the *pl. de Jaude*; an **Opera House**, *blvd Desaix; information, tel: 04 73 37 56 55, bookings: 04 73 36 56 88;* several **theatres** and regular classical music **concerts**.

Shopping

Centre Jaude, a modern mall in the wide expanse of *pl. de Jaude*, is the focus of the main shopping area, which includes *r. Blatin.* Leading north off this large square is *r. de 11 Novembre*, the beginning of the narrow, mostly pedestrianised streets of the old town with speciality and craft shops, fashion boutiques and antique showrooms. In addition to the covered market, **Espace St Pierre** (Mon–Fri 0600–1930, Sat 0500–1930), there are several weekly produce markets and a **flea market**, *cour de la Gare Routière*, every Sun am.

Sightseeing

At the heart of old Clermont, towering blackly over the site of a former Celtic sacred grove, is the Gothic **Cathédrale de Notre Dame de l'Assomption**, *pl. E. Lemaigre* (open daily 0900–1200, 1400–1800). Work began on the east end in 1248, under the eagle eye of architect, Jean Deschamps. After his death, several different architects continued his work, well into the 14th century, astonishingly managing to retain a sense of harmony in the building. The final flourish, the elaborate spires above the west front, were only added in the 19th century by Viollet-le-Duc. Given a somewhat dour impression by its sooty Volvic stone, the cathedral has a number of magnificent 12th- and 13th-century stained-glass windows (including one rare panel, in the Chapel of St Anne, rescued from the previous Romanesque church). Several other chapels have fine 13th century frescos.

Down the hill, an even older church, **Notre-Dame-du-Port**, *r. du Port*, protected both a main city gate and the busy commercial district. This is one of the five great Romanesque churches of the Auvergne, a magnificent creation of elegant stone, whose many carved capitals describe the Book of Life and the epic battle between good and evil.

The surrounding streets of the old town are filled with seemingly austere old houses, many of which are turned inwards around elegant courtyards (you are allowed to push open the doors and peer in). The **Musée du Ranquet**, *34 r. des Gras; tel: 04 73 37 38 63* (bus stop: Gaillard; open daily 1000–1800; FFr.13) is housed in one of the most beautiful, the Fontfreyde Mansion, also known as the

Local Heroes

Clermont-Ferrand has three real local heroes. In 52 BC, the Gallic chieftain **Vercingetorix** (72–46 BC) gathered a massive Celtic army to defeat Julius Caesar at the Battle of Gergovia, the only setback suffered by the emperor in his conquest of Gaul.

In 1095, **Pope Urban II**, at the Council of Clermont, gathered townspeople and delegates alike in a field just outside town to preach the First Crusade.

Blaise Pascal (1623–1662) was a scientist, writer and philosopher who invented a way of measuring air pressure (1648), leading to the creation of modern meteorology, and the first calculating machine, the Pascaline, which can be seen in the Musée Ranquet.

Medallion portraits of these three, embedded in the pavement, mark the route of various walking trails around old Clermont.

Architect's House. It is filled with displays of traditional life in the Auvergne, together with memorabilia of Blaise Pascal and the Napoleonic Général Desaix (1768–1800), another native of the city.

There are also numerous small delights, including several fountains, the finest of which is the **Fontaine d'Amboise**, *pl. de la Poterne*, a Renaissance jewel erected by Jacques Amboise, Bishop of Clermont, in 1515, as a local supply of clean water. The poor arrived with buckets and jugs; the rich ran pipes to their homes.

Just south of old Clermont are three museums, The **Musée Bargoin**, *45 r. Ballainvilliers; tel: 04 73 91 37 31* (bus stop: Baillainvilliers) features archaeological finds from the local area, including prehistoric and Roman remains, such as wooden votive offerings left at the thermal springs in Chamalières. On the second floor of the same building, the **Musée du Tapis d'Art**, *tel: 04 73 90 57 48*, displays a fine collection of 18th–20th century Oriental carpets. Both open Tue–Sun 1000–1800; FFr.22; guided tours of the carpets at 1430, FFr.10 extra.. Nearby, the **Musée Lecoq**, *15 r. Bardoux; tel: 04 73 91 93 78* (bus stop: Baillainvilliers; open Tues–Sat, 1000– 1200, 1400–1700, Sun afternoon (until 1800 May–Sept; closed Mon, Sun morning; FFr.22) showcases regional and global natural history, with fine mineral and fossil collections alongside the stuffed animals.

To the north of the city centre is the unusual **La Fontaine Pétrifiante**, *13 r. du Pérou; tel: 04 73 37 15 58* (open July–Aug daily 0900–1930; Sept–June daily 0900–1200, 1400–1800; free), which offers guided tours of the stalactite-laden mineral springs, with an exhibition gallery and garden filled with life-sized models of people and animals, given an alabaster-like translucence by immersion in the waters.

The first town of **Montferrand** was almost totally destroyed during the 100 Years War, but was rebuilt by a determined Countess with the gridlike layout of a typical bastide (fortified town). The walls have long since come down, but there are still a number of delightful old streets and houses, making this the perfect area for a gentle stroll. On the edge of the district, the **Musée des Beaux-Arts**, *pl. Louis Deteix; tel: 04 73 23 08 49* (bus stop: Montesquieu; open Tues–Sun 1100–1900; guided visits every Sun, Apr–Sept, 1500; FFr.21) began life as an 18th-century convent, now dramatically transformed into a magnificent gallery displaying fine art from medieval ivory and enamels to 20th-century works by Paul Paulin and Ernest Pignon.

Side Tracks From Clermont-Ferrand

ROYAT

Tourist Information: *pl. Allard; tel: 04 73 35 81 87.*

There are several fine old hotels, built on a grand scale at the turn of the century, to accommodate those coming to take the cure. Amongst them are the **Hôtel Métropole**, *2 blvd Vaquez; tel: 04 73 35 80 18; fax: 04 73 35 66 67* (moderate; open May–Sept); the **Castel Hôtel**, *1 pl. du Dr Landouzy; tel: 04 73 35 80 14; fax: 04 73 35 80 49* (moderate; open May–Oct) and the **Hôtel Royal Saint-Mart**, *6 av. de la Gare; tel: 04 73 35 80 01; fax: 04 73 35 75 92* (moderate; open May–Sept). **Campsites**: **L'Oclède**, *rte de Gravenoire, Royat; tel: 04 73 35 97 05* (4-star; open Apr–Oct); **Le Chanset**, *av. Jean Baptiste Marrou, Ceyrat; tel; 04 73 61 30 73* (3-star; open all year).

On the western edge of Clermont, this small town grew around the local thermal springs and is now a slightly faded, but still elegant *Belle Epoque* suburb, filled with magnificent apartment blocks sporting curly wrought iron. The **Etablissement Thermal**, *tel: 04 73 29 51 51*, specialises in the treatment of rheumatism, arthritis, back and heart trouble. It is not possible to visit without taking the cure. The **Grotte du Chien**, beside the Viaduct, *tel: 04 73 19 05 50* (open Apr–Oct daily 1000–1200, 1400–1830; groups all year by appointment) is a cave formed by the lava flow of the 'little Puy de Dôme' (younger relative of the Dome itself) 43,500 years ago. Within the cave are Roman remains, mineral springs, a small museum and audio-visual on its ever-shifting geology.

PARC DES VOLCANS

Tourist Information: **Parc Naturel Régional des Volcans d'Auvergne**, *Château de Montlosier, 63970 Aydat; tel: 04 73 65 67 19. Open daily mid-June–Sept Tue–Sat 0830–1200, 1430–1900.* Parks information, audio-visual and other exhibitions; regular guided walks and lectures.

Covering 395,000 ha, this is the largest regional natural park in France, stretching north-south for 120 km along the volcanic massifs of the Chaîne des Puys, the Monts-Dore, Cézallier and and the Monts du Cantal. Distances are not long, but the roads are mountainous and slow. Stunningly beautiful, the area is hiker's heaven. The Chaîne des Puys alone has two Grand Randonnée walking trails, and over 250 shorter circuits, lasting 1-6 hrs, many also suitable for mountain biking.

PUY DE DÔME

15 km west of Clermont-Ferrand, tel: 04 73 62 21 46. Open daily July–Aug 0830–2000, June, Sept 0900–1900; FFr.23

This famously pudding-shaped peak is the highest (1465m) of the Chaînes des Puys, a series of 80 small volcanoes, only about 10,000 years old, all of which can be seen in a spectacular chain from the summit. Other attractions include the ruins of a Roman Temple to Mercury and a fascinating information centre, with video, exhibition, souvenir shop and excellent restaurant and café.

LE MONT-DORE

Tourist Offices: **Le Mont-Dore**: *av. de la Libération; tel: 04 73 65 22 69*; **Besse**: *pl. du Dr Pipet; tel: 04 73 79 52 84.*

There are some 70 hotels in this busy tourist valley, with a free booking service through the tourist office. In the town centre, try **Le Castelet** (LF), *av. Michel Bertrand; tel: 04 73 65 05 29; fax: 04 73 65 27 95* (moderate). At the foot of the Puy de Sancy is the **Hôtel du Puy-Ferrand** *(LF); tel: 04 73 65 18 99; fax: 04 73 65 28 38* (cheap; food moderate), while 7km north of town, the **Auberge du Lac de Guéry**, *tel: 04 73 65 02 76; fax: 04 73 65 08 78* (cheap–moderate) has excellent food and a superb setting by a mountain lake. For vast portions of excellent, very hearty food, head for **Le Bougnat**, *23 r. G. Clémenceau; tel: 04 73 65 28 19* (moderate). **Campsites**: **L'Esquiladou**, *rte des Cascades; tel: 04 73 65 23 74* (3-star; caravans; open May-Oct); **Les Crouzets**; *tel: 04 73 65 21 60* (2-star; caravans; open all year).

Well-organised and welcoming, Le Mont-Dore is, in summer, a centre for outdoor activities and a thriving spa, with a vastly impressive neo-Byzantine **Établissement Thermal**; *tel: 04 73 65 05 10* (guided tours; FFr.3). In winter, when the mountain air is too cold for asthmatics, it transforms itself into a busy ski resort (ski hotline, *tel: 04 73 65 03 62).*

Just south of town looms the vast bulk of the **Puy de Sancy**, the highest mountain in the Parc des Volcans (1886m), with a **cable car**; *tel: 04 73 65 02 73* (FFr.23 return) up to the summit, from where there are superb views and easy walks. At the foot, near the cable car station, two tiny mountain streams bubble together to form the source of the great Dordogne River.

Just north of the town, the **Musée de la Toinette**, *Murat-le-Quaire; tel: 04 73 81 12 28* (open daily Easter–mid Nov1000–1200, 1400–1900, mid Nov–Easter 1400–1800; FFr.28) uses a dazzling array of audio-visual techniques to paint a portrait of traditional life in the region. A must-see museum.

A ring road leads right round the base of the giant Puy de Sancy and makes an excellent day's drive. En route, stop at the ski resort of **Super-Besse** (ski hotline: *tel: 04 73 79 62 92)* and its lower neighbour, **Besse**. In this charming medieval town, once the fiefdom of Marguerite de Valois, take time for a stroll round the beautiful 12th-century **Church of St-André** and the narrow streets which are still filled with fine 16th-century houses and shops. The **Musée du Ski**, *tel: 04 73 79 57 30* (open daily during school holidays 0900–1200, 1400–1900) has a historic collection of skis and winter sports equipment from throughout Europe. The **Maison de l'Eau et de la Pêche**; *tel: 04 73 79 55 52* (open daily 1000–1200, 1400–1800) has exhibitions and aquaria showing life in the local mountain rivers and lakes.

ST NECTAIRE

Tourist Office: *in the Établissement Thermale; tel: 04 73 8 50 86.*

Chain hotels include *Mc.* **Campsites**: **Camping l'Oasis**, *rte de Granges; tel: 04 73 88 52 68* (2-star; caravans).

This small village 26 km east of Mont-Dore on the D996 is home to a famous cheese, first made popular by Louis XIV in the 16th century. The village is split in two. St-Nectaire-le-Haut, at the top of the cliff, is the old centre, gathered around a magnificent Romanesque **church** (open June–mid Sept daily 1000–1200, 1430–1800, Easter–May, mid Sept–mid Oct

Wed–Sat 1000–1200, 1430–1800, Sun 1430–1800; mid Oct–Easter, restricted hours, ask at Tourist Office). In the valley bottom are a splendid Belle Époque **spa**, *tel: 04 73 88 50 01*, and **casino**; *tel: 04 73 88 54 71*. At the **Maison du St-Nectaire**, *rte de Murol; tel: 04 73 88 51 66* (open mid Feb–Sept daily, Oct–Nov Sun; FFr.16), you can see the cheese being made, taste and buy the proceeds. A little way east is the imposing and highly visible **Château de Murol**; *tel: 04 73 88 67 11* (open Apr–Sept 1000–1230, 1330 1800; Jan–Apr Sat–Sun and holidays 1400–1700; FFr.40). In season, guided tours provide a lively castleful of characters in costume, showing off their skills, from cooking and music to archery. Tours daily except Wed and Sat, every 45 mins in July–Sept; by appointment at other times. Ask the tourist office about other local attractions.

VICHY

Tourist Office: *19 r. de Parc (next to Parc des Sources); tel: 04 70 98 71 94.* Open Jul–Aug Mon–Sat 0900–1930, Sun 0930–1230, 1500–1900; Apr–Jun, Sept Mon–Sat 0900–1230, 1330–1900, Sun 0930–1230, 1500–1900; Oct–Mar Mon–Fri 0900–1200, 1400–1830, Sat 0900–1200, 1400–1800, Sun 1500–1800. Plans, guides and brochures, exchange when banks are shut; walking tours.

For gracious living on a grand scale, try the **Aletti Palace Hotel**, *3 pl. Joseph Aletti, near the opera house; tel: 04 70 31 78 77; fax: 04 70 98 13 82* (expensive). Nearby, the **Hôtel de la Paix**, *13 r. du Parc; tel: 04 70 98 20 56* (moderate) offers a cheaper, but charming alternative, while those on a budget should try **Les Archers**, *32 r. de Paris; tel: 04 70 59 81 82; fax: 04 70 97 03 56*. Chain hotels include: *Ca, Ib, IH, Nv*. **Campsite**: **Les Acacias au Bord du Lac**, *r. Cl.-Décloitre, Bellerive; tel 04 70 32 36 22* (4-star; caravans; open Apr–Oct).

On the shores of the Allier River, Vichy is a one product town – water is its foundation, lifeblood and raison d'être. The little spa town has a population of around 30,000, with over 200 doctors. Amongst the other tourists, over 13,000 people a year flock here to take 'the cure'. There are twelve springs, producing six different types of sodium-bicarbonated mineral waters, three hot and three cold; one bottled commercially, the others used to cure a range of ailments from rheumatism and arthritis to digestive or respiratory problems and migraine.

A full cure lasts 21 days, with most patients currently funded by the French National Health Service. It is possible to buy a one-day or afternoon pass, but you will have to pass a quick medical before being allowed to use the facilities. There has been a town and spa here since Roman times, but it became truly fashionable in the 19th-century under Napoleon III and the town centre is now a delightful *Belle Époque* resort of the sort normally more at home on the coast. It gained another more sombre reputation during World War II when Maréchal Pétain moved the government of the subject État Français to Vichy, suitable because it had modern telephone exchanges and a vast number of hotel rooms. Power returned to Paris only after liberation in 1944. There are few specific sights, but walking through the streets and parks is a joy.

Clermont-Ferrand –Le Puy-en-Velay

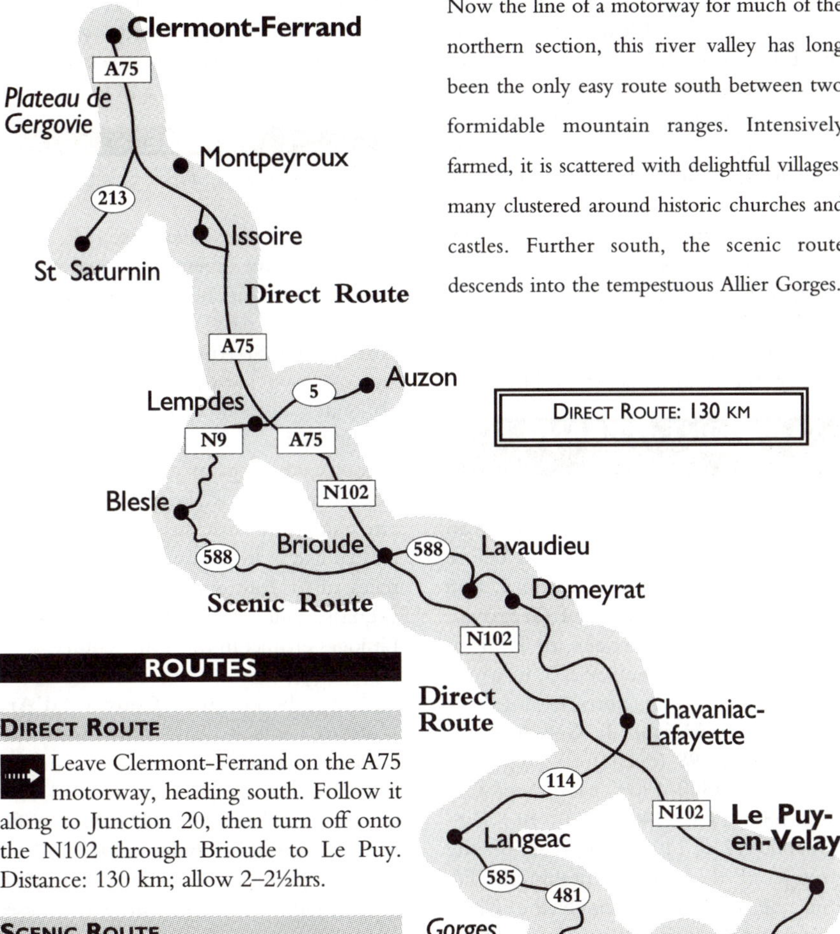

Now the line of a motorway for much of the northern section, this river valley has long been the only easy route south between two formidable mountain ranges. Intensively farmed, it is scattered with delightful villages, many clustered around historic churches and castles. Further south, the scenic route descends into the tempestuous Allier Gorges.

DIRECT ROUTE: 130 KM

ROUTES

DIRECT ROUTE

Leave Clermont-Ferrand on the A75 motorway, heading south. Follow it along to Junction 20, then turn off onto the N102 through Brioude to Le Puy. Distance: 130 km; allow 2–2½hrs.

SCENIC ROUTE

Leave Clermont-Ferrand on the A75 motorway (toll-free), heading south. Turn off at Junction 4 for the **plateau de Gergovie**. Turn off at Junction 5 for **St Saturnin**, at Junction 7 for **Montpeyroux**, and Junction 11 for **Issoire**.

Continue south on the A75 to Lempdes, where you turn left to **Auzon**, before returning to Lempdes and going left onto the N9, which snakes south through the Gorges de l'Alagnon. After 23 km, turn right to **Blesle**.

Return to the N9 and continue south for 3 km, then turn left onto the D588 to **Brioude**. Leave Brioude on the D588, towards La Chaise-Dieu. After 2 km, turn right through Fontannes to **Lavaudieu**, **Domeyrat**, Paul-Haguet and **Chavaniac-Lafayette**, where you turn right onto the D114 to **Langeac**. Leave Langeac heading south on the D585. There is only one main road through the **Gorges de l'Allier**, which then becomes the D48 and D301. From **Monistrol-sur-Allier**, take the D589 east, via St-Privat d'Allier and Montbonnet to Le Puy.

CLERMONT-FERRAND TO ISSOIRE

The easiest way to tackle this first section of the route is to use the motorway as an artery, jumping off to visit sights before continuing south. From Junction 4, you have access to the **plateau of Gergovia**, site of an epic battle between the Romans and Celts in the 1st century AD, in which the local hero, Vercingetorix, emerged triumphant. The **Maison de Gergovie**; *tel: 04 73 79 42 98* (open June–Aug daily 1000–1200, 1400–1900, May, Sept–Oct daily 1000–1200, 1400–1800, Apr Sat–Sun 1000–1230, 1400–1800) describes the geology of the plateau, prehistoric life from the neolothic through the Gallic period, and the battle. A monument to the victory, erected in 1900, stands near the museum, offering a panoramic view back over Clermont-Ferrand.

Further south, the village of **St Saturnin** was the familial home of Catherine de Medici and Marguerite de Valois. It is a charming little place, with attractive old streets, 16th century fountain and imposing 14th–15th century **château** (open daily mid June–mid Sept 1000–1200, 1400–1830, Apr–mid June, p.m. only). The real pearl however is the **Church**, one of the finest Romanesque churches in the region. **Montpeyroux** is a typical little hill village, its streets winding up to a crowning church and tower.

ISSOIRE

Tourist Office: *pl. du Gén. de Gaulle; tel: 04 73 89 15 90.*

A lively market town, Issoire is home to probably the finest of all the superb Romanesque churches in the region, built originally as part of the Benedictine **Abbaye de St-Austremoine**. The east end is a towering pyramid of chapels, its elaborately decorations including the signs of the zodiac. Thanks to 19th-century restorers who repainted the interior in a riot of colour, it is also possible to get a rare glimpse of what the church may have looked like in its heyday. In the crypt, the relics of St Austremoine are held in an exquisite blue and gold casket, made of Limoges enamel in the 13th century.

Nearby, some of the former monastery building house the **Centre d'Art Roman**, which has exhibitions on Romanesque and other art each summer and the surrounding streets are filled with fascinating old buildings. The **Musée de Minéralogie Régionale**; *tel: 04 73 89 92 31* (open June–Sept Tue–Sun 1000–1200, 1500–1900; Oct–May Tue–Sat) houses over 900 specimens of rock collected throughout the Massif Central.

ISSOIRE TO BRIOUDE

Tourist Offices: **Auzon**: *pl. de la Barreyre; tel: 04 71 76 18 11;* **Blesle**: *pl. des 4 Chemins; tel: 04 71 76 26 90.*

Traces of the town walls and feudal castle are still visible in the old fortified village **Auzon**, dramatically sited on a spur of rock. **Blesle** is another pleasing old village, with a great many half-timbered houses. There are two churches worth looking at, the 17th-century **Chapelle de Notre Dame de la Chaigne**, and the 12th-century **Abbaye de St-Pierre**. Nearby, a 13th-century hospital is home to the **Musée de la Coiffe**, *tel: 04 71 76 20 75* (open mid June–mid Sept 1000–1200, 1430–1830), with displays of over 600 historic hats and hairstyles.

BRIOUDE

Tourist Office: *av. Léon Blum; tel: 04 71 74 97 49.*

Accommodation and Food

Most of the best restaurants in the vicinity are out of town. The exception is the **Hôtel de la Poste et Champonne**, *1 blvd Dr Devins, av. Paul Chambriard; tel: 04 71 50 14 62* (cheap) which serves Auvergnat specialities. Eight km west of Brioude, the **Hôtel Le Baudière**, *St-Beauzire; tel: 04 71 76 81 70; fax: 04 71 76 80 66* (cheap) has comfortable rooms, a pool and a fine restaurant, **Le Vieux Four** (moderate), serving nouvelle cuisine. Ten km south, the **Hostellerie St Verny**, *Villeneuve d'Allier; tel: 04 71 74 73 77* (cheap) has simple rooms and an excellent terrace restaurant overlooking the Allier River and Château de Saint-Ilpize. The **Auberge de l'Abbaye**, *Lavaudieu; tel: 04 71 76 44 44* (cheap) serves traditional French cuisine in an old village house. **Campsite**: **La Bageasse**; *tel: 04 71 50 07 70* (2-star; caravans; June–Sept).

Sightseeing

Brioude used to be a major salmon-fishing centre. Few salmon ever struggle the 1000 km up the river these days, and fishing is forbidden, but the town still has a salmon factory and smokehouse, while the **Maison du Saumon**, *tel: 04 71 74 91 43* (open July–Aug daily 1000–1200, 1500–1900, Sept–Jun Sun 1500–2100 or by appointment) is an aquarium and eco-museum dedicated to the fish and the Allier River.

On this route of magnificent churches, one of the finest, and the largest, Romanesque church in the Auvergne, is the imposing and colourful **Basilique de St-Julien**, named after an evangelising saint martyred in Brioude in AD304. The area immediately surrounding the church is a charming district of half-timbered houses. In one of them is the **Hôtel de la Dentelle**, *29/43 r. du 4 Septembre; tel: 04 71 50 27 00*, filled with lace objects from the exquisite to the bizarre (such as a lace shark). It is also a lace-making workshop, with demonstrations and a shop.

BRIOUDE TO LANGEAC

Tourist Office: **Paul-Haguet**: *pl. Lafayette; tel: 04 71 76 62 67.*

This section of the route is marketed locally as part of the Route Historique Lafayette. The first stop is in **Lavaudieu**, still a picture postcard of rural life, down to the hay and chickens in the street. The village is centred on a little **Romanesque church**, founded by St Robert of La Chaise-Dieu in 1057 as part of a Benedictine convent, with a number of fine 14th century frescos and a copy of a head of Christ. Even more magnificent is the only complete remaining Romanesque **cloister** in the Auvergne. Round the corner, the **Carrefour du Vitrail**, *tel: 04 71 76 46 11* (open daily, FFr.25) is a fascinating workshop creating wonderful contemporary stained glass, together with a small museum of historic glass.

Two km on, at **Frugières-le-Pin**, is the **Musée de la Résistance, de la Déportation et de la 2e Guerre Mondiale**; *tel: 04 71 76 42 15* (open June–Sept 1000–1200, 1400–1900, Oct–May Sun 1400–1900 or by appointment; FFr.15), the entrance marked by a couple of American armoured cars.

Three km further, the **Château de Domeyrat**, *tel: 04 71 76 69 12* (open Apr 1000–1700 by appointment, May–June Sun–Fri 1000–1200, 1400–1800 by appointment, July–mid Sept Sun–Fri 1000–1800, with tours every 45 mins and 3 performances daily; FFr.25) is a virtually ruinous 12th-century hilltop fortress, which has been revived by the 'Compagnons de Gabriel', a historical re-enactment group, as the setting for their colourful medieval junketings. A few km beyond this, the **Château de Chavaniac-Lafayette**, *tel: 04 71 77 50 32* (open Apr–Oct daily 0700–1200, 1400–1800, Nov–Mar by appointment; FFr.25) is a huge edifice which looks Victorian (although it is earlier) from the front, and positively medieval, with towers and crenellations, from the back. This was the birthplace of the famous Marquis de la Fayette, who won fame for his role in the American War of Independence. The château is furnished in period and contains memorabilia of the General.

LANGEAC AND THE ALLIER GORGES

Tourist Office: *pl. A. Briand, Langeac; tel: 04 71 77 05 41.*

Right in the centre of Langeac, the **Hôtel de l'Avenue**, *tel: 04 71 77 08 88; fax: 04 71 77 12 03* (cheap) is comfortable and convenient. Beautifully positioned on the edge of town by the river is the **Auberge de l'Ile d'Amour**, *av. de Gévaudan; tel: 04 71 77 00 11* (cheap–moderate). Two km north of Langeac, try the **Hôtel du Val d'Allier** *(LF), Reilhac; tel: 04 71 77 02 11; fax: 04 71 77 19 20* (cheap–moderate) while 12 km south, in the heart of the Gorges, is the charming **Chalet de la Source**, *Prades; tel: 04 71 74 02 39* (cheap–moderate). All four have excellent restaurants. **Campsites**: **Les Gorges d'Allier,** *Langeac; tel: 04 71 77 05 01* (3-star; caravans).

Langeac is a busy little town which acts as the main tourist centre for the Gorges. In the old centre, the huge 15th-century **Collégiale St Gal** is one of few Gothic churches in the Auvergne. Nearby, the **Musée de Jacquemart**, *pl. de l'Église; tel: 04 71 77 02 12* (open July–mid Sept Mon–Sat p.m.; FFr.5) has excellent displays on local lace and the geology of the gorges. The house itself is also worth a look. An offshoot exhibition in the **Chapelle St-Dominique** looks in detail at the work of Jacques de Langeac, a celebrated 15th century illuminator.

The **Allier Gorges** are undoubtedly dramatic, yet the narrow wooded valley and rough cliffs are just small enough to be magnificent without becoming overpowering. Look closely at the cliffs for superb cascades of crystalline basalt formations in the overhanging rocks and redo the drive at night, when many of the buildings are illuminated.

Volvic Adventures, *Site du Pradel, St-Julien-des-Chazes; tel: 04 71 74 04 34,* are organisers of a variety of adventure sports within the gorges, including white water rafting and canoeing, climbing and mountain biking. Adventure sports for children, including canoeing and riding, is available from the **Centre Aéré de Brugiroux**, *École Jules-Ferry, Langeac; tel: 04 71 77 06 15* (July–Aug, ages 4–16; FFr.70 a day).

Clermont-Ferrand–St Étienne

This delightful route is a meander through the past, with old villages, ancient crafts, thickly wooded mountains and river valleys.

Direct Route: 96 km

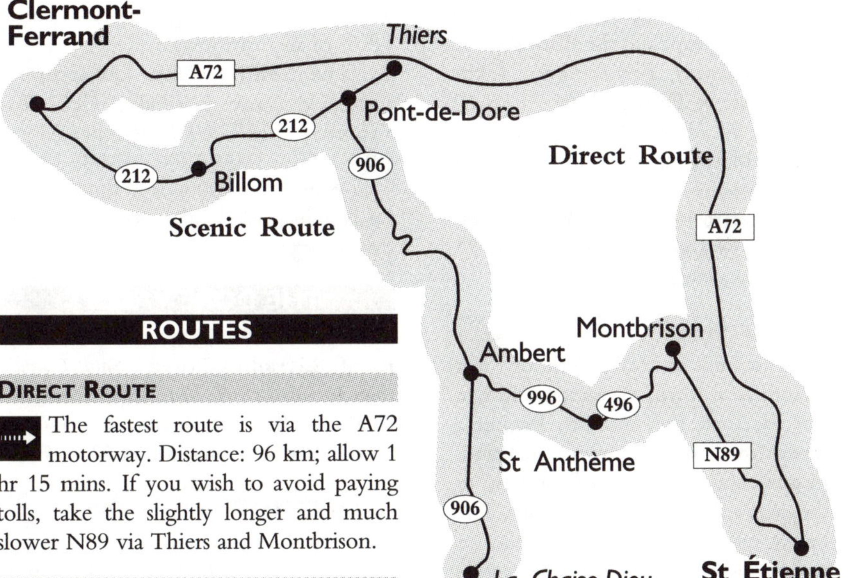

ROUTES

Direct Route

The fastest route is via the A72 motorway. Distance: 96 km; allow 1 hr 15 mins. If you wish to avoid paying tolls, take the slightly longer and much slower N89 via Thiers and Montbrison.

Scenic Route

Leave Clermont-Ferrand on the D212, via Cournon d'Auvergne and follow it for 25 km east to **Billom.** Turn left onto the D229 towards Lezoux, then, 4 km out of town, turn right, back onto the D212. At Pont-de-Dore turn left onto thc D906, which heads right down the Dore Valley to **Ambert.** From Ambert, take the twisting, mountainous D996 to St Anthème, where you join the D496 to Montbrison. At Montbrison, turn right onto the N89 and follow it right through to St Étienne.

BILLOM

Tourist Office: *13 r. Carnot; tel: 04 73 68 39 85.*

For the moment, Billom is that extraordinary find, a perfectly preserved, but totally unrestored, medieval town – so unknown that it has one part-time restaurant and no hotel. A wealthy fortified trading city with a renowned university in the 12th century, it was eclipsed by Clermont-Ferrand and has remained an enchanting backwater.

Side Track from Pont-de-Dore

You can side-track at Pont-de-Dore by taking the N89 a short way to Thiers.

THIERS

Tourist Office: *1 r. des Vieilles-Ecoles; tel: 04 73 80 10 74*.

Accommodation and Food

The **Hostellerie Le Moulin Bleu**, *Courty; tel: 04 73 80 06 22; fax: 04 73 80 08 16* (cheap) and the **Eliotel** *(LF), rte de Maringues, Pont-de-Dore* , 4 km south-west of Thiers*; tel: 04 73 80 10 14; fax: 04 73 80 51 02* (cheap) both have uninspiring surroundings and decor, friendly service and excellent food. **Campsites**: **Les Chanterelles**, *St-Rémy-sur-Durolle; tel: 04 73 94 31 71* (3-star; caravans).

Sightseeing

Thiers is built on a cliff. Although it is an industrial town, the factories lurk at low level on the outskirts, leaving a superb medieval old town, filled with magnificent half-timbered houses, in the centre (below the main road). The tourist office will provide details for walking tours. However, this extraordinary place, ideally situated beside a fast-flowing river which provided copious quantities of both water and hydro-electric power, is really all about knives, a local industry which dates back to 1272, when the first 85 franchises were granted. Today, some 3500 people are still employed by 230 companies making huge numbers of them, from household cutlery to vicious-looking Rambo-worthy monsters. The souvenir shops are more like armouries. One of the most compelling museums in the Auvergne is the **Musée des Couteliers**, *23 and 58 r. de la Coutellerie; tel: 04 73 80 58 86* (open June–Sept daily 1000–1200, 1400–1830, Oct–May Tue–Sun 1000–1200, 1400–1800; FFr.20), with a superb collection of knives, swords and other sharp implements, many of them genuine works of art, as well as demonstrations of how they are made. Just up the road, **St-Rémy-sur-Durolle** claims to be the 'corkscrew capital of the world', manufacturing the gimlets for some 80% of all corkscrews made.

The **Centre d'Art Contemporain**, *le Creux de l'Enfer, Vallée des Usines; tel: 04 73 80 26 56* (open Mon, Wed–Fri 1000–1200, 1400–1800, Sat–Sun 1400–1900) is a modern art gallery in an old knife factory beside the river.

THE DORE VALLEY

Tourist Offices: Parc Naturel Régional Livradois-Forez, *Saint-Gervais-sous-Meymont; tel: 04 73 95 57 57;* **Ambert:** *4 pl. de l'Hôtel de Ville; tel: 04 73 81 61 90;* **Olliergues:** *tel: 04 73 95 50 26.*

Accommodation and Food

Amongst the many hotels in the valley, a few stand out for their affordable comfort and excellent regional cuisine. They are **La Chaumière** *(LF), 41 av. Maréchal Foch, Ambert; tel: 04 73 82 14 94; fax: 04 73 82 33 52* (cheap); the **Hôtel de Voyageurs** *(LF), Vertolaye; tel: 04 73 95 20 16; fax: 04 73 95 23 85* (cheap); the **Hôtel de la Casadei** *(LF), La Chaise-Dieu; tel: 04 71 00 00 58; fax: 04 71 00 01 67* (cheap); and the **Hôtel Monastère et Terminus**, *pl. de la Gare, La Chaise-Dieu; tel: 04 71 00 00 73; fax: 04 71 00 09 18* (cheap).

Sightseeing

The lushly wooded Dore Valley runs

north-south between the two massifs of the Monts du Livradois and the Monts du Forez, which together make up the Parc Régionale de Livradois-Forez, an area of immense natural beauty, little known outside France. Because, for years, this was one of a handful of accessible routes through the mountains, it was heavily built-up with a string of small towns and villages, many of which still have charming old centres. Most warrant a quick stroll even if few have specific attractions. At the château in **Olliergues**, the **Musée des Vieux Métiers**; *tel: 04 73 95 54 90* (open daily June–Sept 1000–1900, Apr–May 1400–1700; FFr.20) encompasses many regional crafts from clog-making to cheese.

Ambert is the largest town in the valley, a busy tourist centre with an attractive old town and several small museums, including the **Musée Agrivap**, *r. de l'Industrie; tel: 04 73 82 60 42* (open daily Mar–Oct; FFr.25), with a range of steam tractors and other farm machinery, and the **Musée des Fromages**; *tel: 04 73 82 49 23* (open July–Aug daily 0900–1200, 1400–1900, Feb–June, Sept–Dec Wed–Mon 0900– 1200, 1400–1900; FFr.23) which demonstrates and makes cheese. This is the home of the excellent Bleu d'Ambert variety.

Side-track from Ambert

You can divert to La Chaise-Dieu by taking the D906 south from Ambert. In high season, a small tourist train with an upstairs observation car, **Le Train de la Découverte**, *tel: 04 73 82 43 88* (details and times on demand; FFr.60–100) runs along the Dore Valley from Courpière, via Ambert to La Chaise-Dieu, along one of the most scenic lines in Europe.

LA CHAISE-DIEU

Tourist Office: La Chaise-Dieu: *tel: 04 71 00 01 16;* **Arlanc:** *pl. Charles de Gaulle; tel: 04 73 95 03 55.*

La Chaise-Dieu, 34 km south of Ambert on the D906, is a thriving town, but is really all about one monument, the vast Benedictine **Abbaye de la Chaise-Dieu**. Founded by Robert de Turlande in 1047, it went on to become one of the richest and most powerful in France, and is still magnificent, with several superb tapestries, a fresco of the Danse Macabre, 14th-century cloisters and the elaborate tomb of Pope Clement VI.

On the way back up to Ambert, stop in at the **Musée de la Dentelle**, *Arlanc; tel: 04 73 95 60 08* (open daily Mar–mid Oct; FFr.15) to learn about lace, and at the Romanesque **Chapelle des Pénitents Blancs**, *Marsac-en-Livradois; tel: 04 73 95 60 08* (open daily June–Sept, by appointment Oct–May; FFr.15) for a museum about this extraordinary masked religious brotherhood.

MONTS DE FOREZ

From Ambert, turn right onto the D496 which leads right over the Monts de Forez. Huge signboards will point you towards Ambert's prize attraction, the **Moulin Richard-de-Bas**; *tel: 04 73 82 03 11* (open daily; FFr.23). This working papermill uses ancient techniques to create magnificent handmade papers. Three km further on, visit the **Musée de l'École 1900**, *St-Martin-des-Olmes; tel: 04 73 82 66 80* (open June–Sept; FFr.18), a carefully restored Victorian school. From here, the road becomes a magnificent mountain drive through the ski resort and outdoor activity centre of **St Anthème** to Montbrison and St Étienne.

Digne–Chorges

This short but interesting route starts in the Réserve Naturelle Géologique, a unique geological reserve where prehistoric fossils can be spotted in rocks in several places near the road as it follows the narrow valley of the River Bès. Later, the route joins the Blanche valley, crossing the Col St Jean (1332 m) before dropping out of the mountains down to the beautiful Lac de Serre-Ponçon, created by damming the River Durance in 1961.

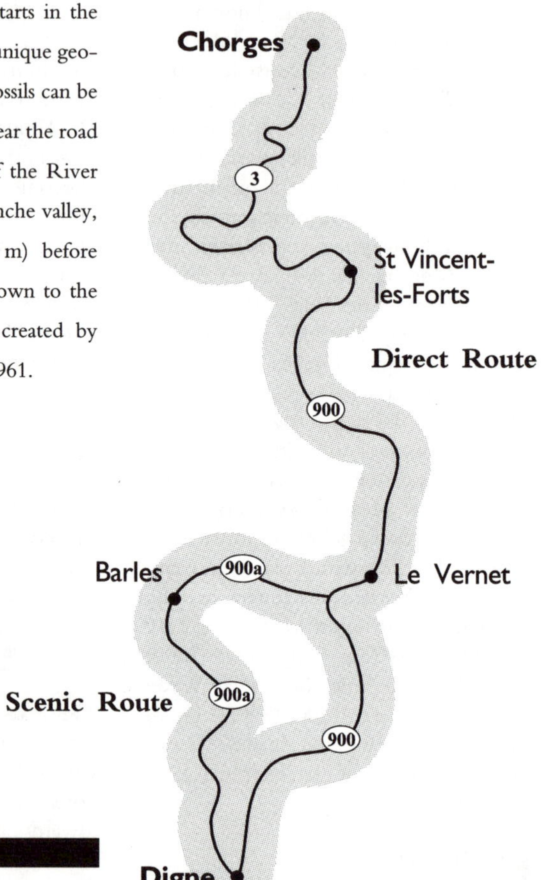

Chorges
3
St Vincent-les-Forts
Direct Route
900
Barles
900a
Le Vernet
Scenic Route
900a
900
Digne

DIRECT ROUTE: 79 KM

ROUTES

Direct Route

The D900 runs north from **Digne-les-Bains**, splitting just after the hillside village of **St-Vincent-les-Forts**. Take the east turn (left) along the south shore of the **Lac de Serre-Ponçon**. On the far side of the bridge over the Durance River, turn right onto the D3 which wriggles north beyond the lake to **Chorges**. Journey time is about 1 hour 30 mins.

Scenic Route

Take the narrow D9004 north from **Digne-les-Bains**, signposted to **Barles**. This follows the course of the River Bès along the **Clues de Barles** and **Clues de Verbaches** until it joins the D900 near **Le Vernet**. Then as above. Total distance: 84 km; journey time about 2 hours.

DIGNE-LES-BAINS

Tourist Office: *le Rond-Point, pl. du Tampinet; tel: 04 92 31 42 73* (on the way into town from the station). Open June–Sept Mon–Sat 0845–1230, 1400–1900, Sun 0900–1200, 1500–1900; Oct–May Mon–Sat 0845–1200, 1400–1800, Sun 1000–1200. Exchange facilities.

Parking: Plenty of space next to the Tourist Office so leave your car there and walk. **Station: Gare de Digne**, *tel: 04 51 50 50 50.* The town centre is a 10-min walk from the station – turn left at the main road. The station is shared – with separate booking offices – between SNCF and the privately-run **Chemins de Fer de la Provence**, *40 r. Clément Roassal, 06007 Nice, tel: 04 93 88 34 72,* which runs four trains a day to, special day excursions, including steam trains between **Puget-Théniers** and **Annot** in summer, and ski-specials in conjunction with the **Val d'Allos** resorts in winter.

Accommodation and Food

Accommodation may be a problem in Digne in high season, so reserve in advance. Clustered around the main street, *blvd Gassendi*, are a number of hotels such as the **Central**, *26 blvd Gassendi; tel: 04 92 31 31 91; fax: 04 92 31 49 78* (cheap). In a quieter position across the river is the family-run **Le Bourgogne (LF)**, *av. de Verdun; tel: 04 92 31 00 19; fax: 04 92 32 30 59* (cheap). **Campsite: Les Eaux Chaudes**, *r. des Thermes; tel: 04 92 32 31 04* (open Apr–Oct; caravans). The best restaurants are attached to the hotels, but fast food can be found on *pl. de Gaulle.*

Events

First week in Aug: **Lavender Festival** with floats decorated with flowers and the streets sprayed with lavender cologne.

Sightseeing

Digne, on the River Bléone, is the 'capital' of the sparsely populated *département* of Alpes-de-Haute-Provence. Surrounded by a necklace of mountains, it nevertheless has a feel of the Midi with plane trees shading the bustling pavements along its long straight main street, *blvd Gassendi.* This is a typical provincial town, unassuming and quiet, decked with flowers in summer and renowned for the purity of its ai.r. Many visitors come for a 'cure' at the thermal baths, others to enjoy its isolation as a base for walking and other outdoor activities.

Pause first in **Parc Bayetti** to admire the gardens and sculptures. Then head down *blvd Gassendi* to the main square, *pl. de Gaulle,* with its glitzy **Hôtel de Ville** and a statue of **Pierre Gassendi**, an erudite 17th-century physicist, philosopher and historian. From here, steps climb up to the **old town** with its narrow somewhat-seedy cobbled streets. At the beginning of *r. de l'Hubac,* a plaque on the wall commemorates Napoleon's 3-hr pause for lunch on 4 March 1815. At the top, the **Cathédrale de St-Jérôme** dates from the 15th century, but has a 19th-century Gothic façade. At the far end of *blvd Gassendi,* a curiosity is the **Grande Fontaine**, a fountain where water flows from a huge mossy face.

Another intriguing attraction is the **Fondation Alexandra David Neel**, *rte de Nice, 27 av. du Mar. Juin; tel: 04 92 31 32 38,* dedicated to the life of one of the world's greatest travellers, Alexandra David Neel. She was a Frenchwoman who set out for India in 1891, at the age of 23, and walked across Tibet. Later a friend of Gandhi and the Dalai Lama, she returned to France at the age of 80 and set up home in Digne, surrounded by her 'Himalayas in miniature'. She was visited by the Dalai Lama before her death in 1969 at the age of 101. Guided tours of the Foundation, include its **Tibetan shop**, daily 1030, 1400, 1530 and 1700 July–Sept; 1030, 1400 and 1600 Oct–June.

If you have more time to spare, you can enjoy relaxing mud baths, inhalation and water massage at Digne's **Thermes** (thermal baths), one mile along the *rte des Thermes, tel: 04 92 32 32 92*, as many French people do, courtesy of the state health service. They were bought by the town in 1975 and modernised. Guided visits Apr–Oct Wed 1400. Also on the edge of the town is the **Musée de la Guerre**, *pl. Paradis, tel: 04 92 31 28 95,* which tells the story of the town's role in World War II (open July–Aug Mon–Fri 1400–1800; Apr–June, Sept–Oct Wed 1400–1800; Nov–Mar1st Wed only).

VALLEY OF THE RIVER BÈS

Four km north of Digne, the **Bléone** is joined by the narrow **River Bès**. The road follows its exciting course as it rushes through the deep wooded ravines of the **Clues de Barles** and **Clues de Verbaches**, hugging the narrow wooded valley beside the water and often passing through narrow cuttings beneath hugh rocks. This is a quiet, distinctly 'untouristy' route, yet it surely ranks as one of the most beautiful anywhere in the South of France. All the way to the village of Barles, you are in the **Réserve Naturelle Géologique de Haute-Provence**, a unique geological reserve.

SEYNE-LES-ALPES

Tourist Office: *pl. d'Armes; tel: 04 92 35 11 00.* Open July–Aug daily 0830–1230, 1500–2000; Sept–June 0900–1200.

Accommodation and Food

La Chaumière *(LF), 33 Grande Rue; tel: 04 92 35 00 48* (cheap) is a small hotel in the centre of the town. **Campsite: La Blanche**, *rte de Chardavon; tel: 04 92 35 02 55* (caravans).

Sightseeing

Situated in the centre of the **Blanche Valley** at a height of 1210m, Seyne is very much a tourist resort with mountains and lakes all around. In summer it offers activities in the great outdoors like walking, riding, rafting and paragliding. In winter, you have easy access to skiing (mainly cross-country) in **Saint Jean de Montclar**, **Le Grand Puy** and **Chabanon-Selonnet**. But Seyne also has a long history, having been a frontier town in the 13th century with a splendid **tower** (indeed its name used to be **Seyne La Grande Tour**) from which signals were sent to Selonnet and Montclar. In the 16th century, this was one of only two towns in Provence that were protestant strongholds. Work started on the **fortress** in 1691, under the auspices of Vauban, as a defence against the kingdom of Savoy. This later fell into ruin but was restored in 1983. The Tourist Office organises guided visits. Beside the main road, the 13th-century Romanesque **Church of Notre-Dame de Nazareth** has a large rose window and typically Alpine bell-tower.

The local **mule fair** in Aug and **horse fair** in Oct are famous throughout the region.

ST-VINCENT-LES-FORTS

Accommodation

Hotel Pension Rolland *(LF), L'Auchette; tel: 04 92 85 50 14* (cheap) is a former farm with outdoor pool about a mile beyond the village; signposted left off the D900, just beyond the road's divide. **Campsite: Camping Municipal du**

Lac; *tel: 04 92 85 51 57* (caravans) is a municipal site with 250 emplacements, situated beside the Lac de Serre-Ponçon.

SIGHTSEEING

Straggling up a hillside just off the main road, this small village is topped by the ruins of a privately-owned **castle**, reached by a footpath from behind the small 13th-century **church**. The view from beside it is well worth the short climb as it stretches over farms, forests and the River Ubaye flowing into the beautiful **Lac de Serre-Ponçon**, Europe's largest reservoir (see p. 119).

As you turn west beside the lake and then climb on the D3 along the edge of **Mont Colombis** (1733m), there are spectacular views down over the lake and its mighty 123.5m high **dam** across the River Durance (visits: *tel: 04 92 54 58 18*; open Mon–Fri 1400–1600).

CHORGES

Tourist Office: *05230 Chorges, tel: 04 92 50 64 25.* Open Mon–Sat 0900–1230, 1430–1900; Sun 0900–1300.

ACCOMMODATION

Campsites: A dozen campsites are dotted around the village, several on the banks of Lac de Serre-Ponçon, including **Le Serre du Lac**, *tel: 04 92 50 67 57* (caravans) and the municipal site, **Baie Saint-Michel**, *tel: 04 92 50 67 72.*

SIGHTSEEING

This small town is well-placed to make the most of the lake's facilities, situated on the N94 and with a rail station on the Paris-Briançon line. A narrow lane leads off the main road to the 12th-century **church** in the somewhat delapidated old village centre. It was here that the first assembly of the Hautes Alpes was elected in 1790.

Réserve Naturelle Géologique de Haute-Provence

This is Europe's largest geological reserve, a natural museum in the open air, where fossils are clearly preserved in slabs of calcium. Four eras of life on Earth around 30 million years ago can be traced through these extraordinary deposits left by plants, marine life, birds and reptiles. Scientists from all over the world come to study them.

The total protection zone, in which all excavation is forbidden, covers over 358,579 acres, stretching from the village of **Barles** in the north to **Castellane** in the south. Eighteen sites in a central 665-acre area are classed as special **Nature Reserves**, showing the fossils of amonites, bird footprints and skeletons. Seven are clearly signposted along the beautiful **Clues de Barles**. Most impressive of all is the limestone 'wall' beside the road where the fossils of 1550 amonites, some as large as a foot across, are particularly well-preserved. Another, a little further up the valley, shows the skeleton of an ichthyosaurus, a marine reptile.

The Geology Centre, *Quartier Saint-Benoît, tel: 04 92 31 51 31* beside the D900A on the edge of Digne, houses an exhibition on the local geology and a library. Open daily 0900–1200 and 1400–1730 (closes 1630 Fri and closed Sat–Sun Nov–Apr). The centre is a 15 min walk from its car-park, or take bus no. 2 from Digne. The **Information Office** of Réserve Naturelle Géologique in Barles is open Sat–Thurs 1030–1230, 1500–1930.

FRÉJUS AND ST RAPHAËL

Barely a kilometre apart, these two resorts have their own individual identities. The historic centre, Fréjus town, is inland, with the new marina, Port-Fréjus, alongside a good sandy beach lined with bars and restaurants. St Raphaël is a more up-market continuation, with its casino, smart hotels, and picturesque old port.

TOURIST INFORMATION

Fréjus: *325 r. J. Jaurès; tel: 04 94 17 19 19.* Open July–Sept daily 0900–1900; Oct–May Mon–Sat 0900–1200, 1400–1800. **St Raphaël:** *r. W. Rousseau; tel: 04 94 19 52 52.* Open mid June–mid Sept daily 0830–1900; mid Sept–mid June Mon–Sat 0830–1200, 1400–1830. Currency exchange Easter–Oct 0900–1200, 1400–1900.

ARRIVING AND DEPARTING

By Car

Parking: In **Fréjus** town, you can usually find space in *pl. P. Vernet*, the large square opposite the tourist office. In **St Raphaël**, there are multi-storey car parks behind the Tourist Office (**Parking Place Coulet**) and next to the station (**Parking de la Gare SNCF**). Otherwise, parking is on a meter; information: *tel: 04 94 40 56 78.*

By Train

Gare de Fréjus: *r. du Capitaine Blazy; tel: 04 94 51 30 53.* **Gare de St Raphaël**: *pl. de la Gare; tel: 04 94 91 50 50*; for reservations, *tel: 04 94 22 39 19.*

GETTING AROUND

St Raphaël's old town, port and beaches are all within easy walking distance of each other. Fréjus is slightly more spread out, and there is the option of a 50-min guided tour aboard **Le Petit Train du Soleil**, *tel: 04 93 09 40 60.* There are regular bus services between the two centres by **Esterel Bus-Forum Cars**; *tel: 04 94 52 00 50* (Fréjus); *04 94 95 16 71* (St Raphaël). **Taxis**: **Fréjus**: Station; *tel: 04 94 51 51 12;* **St Raphaël**: Station; *tel: 04 90 95 04 25; pl. de la Poste, tel: 04 52 32 24.*

STAYING IN FRÉJUS AND ST RAPHAËL

Accommodation

Fréjus: Chain hotels include a *CF*. Others in the centre include the **Aréna**, *139 r. Gen. de Gaulle; tel: 04 94 17 09 40; fax: 04 94 52 01 52* (cheap–moderate), which has attractive rooms; and the **Hôtel-Restaurant La Riviera**, *90 r. Grisolle, tel: 04 51 31 46* (cheap), which has clean, well-kept rooms at budget prices. You can rent studios or apartments on a per-night basis in **Port-Fréjus**, the huge marina complex just near the beach, through **Port-Fréjus Location**, *av. des Forces Françaises Libres; tel: 04 94 17 30 47; fax: 04 94 52 24 74*, with self-catering accommodation ranging from studios (cheap) to penthouse apartments (expensive).

HI: **Auberge de Jeunesse**, *chemin du Counillier; tel: 04 94 53 18 75; fax: 04 94 53 25 86*, 2km from the town centre. **Campsite**: **Camping La Baume**, *r. des Combattants en Afrique du Nord; tel: 04 94 40 87 87; fax: 04 94 40 73 50* (caravans), 5 km from the seaside.

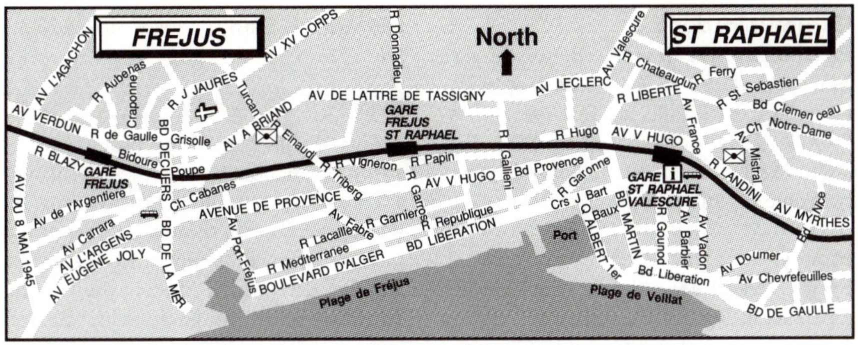

St Raphaël: There is a good selection of hotels both within the town and along the seafront, although even those in the town are within easy reach of the beach. The **Hôtel Moderne**, *331 av. Gen. Leclerc; tel: 04 51 22 16; fax: 04 94 17 19 26* (cheap–moderate) is a convivial little hotel with a rustic flavour. Another good value hotel in the centre is the **Bellevue**, *22 blvd F. Martin; tel: 04 94 95 00 35; fax: 04 94 95 88 41* (cheap–moderate). On the seafront the top hotels are the **Continental**, *100 promenade R. Coty; tel: 04 94 83 87 87; fax: 04 94 19 20 24* (moderate–expensive), which is a three-star property with its own private beach, and the **Excelsior**, *Promenade R. Coty; tel: 04 94 95 02 42; fax: 04 94 95 33 82* (moderate–expensive) which faces the casino and has recently been entirely renovated. If you're looking for total peace and quiet, 7 km behind the town is the **Hôtel du Golf de Valescure**, *av. Paul l'Hermite, Valescure; tel: 04 94 82 40 31; fax: 04 94 82 41 88* (expensive), a long-established, luxury hotel with an 18-hole golf course and a high-class restaurant.

HI: **Centre International du Manoir**, *Boulouris; tel: 04 94 95 20 58; fax: 04 94 83 85 06*, 5 km from St Raphaël, by the sea on *chemin l'Escale,* next to the station at Boulouris.

Eating and Drinking

Fréjus: One of the best restaurants is **Les Potiers**, *135 r. des Potiers; tel: 94 51 33 74* (moderate), which has a long-standing reputation for good food at reasonable prices. The **Restaurant La Romana**, *155 blvd de le Libération; tel: 04 94 51 53 36* (cheap) on the seafront, has good value menus with Provençal specialities as well as pasta and pizzas.

The restaurant at the **Aréna** (see above; moderate), is good for fish and *bouillabaisse* (to order). Other seafood restaurants include **Chez Jo**, *47 blvd de la Libération; tel: 04 94 51 32 47* (moderate), and the **Brasserie des Galoubets**, *pl. des Galoubets, Port-Fréjus; tel: 04 94 17 11 66* (moderate).

St Raphaël: Many of the usual pizzerias, cafés and brasseries are clustered around *pl. de la République* and *pl. V. Hugo.* On the seafront good seafood can be found at **Le Sirocco**, *35 quai Albert 1er; tel: 04 94 95 39 99* (moderate). The long-established **Pastorel**, *54 r. de la Liberté; tel: 04 94 95 02 36* (moderate) serves excellent local dishes such as *aïoli*, *bourride*, and marinaded sardines. **Les Terrasses de l'Orangerie**, *promenade R. Coty; tel: 04 94 83 10 50* (moderate–expensive) is a *belle époque*-style brasserie with a gastronomic menu.

Communications

Post office: Fréjus: La Poste, *38 rue Blériot; tel: 04 94 17 60 60.* **St Raphaël:** Poste du Centre Ville, *av. V. Hugo; tel: 04 94 19 52 00.* Both open Mon–Fri 0830–1830, Sat 0830–1200 and have exchange facilities.

Money

Fréjus: **Crédit Municipal**, *42 av. Verdun* (open Mon 1400–1830, Tues–Fri 0900–1830, Sat 0900–1700) and **Change Fréjusian**, *RN 98, St-Aygulf* (open daily 0930–1300 and 1530–1930) both offer exchange facilities. **St Raphaël**: All the major banks are represented. Most are open Mon–Fri; many stay open through the day until 1800 and some are open on Sat until 1700. **Change Service**, *Centre Commerciale de la Gare; tel: 04 94 95 67 91.*

Entertainment

Fréjus: Several hotels and restaurants offer dinner-dancing, amongst them **Le P'tit Bonheur**, *RN7, La Tour de Mare; tel: 04 94 44 45 97,* and the **Hôtel le Grand Bleu**, *485 av. de Provence; tel: 04 94 40 12 19.* Discos include **La Playa**, *blvd de la Libération; tel: 04 94 52 22 98,* and **L'Odysée**, *blvd de la Libération; tel: 94 53 52 63.* The main cinema is **Le Vox**, *pl. Agricola; tel: 04 94 51 15 11.*

St Raphaël: At the heart of the entertainment here is **Le Grand Casino**, *square de Gand; tel: 04 94 95 10 59* (open 1100–0400; July–Aug until 0500), with roulette, blackjack, slot machines and a piano bar, **Le Madison** (open Wed–Sun 2230–0400; July–Aug until 0500). There are also several piano bars in the *Vieux Port*, including **Le Satellit**; *tel: 04 94 95 42 94*, and the **Coco Club**; *tel: 04 94 95 95 56.* Discos include **L'Embassy**, *186 blvd F. Martin; tel: 04 94 95 02 19,* and **Le Kilt**, *130 r. J. Barbier; tel: 04 94 95 29 20.* Cinema: **Le Lido**, *r. Amiral Baux; tel: 04 94 95 16 63.*

Events

Fréjus: Fréjus has a busy programme of events throughout the summer, detailed in a Tourist Office leaflet, *Arts et Culture.* As well as the Roman theatre, another of the town's unusual venues is the Villa Aurélienne, which hosts the **Nuits Aurélienne** in summer, with classical concerts, plays and films; details, *tel: 04 94 04 76 30.* **St Raphaël**: June: **Fête de la Musique**; July: **International New Orleans Jazz Competition**; Aug: **Fête de la Saint Pierre**, traditional/nautical fun and games.

Shopping

In **Fréjus** there are quite a few art galleries and artisans' workshops, amongst them **Salaun Kellig**, *9 pl. Castelli*, for sculptures and jewellery; **Atelier St François de Paule**, *3 pl. St François de Paule*, for pottery; and the **Centre de Rencontre des Arts Occitans**, *Galerie de la Muscadière, la Tour de Mare,* which groups together several painters, sculptors, ceramicists and *santonniers.* In **St Raphaël**, speciality shops include **L'Ensoleillade**, *pl. Coullet*, for Provençal fabrics; **Nougat Cochet**, *98 blvd F. Martin*; and **Les Delices de Provence**, *35 rue Marius Allongue.*

In addition, St Raphaël's daily **fish market**, *pl. Ortolan,* is fun. Food and flower markets take place every morning in *pl. V. Hugo* and *pl. de la République.*

Sightseeing

Fréjus

Guided visits (two circuits) depart from the Office du Tourisme (June–Sept Tues 1700–1900, Thurs 1000–1200; by appointment out of season; FFr.15).

Fréjus was created by Julius Caesar in 49BC and turned into an important Roman port by Augustus. The Roman remains are scattered: the **Amphithéâtre**, *r. Henri Vadon; tel: 04 94 17 05 60* (open Apr—Sept daily 0930—1200, 1400–1830; Oct-March Wed—Mon 0900–1200, 1400-1630; free) is to the west of the old town. Dating from the 1st–2nd century AD, its upper tiers have been restored but the vaulted galleries are original. Of the **Aqueduct** only a few crumbling arches remain: these are best seen from the **Parc Aurélien**, between *av. du XVème Corps* and *av. Gén. d'Armée J. Calliès*. The **Théâtre Romain**, *r. du Théâtre Romain; tel: 04 94 17 05 60* (open daily April–Sept 0930–1200, 1400-1830; Oct–March 0900–1200, 1400–1630; free) has retained only part of the stage and surrounding walls. Fréjus' most important monument is the fortified **Groupe Épiscopal**, *r. de Fleury; tel: 04 94 51 26 30* open daily Apr–Sept 0900–1900; Oct–Mar 0900–1200, 1400–1700; FFr.25). This comprises the **Cathedrale de St-Léonce**, begun in the 10th century, with a superb set of carved Renaissance doors; the octagonal **baptistry**, which dates from the 4th or 5th century; 12th–13th century **cloisters**, with slender columns supporting a fantastic painted wooden ceiling; and a small **archaeological museum**, which contains an interesting double-headed bust of Hermes.

St Raphaël

Guided visits every Wed 1000 from the Office du Tourisme (FFr.30).

Once a fashionable resort, St Raphaël lost most of its *Belle Époque* seafront buildings during wartime bombing raids. Apart from wandering around the **Vieux Port** or taking part in watersports on the beaches which stretch westwards from the centre, most activities (sightseeing and theme parks) are nearer to Fréjus. In the tiny old quarter behind the railway line there is a small **Musée Archéologique**, *r. des Templiers; tel: 04 94 19 25 75* (open Mon, Wed–Sat; free) which has some interesting displays on underwater archaeology. The town's main beach is the **plage du Veillat,** a 1-km long sandy beach opposite the *promenade des Bains*, which is lined with ice-cream parlours and cafés. The beach has sun-loungers, showers and toilets and is reserved for swimmers only. Beyond this, the **plage du Beaurivage** reaches as far as the Sailing Club at the entrance to Port St Lucia. This 500 m-long shingle beach also has swimming-only areas, with launch ramps for windsurfing and water-skiing.

Fréjus-St Raphaël is a popular family resort area and there are a number of attractions on the outskirts geared to family entertainment. These include the **Parc Zoologique Safari de Fréjus**, *le Capitou; tel: 04 94 40 70 65* (open daily May–Sept 0930–1800; Oct–Apr 1000–1700; FFr.37) where you can drive or walk between the animal enclosures and the **Parc Aquatica**, *RN98; tel: 04 94 53 58 58* (open June–Sept 1000–1800 (July-Aug until 1900); FFr.40).

Out of Town

Just outside Fréjus (1 km north-east on the N7) is the **Villa Aurélienne**, *parc Aurélienne; tel: 04 94 53 11 30* (open summer Tue–Sun 1400–1900; winter Tue–Sun 1400–1800; free). This gracious Palladian mansion, which sits atop a small hill in a large park, was built in the 1880s and acquired by the municipality in 1988. Now fully restored in the Italian Renaissance style, it features a superb entrance hall with a sweeping staircase, dining hall, music room, and library.

FRÉJUS–CANNES

This route traverses the Esterel Massif, which is one of the most dramatic and beautiful sections of France's Mediterranean coast, particularly where the richly coloured rocks of the massif meet the sea below the corniche. The interior of the massif is well worth exploring on foot or by mountain-bike.

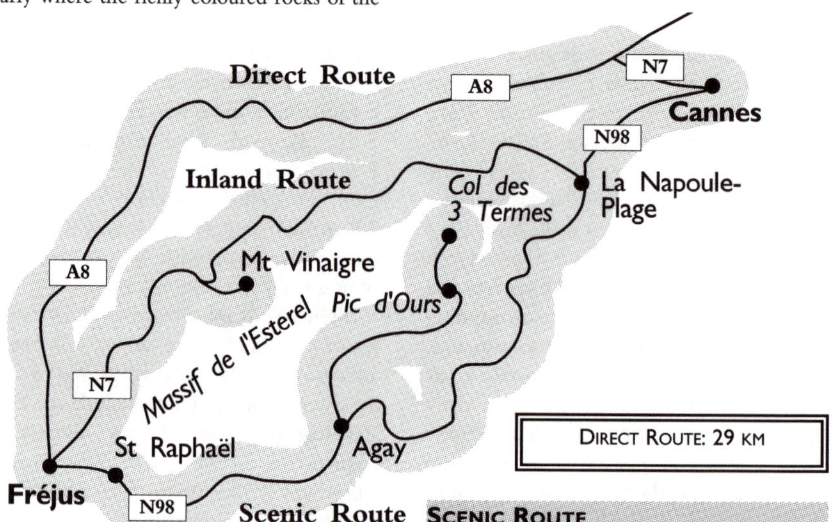

DIRECT ROUTE: 29 KM

ROUTES

DIRECT ROUTE

Follow signs out of central Fréjus for the autoroute, A8, joining the motorway at Junction 38. Distance: 29 km; allow 1 hr.

INLAND ROUTE

Take the N7 out of Fréjus, signposted to Cannes, following it through the Esterel hinterland to **La Napoule-Plage**, and then continuing on the N98 along the seafront into Cannes. Distance: 30 km; allow 2 hrs.

SCENIC ROUTE

Follow the N98 through St Raphaël around the coast to **Agay**, turning inland to the **Aquarium des Roches Rouges**, from where you can side-track north into the interior of the Esterel. Return to the coast and continue along the N98 into **La Napoule-Plage** and Cannes. Distance: 38 km (add 30 km for the sidetrack to Col des Trois Termes); allow 1 day.

Note: The most famous coastal section of this route (between Agay and Théoule-sur-Mer) can become very congested at weekends, with so many cars and coaches pulling over to admire the scenery that it may be impossible to stop at some of the viewpoints. The interior of the Massif can also seem overcrowded at weekends.

INLAND ROUTE

Much of the inland route follows the old **Aurelian Way** *(Via Aurelia)*, which was built by the Romans to link Rome with Arles and was one of the great strategic routes of the Roman Empire. Soon after leaving the outskirts of Fréjus, there are views to the north and north-west, with the wooded hills of the Esterel off to the right; this is the most heavily-wooded part of the massif. After 11 km there is a car park with a track leading to the summit of **Mt Vinaigre** (45 mins return), the massif's highest peak at 618 m, from where there is a superb 360-degree panorama across to Cannes and the Golfe de la Napoule to the east, the Massif des Maures to the west, the uplands of the Var to the north, and across the Esterel itself to the south. Three km further on, after skirting the base of Mt Vinaigre, you reach the **Auberge des Adrets**, *les Adrets-de-l'Esterel; tel: 04 94 40 36 24; fax: 04 94 40 34 06* (moderate–expensive). This hospitable old coaching inn, with lovely rooms and a good restaurant, sits roughly mid-way between Fréjus and Cannes and was once a notorious haunt for the 18th-century highwayman Gaspard de Besse, who would rob the coaches and then take refuge with his gang in a cave behind Mt Vinaigre.

The road continues down towards the Argentière River, emerging at **La Napoule-Plage**, from where it is 4 km along the seafront into Cannes.

SCENIC ROUTE: FRÉJUS TO AGAY

Tourist Office: *blvd de la Plage, Agay; tel: 04 94 82 01 85*; open Mon–Sat 0830–1200, 1330-1800).

The road hugs the coast as it leaves St-Raphaël, passing several small resorts and beaches. Just after the *plage du Dramont* there is a signpost off to the right for the **Sémaphore du Dramont**. Park 100 m further on and walk up (45 mins return) to the signal station, from where there is a panoramic view which encompasses the red porphyry rocks known as the *Lion de Mer* and *Lion de Ter* at the entrance to the Gulf of Fréjus to the west, as well as the Esterel massif to the north-east, and the Bay of Agay below. Descend into the bay and the pleasant little resort of **Agay**, built around a deep natural harbour used centuries ago by the Ligurians, Greeks and Romans. It now has a little marina, with plenty of nautical excursions (including underwater viewing trips) and watersports available.

Turn inland on the D56 (signposted to autoroute A8). After 1.3 km on the left is the **Aquarium des Roches Rouges**, *1387 av. du Gratadis; tel: 04 94 82 77 94* (open Mon–Fri 1400–1900, Sat–Sun 1000–1900 (July–Aug until 2100); FFr.35). This new aquarium has over 40 tanks inside a cavernous warehouse, with around 130 different species from the different oceans and environments (lagoons, mangroves, and so on) around the world. It's a well-presented display, and also has a touch-tank for children.

MASSIF DE L'ESTEREL

Turn right almost immediately after the aquarium and head into the interior of the **Massif de l'Esterel**. Far older than the limestone which dominates much of Provence, the range is composed of vivid red porphyry (volcanic rock) which has created some striking landscapes formed of rust-red canyons, strange rock formations, and jagged peaks. Although the tallest peak, Mt

Vinaigre, is only 618 m high, the relief of the massif, with its dramatic skyline and steep ravines, gives the impression of a much loftier range. Once covered in pines and holm oaks, the Esterel has been subject to numerous fires and the predominant vegetation today is primarily rough scrubland *(maquis)*, consisting of heathers, gorse, lavender, mimosas and other shrubs. The interior of the Esterel is at its best in the Spring, when the wildflowers are in bloom.

There are several options once you are in the interior of the Esterel. Recent road closures mean that it is no longer possible to do an entire circuit by car (many roads have now become tracks for mountain-biking, an activity which is particularly popular here). For one of the most dramatic routes, follow signs for the **Pic de l'Ours**, with a road which winds up and over the massif towards the coast with superb views across to the Golfe de la Napoule and Cannes beyond.

This road continues on towards the **Col des Trois Termes**, with views down into the ravines in the interior of the massif, but you will then have to turn around and come back the same way.

There are two areas are of special interest within the massif: the **Ravin de Perthus** and the **Ravin du Mal-Infernet**. Both these gorges have cold, humid conditions which have produced an exceptional flora unknown elsewhere on the Mediterranean coast, and both are designated Biological Reserves (the ravines are signposted off the main internal road; it takes around 2 hrs rtn on foot to reach the head of the Ravine du Mal-Infernet, but you can make a shorter excursion into either of them).

AGAY TO CANNES

Tourist Office: *blvd de H. Clews, La Napoule-Plage* (on the seafront); *tel: 04 93 49 95 31*. Open summer Mon–Sat 0900–1800; winter Mon–Fri 0900–1700, Sat 0900–1200.

Return to Agay, continuing around the coast road through Anthéor, which is dominated by the peaks of the Cap Roux range, the massif's most seaward hills. Past here, the **Pointe de l'Observatoire** is one of the main scenic stopping points, with the vivid red rocks of the **Pic du Cap Roux** reaching right down to the sea and forming a striking contrast where they meet the deep blue waters of the Mediterranean. The road continues along this magnificent coastal landscape until rounding the headland at la Galére and Théoule-sur-Mer to descend into the **Golfe de la Napoule**.

At the head of the bay is **La Napoule-Plage**, the seaside resort of the town of **Mandelieu**. La Napoule is a medium-sized resort with its own marina, plenty of shops, cafés and restaurants, and several good sandy beaches. At the end the eastern-most beach is the **Château de la Napoule**, *tel: 04 93 49 95 05* (open for guided visits Wed–Mon July–Aug 1500, 1600, 1700; May–June, Sept–Oct 1500, 1600; FFr.15). This unusual château, originally dating from the 14th century, was restored after World War I by the American sculptor Henry Clews (1876–1937). Clews sculpted a menagerie of mythical beasts on the gatehouse and roofs and walls of the buildings within the castle complex, creating a bizarre environment in conjunction with the Gothic and Renaissance remnants of the castle, which now houses an art school, the *Fondation Henry Clews*.

Continue along the seafront into **Cannes**.

GRENOBLE

Home to the great 19th-century writer Stendhal, this historic city at the meeting of the Drac and Isère rivers has moved with the times. Today, its three traditional 'powers' – religion, law and the people – are said to have been replaced by university, research and industry. The university, with 48,000 students, is one of the most famous in Europe for science and engineering and many high-tech industries have settled in the area. Tourism is the other important activity, largely because the city is surrounded by the Alps. Indeed the Tourist Office, which opened in 1889, (the first in France), it concerns itself with both Grenoble and the Dauphine valley area where thousands enjoy skiing in winter and activities from walking to paragliding in summer.

Tourist Information

Tourist Office: *14 r. de la République; tel: 04 76 42 41 41*, in a modern glass building. Open June–Sept daily 0900–1230, 1330–1900; Oct–May, Mon–Sat 0900–1230, 1330–1800; Sun 1000–1200. Excellent maps, the free glossy *Grenoble Magazine*, accommodation booking service, and guided tours of the Old Town (June–Sept, Mon–Sat 1000; FFr.30). **The Centre Informations Montagnes et Sentiers (CIMES)**, based in the Tourist Office, has information on hiking, biking and cross-country skiing. **The Centre Régional d'Information Jeunesse**; *8 r. Voltaire; tel: 04 76 54 70 38*, provides student and youth information.

Arriving and Departing

By Car

Driving around the city centre is difficult because of heavy traffic, long articulated trams and a complex one-way system round the central pedestrianised area. Parking costs more on meters along streets marked with red lines (2 hrs max) than on those with green (8 hrs max). Parking is free 1200–1400, 1900–0900 and on Sun.

By Train

Station: *pl. de la Gare; tel: 08 36 35 35 35.* Information office open Mon–Fri 0830–1830, Sat 0900–1800. Luggage lockers. For the town centre take *av. F Viallet* to the *Jardin de Ville* and turn right onto *r. de la République* (about 15 mins walk).

By Bus

Gare Routière (next to the station), *tel: 04 76 87 90 31* or *76 47 77 77* (maps and information in *pl. de la Gare*).

Getting Around

An efficient **tram and bus** network serves the city. Particularly useful are tram lines A and B which run direct from Gare Europole next to the railway station along *av. Alsace Lorraine*, past the main shops, department stores and Tourist Office. **TAG** (Grenoble transport company): **Station de Tramway Grand' Place**, *av. General de Gaulle.* Open Mon–Fri 0730–1830, Sat and school holidays 0930–1200, 1400–1800. Information *tel:*

04 76 20 66 66, Mon–Fri 0800–1800. Bus/tram tickets are valid for one hour. One journey FFr.7, 10-journey carnet FFr.49, Visitag day pass FFr.22. Single tickets can be bought on buses (not on trams), others at kiosks and machines, and must be validated on board. Alternatively, the Old Town is small enough to manage easily on foot and leads to the promenades beside the river. Parts of the central area are pedestrianised.

Le Petit Train de Grenoble, a motorised road train, is useful for lifts when sightseeing, *tel: 04 07 04 77 44*. The Bastille fortifications on a hill across the river are served by a *télépherique* ('bubble' cars) from *quai S Jay; tel: 04 76 44 33 65*, Apr–Oct 0900–2400 (Mon from 1100, Sun to 1930); Nov–Mar 1030–1830; FFr.33 return; about 3 mins. There is also a comprehensive cycle-path network; map available from Tourist Office.

Taxis: **Taxi Grenoble**, *tel: 04 76 54 42 54*, 24-hr call service.

Staying in Grenoble

Accommodation

Hotel chains include *BW, F1, Ib, Mv*. Top of the list is the modern **Park Hôtel**, *10 pl. P Mistral; tel: 04 76 85 81 23; fax: 04 76 46 49 88* (expensive). To pay less head for the station where you'll find **Hôtel Terminus**, *10 pl. de la Gare; tel: 04 76 87 24 33; fax: 04 76 50 38 28* (moderate) and **Hôtel Alizé**, *1 pl. de la Gare; tel: 04 76 43 12 91; fax: 04 76 47 62 79* (cheap). **Hôtel Victoria**, *17 r. Thiers; tel: 04 76 46 06 36* (cheap) is centrally-placed. **Les Trois Roses**, *32 av. du Grésivaudan, 38700 Grenoble-Corenc; tel: 76 90 35 09; fax: 76 90 71 72* (moderate) is on the attractive north side of the town, 4 km from the centre, in leafy surroundings with views of the Chartreuse mountains.

HI: *18 av. du Grésivaudan; tel: 04 76 09 33 52*. **Campsite**: **Les 3 Pucelles,** *Seyssins; tel: 04 76 96 45 73* (caravans) is 2 km south-west of the centre.

Eating and Drinking

Grenoble offers food from all over the world – regional cuisine, including alpine specialities, North African, Italian, Indian and Vietnamese. The town's speciality is *gratin dauphinois* – sliced potatoes baked in a cream sauce. Also look out for *gateaux aux nois de Grenoble* (nut cake).

Try the streets around the *Jardin de Ville* for regional specialities, or you can find North African cuisine a little further east in the Old Town. There are several Vietnamese restaurants around the station. Cafés and bars abound between *pl. St André* and *pl. Notre Dame*. **La Qantara**, *2 r. Lazare-Carnot; tel: 04 76 47 42 60* (cheap) features Egyptian food and **Le Saphir**, *19 r. de Turenne; tel: 04 76 87 30 02* (cheap) serves Middle-Eastern food.

At **L'Escale La Pierrade**, *4 pl. de Gordes; tel: 04 76 51 65 67* (cheap), try Pierres Chaudes, the Savoyard speciality of thin slices of meat which you cook yourself on a hot stove at the table. **L'Épicurien**, *1 pl. aux Herbes; tel: 04 76 51 96 06* (cheap) also serves regional specialities. For a special occasion it is worth heading 8km out of town on the N90 to **Les Mésanges**, *Montbonnot-St-Martin; tel: 04 76 90 21 57* (moderate) where menus feature local produce and the mountain views are magnificent.

Communications and Money

Post Office, *7 blvd Mar Lyautey; tel: 04 76 43 53 31*. Facilities include poste restante and currency exchange. Open Mon 0800–1800, Tues–Fri 0800–1830, Sat 0800–1200. **Comptoir de Change**, *r. Philis de la Charce*, near the Tourist Office.

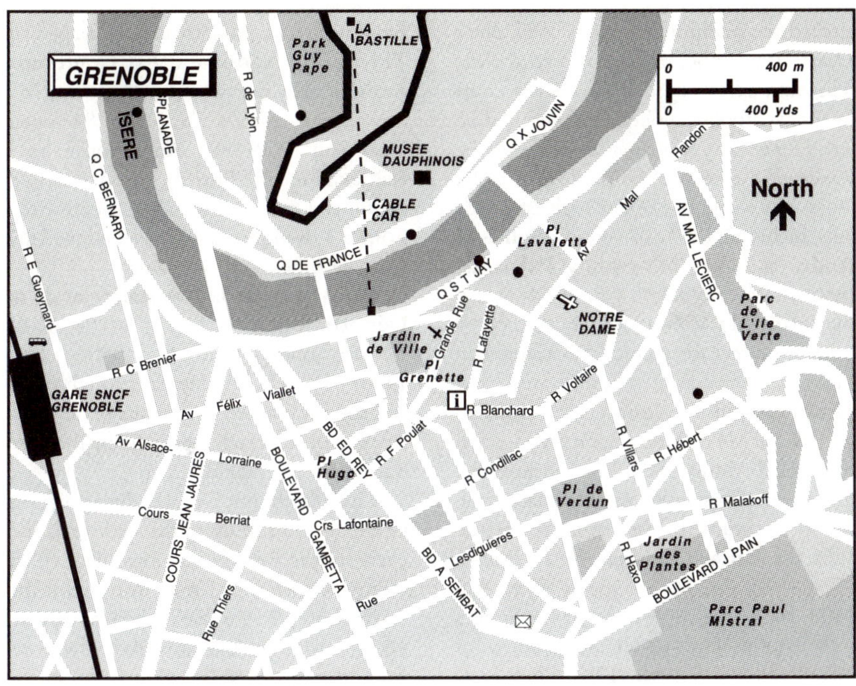

Entertainment

Grenoble is proud of its cultural heritage and there is no shortage of music, theatre and art. To find out what's on, pick up a free copy of *Contact* from the Tourist Office or bookshops. Plays, opera and dance take place at the **Théâtre de Grenoble**, *2 r. H. Berlioz; tel: 04 76 54 03 08*. **Companie Renata Scant** performs at *8 r. P Duclot; tel: 04 76 44 60 92*.

Concerts take place at **Summum**, *Grand'Place; tel: 04 76 39 63 00*.

There is no shortage of clubs and discos – remember this is a university town. Buy *Guide DAHU*, written by Grenoble students, for what's new and improved (FFr.15 from the Tourist Office).

Events

Mid Mar **Jazz Festival**; July **Festival of European Theatre**; late Oct **Six Jours de Grenoble** (cycling competitions and concerts) at Palais des Sports.

Shopping

The main shops line a traffic-free route from *pl. de la Gare* along *av. Alsace Lorraine* and *r. F Poulat*. Several markets are held every day except Mon, plus flea markets on Sun mornings.

Sightseeing

At the heart of the city is the Old Town on the south bank of the river, the so-called **Village St Hugues**, with its impressive **Cathédrale de Notre-Dame**, whose large St Hugues chapel was once the nave of a 13th-century church. Tall 17th- and 18th-century mansions overshadow narrow pedestrianised streets crowded with small shops and restaurants. The three squares are said to symbolise the city's three traditional 'powers' – *pl. Notre Dame*, the cathedral square, symbolises religious power; *pl. St André*, the law court square, symbolises political power; and *pl. aux Herbes*, a typical market-place, is the square of the people. *Pl. St André* is overlooked by some of the city's oldest buildings, including the 13th-century **Eglise St André** and the 15th-century **Palais de Justice**. On the edge of the Old Town, the **Jardin de Ville** is a finely manicured garden, perfect for picnics. Excavations in the old St Laurent church, now the **Musée Archéologique**, *pl. St Laurent, tel: 04 76 44 78 68* (open Wed–Mon 0900–1200, 1400–1800; FFr.15) show the origins of Christianity in the area during the 4th century. In the former Hotel de Ville, the **Musée Stendhal**, *1 r. H. Berlioz, tel: 04 76 54 44 14* (open Tues–Sun 1400–1800, free) is devoted to Grenoble's most famous son, writer and admirer of Napoleon, Henri Beyle (1783–1842), better known as Stendhal, whose most famous novels were *Le Rouge et le Noir* and *La Chartreuse de Parme*. The apartment where he stayed as a child with his grandfather at **Maison Stendhal**, *20 Grande Rue, tel: 04 76 42 02 62* stages exhibitions. (Open Tues–Sun 1000–1200, 1400–1800). A leaflet available from the Tourist Office lists all the Stendhal connections.

Also on the south bank, beyond the Old Town, is the ultra-modern new building which houses the **Musée de Grenoble**, *5 pl. Lavalette, tel: 04 76 63 44 44* (open Wed 1100–2200, Thur–Mon 1100–1900FFr.25). Founded during the Revolution and combining medieval ramparts with modern design, this is one of the biggest museums in Europe, with vast collections of 18th and 19th-century art, including paintings by Rubens, Delacroix, Picasso, Matisse, Miró and Ernst, as well as a collection of Egyptian antiquity. Exhibitions of modern art are staged at The **Centre National d'Art Contemporain**, usually known as **Le Magasin**, *155 cours Berriat; tel: 04 76 21 95 84* (open Tues–Sun 1200–1900. Admission to special exhibitions, FFr.15), a national art centre and museum which was converted from a warehouse originally designed by Gustave Eiffel, of tower fame.

The **Musée de la Résistance et de la Déportation**, *14 r. Hébert; tel: 04 76 42 38 53* (open Wed–Mon 0900–1200, 1400–1800; FFr.15) depicts through sights and sounds the heroic exploits of 30 resistance groups which operated in the area during World War II.

The highlight of sightseeing in Grenoble is a trip up to the stark rock and even starker fortress, **La Bastille**, which looms over the Old Town from across the River Isère. A 'bubble' cable-car whisks you dramatically upwards, over the river from *quai S Jay*. At the top is a restaurant with terraces with a view that extends to the Alps. Half-way down the hill again through the *Parc Guy Pape* and *Jardin des Dauphins* (or 250 steps up from the St Laurent Bridge) is the **Musée Dauphinois**, *30 r. Maurice Gignoux; tel: 04 76 85 19 00* (open Wed–Mon 0900– 1200, 1400–1800; FFr.15) which traces the history and culture of the region from prehistoric times. The building is a 17th-century convent. The top floor is now devoted to an exciting new exhibition on skiing, the only one of its kind in France. Decorated appropriately in crisp white, it traces 4000 years of conquest and adventure on the mountains in wintertime

On the northern side of town, bordering ancient fortifications, is the curious **Casamaures**, *13 bis r. de la Résistance, St Martin-le-Vinoux, tel: 76 47 13 50* (guided visits by arrangement), a Moorish-style palace built in 1886.

GRENOBLE–SISTERON

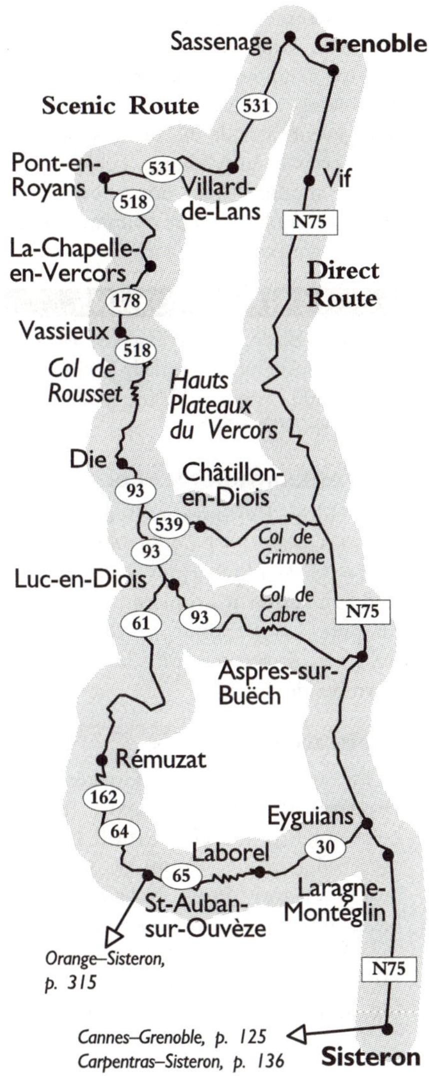

This varied mountain route crosses the high Vercors plateau and the lesser-known Dios and Baronnies ranges. The Vercors, a 30km-wide area of pastures and woods below the distinctive 60km-long ridge of the Montagne de la Lans, is sunny and green. Beyond Die, the quiet countryside, punctuated by farms and hamlets, is at its most colourful in July and August, when fields of lavender are in bloom.

ROUTES

DIRECT ROUTE

Head south from the centre of Grenoble along *cours de la Libération* onto the N75 which goes through **Vif**, **Clelles** and **Aspres-sur-Buëch** to **Sisteron**. Distance 142 km; allow 2½ hrs. 185

SCENIC ROUTE

Head west from the centre of Grenoble along *blvd J. Vallier* onto the N532. At **Sassinage**, turn left onto the D531, through the **Gorges d'Engins** following the River Furon to **Villard-de-Lans**. Continue south-west on the D531 to Pont-en-Royans, then take the D518 to **La Chapelle-en-Vercors**. Take the D178 through **Vassieux**, rejoining the D518 to cross the **Col de Rousset** (1254 m) to **Die**. Leave here on the N93.

To join the Direct Route, turn east on the D539 through **Chatillon** and over the **Col de Grimond** (1318m). Alternatively, remain on the D93 and wriggle east up to the **Col de Cabre** (1180m) and then down to join the Direct Route at **Aspres-sur-Buëch**.

To continue along the scenic route, continue south on the N93 and, just before **Luc-en-Diois**, turn right onto the twisting D61 to **Rémuzat**. Just south of **Rémuzat**, turn right onto the even-more-wriggly D162 and then in succession the D510, D64, D65 and D30 which take you through **St Auban-sur-Ouvèze** and **Laborel** to join the N75 north of **Laragne-Montéglin** and **Sisteron.** Distance 267 km; allow 6 hours.

VILLARD-DE-LANS

Tourist Office: *av. du Gén. de Gaulle; tel: 04 78 95 10 38.* Open daily July–Aug 0900–1230, 1330–1900; Sept–Christmas, Easter–June 0900–1200, 1400–1800; Christmas–Easter 0900–1900.

As part of Villard's growth into a bustling resort, geared to skiers in winter and walkers and sightseers in summer, its accommodation has expanded along the valley, with everything from 3-star hotels to simple auberges. On the edge of the village, the **Hôtel Georges** (*LF*), *av. Gén. de Gaulle; tel: 04 76 95 11 75; fax: 04 76 95 92 66* (cheap) is a family-run chalet-style hotel with 25 rooms, some in an annexe across the road. Facilities include a games room, pool and garden. The town has no shortage of eateries either, though many offer fast food rather than gourmet dining. Menus are adjusted to suit the season. Paul and Geneviève Chabert, who have run la **Petite Auberge**, *r. de la République; tel: 04 76 95 11 53* (cheap) for over 25 years, serve genuine local dishes like potato 'gratin' and ravioles; also raclette in winter. They smoke their own salmon, trout and duck.

Villard (1023 m) is the main base for visiting the beautiful Vercors Regional Park, a broad plateau of meadows and pine forests bordered on the east by a long ridge of mountains, the Montagne de la Lans. The little town spreads attractively along a hillside facing west across the wide Val Molière to forested mountains. The area offers visitors every outdoor activity they care to pursue, notably cross-country skiing, with some downhill in winter, and walking, climbing, horse-riding, mountain-biking and paragliding in summer. Main events include the Vercors long-distance cross-country skiing (Feb) and the Vercors mountain-bike ride (Sept). Villard has an ice-rink, outdoor swimming pools and a wave-pool with slides.

PONT-EN-ROYANS

Tourist Office: *Grande Rue; tel: 04 76 36 09 10.* Open July–Aug daily 0900–1200, 1400–1800 (Sun 1700); Sept–June Mon–Fri 0900–1200.

ACCOMMODATION AND FOOD

The **Hôtel Restaurant Beau Rivage** (*LF*), *r. Gambetta; tel: 04 76 36 00 63; fax: 04 76 36 00 11* (cheap) is scenically situated by the river. **Campsite:** A municipal campsite, **Les Seraines**, *tel: 04 76 36 06 30*, is prettily situated at the bottom of the town beside the river.

SIGHTSEEING

In the steep ravine of the **Gorges de la Bourne**, the Bourne River tumbles below high grey cliffs. A small village is squeezed into the bottom of the gorge, near the narrow **Pont Picard**. The first bridge, constructed in wood, was built in the 13th century as part of the village's fortifications but the road from Villard dates only from 1872. The village itself, around 1000 years old, originally grew around a castle and convent. In medieval times, houses were built into the steep limestone cliffs on each side of the gorge. From the mid 16th to mid 17th centuries, it was the centre of bitter struggles between

Protestants and Catholics. The Bourne is said to have 'run red with blood' and the population dropped from 5000 to only 1500. Now the houses have been renovated and artists have opened galleries along the narrow old streets.

Four kilometres along Gorges de la Bourne from Pont-en-Royans is one of the area's most spectacular caves, the **Grottes de Choranche**, *tel: 04 76 36 09 88* (open daily 1000–1200, 1400–1700 with guided tours every hour (every 20 mins Jul–Aug from 0930–1800); FFr.38).

LA CHAPELLE-EN-VERCORS

Tourist Office: *26420 La Chapelle; tel: 04 75 48 22 54.* Open July–Aug 0900–1230, 1430–1900; Sept–June 1000–1200, 1400–1800. Information office for Vassieux and the Cantonal du Vercors.

It took ten years from 1843 to build a road up the narrow Grand Goulets ravine to link Pont-en-Royans with Die through La Chapelle. The road, blasted through high rocks, provides a drive to remember as it weaves through a series of tunnels and squeezes alongside the fast-flowing river through the Gorge des Barragues de Verains, before the countryside opens out into wide meadows at La Chapelle.

The tiny 13th-century **Chapelle St Antoine** is all that remained of the original village after World War II. Its darkest hour was on 25 July 1944, when 17 young hostages were shot by German soldiers in the courtyard of a farm. A wall and part of a barn have been turned into a poignant memorial.

DIE

Tourist Office: *av. Sadicarnot; tel: 04 75 22 03 03.* Open July–Aug Mon–Sat 0900–1230, 1430–1800, Sun 0900–1230; Sept–June Mon–Fri 0900–1200, 1400–1800, Sat 0900–1200.

Accommodation and Food

The **Hôtel des Alpes**, *87 r. C. Buffardel; tel: 04 75 22 15 83; fax: 04 75 22 09 39* (cheap), and **Hôtel Saint Dominique**,

Resistance in the Vercors

The Vercors was an important Resistance centre during World War II. Its 60 km long ridge of mountains helped form a natural fortress from which the Maquis, local volunteers who knew the territory well, could operate very effectively. In particular, a secret Plan Montagnards was designed to swing into operation like a Trojan Horse when the Allies landed in the South of France. However in July 1944 operations went horribly wrong when allied reinforcements failed to arrive and the Germans launched a massive attack, killing 600 Maquis.

Opened in 1994, a bunker-like museum dedicated to the Maquis, the **Mémorial de la Résistance**, *tel: 04 75 48 26 00* (open daily Apr–Sept 1000–1800; Oct–Mar 1000-1700; closed mid-Nov–mid-Dec; FFr 25) is tucked into the hillside just below the Col de Lachau near Vassieux. The Germans attacked this village in gliders, demolishing the buildings and murdering 73 people, including children. The museum uses tableaux, videos, inter-active screens and artifacts to depict the Maquis' heroic exploits and the villagers' terrible suffering. On the plain below, beside the Maquis cemetery, the **Nécropole de la Résistance** (open daily May–Oct 1000-1200, 1300–1800) has an audio-visual display. In Vassieux, the **Musée de la Résistance Vercors**; *tel: 04 75 48 28 46* (open daily Apr–Nov 0900–1200, 1400–1800; free) is a small private museum created by one of the maquisards.

44 r. C. Buffardel; tel: 04 04 75 22 03 08; fax: 04 75 22 24 48 (cheap) are both in the town centre. On the edge of town, **Le Relais de Chamarges**, *av. de la Clairette; tel: 04 75 22 00 95; fax: 04 75 22 19 34* (cheap) specialises in local cuisine and has a garden and sun terrace. **Campsite: Camping Municipal de Die**, *quartier du Pont Rompu; tel: 04 75 22 14 77* (caravans) is beside the River Drôme.

Sightseeing

Leave your car near the tourist office where parking is free and take a leisurely stroll around the narrow streets of this attractive little town. You will pass several imposing Renaissance mansions on your way to the gleaming white **Cathédrale de Notre-Dame,** *pl. de l'Horloge; tel: 04 75 22 01 13* (open 0900–1900), which you enter through the 12th-century porch of its low square bell tower. Continue to pl. de l'Hôtel de Ville where the **Hôtel de Ville** occupies an ancient episcopal palace. Inside it, **La Chapelle St-Nicolas** (open Mon–Fri 0900–1200, 1330–1700; free) was the private chapel of the bishops and has a well-preserved 12th-century mosaic made with Roman stones.

Two towers still mark one of the town's old Roman gates, the **Porte St Marcel**, *pl. André Chevandier*. From here, you can climb along the remains of the ramparts which encircled the town until the 9th century and later formed part of a citadel. Die's prosperity and fame today is based on its production of Clairette, a sparking white wine made at the **Cave Coopérative**, *rte de Valence; tel: 04 75 22 20 80* (guided tours July–Aug Mon–Fri 1100 and 1500; free).

June sees the **Fête de la Transhumance**, when thousands of sheep are led through the town on their way to summer pastures up in the hills.

LUC-EN-DIOIS

Tourist Office: *pl. la Crois; tel: 04 75 21 34 14*. Open July–Aug Mon–Sat 0930–1200, 1530–1900, Sun 0930–1200; Sept–Jun Tues–Fri 0900–1200.

This is one of the few villages which punctuate this rural drive through hillsides yellow with broom and valleys vivid purple when the lavender is in bloom. To shorten your journey, take any of the scenic roads eastwards to the direct route. Two km south-east of Luc, the busy D93 passes **Le Claps** where, in 1442, the River Drôme suddenly altered its course, having broken through rocks, creating two small lakes and a valley of giant boulders. Today it is a popular spot for picnics and walks.

LARAGNE-MONTÉGLIN

Tourist Office: *pl. des Aires; tel: 04 92 65 09 38*. Open July–Aug Mon–Sat 0900–1800; Sept–Jun Mon–Fri 0900–1730.

The town's small selection of hotels and restaurants offers an alternative to the scattered auberges and chambres d'hôtes on the route from Die. The best bet is **Les Terrasses** (*LF*); *tel: 04 92 65 08 54; fax: 04 92 65 21 08* (cheap), which has 15-rooms and a garden. **Campsite: Les Cigales**; *tel: 04 92 66 20 63*, is a 3-star site, 5 km north in the village of Eyguians.

It comes as a shock to reach this busy little town after joining the direct route on the N75. Thanks to the proximity of the **Montagne de Chabre**, a mountain ridge popular for hang-gliding and paragliding, the town has made them its speciality. The European championships were held there in 1994. Exhibitions are held in the vaulted cellars of the 17th-century castle during the summer months (details from the Tourist Office).

SISTERON

See p. 126.

Le Puy-en-Velay

One of the most dramatic and unusual towns in France, Le Puy is set on a broad plain surrounded by mountains and has been built around a series of enormous volcanic pitons, all topped with religious monuments. Once an important pilgrimage centre (see p. 193) and a centre for lace manufacture, it is today a thriving tourist centre at the heart of the Massif Central.

Tourist Information

Tourist office: *pl. du Breuil; tel: 04 71 09 38 41.* Open daily July–Aug 0830–1930; Easter–June daily 0830–1200, 1345–1830, Sept;Oct–Easter Mon–Sat 0830–1200, 1345–1830 . A wide range of information is available on the town and surrounding region.

Arriving and Departing

Airport

Airport: Aéroport Le Puy-en-Velay-Loudes, *tel: 04 71 08 62 28*, is 12km to the west of the city, with a twice-daily service (Mon–Fri) to Paris Orly-Sud.

By Car

Le Puy is at the junction of the N88 (St Étienne 78km) and N102 (Clermont-Ferrand 132km). There is ample parking around *pl. du Breuil* and *pl. Michelet*; most hotels also have garages. It is not advisable to drive into the old town.

By Train

Station: *av. Charles Dupuy; tel: 36 35 35 35.* About 15 mins walk to the centre, Turn left, follow *av. C. Dupuy* to *sq. Coiffier*, go left on *blvd Mar. Fayolle* to *pl. du Breuil.* There is no bus from the station but lines nos 1 and 3 leave from *sq. Coiffier* (stop: *pl. Michelet*).

By Bus

Bus station: *pl. Mar. Leclerc; tel: 04 71 09 25 60.*

Getting Around

The narrow street layout means that the only practical way to reach the hilltop monuments is on foot, up steep, heavily cobbled streets and seemingly endless stairs. Wear comfortable shoes. For outlying journeys, tickets and timetables for the local **bus** network (TUDIP) are available from the Tourist Office or *tel: 04 71 09 38 41.* Single journey FFr.5.40; ten tickets for FFr.39. **Taxis**: at station, *tel: 04 71 09 21 10*; at *pl. du Breuil, tel: 04 71 05 42 43.*

Guided tours (in French) depart from outside the Tourist Office, daily at 1600 (last two weeks July and 19 Aug–8 Sept); 1000 and 1600 (first three weeks in Aug); FFr.30. Evening walks on Mon, Wed, Fri, 2100 (mid July–Aug); FFr.30.

A **Petit Train**, *tel: 04 71 02 70 70*, runs guided sightseeing tours in July–Aug (daily 1000, 1100, 1400, 1500m 1600, 1700; FFr.20), departing from *pl. Michelet.*

Staying in Le Puy

Accommodation

There is limited but adequate accommodation. There are several hotels near the station, while those near *pl. du Breuil* are only a short walk from the old town. Hotel chains include *Ib*. A good, centrally located hotel is the **Régina**, *39 blvd Mar. Fayolle, tel: 04 71 09 14 71; fax: 04 71 09 18 57* (cheap), housed in a lovely old building with well-equipped, comfortable rooms. Close by is the **Dyke Hôtel**, *37 blvd Mar. Fayolle; tel: 04 71 09 05 30; fax: 04 71 02 58 66* (cheap), which, despite its rather shabby exterior, has been entirely refurbished inside; rooms are slightly on the small side. The old-fashioned **Hôtel Bristol** *(LF), 7 av. Mar. Fayolle; tel: 04 71 09 13 38; fax: 04 71 09 51 70* (cheap) has 40 rooms and a pleasant garden. The slightly more upmarket **Hôtel Christel**, *15 blvd A. Clair, tel: 04 71 02 24 44; fax: 04 71 02 71 31* (cheap–moderate) has 30 rooms and is not far from the centre. On the outskirts of town (direction Mende-Aubenas) is the **Val Vert** *(LF), 6 av. B. Marcet; tel: 04 71 09 09 30; fax: 04 71 09 36 49* (cheap), which has a welcoming atmosphere and just 23 well-kept rooms; the ones at the back are quieter. Pilgrims en route to Santiago should try the **Maison Saint François**, *r. St Mayol; tel: 04 71 05 98 86; fax: 04 71 05 43 42* (cheap), a *gîte d'étape* following a tradition over 1,000 years old. **HI: Centre Pierre Cardinal**, *9 r. J. Vallès; tel: 04 71 05 52 40; fax: 04 71 02 62 08* (15-min walk from the station, near the cathedral). **Camping: Bouthezard** 2-star, *ch. de Roderie, tel: 04 71 09 55 09* (caravans).

History

Le Puy stands on a site which was once a Celtic place of worship (there are the remains of a 1st-century sanctuary in the foundations of the cathedral), which became christianised during the 3rd century. Apparitions of the Virgin and the miraculous healing powers attributed to the flagstone from a local dolmen (later known as the 'fever stone', it can still be seen in the cathedral) led to the establishment of a bishopric and the building of the first cathedral. Le Puy soon eclipsed St Paulien, the Roman capital of Velay, especially with the development of the pilgrim route to Santiago (see p. 193). During the 12th century the security of the pilgrims (and so the prosperity of Le Puy) became seriously threatened by marauding bands known as *Les Cotereaux*. A carpenter named Durand had a vision of the Virgin and set about organising a vigilante war against the Cotereaux, pursuing them into the countryside and hanging them *en masse*. Unfortunately the vigilantes got a taste for brigandry themselves and were in turn massacred by royal troops.

Eating and Drinking

There is a good choice of restaurants, many featuring local specialities, with some offering set price menus from FFr.55 in the *pl. de la Halle* and *blvd St Louis*. For a choice of brasseries or pizzerias, try *pl. du Breuil*, and there are good crêperies in *r. Vibert*. From salads to casseroles, many dishes feature the green Puy lentil, a plant which thrives in the volcanic soil of the Velay region. Recommended restaurants include **Marc et Éric Tournaye**, *12 r. Chênebouterie, tel: 04 71 09 58 94* (moderate–expensive), housed in a lovely vaulted chamber in a 16th-century mansion, with excellent service and imaginative menus. A similar ambience is found at **A l'Ecu d'Or**, *59 and 61 r. Pannessac, tel: 04 71 02 19 36* (moderate–expensive), which features classic French cuisine. **Le Bateau Ivre**, *5 r. Portail d'Avignon, tel: 04 71 09 67 20* (moderate–expensive) has an extensive menu with regional specialities and fantastic desserts. A good budget alternative is **le**

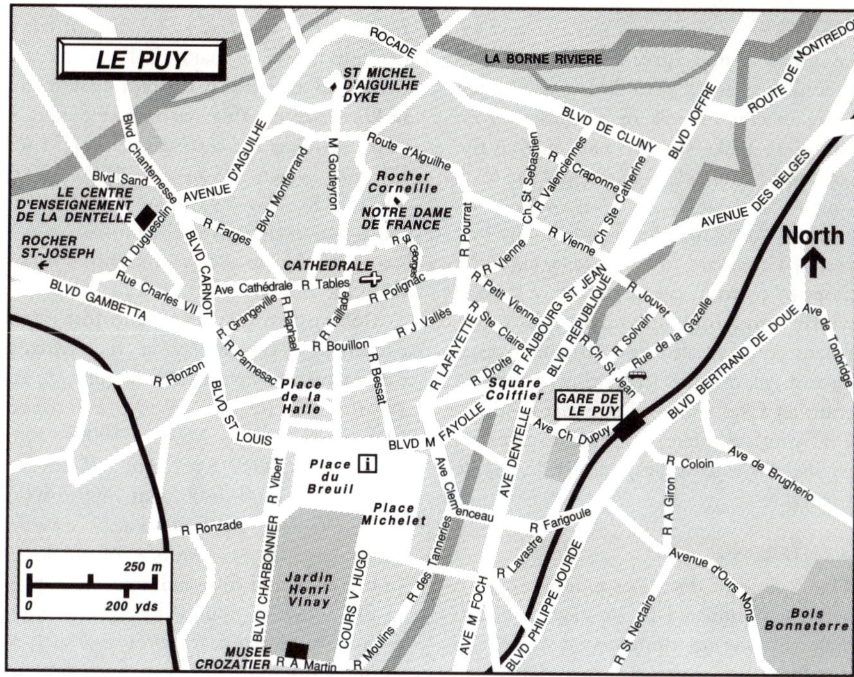

Chat Botté, *8 ave de la Cathédrale, tel: 04 71 02 83 00* (cheap), a small corner restaurant with a cosy, bistro atmosphere and generous portions.

Communications

Post Office: *8 av. de la Dentelle; tel: 04 71 07 02 00.*

Money

Most major French banks have branches here with exchange facilities, many of them on the *pl. du Breuil* and *pl. Michelet.*

Entertainment

There are two cinemas (*pl. du Breuil* and *r. Vibert*). A variety of exhibitions (books, paintings, costumes etc.) are held at either the **Commanderie St Jean**, *r. de Vienne*, or the **Centre Pierre Cardinal**, *9 r. J. Vallès,* throughout the year; *tel: 04 71 05 52 40* for both. There is also a **Théâtre Municipal**, *pl. du Breuil, tel: 04 71 09 03 45.*

Events

The spectacular **Fêtes Renaissance du Roi de l'Oiseau** (The Bird King Renaissance Festival) dates back to an archery competition in 1524. A free special supplement, in French, details the varied events including concerts, exhibitions and re-enactments involving costumed performers and residents. The festival takes place anytime from mid Aug to mid Sept. Besides the Tourist Office, information is available from **Boutique Renaissance**, *44 r. Raphaël; tel: 04 71 09 23 78.* Other festivals include a musical gathering of street musicians in June and a folklore celebration with costumed performers and fireworks in mid-July.

Shopping

Le Puy's famous green lentils are sold everywhere, as is a great deal of lace (much of it machine-made or imported from China, so make sure you are buying the real local handmade version) and the local liqueur, *la Verveine du Velay*, which has been produced here for over two hundred years. There are some interesting little shops in narrow streets such as *r. Raphaël* which wind round the hilly old town, where you will also find a small covered market *(pl. Marché Couvert)* with several gourmet food stalls and regional produce. On Saturdays, there is a general market in *pl. du Plot* and a flea market in *pl. du Clauzel.*

Sightseeing

The skyline of this most unusual town is striking, dominated by its massive cathedral, its towering monumental statues and its solitary 10th-century chapel, all perched high on pinnacles of craggy, volcanic rock. Spread out flat, it would be easy to visit Le Puy's attractions in an afternoon, but the many steep climbs can be punishing and set a slow pace, albeit in a historically evocative setting.

A free brochure, *Historical Visits*, printed in English, is available from the Tourist Office. It outlines two walking routes of 2–3 hrs plus a 2-hr evening one, which pass all the historic sites. For those wanting to do several sights, **combined tickets** for the cloister, the statue, the chapel and the museum (Apr–Sept; FFr.33 instead of FFr.55) are sold at the Tourist Office and the attractions.

Meandering through the little streets of the old town is always fascinating, especially since a turn of a corner often means coming across a lacemaker sitting outside a shop, bobbins clicking over intricate dentelle (lace) spread on a cushion (*r. St Georges* or *r. du Table*). Traditional lace-making is still a major industry in the town. **Le Centre d'Enseignement de la Dentelle du Puy** (lace-making education centre), *2 r. Duguesclin; tel: 04 71 02 01 68* (open Mon–Fri 1000–1200, 1400–1730; also Sat, June–Sept; FFr.10) trains new craftsmen in the profession and has an exhibition and demonstration room open for viewing.

Bobbin lace work from the 16th–20th centuries is on display at the **Musée Crozatier**, *Jardin H. Vinay* (off *pl. du Breuil*); *tel: 04 71 09 38 90* (open May–Sept Wed–Mon 1000–1200, 1400–1800; Oct–Apr Mon, Wed–Sat 1000–1200, 1400–1600, Sun 1400–1600 ; FFr.12.50; free on Sun, out of season). There are also collections of geology, archaeology and folk traditions on display in this museum, founded in 1828, along with early mechanical prototypes, such as a sewing machine, and many fine paintings from the 15th–18th centuries, medieval sculptures and furniture.

The real gems of the city are its peak-top attractions, all of which give breath-taking views. On **Rocher Corneille** (Corneille Rock), the statue of **Notre–Dame de France** (Our Lady of France) is reached via an internal staircase. An engineering feat completed in 1859, using iron from 213 cannon captured at the battle of Sebastopol in Crimea, the Mother holds the Child blessing the town. The unusual red colour was chosen to make it even more visible from a distance (a success) and to match the red roofs of the houses of the town (a failure). The statue's dimensions are colossal. The hair is 7m long; its foot rests on a serpent 17m long; the crowned head weights 110 tons; and 18 people can fit inside the chest. Open May–Jun, Sept daily 0900–1800; Mar–Apr 0900–1900; July–Aug

0930–2000; Oct–Nov, Mar 1000–1700; Dec–Jan Sun 1400–1700; FFr.10.50.

There are 268 steps to **St Michel d'Aiguile Dyke** (St Michael on a Needle), the tiny 10th century chapel built to commemorate the first French pilgrimage to Santiago de Compostela. Open daily end Feb–mid Mar 1400–1600; last two weeks Mar 1000–1200, 1400–1700; Apr–May 1000–1200, 1400–1800; first two weeks June 0900–1200, 1400–1900; mid June–mid Sept 0900–1900; mid Sept–mid Nov 0930–1200, 1400–1730; FFr.10.

To reach the striped **Cathédrale de Notre-Dame du Puy**, with its magnificent frescos and carved capitals, follow *r. des Tables* to the 134 steps leading to the massive arched entrance, with carvings of the nativity and the death of Christ on the grand door within the porch. The first cathedral was built on this sacred Celtic site as a pilgrimage centre in the 5th century, following a series of miraculous visions of the Virgin. It later became one of the most important stops of the great trans-European pilgrimages (see box). One of the cathedral's famous objects is the Black Madonna, a 19th-century copy of a statue carved in dark cedar wood, said to have been an Egyptian representation of Isis brought back from the Crusades by King Louis IX (St Louis). The original was burned during the Revolution. The High Altar serves as its pedestal and the statue is carried in a procession during the mid-Aug Feast of the Assumption. The fine Romanesque **Cloître** (cloister) (open daily Apr–June 0930–1230, 1400–1800; July–Sept 0930–1930; Mon–Sat 0930–1200, Oct–Mar 1400–1600, and Sun 0930–1600; FFr.22) includes a museum of sacred art.

At Espaly St Marcel, 2 km away, is the **Rocher St Joseph** (Rock of St Joseph), with a diorama and another giant figure (open July–Sept daily 1400–1900; FFr.11; bus no. 4 from *pl. Michelet* to stop: *Arbrouset* in Espaly).

Pilgrims' Route to Santiago

After the Ascension, St James the Apostle left Palestine and journeyed to Galicia in Northern Spain. In 44AD, he returned home and was beheaded by Herod but his body was returned to Spain for burial. During the 8th–9th centuries, he was said to have appeared at critical moments on the battlefield as the Christians fought the encroaching Moors. His fame spread as Santiago Matamore (St James, Slayer of the Moors) until, in 813, his grave was rediscovered at what is now Santiago de Compostela. The pilgrimages began almost immediately, with people flocking in by the thousands from all across Europe. Magnificent churches sprang up in Santiago, and all along the pilgrim routes, from Le Puy, Paris, Vezelay and Arles, spreading the new Romanesque architectural style. By the 11th century, Santiago was declared the world's third Holy City and some 2 million people were making the trek each year, wearing the cockleshell emblem of St James. Today, people are still walking the route, aiming to arrive on the 25th July, the saint's festival .

Out of Town

Guided excursions (in French) to the Velay region depart Tues 1400 (July–Aug) offering three routes, each 2 hrs 30 mins, to explore the volcanic landscape. They leave from the Tourist Office which sells the tickets and are a combination of bus travel and walks to volcano tops such as Cheyrac and La Denise.

LE PUY–MONTÉLIMAR

Spectacular views of the gorges of the Haute Loire valley mark the start of this route, which then crosses the massif before descending into the upper Ardèche valley. From Aubenas to Montélimar the route encompasses antiquities spanning the Roman and medieval eras.

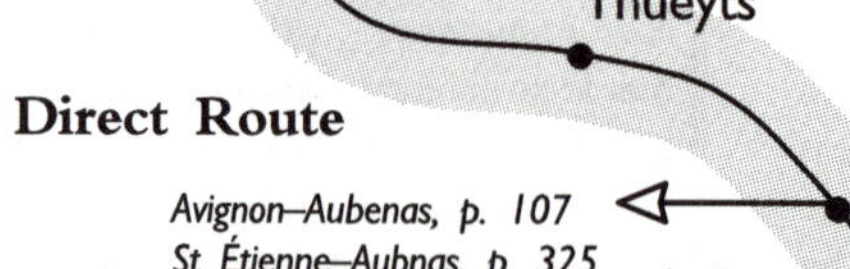

DIRECT ROUTE: 91 KM

ROUTES

DIRECT ROUTE

Leave Le Puy on the N88 south, signposted towards Aubenas and Mende. After 33km, take the left-hand fork onto the N102 through Aubenas (58 km on) and continue on the N102 to Montélimar (43km further). Alternatively, head east to Valence (see p. 212) where you can pick up the motorway or the N7 south to Montélimar. Allow 3 hrs.

SCENIC ROUTE

From Le Puy take the N88 south, turning left at Les Baraques onto the D27 to Solignac, following through to Le Monastier-sur-Gazeille. Leave on the D500 signposted to Pradelles, turning right on the D49 towards St Martin-de-Fugères and Goudet; 4km past Goudet take the D54 left to Arlempdes. Continue on the D54, turning right and following the

D500 until it meets the N102, where you turn left to Thueyts and Aubenas. Leave Aubenas on the N102, and turn left onto the D258 to Mirabel, then return on D258 and take a left on the D458 to St Jean-le-Centenier, following signposts along the D7 to the Grottes de Montbrun. Return to the N102, turning left and then right on the D107 to Alba, and then continue on to Viviers. From Viviers, cross the Rhône and follow the signs for Montélimar. Allow 1 day.

LE MONASTIER-SUR-GAZEILLE

Tourist Office: *30 r. St Pierre; tel: 04 71 08 37 76*, open Mon–Sat 1000–1200.

Sightseeing

Named after a 7th-century Benedictine monastery, Le Monastier still has an unusual **abbey church**, hidden away behind the small town's one km-long main street. Largely dating from the 15th-century, its colourful and elaborate 11th-century façade with intricate brickwork is rightly considered a masterpiece of the Romanesque in the region. Inside, there is a dramatic contrast between the austere granite pillars and flamboyant choir, highlighted by the superb organ (1518, but later restored). Behind the church is a **château**, flanked by four massive round towers, which dates from the mid 16th-century: the basement and ground floor house a **Museum** (open Tues–Sun, July–Aug 1030–1200, 1500–1900; Sept–June 1030–1200, 1430–1700), with displays on prehistory, local costumes and lacemaking, and a room devoted to Robert Louis Stevenson. Stevenson set out from here on his travels by donkey across the Cévennes (see p. 149), an event commemorated by a small stone memorial in front of the post office on *r. St Pierre*.

ARLEMPDES

As the D54 descends into the Loire Gorges, look out for the extraordinary village of Arlempdes. Perched 80m above a bend in the river on a volcanic piton, this ruined medieval château with a tiny village clustered at its base is one of the most remarkable – and photogenic – sites in the region.

Accommodation and Food

The welcoming **Hotel du Manoir**, *tel: 04 71 57 17 14* (cheap–moderate) is in the centre of the hamlet to the right of the old gateway. Past the gate is the **Auberge la Gentilhommiere**, a restaurant/salon de thé, *tel: 04 71 57 10 26* (moderate).

Sightseeing

In the middle of the village an 11th-century fortified gateway leads up to the **château**, built by the seigneurs of Montlaur in the 13th century and subsequently repeatedly sacked, despite its seemingly impenetrable position. Within the walls there is a tiny chapel, built from red volcanic rock; the view of the gorges from beside the chapel is superb. Collect the key to the château from the Hôtel du Manoir, or take a guided visit (FFr.20) every 30 mins, 1430–1800 daily, July–Aug, closed Tues.

THUEYTS

Tourist Office: *pl. du Champ de Mars, tel: 04 75 36 46 79*. Open Mon–Sat 1000–1215, 1600–1830.

Sightseeing

A characterful little town on the edge of an ancient lava flow jutting out across the Ardèche valley, Thueyts is surrounded by orchards and is a popular stopping point along this route, with craft shops, fruit stalls, and several cafés and restaurants.

Surrounding the main square, *pl. du Champ de Mars*, there are several 18th-century houses, one of which contains the **Musée de l'Ardèche Autrefois** (open daily 0900-1200, 1400-1800 in summer; by appointment in winter), which has displays and tableaux depicting traditional regional peasant life through the seasons.

Leaving the village on the N102, there is a viewpoint back down to the **Pont du Diable**, a remarkable stone arch framing the Ardèche as it squeezes between the volcanic rocks. There is also a walking trail (1hr 30mins circuit) alongside the river and up again via the narrow steps of the Échelle du Roi to the village.

AUBENAS

Tourist Office: *4 blvd Gambetta, 07204 Aubenas; tel: 04 75 35 24 87*, open Mon–Sat 0900–1200 and 1400–1800.

Accommodation and Food

Aubenas is well served with two-star hotel-restaurants, including the **Hôtel Ponson**, *quartier Ponson; tel: 04 75 35 07 78; fax: 04 75 93 86 61* (cheap) and the **Hôtel le Panoramic de l'Escrinet (LF)**, *col de l'Escrinet; tel: 04 75 87 10 11; fax: 04 75 87 10 34* (moderate). The **Hôtel-Restaurant Le Pinede**, *route du Camping; tel: 04 75 35 25 88; fax: 04 75 93 06 42* (cheap–moderate), has a lovely, quiet position on a hilltop behind the town, a pool and a reputable restaurant (moderate), while the old-fashioned **Hôtel les Negociants**, *pl. du Château, 3 r. J. Jaurès; tel: 04 75 35 18 74* (cheap), directly opposite the chateau, serves a broadly-based regional menu.

The **Hôtel-Restaurant Chez Jacques**, *9 r. Beranger de la Tour; tel: 04 75 93 88 74; fax: 04 75 35 37 54* (cheap), has a few, simple rooms and pleasant food. **Le Fournil**, *34 r. du 4 Septembre; tel: 04 75 93 58 68* (moderate–expensive) has gastronomic menus. Chain hotels include *Hf and Ib.*

Campsites: **Plan d'Eau**, *rte de Lussas; tel: 04 75 35 44 98* (caravans); **Camping La Chareyrasse**, *St Pierre-sous-Aubenas; tel: 04 75 35 14 59* (no caravans), and **Domaine de Gil**, *rte de Vals-les-Bains; tel: 04 75 94 63 63* (caravans).

Events

There is a market on *pl. du Château* on Sat, and *quartier des Oliviers* on Tues. The *Foire de l'Ardèche Méridionale* is held in the last week in June, with over 100 regional producers displaying their wares, a car and motorbike rally, and mock bull fights (*cours à la Camarguais*) with visiting *Gardians* from the Camargue (see p.87). For information, ask the Tourist Office for a copy of *Le Tambour.*

Sightseeing

A busy town perched on a clifftop high above the Ardèche river, Aubenas is surrounded by industrialized suburbs but its inner core, the *vieille ville*, is particularly attractive. At the centre of a network of cobbled streets sits the imposing **Château**, a hotch-potch of styles added principally between the 11th- and 18th-centuries. It now houses the *Hôtel de Ville* and the interior (which has several wood-panelled reception rooms furnished in 18th-century style) can only be visited on a guided tour (daily 1100, 1500, 1600, 1700, 1800 July–Aug, Tues–Sat 1100, 1500, 1600 June–Sept, Tues–Sat 1500 and 1600 Oct–May; FFr.15).

The finest church in town is the hexagonal 17th–18th-century **Dôme St-Benoit**, *r. du Dôme*. Next to the Tourist Office, an **orientation table**, *blvd Gambetta*, offers sweeping views across the Ardèche and the surrounding mountains.

PLATEAU DE CORION

Separating the Lower from the Higher Vivarais, the plateau du Corion comprises a series of volcanic cliffs and plateaux characterised by basalt ridges and eroded peaks (known locally as *dykes* and *necks* respectively). Thanks to its strategic position on the route between the Rhône and the Cévennes, **Mirabel** was once an important fortified town, although the fortress itself was torn down in 1628. All that remains is an impressive **tower** (private property, but you can walk round the outside) perched on the edge of a ridge above the village. From the tower there is a stunning panorama across the Lower Vivarais, the Auzon valley and the Ardèche gap.

In the neighbouring valley, the **Grottes des Montbrun** present an interesting spectacle: park at the farm on top of the plateau and follow the signs down the left-hand ravine to the grottos (open access, 40 mins rtn), which have been carved out of the cliff face on both sides of the ravine. Some of these ancient troglodyte dwellings are vast, with beds carved out of the walls and pens for animals; some even have two floors. There's absolutely no indication of their age – they could be anything from prehistoric to medieval – which adds to their aura of mystery.

ALBA-LA-ROMAINE

Tourist Office: **Alba Information**, *la Grande Rue, 07400 Alba-la-Romaine; tel: 04 75 52 45 86*, open daily 1000–1200 and Mon–Sat 1400–1800 (summer), 1500–1900 (winter).

Accommodation and Food

There are no hotels in Alba but the village's one *chambre d'hôte* receives rave reviews. Marie Françoise and Maurice Arlaud's **Le Jeu du Mail**, *tel: 04 75 52 41 59* (cheap), is an ancient farmhouse with very comfortable rooms, surrounded by vineyards, on the outskirts of the village. Alba has three restaurants, a bar and pizzeria. *GF* is represented here.

Sightseeing

During the Gallo-Roman period Alba was an important regional capital, *Alba Helviorum*, with jurisdiction over most of the lower Vivarais. It had all the trappings of a typical Roman city, including a forum, baths, amphitheatre, aqueduct, thermal baths and several temples. It became a bishopric in the 4th century but in the middle of the 5th century lost this role to Viviers, after which it went into decline and was eventually sacked during the barbarian invasions.

It was not until the Middle Ages that a new settlement arose on the site of the present-day village. The most accessible of the Roman remains is the **amphitheatre**, open continuously, on the east side of the D107 just below the village. Within Alba there is also a **Centre de Documentation Archaeologique**, *r. du Chabrol, tel: 04 75 52 46 42*, open daily 1400–1800 July–Aug, with finds from local archaeological digs.

The old town has a number of 15th-century houses and vaulted passageways, with the **Château d'Alba** (open daily 1000–1200 and 1500–1900, mid June–Sept) perched on a volcanic outcrop on its eastern flank. Rebuilt in the 17th century, on the site of an 11th-century keep, it features several restored rooms and temporary art exhibits.

VIVIERS

See p. 215.

MONTÉLIMAR

See p. 214.

LE PUY–VALENCE

This route traverses the Vivarais plateau, connecting the Auvergne with the Rhône valley. There are good views across rolling countryside, pastures and pine forests, and several pleasant villages along the route, but little in the way of demanding sightseeing.

DIRECT ROUTE: 107 KM

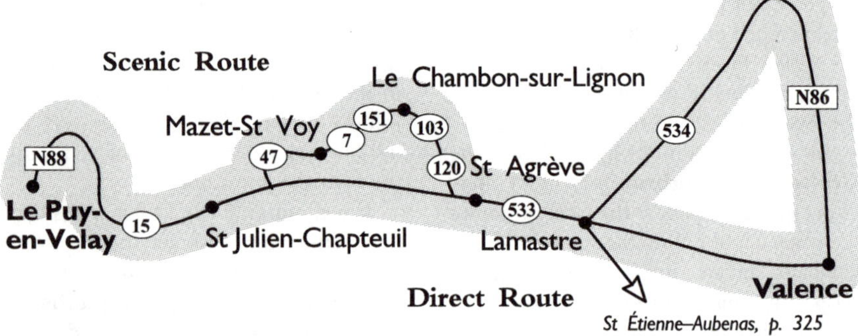

ROUTES

DIRECT ROUTE

Leave Le Puy on the N88 north signposted **St Étienne**, forking right on the outskirts of town, on to the D15 signposted **Valence**. At **St Agrève**, take the D533, which continues across the Rhône into Valence. Allow 2 hrs.

SCENIC ROUTE

Leave Le Puy on the N88 signposted **St Étienne**, forking right on the outskirts of town on to the D15 signposted **Valence**. The road passes through **St Julien-Chapteuil** before climbing up on to the plateau from where the **Pic du Lisieux** is indicated down the D47 on the left at La Chèze. Follow the road around on to the D7 then the D500 to enter **Mazet-St-Voy**, exiting on the D7 and then turning left on the D151 to **le Chambon-sur-Lignon**. Take the D103 and D120 to rejoin the D15 and enter **St Agrève**. From St Agrève follow the D533 to **Lamastre**, turn left onto the D534 to Tournon, from where you can head south to **Valence** on the N86, N7 or A7. Allow 1 day.

ST-JULIEN-CHAPTEUIL

Tourist Office: *pl. St. Robert, tel: 04 71 08 77 70.* Open Mon and Wed 0900–1200, Tues 1400–1730, Thurs 0900–1200 and 1400–1730, Fri 1000–1200 and 1430–1800, Sat 1000–1200 and 1430–1800.

Accommodation and Food

The friendly 2-star **Hôtel Barriol** (*LF*), *pl. du Marché, tel: 04 71 08 70 17; fax: 04 71 08 74 19* (cheap) run by the same family for four generations, also has a restaurant. Opposite, in the **Restaurant Vidal**, *pl. du Marché; tel: 04 71 08 70 50* (expensive) the chef, Jean-Pierre Vidal, is one of the rising stars of the region, serving imaginative regional specialities with a light touch, complemented by an extensive cellar. The restaurant is not atmospheric, but service is courteous. The main street, *r. Chaussade*, has several epiciers with home-made regional charcuterie.

Sightseeing

Dominating the village, the **parish church** of St Julien was built in the 11th century but has many later additions and alterations. From the platform behind it, there is a good view over the valley and the surrounding volcanic peaks, most notably the Suc de Monac and le Suc de Chapteuil. The village houses have the characteristic slate roofs of the region. Above the Tourist Office is a small **museum** (opening hours variable: enquire at desk) dedicated to **Jules Romains**, a local dramatist and essayist who achieved public recognition during the inter-war period.

MAZET-ST-VOY

Tourist Office: *La Halle Fermière; tel: 04 71 65 07 32.* Located in a purpose-built farmers' market on the outskirts of the village, with 18 different artisans and other local producers grouped together under its circular roof. As well as regional specialities (honey, cheeses, fruits, charcuterie and *paté des pigeons* amongst them) it also features craft demonstrations and exhibitions on the local environment and heritage, and a small botanical garden.

Accommodation and Food

Amongst the handful of hotels and restaurants in the village, the best is the small **Hôtel L'Escuelle**; *tel: 04 71 65 00 51.* Just outside the village (direction Fay-sur-Lignon) is the **Restaurant Odette-Ruel**, *Malagayte; tel: 04 71 65 02 33* (cheap) which houses a bakery, epicerie, café and restaurant; advance booking is recommended at weekends.

Sightseeing

The 11th-century **Église St Voy**, 1km to the south, is a charming rural chapel, built of granite with a slate tiled roof. During the 16th century it was an staunch outpost of Protestantism, as was neighbouring Chambon-sur-Lignon.

LE CHAMBON-SUR-LIGNON

Tourist Office: *1 la Place; tel: 04 71 59 71 56.* Open: Mon–Sat 0900–1200 and 1500–1830, Sun and holidays 1100–1200. Hotel and transport bookings. The town has long been established as a *station touristique* (principally for activities in the surrounding countryside such as golf, fishing, mountain-biking, cycling and walking) and consequently has a reasonable selection of hotels.

Echoing Sucs

One of the most notable features of this drive across the plateau is the presence of numerous volcanic pitons, known as *sucs*, which jut up like pimples from the eroded walls of ancient craters.

Many of these curious *sucs* are made up of fine-grained rock which is phonolithic, so that when you bang on the ground the noise resonates as if from a sounding board.

Despite its name the **Hôtel de la Plage** (*LF*), *r. de la Grande Fontaine; tel: 04 71 59 70 56;* is not on a beach but has two terraces overlooking the river and clean, well-kept rooms. Other possibilities include the **Hôtel Bel Horizon**, *24, chemin de la Molle; tel: 04 71 59 74 39;* (cheap–moderate) and the **Hôtel Clair Matin**, *les Barandons; tel: 04 71 59 73 03; fax: 04 71 65 87 86* (moderate).

ST AGRÈVE

Tourist Office: *Hôtel de Ville; tel: 04 75 30 15 06.*

Accommodation and Food

The centrally-placed **Hôtel Restaurant des Cevennes** (*LF*), *10 pl. de la Republique; tel: 04 75 30 10 22;* (cheap) has just ten rooms and a restaurant. The **Hotel Restaurant au Bois Sauvage** (*LF*), *rte de Valence; tel: 04 75 30 15 15; fax: 04 75 30 12 02* (cheap) is in a quiet position 500m from the centre, with a range of outdoor activities on offer. Just under 1km to the south-east the **Hôtel Clair Logis** (*LF*), *rte du Cheylard; tel: 04 75 30 13 24; fax: 04 75 30 22 05* (cheap) is built in mountain-chalet style, with a lovely situation overlooking a lake.

Campsites: the **Château Lacour**; *tel: 04 75 30 27 09* (caravan); the **Camping-Caravanning du Lac de Devesset**, *07320 Devesset; tel: 04 75 30 00 37* (caravan), both of which are two-stars, plus the three-star **Camping-Caravanning du Riou La Selle**, *le Riou La Selle; tel: 04 75 30 29 28* (caravan). Good food can be found at the **Hôtel Restaurant Boissy-Teyssier**, *pl. de Verdun; tel: 04 75 30 12 43* (cheap).

Sightseeing

The village styles itself *belvédère des Cévennes* with good reason, as you will discover by following the signposts to the *table d'orientation* at the top of Mount Chiniac (1120m) just behind the village centre, from where there is a superb panorama of the Cévennes chain, Gerbier de Jonc, the Pilat massif, and the Monts d'Auvergne.

LAMASTRE

See p.327.

GORGES DU DOUX

To the north of Lamastre, the route winds through the picturesque Doux river gorges, lined with vineyards and orchards. One of the best ways to see them is on the **Vivarais Railway**, built as part of the Ardèche and Haute-Loire network between 1868 and 1891 but run as a private concern since 1969.

A regular service now runs between Lamastre and Tournon, with at least one service in each direction using steam engines every day, with other trains (daily on weekdays and up to three in each direction on weekends) pulled by autorail.

From Lamastre the train descends towards Monteil, crossing the viaduct Garnier and the viaduct du Banchet before arriving in the picturesque village of **Boucieu-le-Roi**. From here it enters into the gorges until emerging by the **Clauzel Dam**, from where it runs alongside the **Canal des Allemands** (so called because it was built by prisoners of war), through a tunnel and into the **Gorge de Mondane**.

A steep descent brings the track down to an ancient stone bridge (when it was built in 1538 its 31m arch was the longest in the world) and a halt at Douce Plage. From here, the train winds its way alongside the Doux to St-Jean-de-Muzols and, finally, Tournon. For information contact: **Société CFTM**, *2 quai Jean Moulin, 69001 Lyon; tel: 04 78 28 83 34.*

Lyon

France's second city has long been forgotten by the powers-that-be in Paris. The people of the city (the Lyonnais) are reputed by their fellow citizens to be the unfriendliest in France. For many French people, Lyon is just somewhere to get through on their way south. But once they take a closer look, they invariably want to return. For this great metropolis at the junction of two of Europe's mightiest rivers – the Saône and Rhône – is very inviting. The people are hard-working and proud (this was the centre of the French Resistance during World War II), but also courteous and sociable. Lyon has been a crossroads since early Roman occupation in 43BC and is used to greeting strangers. The bustling city has much to offer the visitor – in particular its cuisine, served in traditional *bouchons* (inns). Many consider the city to be the capital of gastronomy. Lyon can also offer you the largest Renaissance quarter in France, museums galore and a thriving student-oriented nightlife. And everywhere the ambience seems distinctly southern, a reminder that the Mediterranean is not too far away.

Tourist Information

Tourist Office: *Pavilion du Tourisme, pl. Bellecour, 69000 Lyon* (east of *Lyon-Perrache* rail station); *tel: 04 72 77 69 69*. It provides free guides and maps to the city. Open June–mid Sept Mon–Fri 0900–1900, Sat 0900–1800; mid Sept–May Mon–Fri 0900–1800, Sat 0900–1700. Multi-lingual guides can be booked for tours. **Branches**: *pl. St Jean, av. A. Max; tel: 04 72 77 69 69*, just across the Saône from *pl. Bellecour*. Open June–mid Sept Mon–Sat 1000–1900, Sun 1000–1800; mid Sept–May Mon–Fri 0900–1300 and 1400–1800, Sat 0900–1700, Sun 1000–1700. **Centre d'Échanges**, *Perrache* rail station, with money exchange and accommodation service, maps etc. Open June–mid Sept Mon–Fri 0900–1800, Sat 0900–1700; mid Sept–May Mon–Fri 0900–1300 and 1400–1800, Sat 0900–1700. **Fourvière Esplanade** during the holiday season. Open Easter–mid June Tues–Sun 1000–1300 and 1330–1800; mid June–mid Sept Tues–Sun 1000–1250 and 1400–1900.

Centre Régional d'Information Jeunesse: *9 quai des Célestins; tel: 04 72 77 00 66*. Open Mon 1200–1900, Tues–Fri 1000–1900, Sat (Sept–June) 1000–1700. Closed end July–mid Aug. For student and youth information including jobs, accommodation, transport.

Arriving and Departing

Airport

Aéroport Lyon-Satolas: *32 km east of Lyon; tel: 04 72 22 72 21*. Facilities include restaurants, exchange office and tourist information. From the airport a regular bus service runs every 20 mins (30 mins on Sun) between 0600 and 2300 to and from *Perrache* rail station (via *Part-Dieu* rail station); FFr.50.

By Car

Thanks to recent investment in underground car parks, parking is somewhat easier then it used to be, particularly in central areas. Now there is as much space in multi-storeys as at parking meters on the streets. Central car parks include ones on *pl. des Celestins*, *pl. A.Poncet*, *r, de la République* (at *pl. le Viste*), *pl. des Terraux* and *quai R.Rolland*. Information from **Lyon Parc Auto**, *tel: 04 72 41 65 25*. It makes sense to park your car and sightsee by public transport.

By Bus

Perrache Bus Station: near the train station; *tel: 04 78 71 70 00*. Open 0630–1700. Services to Vienne, Annecy and Grenoble.

By Train

There are two mainline stations. Many trains stop at both, so check on your final destination. **Lyon-Perrache** is the more central, *tel: 08 36 35 35 35*. It provides tourist information and money exchange offices, luggage lockers, a restaurant and bar as well as **SOS Voyageurs** – an information and practical assistance service for passengers, *tel: 04 78 37 03 31* (open 0800–2000). The station is closed 0000–0500. For the town centre, head north from *pl. Carnot*; then a 5-min walk along *av. V.Hugo* to *pl. Bellecour*. **Lyon-Part-Dieu** station is on the east bank of the *Rhône* and serves the business district (same telephone number as *Lyon-Perrache* for information). It has a restaurant and luggage lockers. **SOS Voyageurs** open 0800–2200; *tel: 04 72 34 12 16*. Station closed 0130–0445.

Getting Around

Lyon is big (population 1.5 million). Nature, in the form of the two rivers, the **Saône** and the **Rhône**, has divided it into three distinct sections.

On the west bank of the *Saône* is **Vieux Lyon (Old Lyon)**, an area of attractive Renaissance streets. On the east bank of the *Rhône* is the **business area**, with *Part-Dieu* rail station, its big shopping centre and many of the city's high-rise offices and apartment blocks. In between, bordered by the *Saône* and *Rhône*, is the partly-pedestrianised **centre** of the city, running from *Perrache* railway station to *pl. Bellecour,* the **Hôtel de Ville** and the ancient quarters of **Les Terreaux**. Beyond is **La Croix-Rousse**, centre of the city's silk weaving industry in the 15th century. This area and **Vieux Lyon** across the *Saône* are manageable on foot.

To go further afield, take a bus, funicular *(funiculaire)* or underground train *(métro)* which are all run by **TCL** *(Transports en Commun Lyonnais)*; *tel: 04 78 71 70 70*. Information booths can be found everywhere, including the rail stations and main metro stops. Get the transport map (*plan de réseau*) from the tourist office or any *TCL* branch.

Lyon is a relatively safe city. Wander anywhere during the day. At night some care is needed around Perrache station.

Tickets

Tickets for buses and the underground are valid for 1 hour (FFr.7.80). A carnet of 10 costs FFr.66.50, students FFr.54. A **Ticket Liberté** (FFr.23.50) provides unlimited travel for one day on all *TCL* services; available from tourist offices, *TCL* booths or automatic vending machines (which take coins or credit cards).

The **Metro** is modern, clean and safe. Its four lines, unimaginatively named A, B, C and D, criss-cross the city, operating 0500–0000.

Funiculaires depart every 10 mins

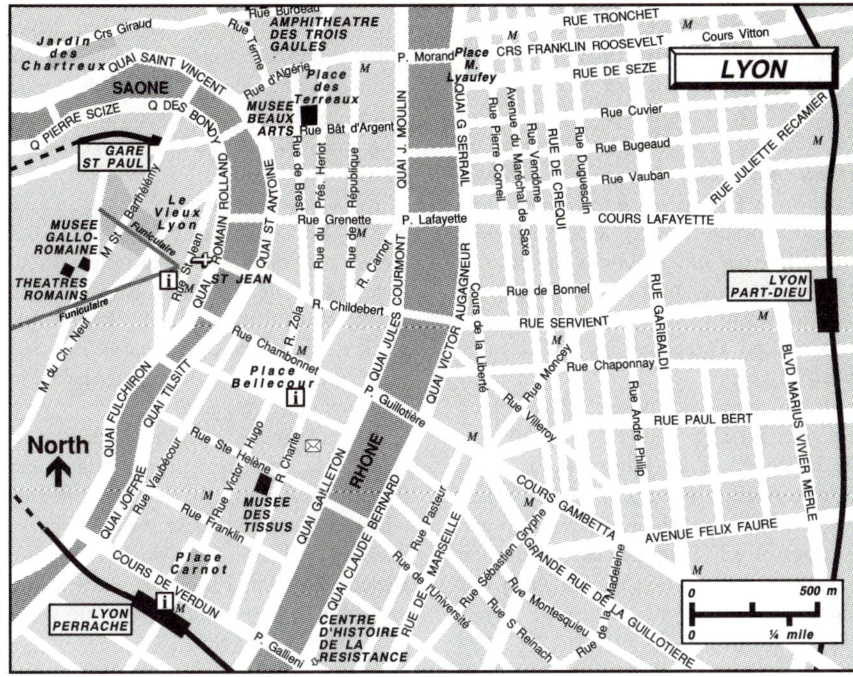

from *Vieux Lyon* metro station, pulled by cables up steep, curving tracks to the **Roman theatre** at *St Just* (0545–2400) and the **Fourvière Esplanade** high above the city (0600–2200).

Buses cover every corner of Lyon, 0500–2400 with a limited night bus service. Same ticket price as above.

For 24-hr **taxis**, *tel: 04 78 28 23 23.* Fare to the airport about FFr.250.

Car Hire: **Avis**, *Lyon-Perrache station, tel: 04 78 37 14 23*; also at *Part-Dieu station, tel: 04 72 33 37 19*, and the *airport, tel: 04 72 22 75 25.* **Budget**, *201 av. Berthelot, tel: 04 78 72 46 09*; also at *Part-Dieu station, tel: 04 72 31 61 55*, and the *airport, tel: 04 72 22 74 74.*

Bike Hire: **Crit Neway VTT**, *85 cours Gambetta, tel: 04 78 95 37 09.* **Gitane Espace**, *139 av. du Mar de Saxe, tel: 04 78 60 46 40.*

Staying in Lyon

Accommodation

Central Bookings (Allotel), *tel: 04 78 38 29 29.*

Lyon is a business town and filled during the week with briefcases and expense-accounts. The central hotels are often booked out Mon–Thur but this is a big city and you can always find a room somewhere. Chain hotels include *Ca, Cn, CL, CS, Et, F1, Hf, Ho, Ib, IH, Me, Mc, MO, Nv, Pu, RC* and *Sf.*

La Cour des Loges, *6 r. du Boeuf, tel: 04 78 42 75 75, fax: 04 72 40 93 61* (expensive) occupies a graceful Renaissance mansion in the heart of the old town. **Hôtel Plaza République**, *5 r. Stella; tel: 04 78 37 50 50, fax: 04 78 42 33 34* (moderate–expensive), centrally-situated near *pl. Bellecour*, is small but smart and has efficient friendly service. The nearby **Hôtel-des-Beaux-Arts**, *75 r. du Président Herriot; tel: 04 78 38 09 50, fax: 04 78 42 19 19* (moderate–expensive) has 79 rooms. For a budget alternative, try **Hôtel Moderne**, *15 r. Dubois, 69005 Lyon, tel: 04 78 42 21 83, fax: 04 77 41 04 40* (cheap). Budget accommodation abounds – for other options, try *cours de Verdun, r. V. Hugo* near **Perrache station**; *pl. Croix-Paquet* and around the *Hôtel de Ville* in **Les Terreaux**; and *r. Lainerie* in **Vieux Lyon**.

If you prefer to stay out of town, go 6 km west on D75 to the 2-star **Auberge de la Vallée et Le Fleury (LF)**, *39 av. Chater, Francheville, 69340 Rhône, tel: 04 78 59 11 88, fax: 04 78 59 47 16* (cheap).

Alternatively, the grandest and most expensive of all is the **Château de Bagnols**, *Amanresorts Le Bourg, 69620 Bagnols; tel: 04 74 71 40 00; fax: 04 74 71 40 49* (expensive), 24km north-west of the city on the D38 (off the D485).

HI: *51 r. R. Salengro, 69200 Vénissieux; tel: 04 78 76 39 23.* Just outside the city – take bus no. 35 (last bus at 2100) from *pl. Bellecour* to *George-Lévy* (30-mins).

Centre International de Séjour: *46 r. du Commandant Pegoud; tel: 04 78 01 23 45* (take bus no. 53 from *Perrache*, direction *St Priest*, to stop: *États-Unis Beauvisage.*

Campsite: **Camping International de Lyon**, *Porte de Lyon, 69570 Dardill, tel: 04 78 35 64 55* (caravans; open year-round). Take bus nos 3 or 19 from the *Hôtel de Ville*, direction *Ecully-Dardilly* to *Parc d' Affaires*.

Eating and Drinking

Lyon boasts some of the best restaurants in France and more famous chefs than almost any other city in Europe. Some visitors come just for the food which is undeniably rich and full of flavour. Throughout the city, but especially in *Vieux Lyon*, tables spill out onto the streets, offering you the bonus of being able to watch all the varied passers-by during your meal and probably long afterwards as you linger over the last glass of wine.

Even on a tight budget you can eat very well. The cuisine is rarely fancy, but always presented with great attention to detail. Meals are very much based on meat dishes, particularly pork, the local *Bresse* chicken, plump sausages (*andouillettes*) and tripe, often served with potatoes baked in a creamy sauce (*gratinées*).

You might like to try local dishes like *la morue à la lyonnaise* (salt cod flaked and fried with onions), *la poularde demi-deuil* (chicken with truffles) or even *la matelote d'anguille* (eel stew with wine and herbs). Expect also to find hot *pâtés* and seafood, invariably with accompanying sauces and lots of fresh vegetables.

Countless small cafés serve imaginative *plats du jour*, the chef's whim of the day.

The most traditional Lyonnais restaurants are the *bouchons* (travellers' inns), mainly in *Les Terreaux* and *Vieux Lyon*. Twenty or so survive, serving hearty meals based on tripe, pork and sausages washed down with local Beaujolais wines. The oldest is **Le Soleil**, *2 r. St Georges; tel: 04 78 37 60 02*, in *Vieux Lyon.*

For a really memorable meal, head for **Léon de Lyon (RC)** *1 r. Pleney; tel: 04 78 28 11 33* (expensive). Decorated in old Lyonnais style, it has elegant panelling and stained glass, while its chef-owner, **Jean-Paul la Combe**, has one of the best reputations in town, as well as owning a cellar of 40,000 bottles.

For good eateries in **Vieux Lyon**, head for *pl. Neuve St Jean* and *pl. de la Baleine.* Try **L'Amphitryon**, *33 r. St Jean, tel: 04 78 37 23 68* (cheap), for inexpensive menus and outside tables. Away from this busy tourist area, the *r. des Marroniers* just to the east of *pl. Bellecour,* off *pl. Antonin Poncet*, is a good bet. **Les Trois Tonneaux**, *3 r. des Marronniers; tel: 04 78 37 34 72* (cheap) includes traditional *Lyonnais* dishes in its menus. Or try the streets around *Cordeliers* metro, including *r. Mercière*, which is devoted to restaurants.

Communications

Post Office: *pl. A. Poncet; tel: 04 72 40 65 22,* next to *pl. Bellecour.* Facilities include poste restante, photocopying, telephones and currency exchange. Open Mon–Fri 0800–1900, Sat 0800–1200.

Money

There are **Thomas Cook bureaux de change** at both *Part-Dieu* and *Perrache* stations. The bureaux at *Part-Dieu, tel: 04 72 33 48 55*, is open daily 0800–1900. *Perrache, tel: 04 78 38 38 84*, opens daily 0830–1200, 1300–1845. **AOC** money exchange has 8 branches, including the airport and *St Jean* tourist office, *av.A. Max*. **BNP** has branches with exchange facilties at *4 pl. le Viste, 37 r. Victor Hugo;* and *145 cours Lafayette* (near *Part-Dieu* station).

Consulates

Canada: *74 r. de Bonnel; tel: 04 72 61 15 25*, near Part-Dieu. Open Mon–Fri 1000–1200.
UK: *24 r. Childebert; tel: 04 78 37 59 67.* Follow *r. de la République* to metro *Bellecour.* Open Mon–Fri 1000–1230 and 1400–1730.

Entertainment

Theatres, a resident opera company, film, ballet and dancing late into the night – Lyon has all the big-city attractions. The weekly publication, *Lyon Poche,* lists the week's events (FFr.7 from news-stands).

Minute Movies

The famous cinema pioneers, Auguste and Louis Lumière, grew up in Lyon. Their photographer father, Auguste, moved the family there in 1870 when they were 8 and 6 years old. After living first in *r. de l'Hôtel de Ville*, he had a small château built in the *Monplaisir* district just south of *Part-Dieu*. Today it houses the **Institut Lumière**.

The brothers attended *La Martinière* technical *lycée* where Louis developed the *Etiquette Bleue*, a dry photographic plate which the family's small factory at *Monplaisir* began manufacturing. Further experiments led to the first 'moving pictures' when they used a hand-operated camera to film the factory's workers coming out on a bright sunny day in 1895. *Sortie des Usines Lumière* only lasted 41 seconds but caused a sensation when it was premiered at a national photography congress in Lyon shortly afterwards.

Cinema

Lyon was birthplace of the cinema; the **Lumière** brothers invented moving pictures while working with their father, a local photographer. Their legacy remains in the city's numerous cinemas, as well as the **Institut Lumière**, *r. du Premier Film; tel: 04 78 78 18 95,* south-east of the centre in *Montplaisir* (metro: *Montplaisir-Lumière*). It shows films free on Tues and Thur during the summer on the square outside.

Clubs

Lyon is a student city so clubs and discos abound. The best areas are near the Hôtel de Ville in *r. Algérie* and *pl. des Terreaux*, or along *quai Pierre Scize* on the *Vieux Lyon* side of the *Saône*. These do not get going until after midnight so head to a bar first. Most discos/clubs charge entry, up to FFr.100 at weekends (including your first drink).

Dance and Opera

Maison de la Danse, *Théâtre du 8ème, 8 av. J.Mermoz; tel: 04 78 75 88 88*, for modern dance, Latin and African, as well as classical ballet.

The 1200-seat **Lyon Opera House**, *9 quai J.Moulin*, just east of the *Hôtel de Ville*, soars up to 18 different seating levels. Under the orchestral direction of Kent Nagano, the company is now one of Europe's finest. Reservations: *tel: 04 72 00 45 45*, from 1100–1900. Seats cost FFr.70–360.

Puppets

Lyon was birthplace of **Guignol**, the French equivalent of *Mr Punch,* who proceeds through a series of stock adventures, beating fellow puppets over the head as he goes.

The **Guignol de Lyon** theatre, *2 r. Louis Carrand; tel: 04 78 28 92 57*, in Vieux Lyon, puts on classical performances for children and adults alike.

Theatre

The Lyonnais love their theatre and boast 15 different stages throughout the city. The most illustrious is the Italianate **Théâtre des Célestins**, *4 r. C.Dullin; tel: 04 78 37 50 51*, just north-west of *pl. Bellecour.* Tickets cost from FFr.70–250; the cheapest are on sale the evening of the performance.

Events

May: **Biennale Theatre Jeune Public**; *tel: 04 78 64 14 24*, an international festival of improvisation.

May–June: **Festival Estival du Vieux Lyon**; *tel: 04 78 42 39 04*. Chamber music.

May–Sept: **Summer festival of music and theatre**; *tel: 04 72 10 30 30.*

Sept: **Les Musicades festival of chamber music**; *tel: 04 78 39 28 41* and **Biennale de la Dance**; *tel: 04 72 40 26 26* (alternates with a **modern art festival**).

Oct: **Grand Prix de Tennis**, *Palais des Sports; tel: 04 78 23 45 45.*

Nov: **Festival de Musique du Vieux Lyon**: *tel: 04 78 42 39 04*. Sacred music takes over the churches with Gregorian chanting and organ recitals.

8 Dec: **Fête des Lumières** when everyone places a lit candle in their window following a tradition started on 8 Dec 1852 when a statue of the Virgin Mary was unveiled on *Fourvière Esplanade.*

Puppet Monster

Lyon's famous puppet character, Guignol, was created by Laurent Mourguet who was born into a family of silk workers in the *St Georges* district in 1768. As a child he loved going to the theatre and became fascinated by puppets. Though his first job was as a tooth-puller, he gave puppet shows both outdoors and in a theatre in *r. Lainerie*.

His rise to fame came when he invented a glove puppet activated by three fingers. Being much easier to operate than the conventional string one, it enabled him to create larger-than-life characters, which he invariably based on real people. The first was a Beaujolais-swigging cobbler called Gnafron, but the most famous was the witty Guignol who constantly poked fun at the authorities and the failings of his friends.

Shopping

The poshest shops for haute couture, jewellery and china are grouped along *r. E. Zola, r. Gasparin* and *r. Président Herriot* between *p. Bellecour* and *p. des Jacobins*. For less exhalted purchases, take a short detour east along *r. de la République* to department stores like **Printemps**, **Prisunic-Grand Bazar** and **Galeries Lafayette**. Antique shops are gathered along *r. A. Comte* beyond *Perrache* station. The **Part-Dieu** station complex houses 260 shops on four levels, one of the largest shopping centres in Europe.

To discover where all the wonderful fresh produce comes from, wander round Lyon's great markets, open daily except Mon. The largest and most animated are at *quai St Antoine* on the *Saône*, west of *Cordeliers* metro, and along *blvd de la Croix-Rousse*, north of *Les Terreaux*.

The covered market at **Les Halles** is grandiose and expensive, but more varied, with meat joining the fruit and vegetables. Don't miss the **Renée et Renée** cheese shop in the market – it's one of the best in France; *tel: 04 78 62 30 78*.

Sightseeing

Like Paris, the best way to see Lyon is to stroll. Two hour **guided walks** in English with themes like *Vieux-Lyon, Modern Lyon* and *Museums* are available on Saturdays from the Tourist Office, *pl. Bellecour,* departing 1430; also Sun Apr–Oct at 1530 (FFr.51). For **coach tours** to local gardens and around Lyon by night; *tel: 04 78 42 25 75*. A general **bus tour** of the city operates Apr–Oct; contact **Cars Philibert**, *tel: 04 78 98 56 98*.

One of the most pleasant ways to see Lyon is from the river, especially after dark when over 100 buildings are floodlit. **Boat trips** run throughout the year from *quai C. Bernard* operated by **Naviginter**, *13 bis quai Rambaud, tel: 04 78 42 96 81,* lasting 1hr–1hr 20 mins (FFr.42); lunch and dinner cruises from FFr.200.

Museums

To see more than one museum, a 3-day **Key to Lyon** chequebook, available from Tourist Offices (FFr.90), includes a conducted or audio-guided city tour, admission to six museums and one-day travel pass.

Pl. des Terreaux, a bustling landmark, boasts the best museum in the city – **Musée des Beaux Arts,** *20 pl. des Terreaux; tel: 04 72 10 17 40* (open Wed–Sun 1030–1800; FFr.20). France's second-largest fine arts museum, after the Louvre, it occupies the former **Abbaye des Dames de St Pierre**, a 17th-century Benedictine convent, and contains French, Italian, Spanish, Flemish and Dutch paintings from the Middle Ages up to the present day. Sculpture and tapestries are on show, as well as antiquities from places such as Egypt and Cyprus.

The **Musée d'Art Contemporain**, *Cité Internationale, quai C. de Gaulle; tel: 04 72 69 17 17* (open Wed–Sun 1200–1800; FFr.20) is housed in a specially-designed building opened in 1995, and contains post-1960 works.

Just across **Pont Gallieni** from the Bellecour Tourist Office, **Le Centre d'Histoire de la Résistance et de la Déportation**, *14 av. Berthelot; tel: 04 78 72 23 11* (open Wed–Sun 0900–1730; FFr.20) is the most poignant museum in Lyon. It marks the history of Lyon during the German occupation in World War II when the city was the capital of the French Resistance. Five times a day, it shows a film, *Procès Barbie, Justice pour la mémoire et l'histoire*, about the trial of the reviled Nazi, Claus Barbie, which took place in the city in 1987.

Silk Capital of Europe

The hilly **Croix-Rousse** quarter was the centre of Lyon's silk industry which made the city one of the wealthiest in Europe in the 15th century. The weavers (*canuts*) operated no less than 28,000 looms. Narrow passageways called *trabules* (from the Latin word *transambulare* (walk across)), which enabled them to carry their fabrics from one street to another, run through many of the buildings. Old looms are still in use at **Maison des Canuts**, *10–12 r. d'Ivry; tel: 04 78 28 62 04* (open Mon–Fri 0830–1200, 1400–1830; Sat 0900–1200, 1400–1800; FFr.6). The **Musée des Tissus**, *34 r. de la Charité; tel: 04 78 37 15 05* (open Tues–Sun 1000–1730; FFr.26) in the 18th-century Hôtel de Villeroy, south of *pl. Bellecour,* is another reminder of Lyon's textile industry.

Old Town

Renovated mansions abound in the **St Jean, St Paul** and **St Georges** quarters of the **Vieux Ville** leading back from the west bank of the *Sôane*. The best preserved Renaissance area in France, it was the first urban district in the country to be officially designated as a conservation area and is still the largest. The elegant old façades include features like mullioned windows, galleries and towers with spiral staircases. The **Cathédrale St Jean**, started in 1180, is a mixture of styles and has a 14th-century astronomical clock which shows feast days well into the 21st century. Beside it are the remains of an 11th-century **cloister**.

Roman Lyon

Julius Caesar was responsible for developing the Roman town of *Lugdunum*, capital of the Three Gauls, centred on the hillside of **Fourvière** above the old town. The funicular from *Vieux Lyon* metro station climbs the hill to the **Esplanade** from where you get a superb view over the city and its two rivers. The **Basilica de Notre Dame-de-Fourvière**, whose turrets and ornate interior are typical of late 19th-century architecture, occupies a commanding position on the hillside. Nearby is the underground **Musée de la Civilisation Gallo-Romain** *17 r. Cléberg; tel: 04 78 25 94 68* (open Wed–Sun 0930–1200, 1400–1800; FFr.20) opened in 1975 in the *Fourvière Archaeological Park*. Cleverly designed to embrace the contours of the hill, it vividly evokes Roman times during the first four centuries AD. The outstanding collection includes a rare and beautiful mosaic, coins, pottery and swords. The park's other notable features, just down the hill from the museum, are the two **Théâtres Romains**, *8 r. de l'Antiquaille* (open 0900 to dusk; free). Both still have much of their seating intact and the remains of gigantic columns. The **Grand Théâtre** (108m in diameter) is the oldest amphitheatre in France. Built in 15BC to seat 10,000 spectators, it is still used for summer events and spectacles. The smaller **Odéon** (theatre) has a mosaic floor.

North of *pl. des Terreaux* in *Croix Rousse* is another vestige of the city's Roman past – **L'Amphithéâtre des Trois Gaules**, *Jardin des Plantes* (open dawn–dusk; free), built in 19AD, is the site of an altar built for Emperor Augustus, the founder of Lyon.

Modern Lyon

The most modern part of the city, east of the *Rhône*, includes the university area to the south and a new campus, the **Cité Internationale**, north of the **Parc de la Tête d'Or**, which houses Interpol's HQ. In between, the city's commercial centre lies around the new **Part-Dieu** development.

LYON–AVIGNON

This route follows the massive River Rhône as it descends from Lyon into Provence, through a broad corridor wedged between the Préalpes and the Massif Central. The great river is a constant presence but the landscapes change with the passing miles, encompassing scenery as diverse as fertile vineyards and orchards, feudal ruins perched high above the plain, towns and cities spreading across the river's embankments, and the great industrial enterprises of the valley.

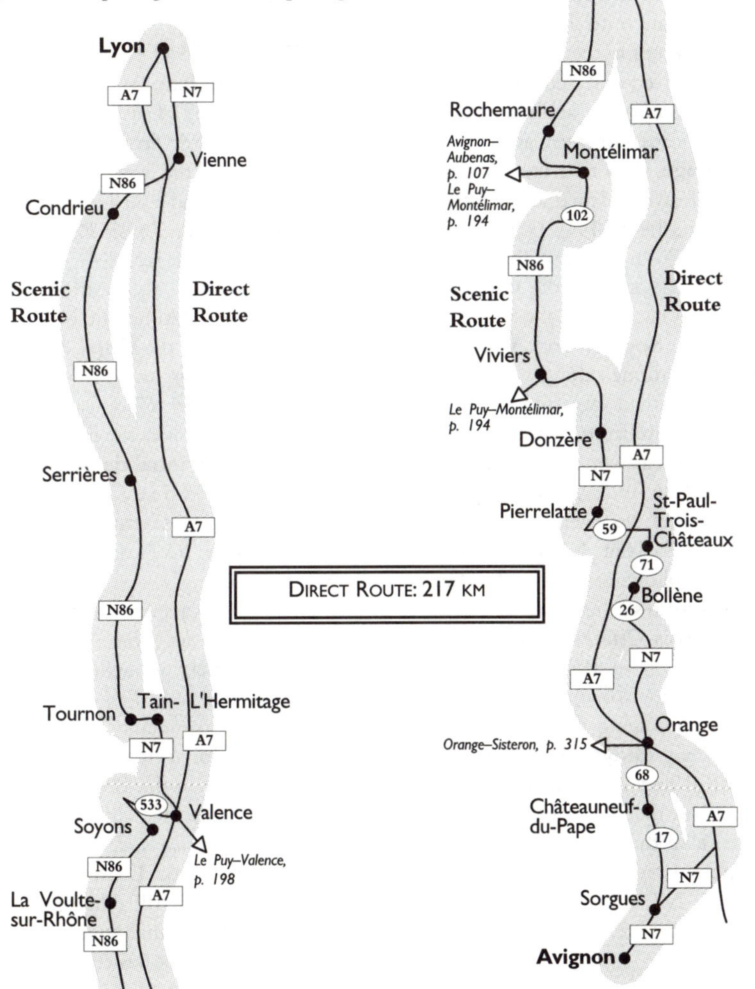

209

ROUTES

DIRECT ROUTE

Leave Lyon on autoroute A7, following it all the way south until the main Avignon turn-off at junction 23. Distance: 217 km; allow 3–4 hrs.

SCENIC ROUTE

Follow signs out of Lyon centre for autoroute A7 to Marseilles, taking the Solaize exit and going through the village to turn right onto the N7. Follow this through to **Vienne**, then cross the Rhône to St Roman-en-Gal and take the N86 through Condrieu and Serriére to **Tournon**. Cross the river again to **Tain L'Hermitage**, then take the N7 south to **Valence**. Leave Valence across the Pont F. Mistral on the N532 to Le Puy, turning onto the D533 in St Péray, then immediately left at the sign for the **Château de Crussol**. Go back down the hill and take the N86 to **Soyons** and **Voulte-sur-Rhône**. Continue along the N86 to Rochemaure, then cross the river on the D11 into **Montélimar**.

Leave the city on the N102, turning left on the N86 through **Viviers** and then left back across the river on the D486 to Donzère. Take the N7 down through Pierrelatte, following signs to **La Ferme aux Crocodiles**, then take the D59 to **St-Paul-Trois-Châteaux**. Take the D71 in the direction of Bollène, turning left (1.5 km before town) at the Église St Pierre and following signs up the hill to the **Site Trogolodyte de Barry**. Return to the road and continue into **Bollène**. Continue on the N7 through to Orange and then take the D68 to **Châteauneuf-du-Pape**. Leave here on the D17 and rejoin the N7 at Sorgues to arrive in Avignon. Distance: 287 km; allow 2–3 days.

VIENNE

Tourist Office: *cours Brillier; tel: 04 74 85 12 62*. Open mid June–mid Sept Mon–Sat 0900–1230, 1330–1900, Sun 1000–1200, 1430–1800; mid Sept–mid June Mon–Sat 0830–1200, 1400-1800. Comprehensive brochures detailing Vienne's history, attractions, hotels and restaurants. **Guided visits** July–Aug depart from the tourist office Mon–Fri 1000, 1500; Sat–Sun departures from the Théâtre Antique at 1500; FFr 40.

ACCOMMODATION AND FOOD

Chain hotels include *Ib*. Vienne's top hotel is **La Pyramide**, *14 blvd Fernand-Point; tel: 04 74 53 01 96; fax: 04 74 85 69 73* (expensive) on the south side of town, with 20 rooms and a well-regarded restaurant. **Le Central**, *7 r. de l'Archevêche; tel: 04 74 85 18 38; fax: 04 74 31 96 33* (cheap) is bang in the heart of the city, with 25 rooms. Although old-fashioned and slightly stuffy, the **Hôtel de la Poste**, *47 cours Romestang; tel: 04 74 85 02 04; fax: 04 74 85 16 17* (cheap), has good value rooms and is centrally located. **HI**: **Centre International de Séjour**, *11 quai Riondet; tel: 04 74 53 21 97; fax: 04 74 31 98 93*. **Campsite**: **Camping de Leveau**, *rte de Leveau; tel: 04 74 85 23 15* (caravans; open Apr–Sept).

Vienne offers plenty of choice for eating out, with *r. des Clercs* a good street for browsing a variety of menus. At the end of the road, the *r. de la Table Ronde* has two good restaurants, notably the cheerful **Au Petit Chez Soi** at *no.6; tel: 04 74 85 19 77* (cheap), where the Belgian chef serves moules in numerous different sauces as well as *carbonade flamande* and other well-prepared dishes, and **L'Estancot** at *no.4; tel: 04 74 85 12 09* (cheap), which is slightly more formal, with inventive menus and excellent desserts.

SIGHTSEEING

Vienne was a major colony under Roman rule, and with some 30,000 inhabitants one of the largest towns in Gaul. During the 4th and 5th centuries it again flourished as the capital of a vast diocese and one of the residences of the Burgundy dynasty, but its true golden age was in the 7th century, when it had 12 monasteries and became known as Holy Vienne. In 1450 it was annexed by the French crown and gradually eclipsed as a commercial centre by its northern neighbour Lyon.

Vienne's historical attractions are scattered liberally throughout the old city centre: at its heart is a superb temple, the **Temple Auguste et Livie**, on *pl. du Palais*, once part of the forum, whilst slightly to the north the **Jardin Archéologique du Cybèle**, off *pl. Miremont* (open access), contains the remains of a Cybeline temple and two imposing archways. A steep walk up from the centre brings you to the vast **Théâtre Antique**, *r. du Cirque* (open May–Aug daily 0930–1300, 1400–1800; Oct–Mar Wed–Sat 1000–1200, 1400–1700, Sun 1400–1800; FFr. 10; admission on a combined ticket with the cloister and two museums, FFr. 20). There are superb views of the town and the Rhône from the top tiers of the theatre. Vienne's main museum, the **Musée des Beaux-Arts et d'Archéologie**, is on the first floor of the old Halle à Grains, *pl. Miremont; tel: 04 74 85 50 42* (open Apr–mid Oct Wed–Mon 0930–1300, 1400–1800; mid Oct–Mar Wed–Sat 1000–1200, 1400-1700, Sun 1400–1800; prices as for Théâtre). Although this fairly extensive collection spans the centuries from prehistoric artefacts to 18th-century faïence, it is unimaginatively presented and the atmosphere is that of a dull, dusty provincial museum; the best pieces are the Roman silverware dating from the 3rd century AD. Further down towards the river the **Église-Musée St-Pierre**, *pl. St Pierre* (same hours and prices as Musée des Beaux-Arts), houses the town's lapidary collection (tombstones, statues and so on) inside a 5th-century church which lays claim to being one of the earliest cathedrals in France and was the traditional burial place of the bishops of Vienne. Although much altered over the centuries, the interior (with a timber-roofed nave) is still worth seeing.

More funerary monuments are to be found in the **Église et Cloître de St-André-le-Bas**, *r. des Clercs* (hours and prices as above). Once part of a 6th-century abbey, parts of the complex date from the 9th century but most, including the small cloister, belongs to the 12th century. Both church and cloisters are rich with imaginatively decorated capitals. Finally, the 12th–16th-century **Cathédrale St-Maurice**, *r. Boson; tel: 04 74 85 18 43,* features a Flamboyant west front with three elaborately decorated portals and a soaring Gothic vaulted nave surrounded by Romanesque chapels, many filled with fine statues.

VIENNE TO VALENCE

Tourist Offices: **Tournon:** *Hôtel de la Tourette, quai Farconnet* (opposite the large car park)*; tel: 04 75 08 10 23* (open summer Mon–Sat 0930–1200, 1400–1900; winter Tue–Sat 0930–1200, 1400-1830; **Tain-l'Hermitage**: *70 ave J. Jaurès; tel: 04 75 08 06 81* (open Mon–Sat 0900–1200, 1400-1800).

Crossing over the Rhône from Vienne, you will immediately encounter the extensive Roman ruins of **St-Roman-en-Gal** to the right after the bridge (open Apr–Sept daily 0900–1200, 1400–1900; Oct–Mar daily 0900–1200, 1400–1700; FFr.8; the main car park is on the left).

This mainly 1st-3rd century AD Roman settlement covers a large site, with villas, workshops, shops and warehouses. Particularly notable is the **Maison des Dieux Océans** (House of the Sea Gods), with mosaics comprising images of Neptune and other marine deities. A new archaeological museum, with mosaics previously housed in the Église-Musée St-Pierre, opened here in late 1996.

Continuing south along the west bank of the Rhône the scenery is still primarily industrial, but squeezed between the river and the approaching flanks of the Parc Régional du Pilat are several tiny but highly renowned vineyards, such as Côte Rotie, Condrieu, Croze-Hermitage and Hermitage. There are plenty of opportunities to stop at *caveaux* along the way to pick up a bottle (or even a case) or two of these excellent wines. Beyond Serrières, the route runs closer to the river itself and becomes more scenic, with vineyards giving way to orchards (roadside fruit stalls are plentiful), until you arrive at the attractive riverside town of **Tournon.** Rising up a few paces away from the tourist office is the forbidding-looking **Château-Musée de Tournon**, *pl. A. Faure; tel: 04 75 08 10 30* (open daily June-Aug 1000–1200, 1400–1800; Apr, May, Sept 1400–1800; Oct Wed–Mon 1400–1700; FFr.20). Inside, the museum features local history (including a room devoted to Marc Seguin, who built the first ever suspension bridge across the Rhône at Tournon in 1825), paintings, sculptures, and a charming Renaissance chapel alongside a rooftop garden overlooking the river. The main terrace, reached as you follow the exit route, is equally dramatic, with views across to the vineyards of Tain L'Hermitage opposite.

These vineyards are, in fact, the principal attraction of **Tain-l'Hermitage**, which is reached via the Pont Gustave Toursier from Tournon. The Tourist Office provides leaflets on the vineyards and surrounding attractions. Several blocks back from the river front is the **Cave de Tain-l'Hermitage**, *22 rte de Larnage; tel: 04 75 08 20 87* (open daily 0900–1200, 1400-1800) where you can sample (and buy) their superb wines as well as those from the equally famous St Joseph region across the river and others nearby.

VALENCE

Tourist Office: *Parvis de la Gare; tel: 04 75 44 90 40.* Open June–Aug Mon–Sat 0900–1900, Sun 0900–1200; Sept–May Mon–Sat 0900–1230, 1400–1830, Sun 0900–1200.

Accommodation and Food

Chains include *Ca, Ib, Nv.* Within the centre there are plenty of reasonably-priced options including the quietly-situated **Saint-Jacques** *(LF), 9 fauborg St Jacques; tel: 04 75 42 44 60; fax: 04 75 42 70 88* (cheap) and the recently-renovated **Hôtel de l'Europe**, *15 av. F. Faure; tel: 04 75 43 02 16; fax: 04 75 55 43 61 75* (cheap–moderate), which has 26 rooms. One of the best central hotels is the new **Hôtel Atrium**, *r. J.-L. Barrault; tel: 04 75 55 53 62; fax: 04 75 55 53 68* (cheap–moderate), which has spacious, attractive rooms with their own kitchenettes. **Campsite**: **Camping Municipal de l'Eperviere**, 1 km south of town centre off N7*; tel: 04 75 42 32 00* (caravans).

The town's top gourmet restaurant is **Restaurant Pic**, *285 av. V. Hugo; tel: 04 75 44 15 32* (expensive), where specialities include *filet de loup avec caviare*, lobster with truffles, and other gastronomic delights. A cheaper option is **L'Épicerie**, *18 pl. Belat; tel: 04 75 42 74 46* (cheap–moderate), which has a convivial atmosphere and some interesting regional dishes. Valence also has plenty of pizzerias and snack bars as well as Moroccan, Vietnamese, Chinese, Lebanese and Greek restaurants.

Sightseeing

Valence has an extensive *vieille ville*, mostly pedestrianised and criss-crossed by narrow streets known as *côtes* (one of the best preserved is *Côte St Martin*). At the centre of the old town is the **Cathédrale St Appolinaire**, founded in the 11th century but largely rebuilt in the 17th after being damaged during the Wars of Religion, and with a neo-Romanesque tower added in the 19th. The interior, however, has largely retained its original Romanesque style. Of more interest are the Renaissance façades on town houses, notably **La Maison des Têtes**, *57 Grand-Rue*, built in 1530 and ornamented with peculiar statuary, and the **Maison Dupré-Latour**, *77 r. Pérollerie,* with a sculpted doorway and courtyard featuring a spiral staircase. Near the cathedral is the **Musée de Valence**, *pl. des Ormeaux; tel: 04 75 79 20 80* (open Wed, Sat, Sun 0900–1200, 1400–1800; Mon, Tues, Thurs, Fri 1400–1800; FFr.12). The museum contains Gallo-Roman mosaics, a large collection of paintings from the 16th–19th centuries, and a collection of pencil drawings by the artist Hubert Robert (1733–1808).

VALENCE TO MONTÉLIMAR

Tourist Office: La Voulte-sur-Rhône: *r. Rampon* (in the main square); *tel: 04 75 62 44 36.* Open Mon–Sat 0900–1200, 1400–1800.

Perched some 230m above St Péray, the **Château de Crussol** is one of the most celebrated of the Rhône valley chateaux, with its white stone walls rising up dramatically from the rocks upon which it was built during the 12th century. Parking by the *crêperie* past a towering statue of the Virgin, it is a 60-min walk there and back. Surrounding the château walls are the remains of the hundred or so houses which clung to it for support, whilst from the keep there is an extraordinary view across the plain and the confluence of the Rhône and the Isère.

The small village of **Soyons**, nestling between a limestone escarpment and the river, may look unpretentious but a different story is revealed in its small **Musée**, one street back from the main road; *tel: 04 75 60 88 86* (open July–Aug daily 1000–1200, 1400–1800; May, June, Sept Wed–Sun 1000–1200, 1400–1800; Oct–Apr Wed–Sun 1400–1700; FFr.25). Featuring finds from a 30-hectare archaeological site covering the hills behind the village, the museum charts the occupation of this area from paleolithic times onwards – in fact, it is unique in the Rhônes-Alpes region in that it presents a panorama of history from the paleolithic and neolithic through to the Gallo-Roman and medieval eras, reflecting Soyons' position at the cross-roads of both the north-south Rhône valley and also the east–west Drôme–Ardèche routes. The four small rooms of the museum contain some fascinating items, including a neolithic necklace, Greek coins, and the remains of cave bears, lions, and a mammoth which was butchered in one of the 40 grottos behind the village. The **grottos and archaeological site** can also be visited (July–Aug daily 1400–1800; Sept–June Wed, Sun 1400–1700; combined ticket FFr.40).

Just outside Soyons, on the main road (1.5 km) is **Ardèche Miniatures**, *tel: 04 75 60 96 58* (open June–Sept daily 1000–1900; Oct–Nov, Mar–May Mon–Sat 1400–1800, Sun 1000–1800; FFr.33). This painstakingly created miniature landscape features many typical Ardèchois scenes – small villages, quarries, farms, forests, waterfalls and mountains – with seven different kinds of miniature trains running around a track which encompasses viaducts, tunnels, bridges, rural stations, and the like.

La Voulte-sur-Rhône is a substantial town, built on the textile and fishing trades, with the obligatory **Château** perched high above it (open for guided visits (75 mins) July–Aug only, Mon–Fri 1100 depart tourist office; 1500, 1600, 1700, at the château; FFr.10). The château, built between the 14th and 16th centuries, was badly damaged during World War II but still retains a set of attractive mullioned windows, a grand staircase leading down into the courtyard, sculpted architraves, and a flamboyant Renaissance chapel. Just a few paces along the river bank from the main square is the extraordinary **Musée de Paléontologie**, *4 quai Anatole France; tel: 04 75 62 44 94* (open Sun–Fri July–Aug 1000–1900; Sept–Dec, Feb–June 1400–1800; closed Jan; FFr.22). The result of over 25 years work in the region by paleontologist Bernard Riou, who set up this museum in 1989, this astonishing display includes a fossil of the oldest octopus in the world, dating back 155 million years, which is not only twice as old as the previous record-holder but also had to have a whole new genus created for it. Here too is a hipparion (ancestor to the horse), just over 1 m tall and 1.5 m long, with a perfectly preserved foetus clearly visible inside it's fossilised skeleton. It took 1500 hours of patient work to reveal this graceful animal as we see it today. Alongside it stand two Microstonyx Major, predecessors to wild boar, displayed side-by-side as they were found, and there is also a snake with the half-digested remains of a mouse visible in its belly. The delicacy of these and many other ancient life forms, preserved in perfect detail, is astounding, and this museum should definitely not be missed. An audio-visual (in French, German, Dutch and English) gives a good background to these finds, which have cemented Bernard Riou's reputation worldwide.

Beyond here, the N86 runs beside the Rhône down through Le Pouzin and the heavily industrialised zone around Cruas, until Rochemaure, where the D11 crosses the river into Montélimar.

MONTÉLIMAR

Tourist Office: *Allée Provençales; tel: 04 75 01 00 20.* Open Mon–Sat 0900–1200, 1400–1730.

Accommodation and Food

Chains include *LF, Ct.* Recommended hotels include the **Logis Dauphiné-Provence** *(LF), 41 av. Gén. de Gaulle; tel: 04 75 01 24 08; fax: 04 75 53 08 29* (cheap), a classic old hotel right in the centre; and, just nearby, **Le Relais de l'Empereur**, *1 pl. M. Dormoy; tel: 04 75 01 29 00; fax: 04 75 01 32 21* (cheap–moderate). In the old town, the **Hôtel Pierre**, *7 pl. des Clercs; tel: 04 75 01 33 16* (cheap) is housed in a converted 16th-century mansion. Five km out of town, the **Château de Montboucher Le Castel**, *Monboucher-sur-Jabron; tel: 04 75 46 08 16; fax: 04 75 01 44 09* (moderate–expensive) is an elegantly-appointed 13th-century château with spacious rooms, swimming pool, and gourmet restaurant in a lovely vaulted room. **Campsite**: **Les Deux Saisons**, *chemin des Deux Saisons; tel: 04 75 01 88 99* (caravans; open Mar–Nov).

Montélimar has almost as many restaurants as *confiseries* (sweet shops). Amongst those which are good value are **Le Bistro Latin**, *3 r. du Collège; tel: 04 75 51 90 76* (cheap–moderate); **Le Grillon**, *40 r. Cuiraterie; tel: 04 75 01 79 02* (cheap–moderate), which specialises in regional cuisine such as *suprême de pintade au jus de truffes;* and **Le Lion d'Or**, *5 r. Lion d'Or; tel: 75 53 72 29* (cheap) for pizzas and nourishing *plats du jour.* On the outskirts, the **Restaurant Francis**, *202 rte de Marseille; tel: 04 75 01 43 82* (moderate) is a gastronomic haven popular with locals (reservations advisable at weekends), with an extensive and imaginative menu at reasonable prices.

Sightseeing

Montélimar is famous as the 'Nougat Capital'; this sticky confection of honey, almonds, pistachios, and vanilla has been made here since the 17th century. There are around a dozen manufacturers in town, most of which can be visited (details on *Fabriques de Nougat* are available from the tourist office) or you can taste and buy at shops along the *Allées Provençales* or in the old town.

Montélimar has a pleasant *vieille ville,* centred around the 15th-century **Église St Croix**, its old streets lined with 16th-17th century townhouses leading down to the busy boulevards known as the *Allées Provençales.* To the east of the old town is the **Château des Adhémar**, *r. du Château; tel: 04 75 01 07 85* (open July–Aug daily 0930–1130, 1400–1800; Apr–June, Sept–Oct 0930–1130, 1400–1730; Nov-March, Wed–Mon 0930–1130, 1400–1730; free). Built by thc Adhémar family in the 12th century, on a hilltop above the town which bears their name (Montélimar is a contraction of 'mont' of the Adhémars), it is one of the largest medieval castles of the Middle Rhône; within the castle are a lodge with beautifully-decorated Romanesque capitals and an 11th-century chapel.

One of the newest attractions in town is the excellent **Musée de la Miniature**, *19 r. P. Julien; tel: 04 75 53 79 24* (open June–mid Sept daily 1000–1800; mid Sept–May Wed–Sun 1400–1800; closed Jan; FFr.30). The magnifying glasses positioned over the exhibits are essential to viewing some of these astonishing works of art, such as portraits, poems and other texts engraved on rice grains; there are also superb miniature models of musical instruments, chess sets, house interiors and much more.

Out of town, at *Montboucher-sur-Jabron,* the **Musée de la Soie**, *rte de Dieulefit; tel: 04 75 01 47 40* (open Mon–Fri 0930–1130, 1430–1830, Sun 1430–1830, July–Aug only Sat 0930–1130, 1430–1830; FFr.28) is housed in an old mill and traces the history of the silk-rearing and weaving industry (once so important in Provence) from the 17th century onwards.

Viviers

Tourist Office: *pl. Riquet; tel: 04 75 52 77 00.* Open Mon–Sat 0930–1230, 1430–1800. Accommodation bookings, guided visits of the old town year round (Fr.15 per person, minimum 10 people).

Accommodation and Food

The town's main hotel, **Le Provence**, recently lost its *LF* affiliation. Just outside town, at St Alban, there is a friendly and hospitable *gîte d'étape*, **Le Mas**: *tel: 04 75 52 69 94* (cheap). Restaurants include the traditional **Café l'Horloge**,*tel: 04 75 52 62 43*; the **Auberge du Sauvage**, *tel: 04 75 52 69 31*, good value for grills and salads; and the more up-market **Carpe Diem**, *pl. de la Roubine; tel: 04 75 52 79 43* (expensive, but worth it). Outside town on the *route d'Aubenas* the **Auberge**

du Pont Romain; *tel: 04 75 52 60 84* (moderate) specialises in regional cuisine.

Sightseeing

Viviers became the episcopal capital of the province of Vivarais (to which it gave its name) during the 5th century, when a cathedral was built on a rocky promontory overlooking the Rhône valley. The fortified **citadel** is entered by one of two massive gateways, the *porte de la Gâche* and the *porte de l'Abri*, from where the narrow streets (one of which, *r. Châteauvieux*, is vaulted) lead up to the **Cathédrale St Vincent**. The porch and façade are 12th-century Romanesque, whilst the interior boasts a magnificent 15th-century vaulted ceiling and several Gobelin tapestries. To the north of the cathedral an open space leads to the **Belvédère du Châteauvieux**, an extraordinary viewpoint perched 40 m above the square, with sweeping views across the tiled roofs of the old town and east across the Rhône valley. Below the citadel the **old town** features several 18th-century *grands hôtels*, including the **Hôtel de Ville**, built as the Bishop's Palace in 1732. The most remarkable building of all is the elaborate **Maison des Chevaliers**, *r. de la République* (1546–48), whose florid Renaissance façade is France's most outstanding example of 16th-century domestic architecture. The weekly market takes place in *pl.Roubine* (Tues a.m.).

VIVIERS TO ORANGE

Tourist Office: **St Paul-Trois-Châteaux:** *Maison de la Truffe et du Tricastin*, see below for details; **Bollène**: *pl. Reynaud de la Gardette; tel: 04 90 40 51 44* (open summer Mon–Sat 0830–1200, 1400–1930; winter Mon–Sat 0830–1200, 1500–1730).

From Viviers the N98 runs alongside the river and then crosses it towards Donzère. From the bridge there is a good view of the Rhône and the **Defile de Donzère**, a narrow passage flanked on the left bank by a series of rocky peaks (one of which is topped off by a statue of St Michel, patron saint of mariners). This passage is traditionally considered as the entrance to Provence for mariners.

To the south of Pierrelatte, within sight of the Tricastin nuclear centre is **La Ferme aux Crocodiles**, *quartier de Faveyrolles; tel: 04 75 04 33 73* (open June–Sept daily 0930–1900; Oct–May 0930–1700; FFr.32). Warmed by waste heat from Tricastin, this large exhibition features crocodiles from all over the world, the main glass enclosure housing over 300 Nile crocodiles. Walkways lead between tropical vegetation over and around the crocodile pools, with multi-lingual explanatory panels.

Overlooking the Rhône from a small hill, **St-Paul-Trois-Châteaux** is an attractive old village with a Romanesque **Cathedral** at its heart. Behind the cathedral is the **Maison de la Truffe et du Tricastin**, *r. de la République; tel: 04 75 96 61 29* (open May–Sept Mon 1500–1900, Tue–Sat 0900–1200, 1500–1900, Sun 1000–1200, 1500–1900; Apr, Oct Mon 1400–1800, Tue–Sat 0900–1200, 1400–1800, Sun 1000–1200, 1400-1800; Nov–Mar Mon 1400–1800, Tue–Sat 0900-1200, 1400–1800. The tourist office represents the Tricastin region and there are tastings and sales of Tricastin wines; most of the building, however, is devoted to black truffles, a Tricastin speciality, with an extensive display and videos covering life cycles, harvesting, truffle dealers and more. In season (Nov–Mar), there is a truffle market in the *pl. de la Libération* (Tues and Sat a.m.) and a Truffle Festival (2nd weekend in Feb).

Rhône Wines

The Rhône Valley has been an important wine-producing area since Roman times, although the majority of vineyards were planted in the mid19th century following the decline of the silkworm industry. Today the vineyards cover around 160,000 hectares and produce 2,500,000hl of *appellation controllée* wines, accounting for nearly 15 percent of fine wine production in France. The Côte du Rhône *appellation* embraces a wide variety of types of wine because of differences in the soil over this vast area, as well as the many varietals of grapes grown. For the whites, Marsanne and Viognier are the most frequently used, with Syrah and Grenache, as well as some Mourvèdre and Cinsault for the reds. The reds are typically robust, full-flavoured wines which develop considerably in depth and subtlety if left to mature (preferably for at least five or six years). Some of the most famous vineyards to look out for are those of the **Côte Rotie, Condrieu** and **Château-Grillet** to the south of Vienne; **Crozes-Hermitage, Hermitage, St Joseph, Cornas** and **St Péray** to the north of Valence; **Lirac, Tavel, Laudun**, and **Chusclan** on the west bank and **Châteauneuf-du-Pape** on the east bank near Orange; and **Rasteau, Beaumes-de-Venise, Vacqueyras**, and **Gigondas** between Orange and Vaison-la-Romaine.

On the outskirts of Bollène is the **Site Troglodyte de Barry** (open access; guided visits from Bollène by appointment; FFr.25), an unusual cave village which was occupied continuously from prehistoric times up until World War II. The houses have stone façades but the rooms have simply been carved out of the rocks behind, and there are also a small chapel, fountains and a *lavoir* (wash house). Above the village are the ruins of a feudal **château**, from where there are good views across the Rhône valley.

On the left bank of the Canal Donzère-Mondragon, the major agricultural town of **Bollène** has also developed economically thanks to the André Blondel hydro-electric plant on the canal, and the Tricastin nuclear centre.

From the terrace of the **Collégiale St Martin** above the town the views extend across these industrial suburbs towards the Bas Vivarais and the Ardèche hills. The church, built between the 12th and 16th centuries, has an impressive timbered saddleback roof (the interior can be seen on guided tours from the Tourist Office which also include the old town; FFr.25, by appointment). Next to the church is a small garden, the **Belvédère Pasteur**, with a bust of Pasteur commemorating the fact that he discovered an innoculation against swine fever whilst staying in Bollène in 1882. Within the old town is the **Maison de la Culture Provençale**, *r. de St Sacrement; tel: 04 90 30 41 39* (open Sat 1430–1730 or by appointment; free) which contains over 1,800 works on every aspect of Provençal life and history.

The old town has some nice old doorways, Renaissance townhouses, and other architectural features; a leaflet describing two walking tours, *Bollène Balades*, is available from the Tourist Office. There is a Provençal market on *pl. 18 Juin* (Sat am).

CHÂTEAUNEUF-DU-PAPE

Tourist Office: *pl.du Portail; tel: 04 90 83 71 08.* Open July–Aug Mon–Sat 0900–1900, Sun 1000–1700; Sept–June Mon–Sat 0900–1230, 1400–1800.

Accommodation and Food

The village has several fine hotels, none of them cheap. The top establishment, standing amidst of its own vineyards, is the nearby **Hostellerie Château Fines Roches**, 3 km along the D17; *tel: 04 90 83 70 23; fax: 04 90 83 78 42* (expensive), which was built by the Marquis de Baroncelli in mock-medieval style; there are just seven, antique-furnished rooms and a gourmet restaurant. An alternative is the **Logis d'Arnavel**, *rte du Roquemare, tel: 04 90 83 73 22* (moderate–expensive), a converted farmhouse in quiet surroundings, with its own pool. There are several good restaurants, including the long-standing **La Mère Germaine**, *pl. Fontaine; tel: 04 90 83 70 72* (moderate–expensive), which has a wonderful atmosphere and offers good value lunchtime menus.

Sightseeing

This famous wine village, the 'Pope's new castle', takes its name from the **Château des Papes** (open access) whose ruins tower above it. Built by Pope John XVII in the 14th century, it was mostly burned down during the Wars of Religion and finally blown up by the retreating Germans in 1944; only the keep and some walls survive, but it commands excellent views of the Rhône Valley, Avignon and the Alpilles, the Vaucluse Plateau, and Mt Ventoux. The village was renowned for its wines even during the Middle Ages, to the extent that when Urban X suggested moving the Papacy back to Rome there was strident opposition from his cardinals, reluctant to leave a summer residence which produced such exquisite vintages. The poet Petrarch, on hearing this, remarked that 'the princes of the church value the wines of Provence and know that French wines are rarer at the Vatican than Holy Water'. After the vineyards were destroyed by phyloxera in the 1880s they were entirely replanted; in 1923 the winegrowers association decided to implement stringent quality controls (regarding the management of vineyards, grape selection, harvest times and so on) which later came to form the basis for the national system of *appelations contrôlées*.

Approaching Chateauneuf-du-Pape the first thing you notice about the vines is that they seem to be growing out of a bed of pebbles; this surface layer of alluvial shingle magnifies the heat of the sun by day and heats them into the night, resulting in a wine with one of the highest minimum strengths (12.5 per cent alcohol) of all French wines. The characteristically full-bodied, deep red wines can be sampled at several *caves* in the village, such as **Prestige et Tradition**, *3 r. de la République*, or the Tourist Office can provide a list of the domaines to visit.

At the bottom of the village is the **Musée des Outils de Vignerons**, *Cave Pèrre Anselme, av. Bienheureux-Pierre-de-Luxembourg; tel: 04 90 83 70 07* (open daily mid June–mid Sept 0900–1930; mid Sept–mid June 0900–1200, 1400–1900; FFr.15). The displays follow the production of wine from tending the vineyards through to harvesting, pressing, and bottling, with historical documentation, a 16th-century wine press and an enormous 14th-century barrel.

During the annual **Fête de la Véraison** (first weekend in Aug) which celebrates the grapes reaching maturity, there are *dégustation* stalls throughout the village, as well as food stalls, a medieval parade, folklore dances, and other festivities.

ORANGE

See p. 311

LYON–GRENOBLE

This scenic route could scarcely be in bigger contrast to the direct motorway dash across flat farming country. Keeping well north of the motorway, it meets the mountains shortly before the slender Lac du Bourget where Aix-les-Bains, the gracious lakeside spa on the far bank, beckons for a pleasant short detour before continuing due south to Chambéry. The road then climbs over the Grande Chartreuse, one of the most famous and beautiful mountain ranges in the whole of France.

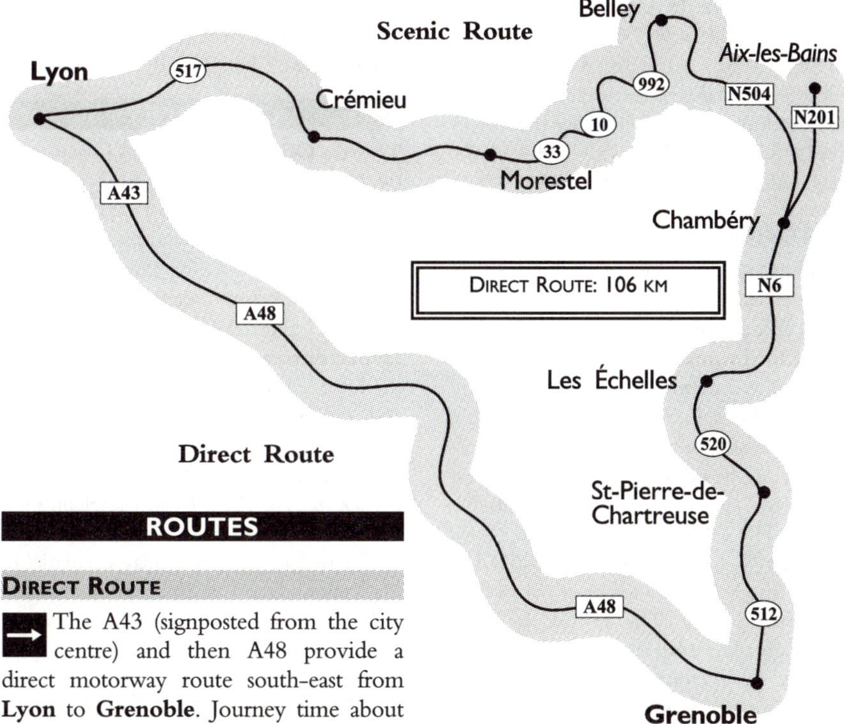

ROUTES

Direct Route

The A43 (signposted from the city centre) and then A48 provide a direct motorway route south-east from **Lyon** to **Grenoble**. Journey time about 75 mins.

Scenic Route

From **Lyon**, follow D517 east through **Crémieu** to **Morestel**. From there, take the D33, D10 and then D992 to **Belley**. Next, turn south on the N504, crossing the Rhône to emerge later from the **Mont du Chat** tunnel high above **Lac du Bourget**. Continue on the N504 past the southern end of the lake, to **Chambéry**. Return to the **Lac du Bourget** and take the N6 south-west to **Les Échelles**, where you turn onto D520 through the **Gorges du Guiers Mort** to **St-Pierre-de-Chartreuse**. Finally the wriggling D512 takes you into **Grenoble**. Total distance is about 190 km; with sightseeing, allow about 2 days.

CRÉMIEU

Tourist Office: *pl. de la Nation C. de Gaulle; tel: 04 74 90 45 13.* Open daily 1000–1200, 1400–1730.

Accommodation and Food

L'Auberge de la Chiate (*LF*), *38460 Crémieu, tel: 04 74 90 76 63, fax: 04 74 90 88 08* (cheap), is the town's only hotel, but there are a dozen restaurants, including one outdoors in summer under the hotel's trees (cheap) and two with tables in the open-sided medieval market hall.

Sightseeing

Nestling at the foot of a hilly ridge, Crémieu dates back to medieval times. Only 36km from Lyon, it is the obvious choice for Lyonnais wanting a peaceful little town as a commuter base or weekend retreat. The *cours Baron Raverat,* running along one side, takes the brunt of the traffic, leaving the narrow old streets and their 13th–19th century houses largely undisturbed. The central square, *pl. de la Nation C. de Gaulle*, has recently been stripped of all cars and refurbished with flower-boxes and smart paving. The **Hôtel de Ville** was originally a 14th-century convent and its beige stone cloister and church remain intact. But the town's real gem, built in 1315, is the original market hall, **La Halle**, *r. Mulet.* (60m long and 20m wide), with rows of wooden pillars supporting the beams under its red tiled roof. For local produce, the bustling Wednesday morning market is not to be missed.

A footpath path leads up to the remains of an ancient priory on the hillside overlooking the town – a splendid viewpoint.

BELLEY

Tourist Office: *34 Grand-Rue tel: 04 79 81 29 06.* Open daily Mon–Sat 0930–1200, 1400–1800 (until 1900 Apr–Oct).

Sightseeing

The main sights in this busy little town, formerly the capital of the Bugey region, are the gleaming white **Cathédrale de St Jean** – the façade is 19th-century Gothic but the beautiful rose windows are 15th-century – and an 18th-century **episcopal palace**, now taken over by the council.

CHAMBÉRY

Tourist Office: *24 blvd de la Colonne; tel: 04 79 33 42 47.* Open mid June–mid Sept Mon–Sat 0900–1230, 1330–1830, Sun 1000–1230; mid Sept–mid June, Mon–Sat 0900–1200, 1330–1800. English-speaking staff, walking-tour maps. In the same building the **Agence Touristique Départementale de Savoie**; *tel: 04 79 85 12 45*, has information on ski resorts and summer hiking. **Youth information**: **CIDJ**, *4 pl. de la Gare; tel: 04 79 62 66 87.* **Post office**: *pl. Paul Vidal; tel: 04 79 69 92 10. Poste Restante*, telephones, and currency exchange facilities.

There are pay and display car parks in the central area but free parking within walking distance of the main sights and shops.

Accommodation and Food

Never as crowded as neighbouring Aix-les-Bains, the town has a good selection of attractive hotels. Chain hotels (all on the outskirts) include: *Ca, Ib, F1, Me, Nv.* Hotels in the central area are surprisingly affordable; near the château try *pl. St Léger* and *pl. Hôtel de Ville.*

The heartland of **Savoie**, Chambéry

offers fine regional cuisine. Salamis, hams and various other salted meats are specialities and cheese is the basis of many dishes, particularly the sociable *fondue Savoyarde* eaten from a communal pot. There are numerous low-priced restaurants throughout the **old town** – try *pl. Monge, pl. Hôtel de Ville* and *r. Croix d'Or.* **La Chaumière,** *14 r. Denfert-Rochereau; tel: 04 79 33 16 26* (cheap) is a cosy restaurant offering traditional dishes.

Sightseeing

Ancient capital of Savoie, Chambéry is the epitome of an Alpine town. Most of the main sights are within the central partly-pedestianised area. Guided tours of the **château** and the old town, daily May–Sept (FFr.25). Also an **Old Town By Night tour** mid July–Aug at 2100, and other themed visits.

Chambéry's role as home to the Dukes of Savoy brought it great riches. The **old town** abounds with magnificent mansions, especially along *r. Croix d'Or.*

The **Château des Ducs de Savoie**, *pl. du Château* is the highlight. Built in the 15th century and updated in the 19th, most of it is now occcupied by the *Préfecture de Police*, but a small section can be visited, including its late-Gothic **Sainte Chapelle**. The town's most distinctive landmark is the **Fontaine des Éléphants**, a fountain with four large black elephants' heads, each peering down the street ahead. It was erected in 1838 in honour of Général de Boigne, a former resident who presented the town with some of the fortune he made in India. There are two museums worth seeing. The **Musée des Beaux Arts**, *pl. du Palais de Justice; tel: 04 79 33 75 03*, has the best collection of Italian paintings in France outside the Louvre, while the **Musée Savoisien**, *blvd du Théâtre; tel: 04 79 33 44 48*, in a former convent, covers local history. Both open Wed–Mon 1000–1200 and 1400–1800.

Two km south-east of the centre along a marked trail, *Sentier J-J. Rousseau*, the **Musée Rousseau**, *Chemin des Charmettes, tel: 04 79 33 39 44* (open Wed–Mon 1000–1200 and 1400–1800 (until 1630 Oct–Mar); FFr.20) occupies the beautiful 17th-century country house where this famous French philosopher lived. Plenty of his memorabilia are on show, but the real attraction is the botanic garden.

Side Track from Chambéry

From Chambéry, you can take the N102 north for 18 km to visit the spa of Aix-les-Bains.

AIX-LES-BAINS

Tourist Office: *pl. M. Mollard, 73100 Aix-les-Bains; tel: 04 79 35 05 92.* Housed in a national monument, once a Roman temple. Excellent information service, free map and guide to town in English. Open Mon–Sat 0845–1200, 1400–1830; also Sun 0915–1215, 1400–1800 in summer. Guided tours of the town, the various baths and local wine country operate throughout the year, but mainly June–Sept.

Station: **Gare SNCF**, *pl. de la Gare; tel: 08 36 35 35 35.* Central sights are easily accessible by foot. The lake is a short drive – or 30 mins on foot. The **bus** service is highly efficient (for the lake, take bus no. 2 from the centre except Sun) A single journey costs FFr.7. For **taxis**, *tel: 04 79 35 08 05.* **Post Office**: *av. Victoria; tel: 04 79 33 15 15.* Open Mon–Fri 0800–1900, Sat 0800–1200. *Poste restante* facilities available just round the corner at *av. M. de Solms.*

Accommodation and Food

Despite its reputation as a de luxe spa town, Aix boasts a pleasant selection of budget hotels. Easter and high summer season are always crowded. Budget accommodation is plentiful along *blvd Wilson* and *av. du Tresserve* (to the east of the station).

HI: *promenade de Sierroz; tel: 04 79 88 32 88*. Reservations necessary, as it fills up with groups. Reception 0700–1000 and 1800–2200. **Campsites**: **Camping Municipal Sierroz**, *promenade de Sierroz; tel; 79 61 21 43*. (caravans; open mid Mar–mid Nov). Aix has a wide range of eateries.

Bars are expensive. For an introduction to local wines, the tourist office runs tours of the **vineyards**.

Entertainment

The *Aix Poche* listings guide is available free from the tourist office. In July, there is opera at the **Casino**; for information, *tel: 04 79 88 09 99*. Classical music is performed throughout the summer at the **Théâtre de Verdure**, with larger concerts at the **Palais du Congrès**. In autumn, a **Berlioz** concert opens the **Festival des Nuits Romantiques**, while winter sees theatre and music continue at the **Palais du Congrès** and **Casino** (*18 r. du Casino; tel: 04 79 35 16 16*, open for gambling to over-18s only).

Sightseeing

The Romans first built thermal baths here 2000 years ago. The rich and famous from all over world patronised them right up to World War II. A bust of Queen Victoria in *pl. du Revard* commemorates her three visits in the 1880s. Now the **Thermes Nationaux**, *pl Maurice Mollard; tel: 04 79 35 38 50* (open Mon–Sat; tours Tues–Sat 1500, FFr.15), inaugurated in 1784, attract a far wider clientèle as some treatments are covered by the French national health service. Lesser baths include **Les Thermes d'Aix-Marlioz**, *av. de Marlioz; tel: 04 79 61 00 91*, to the east of the centre.

The **Musée Faure**, *blvd des Côtes; tel: 04 76 61 06 57*, on a small hill west of the centre, contains Rodin statues and an impressive array of Impressionist art, including works by Cézanne, Sisley, Degas, Bonnard and Renoir.

Lac du Bourget, to the west, is the largest natural lake in France (10 miles long), with wooded hills rising steeply on the far side. If you wonder what lives in the lake, the **Aquarium d'Aix**, *Le Petit Port; tel: 04 79 61 08 22* (open Tues–Sun 1000–1800; FFr.20) has 42 fish species on display.

No trip to Aix is complete without a boat ride across the lake to **L'Abbaye d'Hautecombe**, (open Mon and Wed–Sat 1000–1130, 1400–1700; Sun 1400–1700; boats leave from *le Grand Port;* FFr.50), a mystical monastery on the far shore. The building houses the tombs of the Dukes of Savoy. Other boat tours are available with **Bateaux du Lac du Bourget**; *Le Grand Port, Les Belles Rives; tel: 04 79 63 45 00.*

MASSIF DE LA CHARTREUSE

The mountains which dominate the landscape between Chambéry and Grenoble, bordered by the River Isère to the east, are as spectacular as any in the Alps, notable for their steep wooded hillsides and deep gorges. Officially designated as a **Regional Natural Park** in 1995, it is a great area for walking and also more specialised pursuits such as caving, paragliding and canyoning.

LES ÉCHELLES

Tourist Office: *r. Stendhal tel: 04 79 36 60 49*. Open daily 1000–1200, 1400–1800 (closed Sun afternoon).

This little town on the northern edge of the Chartreuse mountains makes a convenient base for exploring the area. Stay at the **Auberge du Morge**, *tel: 04 79 36 62 76* (cheap), or at one of its three **campsites**, such as **Arc-en-Ciel**, *Entre-Deux-Guiers, tel: 04 79 65 70 14* (caravans).

From the town, roads climb through deep gorges into the mountains. The **Gorges du Guiers Mort** lead past the **Monastère de la Grande Chartreuse**, the famous monastery where Carthusian monks live and pray in solitude and silence. Though not open to visitors, the outside can be seen after an hour's walk through the woods, from **La Correrie**, which was formerly the Brothers' hospital. It now houses a museum, **La Correrie de la Grande Chartreuse**, *tel: 04 76 88 60 45* (open Apr–Oct daily 1000–1200, 1400–1800 (slightly longer July–Aug); FFr.12) about the history of the Brotherhood created by St Bruno over 900 years ago in *Le Desert*, the heart of the Chartreuse mountains, an area chosen because of its inaccessibility and utter peace. The museum explains the Carthusian way of life. There is also a small 12th-century chapel. Chartreuse, the liqueur which has made a name for the monks worldwide, is now produced in **Voiron** (just off the *Lyon-Grenoble* motorway); *tel: 04 76 05 81 77* (guided visits daily). It is made from 130 plants, using a secret recipe presented to the Brothers by Maréchal d'Estrées in 1605.

ST-PIERRE-DE-CHARTREUSE

Tourist Office: *pl. de la Mairie; tel: 04 76 88 62 08*. Open July–Aug daily 0900–1200, 1400–1800; Sept–Dec and Apr–June Wed–Mon 0900–1200, 1330–1730; Jan–Mar (ski season) daily 0900–1200, 1330–1730. Guided walks daily July–Aug. Information on the park is available from the **Parc Naturel Regional de Chartreuse**, *pl. de la Mairie, tel: 04 76 88 65 07*.

Accommodation

Most accommodation is self-catering but there are several hotels including four Logis. The **Beau Site** (*LF*), *tel: 0476 88 64 69; fax: 76 88 64 69* (cheap) is in the centre, with a heated outdoor pool.

Sightseeing

At the end of the **Gorges du Guiers Mort** and surrounded by peaks, St Pierre has a magnificent location, making it a bustling little holiday resort, popular with walkers in summer and skiers in winter. Organised walks with mountain guides (July–Aug) include a nature watch on **Mont Blanc** at dawn, the **St Même Waterfalls** and the **Chartreuse monastery woods**.

Three km south of the village, the wayside **Église St Hugues de Chartreuse**, *tel: 04 76 88 65 01* (open Apr–Sept Tues–Sun 0900–1200, 1400–1900; Oct–Mar Wed–Mon 1000–1200, 1400–1730; closed Feb) has striking modern decor inside. In 1953 the artist Arcabus, then only 25, happened to meet the priest and got a commission to restore the interior. It became an all-consuming task which took him until 1991. He conceived it as a whole, so the decoration – red ribbing across beige walls and vaulted ceiling – is complemented by modern furniture and ornaments. There is a red hessian frieze around the walls, striking stained glass windows, bronze font and metal sculptures. Even non-Christians are moved by its simple beauty. Services on alternate Sun at 1000.

LYON–ST ÉTIENNE

This route meanders gently around the Monts du Lyonnais, whose rolling farmlands and forests are scattered with peaceful villages. Crossing to the east side of the A7 autoroute it then circles Mont Pilat, a delightful (mostly forested) area with stunning views across the Rhône Valley.

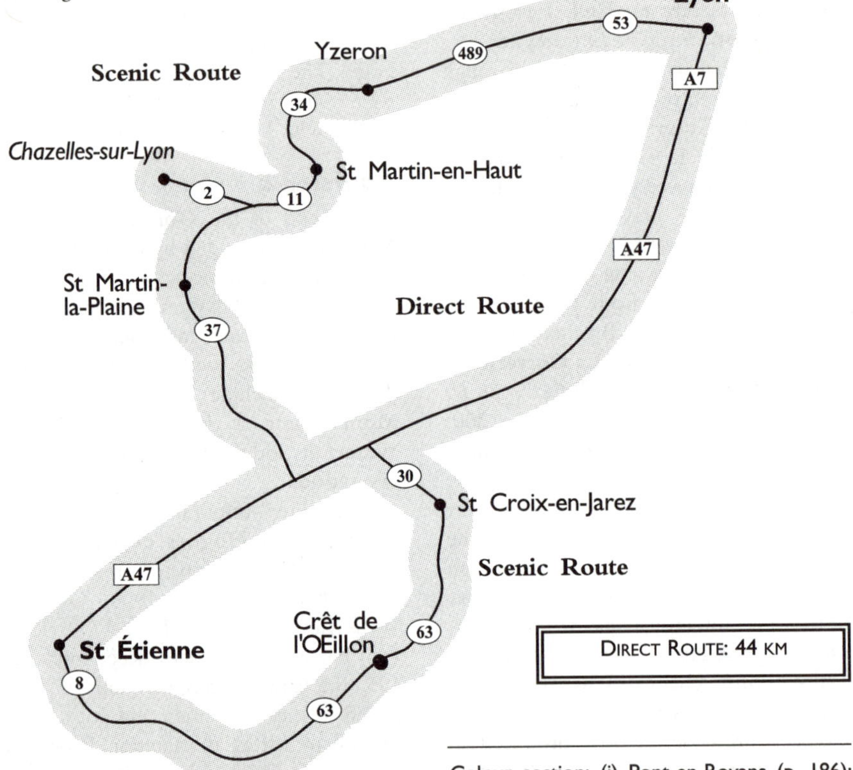

Direct Route: 44 km

ROUTES

Direct Route

The A7 autoroute southbound is well sign-posted out of central Lyon; follow direction Vienne/Valence. At Givors (19 km south of Lyon) take the A47 signposted St Étienne. Allow 1 hr.

Colour section: (i) Pont-en-Royans (p. 186); Marseille, the Vieux Port (p. 228).
(ii) Nîmes, the Maison Carré and in the background the Carré des Arts (p. 306); Salon-de-Provence – 18th-century 'tree' fountain and House of Nostradamus (p. 238).
(iii) Cassis – the harbour and café life (p. 244).
(iv) Vineyards are one of the visual joys of a Provençal autumn. This one is in the Var region.

MA308247

PIZZAS

YAMAHA
SPÉCIALITÉ
FRUITS
DE
MER

Scenic Route

Heading west out of central Lyon on the D53 follow signs for Tassin la-Demi-Lune, then turn right onto the D489 through Craponne. Continue on to **Yzeron**, then rejoin the D489 to pass over the Col des Brosses (867m). In Duerne take a left turn on the D34 to **St Martin-en-Haut**, leaving by the D11 to St Symphorien-sur-Coise. Take the D2 to **Chazelles-sur-Lyon**, then backtrack to St Symphorien-sur-Coise and take the D4 and D3 to Grammond, then the D6 left to St Christo-en-Jarez and the Col de la Gachet (748m). At the Col, take the D37 to **St Martin-la-Plaine**, then follow signs to autoroute A47.

Cross the autoroute into Rive-de-Gier, and then take the D30, signposted to **St Croix-en-Jarez**. Continue on the D30 to the **Parc Regional du Pilat** and the **Maison du Parc** in Pelussin. Leave the village by the same route, turning left just outside onto the D36 signposted Col de l'Œillon. At the *col*, turn right to the **Crêt de l'Œillon**, parking at the base of the peak to walk (30–40 mins rtn) to the summit. Continue on the D63 to le Bessat, then follow the D8 into **St Étienne**. Allow 1–2 days.

YZERON

Tourist Office: *pl. Centrale; tel: 04 78 81 01 52*. Perched on a rocky promontory 800m above the valley floor, Yzeron is surrounded by the peaks of Py-Froid (870m), les Bruyères (840m) and les Brosses (910m).

A leaflet available from the tourist office describes marked trails around these peaks and up to a Madonna (859m) above the village.

Relief for thirsty hikers is provided by the many restaurants and bars in the village, most surrounding the central square. Amongst them are the quaint **Auberge du Tonton**, *tel: 04 78 81 01 42*, the **Restaurant des Touristes**, *tel: 04 78 81 00 18*, the **Café du Midi**, *tel: 04 78 81 01 81*, and **L'Échaugette**, *tel: 04 78 81 01 40* (all cheap).

Rooms are available at the **Auberge du Tonton** and the **Hôtel-Restaurant La Randonnière**, *tel: 04 78 81 00 09* (both cheap).

The village has a 15th-century **church**, beside which is an **orientation table** from where there are fabulous views down across the wooded slopes of the Monts Lyonnais to Lyon itself, some 20km in the distance.

ST MARTIN-EN-HAUT

Tourist Office: *pl. de l'Église; tel: 04 78 48 64 32*, open Tues–Sat 0900–1200 and 1400–1800, Sun 1000–1200.

This large village was once an important cross-roads on the pilgrim route to Santiago de Compostella (see p. 193), and boasts a Romanesque church of almost cathedral-like proportions. Surrounding the attractive square there are several good restaurants. **Les 4 Saisons**, *pl. de l'Église; tel: 04 78 48 69 12* (cheap–moderate) has a bar (snack menu) and an old-fashioned dining room with a surprisingly inventive menu, serving seasonal specialities in generous proportions.

Another good choice is **Le P'tit Machon**, *59, Grande Rue; tel: 04 78 48 63 90* (cheap) which has a rustic atmosphere and interesting menus. The comfortable **Relais des Bergers (LF)**, *2, pl. Neuve; tel: 04 78 48 51 22* (cheap–moderate), just off the main square, has 20 rooms and an agreeable restaurant with wide-ranging menu.

There is also a 2-star **Municipal Camping**, *les Verpillières; tel: 04 78 48 62 16,* to the south-west of the village.

Side Track from St Martin-en-Haut

Continuing on the D11 from St Martin-en-Haut, take the D2 at St Symphorien-sur-Coise.

CHAZELLES-SUR-LYON

Tourist Office: *9 pl. J.B. Galland; tel: 04 77 94 22 15*, open Mon 1400–1800, Tues, Fri, Sat 0900–1200 and 1400–1800; Wed–Thurs 1400–1800.

Accommodation and Food

The 2-star **Château Blanchard (LF)**, *36 rte de St Galmier, tel: 04 77 54 28 88; fax: 04 77 54 36 03* (moderate), just 50 m from the hat museum in a quiet garden, is a former hat maker's residence, restored to its original 1930s style which features 12 individually-decorated rooms and a gastronomic restaurant (expensive). Restaurants in town include **Le Couvre-Chef**, *7 r J.Jaurès; tel: 04 77 94 20 20* (cheap), the **Restaurant de la Coise**, *rte de Chevrières; tel: 04 77 54 22 13* (cheap) and **Chez Françoise**, *11 Carrefour St Roche; tel: 04 77 54 95 45* (cheap). There are also several pizzerias and snack bars around the central *pl. J. B. Galland*.

Sightseeing

Chazelles-sur-Lyon is a large town which owes its prosperity to four centuries of felt hat-making. Legend has it that the techniques were imported from the Middle East at the time of the Crusades in the 12th century, although historical sources place the industry's beginnings in the 16th century. The manufacture of hats (which became mechanised in the middle of the 19th century) reached its peak in the 1930s, when 2500 craftsmen were employed in 28 factories. Post war fashions heralded the decline of felt hats, and today only one factory is still in operation. The history of hat-making is documented in the excellent **Musée du Chapeau**, *16 rte de St Galmier; tel: 04 77 94 23 29* (open Sept–June Wed–Mon, 1400–1800, closed Tues; FFr.17). Housed in a former factory, this lively museum provides an insight into this ancient craft, from the pressing of rabbits' and hares' hair into felt cones through to dying, moulding and finishing. The tour also includes audio-visual presentations, demonstrations, and a fashion museum with hundreds of unusual hats.

ST-MARTIN-LA-PLAINE

This was once a Roman encampment (traces of the old aquaduct still remain) and developed an ironworking industry in the 12th century thanks to the discovery of coal deposits nearby. The village features a handful of ancient buildings but for most visitors (around 120,000 annually) the chief attraction is the extensive **Espace Zoologique**, *tel: 04 77 83 87 87* (open summer 0900-1900, winter 0900-dusk; adults FFr.42, children FFr.27) on the D37 just to the west of the village.

Featuring around 60 different species of animals and birds, the park specialises in breeding programmes for rare and endangered species, including gorillas, gibbons, macaques, wolves and Siberian tigers. A recently-built aviary also houses parrots and rare cockatoos from the Philippines. Wallabies, bears, lions, kangaroos, emus, and panthers are some of the other species to see; you can also help with gorilla feeding (1400 daily).

ST-CROIX-EN-JAREZ

Tourist Office: *Chartreuse-de-Ste-Croix; tel: 04 77 20 20 81*. Located just on the left of the main gateway. Guided tours by arrangement.

Hidden away in a fold in the hills on the north slopes of Mt Pilat, the **Chartreuse-de-St Croix** is an unusual monastery which has since become a self-contained village. Founded by Béatrix de Roussillon in 1280, it was home to a small Carthusian order for nearly five centuries until just after the Revolution, with the last monks being forced to leave in 1792. It was then sold to the neighbouring commune of Pavezin, whose inhabitants took up residence in 1888 to live in what became France's only village inside a monastery, classified as one of the most beautiful villages in France.

The **Monastery** (open access), is entered via a monumental gateway, flanked by circular granite towers, which leads into the first courtyard, the *Cour des Frères*. This vast courtyard is flanked by homes which once housed the bakery, forge, and other workshops. A covered passageway leads through to the **chapel** (open Oct–Mar Sun 1400–1800, Apr–May daily 1500–1700, June–Sept daily 1500–1800), which has 16th-century panelling and elaborately-carved 14th-century choir stalls. Beyond is a second massive courtyard, the *Cour des Pères*, surrounded by the monks' cells – now converted into houses. In the right hand tower of the main gateway is a charming auberge, **Le Prieuré**, *42800 St Croix-en-Jarez; tel: 04 77 20 20 09*; (cheap–moderate) which has just four comfortable and tastefully converted rooms within the tower; the vaulted restaurant (cheap) is also recommended.

PARC RÉGIONAL DU PILAT

Tourist Office: *Maison du Parc, Moulin de Virieu, 42410 Pelussin; tel: 74 87 52 00.* Provides a free schematic map of the park as well as selling more detailed guides to the park's 560km of marked walking paths, 600km of marked mountain-bike tracks, 420kms of bridlepaths, and climbing sites. A permanent display features the cultural and natural heritage of the region. The **Maison du Parc** is housed in a former mill (once used for spinning silk) and, outside, the various hydraulic works are now surrounded by a charming garden with fruit trees and native species found in the park. Alongside the garden are the old château and ramparts, from where there are superb views of the Pilat peaks to the west and the Alps to the east.

The Pilat Régional Park is a patchwork of small districts, each with its own characteristic landscapes and attractions, which forms an elongated shape stretching from the banks of the Rhône in the north-east to the boundaries of the Haute-Loire to the south-west of St Étienne. Rich in flora and fauna, it is dominated by the bulk of Mount Pilat, with the most panoramic views – encompassing the Jura and Mt Ventoux to the east – easily accessible on this route from the **Crêt d'Œillon**.

Pilat Ecology

The Pilat *massif* was originally completely forested. Although most of it is now covered by conifer plantations there are still pockets of ancient beech woods. Ferns and pink willow-herb grow in the well-lit clearings, and black woodpeckers, wrens and crested coal tits are often seen here. Above the forest line, the rock and screes (known locally as *chirats*) are home to eagle owls and the short-toed eagle. The southern slopes, where forests give way to heath, are used for raising goats whilst to the south-west extensive pastures are used for dairy farming. Cornflowers, orchids and rare delphiniums are among the flowers found here.

Marseille

Marseille is France's secret city. Most people expect it to be dirty, run-down and dangerous, a port town of slums and drugs. Forget this, it is wonderful, surprising and invigorating. The old queen of the Mediterranean is a place to explore, with fine museums, opera halls and theatres to rival Paris, traditions, cuisines and languages from around the world.

One of the oldest settlements in Europe, Marseille dates back over 2600 years to the Phocaean Greek settlement of Massalia, set up to trade with the local Celtic Ligurians. The city suffered badly when it took the wrong side in the cataclysmic battle between Julius Caesar and Pompey in 49BC and didn't really have another moment of glory until Louis XIV began building here in the 17th century. A third time of triumph came during the rapid colonial expansion of the 19th-century Second Empire under Napoleon III.

Today, the city has a population of 820,000 (about 1 million including the surrounding area), is the capital of the Provence-Côte d'Azur-Alpes region, and is fighting an ongoing battle with Lyon over which is the second largest city in France.

Throughout its long life, Marseille has been ruled by the sea. It is, without question, the largest port in France (the second largest in Europe, following Rotterdam) the docks stretching intermittently for nearly 60km between the city centre and the vast purpose-built industrial complex of Fos (see p. 242). Even the marinas can house over 8000 boats, the many beaches in the suburbs offer a wide range of watersports while boat trips from the Vieux Port offer a perfect way to idle away a sunfilled day.

Tourist Information

Main Tourist Office: *4 La Canebière, 13001 Marseille; tel: 04 91 54 91 11.* Open 16 Jun–14 Sept, daily 0830–2000; 15 Sept–15 Jun, Mon–Sat 0900–1915, Sun 1000–1700. Very helpful, with information on the surrounding area as well as the city; book here for city tours, exhibitions and museums. **Branch**: *Gare St Charles, tel: 04 91 50 59 18.* Open Mon–Sat 1000–1430 and 1530–1900 (July–Aug); Mon–Fri 1000–1300 and 1330–1800 (Sept–June). There are also information kiosks at the airport and in various key tourist areas (summer only). **Student and youth information**: **Centre Information Jeunesse**: *4, r. de la Visitation; tel: 04 91 49 91 55.*

Arriving and Departing

Airport

Marseille-Provence Airport: *tel: 04 42 89 09 74.* At Marignane, 22km north-west of town. Direct flights to over 80 cities in 34 countries, with over 20 flights a day to Paris. Terminal 1 handles international flights. A shuttle bus, *tel: 04 42 89 03 65*, runs between the airport and St

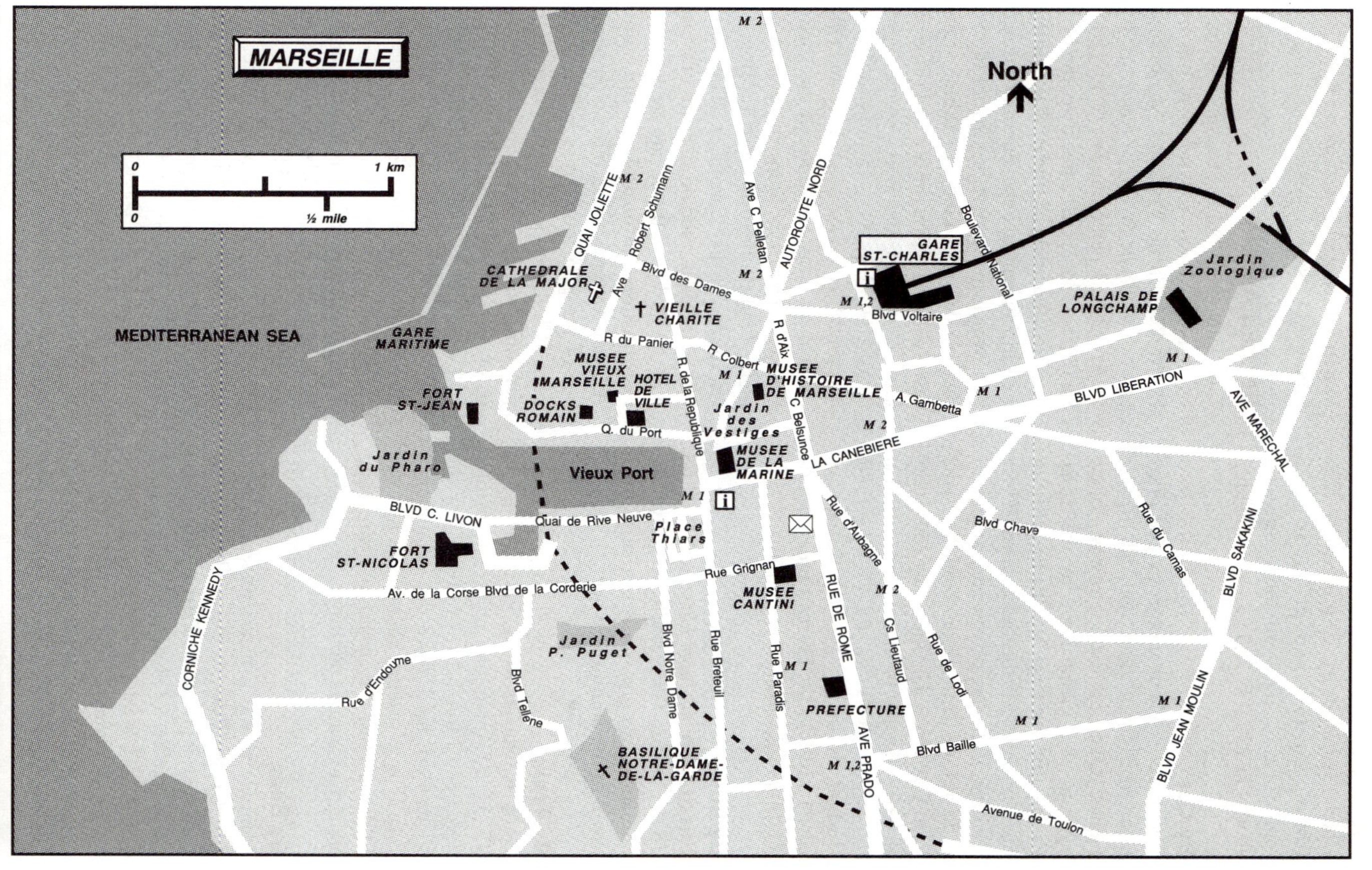
MARSEILLE
0
1 km
0
½ mile
North
MEDITERRANEAN SEA
GARE MARITIME
CATHEDRALE DE LA MAJOR
QUAI JOLIETTE
Ave Robert Schumann
Blvd des Dames
VIEILLE CHARITE
Ave C Pelletan
AUTOROUTE NORD
GARE ST-CHARLES
Boulevard National
Blvd Voltaire
Jardin Zoologique
PALAIS DE LONGCHAMP
R du Panier
R. Colbert
R d'Aix
MUSEE VIEUX MARSEILLE
HOTEL DE VILLE
MUSEE D'HISTOIRE DE MARSEILLE
A. Gambetta
BLVD LIBERATION
AVE MARECHAL
FORT ST-JEAN
DOCKS ROMAIN
R. de la Republique
Jardin des Vestiges
C Belsunce
Q. du Port
MUSEE DE LA MARINE
LA CANEBIERE
Jardin du Pharo
Vieux Port
BLVD C. LIVON
Quai de Rive Neuve
Place Thiars
Rue d'Aubagne
Blvd Chave
Rue du Camas
BLVD SAKAKINI
FORT ST-NICOLAS
Rue Grignan
MUSEE CANTINI
RUE DE ROME
Cs Lieutaud
Rue de Lodi
Av. de la Corse Blvd de la Corderie
CORNICHE KENNEDY
Jardin P. Puget
Blvd Notre Dame
Rue Breteuil
Rue Paradis
PREFECTURE
AVE PRADO
Blvd Baille
BLVD JEAN MOULIN
Rue d'Endoume
Blvd Tellene
BASILIQUE NOTRE-DAME-DE-LA-GARDE
Avenue de Toulon
M 1
M 2
M 1,2

229

Charles station every 20 mins 0620–2250 (last bus out to airport 2150), taking 25 mins (FFr.38). Taxis to the centre cost about FFr.220 (FFr.290 Sun and at night).

By Car

There are excellent motorway and other main road connections with all parts of France. Once off the motorway, follow signs to the Vieux Port; to the *Cinqs Avenue* (for the Gare St Charles area); or the Corniche (for the beach area). There are large, well-signposted underground car parks at the Centre Bourse and the Vieux Port. **Car Hire:** The following companies all have branches in the city centre and at the airport: **Avis**, *tel: 04 91 08 41 80*; **Budget**, *tel: 04 91 71 75 00*; **EuropCar**, *tel: 04 91 90 11 00*; **Hertz France**, *tel: 04 91 14 04 22*.

By Bus

Bus Station: *pl. Victor Hugo; tel: 04 91 08 16 40*, next to Gare St Charles (leave station and turn right). Connections to most towns in the South of France.

By Train

Gare St Charles: *av. P. Semard; tel: 04 36 35 35 35* (premium rate); information desk open Mon–Sat 0900–1900. For the Vieux-Port, head down the monumental 'Marseillaise' steps, straight along *blvd D'Athènes/blvd Dugommier* and turn right along *La Canebière* (800m).

By Boat

Marseille is also a major passenger port. The **Cruise Port**, to the northern end of the docks, is part of the **Porte Autonome de Marseille**, *23 pl. de la Joliette; tel: 04 91 39 40 00*. For information about ferries to Corsica, Sardinia, Algeria and Tunisia, contact **SNCM**, *61 blvd des Dames* (métro: *Joliette*); *tel: 04 91 56 30 10*. For the **Gare Maritime**, continue west along the coast from the Docks de la Joliette.

Getting Around

The integrated public transport system with métro, buses and trams is run by **RTM** (Réseau de Transport Marseillais), *opp. Centre Bourse, 6–8 r. de Fabres; tel: 04 91 91 92 10* (open Mon–Fri, 0830–1800, Sat 0900–1730; ask for a free map, the *Plan du Réseau*, covering all routes). The **métro** is clean, efficient and safe, but only has two lines which intersect at St Charles (down the escalators). Line 1 (blue) runs east–west, and serves the Vieux Port area; Line 2 (orange) runs north–south (open 0500–2100, then every 15 mins to 0030). The local **bus** service is extensive and efficient; most buses pass through the Vieux Port/Canebière area. Some run until midnight. Night buses run from La Bourse, just north of La Canebière. The same FFr.8.50 tickets, valid on all forms of transport for 1 hr of travel, are available at métro stations, on board buses and trams. A **Carte Liberté** which offers a set number of pre-paid journeys is better value, from RTM kiosks or métro stations. A day-long **tourist ticket** usable on all transport costs FFr.25.

Taxis are available from the station exit, or *tel: 04 91 03 60 03*. Taxi ranks are found throughout the city. Taxis are expensive and overcharging is common. **Taxis Tourisme** offer organised tours by taxi, with an audio guide, from FFr.145 for 1hr 30 mins to FFr.515 for a 4hr circuit; book through the tourist office. For **guided walks**, ask at the tourist office. Two **Petit Trains** run guided tours from the Vieux Port to Le Panier and the Basilique de Notre-Dame (50-mins; daily, 1 per hour, July–Aug, 1030–1815; limited hours through the rest of the year, enquire at the tourist office).

Staying in Marseille

Accommodation

There is accommodation to suit all pockets and the main tourist office provides a free booking service. Hotels are busier in summer months, but this is a business city and business is brisk year round. Hotel chains include *Ba, BW, Ca, Ch, Cn, Et, F1, Hd, Ib, IH, Mc, Nv, Pu, RC* and *Sf*, New Hotel.

The best places to find a hotel are around the Vieux Port, in the heart of the city, or along the corniche, with easy access to the beach. Three of the best-value options around Vieux Port are chain hotels. The 4-star **Sofitel**, *36 blvd Charles Livon; tel: 04 91 52 90 19; fax: 04 91 31 46 52* (expensive) is right beside the harbour entrance, with magnificent views and a fine gourmet restaurant, **Les Trois Forts**. The 3-star **Mercure Marseille Centre**, *r. Neuve Saint Martin, 13001 Marseille; tel: 04 91 39 20 00; fax: 04 91 56 24 57* (moderate) is a modern tower-block in the business district, an easy walk from the Vieux Port. It has two excellent restaurants, the traditional **L'Oursinade**, and regional **L'Oliveraie** (closed Sun lunchtime). The 3-star **St Ferreol's Hotel**, *19 r. Pisançon; tel: 04 91 33 12 21; fax: 04 91 54 29 97* (moderate) has only 20 rooms, each decorated differently and named after an artist. The **New Hotel Vieux-Port**, *3bis r. Reine-Elisabeth, 13001 Marseille; tel: 04 91 90 51 42; fax: 04 91 90 76 24* (cheap) is perfectly positioned, right beside the harbour, in a pleasant old building with comfortable, airy rooms.

Along the corniche, look for unabashed luxury at the 4-star **Petit Nice (RC)**, *Corniche Kennedy; tel: 04 91 59 25 92; fax: 04 91 59 28 08* (expensive), whose restaurant, **Le Petit Nice**, is one of the finest in the city (expensive, closed Sat lunch, and Sun, Oct–Mar). The 3-star **New Hôtel Bompard**, *2 r. des Flots Bleus; tel: 04 91 52 10 93; fax: 04 91 31 02 14* (moderate) is a charming old villa overlooking the corniche, with rooms and bungalows opening on to lush gardens.

In the suburb of Mazargues, towards the Calanques, **Le Cigale et la Foumi**, *19 r. Théophile Boudier; tel: 04 91 40 05 12* (cheap) is a delighfully decorated, tranquil guesthouse.

For very cheap, functional hotels, try the areas between *blvd Garibaldi* and *allée Léon Gambetta*, and around the Préfecture *(r. Montgrand)*. Avoid streets to the south-west of the station (roughly between St Charles and La Canebière) which can be a bit rough at night.

HI: there are two youth hostels. The more attractive and less expensive is the **Château de Bois-Luzy**, *allée des Primevères; tel: 04 91 49 06 18* (bus no. 6: *J-Thierry/M-Richard*), 8.5km north-east of the city centre, which overlooks the sea. **Bonneveine**, *47 av. J. Vidal (Impasse du Dr Bonfils); tel: 04 91 73 21 81*, is 6km south, in a residential district near the beach (métro: *Prado*; or bus no. 44: *pl. Bonnefons*). **Campsite**: **Jai** (2-star), *95 av. Henri Fabre, Plage du Jaï, Marignane; tel: 04 42 09 13 07*.

Eating and Drinking

Marseille offers cuisine for all tastes and all pockets, from street vendors to lavish belle époque restaurants, with a staggering array of ethnic eating places – North African, Vietnamese, Italian, Russian, Indian, Mongolian and even Corsican.

Markets and delicatessens abound from which to stock up for picnics, while for food on-the-hoof, most street corners host pizza vans which cook fresh pizzas to order on charcoal ovens. For hotel restaurants, see Accommodation.

Restaurants and cafés line the quays of the Vieux Port, but they are a mixed bag. Do stop at **La Samaritaine**, *2 quai du Port; tel: 04 91 90 44 95*, a café with a long pedigree, live music and, once a month, philosophical debate. A rather better selection can be found around *pl. Thiars, pl. aux Huiles* and *cours D'Estienne d'Orves* behind the south quay. Among them are **Le Patalain**, *49 r. Sainte; tel: 04 91 55 02 78* (closed Sat lunch and Sun); **Bistros Gambas**, *29 pl. aux Huiles; tel: 04 91 33 26 44*; **Le Caribou**, *38 pl. Thiars; tel: 04 91 33 22 63*; **L'Atelier Chocolat**, *18 pl. aux Huiles; tel: 04 91 33 55 00* and **L'Oliveraie**, *10 pl. aux Huiles, tel: 04 91 33 34 41*; all moderate. On the hill above, try a light lunch *al fresco* at the **Buvette de Chalet**, *Jardin de Pharo, blvd Charles Livon; tel: 04 91 52 80 11* (cheap), little more than a snack bar in the park, but with good food at lunchtime and a spectacular view over the Vieux Port.

Directly opposite, in Le Panier are seafood-based **Le Chaudron Provençal**, *48 r. Caisserie, tel: 04 91 91 02 37* (moderate) and **Le Panier des Arts**, *3 r. du Petit Puits, tel: 04 91 56 02 32* (cheap). More opulent restaurants are found along the Corniche J. F. Kennedy.

Drinking is a subject close to Marseille's heart: the life-blood of the city is the aniseed-flavoured pastis, produced by local firm Ricard. The bars and cafés of the Vieux Port house an older crowd, the young and hip head to *pl. Thiars* and *cours Julien*.

Communications

Post Office: *pl. de l'Hôtel des Postes; tel: 04 91 15 47 04*, near the Bourse (for poste restante and currency exchange; open Mon–Fri 0800–1900, Sat 0800–1200). Also *1 sq Canebière, tel: 04 91 11 01 80; 50 r. de Rome, tel: 04 91 13 6020* and *2 pl. Félix Baret, tel: 04 91 00 39 00.*

Money

There is no shortage of money-changing facilities in Marseille. Several major banks, including Société Générale can be found along *La Canebière*. **Bureaux de change** (open until 1800/1830) can be found at **la Bourse**, *3 pl. du Général de Gaulle, tel: 04 91 54 10 13*; **39, La Canabière**, *tel: 04 91 13 71 26*; **le Port**, *35 r. Vacon, tel: 04 91 55 62 15* and **Gare St Charles**, *tel: 04 91 84 68 88.*

Consulates

Canada: *24 av. du Prado; tel: 04 91 37 19 37*. Open 0900–1200 and 1400–1700.
Ireland: *148 r. Sainte; tel: 04 91 54 92 29*. Open 0900–1230 and 1430–1700.
UK: *24 av. du Prado; tel: 04 91 15 72 10*. Open 0900–1200 and 1400–1700.
USA: *12 blvd Paul Peytral; tel: 04 91 54 92 00*. Open 0900–1200 and 1400–1730.

Entertainment

Marseille rarely lives up to its gritty reputation and its nightlife is safe and notoriously dull. To be extra cautious, avoid streets to the south-west of the rail station (north of La Canebière). The *Opéra* district is Marseille's historical red-light venue – often lively but not dangerous. *Cours Julien* and *pl. Thiars*, off the Vieux Port, are the centres of nocturnal festivities, with trendy bars, restaurants and mediocre night-clubs.

The city's football team – L'Olympique de Marseille – is Marseille's number one obsession. On match days, the city is a ghost town until the final whistle. Tickets start around FFr.50, from **Stade Vélodrome**, *blvd Michelet; tel: 04 91 07 77 28*, (métro: *Rond Point du Prado*).

For all listings, pick up *A Tout Marseille* from the tourist office, or look in the pages of *La Marseillaise*, *Le Provençal* or the Wed

Bouillabaisse

Bouillabaisse is almost synonymous with Marseille and really should be tried. A traditional fisherman's stew, based originally on the day's catch, it is on offer in virtually every restaurant. Few however produce an authentic version with at least four different fish, such as mussels, lobster, eel and rascasse, an ugly red fish only found in the Mediterranean. You eat the soup first, with croutons and *aïoli* (garlic mayonnaise), followed by the fish. True devotees have banded together to form 'La Charte de la Bouillabaisse', an association guaranteeing quality. This does not come cheap, at up to FFr.300 a head, but bouillabaisse is a meal in itself. There are several charter members in Marseille (a leaflet listing them all is available from the tourist office), but two of the best are **Le Miramar**, *12 quai du Port; tel: 04 91 91 10 40*, on the Vieux Port, and **Chez Fonfon**, *140 Vallon des Auffes; tel: 04 91 52 14 38*, off the Corniche. It's advisable to book at both places.

edition of *Le Méridional*. For tickets, try **fnac**, *Centre Bourse; tel: 04 91 39 94 00.*

Music

The **Opéra Municipal**, *pl. Reyer; tel: 04 91 54 70 54*, has a magnificent opera company as well as classical concerts. The **Abbaye St-Victor**, *pl. St-Victor; tel: 04 91 33 25 86*, hosts classical music concerts. All types of music, from classical to jazz and rock are on offer at **Espace Julien**, *39 cours Julien; tel: 04 91 47 09 64*, and the **Cité de la Musique**, *4 r. Bernard du Bois; tel: 04 91 39 29 29.*

Theatre

Amongst the city's 32 theatres, the most important are the world-class **Théâtre National de Marseille la Criée**, *30 r. de Rive-Neuve; tel: 04 91 54 70 54* and the **Théâtre du Gymnase**, *4 r. du Théâtre Français; tel: 04 91 24 35 24.*

Cinema

There are 57 cinemas. The **Breteuil**, *120 blvd de Notre-Dame; tel: 04 91 37 88 18*, and the **Paris**, *29 r. Pavillon; tel: 04 91 33 15 59*, both show films both in French (indicated by V.F. – *Version Française*) and English (V.O. – *Version Originale*). The **Alhambra**, *2 r. du Cinéma; tel: 04 91 03 84 66*, is a good arts cinema.

Festivals

The summer sees non-stop festivities, which culminate in the **Festival de Marseille**, a 2-week whirlwind of culture in July. For information, *tel: 04 91 55 57 23*. The **Festival des Isles** (July) takes music from classical to rap, out to two small islands off the coast, access by boat or helicopter – great for summer evenings.

Shopping

For mainstream shopping, try the **Centre Bourse**, a large modern mall just behind the Vieux-Port, also home to **fnac**, which has a huge array of tapes, CDs and books, including some in English. For typically Provençal gifts, try **Label Bleu**, *216 r. Breteuil; tel: 04 91 81 61 76.* **Santons Jacques Flore**, *48 r. du Lacydon; tel: 04 91 90 67 56*, offers a wide range of the little terracotta figures, while **Santons de Marcel Carbonel**, *47 r. Neuve Ste-Catherine; tel: 04 91 54 26 58* , also offers guided tours and a small museum. The **Savonnerie Le Serail**, *50 blvd Anatole de la Forge; tel: 04 91 98 28 25*, is the last family workshop in Marseille producing the city's famous soap (the purest in the world, with 72% pure vegetable oil, no colouring or preservatives). **La Chocolatière**, *pl. des Treize Coins; tel: 04 91 91 67 66*, is a true chocoholics' paradise with no less than 85 different flavours of superlative chocolate. **Les Arcenaulx**, *25 cours d'Estienne d'Orves; tel: 04 91 54 39 67,* (moderate) is a delightful complex near the Vieux Port, with a restaurant inside a book and gift shop.

A daily market enlivens the *pl. des Capucins* (métro: *Noailles*). On the *quai des Belges* (métro: *Vieux Port*), the fish market is always vibrant and a glimpse of Marseillais temperament at its most entertaining. There is a flea market on the 2nd Sun of each month, a garlic market in late June–early July, and a santons market in Dec.

Sightseeing

Many of Marseille's museums synchronise their hours and are open Tues–Sun, June–end Sept 1100–1800, Oct–end May 1000–1700; admission FFr.10; free under 5. Details have been listed below only when they deviate from this pattern.

Vieux Port

The undisputed focus of the city is the Vieux Port, probably in use even before the Greeks arrived in about 600BC. Today, it is a small-boats harbour, guarded by two formidable 17th-century fortresses, St-Jean to the north and St-Nicholas to the south. Both were built by Vauban on behalf of Louis XIV. Remains of the original Greek harbour (Massalia) and 1st–3rd century BC walls can be seen in the pretty sunken garden, **Jardin des Vestiges**, beside the Centre Bourse shopping complex. This also houses the wonderful **Musée d'Histoire de Marseille**, *12 r. Henri Barbusse; tel: 04 91 90 42 22* (métro: *Vieux Port*; open 1200–1900, closed Sun), where Marseille's turbulent history is beautifully laid out and explained. In pride of place is a 3rd century AD Roman ship recovered from the harbour.

Following the line of an old river, **La Canebière** is one of the most famous streets in France. Named after a former hemp factory (hemp is also known as cannabis; *canébé* in Provençal), the street was nicknamed 'Can o' beer' by English sailors in the last century. The vast central hall of the 19th-century Imperial **Palais de la Bourse** charts the entire history of Marseille and also houses the **Musée de la Marine**, *7 La Canebière; tel: 04 91 39 33 33* (open 1000–1200 and 1400–1900, closed Tues, free) which honours Marseille's relationship with the sea, with a series of paintings, carvings and models.

The **Musée de la Mode**, *11 La Canabière; tel: 04 91 14 92 00* (open Tues–Sun, 1200–1900) has more than 2000 outfits charting fashion from the 1930s to the present. Nearby the **Musée Cantini**, *19 r. Grignan, tel: 04 91 54 77 75* (métro: *Estrangin-Préfecture*) boasts a fine assemblage of 20th-century art in an impressively opulent 17th-century mansion, with works by Picasso, Miro, Bacon and Ernst.

Boats depart regularly from *quai des Belges* for a 15-min journey to the **Château d'If**, *tel: 04 91 59 02 30* . This skeletal island fortress was built by François Ier in 1531, but later became a notorious prison, and the setting for Dumas' great novel, *The Count of Monte Cristo*. The 'Man in the Iron Mask' is also said to have been held here. The neighbouring **Isle de Frioul** houses Marseille's former leper colony, now being converted into a museum. There are also regular boats trips to the Calanques and a small ferry shuttles backwards and forwards across the harbour between the quai de la Rive Neuve and the Hôtel de Ville (FFr.2.50).

South of the Vieux Port

The city's oldest church, **St-Victor**, *pl. St-Victor; tel: 04 91 33 25 86* (open 0800–1200, 1400–1800; free, FFr.10 for the crypt) is a fascinating mixture of church and fortress, a former abbey of enormous power, which produced two Popes before being disbanded during the Revolution. Still preserving its Romanesque design, the achingly beautiful crypt includes the first rough 5th century chapel and many early sarcophagi. The Black Madonna is the centre of a popular pilgrimage cult.

Towering over the entire city, on a 154-m hill, once the site of a 13th-century hermitage and 18th-century watch-tower, is the **Basilique Notre-Dame-de-la-Garde**, a large striped neo-Byzantine church (open summer, 0700–1930, winter 0730–1730; free; bus no. 60 from Vieux Port). Built by Henri Espérandieu and consecrated in 1864, it is topped by a 6m-high gold-leafed Virgin, *La Bonne Mère*, who casts her benign influence over the city and the sea. Sailors come here to give thanks for surviving shipwrecks, and paintings of their ordeals and models of the ships that went down, decorate the church interior, along with a riot of mosaic, gilt and paint. The view from the terrace encompasses the whole vast sprawl of Marseille. In the distance, you can just glimpse Le Corbusier's **Unité d'Habitation**, *blvd Michelet*, a giant minimalist apartment complex built in 1952 (see also p. 331).

Le Panier

One of the oldest quarters in Marseille, on the north shore of the Vieux Port, Le Panier is a maze of narrow tortuous streets which had reached slum condition by the time they were used to film *The French Connection*. Since then, money has been poured in to restore what is, in many ways, the real heart of Marseille. The Résistance was based here during the German Occupation in World War II, and extensive modern concrete near the waterfront serves as a reminder of the Nazis' vengeful destruction, which also involved the forcible removal of up to 40,000 people. Some handsome old buildings did survive, however, notably the 17th-century **Hôtel de Ville**, **Hôtel de Cabre** and the oddly decorated 16th-century **Maison Diamantée**. An unexpected bonus of a German explosion in 1943 was the discovery of the remains of the Roman warehouses, complete with pots and wine casks, which can be seen *in situ* at the **Musée des Docks Romains**, *28 pl. Vivaux; tel: 04 91 91 24 62* (métro: *Vieux-Port*), which covers a thousand years of commercial life, from 600BC–400AD.

The foot of the hill is dominated by the huge 19th-century **Cathédrale de la Major**, *pl. de la Major*, built by the ubiquitous Henri Espérandieu. Tucked into its shadow are the tiny, truncated remnants of the elegant Romanesque **Ancienne Cathédrale de la Major**. Above, the **Centre de La Vieille Charité**, *2 r. de la Vieille Charité, tel: 04 91 56 28 38* (métro: *Joliette*) is a 17th-century workhouse and lunatic asylum with a fine baroque church, designed by local luminary, Pierre Puget. Recently restored, it has now become an innovative art centre with exhibitions, museums and performance space. The **Musée d'Archéologie Méditerranienne** has a rich collection of protohistoric and classical exhibits from around the sea, with a particular emphasis on Egypt. The **Musée d'Arts Africains, Océaniens and Amérindiens** has a superb collection of the ethnic art of three continents.

A little further along, in the carefully restored warehouses of the old docks is the

Grotte Henri Cosquer, *Sanctuaire Englouti, Les Docks de la Joliette; tel: 04 91 13 89 00* (open daily 1000–1800; guided tours on Mon and Sat at 1500; FFr.30/20). This fascinating exhibition, using photographs, audio-visual and, eventually, virtual reality, is the only opportunity you will have to see one of the most exciting discoveries of recent years: a magnificent series of prehistoric cave paintings, as dramatic as those of Lascaux, hidden deep inside a flooded cave system in the Calanques.

Longchamp

Some way east of the port (métro: *Longchamp-Cinq Avenues*) the **Palais Longchamp** is a magnificent building built in 1869 by Henri Espérandieu, designed originally to honour the arrival of a much-needed fresh water supply – and disguise a massive cistern. At the centre is a monumental arcade with tumbling cascades of water; in the left wing is Marseille's finest museum, the **Musée des Beaux Arts**, *tel: 04 91 62 21 17*, which offers an interesting mix of stoically classical works and lively impressionists, including such famous names as Rubens, David, Corrot, Ingres. The right wing contains the **Musée d'Histoire Naturelle** (Natural History), *tel: 04 91 62 30 78*, and an aquarium of local sealife. Nearby, the **Musée Grobet-Labadié**, *140 blvd Longchamp; tel: 04 91 62 21 82* is a 19th-century mansion, well-furnished with a collection of sculptures, tapestries, furniture and ceramics, some dating back to the 13th century. The **Musée d'Art Contemporain**, *69 av. de Haifa; tel: 04 91 25 01 07*, is a new museum at the cutting edge of modern art, with permanent and temporary exhibitions and works by César, Tingueley, Viallet, Buren and many others.

Other Museums

The **Musée de la Faïence**, *Château Pastré, 157 av. de Montredon; tel: 04 91 72 43 47* (pottery from the Neolithic to the present, in a 19th-century château); **Musée des Arts et Traditions Populaires du Terroir Marseillais**, *5 pl. des Héros, Château Gombert; tel: 04 91 68 14 38* (traditional Provençal life from the 17th to 19th centuries; open Wed–Mon, 1430–1830); the **Galerie des Transports**, *pl. du Marché des Capucins; tel: 04 91 54 15 15* (transport in Marseille through the ages; open Wed–Sat 1000–1700); **Musée du Santon**, *47 r. Neuve Ste-Catherine; tel: 04 91 54 26 58* (small museum of santon figurines (see p. 76); open Mon–Sat 0900–1200, 1430– 1900);

Musée de la Moto, *Traverse St-Paul, Le Merlan; tel: 04 91 02 29 55,* (motorcycles from 1898 to the present; open Tues–Sun 1000–1800); the **Musée Provençal du Cinéma**, *64 r. de la Joliette; tel: 04 91 90 24 54* (cinema, from film sets and costumes to photos and autographs; open by appointment); and **Le Préau des Accoules**, *29 Montée des Accoules; tel: 04 91 91 52 06* (regular special exhibitions for children; open Wed and Sat summer 1400–1800, winter 1300–1700).

At the time of writing, there were also several museums under restoration or construction, including the **Musée du Vieux Marseille**, *r. de la Prison; tel: 04 91 55 10 19*, with two centuries worth of Marseille's fascinating junk in the 16th-century Maison Diamantée, the **Musée César**, *pl. du Mazeau* (to house works donated to the city by the artist himself), the **Musée des Arts Décoratifs**, *Château Borély, av. Clot-Bey* (for furniture, ceramics, and objets d'art) and the **Forteresse de St-Jean**, *Vieux-Port* (a museum of French colonies).

MARSEILLE–ARLES

There are two very different routes out of Marseille, the first heading inland through the rolling heartland of Provence, the second skirting the coast through the pine trees and sandy beaches of the Côte Bleue. Both have charm and a great deal of interest and a surprising amount of greenery; both are fast if you don't stop or turn off. Allow 1 hr 30 mins without stops; 1 day with sightseeing on either route.

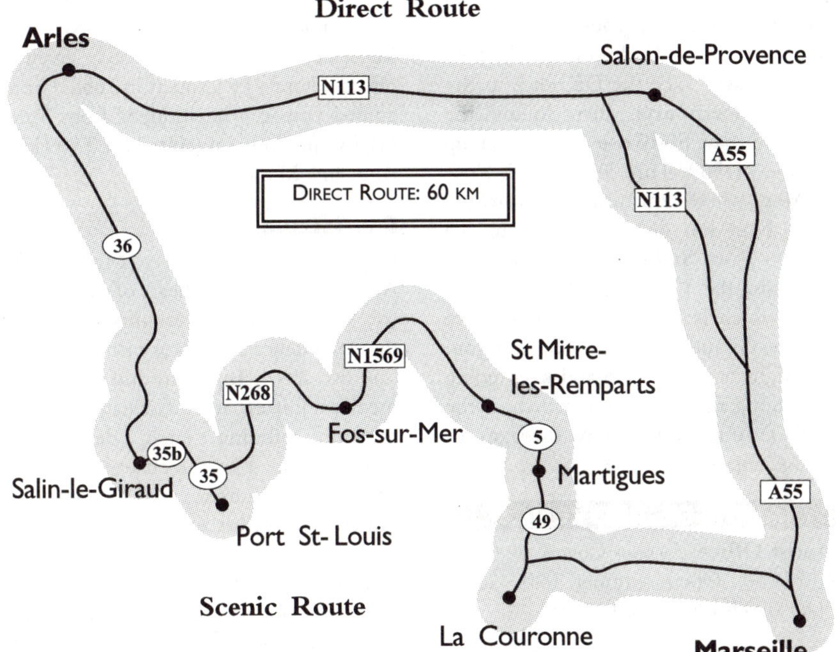

ROUTES

DIRECT ROUTE

➡ Leave Marseille on the A55 motorway, heading north towards Avignon. If you want to get off the toll road, take the exit for Marignane Airport which will lead you onto the N113. Both lead to **Salon-de-Provence**, from where you continue along the N113 or A54 via St-Martin-de-Crau to **Arles**.

For a fast alternative, leave Marseille on the A55 (the *Autoroute du Littorale)*. From Fos-sur-Mer, take the N568 which connects up with the N113 for the last segment through to Arles.

Scenic Route

If you want the scenic option, again take the A55 towards Fos, past the docks and fishing port, then take the Estaque exit (Junction 5). In **Estaque**, fork left round the harbour (signposted Gignac) on the N568 and keep going to Le Douard, where you turn left again onto the D5. Beyond Ensuès-la-Redonne, fork left again onto the small, hilly coast road to Carry-le-Rouet. This wriggles along the coast through Saussets-les-Pins to **La Couronne**. Retrace your path to the main junction and head north on the D49 to **Martigues**. Take the D5 north to **St-Mitre-les-Remparts**, then follow the small D51 past **St-Blaise** to connect up with the N1569. Turn left towards **Fos-sur-Mer**, where you turn right onto the N568. Four km on, turn left onto the N268 to **Port St-Louis**. From here, go right onto the D35, then left onto the D35B which leads across the Rhône to Salin-de-Giraud and the **Camargue**. Turn right onto the D36 and keep going north along the river until you meet the D570. Turn right and follow the signs for **Arles-Centre**.

SALON-DE-PROVENCE

Tourist Office: *56 cours Gimon; tel: 04 90 56 27 60.* Open summer 0900–2000; winter 0900–1200, 1400–1830.

Accommodation and Food

Chain hotels include *Ib*. The **Abbaye de Ste-Croix** *(RC), rte du Val de Cuech; tel: 04 90 56 24 55; fax: 04 90 56 31 12* (expensive) is a 12th-century Romanesque abbey in the foothills of the Alpilles, with lovely views, antique furnishings and a prestigious gourmet restaurant (expensive; closed Mon lunchtime) blending classic French and Provençal cuisine. Alternatively, try the **Mas du Soleil**, *36 chemin Saint-Côme; tel: 04 90 58 06 53; fax: 04 90 56 21 52* (moderate) or the **Domaine Roquerousse**, *rte d'Avignon; tel: 04 90 59 50 11; fax: 04 90 59 53 75* (2-star; cheap). **Campsite: Camping Nostradamus**, *rte d'Eyguières; tel: 04 90 56 08 36* (3-star; caravans).

Shopping

The **Établissement Marius Fabre Jeune**, *148 av. de Grans, 13300 Salon de Provence; tel: 04 90 53 24 77*, is one of the last traditional manufacturers of Savon de Marseille, a pure vegetable soap given its official identity by Colbert in 1688. Group guided visits can be arranged from Mon–Fri, by appointment (closed for 3 weeks in Aug, and 23 Dec–3 Jan).

Sightseeing

Roughly halfway between Marseille and Arles, Salon is in the heart of olive country, the surrounding countryside shaded the same delicate green as first pressing oil (see p. 294). Built around a massive medieval fortress, it is a fascinating stop for tourists, offering such delights as Napoleon's bed (in the château), a waxen Manon des Sources, and a Coca Cola museum, as well as abundant history.

The town centre boasts the oldest clock-tower in Provence. In the square near the *Porte d'Horloge* stands a curiosity dating from the early 18th century. This fountain appears from a distance to be a tree dripping water continually from its branches; closer inspection reveals a mushroom shape of weathered solid stone with a fern-covered top. Through the archway of the *Porte d'Horloge* the giant mural of Nostradamus beckons the visitor to explore the café-lined *r. de l'Horloge* and the largely pedestrianised old town.

In the town centre, with parking

nearby, are several museums of more than passing interest. The **Château de l'Empéri**, *Monté du Puech; tel: 04 90 56 22 36* (open Wed–Mon, 1000–1200, 1430–1830 Apr–Sept; 1000–1200, 1400–1800 Oct–Mar; FFr.25) is the oldest and largest medieval fortress in Provence, built originally for the Archbishops of Arles, but largely reconstructed in the 13th century. Inside, the **Musée de l'Art et l'Histoire Militaire** is a world-class collection, covering the history of the French Army from Louis XIV to 1918, with 10,000 exhibits arranged in lively tableaux.

Housed in the former home of shadowy Michel de Nostredame, the world's most famous fortune-teller, the fascinating **Maison de Nostradamus**, *11 r. Nostradamus; tel: 04 90 56 64 31* (FFr.25) covers a whole range of Renaissance discoveries and philosophies. The **Musée Grévin de la Provence**, *pl. du Puits de Jacob* and *pl. des Centuries; tel: 04 90 56 36 30* (FFr.30) covers 2500 years of Provençal history, together with the area's most enduring legends, in a series of waxwork scenes. Both open daily 1000–1200, 1500–2000 15 June–15 Sept; 1000–1200, 1400–1800 16 Sept–14 June; audio guides in English and other languages; ticket for both FFr.45.

Five mins walk away, an 18th-century mansion houses the **Musée de Salon et de la Crau**, *av. Donnadieu, tel: 04 90 56 28 37* (open 1000–1200, 1400–1830 closed Tues, Sat am, Sun am; FFr.15) which features strong collections of Provençal art, furniture and lifestyle, together with a natural history gallery containing animals from la Crau, the last natural desert in Europe. The **Musée de Coca Cola**, *39 r. St-François; tel: 04 90 56 46 23* (open daily 0900–1900 June–Sept; 1400–1900 Oct–May; FFr.25) is Europe's one and only museum dedicated to the sticky fizzy drink, with an array of posters, bottles etc.

Nostradamus died in Salon in 1566 and is buried in the elegant Gothic **Church of St-Laurent**, *r. Maréchal Joffre*, while the 13th-century **Church of St-Michel**, beside the château, is also worth a visit. There is a major jazz festival at the château each July. Finally, keep looking up, this is the home of the French air display unit and aerobatics teams.

Nostradamus

Michel de Nostredame was born in St-Rémy-de-Provence on 14 December, 1503. He became a doctor of medicine in 1529 and practised in several towns before marrying a girl from Salon and setting up there as an astrologer and prophet in 1547. In 1555–58, he published *Centuries*, two volumes of predictions written in rhyming quatrains, which became instant bestsellers although they were banned by the Pope, while he narrowly escaped being burnt for witchcraft. In 1560, he became court physician to Charles IX, but died in 1566. His mysterious prophecies are still widely read and believed, adapted to fit current events by each new generation.

SALON TO ARLES

Beyond Salon, the road crosses the bleak stony scrubland of the **Plain de Crau**, left behind when the Durance River changed course. Legend blames the gods. When Hercules was on his way home with the cattle of Geryon (his 10th Labour), he passed through Ligurian territory. The locals tried to steal his herd, but Zeus sent down a shower of stones which our hero used to defeat his enemies and win the day. The stones were left lying around.

CÔTE BLEUE

Tourist Offices: *av. A. Briand, Carry-le-Rouet; tel: 04 42 13 20 36* (open Mon–Sat 0900–1200, 1400–1700, Sat 1000–1200 Sept–June; Mon–Sat 0900–1200, 1400–1800, Sun 1000–1200 July–Aug); and *blvd Charles Roux, Sausset-Les-Pins; tel: 04 42 44 71 48* (open Mon–Fri 0900–1200, 1500–1800, Sat–Sun 0900–1200, 1500–1900 July–Aug; Mon–Fri 0900–1200, 1500–1800 Sept–June).

Accommodation and Food

Much of the accommodation in this area is in self-catering holiday cottages, but there are a number of pleasant small hotel-restaurants, such as **La Tuilière** *(LF), 34 av. Draio de la Mar, Carry-le-Rouet; tel: 04 42 44 79 79; fax: 04 42 44 74 40* (cheap); **Le Paradou**, *Le Port, Sausset-Les-Pins; tel: 04 42 44 76 76; fax: 04 42 44 78 48* (moderate); and the **Auberge à la Folie**, *rte St Julien, Sausset-Les-Pins; tel: 04 42 45 06 87; fax: 04 42 44 56 60* (cheap). **Campsites: Arquet**, *chemin de la Batterie, La Couronne; tel: 04 42 42 81 00* (3-star); **Mas**, *plage de Ste Croix, La Couronne; tel: 04 42 80 70 34* (3-star; caravans); **Marius**, *plage de la Saulce, La Couronne; tel: 04 42 80 70 29* (2-star; caravans); plus 7 more in the Martigues/La Couronne area.

For a gourmet seafood meal, try **L'Escale**, *promenade du Port, Carry-le-Rouet; tel: 04 42 45 00 47* (expensive) or **Les Girelles**, *r. Frédéric Mistral, Sausset-Les-Pins; tel: 04 42 45 26 16* (moderate). If you prefer regional cuisine at an affordable price, try **Les Pins**, *av. de la Gare, La Couronne; tel: 04 42 80 70 76*, or **Thalassa**, *pl. du Verdon, La Couronne; tel: 04 42 42 85 34* (both cheap).

Sightseeing

Not quite as ambitious as its larger sister, the Côte d'Azur, the relatively unknown Côte Bleue is a 30km stretch from the western suburbs of Marseille to Martigues. Astonishingly, it still has charming little villages, hidden coves and abandoned headlands.

The area begins in **Estaque**, once a pretty little fishing village on the southern slopes of the Chaîne de l'Estaque, a small but beautiful chain of coastal hills. Estaque has been swallowed by suburban Marseille, yet it does still have a distinctive and pleasant character, and remains famous thanks to the many painters, including Cézanne, Braque, Dufy and Renoir, who immortalised the harbour, church and railway viaduct. As the buildings give way to pine forests and the brilliant yellow of flowering broom, there is access to some fine beaches and magnificent views back across Marseille. A series of small side roads to the left lead down to cheerful Mediterranean holiday villages, with orange tiles, apricot walls and cobalt shutters, such as **Ensuès-La Redonne**, from where an even smaller road leads steeply down to the minute fishing hamlet of **Madrague-de-Gignac** (difficult to turn round here) and the little town of **Carry-le-Rouet**, where an 85-hectare area of the shore has been protected as the **Parc Marine Régional de la Côte Bleue**, *tel: 04 42 45 45 07*. Those in search of entertainment should head for the **Casino**, *blvd des Moulins; tel: 04 42 45 01 58* (open daily 1200–0200). From here, you are on a true coast road with magnificent views over a peacock sea and small sandy bays, with much of the road loosely lined by Mediterranean-style villas with arched verandahs. At the end **La Couronne** is one of the prettiest of all the local villages, with a road leading round the marina to its smaller satellite, **Cap Couronne**, both of which have good beaches well-equipped with ice-creams, buckets and spades and similar essentials.

MARTIGUES

Tourist Office: *2 quai Paul Doumer,* beside the iron bridge; *tel: 04 42 80 30 72.* Open daily 0900–1900 July–Aug; Mon–Sat 0830–1200, 1400–1830, Sun 1000–1200 Easter–June, early Sept; Mon–Sat 0830–1200, 1400–1830, Sun 1000–1200 mid Sept–Easter. Information, brochures and bookings for **boat trips** on the **Grand Bleu**; *tel: 04 42 80 30 72* (FFr.100–160, depending on the itinerary). Ask about the **Pass Nautiques**, a passport ticket for a whole raft of different watersports available locally.

Accommodation and Food

Chain hotels include *Ba, Ca, F1.* Alternatively, try the **Saint Roch**, *Le Moulin de Paradis; tel: 04 42 80 19 73; fax: 04 42 80 01 80* (moderate), or the **Hôtel Eden**, *blvd E. Zola; tel: 04 42 07 36 37; fax: 04 42 07 10 55* (cheap).

For good regional cuisine, try **Chez Marraine**, *6 r. des Cordonniers; tel: 04 42 49 37 48*; **Hostellerie Pascal**, *quai L. Toulmond; tel: 04 42 42 16 89;* **Le Capoulié**, *pl. F. Gras; tel: 04 42 49 26 52;* or **Le Miroir**, *quai Brescon; tel: 04 42 80 50 45* (all cheap–moderate). For a gastronomic extravaganza of classic Lyonnais cooking, head for **Berjac Bouchon à la Mer**, *19 quai Toulmond; tel: 04 42 80 38 60* (expensive).

Sightseeing

A little way inland, Martigues is a delightful market and fishing town which straddles the canal linking the huge grey Etang de Berre to the open sea. The town was founded in 1581 by the amalgamation of three smaller communities, Jonquières (founded 950); l'Ile du Pont St-Geniès (1226) and Ferrières (1250).

Beloved by painters for the last century and now also a popular holiday resort, it has a truly Mediterranean feel, with pastel houses and arched footbridges reflected in the still blue water between the multi-coloured fishing boats. The **Musée Ziem**, *blvd du 14 Juillet; tel: 04 42 80 66 06* (open Wed–Mon 1000–1200, 1430–1830 July–Aug; Wed–Sun 1430–1830 Sept–June; FFr.10, free on Sat–Sun pm) was founded in 1908 when Félix Ziem, one of many artists drawn to the area, donated a painting to the town. It now has a number of excellent works by Provençal artists, as well as archaeological finds from nearby digs and displays on the local fishing trade. The **Maison de Charles Maurras**, *chemin de Paradis; tel: 04 42 80 30 72* (open on request; free) is an 18th-century country house, with memorabilia of its previous owner, Charles Maurras, a local writer and member of the *Académie Française.* The **Vitrine Archéologique**, *pl. Maritima; tel: 04 42 42 18 43* (open daily; free) is a collection of 4th-century Gallic huts, rebuilt on their original foundations.

Amongst a great many fine historic houses in the narrow streets, the **Chapelle de l'Annonciade**, *r. du Dr Sérieux*, is a magnificent baroque creation, belonging to the Pénitants Blancs. The heavily decorated ceiling was painted in 1688, the frescos in 1734. The baroque **Church of La Madeleine**, *quartier de l'Isle* (open for mass or on request), built in 1668, is also worth a quick stop. The thriving local theatre, the **Théâtre des Salins**, *quai Paul Doumer; tel: 04 42 44 36 00*, has exhibitions, concerts, a restaurant and *salon de thé.* The town hosts a major international arts festival in early Aug. Information from the **Bureau de Festival de Martigues**, *r. Colonel Denfert; tel: 04 42 42 12 01.*

A few kilometres out of town, at **Châteauneuf-les-Martigues**, are two stops for the children. **El Dorado City**, *tel: 04 42 79 86 90* (open from 1100, daily June–mid Sept; Wed, Sat–Sun mid Mar–May; Sat–Sun mid Sept–mid Nov; closed mid Nov–mid Mar; FFr.45) reconstructs the Wild West, with events and entertainment. **La Vallée des Fauves**, *tel: 04 42 79 92 04* (open daily 1000–1900, closed Dec; FFr.50) is an animal park with animals ranging from lions to sea lions.

ST-MITRE-LES-REMPARTS

Tourist Information: *pl. Neuve; tel: 04 42 49 18 93.* Open Mon–Fri 0830–1200, 1330–1730.

First founded in about 700BC, St-Mitre has a long, if not wildly distinguished history. The ramparts of its name were built in the 16th century following a siege by Raymond of Turenne, and are still firmly in place, with two **gateways** leading into a maze of tiny pedestrianised streets in the old town centre. Use the large carparks outside the walls and walk. The delightful little 17th–18th-century **church** has several fine paintings, a Roman font and modern stained glass.

A couple of kilometres west of the town, the **Oppidum St Blaise** (open Wed–Mon 0900–1200, 1400–1800) is the site of the ancient town, with the earliest signs of habitation going back 5000 years. The first formal settlement, founded by Etruscan traders in the 7th century BC was destroyed by Saracen invaders in the 9th century AD, but struggled on intermittently until 1390. The long rocky spur, reinforced by numerous layers of defensive walls, is a fascinating slice of layered time, including Hellenic ramparts, a 5th-century enclosure, two ruined churches, a necropolis and many other smaller remains. With the remains scattered through the woods, the poorly signed site can be surprisingly difficult to find.

FOS-SUR -MER

Tourist Office: *av. J. Jaurès; tel: 04 42 47 71 96.* Open Mon–Sat 0900–1900, Sun 0900–1200, 1400–1900 July–Aug; Mon–Fri 0900–1200, 1300–1800, Sat 0900–1200, 1400–1800 Sept–June.

Astonishingly, Fos has pretentions as a holiday resort, with a pretty marina, fine sandy beach and attractive village houses huddled around **L'Hauteur**, a huge 39m rock topped by large, well-preserved 10th century fortress.

A parapet walk leads around the ramparts which enclose a huddled medieval village and the 12th-century **Church of St Sauveur**. The little **Chapelle de Notre-Dame de la Mer** is now home to a small **museum**, *tel: 04 42 05 01 22*, dedicated to the 1st century BC Roman port of Anse de Saint-Gervais.

The old centre is swamped however by the staggeringly vast industrial complex and container port belching smoke in 16 shades of grey. Created in the 1960s, and catering mainly for the oil and gas industry, with its many by-products, the complex covers over 10,000 hectares and employs about 21,000 people). It is not beautiful, but it is deeply impressive. Ask the Tourist Office about factory and harbour tours. Chain hotels include *Mc.*

The far end of the 19km-long zone is marked by **Port St Louis** (**Tourist Office**: *Tour Saint-Louis; tel: 04 42 86 01 21.* Open Mon–Sat 0900–1200, 1500–1900, Sun 0900–1200) another small town struggling to find the remnants of a prettier past. From here, the road leads to the **Bac de Barcarin**, a small car ferry across the Grand Rhône (shuttle service until 0100 daily; FFr.28) to Salins-de-Giraud and the Camargue (see pp. 87–89).

Marseille–Toulon

If you have just landed or driven to Marseille, this route offers the first real taste of Mediterranean France, heading east from the city along a coastal route which encompasses one of the most dramatic *corniches* in Provence, as well as a trio of delightful seaside resorts. The inland route offers an interesting alternative.

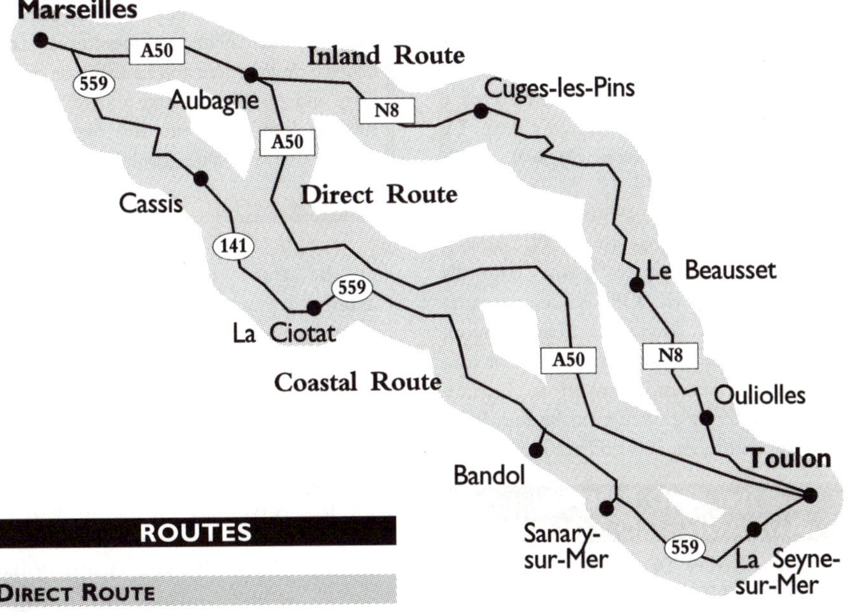

ROUTES

Direct Route

Leave Marseille on the Autoroute A50, following it past Aubagne and through the coastal hinterland behind Cassis, Bandol and Sanary to reach Toulon. Distance: 70 km; allow 2 hrs.

Direct Route: 70 km

Inland Route

Leave Marseille on the Autoroute A50, exiting after 21 km at **Aubagne**. From Aubagne, take the N8 through Cuges-les-Pins, Le Beausset, and Ollioules to Toulon. Distance: 67 km; allow 3–4 hrs.

Coastal Route

Leave Marseille on the D559, following it through to **Cassis**. From Cassis take the D141, the **Corniche des Crêtes**, to **La Ciotat**, and then the D559 to **Bandol** and **Sanary**. Continue along the D559 through La Seyne into Toulon. Distance: 78 km; allow 1–2 days.

AUBAGNE

Tourist Office: *av. A. Boyer; tel: 04 42 03 49 98*. Open Mon–Sat 0900–1200, 1400–1800.

Dominated by the limestone peaks of the Chaîne de l'Etoile, Aubagne is a major agricultural and pottery centre. Local potteries specialise in santons and beautiful pots, vases and other ceramic ware, and there are two major **ceramics fairs** (mid July–early-Sept and Dec) as well as the **Argile** (from *argilla*, the Latin for clay), which is France's largest ceramics market (biennial, Aug).

Aubagne is also famous as the birthplace of Marcel Pagnol. In the town centre, **Le Petit Monde de Marcel Pagnol**, *av. A. Boyer; tel: 04 42 84 10 22* (open mid Feb–mid Nov Tues–Sun 0900–1200, 1400–1800; free) has over 200 santons representing characters from Pagnol's works. The Tourist Office issues a pamphlet, *Sur Les Traces de Marcel Pagnol*, which describes several routes in the surrounding countryside linked to Pagnol, and offers 2½-hr guided visits by bus, July-Aug Wed and Sat 1600; FFr.30.

Marcel Pagnol

The birthplace of the great writer and film-maker Marcel Pagnol is marked by a plaque at *16, cours Barthélemy* in Aubagne. Born on 28 February 1895, Pagnol grew up in the village of La Treille, to the north-west of Aubagne. He eventually returned to spend his last years there and died in the village in 1974. The surrounding countryside and the rural Provençaux inspired early books such as his childhood memoires, *Le Château de ma Mère* and *La Gloire de mon Père*, and his later, better-known books such as *Jean de Florette* and *Manon des Sources* which, as films, gained world-wide renown.

INLAND ROUTE: AUBAGNE TO TOULON

Tourist Office: *16 r. Nationale, Ollioules; tel: 04 94 63 11 74* (open July–Aug daily 0900–1800; Sept–June Mon–Sat 0900–1200).

After traversing the Plaine des Cuges and the village of Cuges-les-Pins (19 km from Aubagne), the route starts to climb up through pine forests, with the massif of St-Baume in the background, before reaching the **Parc d'Attractions OK Corral**; *tel: 04 42 73 80 05* (open daily June–Aug 1000–1800; Apr, May, Sept Wed and Sat 1000–1730, Sun 1000–1800; FFr.73). The park has rides and Western-style amusements. Eight km further, you pass the **Paul Ricard Circuit du Castellet**, a grand prix racing circuit, then a panorama of the valley unfolds as the road descends into the large town of Le Beausset. From Le Beausset, the N8 passes through Ste Anne-d'Evenos and then winds its way through the lovely Gorges d'Ollioules to reach Ollioules. This pleasant village is typically Provençal, with an economy based on vines, olives and wholesale flowers. It has a charming old quarter, with fountains and cobbled streets, and is dominated by the ruins of an 11th-century château.

From here, it is 7 km along the N8 into Toulon.

CASSIS

Tourist Office: Maison de Cassis, *pl. P. Baragnon; tel: 04 42 01 71 17*. Open daily July–Aug 0900–1930; June Mon–Sat 0900–1800, Sun 0900–1230; Sept Mon–Sat 0900–1930, Sun 0900–1230; Oct–May Mon–Sat 0900–1300, 1400–1800, Sun 0900–1230.

Accommodation and Food

Cassis has some excellent hotels, amongst them **Le Jardin de Cassis**, *av. A. Favier; tel: 04 42 01 84 85; fax: 04 42 01 32 38* (moderate–expensive), a stylish hotel with gardens and a pool; **Les Roches Blancs**, *av. des Calanques; tel: 04 42 01 09 30; fax: 04 42 01 94 23* (expensive), 1 km from town on a promontory with fine sea views, beach, and pool; and **Le Clos des Aromes**, *r. Agostini; tel: 04 42 01 71 84; fax: 04 42 01 31 76* (moderate), which has a charming courtyard.

There are plenty of good restaurants along the quay. **Le Dauphin**, *3 r. S.Icard; tel: 04 42 01 10 00* (cheap), is hidden away in a back street and very good value.

Sightseeing

Even if its reputation is quite overblown (Mistral wrote 'Qui a vist Paris è noun Cassis a ren vist' – 'he who was seen Paris but not Cassis has seen nothing'), Cassis is still an enchanting little port, set in a picture-postcard location between the escarpment of Cap Canaille to the east and the Gardiole heights to the west.

As well as its setting, Cassis is famous for its light, fruity wines (there is no central *cave* but the Tourist Office provides a map and list of domaines which can be visited) which go so well with the seafood dishes – particularly the local speciality of *oursins* (sea urchins) – which are served up in copious quantities in the numerous restaurants which line the quayside. Within the town there is a **Musée d'Arts et Traditions Populaires**, *r. Xavier d'Authier; tel: 04 42 01 88 66 (*open Wed, Thurs, Sat summer 1530–1830; winter 1430–1730; free). This small museum contains Gallo-Roman artefacts, as well as local paintings and sculpture.

The other great attraction of Cassis is as the main entry point to the magnificent **Calanques**, the deep sea inlets which have been eroded from the limestone cliffs of the Gardiole. The main calanques are **Port Miou** (a former quarry, now sheltering a small marina), **Port Pin** (shallower, but with a little beach and superb swimming in the limpid waters), and **D'En Vau** (the most dramatic, with steep cliffs plunging down into the sea). They can easily be reached on foot (from 1 to 3 hrs return), but the preferred method – particularly after a long, lazy lunch on the quayside – is to take a trip on one of the dozen or so boats which tout for business in the port (regular departures daily between 0900–1800; FFr.45).

Coastal Route: Cassis to Bandol

Tourist Office: *blvd Anatole France, La Ciotat; tel: 04 42 08 61 32.* Open Mon–Sat 0900–1200, 1430–1800.

From Cassis the road climbs steeply upwards towards the **Corniche des Crêtes**, a superb coastal route which traverses the top of the Canaille range, a limestone outcrop which rises straight up from the sea in a series of dizzying white cliffs. At Pas de la Colle, turn right to the **Mont de la Saoupe**, from where there is a panoramic view across Cassis out to the Île de Riou (west), the Chaîne de l'Etoile and Massif de Ste-Baume (north) and La Ciotat (east). Return to the pass and continue on to Cap Canaille, where the highest coastal cliff in France reaches a formidable 362 m. A viewpoint reveals the sheer drop of the cliffs to the sea below. As the road twists and turns around the headlands there is an ever-widening view of Cassis and La Ciotat, with another superb coastal panorama visible from the Lighthouse (500 m off to the right) after Grand Tête. It then descends into La Ciotat.

LA CIOTAT

A prosperous ship-building port since Roman times, La Ciotat has had to re-adjust since the closure of the shipyards in the 1990s. Derelict gantries still dominate the small harbour, but tourism is now a primary goal. The town is the birthplace of the appropriately-named Lumière brothers, Auguste and Louis, who invented the technique of piercing the edge of a roll of film with holes and running it over a toothed mechanism attached to a projector – thus giving birth to modern cinema (see p. 205). The world's first 'motion picture' was shown here in September 1895, two months before it stunned Parisian audiences. There is now an annual Film Festival (second half of July).

From La Ciotat, the road follows the coast through the resort of **Les Lecques** (good sandy beaches), before cutting across inland to Bandol.

BANDOL

Tourist Office: *allées Vivien; tel: 04 94 29 41 35.* Open July–Aug daily 0900–1300, 1400–1900; Sept–June Mon–Sat 0900–1200, 1400-1800.

A popular family resort with a pleasant, palm tree-lined promenade alongside the harbour, Bandol has several beaches and a good selection of shops, restaurants and cafés. At the turn of the century the resort was frequented by literati such as Thomas Mann, Aldous Huxley and Katherine Mansfield, as well as being known for its tuna fisheries. The quayside today is lined with craft offering various sea-based activities from deep sea fishing to scuba diving, underwater viewing or simply promenades en mer. A popular excursion is to the off-shore **Île de Bendor**.

Just outside Bandol is the **Musée de l'Automobile Sportive**, *4303 Ancien Chemin de Toulon; tel: 04 94 29 63 63* (open Tue–Sun Apr–Sept 0900–1200, 1400–2000; Oct–Mar 0900–1200, 1400–1800; FFr.45). This nostalgic collection features over 60 pristine roadsters and racing cars from Europe and America.

Bandol is known for its fine red wines, the quality of which is enchanced by the Mourvèdre grapes which thrive in this sunny, protected region; ask at the Tourist Office for the Route des Vins de Bandol, which gives details of around 50 domaines which can be visited.

SANARY

Tourist Office: *Jardin de la Ville; tel: 04 94 74 01 04.* Open July–Aug daily 0900–1200, 1400-1900; Sept–June Mon–Sat 0900–1200, 1400–1800.

Accommodation and Food

Sanary's top hotel is the **Grand Hôtel des Bains**, *av. E. d'Orves; tel: 04 94 74 13 47; fax: 04 94 88 14 02* (moderate), which is right on the seafront with 34 rooms. Other good hotels include the **Primavera**, *324 av. de Portissol; tel: 04 94 74 00 36* (moderate), and the **Hôtel du Parc**, *av. Europe Unie; tel: 04 94 25 80 08; fax: 04 94 25 56 65* (moderate). There are half-a-dozen seafood restaurants around the port as well as numerous traditional restaurants, pizzerias, and crêperies.

Sightseeing

Sanary is sheltered by the wooded hills of the Gros Cervau from the Mistral and has a charming port area surrounded by pastel-coloured houses. The 14th-century Tower on the quayside is now part of a hotel. In the backstreets, the 16th-century **Chapel of Notre-Dame de Pitié**, *r. Marcellin-Siat* (open 0950–1900; free) contains some curious ex-votos and a splendid 16th-century piéta.

MENDE–MONTPELLIER

This is one of the most spectacularly beautiful and entertaining routes in the whole region, twisting through the the Gorges of the Tarn, Jonte and Hérault Rivers, crossing mountain passes around the base of massive Mont Aigoual. The driving is slow and often hard and the area is so crammed with activity and history that you should allow plenty of time.

ROUTE: 255 KM

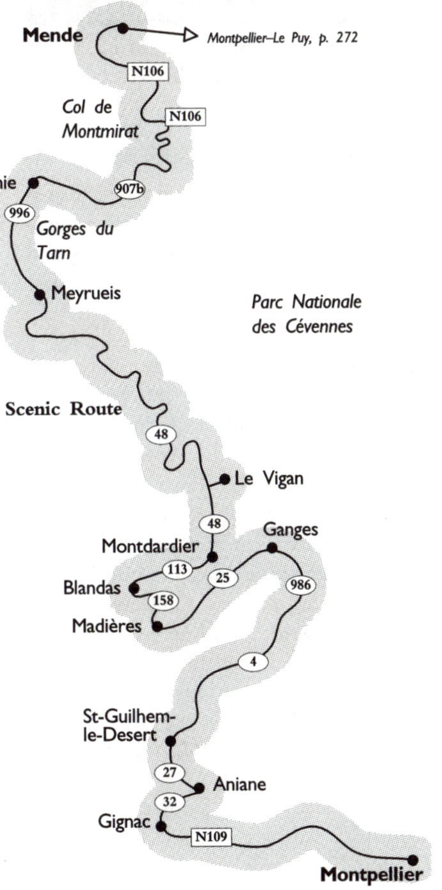

ROUTE

Leave Mende heading south towards Florac on the N106. After 35 km and crossing the Col de Montmirat, turn right onto the D907bis, clearly marked to the **Gorges du Tarn**. Keep on this through **Ste Énimie** and the gorges to **Le Rozier**, where you turn left onto the D996 to **Meyrueis**. From here, the D986 wriggles south, climbing up to the Col de la Sereyrède, which is the access point for **Mont Aigoual**. Turn right and take the D48, then the D999 to **Le Vigan**. Retrace your steps to the edge of town and crossing the old bridge, take the D48 through **Montdardier**, and turn right onto the D113. At Blandas, turn left onto the D158, then right onto the D173 to the **Cirque de Navacelles**. Return to the D158 and turn turn right towards Madières, where you join the D25 to **Ganges**. Rejoin the D986 heading south to St-Bauzille-de-Putois, then turn right onto the smaller D4 which heads south via Causse-de-la-Selle to the **Gorges de l'Hérault**, **St-Guilhem-le-Désert** and the Pont du Diable, where you fork left onto the D27 to **Aniane**. Turn right onto the D32 to **Gignac** and, from here, turn left onto the N109 (E11) for a fast run into Montpellier. Allow a minimum of 2 days, preferably 4.

Note: A direct route from Mende to Montpellier is provided by the first section of the Montpellier–Le Puy route, p. 272.

MENDE

See p. 275.

GORGES DU TARN

Tourist Offices: **Ispagnac**: *Mairie; tel: 04 66 44 20 50;* **Ste Énimie**: *tel: 04 66 48 53 44.*

Accommodation and Food

Sainte-Énemie is probably the best base at the eastern end of the gorges, with a number of small hotels, restaurants, bars and crêperies. Amongst the best is the **Auberge du Moulin**, *tel: 04 66 48 53 08; fax: 04 66 48 58 16* (moderate), a small traditional inn beside the Tarn, refurbished into a comfortable hotel with good restaurant and shady terrace. Just beyond Ste Énimie, the **Auberge de la Cascade**, *St-Chély-du-Tarn; tel: 04 66 48 52 82; fax: 04 66 48 52 45* (cheap) is a pretty riverfront inn with a shady terrace and pool. Halfway along the gorge is the romantic 15th-century **Château de la Caze**, *La Malène; tel: 04 66 48 51 01; fax: 04 66 48 55 75* (expensive), now transformed into a luxurious hotel with a gourmet restaurant. Nearby, the **Manoir de Montesquiou**, *La Malène; tel: 04 66 48 51 12; fax: 04 66 48 50 47* (moderate–expensive) is a similarly restored 15th–16th century manor house with comfortable rooms and traditional local cuisine. **Campsites**: **Camping Municipal du Pré Morjal**, *Ispagnac; tel: 04 66 44 23 77* (3-star; caravans; open Apr–Oct); **Camping Couderc**, *Ste Énimie; tel: 04 66 48 50 53* (3-star; caravans; open Apr–Sept); **Le Site Castelbouc**, *Ste Énimie; tel: 04 66 48 58 08* (2-star; caravans; open Apr–Sept).

Cruising the Gorges

The best possible way to see the Gorges du Tarn is from the river. There are numerous opportunities to do so. The laziest is with **Les Bateliers de la Malène**; tel: 04 66 48 51 10 (open daily Apr–Oct; FFr.95) who waft you downstream for 8 km to the Cirque des Baumes on flat-bottomed boats.

Those who would also like a little exercise, there are plentiful opportunities to hire a canoe or kayak. You are given a short training session and can go either accompanied by a guide or on your own. **Canoë 2000**, *La Malène; tel: 04 66 48 51 28*, run trips to the Cirque des Baumes from La Malène, St Chely du Tarn, Ste Énimie and Montbrun. Other companies include **Ispa Canoë**, *Ispagnac; tel: 04 66 44 20 73*, **Canoë Paradan**, *Ste Énimie; tel: 04 66 48 56 90* and **Euro-Canoë**, *Ste Énimie; tel: 04 66 48 52 89*. Prices range from about FFr.75–250, dependent on what and how long you want and include a return trip by minibus to where you left your car. The light is best in the morning.

Sightseeing

The gorges begin officially at **Ispagnac**, which received its name from a colony of Spaniards who settled here in Roman times. Today, it is a pretty little village with a charming 12th-century Romanesque church, a 14th-century bridge, an Ursuline monastery with a fine 17th-century stone door and a number of handsome Renaissance buildings. It is also a 'Station Verte', with numerous opportunities for outdoor activities.

From here, the road drops ever further down between sheer and even overhanging granite walls as the full impact of these magnificent gorges takes hold. You pass the little village and Château of **Prades** (floodlit 2100–2300 each evening) before reaching the enchanting medieval town of **Ste Énimie**, now also the heart of the Tarn tourist trade, named after a Merovingian princess who prayed to be made ugly to fend off her suitors and was struck down with leprosy. She changed her mind and came here to cure her illness, but it returned every time she tried to leave. Eventually she gave up and founded a monastery. Its remains are still evident within the narrow cobbled streets, together with a lovely 12th-century Romanesque church, and a fountain gushing the spring water which cured her. The **Musée Le Vieux Logis**; *tel: 04 66 48 53 44* (open Apr–Jun, Sept 1000–1200, 1430–1800; July–Aug 1000–1230, 1400–1900) is a careful reconstruction of a medieval lodging. Walking tour brochures are available from the tourist office.

As the road winds on through **St-Chély-du-Tarn** and **La Malène**, the road becomes ever more spectacular, twisting under giant overhangs and through tunnels blasted out of sheer rock. The whole way along, the clear, dark green river wriggles alongside and there are regular parking places at the most scenic viewpoints.

At la Malène, a road (D18) leads across the river up the canyon wall to the **Roc des Hourtous**, above the rocky bowl of the **Cirque des Baumes**, end point for most canoe trips. A little further on, at Les Vignes, a road (D995) on the right leads up the north bank to **Point Sublime**, a dizzyingly high and magnificent viewpoint, reached by dizzying hairpin bends. Back down on the main road, the last stretch of the gorges becomes much wilder and less developed as the river heads towards **Le Rozier** and its confluence with the Jonte.

GORGES DE LA JONTE

Tourist Office: Meyrueis: *tel: 04 66 45 60 33.*

Accommodation and Food

Meyrueis is the main centre for this area, with a number of hotels and restaurants. Amongst the best are the **Hôtel La Renaissance**, *tel: 04 66 45 60 19; fax: 04 66 45 65 94* (moderate), created out of two 16th and 18th century houses; and the **Château d'Ayres**, *tel: 04 66 45 60 10; fax: 04 66 45 62 26* (moderate) which began life as a 12th-century fortified abbey. For something cheaper, try **Le Mont Aigoual** *(LF), r. de la Barrière; tel: 04 66 45 65 61; fax: 04 66 45 64 25* (cheap–moderate).

Campsites: **Camping de Capelan**; *tel: 04 66 45 60 50* (3-star; caravans; open May–Sept); **Le Champ d'Ayres**; *tel: 04 66 45 60 51* (3-star; caravans; open Apr–Sept).

Sightseeing

The 21 km Gorges de la Jonte are also extremely dramatic, a huge, sheer gash in the plateau, with heavily wooded V-shaped slopes often hiding the river from view. There are very few stopping places and no points of access to the river.

At the far end, **Meyrueis** is a lively small town with a large number of hotels and restaurants and a pretty centre built on three rivers. From here, a road to the left leads back 15 km to a show cave, the **Aven Armand**; *tel: 04 66 45 61 31* (open: Jul–Aug daily 0900–1900; Apr, May, Jun, Sept daily 0900–1200, 1330–1800; Oct daily1000–1200, 1330–1700; Nov–Mar by prior arrangement (groups only); FFr.43). A road (D39) to the right doubles back along the south bank for 8 km to the **Grotte de Dargilan**; *tel: (in season) 04 66 45 60 20; (out of season) 04 66*

45 64 35 (open: Jul–Aug daily 0900–1900; Apr, May, Jun, Sept daily 0900–1200, 1330–1800; Oct daily1000–1200, 1330–1700; Nov–Mar by prior arrangement, groups only; FFr.36), the first cave in France to be opened to the public, in 1888. Both systems rank amongst the largest and most flamboyant show caves in France. Two km south of town is the 15th–16th-century **Château de Roquedols**, which now houses an information office for the Parc des Cévennes (see p. 149).

From here, the road climbs over the Col de Montjardin to Mont Aigoual.

MONT AIGOUAL

Tourist Office: **Maison Georges Fabre**, *Le Pont du Moulin, Cambrieu; tel: 04 67 82 64 67*. Open July–Aug daily 1000–1300, 1400–1900; May–June, Sept daily 1000–1230, 1400–1730; Oct–Apr, Sat–Sun, school holidays 1000–1200, 1400–1700. Exhibition on the forest of Aigoual; FFr.10.

ACCOMMODATION AND FOOD

The **Grand Hôtel du Parc et de l'Esperou** *(LF), L'Esperou; tel: 04 67 82 60 05; fax: 04 67 82 62 12* (cheap–moderate) and the **Hôtel du Touring et l'Observatoire**, *L'Esperou; tel: 04 67 82 60 04* (cheap) face each other in this quiet village waiting for winter snow and the ski crowd. **Campsite**: **Camping Le Terondel**, *Camprieu; tel: 04 67 82 61 89* (caravans).

SIGHTSEEING

The Aigoual Massif is one of the largest and certainly the highest mountain in the Cévennes. At the summit (1567m), an extraordinary neo-Gothic castle, bristling with antennae, houses the **Observatoire Météorologique**; *tel: 04 67 82 60 01* (open June–Sept daily 1000–1900; free), a working weather station which also houses a fascinating exhibition on meteorology, together with stunning photographs taken by the staff. There is plenty of weather to be observed up here, with the highest rainfall in France (2.50 m annually), whistling winds year round and heavy frosts and snow in winter, so wrap up warmly.

In winter, the ski resort of **Prat Peyrot**; *tel: 04 67 82 60 17*, comes to life, with 208 km of cross-country ski trails, 10 lifts and 14 pistes for downhill enthusiasts.

At the foot of the mountain, an underground river has carved out a huge, echoing chasm, the **Abîme du Bramabiau**, *on the D986, Camprieu; tel: 04 67 82 60 78* (open Apr–mid Nov; FFr.32). Its name means 'the ox that bellows' in Occitan, after the thunderous noise it makes.

Just off the route, at *Lanuéjols*, **Randals Bison**, *tel: 04 67 82 73 74* (open June–Sept daily 1000–1900; Oct–Dec, Mar–Jun Sun 1400–1700) is a breeding farm for American bison. You can visit the bison, then eat them, on the spot or as a take-away. Nearby is also a **deer farm**; *tel: 04 67 82 71 74*.

MONT AIGOUAL TO GANGES

Tourist Office: **Le Vigan**: *Maison de Pays, pl. du Marché; tel: 04 67 81 01 72*.

ACCOMMODATION AND FOOD

The **Auberge de la Cascade**, *St-Maurice-Navacelles; tel: 04 67 81 50 95* (moderate) is a gourmet restaurant with a few rooms in a superb setting by the Cirque de Navacelles. The **Château d'Isis**, *St-Julien-de-la-Nef-en-Cévennes (on the D999 between L'Hérault and Ganges); tel/fax: 04 67 73 56 22* (cheap) is a magnificent farmhouse B&B in a 14th-century château, serving gastronomic food.

Sightseeing

The road now winds through the southern tip of the Cévennes, crossing the Col du Minier before dropping off the edge of the massif. At the bottom, **Le Vigan** is home to the **Musée Cévenol**, *r. des Calquières; tel: 04 67 81 06 86* (open Apr–Oct Wed–Mon 1000–1200, 1400–1800; Nov–Mar, Wed 1000–1200, 1400–1800), an excellent rural life museum, with tableaux of everyday life and displays on traditional crafts and industries (including silk production), local artists and writers. **La Maison des Magnans**, *CAT Molières-Cavaillac; tel: 04 67 81 05 06* (open mid May–mid-Sept Mon–Fri), is one of a handful of silk farms still in production Tours include cultivation, spinning and weaving, with silk items on sale.

The road now climbs back onto the plateau, to the little stone village of **Montdardier**, built around a glamorous château (not open to the public). Beyond the village, keep a lookout to the right for a large, but totally unmarked, ring of pre-historic standing stones.

The **Cirque de Navacelles** is one of the most extraordinary and dramatic natural sights in the region. An oxbow loop in the little Vis River has over the millenia, carved a vast, almost perfect bowl (1200 m across and 400 m deep) in the limestone plateau. The view is spectacular. Those with time can wind down and take the road along the **Gorges de la Vis** via St-Maurice-Navacelles. Others should return take the road through flowering grasslands and cornfields towards la Madières, where a delightful drive allows intermittent views of the gorge before dropping down to follow the river into Ganges.

GANGES TO GIGNAC

Tourist Offices: Gignac: *Hôtel de Laurès, pl. du Général Claparède; tel: 04 67 57 58 83.* Open July–Aug Mon–Sat 0930–1230, 1500–1900, Sun 1000–1230, 1600–1800; Sept–June Mon–Fri 0900–1200, 1400–1800, Sat 1000–1200, 1500–1700; **Aniane**: *2 av. de St-Guilhem; tel: 04 67 57 01 42* (July–Aug only); **St-Guilhem-le-Désert**: *9 r. Font-Portal; tel: 04 67 57 44 33.*

Accommodation and Food

The **Hostellerie St Benoit** *(LF), rte de St-Guilhem, Aniane; tel: 04 67 57 71 63; fax: 04 67 57 47 10* (cheap) is a peaceful hotel and restaurant near the river, with its own pool and pétanque. Another reasonable option is the **Motel-Restaurant du Vieux Moulin** *(LF), chemin de l'Auberge, blvd du Moulin, Gignac; tel: 04 67 57 57 95; fax: 04 67 57 69 19* (cheap–moderate), a comfortable modern motel, with a pool and good food. **Campsites: Camping du Pont**, *730 blvd du Moulin, Gignac; tel: 04 67 57 52 40* (2-star; caravans; open all year); **Camping Municipal la Meuse**, *chemin de la Meuse, Gignac; tel: 04 67 57 92 97* (3-star; caravans; open June–Sept).

Sightseeing

Ganges is a small industrial town with the remnants of an fine old quarter with 'traverses' (narrow alleys) linking courtyards, hanging gardens and cellars. From the little medieval village of **Laroque**, just south of Ganges, a road train winds up to the entrance of the **Grotte des Lauriers**; *tel: 04 67 73 55 57* (open daily July–Aug 1000–1830, Apr–Jun 1400–1700, Sept 1400–1800, Oct–Mar by appointment), the first of several cave systems in the area. A little further south, turn left on the D108 to the **Grotte de Demoiselle**, *St-Bauzille-du-Putois; tel: 04 67 73 70 02* (open daily July–Aug 0900–1900, Apr–Jun, Sept 0900–1200, 1400–1900, Oct–

Mar 0930–1200, 1400–1700; FFr.38), once used as a hide-out by Camisard rebels during the Wars of Religion. The entrance is through a tunnel in a towering cliff with wonderful views over the Hérault Valley and a thriving Mediterranean garden. A funicular whisks visitors up to the start of the tour. Both cave systems have magnificent arrays of stalactites and stalagmites.

The Hérault River is one of the more important rivers in the south of France, rising on Mont Aigoual before making a rapid dash for the coast 150 km south. En route, about 10 km south of Causse-de-la-Selle, it has carved the last set of gorges on this tempestuous route. The **Gorges de l'Hérault** are on the whole are more gentle than their northern counterparts, with languid curves and richly flowered slopes. The view from the bank is good, but imperfect, and the best way to see them in their true glory is from the water. Canoes can be hired through **Rapido**; *tel: 04 67 55 75 75.*

At the southern entrance to the gorges, the delightful village and abbey of **St-Guilhem-le-Désert** was founded in 806 by Guilhem, Duc d'Aquitaine, a companion of Charlemagne and soon became a popular pilgrim destination, both as a stop on the road to Santiago de Compostela (see p. 193) and for its relic of the True Cross. The existing abbey church, built in the 11th–13th centuries, is one of the finest Romanesque structures in the Languedoc. The abbey refectory houses a small museum (open July–Aug Mon–Sat 1000–1200, 1430–1800, Sun 1430–1800; Apr–Jun, Sept–Nov Mon–Tue, Thur–Sat 1400–1730, Sun 1430–1700; Dec–Mar Mon–Tue, Thur–Sun 1400–1700; FFr.10).

Nearby are the **Grottes de Clamouse**; *tel: 04 67 57 71 05* (open daily July–Aug 1000–1900, Sept–June 1000–1700), yet another superb set of caves, distinguished by the extraordinarily beautiful feathery crystals growing on its stalactites, and the 11th-century **Pont du Diable** (Devil's Bridge), crossing the Hérault.

In **Aniane**, stop for a look at the imposing 17th-century churches of **St Sauveur**, on the site of the original 8th century monastery of St Benoît, and **St Jean-Baptiste**, both surrounded by a huddle of pretty old houses and alleys. Just out of town, the 100-hectare **Géospace**, *rte de la Boissière; tel: 04 67 03 49 49* (open July–Aug Tue–Sun 1000–1200, 1400–1800) is above all, a working science park but also hosts a range of fascinating tours and events, including regular public night sessions in the observatory. A few km on, the **Maison du Fleuve**, *Barrage de la Meuse; tel: 04 67 57 99 00* (open July–Aug and school holidays daily 1000–1200, 1400–1900, Sept–June Wed, Sat 1400–1800, Sun 1000–1200, 1400–1800) is a well-stocked information centre with a freshwater aquarium and exhibitions on the Hérault River, marking the southern end of the gorges.

Just beyond that, **Gignac** is a small fortified town dating back to the 8th century, with a number of fine old houses, most of the 17th century. There is also a particularly graceful 18th century bridge. Three km from town, **Florilab**, *rte de Pézenas (D32); tel: 04 67 57 51 35* (open school terms Mon–Fri 0900–1200, 1330–1630, at other times by appointment) is much more than a botanic laboratory, filled with magnificent plants and gardens to gladden the heart of anyone with green fingers. The area is also home to a great many vineyards, producing highly drinkable Vin de Pays d'Oc.

MENTON–BARCELONNETTE

SHORTEST ROUTE: 185 KM

The hustle and traffic of the Riviera is quickly left behind as this scenic route heads inland, up into the quiet Alpes-Maritimes, hairpinning around the hillsides and hugging the sides of deep gorges.

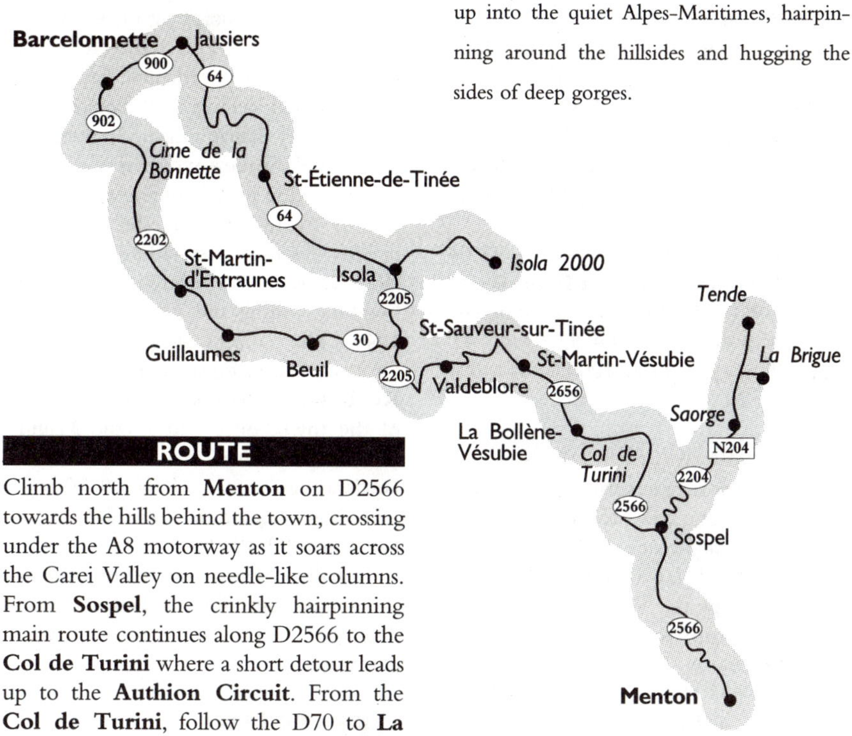

ROUTE

Climb north from **Menton** on D2566 towards the hills behind the town, crossing under the A8 motorway as it soars across the Carei Valley on needle-like columns. From **Sospel**, the crinkly hairpinning main route continues along D2566 to the **Col de Turini** where a short detour leads up to the **Authion Circuit**. From the **Col de Turini**, follow the D70 to **La Bollène-Vésubie**. There turn onto D2565 and go through **St-Martin-Vésubie** to join D2205 into **St Sauveur-sur-Tinée**. Here the route splits.

You can continue north on the D2205 (with the option of a side-track up to **Isola 2000**; 17km each way) and then take the D64 over the lonely **Cime de la Bonette** summit. The final stretch into **Barcelonnette** is on the D900.

The alternative route from **St-Sauveur** follows the D30 through several short tunnels to **Beuil**, then takes the D28 to **Guillaumes** where there is a side-track south through **Gorges de Dalius**; 12km each way. From Guillaumes, the D2202 and then the D902 lead to **Barcelonnette**.

As the crow flies, Barcelonnette is only 97km from Menton, but this mountainous route has so many bends that, even without the side-tracks, it stretches for 185km via Cime de la Bonette or 206km via Guilllaumes.

Allow 3 days – but if possible take more time as both sections from St Saveur-sur-

Tinée to Barcelonnette are well worth doing. There is no more direct or faster route. To do the journey non-stop, allow 3–4 hrs.

SOSPEL

Tourist Office: *Vieux Pont; tel: 04 93 04 15 80.* Open daily July–Aug 0900–1200, 1430–1830; Sept–June 0900–1200, 1400–1700. The office shares the little tower in the middle of the **Vieux Pont** across the **River Brévéra** with the **Mercantour National Park Information Office**. Open daily July–Aug 0900–1300, 1400–1800.

Station: *rte de Castillon, tel: 04 93 04 00 17.* Four opulent **Orient Express** carriages from the *Belle Époque* era can be visited in the sidings; *tel: 04 93 04 00 43.* Open Tues–Sun 1100–1200 and 1400–1700; FFr.20.

Accommodation and Food

The town has several small hotels including three Logis. The **Hôtel de France** *(LF), 9 bvld de Verdun, 06380 Sospel; tel: 04 93 04 00 01, fax: 04 93 04 20 46,* has been owned by the Volle family for over 35 years. **Campsite**: 5 sites including the 3-star **Domaine Ste Madeleine**, *rte de Moulinet, 06380 Sospel, tel: 04 93 04 10 48* (caravans), a family-run site with 90 emplacements, 4km north-east of the town.

Sightseeing

In its beautiful location surrounded by hills, **Sospel** is one of the best walking bases in the Alps, with marked trails of various lengths and difficulties all around. It is also a pretty town, spanning the **River Bévéra**, with a tree-lined waterside terrace and interesting old streets.

Situated on the salt route which ran from Nice to Turin at the end of the 16th century, its most distinctive feature is the **medieval bridge** which all traffic had to use to get over the river. The original wooden bridge, built in the 10th century, was replaced by a stone one in the 15th century. The little tower in the middle where everyone crossing had to pay a toll now houses the tourist information office and exhibitions. The **Church of St Michel**, formerly a cathedral, has magnificent painted ceilings and boasts a rare 19th-century Italian organ. It dominates **St Michel Square** which is covered by cobbles laid in neat coloured stripes.

The town (including the toll tower) needed extensive restoration after World War II, as it was severely damaged by bombing during the German retreat in 1944. The citizens were awarded the Croix de Guerre for their bravery. **Fort St Roch**, beside the Nice road on the edge of the town, once part of the Maginot Line, now houses the **Musée de la Resistance**, *tel: 04 93 04 00 70* (open July–Aug Tues–Sun 1400–1800; June Sat–Sun 1400–1800).

Mid-June sees a competition amongst the shopkeepers for the best scarecrow. They remain on show for several weeks afterwards.

Side Track from Sospel

At **Sospel**, the sidetrack through **Soarge** to the **Vallée des Merveilles** in the **Mercantour National Park** follows the wriggling D2204 to **Breil-sur-Roya** and then takes the N204 through **Soarge** to **Tende** (47km each way).

THE ROYA VALLEY

The countryside is increasingly remote as the road and railway make their way up the deep, often wooded **Roya**

Valley below mountain ridges towards the Italian border. Ancient villages, once on the Nice–Turin salt route, punctuate the journey. Marked footpaths, including the GR 58 long-distance path which crosses the Alps through Chamonix, beckon walkers up the hillsides, and mountain bike – V.T.T. – trails are also marked from each of the villages.

BREIL-SUR-ROYA

Tourist Office: *Place Brancherie; tel: 04 93 04 99 76.* Open June–Sept 1000–1200, 1400–1800; closed Tues am and Sun pm.

ACCOMMODATION

Le Castel du Roy (*LF*), *rte de Tende; tel: 04 93 04 43 66, fax: 04 93 04 91 83* (cheap), is a family-run riverside hotel with a pool and a good reputation for food. **Campsite**: **Camping-Caravaning U.S.B.T.P**, *tel: 04 93 04 46 66*, is also near the river with a pool. Open all year.

SIGHTSEEING

Breil is nicknamed the *Pays des Oliviers* as the hills around are covered in olive trees. A lively village, it stages various festivities during the summer months. Every four years, the **Astacado d'Brei** is a costumed re-enactment of the peasants' revolt in the Middle Ages against *Cuissage* (permission from the Seigneur to get married).

With tall buildings towering over its single narrow main street, the village feels distinctly Italian, a reminder that this haute Roya area was indeed part of Italy until 16 September 1947 when the local people voted in a referendum to become part of France. The date is commemorated in the street names of several local villages. The **Ecomusée du Haut Pays**, in a former SNCF depot, *tel: 04 93 04 99 76* (open June–Sept Wed–Mon 1000–1200, 1530–1830; Oct–May Sat–Sun 1000–1200, 1530–1830)brings the history of the valley and its railways to life. It has an old steam locomotive, railcars, carriages and a model layout showing how tunnels on the lines from Breil down to Nice and Ventimiglia twice cross each other inside the mountains, an extraordinary feat of engineering and certainly a memorable feature of the rail journey along the valley. Breil's grand orange-pink stone **station** with its row of arches seems incongruously large and ornate for a small village. Like the others along this section of the Nice–Turin line, it was built in the 1930s by Mussolini (whose family came from the area) to encourage the villagers' loyalty to Italy. During World War II the line was so severely damaged that it did not fully reopen until 1979.

SAORGE

Tourist Office: Information from the **Mairie**, *av. Dr Davéo; tel: 04 93 04 51 23.* Mon–Fri 1000–1200, 1400–1700.

This medieval fortified village is the most attractive in the valley. Clinging to the hillside, it has narrow streets, 500-year old houses, three **chapels**, a **church**, a **Franciscan convent** and wonderful views. The **Église St Sauveur** contains one of the valley's 5 historic organs, built by master organists from Tuscany and Lombardy in the 18th and 19th centuries when it was a matter of local honour to boast a fine organ. During the summer, concerts are given on them. Details from the **Mairie** or organist Mme Renate Duffey, *tel: 04 93 04 50 47.*

LA BRIGUE

Tourist Office: *pl. de Nice; tel: 04 93 04 61 01* and at the *Mairie, pl. St. Martin*. Open Mon–Fri 0900–1200, 1700–1800.

Accommodation

Le Mirval, *06430 Tende, tel: 04 93 04 63 71, fax: 04 93 04 79 81* (cheap), is a comfortable family-run hotel with lovely views.

Sightseeing

This attractive little town beside the River Levense is surrounded by wooded hillsides and, at 800m high, has a distinctly Alpine feel. In the Middle Ages it was a thriving cattle and wool centre and its narrow streets are lined with houses dating back to the 14th and 15th centuries, built in the local green stone. The 13th-century **Church of St Martin** is crowned by a fine Italianate belfry, but the real gem is **Notre-Dame-des-Fontaines**, a tiny 13th-century chapel built at the source of a 'miraculous' spring in woods, 5km further up the valley (key available at *Auberge St Martin, pl. de l'Eglise)*. The spring was considered miraculous because it flows intermittently, though this is now known to depend on the rainfall and a syphon system in the rocks below. The chapel's interior is completely covered in a series of colourful square murals, some jolly, some gruesome, depicting the life of the Virgin Mary and the Passion of Christ.

TENDE

Tourist Office: *av. du 16 Septembre; tel: 04 93 04 73 71*. Open 0900–1200, 1400–1800; closed Sun pm and Thurs.

This small town of tall medieval slate-roofed houses is built in tiers on the mountainside below the ruined **castle** of the Counts of Lascarris. The **Church of Notre Dame-de-l'Assomption**, dating back to the 15th-century, is on the main street which slopes down from the railway station.

The new **Musée des Merveilles**, *tel: 04 93 04 32 50* (open Wed–Mon 1030–1830; Sat until 2100; FFr.30) has dioramas and models which bring to life the history of the remarkable **Valleé des Merveilles** in the nearby Mercantour National Park. Pre-historic archaeological finds, and photographs of the valley's extraordinary rock engravings, are on show.

You have to have a guide to visit certain parts of the Valley. Guided walks take place daily during July–Aug and on Sun in June, Sept and Oct; FFr 35. Details from the **Bureau des Guides** at the Tourist Office. Also jeep tours by authorised guides, but only as far as the 2111m-high mountain **Refuge des Merveilles**. Information at the **Hotel le Mirval**, *La Brigue; tel: 04 93 04 63 71*. On foot, the refuge is a 2 hr 30 min climb from the **Lac des Mesces**. It has space for 64 people to stay overnight (advance booking essential); *tel: 04 93 04 67 00*. **Camping** is also permitted for one night, only if you are more than one hour's walk inside the National Park's boundary; all fires are forbidden.

COL DE TURINI

After climbing up the **Bévéra Valley** in a series of tight hairpin bends, through woods and skirting deep ravines, the road reaches the **Col de Turini**.

With no building to mar the wide views of mountains and valleys, the twist-

The Vallée des Merveilles

Are they doodles made by bored shepherds or the religious symbols of pagan worshippers? All sorts of theories exist about the ancient rock markings in the Vallée des Merveilles (Valley of Marvels) in the Mercantour National Park, west of la Brigue and Tende. It is an awe-inspiring place, surrounded by smooth sand-coloured ridges of granite and dotted with pine trees. Even the colours of the rocks are remarkable, with shades of grey streaked with browns, purples and turquoise and often covered with patches of vivid green lichens. Altogether, over 30,000 ancient rock engravings have been found, thought to date back to at least 1800 BC. Though they have been known since the 15th century, they were first brought to public attention by an English priest and botanist, Clarence Bignell, at the turn of the century. He was on a week's study tour in the area, looking particularly for the rare saxifrage, a rock plant which only flowers every 10 years and then dies. But he became so fascinated by the primitive outlines he discovered etched on the rocks, each about six inches high, that he decided to move to nearby Casterino and lived there until he died in 1918.

The markings have intrigued archaeologists ever since but no-one has been able to say definitely why they are there or what they depict. Once you know what you are looking for, they are not difficult to spot on the boulders spread over the rocky valley.

Park Information Office, *23 r. d'Italie, 06006 Nice; tel: 04 93 16 78 88*. Tourist offices in the Roya Valley have leaflets and details of guided walks.

ing one-way road leads to **Cabannes Vieilles**, an isolated group of ruined barracks (2080m high).

In 1794, Napoleon's troops were the first to occupy this strategically important spot, commanding access to the coast across the Alps. The French army also made use of them in 1870. New fortifications were constructed in 1933 which the Italian and German armies used during World War II when 30,000 troops were stationed in the area. The buildings were finally evacuated in April 1945 after a bloody attack in which the lst Divison Française Libre lost 273 soldiers. Today only the occasional car and a handful of walkers disturb the peace of these remote hillsides dotted with wild flowers. The narrow road is bordered by broom and dog roses.

LA BOLLÈNE-VÉSUBIE

As the road drops down from the Col de Turini, **La Bollène** crowns a small hill, its red rooftops providing a distinctive landmark against the green backcloth of woods and fields. A large map painted on a wall beside *pl. Jean-Ange Bosio* makes an attractive guide to the area. Narrow streets lead up to **Sancto Laurentio**, a cream-coloured church with coloured tiled roof.

ST-MARTIN-VÉSUBIE

Tourist Office: *pl. F. Faure; tel: 04 93 03 21 28*. Open daily July–Aug 0900–1230, 1430–1900; Sept–June, Mon–Sat 0930–1200, 1500–1800, Sun 0930–1200.

ACCOMMODATION

Catering for an influx of walkers, climbers, mountain-bikers and riders in summer and cross-country skiers in winter, the village boasts 9 small hotels including **Hôtel la Bonne Auberge**, *allée de Verdun; tel: 04 93 03 20 49; fax: 04 93 03 20 69* (cheap), as well as *chambres d'hôte*. **Campsites**:

there are 4 campsites including **Le Touron**, *rte de Nice, tel: 04 93 03 21 32* (2-star; caravans).

Sightseeing

Set 975 m high between two wooded valleys, this small town expanded – slightly – beyond its medieval centre about 100 years ago. It retained its 12th-century church, built by the Templars, but lost all but one of its old gateways. In 1893 it had the distinction of being only the second village in France (after La Roche-sur-Foron) of installing electricity.

The River Vésubie tumbles down its wooded valley, fed by the small Madone de Fenestre and Boreon streams which meet in the village. Each year a statue of Notre-Dame-de-Fenestre is carried from the **Church of St Martin** to a remote chapel high in the hills 12km away, to spend the summer months.

VALDEBLORE

Tourist Office: *06420 La Roche, Valdeblore, tel: 04 93 02 88 59.* Open daily 0930–1200 and 1430–1730.

Once you have passed over the Col St Martin into the **Valdeblore Valley**, the scenery changes noticeably from Mediterranean to Alpine, with slate replacing red tiles on roofs. The hillsides, covered in olives and figs, are patched with red sandstone rocks which become an unusual purple when the route turns up the **Tinée Valley** to **St Sauveur**. On the way look out for the bleak **Frassinea Bunker** (open Sat–Sun 1400–1700). Built into the roadside rock, and left over from less peaceful times, this formed part of the Maginot Line.

ROUTE IMPERIALE

This section of the route, much of which is in the Mercantour National Park, forms part of the *Route Imperiale* built by Napoleon III in the 1860s to link Nice with Briançon for military purposes. At first the fast winding road accompanies the River Tinée to Isola through a gorge beneath steep wooded hillsides and grey peaks.

ISOLA

Tourist Office: *Chalet d'Acceuil; tel: 04 93 23 15 15*, in a small wooden chalet beside the bridge over the River Guerche, just before it joins the Tinée. Also houses the **Bureau des Guides**, *tel: 04 93 02 16 31*, for walking information.

The square 12th-century *Romanesque* bell tower of Isola's church, a picturesque landmark beside the river, is characteristic of the valley.

ISOLA 2000

Tourist Office: *06420 Isola 2000; tel: 04 93 23 15 15.* Open 0900–1200 and 1400–1830; closed weekends May and Sept–Dec.

A twisting 25-min drive up the D94 beside the River Guerche towards the **Col de Lombade** leads to **Isola 2000**, the ski resort created in 1970, just 3 km from the Italian border. The most southerly in France, it is the highest in the Southern Alps. Its setting in a hollow under the majestic Col is striking. Pity about the buildings! The skiing extends to a height of between 1800m and 2610m.

ST-ÉTIENNE-DE-TINÉE

Tourist Office: *place Centrale; tel: 04 93 23 02 66.* Open daily 0830–1200, 1400–1700; later during ski season and July–Aug.

The **Tinée Valley** wriggles up to this attractive village, set in a bowl of mountains, which is popular with climbers, walkers and skiers, though the main downhill pistes are at **Auron**, 7 km south. The parish church has a fine beige stone Romanesque-style tower built in 1784 with tiers of arches and a spire. Inside is a fine collection of 19th-century silver crosses and chalices. The village also has three ancient **chapels** with 15th and 17th-century frescos (visits by arrangement with the tourist office).

Nine km up the winding valley road, you pass **Le Pra**, the ruins of a village destroyed by a torrent cascading off the **Cirque du Salso Moreno** mountain bowl in both 1860 and 1960. Now a dam of grey stones keeps the water in check. Hard to believe, but this was once a major smuggling centre, less than four km from the Italian border. The authorities even posted a permanent contraband officer there.

CIME DE LA BONETTE

As you continue slowly up the valley, the countryside becomes more and more awesome and desolate. Wide expanses of grassy hillsides populated only by sheep lead up to jagged ridges from which waterfalls tumble as white streaks. Even at the height of summer, patches of snow linger in crevices beside the road. This is the highest road in Europe, crossing from the Tinée Valley to the softer Ubaye Valley, over the **Col de Granges** (2505 m) and **Col de Restefond**, passing the ruins of former military installations. In 1961, a side road was built to circle the **Cime de la Bonette** (2802m). From its viewpoint, the mountainous landscape spreads out beneath you like a contour map. If you climb up to the summit, a 10-min walk, the views stretch for many more miles – a *'panorama géant sur toutes les Alpes'* according to the sign. This also warns that the walk should not be attempted if the weather looks at all stormy because of the risk of being struck by lightning!

Descending in tight loops to the wide **Ubaye Valley** where sheep graze peacefully, with bells tinging around their necks, you reach civilization once more in the hamlet of **Villard**, just before Jausiers.

JAUSIERS

Tourist Office: *04850 Jausiers; tel: 04 92 81 21 45.* Open July–Aug Mon–Fri 0900–1230 and 1400–1830, Sat 0900–1230 and 1500–1930, Sun 1000–1200 and 1600–1800; Sept–June Mon–Fri 0900–1200 and 1400–1830, Sat 0900–1200 and 1500–1800. Exchange facilities.

ACCOMMODATION

Catering very much for lovers of the great outdoors, both in winter and summer, most accommodation is in modern self-catering apartments. The **Bel Air**, *04850 Jausiers, tel: 04 92 81 06 35; fax: ???* (cheap), is a small family-run hotel serving country fare. **HI: Le Mas Des Loups**, *04850 Jausiers; tel: 04 92 81 06 49.* **Campsite**: **Le Planet**, *tel: 04 92 81 06 57* (2-star; caravans).

The only man-made 'sight' is the 17th-century baroque **Church of Saint-Nicholas-de-Myre**, but the wonders of nature are all around and the Tourist Office can offer plenty of suggestions on how to make the most of them on foot, mountain-bike or horseback or in the air by paragliding. From the village, a fast straight road runs through a belt of forest beneath jagged ridges to Barcelonnette.

ROUTE DES GRANDES ALPES

The alternative route north from St

Sauveur begins by twisting around the wooded hillsides of **Montagne de l'Alp**, past Alpine villages like **Beuil**, **Les Launes** and **Valberg**, a ski resort, to Guillaumes.

GUILLAUMES

Tourist Office: *Chalet du Tourisme; tel: 04 93 05 57 76.* Open July–Aug daily 1000–1200,1600–1800; Sept–June at *the Mairie, tel: 04 93 05 52 23*, same times but closed Sat afternoon and Sun.

This small village by the broad **River Var** is scenically situated at the foot of craggy ruins and still has houses dating back to its medieval beginnings. For comfortable accommodation, try the family-run **Hôtel les Chaudrons** (*LF*), *pl. de Provence; tel: 04 93 05 50 01* (cheap).

SIDE TRACK FROM GUILLAUMES

GORGES DE DALUIS

The River Var gushes south from Guillaumes down this long deep gorge, nicknamed *Le Petit Colorado Niçois*. One of the most spectacular in the Alpes-Maritimes, it runs beneath wooded hills.

Beyond the 70m high **Pont de la Mariée** (a favourite spot for bungee jumping), the steep sides become red sandstone, a dramatic contrast to the earlier grey rocks. The road snakes around them, passing waterfalls and diving in and out of tunnels cut through the sheerest edges. After 11 km, the hamlet of **Daluis** peeps down to the road from its lofty perch above.

ST-MARTIN- D'ENTRAUNES

Continuing up the **Var Valley**, the mountainsides are often less than picturesque, becoming bare and black as slag heaps.

At St-Martin d'Entraunes, whose Alpine chalets have window-boxes trailing with geraniums in summer, the valley widens into meadows covered in wild flowers. The small **Hostellerie de la Vallière**, *06470 St-Martin d'Entraunes; tel: 04 93 05 59 59; fax: 04 93 05 59 60* (cheap) has a pleasant garden and beautiful mountain views. The source of the Var is in ponds around **Estenc**, further along the route. In winter this is a popular area for cross-country skiing.

COL DE LA CAYOLLE AND GORGES DU BACHELARD

This lofty pass (2360m) is in the heart of the Mercantour National Park. Beyond it you enter a different, gentler landscape of limestone rocks which make the mountain ridges softer and the boulders, scattered across the grassy pastures, whiter. The foliage is prettier too – the pines turning a delicate lime green. Streams ripple noisily over pebbles between grassy banks and the wayside flowers are prettier than any picture. This is a place to linger and savour the beauty and peace. Park guides lead walks to lakes high in the mountains (departures from the **Col Refuge**; July–Aug, Fri 0900; information: *tel: 04 93 05 53 07* from 1500–1900; FFr.??).

As you continue north, the mountain streams swell into a proper river, the Bachelard. Beyond the village of **Bayasse**, this dives through a lush narrow gorge fed by waterfalls, beneath pine forests and sheer rocks patterned with herringbone strata. The road crosses and recrosses the river along the last stretch of the road into Barcelonnette.

BARCELONNETTE

See p. 118.

MONACO

The tiny but wealthy Principality of Monaco, covering just one square mile, is the world's smallest sovereign state after the Vatican. Though independent, with its own police force and laws, it feels like an extension of France – which surrounds it. There are no border controls and it uses the same currency and postal services.

The state first grew rich from taxes on the lemons and olives grown in Menton but the Mentonnais broke away in 1848. Faced with bankruptcy, the then Prince of Monaco, Charles III, decided to open a casino. Its profits soon enabled taxes to be abolished and the grateful citizens renamed the hill by the casino 'Monte-Carlo' (Mount Charles). Today it is still a glitzy place, the home of the famous and very, very rich. You may even catch a glimpse of royalty in the street.

TOURIST INFORMATION

Office du Tourisme: *2A blvd des Moulins, 98030 Monaco*, near the Casino; *tel: 92 166 166*. Open Mon–Sat 0900–1900, Sun 0900–1200. **Branch**: at the railway station, *av. Prince-Pierre*. Open daily 0800–2000.

ARRIVING AND DEPARTING

Airport

Regular helicopter services operate from Nice airport, a 7-min flight.

By Car

On A8 Autoroute, from France take the Monaco-La Turbie exit, or from Italy the Monaco-Roquebrune exit. From Nice, there is a choice of three main roads along the hilly coast – the Basse Corniche (low), Moyenne Corniche (middle) and Grande Corniche (high).

Parking: Driving around the principality is not recommended, as the streets are busy and confusingly laid out around the hills. Only local cars are allowed into Monaco-Ville. Head straight to one of the many car-parks where parking is free for the first hour. *Multi-carte Parking* cards are available; *tel: 93 15 80 00.*

By Train

Station: *pl. de la Gare, av. Prince-Pierre; tel: 93 87 50 50* (closed 0100-0530). Information 0900–1845.

GETTING AROUND

Monaco comprises a narrow 4 km waterfront of glossy buildings stretching up a hillside overlooking a solid phalanx of even glossier yachts. Though small, the diminutive state is very steep in places. It divides into six areas: **Monte-Carlo,** in the centre; **Monaco-Ville**, the old town on the Rock, a headland to the west; the **Condamine** around the port; **Fontvielle**, a port and exhibition area on reclaimed land; **Moneghetti** on the steep hillside to the west; and the **Larvotto** beaches at the east end.

A small motorised **road train** offers hourly tours, encompassing all the major sights. You can get on and off at will. Otherwise the local bus service is very efficient. For those overwhelmed by the cliff-like hills, a series of free public lifts and escalators whisk pedestrians between the different levels of streets.

Boat trips: 55-minute boat trips operate from *Quai des Etats-Unis, port d'Hercule, tel: 92 16 15 15*, including a stop to look at the sea-bed; Apr–Sept, FFr.70.

Taxis: 24-hour radio taxis: *tel: 93 15 01 01* or *93 50 56 28*. Expect them to be more expensive than anywhere in France.

Staying in Monaco

Accommodation

As nearly 80% of the hotels are in the top 4-star de luxe category, budget accommodation in the millionaire Principality is inevitably scarce, although not impossible to find.

The rich and famous head for the **Hôtel de Paris**, *pl. du Casino, Monte-Carlo 98000; tel: 92 16 30 00, fax: 92 16 36 36* (expensive). One of Europe's most extravagant hotels, it has 141 splendid air-conditioned rooms and 59 suites, all sumptuously furnished. Drinks in the bar cost almost as much as a room in a normal hotel, but are worth it to see the glittering décor.

Just around the corner is its *Belle Époque* rival, **L'Hermitage**, *Square Beaumarchais; Monte-Carlo 98000, tel: 92 16 40 00, fax: 93 50 47 12* (expensive), which has spectacular views over the port from its bar-terrace. Both are owned by the *Société des Bains de Mer* (which also owns the **Mirabeau** and **Monte-Carlo Beach** hotels (central booking *tel: 92 16 36 36)*, whose Gold Card provides guests with perks like free entry to the Casino.

For less ruinous prices, try *r. de la Turbie* and *av. Prince-Pierre* near the station, where there are several good low-budget hotels including the **Hôtel de France**, *6 r.de la Turbie, Monte-Carlo 98000, tel: 93 30 24 64* (moderate). **HI: Centre de la Jeunesse**, *24 av. Prince-Pierre; tel: 93 50 83 20, fax: 93 25 29 82*, 100 m from the railway station. This excellent hostel, for 16 –26 year olds and students up to 31, is a godsend, although as with all low-budget accommodation here, it fills up rapidly in summer months. Arrive after 0900 and you will not get a bed.

Eating and Drinking

You can eat like a prince in Monaco, although usually at a price. However the range of restaurants is wide, from some of the most luxurious in Europe to simple Italian trattorie.

True local fare includes *Barbagiuan*, a vegetable and rice-filled deep-fried pasty, *Stocafi*, a thick stockfish soup, and *Fugassa de Munegu*, a nutty pastry. If you win big at the casino, head across the road to **Restaurant Louis XV** at the **Hôtel de Paris**, *tel: 92 16 30 01* (expensive) where Alain Ducasse, one of the world's top chefs, masterminds menus fit for royalty. This was the favourite dining room of Edward VII when he was Prince of Wales. Present-day patrons include Pavarotti and Sting, not to mention Monaco's own Princesses, Stephanie and Caroline.

Yet eating with royalty is not the preserve of the wealthy. **Le Texan**, *4 r. Suffren, tel: 93 30 34 54* (cheap), up from the port, is a Tex-Mex restaurant and bar with the cheapest beers in the Principality, good food and the possibility of brushing shoulders with the likes of Prince Albert or Boris Becker. Indeed, inexpensive food is not too hard to come by.

Proximity to the Italian border means pizzas – again *r. de la Turbie* beckons. For lunchtime fare in the sun by the port, head to the terrace bar-restaurants along *quai Albert 1er*. Up on the Rock in the old

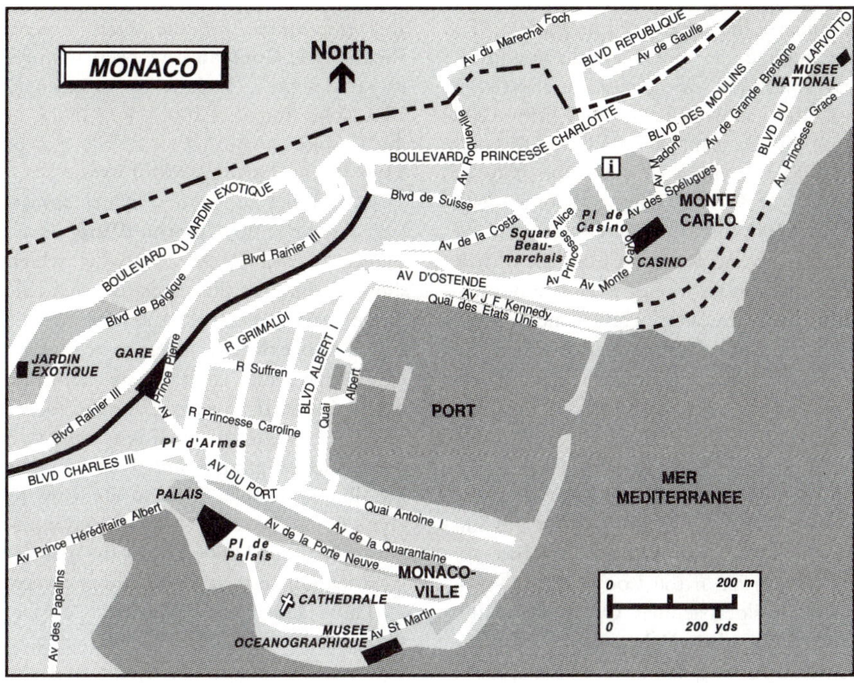

town, numerous small restaurants also offer inexpensive set menus. Try **Tarte au Poivre**, *23 r. Comte Félix Gastaldi, Monaco-Ville, tel: 93 30 29 10* (closed Sat).

Communications

Post Office: *pl. Beaumarchais; tel: 93 50 69 87*. Open Mon–Fri 0800 –1900, Sat 0800–1200. You can buy Monaco's own stamps here, though French ones are also on sale. **Telephones**: Monaco now has its own international code, (00) 377, and its numbers have *not* been changed by the addition of 04 as in south-east France.

Money

Compagnie Monégasque de Change, *av. la Quarantine; tel: 93 25 02 50* (closed Wed and Nov–Dec). A bank is never far away but *blvd des Moulins* has more than its fair share.

Consulates

Belgium: *26 bis blvd Princesse Charlotte; tel: 93 50 59 89*.
France: *1 r. du Téao; tel: 92 16 54 60*.
Germany: *2 r. des Giroflées; tel: 93 30 19 49*.
Ireland: *pl. Sainte Dévote; tel: 93 15 70 00*.
South Africa: *30 blvd Princesse Charlotte; tel: 93 25 24 26*.
United Kingdom: *33 blvd Princesse Charlotte; tel: 93 50 99 66*.

Entertainment

Monaco is synonymous with gambling. There are five casinos serving all tastes but you must be over 21 (they check, so take your passport if necessary) and be smartly dressed. Doyen of them all is the most famous casino in the world, the **Casino de Monte-Carlo**, *pl. du Casino, tel: 92 16 23 00*. Adorned with flags and gold leaf, it dominates the square and its gardens. To get beyond the entrance hall, you must pay FFr.50 just for the pleasure of walking into the hallowed halls (open from 1200 until the last gambler goes home to bed). Add FFr.50 more to enter the holy of holies, the Private Gaming Rooms, open from 1500, and English Club, open for Black Jack and Roulette from 2200. It is here that serious money is won and lost – more likely the latter! The second money-pit is the **Café de Paris** next door, *tel: 92 16 23 00*. It has no entrance fee, but is definitely more tacky, with banks of slots, Las Vegas-style. Open from 1000; gaming tables open from 1700. **Sun Casino**, *12 av. des Spélugues, tel: 92 16 23 00*, is glossy and modern, open from 1700, Sat and Sun 1600. The adjoining **Loews Casino**, *tel: 93 59 65 00*, in the **Loews Hotel** specialises in slot machines. Open from 1100. The **Salle des Palmiers** in **Monte-Carlo Sporting Club**, *av. Princesse Grace; tel: 92 16 21 25*, is open July–mid Sept from 2200.

Bars in Monaco are fun but usually expensive. Try side streets off *r. Grimaldi* behind the port. Monaco is an enjoyable wandering ground at night, and watching is free.

To catch a glitzy cabaret, head for **La Salle des Etoiles** at the **Monte-Carlo Sporting Club**, *av. Princesse Grace, tel: 92 16 22 44*. Monaco's number one club, **Jimmy Z's**, is also in the *Sporting Club, tel: 92 16 22 77*. It has a strict dress code but free entry. Open 2330 to dawn. Once inside you are expected to buy a drink, at around FFr.100 a shot.

Culturally, Monaco gets the best of the lot. In the **Salle Garnier**, *tel: 92 16 22 99*, part of the **Casino de Paris**, the world's opera stars join the resident **Ballet Russe de Monte Carlo**. This opulent theatre was built by **Charles Garnier**, who was also responsible for the Paris Opéra. **Picasso** and **Cocteau** have been amongst its set designers. Tickets are surprisingly affordable, from FFr.100 – box office in the Casino entrance. Open daily except Mon 1000–1230 and 1400–1700.

In summer, open-air cinema attracts large crowds at the **Cinema d'Été**, *26 av. Princesse Grace, tel: 93 25 86 80*, which shows a different film in its original language every evening at 2130 June –Sept.

For **football** fans, Monaco boasts one of Europe's top clubs at the futuristic **Stade Louis II**, 7 *av.des Castelans, tel: 92 05 40 11*, where the pitch is actually two storeys above ground and there are seats for 40,000 people. Tickets are easy to come by, as the team's usual crowd numbers only about 3,000, turning the magnificent stadium into an almost empty cavern.

The **Thermes Marins**, *2 av. d'Ostende; tel: 92 16 40 40*, situated between the **Hotel de Paris** and the **Hermitage**, is a thalassotherapy centre with a pool, Turkish baths, sauna and fitness rooms where you can indulge in envigorating sea-water treatments or simply relax on sunbeds looking out to sea. Day pass FFr. 400, treatments extra.

Events

In Jan the **Monte-Carlo** car rally takes place, including exciting stages in the *Alpes Maritimes* behind Monaco. Stands are erected in the Port area to enable spectactors to see the cars start and finish their gruelling 5–day journey. Seasts can be reserved through the **Automobile Club**, *23 blvd Albert 1ère, 98012 Monaco; tel: 93 115 26 00*.

In mid May the **Grand Prix** motor races take over many of the streets for four days, the only circuit in the world in the centre of a town. **Formula 1** and **Formula 3** trails begin on the Thurs, with

Monaco's Royal Family

The marriage of the beautiful film-star Grace Kelly to Monaco's Prince Rainier III in 1956 captivated the world. Tragically the fairytale came to a sudden end in 1982 when Princess Grace was killed in a car accident on one of the steep roads which wind down into the Principality. Now it is the social life of their three children, Prince Albert and the Princesses Stephanie and Caroline, which capture the attention of the world's press.

Yet the Monaco royal family, the House of Grimaldi, has more serious claims to fame. It is the world's oldest reigning family, dating back to 1297, when François Grimaldi, disguised as a monk, infiltrated and seized the fortress built on the Rock of Monaco. Fifty years later the Grimaldis acquired more land, the 'seigneuries' of Menton and Roquebrune on either side of the Rock.

Monaco itself was officially recognised as an independent seigneurie in 1489 by Charles VIII of France and the Duke of Savoy. However it came under the 'protection' of Spain in 1525 and it was not until 1641 that the Spaniards were chased away with the help of the French king, Louis VIII. Thus began the Principality's close links with France. Alas! During the French Revolution it was down-graded to a mere town called Fort Hercule, the prince was arrested and the Palace converted to a workhouse.

The Grimaldis' rights were restored by the Treaty of Paris in 1814. Menton and Roquebrune subsequently decided to break away (in 1848) and Monaco became the independent state as we know it today in 1861. Five years later, under Prince Charles III, the famous *Société des Bains de Mer* was formed to run the Casino which was to transform the Principality's fortunes. Sited below the Rock, the area was renamed Monte-Carlo in honour of the prince.

Prince Rainier's great-grandfather, Albert I, an adventurous sailor and scientist, founded the Oceanographic Institute for the study of marine science in 1906 as well as several other research bodies. He also created the Jardin Exotique. Prince Rainier succeeded his grandfather, Louis II, to the throne in 1949, aged 25.

the Formula 3 Championship itself on Sat and the Formula 1 on Sun afternoon. Tickets, costing FFr.200–FFr.1500, go on sale immediately after the previous year's races and most sell out within six months. However, some may be available at the last minute from the **Automobile Club** (see above), including standing spaces in the Old Town, from FFr.100 for a bird's-eye view. The smartest place to watch is the terrace of the **Hermitage Hotel** restaurant (even if lunch costs you more than a ticket and gets equally heavily booked), as it overlooks one of the few sections of the circuit where drivers can overtake. Other streets remain open to traffic but get very congested, so stay out of town. Less racy events include the **International Circus Festival**.

In Feb the **Monte-Carlo Tennis Open** features top ATP players from around the world, and there is an **International Fireworks Festival** at the Port with weekly displays followed by a concert during July and Aug.

Shopping

The small shops along the narrow streets of the **Old Town** are best for interesting souvenirs. For more serious shopping, head for *blvd des Moulins, av. de la Costa* and *av. des Beaux-arts* in Monte-Carlo.

Near the Port, the **Condamine** covered market on the *pl. d'Armes* sells fresh meat, cheese and other food, plus fruit and vegetable stalls around the edge outside. The boutiques in the flower-decked *r. Princesse Caroline* pedestrian area are just a few steps away. The glossy new shopping mall under the **Metropole Palace hotel**, *av. de la Madone*, is another shopper's heaven.

Sightseeing

Flash, fast and finely manicured, Monaco always lives up to your expectations. Do not expect a visit to the Principality to be cheap but it costs nothing to wander, look and brush with opulence. In particular, stroll around the narrow streets of the **Old Town** and along the quays of the marina to ogle at the ridiculously large yachts and cruisers and wonder who they belong to.

The **Casino** is the heart of Monte-Carlo. Whether or not you are a gambler, visit the entrance hall at the very least, to see its atrium paved in marble and surrounded by 28 Ionic columns in onyx. The gaming rooms are adorned with stained glass, brass lamps, sculptures, vast paintings and endless gilt. Similarly the *Salle Garnier* is decorated in red and gold with a profusion of frescoes and sculptures.

High up on the Rock in **Monaco-Ville**, the **Royal Palace** is small but regal. Be there punctually to see the **Changing of the Guard** ceremony which takes place at daily at 1155 precisely. The **State Apartments**, *tel: 93 25 18 31* (open 0930 –1830 Jun-Sept, 1000–1700 Oct; FFr.30) are sumptuous. The **Wax Museum of the Princes of Monaco**, *27 r. Basse, tel: 93 30 39 05* (open 0930–1900 Feb–Oct, 1030–1700 Nov–Jan; FFr 24) features waxen Stephanies and Carolines, though you could well see them in the flesh emerging from the Palace opposite.

The **Musée Nationale**, *17 av. Princesse Grace, tel: 93 30 91 26* (open 1000–1830 Easter–Sept, 1000–1215 and 1430–1830 Oct–Easter; FFr.26) is stuffed full of dolls and working models, which are demonstrated regularly. On the southern edge of the rock, Monaco's most stimulating attraction is the **Musée Océanographique**, *av. St-Martin; tel: 93 15 36 00* (open 0930–2000 July–Aug, 0930–1900 Sept–June; FFr.60). Created by Prince Albert I in 1910, it is both an architectural masterpiece, rising on a sheer cliff above the sea, and a remarkable museum which houses specimens which the prince collected on his seafaring expeditions around the world. Its excellent aquarium in the basement was developed by Jacques Cousteau and some of his famous underwater films are screened in the conference hall.

Monaco Cathedral, *4 r. Colonel Bellando de Castro; tel: 93 30 88 13*, built in 1875 in white stone from nearby La Turbie, houses the tombs of former Princes of Monaco and of Princess Grace.

Above the skyscrapers at the back of town in **Moneghetti**, Monaco's botanical garden, the **Jardin Exotique**, *tel: 93 30 33 65* (open 0900–1800 (to 1900 mid May–mid Sept); FFr.37; accessible by public elevator and lift or take bus no 2) sprouts 7000 different kinds of cactus. Also included are the imaginatively illuminated Observatory Caves, 60m velow the gardens, and the Museum of Prehistoric Anthropology, displaying rare animal remains dating back to the Bronze Age (open 0900–1800, mid May–mid Sept 0900–1900, FFr.37). **Musée National Automates et Poupées d'Autrefois**, *17 av. Charles Garnier*, displays 400 dolls in period costumes and mechanical toys which are demonstrated several times a day. Open 1000–1830, Oct–Easter closed 1215–1400, FFr.26).

MONTPELLIER

The inhabitants of Montpellier have a reputation for being sociable and good-tempered. The *place de la Comédie*, an enormous square surrounded by cafés and restaurants, is a popular place to chat over a glass or two of local Languedoc wine. A high proportion of those who gravitate there each evening are young – the city has a student population of nearly 50,000 who add to the general atmosphere of liveliness and relaxation, swelled by an influx of visitors throughout the hot summer months. Indeed Montpellier first made its mark on the world through its medical school – founded in 1220 and still highly-regarded – having developed earlier as a result of its spice trade with the Middle East. Today the city is reputed for being forward-looking, epitomised by the arrival of Antigone, a daring post-modern housing development in pseudo-classical style.

TOURIST INFORMATION

Tourist Office: **Le Triangle**, *allée du Tourisme, pl. de la Comédie; tel: 04 67 58 67 58*. **Branch**: *Moulin de l'Evêque, av. du Pirée; tel: 04 67 22 06 16*, in the Antigone quarter. Both open Mon–Sat 0900–1900, Sun 1000–1300, 1400–1800 (closed Sun mid Sept–mid June). Also at the **rail station**; *tel: 04 67 92 90 03*, and **Prés d'Arènes**; *tel: 04 67 22 08 80*, at the south exit off the autoroute. Both open mid June–mid Sept Mon–Fri 0900–1300, 1530–1900. **Languedoc-Roussillon regional information office**: *20 r. de la République; tel: 04 67 22 81 00*. Open Mon–Fri 0845–1245, 1400– 1800.

ARRIVING AND DEPARTING

Airport

Aéroport Montpellier Mediterranée, 8 km east of town centre; information, *tel: 04 67 20 85 00*. As you fly in, watch out for the view over a lagoon which is home to 4000 flamingos. Airport facilities include car-hire, hotel reservations (*tel: 04 67 20 07 08*), restaurants, nursery, local products shop (*Pais d'Oc*) and bureau de change (open for international flights). Buses from the airport to the town centre and bus station run every 30–50 mins (depending on time and day); information, *tel: 04 67 20 85 00*; journey time 15 mins; fare FFr. 25.

By Car

The city centre is busy and difficult to find your way around as the central area, **Centre Historique**, nicknamed the *Écusson* (coat of arms) because of its shape, is pedestrianised. The new Antigone district on the eastern edge of the centre is particularly difficult to locate and worse to get into, especially from the south and west, due to its one-way streets and traffic-free layout. For sightseeing, head for a parking meter or one of the six car parks in the **Antigone** area, then walk. But be warned that to get to the car parks, you need to crack the one-way, almost bus-only street layout which even the locals find difficult to explain if you ask for directions. **Car Hire: Hertz** at the *airport; tel: 04 67 20 04 64, and 11 r. Jules Ferry (Parking des Gares); tel: 04 67 58 65 18.*

By Bus and Train

Bus Station: *r. Jules Ferry; tel: 04 67 92 01 43*, for services to beaches including Carnon, La Grand Motte and Palavas-les-Flots. Linked by escalators to the **Rail Station:** *pl. Auguste-Gibert; tel: 04 36 35 35 35.*

Getting Around

The Centre Historique is pedestrianised and easily accessible on foot from the modern Antigone area via the Polygone shopping mall. Information on local buses can be obtained from **SMTU**, *23bis r. Maguelone; tel: 04 67 22 87 87.* Single journey fare including changes, FFr.6. One route, Petibus, goes round Centre Historique.

Taxis: Ranks beside *pl. de la Comédie* and outside the rail station; 24-hour, *tel: 04 67 58 10 10.* **Bikes** can be borrowed, free with a FFr.800 deposit, at the Bosc kiosk on the *Esplanade Charles de Gaulle.*

Guided tours of the Centre Historique start from the tourist office; July–Sept Wed, Sat 1000 and 1500; FFr.50 (French only). From the *Esplanade Charles de Gaulle*, the **Petit Train** (road train) sets off on a tour of the town every 45 mins from 1400; FFr.25.

Staying in Montpellier

Accommodation and Food

There are hotels in all price ranges. Chains include: *Ca, CI, F1, Ib, IH, Mc, Nv, Sf.* For a wide selection, check the streets around the railway station – *r. de la République, r. de Verdun, r. Maguelone.* In the Antigone area are several good hotels such as **Sofitel** (*Sf*), *1 r. des Pertuisanes; tel: 04 67 65 62 63; fax: 04 67 65 17 50* (moderate) and the apartment hotel, **Citadines**, *588 blvd Antigone; tel: 04 67 20 70 70; fax: 04 67 64 54 64* (cheap). On the edge of town, not far from the airport, the elegant **Maison Blanche**, *1796 av. de la Pompignane; tel: 04 67 69 60 20; fax: 04 67 79 53 39* (moderate) stands in lush gardens. **HI:** *r. des Écoles Laïques; tel: 04 67 60 32 22.*

As a university town with thousands of students, Montpellier abounds with inexpensive good-quality eating places as well as smart establishments. Restaurants in all price ranges enliven many streets, especially *r. de l'Ancien Courrier, r. Roucher* and the top end of *r. des Écoles Laïques.* **La Digilence**, *2 pl. Pétrarque; tel: 04 67 66 12 21* (cheap) is typical of the many interesting little restaurants lurking in old buildings. For classic French fare, the brasserie **Le César**, *pl. du Nombre d'Or; tel: 04 67 64 87 87* (cheap), is one of several specialist restaurants in the Antigone area.

Communications

Post Office: *pl. Martyrs de la Résistance; tel: 04 67 60 03 60.* Poste restante. Open Mon–Fri 0800–1900, Sat 0800–1200.

Money

The main banks are in *allée Paul Riquet*, including Crédit Lyonnais at *16bis; tel: 04 67 49 85 30.* There are bureaux de change in the rail station and *pl. de la Comédie.*

Entertainment

Much evening entertainment consists of strolling the old streets, sitting at cafés and watching street performers from buskers to jugglers. *Pl. de la Comédie*, the largest traffic-free square in France, gets crowded on summer evenings. More formal entertainment is provided by 10 theatres, notably

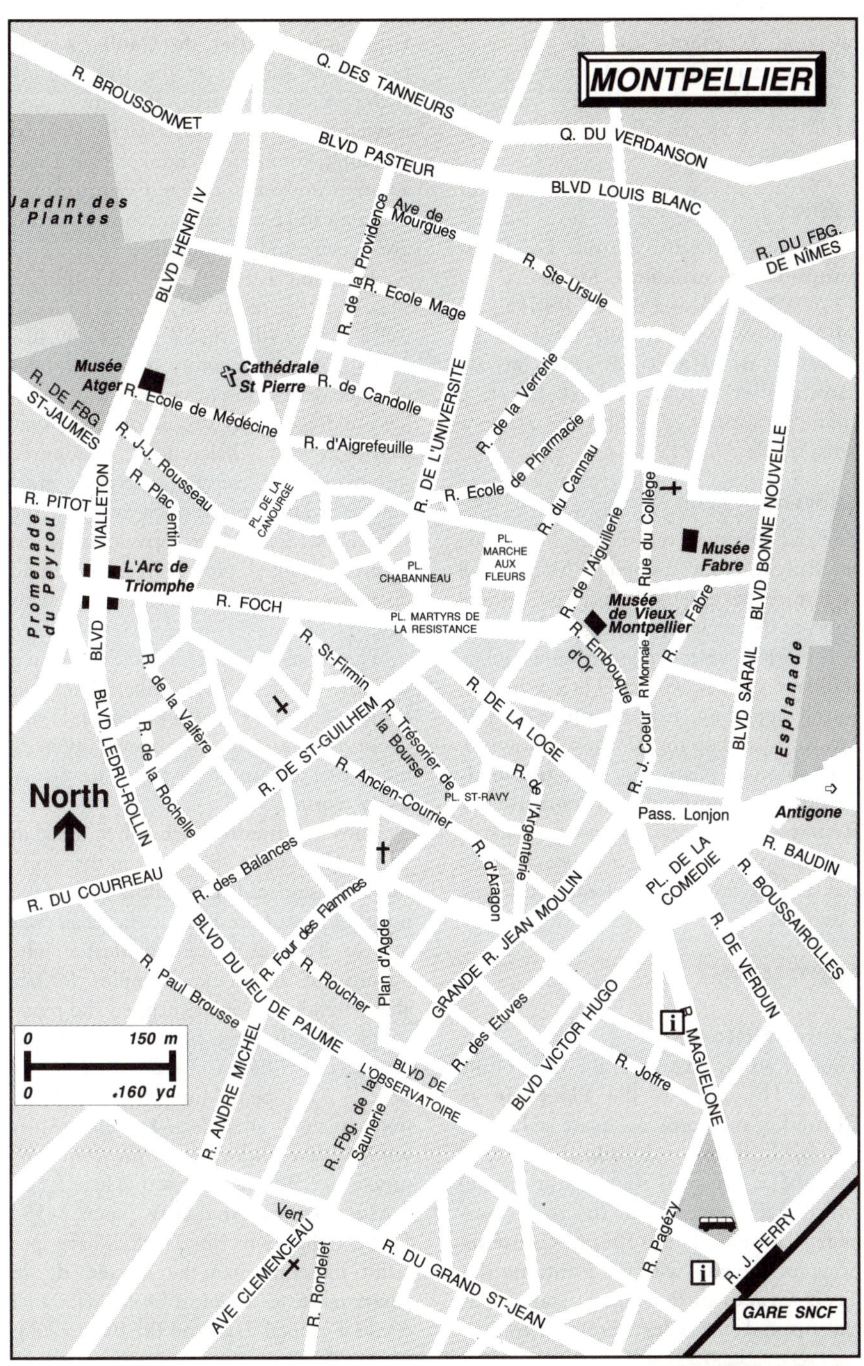
MONTPELLIER
R. BROUSSONNET
Q. DES TANNEURS
BLVD PASTEUR
Q. DU VERDANSON
BLVD LOUIS BLANC
R. DU FBG. DE NÎMES
Jardin des Plantes
BLVD HENRI IV
Ave de Mourgues
R. de la Providence
R. Ste-Ursule
R. Ecole Mage
Musée Atger
Cathédrale St Pierre
R. de Candolle
R. DE L'UNIVERSITE
R. de la Verrerie
R. DE FBG. ST-JAUMES
R. Ecole de Médécine
R. d'Aigrefeuille
R. de Pharmacie
R. J.-J. Rousseau
R. Ecole
R. du Cannau
R. PITOT
VIALLETON
R. Placentin
PL. DE LA CANOURGE
Rue du Collège
Musée Fabre
L'Arc de Triomphe
PL. CHABANNEAU
PL. MARCHE AUX FLEURS
R. de l'Aiguillerie
BLVD BONNE NOUVELLE
Promenade du Peyrou
R. FOCH
PL. MARTYRS DE LA RESISTANCE
Musée de Vieux Montpellier
R. Fabre
BLVD
R. St-Firmin
R. Embouque d'Or
R Monnaie
BLVD SARAIL
Esplanade
R. de la Valfère
R. DE LA LOGE
R. J. Coeur
BLVD LEDRU-ROLLIN
R. de la Rochelle
R. DE ST-GUILHEM
R. Trésorier de la Bourse
R. de l'Argenterie
North
R. Ancien-Courrier
PL. ST-RAVY
Pass. Lonjon
Antigone
R. des Balances
R. d'Aragon
R. BAUDIN
R. DU COURREAU
PL. DE LA COMEDIE
R. BOUSSAIROLLES
R. Four des Flammes
GRANDE R. JEAN MOULIN
R. DE VERDUN
BLVD DU JEU DE PAUME
R. Roucher
Plan d'Agde
R. Paul Brousse
R. des Etuves
BLVD VICTOR HUGO
R. MAGUELONE
0 150 m
0 .160 yd
R. ANDRE MICHEL
BLVD DE L'OBSERVATOIRE
R. Joffre
R. Fbg. de la Saunerie
Vert
AVE CLEMENCEAU
R. Rondelet
R. DU GRAND ST-JEAN
R. Pagézy
R. J. FERRY
GARE SNCF

opera at **L'Opéra-Comédie**, *pl de la Comédie*, and **Opéra Berlioz** in the Corum building. Box office for both, *tel: 04 67 60 19 99*. Tickets cost from FFr.80 to FFr.260.

Events

June: Spring theatre festival, **Le Printemps des Comédiens**. (details, *tel: 04 67 61 06 30*). Also a **dance festival**; *tel: 04 67 60 83 60*, mid July for 3 weeks: **Festival de Radio France et de Montpellier**: music festival featuring young performers, including free jazz concerts; *tel: 04 67 621 66 81.*

Shopping

The old streets in the Centre Historique are delightful for shopping. Many small boutiques have settled into the ground floors of the ancient buildings – those in *r. de l'Ancien Courrier* occupy a former abbey and have vaulted ceilings. Their wares are equally appealing, as in **Bernice**, 7 *r. Jean Moulin*, a hat shop for men and women; an old-fashioned pharmacy, **Droguerie J. Estoul**, *pl. Castellane*, and **Pomme de Reinette**, *33 r. de l'Aiguillerie*, which is crammed with toys old and new. There's also a daily covered food market on *pl. Castellane*.

Sightseeing

Centre Historique

Though on the edge of it, the heart of the Centre Historique is the **Place de la Comédie**, an enormous square laid out in the 18th century and nicknamed *l'Oeuf* after the egg-shaped roundabout around which traffic raced until the square was pedestrianised. The **Opéra Comédie** occupies one end, with the **Fontaine des Trois-Graces** in the middle and restaurants round the edge. From here, the **Esplanade Charles de Gaulle**, a wide promenade laid out in the 18th century with avenues of trees, flowerbeds and fountains, runs to the modern **Corum** building, an unloved bunker-like 1980s addition to the city centre. Constructed in concrete and pink granite, it houses a congress centre and opera house.

Along the narrow streets and intimate squares of the old town, which the locals call *lou clapas* (the rubble), are many fine 17th- and 18th-century mansions built after the destruction of virtually all the earlier buildings during various religious wars. Wrought-iron balconies, decorative stonework and elegant courtyards greet you at every turn, though most of the splendid *hôtels particuliers* (private mansions) connot be visited. However, some ground floors are occupied by shops and restaurants.

The whole area is a delight, embracing the true spirit of Montpellier, but *r. de l'Ancien-Courrier*, *r. de l'Argenterie* and *r. des Trésoriers-de-la-Bourse*, filled with interesting old façades and courtyards, are particularly worth a stroll.

The city's **medical school**, founded in 1220, claims to be the oldest in the world still in existence. It is certainly one of the most respected in France. Rabelais was one of its most famous graduates. The Faculty of Medicine occupies former abbey buildings, much enlarged and renovated, which also house the **Musée Atger**, *r. de l'École de Médicine; tel: 04 67 66 27 77* (open Mon–Fri 1330–1630; free), named after Jean-François Atger who collected drawings in the 18th century. Over 500 are displayed. There is also a **Museum of Anatomy** (open 1415–1700). Other university faculties have specialist museums like the **Musée de la Pharmacie**, *av. Charles Flahault; tel: 04 67 63 20 47* (open Tues and Fri 1000–1200).

Beside the medical faculty stands the **Cathédrale St Pierre**, *pl. St Pierre; tel: 04 67 66 07 44* (open daily 0900–1200, 1430–1900; closed Sun pm) started in the 14th century but not completed until the 19th, which you enter through an immense Gothic porch.

Nearby, across the busy wide blvd Henri IV, the **Jardin des Plantes**, *163 r. Auguste Broussonnet; tel: 04 67 63 43 22* (open Mon–Sat 0800–1200, 1400–1800, until 1730 Nov–Mar; free) is France's oldest botanical garden, planted in 1593 to enable the medical students to study medicinal plants. A specimen of the tree *Phillyrea latifolia* dating from that time is among its treasures. Statues of eminent botanists grace paths leading to an orangery, conservatories and ponds.

On the edge of the Centre Historique stands the **Porte du Peyrou**, a grand triumphal arch erected in honour of Louis XIV in 1691. It leads to the **Promenade du Peyrou**, with terraces laid out in the 18th century, and a splendid watertower like a mini-castle with pillars, arches and carved pediments beside the old aqueduct which once served the city. From here you get a good view over the city with the River Garrigue on its east side and both mountains and sea in the distance.

Museums

The city's main museum, **Musée Fabre**, *39 blvd Bonne Nouvelle; tel: 04 67 16 83 00* (open Tues–Fri 0900–1730; Sat–Sun 0900–1700; FFr.18) occupies a fine mansion facing the Esplanade which was a Jesuit college in the 15th and 16th centuries. It has six floors of paintings, rising to the 20th century at the top. The majority are French but there are also Dutch, Italian and Spanish works by 16th and 17th century masters. One section is devoted to pottery and sculpture.

The **Musée Languedocien et de la Societé Archéologique**, 7 *r. Jacques-Coeur; tel: 04 67 52 93 03* (open Mon–Sat 1400–1700; FFr.20) is housed in another nicely restored 15th-century mansion and displays prehistoric objects and classical artefacts from ancient Greece and Egypt.

The **Musée du Vieux Montpellier** in the Hôtel de Varenne, *pl. Pétrarque; tel: 04 67 66 02 94* (open Tues–Sat 0930–1200, 1330–1700; free) conjures up Montpellier as it used to be, through pictures, old maps and furniture. On its top floor, the small **Musée du Fougau** (open Wed, Thurs 1500–1700) run by volunteers, displays traditional costumes, old sewing machines and local crafts.

Antigone

Only the French could have dared to sanction such a startling new quarter only a few steps away from the historic centre. As the name suggests, this is Classical Greece and Rome recreated, a post-modern development of apartments, offices, hotels and shops. It was conceived in 1980 by a Catalan architect, Ricardo Bofill, to provide housing on a site vacated by the army.

Whether you come to it on foot through the Polygone shopping mall or approach it from the side, Antigone comes as a surprise. The tall beige buildings, with columns, arches and pediments, face wide circular symmetrically-tiled piazzas. Avenues of trees, window-boxes and giant pots trailing with geraniums add softness, but the area has yet to come alive, probably because all of Montpellier is out gossiping on the *pl. de la Comédie*.

Connection from Montpellier

To reach **Nîmes**, and join the Nîmes–Avignon route (p. 115), take the A9 or N113 north-east; 54 km.

MONTPELLIER–LE PUY

This long, meandering road heads upwards from the coast at Montpellier, through the vineyards of Languedoc and the wild mountains of the remote Cévennes. The main road is good but mountainous; the scenery is beautiful and the region little known.

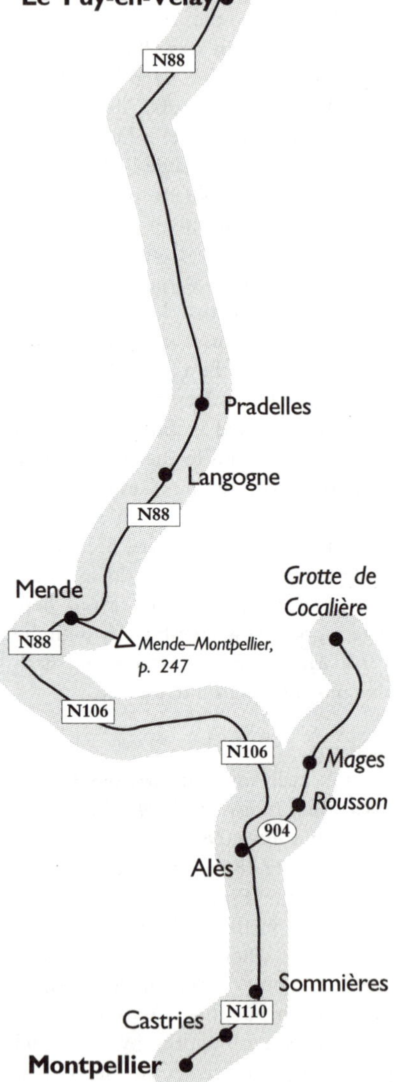

ROUTE: 229 KM

ROUTE

Leave Montpellier, heading north on the N110, stopping in **Castries** and **Sommières** before reaching Alès. From here, take the N106 to **Mende**. The Mende–Montpellier route (p. 247) serves as a scenic (but slow) alternative as far as Mende. From Mende, fork right onto the N88, up through Langogne and Pradelles to Le Puy. Both Alès and Mende are gateways to the Parc National des Cévennes (see p. 149). Allow about 2 hrs 30 mins non-stop; 1–2 days with sightseeing.

MONTPELLIER TO ALÈS

Tourist Office: **Sommières**: *av. du Général Bruyère; tel: 04 66 80 99 30.*

This early stretch of the journey heads over open, rolling countryside, dotted by tiny hill villages and vineyards, with only the occasional larger town. **Castries** takes its name from the Roman *castrum* which once stood guard over the Via Domitia between Italy and Spain. Today, there is a fortified village topped by a medieval church and a **château** (currently under restoration) with a Renaissance façade and gardens designed by Le Notre. As you leave town, you pass an imposing **aqueduct** built by Paul Riquet (who also built the Canal du Midi) in 1720.

About 20 km on, **Sommières** is a pretty market town built along a bluff beside the Vidourle River, reached via a splendid Roman bridge, first built in the early 1st century AD, although heavily restored in the 18th century and again recently. Steep narrow alleys connect the two medieval market centres beside the river, and on the hill, near the castle, from where there are fine views.

Further north, shortly before reaching Alès, the **Château de Ribaute**, *Ribaute-les-Tavernes; tel: 04 66 83 01 66* (open 1500–1900, July–Aug daily, Apr–Sept Sun only; guided tours; FFr.20) is now a B&B, but you can also visit. Its décor and furnishings still reflect the charm of the 18th century. Next, stop briefly in **St-Christol-les-Alès** to visit the **Musée du Scribe**, *42 r. du Clocher; tel: 04 66 60 88 10* (open 1430–1900, July–Aug daily; June, Sept, Sat–Sun; FFr.20) a charming museum in a 17th-century house, covering everything needed for writing, from paper and parchment to pens and ink.

ALÈS

Tourist Office: *pl. Gabriel Péri; tel: 04 66 52 32 15.*

Accommodation and Food

There are a few hotels in town, but those with transport would do well to stay out of town (see below, Alès–Mende). **Campsite**: **Camping Municipal Les Chataigniers**, *chemin des Sports; tel: 04 66 52 53 57* (2-star; open Jun–Sept).

Sightseeing

The largest town in the area, Alès is an ancient settlement, dating back to a Celtic *oppidum*, while Benedictine monks first worked coal in the Montaud hills in 1230AD, but the town really began to grow rapidly with the development of industrial mining in about 1840. Today, the centre is infinitely better than the surrounding series of less-than-lovely modern tower blocks, but the whole town provides a sharp contrast to the fabulous landscapes of the neighbouring Cévennes (see p.149). Nevertheless, it is worth a stop for its handful of fine museums and the curious **Cathédrale St-Jean-Baptiste**, with a Romanesque façade and Gothic porch now attached to a plumply round 18th century church.

The **Mine-Témoin**, *chemin de la Cité Sainte-Marie, Rochebelle; tel: 04 66 30 45 15* (open daily Jun–Aug 0930-1900; Apr–May, Sept–Nov 0900–1230, 1400–1730; FFr.35), is dedicated to coal, with some 650 m of underground galleries housing exhibits on mining over the last century. Tours last 1 hr 20 mins; wear sensible shoes and take a jumper (the temperature remains a constant 13-15°C). The tour is undemanding and suitable for all physical abilities. In the town centre, the **Musée Minéralogique**, *6 av. de Clavières; tel: 04 66 78 51 69* (open June–Sept Mon–Fri 1400–1800; FFr.25), attached to the School of Mining Engineering, is one of France's finest collections of minerals, rocks and fossils.

The **Musée-Bibliothèque Pierre-André Benoit**, *Montée des Lauriers, Rochebelle; tel: 04 66 86 98 69* (open Jul–Aug daily 1200–1900; Sept–Jan, Mar–June Wed–Sun, 1200–1900; FFr.20) has an excellent collection of contemporary art and books, including works by Picasso, Braque and Miró. The **Musée de Colombier**, *Château de Colombier, Carrefour d'Auvergne; tel: 04 66 86 30 40* (open Wed–Mon 1000–1200, 1400–1700; FFr.12) has paintings from the 16th–20th centuries as well as a collection of local archaeological finds.

On the edge of town, a narrow road winds up a steep hill to a tiny **hermitage**, now topped by a vast statue of the Virgin Mary, where there are good picnic sites and superb views.

Side-track from Alès

Head north along the N904 towards Aubenas for a whole collection of family-friendly attractions. About 10 km from Alès is the **Château de Rousson**, *Rousson; tel: 04 66 85 60 31* (open July–Aug daily 1000–1900, Easter–June, Sept; guided tours 30 mins; FFr.25) which remains remarkably unaltered since it was built in 1600–1615. It is filled with fine Louis XIII and Louis XIV furniture. The **Préhistorama**, *La Croix de Fauvie, Rousson; tel: 04 66 85 86 96* (open June–Aug daily 1000– 1900; shorter hours other months; FFr.30) is a carefully reconstructed account of prehistoric development from the origins of life itself to the emergence of early man.

Five kms further, a turning on the left leads to the **Domaine de Villaret**, *Larnac, Les Mages; tel: 04 66 25 73 08* (open July–Aug daily 1500–1900; June daily 1700–1900; guided visits last 1 hr; FFr.25) where you can find the **Musée de Statues d'Enfants**, a permanent exhibition of charming sculptures of children set in an ancient domaine.

Turn right at Les Mages on the D132 and it leads you through St Julien de-Cassagnas to the **Parc Ornithologique des Isles**; *tel: 04 66 25 66 13* (open daily Jul–Aug 0900–1900; FFr.30) with a collection of birds from across the world.

Twenty-five km north of Alès, the **Grotte de Cocalière**, *Courry, on the D904; tel: 04 66 24 01 57* (open July–Aug daily 1000–1800; Apr–June, Sept–Oct daily 1000–1200, 1400–1700; guided tour 1 hr; FFr.42) is one of the many dramatically beautiful cave systems which honeycomb this region, distinguished by its underground river and, bizarrely, the possibility of underground cycle racing.

ALÈS TO MENDE

Tourist Offices: **Cendras**: *Mairie; tel: 04 66 30 21 83;* **La Grand-Combe:** *pl. J. Jaurès; tel: 04 66 54 90 00;* **Florac**: *Château de Florac; tel: 04 66 45 01 14* (see also p. 275).

Accommodation and Food

À l'Auberge Cévenole, *La Favède, Les Salles-du-Gardon; tel: 04 66 34 12 13; fax: 04 66 34 50 50* (moderate; restaurant expensive) is a 1950s villa set in spectacular gardens in the hills near La Grand-Combe. Further on, try the **Grand Hôtel du Parc**, *Florac; tel: 04 66 45 03 05; fax: 04 66 45 11 81* (cheap; restaurant moderate), a large, modern, but pleasant hotel with comfortable rooms. Two km beyond Florac , **Le Rochefort** *(LF), rte de Mende (N106), ; tel: 04 66 45 02 57; fax: 04 66 45 25 85* (cheap) is a smaller, family-run establishment. Both have good restaurants. For an unusual meal involving haut cuisine bison or ostrich in an Art Deco setting, try **La Source du Pêcheur**, *1 r. du Remuret, Florac; tel: 04 66 45 03 01* (expensive).

Campsites: **Camping La Croix Clementine**, *Cendras; tel: 04 66 86 52 69* (4-star; caravans; open Apr–Sept); **Camping Municipal Font de Merle**, *rte de Florac, La Grand-Combe; tel: 04 66 34 55 82* (2-star; open May–Sept); **Camping Municipal Le Pont du Tarn**, *rte de Pont-de-Montvert (N106), Florac; tel: 04 66 45 18 26* (2-star; caravans; open Apr–Oct).

Sightseeing

Almost as soon as you leave Alès, the landscape closes in and becomes wilder as the road plunges into the deep valleys of the Cévennes. The **Eco-Musée de la Vallée du Galeizon**, *Mairie, Cendras; tel: 04 66 30 21 83* (open Tues, Thur–Sun year round) has a small permanent exhibition on life in a Cévenol valley. **La Grand-Combe** is chiefly marked by its vast mines, producing iron, lead, zinc and asphalt. The **Musée du Mineur**, *Vallée Ricard; tel: 04 66 34 28 93* (open daily 0900–1200, 1400–1730) displays a wide selection of objects associated with the local mines over the last century.

The pretty village of **Florac**, in the Tarnon River valley, is the official capital of the National Park, at the meeting point of four geological systems – the Causse Méjean (limestone), Cévennes (schiste), Mont Lozère (granite) and the Aigoual Massif (granite and schiste). With the park headquarters and information in the local château, together with a whole variety of outdoor activities, from canoeing to to rambling, on offer, it makes a good base for exploring the surrounding magnificent and scenery. The **Château de Florac**; *tel: 04 66 49 53 01* (open July–Aug daily 0900–1900; more restricted hours other months; information free; exhibitions FFr.10) was built in 1683 after the Wars of Religion, on the site of a 13th-century fortress. It now houses both the town tourist office and the headquarters and information office of the Parc National des Cévennes (see p. 149) as well as exhibitions and audio-visual presentations on the park.

MENDE

Tourist Office: *14 blvd H. Bourrillon; tel: 04 66 65 02 69.* Open daily Jul–Aug 0830–2000; Easter–June, Sept, Mon–Fri 0830–1230, 1400–1900, Sat 0900–1200; Oct–Easter Mon–Fri 0830–1230, 1400–1800, Sat 0900–1200. Information about the town and region and a brochure outlining two walking tours of the old town. **Lozère Regional Office**: **CDT**, *14 blvd Henri-Bourillon; tel: 04 66 65 60 00.* Open Mon–Fri 0900–1230, 1300–1800, Sat (Jan–Jun) 0900–1600. Details of sightseeing, hiking, mountain biking and other outdoor activities throughout the region.

Accommodation and Food

The **Lion d'Or** *(BW), tel: 04 66 49 16 46; fax: 04 66 49 23 31* (moderate) is a large, attractive hotel set in gardens, with a pool. The **Hôtel du Pont Roupt** *(LF), 2 av. du 11 Novembre; tel: 04 66 65 01 43; fax: 04 66 65 22 96* (moderate) is modern and attractive, with a good restaurant, on the banks of the River Lot, 5 mins walk from the town centre. **Campsite**: **Le Tivoli**, beside the river, 2km from the town centre; *tel: 04 66 65 00 38* (2-star; caravans; open all year).

Sightseeing

Founded in 1368 on the site of a 4th-century hermitage, but largely rebuilt in 1620 after the Wars of Religion, the uneven towers of the **Cathédrale de St-Pierre**, *pl. Urbain V*, dominate this thriving market town. Inside are a Black Madonna, thought to have been brought back by the Crusaders, a magnificent organ (1624) and eight fine Aubusson tapestries.

Around it, old streets such as *pl. du Mazel, r. l'Orange* and *r. des Mulets* , are filled with interesting houses, many dating from the 17th–18th centuries. The **Musée Ignon-Fabre**, *3 r. de l'Épine, tel: 04 66 65 05 02* (currently closed for restoration) is a typical small town museum bursting with local history, geology and culture.

MONTPELLIER–PERPIGNAN

There's a scent of pines and herbs after the route leaves busy Montpellier to head south-west towards the Spanish border. Along the coast, a string of modern resorts, has colonised the long sandy beaches. Inland the country-side is mountainous with ruined castles crowning many of the hilltops.

DIRECT ROUTE: 117 KM

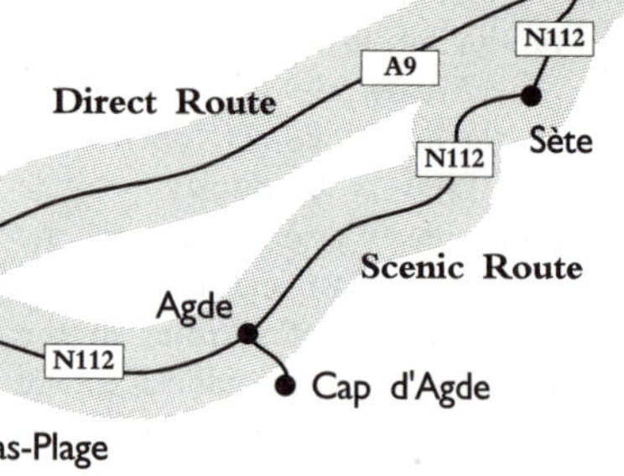

ROUTES

DIRECT ROUTE

The A9 motorway goes direct from Montpellier to Perpignan, bypassing Béziers, Narbonne and the coastal resorts. Distance: 177 km; driving time about 90 min.

SCENIC ROUTE

Leave **Montpellier** heading west on the N113, then soon afterwards branch off to the south on the N112, which reaches the coast just before **Sète**. It then runs along a broad causeway beside the **Bassin de Thau** to **Agde** where it swings inland towards **Béziers**. Turn left onto the D64, across the **Canal du Midi**, to return to the sea at **Valras Plage**. Follow the D37 across the River Aude, and then take the D718 inland to **Fleury,** as there is no coast road. Return to the sea again at **Narbonne Plage** on the D1118, then follow the D332 to **Narbonne**. Leave town heading south on the N9, branching left at **Caves** onto the D627, which runs between the sea and **Étang de Leucate ou de Salses** towards **Perpignan**. Distance: 215 km; allow about 4 hours.

SÈTE

Tourist Office: *60 Grand'Rue Mario Roustan; tel: 04 67 74 71 71.* Open daily July-Aug 0900–2000; Sept–June 0900–1200, 1400–1800.

ACCOMMODATION AND FOOD

There are several small hotels on the bustling canalside quays. Head along the *Corniche* for quieter locations nearer the sea such as **La Conga**, *plage de la Corniche; tel: 04 67 53 02 57, fax: 04 67 51 40 41* (cheap). Canalside dining is plentiful and lively.

SIGHTSEEING

As a major fishing (sardines and tuna) and industrial port with docks and a regular car-ferry to Tangier, the town has its own distinct character and a life independent of tourists. Traffic can be very heavy along the quays of the **Canal Royal** and on the hilly streets which climb from here into the town centre. Highlight of the day is the fish auction at 3pm beside the **Old Port**. Pastel-coloured Italianate houses line the busy **Canal Royal** and steep narrow streets climb from it, giving way to parks and woods at the top of **Mont St Clair**, 183m up. The **Richelieu Citadel** was built on the hill in 1744. The **Sailors' Cemetery** below was immortalised by the poet, Paul Valéry, who was born in the town and is buried in the cemetery. On the far side of the hill, **Le Vignerai**, *blvd Camille Blanc; tel: 04 67 51 17 12* (open Jul–Aug daily 1000–1900; May–June, Sept–Nov Tue–Sun 1000–1900; FFr.28) the process of wine-making from vine to bottle is explained in underground galleries stretching for 1400m.

July: the **Sète Festival**, *tel: 04 67 74 66 97*, dates back to 1666 when the port was built, and includes waterborne jousting, open-air plays in the grounds of Vauban's fort, and music and dancing.

Twice-weekly ferry services to **Tangiers** are operated by **SNCM**, *4 quai des Algers; tel: 04 67 46 68 00.* Also numerous boat excursions on the sea and canals, including day-trips operated by **Sète Croisières**, *quai Gén. Durand; tel: 04 67 46 00 46*, to see shellfish production in the Bassin de Thau (FFr.140).

AGDE AND CAP D'AGDE

Tourist Office: Agde: *Espace Molière (near pl. Molière); tel: 04 67 94 29 68.*

Canal du Midi

This 240 km canal linking **Sète** and **Toulouse** was the brainchild of a prosperous salt-tax inspector, Paul Riquet. In 1667, he persuaded Louis XIV to support ambitious vision of linking the Mediterranean and the Atlantic to avoid the long voyage around Gibraltar. It took him 14 years, using 15,000 labourers, and he bankrupted himself in the process, but the project was a success. The canal, fed by a complicated system of smaller canals and reservoirs and punctuated by locks, aqueducts and tunnels, used pioneering hydraulic technology. One of the most remarkable features is the staircase of 9 locks at Fonserannes near Béziers which lift the water 21.5 m up a hill. Boat excursions (daily Jul–Aug) start from the locks and also from **Agde, Marseillan** and **Portiragnes**, operated by **Bateaux du Soleil**; *tel: 04 67 94 08 79*. Or you can hire a self-drive cruiser for longer trips from **Crown Blue Line** bases at **Port Cassisifière** in **Portiragnes**; *tel: 04 67 90 91 70.* A tiny restaurant, one of the best for miles, occupies a former stables on a lonely stretch east of Capestang: **Le Pourquoi Pas?**, *Pont de Malviès; tel: 04 67 93 37 94* (moderate).

Open Mon–Sat 0900–1800 and (mid Jun–mid Sept) Sun 1000–1200; . Several information offices are situated around **Cap d'Agde**.

ACCOMMODATION AND FOOD

Most visitors choose to stay near the sea in **Cap d'Agde**, where much of the accommodation is self-catering. In Agde, **Hôtel Le Donjon**, *pl J. Jaurès; tel: 04 67 21 12 32, fax: 04 67 94 34 54* (cheap) is centrally-placed and has a pool. The restaurant (expensive) at **La Tamirissière**, *21 quai Théophile Cornu; tel: 04 67 94 20 87* (moderate), a 27-room hotel beside the sea, has been serving gourmet cuisine for over 100 years (closed Jan–mid Mar). **Campsites**: there are numerous options, the top-rated one being **Les Champs Blancs**, *rte. de Rochelongue; tel: 04 67 94 23 42* (caravans).

Activities

As befits a purpose-built seaside resort, **Cap d'Agde** has a club for every activity, particularly tennis, golf, squash and horse-riding, but also scrabble, bridge and snooker. To keep children happy, **Aqualand**, *av. des Îles d'Amérique; tel: 04 67 26 85 94* (open daily Jul–Aug 1000–2000; June, Sept 1000–1800; FFr.90), which was Europe's first water-park, has chutes and slides and there's a **Club Mickey** beach club, *Parking Plage Richelieu Centre; tel: 04 67 26 76 93* for 3–14-year-olds (open Jul–Aug Mon–Sat 1000–1800, Sun 1400–1800; May–June Sat and Sun only). A casino, **Île des Loisirs**, *r. des Sans-Soucis, Ile des Loisirs; tel: 04 67 26 82 82*, and two dozen nightclubs take over after dark, including **Le Feeling** (couples only), *quai du Chapitre; tel: 04 67 94 88 62*.

SIGHTSEEING

Agde, an attractive walled town with narrow streets beside the Hérault River, was first developed as a port by the ancient Greeks. Yachts and fishing boats now line its quays. Many of the buildings are built in sombre-looking black basalt, including the 12th-century **Cathédrale de St Étienne**, *r. L. Bages* (open for services and guided tours; apply at tourist office opposite; FFr.6) whose sturdy tower and sparse windows make it look like a fortress. The **Musée Agathois**, *r. de la Fraternité, tel: 04 67 94 82 51* (open Jul–Aug daily 1000–1200, 1400–1800; Sept–Jun Wed–Mon; FFr.12), housed in a 17th-century mansion, shows Agde's development from prehistoric times to the present day.

Cap d'Agde, 2 km away beside the sea, could scarcely be more different. Developed in the 1960s as a holiday playground around a large marina, it has smart honey-coloured apartments and shops with broad avenues, parks and a golf course. The most famous of its long sandy beaches is the *plage Naturiste*, beside Europe's largest naturist village.

BÉZIERS

Tourist Office: *Hôtel du Lac, 27 r. 4 Septembre, off pl. G. Péri; tel: 04 67 49 24 19*. Open July–Aug daily 0900–1900, Sun 1000–1200; no Sun opening Sept–Jun.

ACCOMMODATION AND FOOD

Centrally located hotels include the 3-star **Imperator**, *28 allées P. Riquet; tel: 04 67 49 02 25, fax: 04 67 28 92 30* (moderate). The **Grand Hôtel du Nord**, *15 pl. J. Jaurès; tel: 04 67 28 34 09; fax: 04 67 49 00 37* (moderate) has a good view of the river. The top restaurant in town is **Le Framboisier**, *12 r. Boiëldieu; tel: 04 67 49 90 00* (expensive; closed 2nd-half Aug). For cheaper fare, try **Le Bistro des Halles**, *pl. de la Madeleine; tel: 04 67 28 30 46* (closed Sun–Mon).

Sightseeing

This is a lively town in an attractive hillside setting surrounded by vineyards above the River Orb and Canal du Midi. Its centrepiece is the **Allées Paul Riquet,** an acacia-shaded promenade created in honour of its famous engineering son. Everyone gathers there to gossip, stroll and browse amongst the flower and bric-a-brac stalls. One end slopes up to the town's grand 150-year old theatre. At the other is the **Plateau des Poêtes**, a park with ornate sculptures and small lake surrounded by trees. Narrow streets punctuated by intimate squares lead to the fortress-like 12th–14th-century **Cathédrale de St Nazaire**, *pl. de la Révolution; tel: 04 67 28 22 89* (open daily 0900–1200, 1430–1900), a landmark for miles around. The views down from its wide terrace are superb. In the former Royal Barracks, the **Musée St Jacques,** *Rampe du 96ème; tel: 04 67 36 71 01* (open Tue–Sun 0900–1200, 1400–1800; FFr.10) covers the town's history and the building of the canal.

NARBONNE

Tourist Office: *pl. Salengro; tel: 04 68 49 84 86.* Open daily 1000–1200 and 1400–1730.

Accommodation and Food

Some of the older hotels in the heart of the town are now well past their prime. A good alternative only a few minutes walk away is the small **Hôtel de France**, *6 r. Rossini; tel: 04 68 32 09 75* (cheap) in a side street near the canal and market hall. **Grand Hôtel du Languedoc**, *22 blvd Gambetta; tel: 04 68 65 14 74; fax: 04 68 65 81 48* (moderate) is bigger and more prestigious with ornate stonework and wrought-iron balconies decorating its facade. Chain hotels include *Ib* and *Nv*. **HI**: *pl. Salengro; tel: 04 68 32 01 00*, has a self-service restaurant. **Campsite**: **Camping Les Mimosas**, *Chaussée de Mandirac; tel: 04 68 49 03 72*, is a large site with pool and tennis (caravans; open Apr–Oct). Seafood cassoulet is served at **Aux Trois Caves**, *r. B. Crémieux; tel: 04 68 65 28 60* (moderate), a small restaurant in old vaulted cellars. Seafood is also the speciality at **L'Estagnol**, *cours Mirabeau; tel: 04 68 65 09 27* (cheap).

Sightseeing

Edged by vineyards and within easy reach of several good beaches, Narbonne is divided by the **Canal de la Robine**. The town centre is dominated by the magnificent 13th–14th-century Gothic **Cathédrale St Just et St Pasteur**, *r. Armand Gauthier; tel: 04 68 90 30 30* (open Mon–Sat 0900–1150, 1400–1750, Sun 0900–1200) which was intended to be one of the biggest churches in Christendom. However it was never finished because the authorities refused to allow the town walls to be pulled down to make way for the nave. It has lovely stained glass and superb views from the towers. Next door the opulent **Palais des Archevêques** (Archbishops' Palace); *tel: 04 68 90 30 30* (open Tues–Sun 1000–1150, 1400–1800; FFr.25) houses an art and archaeology museum. **L'Horreum**, *16 r. Rouget-de-l'Isle; tel: 04 68 32 45 30* (open Tues–Sun 1000–1150, 1400–1800; FFr.25) is a well-preserved underground Roman granary, with a warren of vaulted cellars.

Side Track from Narbonne

Leave **Narbonne** on the A61 (Autoroute des 2 Mars) or N113 which is almost as direct; about 45 mins drive to **Carcassonne**. From Carcassonne, you can make your way on to

Perpignan across the **Corbières Mountains**, where limestone crags peep through wooded hillsides, often topped by the ruins of a castle. This is the **Pays des Cathares**, the stronghold of the Cathar sect which rebelled against the Catholic church in the 12th and 13th centuries, believing it to be out of touch with true Christianity.

CARCASSONNE

Tourist Offices: In the **Ville Basse** (lower town): *15 blvd Camille-Pelletan; tel: 04 68 25 07 04* (open July–Aug Mon–Sat 0900–1900, Sun 1000–1200; Sept–June Mon-Sat 0900–1200, 1400–1900); in **La Cité** (old town): *Tours Narbonnaises; tel: 04 68 25 68 81* (open daily July–Aug 0900–1900; Sept–June 0900–1200, 1400–1730).

Accommodation and Food

The few hotels in the Cité cost more than those in the lower town, where there is a reasonable choice, particularly in *r. de la Liberté* and *r. de Verdun*. A modern hotel with good views up to the Cité is **Des Trois Couronnes**, *2 r. des Trois Couronnes; tel: 04 68 25 36 10; fax: 04 68 25 92 92* (moderate). In the Cité, the **Du Donjon**, *2 r. Comte Roger; tel: 04 68 71 08 80, fax: 04 68 25 06 60* (moderate), has lots of character, though to rub shoulders with the likes of **Princess Di** and **Michael Jackson** you need to book into the exclusive **Hotel de la Cité**, *pl. St-Nazaire; tel: 04 68 25 03 34; fax: 04 68 71 50 15* (expensive). Chains include: *BW*, *Ca*, *Cl*, *F1*, *Ib*, *LF* and *Mc*. **HI**: *r. du Vicomte Trencavel; tel: 04 68 25 23 16*, is in the Cité (open Feb–Nov). **Campsite: Cité Campeole**, *rte de Ste-Hilaire; tel: 04 68 25 11 77*, is 2 km away (caravans; open Mar–Sept).

Restaurants are plentiful in the Cité. **La Marquiére**, *13 r. St-Jean; tel: 04 68 71 52 00* (moderate) is in one of the quieter streets. In the lower town, **Le Relais d'Aymeric**, *290 av. du Gén. Leclerc; tel: 04 68 71 83 83* (moderate) has a good reputation for local dishes.

Sightseeing

When visiting the Cité, you have to leave your car outside the walls, though hotel guests can drive in after 1800. Bus No 4 links it with the lower town. A free '**road train**' operates July–Aug. **Guided tours**, including two a day in English (June–Sept) start at the castle; FFr 32.

There are two distinct towns separated by the River Aude. The 'modern' **Ville Basse** (Lower Town) on the west bank actually dates back to the 13th century. **La Cité**, perched on a crag and floodlit at night, is a convincing 19th-century reconstruction of the medieval fortified town with 50 towers, high double walls and a population of just 200. It becomes a real honeypot in summer when all its small shops (mostly souvenirs) are crowded out. **St Nazaire**, its beautiful church, has an 11th-century nave and fine 14th–15th century stained glass. The 12th-century fortress, **Château Comtal**, *r. Viollet-le-Duc; tel: 04 68 25 01 66*, has a moat and five sturdy towers linked by walls with wooden galleries at the top. Inside it, the **Musée Lapidaire** (open June–Sept daily 0900–1900; Oct–Mar daily 1000–1200, 1400–1700; guided tours only (in English June–Sept); FFr. 32) has a collection of Roman relics and medieval stone missiles. Events include **Cité en Scène** (July), medieval tournaments and fireworks, and a **Son et Lumière** in Aug.

Nice

Nice has been the Queen of the Riviera ever since Russian princes and British aristocracy began to grace its opulent hotels in the mid-19th century. Today it is as vibrant as ever, attracting 3 million visitors a year who come to enjoy its long hours of sunshine. Second only to Paris as a tourist centre, backpackers of the world converge on the long beach throughout the summer months, joining those who can afford to holiday in its stylish hotels or cruise into the port. Out of season it is, not surprisingly, a popular venue for conferences and exhibitions.

Yet Nice is also a place in which people live and work. It is France's fifth most important city and has a burgeoning research industry, university and advanced technology centre. Buzzing with traffic and rapidly expanding into the hills around, it has a thriving life beyond tourism.

Tourist Information

Tourist Office: *av. Thiers; tel: 04 93 87 07 07* (just to the left of the train station). Open June–Sept daily 0800–2000; Oct–May daily 0800–1900. **Branches**: *5 promenade des Anglais, tel: 04 93 87 60 60*, and at the western end of *promenade des Anglais* near the airport, *tel: 04 93 83 32 64*. Both open June–Sept, Mon–Sat 0800–2000, Sun 0800–1200; Oct–May Mon–Sat 0800–1800. Ample brochures on Nice and the surrounding area.

Arriving and Departing

Airport

Nice Côte d'Azur: *promenade des Anglais*, 7 km west of the city. Airport information: *tel: 04 93 21 30 12*. Terminal One handles international, Air Littoral and TAT flights. Terminal Two handles domestic flights. Taxis to the centre cost about FFr.200. The no. 23 bus runs along *promenade des Anglais* to the railway station every 30 mins; the 20-min journey costs FFr.8. **Héli Inter**, *tel: 04 93 21 46 46* offers helicopter transits every 20 mins to Monte Carlo (15 mins) and seven flights a day to St Tropez during the summer.

By Car

Driving is like a race-track in this busy city, particularly on the *promenade des Anglais*, the 5-km multi-lane dual-carriageway along the seafront. **Parking**: there are street meters and three dozen car-parks, including four along the *promenade des Anglais*, for the faint-hearted.

By Bus

Gare Routière (bus station): *promenade du Paillon; tel: 04 93 85 61 81*.

By Train

Station: **Nice-Ville**, *av. Thiers; tel: 08 36 35 35 35*. Information open Mon–Sat 0830–1830; Sun 0830–1115, 1400–1700. Excellent TGV connections with the rest of France and frequent services to all nearby resorts.

By Boat

Ferries: **SNCM-Ferryterranée**, *quai du*

Commerce (on the east side of the port); *tel: 04 93 13 66 66/59*. Regular crossings to Corsica. **Bateaux Trans Côte d'Azur**, *quai de Lunel, tel: 04 92 00 42 30*, operate boat trips to other resorts and the Iles de Lérins (June–Sept, daily 1500– 1700; Oct–May, Tues, Wed, Fri and Sun at 1500).

Getting Around

Nice is a big sprawling city. Broad avenues stretch back from the *promenade des Anglais* along the seafront and its eastern extension, the shorter *quai des États-Unis*. The Old Town quarter is manageable on foot.

Car and motor-bike hire: **Nicea**, *9 av. Thiers* (near the railway station); *tel: 04 93 82 42 71*; **Budget**: *Airport, Terminal 1, tel: 04 93 21 36 50, Terminal 2, tel: 04 93 21 42 51*; **Europcar**: *Airport, Terminal 1, tel: 04 93 21 36 44, Terminal 2, tel: 04 93 21 36 72*; **Hertz**: *Airport, Terminal 1 04 93 21 36 72, Terminal 2, tel: 04 93 21 42 72, Station, tel: 04 93 82 42 71*.

Bus services are good, including four night services until 0110. Most radiate from *pl. Masséna*. Buy tickets on board; FFr.8. A carnet of 5 costs FFr.32.50; one, five and seven-day passes are also available. Information: **Sunbus**, *10 r. F Faure; tel: 04 93 16 52 10*. A 40-min circuit on a **road train** takes you to and from *Esplanade Albert 1er* on the seafront, around the old town and up to the castle gardens; *tel: 04 93 18 81 58* (FFr. 30).

Taxis are plentiful but expensive. Expect to pay FFr.50 for even the shortest trip. For 24-hour service, *tel: 04 93 80 70 70*. **Bicycle hire**: *Arnaud, 4 pl. Grimaldi; tel: 04 93 87 88 55*.

Staying in Nice

Accommodation

As Nice is one of Europe's most popular destinations, it offers a wide range of accommodation but do not expect well-located hotels to come cheap. Hotel chains include *Bw, Ca, Cn, Cs, Ho, Ib, Ih, Mc, Md, Mo, Nv*, and *Sf*. Early Feb is busy during Nice Carnival.

The best address in town is the *promenade des Anglais*; at no. 37 you will find one of the world's most prestigious hotels, the **Négresco**, *tel: 04 93 16 64 00, fax: 04 93 88 35 68* (expensive). This white and pink palace topped by a large dome was built in 1912 for Henri Négresco who had originally been a Romanian gypsy violinist. The same architect designed the Moulin Rouge and Folies Bergères in Paris and it abounds with extravagant furnishings. Those who cannot afford a room (FFr.1250–2350 per night) should at least tiptoe past the reception desk to see the Salon Royal, a grand drawing room adorned with portraits, pillars, a 16,000-crystal Baccarat chandelier and the biggest Aubusson carpet in the world – round and red.

A simpler, but well-placed, hotel which will not totally break the bank despite its sea views is the **Mercure**, *2 r. Halévy* (corner of *promenade des Anglais* near *pl. Masséna*); *tel: 04 93 82 30 88; fax: 04 93 82 18 20* (expensive). **Hôtel Alexandra**, *41 r. Lamartine; tel: 04 93 62 14 43, fax: 04 93 62 30 34* (moderate), is a short walk from the sea in the heart of the town. For the budget-conscious, good-value accommodation is available near the station – try *r. de Suisse, av. Durante* or *r. d'Alsace-Lorraine*. **La Belle Meunière**, *21 av. Durante; tel: 04 93 88 66 15*, **Hôtel Interlaken**, *26 av. Durante; tel: 04 93 88 30 15*, and **Hôtel Orangers**, *10 bis av. Durante; tel: 04 93 87 51 41*, are all relatively inexpensive. Or try in Old Nice around *pl. St François*. High above the town, next to the Parc Écologique on the

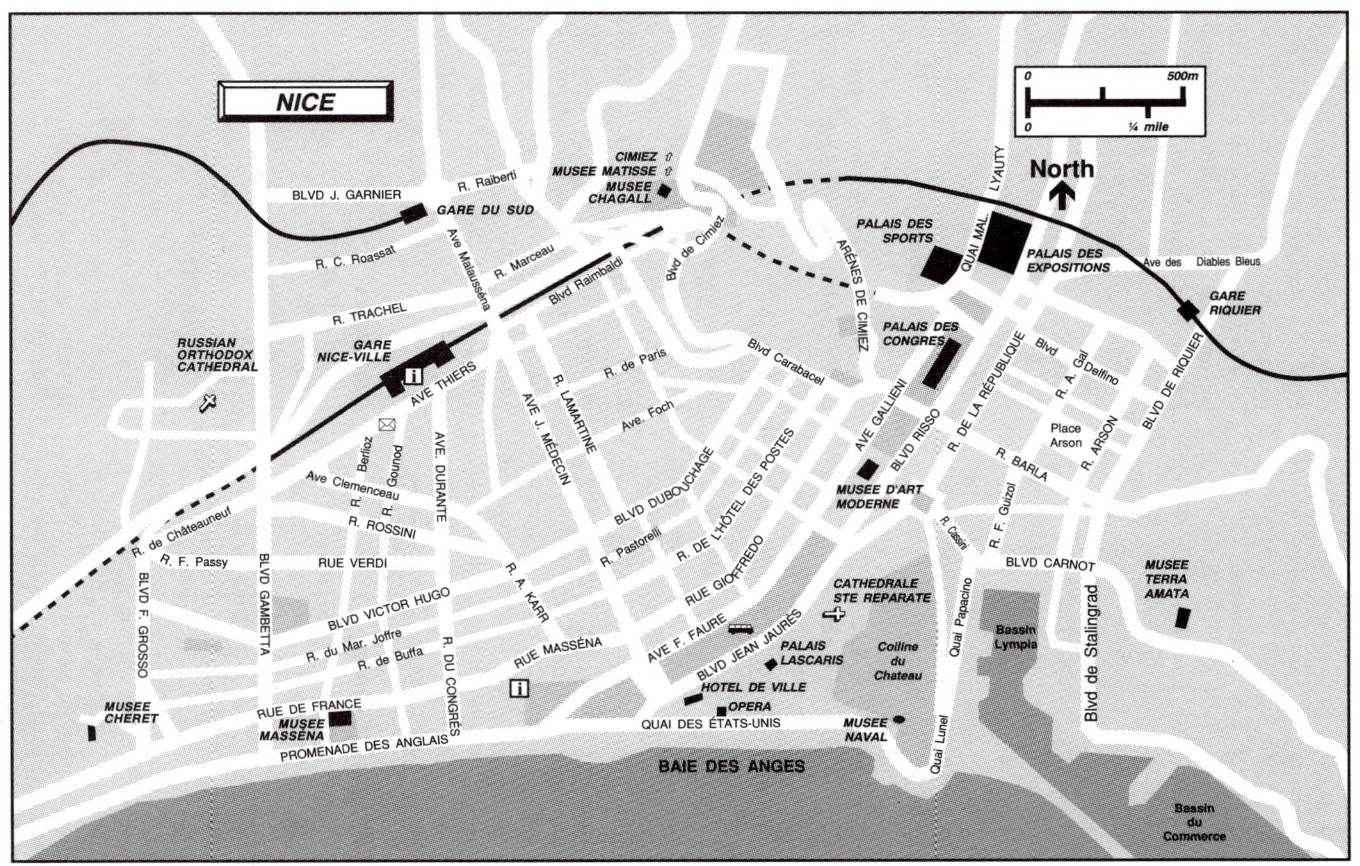
NICE
0
500m
0
¼ mile
North
CIMIEZ
MUSEE MATISSE
MUSEE CHAGALL
BLVD J. GARNIER
R. Raiberti
GARE DU SUD
R. C. Roassat
Ave Malausséna
R. Marceau
R. TRACHEL
Blvd Raimbaldi
Blvd de Cimiez
ARÈNES DE CIMIEZ
PALAIS DES SPORTS
QUAI MAL. LYAUTY
PALAIS DES EXPOSITIONS
Ave des Diables Bleus
GARE RIQUIER
RUSSIAN ORTHODOX CATHEDRAL
GARE NICE-VILLE
AVE THIERS
R. de Paris
Blvd Carabacel
PALAIS DES CONGRES
Blvd Gal Delfino
R. A.
BLVD DE RIQUIER
Ave. Foch
R. LAMARTINE
AVE J. MÉDECIN
AVE GALLIENI
BLVD RISSO
R. DE LA RÉPUBLIQUE
Place Arson
R. ARSON
R. BARLA
Berlioz
Gounod
R.
R.
AVE. DURANTE
Ave Clemenceau
R. ROSSINI
BLVD DUBOUCHAGE
R. DE L'HÔTEL DES POSTES
MUSEE D'ART MODERNE
R. Cassini
R. F. Guizol
R. de Châteauneuf
R. F. Passy
RUE VERDI
BLVD GAMBETTA
BLVD F. GROSSO
R. Pastorelli
R. A. KARR
RUE GIOFFREDO
BLVD CARNOT
MUSEE TERRA AMATA
CATHEDRALE STE REPARATE
Quai Papacino
Bassin Lympia
Blvd de Stalingrad
BLVD VICTOR HUGO
R. du Mar. Joffre
R. de Buffa
R. DU CONGRÉS
RUE MASSÉNA
AVE F. FAURE
BLVD JEAN JAURÈS
PALAIS LASCARIS
Colline du Chateau
HOTEL DE VILLE
OPERA
MUSEE CHERET
RUE DE FRANCE
MUSEE MASSENA
PROMENADE DES ANGLAIS
QUAI DES ÉTATS-UNIS
MUSEE NAVAL
Quai Lunel
BAIE DES ANGES
Bassin du Commerce

Grande Corniche to the north-east, **Hôtel Panoramic**, *107 blvd Bischoffeim; tel: 04 93 89 12 46; fax: 04 93 89 76 51* (cheap) and **Hôtel Les Gemeaux**, *149 blvd Observatoire; tel: 04 93 89 03 60; fax: 04 93 26 90 38* (cheap) provide a breath of fresh air well away from the seafront melée.

HI: Nice has three youth hostels although none are central. **Mt-Alban**, *rte de Mont-Alban; tel: 04 93 89 23 64*, is 4km out of town uphill! (bus no. 5 from the station to *blvd J Jaurès*, then no. 14 to hostel). No reservations, open from 1000. Good view over the city. **Clairvallon Youth Hostel**, *av. Scudéri; tel: 04 93 81 27 63*, is up in Cimiez to the north of the centre (bus nos 15 or 22 to Scudéri); located in a park with pool. **Magnan** *31 r. Louis-de-Coppet* (near the airport); *tel: 04 93 86 28 75* (bus no. 23 from the station or 9, 10 or 12 from *pl. Grimaldi*).

Campsites: The nearest campsites, at Cagnes-sur-Mer to the west beyond the airport, include **Camping Horizon Azur**, *Ancienne Route Vence; tel: 04 93 20 62 02* (caravans), and **Camping La Rivière**, *chemin Salles; tel: 04 93 20 62 27* (caravans). Sleeping on the beach is not allowed, but groups of young people sit chatting there on hot summer nights until long after midnight. Those who stay too long can expect a hosing down at dawn.

Eating and Drinking

A culinary paradise, Nice is influenced both by its neighbour, Italy, and Provence whose cooking combines local vegetables like peppers and aubergines with delicately-flavoured herbs.

Vieux Nice (the old town) is the best area for eating – particularly *cours Saleya*, which is covered with open-air tables in summer, *r. Ste Répararte* and the other narrow side-streets around the cathedral, where it is still possible to eat inexpensively. For really good value, try **P'as de Pot?**, *2 r. Barillerie; tel: 04 93 85 79 32* (inexpensive). **L'Acchiardo**, *38 r. Droite; tel: 04 93 85 51 16* (cheap) is an authentic bar-restaurant. For a real treat, **le Grande Pavois**, *11 r. Meyerbeer, tel: 04 93 88 77 42* (expensive) is widely regarded as the town's top fish restaurant. North of the Old Town, *pl. Garibaldi* boasts the best shellfish, notably at the inexpensive **Café de Turin**, and good *socca*. The Zone Piétonne (pedestrian zone), around *av. J Médecin*, is the place for pizzas.

Communications

Post Office, *23 av. Thiers; tel: 04 93 82 65 00*. Facilities include poste restante, and fax. Open Mon–Fri 0800–1900, Sat 0800–1200.

Money

Banks are scattered throughout the city, but *av. Thiers* is a good place to start. **Office Provençal**, *17 av. Thiers; tel: 04 93 88 56 80* (open 0700–0000) and *10 r. de France; tel: 04 93 82 16 55* (open 0800–2000). **Thomas Cook Bureaux de Change:** *12 av. Thiers, tel: 04 93 82 13 00* (open 0700–2300), at the station; *13 av. Thiers, tel: 04 93 88 59 99* (open 0800–2230), across the road; *2 pl. Magenta, tel: 04 93 88 49 88* (open 0900–2300).

Consulates

United Kingdom, *11 r. Paradis; tel: 04 93 82 32 04.*

United States, *31 r. Mar. Joffre; tel: 04 93 88 89 55.*

Entertainment

Nice is the cultural and social capital of the south-east offering a wide choice of opera, concerts and plays. Head to **Fnac**, Nice Étoile shopping mall, *av. J. Médecin; tel: 04 93 21 00 00,* for tickets.

Opera, Music and Theatre

Nice Opéra, *4 r. St-François-de-Paule; tel: 04 93 85 67 31*, is one of the best in France, staging opera and concerts. The **Théâtre de Nice**, *promenade des Arts; tel: 04 93 80 52 60*, in the huge Acropolis, part of the Palais des Congrès, stages opera, ballet and concerts. There are concerts of chamber and sacred music at the **Cathédrale Ste Réparate**; **CEDAC de Cimiez**, *49 av. de la Marne; tel: 04 93 81 09 09*, is a major venue for jazz. In summer the **Théâtre de Verdure**, *Jardin Albert I; tel: 04 93 82 38 68*, stages rock, jazz and other concerts in a marquee. The **Théâtre de l'Alphabet**, *10 blvd Carabacel; tel: 04 93 13 08 88*, offers classical theatre productions.

Bars and Nightlife

In summer Nice grinds on long after midnight, thanks to its many piano bars, discos and small clubs with live music, though it lacks sophisticated nightclubs. The young gravitate to the beach. Gamblers head for **Casino Ruhl**, *1 promenade des Anglais; tel: 04 93 87 95 87*. Many simply stroll along the *promenade des Anglais* or sit on the *cours Saleya* and watch the world go by.

Events

Jan: **Festival of Costumed Dolls** and **Bird Show**; Feb: **Nice Carnival** and **Battles of the Flowers** involve parades of dozens of giant floats, nights with bands and dancing, fireworks and the burning of the Carnival King (see box); Apr: **International Dog Show**, **International Tennis Tournament** and **Festin des Cougoudrons** – a festival of folklore and sculpted gourds with processions and stalls; June: **Festival of Church Music**; July: International stars perform in the **Jazz Festival** in the Roman amphitheatre and gardens at Cimiez (tickets from Fnac and tourist offices); Sept: **Wine Festival**; Oct: **International Marathon**; Nov: **International Cat Show**; Dec (first Sun after Christmas): **Bain de Noel** – skinny dipping in the sea.

Shopping

The outdoor markets and little shops in Vieux Nice are good places to shop for art, cheap clothes and fresh food. In *cours Saleya*, the food and flower market (0600–1730 except Sun afternoon and Mon) is replaced by a flea market on Mon (0800–1700). Craft stalls arrive on summer

Carnival

Held during the two weeks before Lent, the Carnival is a tradition which has surprisingly authentic origins since it seems tailor-made for tourists. It dates back at least to the 14th century and may be very much older if, as suspected, it derives from pagan springtime rites. The burning of the Carnival King, *Sa Majesté Carnaval*, may even be an echo of the human sacrifice which was associated with such rituals in other parts of pre-Christian Europe. By the beginning of the 19th century the carnival had fallen into decline but it was revived by the Russian community. Now it is the largest pre-Lent carnival in France, using a format established by a local artist, Alexis Massa, in 1873. Festivities begin three weeks before *Mardi Gras* ('fat Tuesday') when the King is wheeled onto the streets. Costumed balls are held in many of the hotels and impromptu parties develop in most bars. At the weekends, colourful flower-decked floats parade along a 2 km route around Jardin Albert 1er, accompanied by bands, horsemen and showers of confetti. The climax comes on Shrove Tuesday with the ceremonial burning of the king and a brilliant fireworks display.

evenings. For clothes and gift shops, head for the pedestrian area behind *pl. Masséna.* The Galeries Lafayette store and Nice Étoile shopping mall are in *av. J Médecin.*

Sightseeing

The *promenade des Anglais* sweeps along the 5km seafront from the centre of the **Baie des Anges** (Bay of Angels) to the airport. Originally a 2m-wide path, this famous boulevard, lined with palm trees and always decked with flowers, was built in the 1830s with funds raised by the English colony, led by a clergyman, Rev. Lewis Way. Though now an 8-lane highway invariably choked with impatient drivers, it still retains much of its old character and the seafront promenade is a wonderful place to watch the world go by. The gardens behind it were created in the late 19th century when the River Paillon was covered over. The first section, **Jardin Albert 1er**, leads to the wide *pl. Masséna* where a huge fountain plays over bronzes of the solar sytem. Designed in 1834, the place is regarded as the heart of Nice.

With its tall shuttered buildings and ornate balconies, **Vieux Nice**, at the eastern end of town, seems almost more Italian than French (indeed it was handed over to the King of Sicily in 1713 and only reunited with the rest of France in 1860). Wander the narrow streets around *pl. Rossetti* (in front of the cathedral) whose terrace restaurants and ice-cream parlours make it one of the liveliest parts of town. **Palais Lascaris**, *15 r. Droite; tel: 04 93 62 05 54* (open Tues–Sat 1000–1200, 1400–1800) is a 17th-century palace with a magnificent grand staircase and a salon hung with Flemish tapestries. An 18th-century pharmacy has been recreated on the ground floor. Beyond it, steps lead up to the remains of the Château, a colourful park, small naval museum and breathtaking views. At sunset, stroll the *promenade des Anglais* as the lights begin to shimmer and the Négresco lights up to look like an elaborate wedding cake.

Museums

Nice boasts some of the best museums and art galleries in France, 18 in all, reflecting the city's long history and its connections with great artists like Matisse, Chagall and Dufy. Admission to nearly all of them is free and most are easily accessible by bus. Best of all, in the Cimiez district 2km back from the sea, is the newly refurbished **Musée Matisse**, *164 av. des Arènes de Cimiez; tel: 04 93 81 08 08* (bus nos 15, 17, 20, 22 from *pl. Masséna;* open Apr–Sept 1000–1800; Oct–Apr 1000–1700, closed Tues; admission charge for special exhibitions only). This 17th-century Genoese-style villa with trompe-l'oeil façade and a modern extension houses Matisse's personal collection of paintings and sculptures in a beautiful setting. Next door, the **Musée Archéologique**, *160 av. des Arènes de Cimiez; tel: 04 93 81 59 57* (bus nos 15, 17, 20, 22 to Arènes; open Tues–Sun, Apr–Sept 1000–1200, 1400–1800; Oct–Mar 1000–1300, 1400–1700; FFr. 15) exhibits the copious finds made while excavating the Roman arenas at Cimiez. Matisse and fellow artist Raoul Dufy are buried in the neighbouring **Couvent des Frères Mineurs**, with a fine view across Nice to the sea. Also in Cimiez, the **Musée Marc Chagall**, *av. du Dr. Ménard; tel: 04 93 81 75 75* (bus no. 15; open Wed–Sun July–Sept 1000–1800, Oct–June 1000–1700; FFr. 28) is a graceful temple to Chagall's genius – beautifully lit to display 17 huge Biblical canvases he painted between 1954 and 1967 as well as stained-glass windows, engravings, sculptures and ceramics.

In the centre of town, the **Musée**

d'Art Moderne et d'Art Contemporain; *promenade des Arts; tel: 04 93 62 61 62* (open Wed–Mon 1100–1800, until 2200 Fri) is unmistakable. A dramatic white marble cliff rising above the street, it is filled with striking pop art including squashed cars in the gardens , from where there is also an exceptional view. The **Musée d'Histoire Naturelle**, *60 bis blvd Risso, tel: 04 93 55 15 24* (open Wed–Mon 1000–1200, 1400–1800) is famous for its vast global shell collection. The **Musée d'Art et d'Histoire**, *Palais Masséna, 65 r. de France, tel: 04 93 88 11 34* (open Tues–Sun 1000–1200, 1400–1800) is a splendid 19th-century Italianate villa adorned with antiques, traditional artefacts, paintings by Renoir and local artists and interior decor redolent of the *Belle Époque*.

Near the port (bus nos 1, 2, 7, 9, 10, 20), on the site of an ancient hunters' encampment, the **Musée de Terra Amata**, *25 blvd Carnot; tel: 04 93 55 59 93* (open Tues–Sun 1000–1200, 1400–1800) has displays on the prehistoric inhabitants of Nice from 400,000 years ago. Overlooking the port, the **Musée Naval**, in the historic Bellanda Tower, *parc du Château; tel: 04 93 80 47 61* (open Wed–Sun Jun–Sept 1000–1200, 1400–1900; Oct–May 1000–1200, 1400–1700) displays weapons, model ships and instruments. Hector Berlioz lived there for a short time. At the far west end of the *promenade des Anglais*, the tropical conservatories of **Parc Floral Phoenix**, *405 promenade des Anglais; tel: 04 93 18 03 33*, contain species of exotic fish, birds and butterflies.

Churches

Nice has two cathedrals, each in its own way tracing the resort's cosmopolitan history. In the Old Town, the **Cathédrale de Ste Réparate**; *pl. Rossetti*, is an impressive 17th-century Catholic masterpiece built with Italian money and dedicated to the town's patron saint. The interior is lavishly decorated with marble and plasterwork.

To the west of the railway station, the **Cathédrale Orthodoxe Russe St Nicolas**, *17 blvd du Tzarévitch; tel: 04 93 96 88 02* (open 0930–1200, 1430–1700, closed Sun am) is a mighty Russian Orthodox church built by Tsar Nicolas II on the site of a villa where the young Tsarevich Nicolas died. Completed in 1912, just five years before the Russian Revolution, it remains a symbol of the aristocratic opulence that characterises the Riviera. Topped by six distinctive onion-shaped cupolas, it is a subtle mixture of pink brick, grey marble and richly-coloured ceramics and contains suberb icons, woodwork and frescos.

Beaches

Nice has pebbly beaches but this does not deter the sun-worshippers from crowding onto the long **Baie des Anges** beach below the *promenade des Anglais* all summer long. Access to most of the beach is free, but private beach clubs cover some central sections, charging around FFr.100 for a day's hire of lounger and umbrella. Hotels make special arrangements for their guests to use the facilities. A series of modern white pergolas provide shade on the promenade for those who want to pause while strolling. For less hectic sun-worshipping, seek out the long stretch of beach between Cagnes-sur-Mer and Antibes to the west. However the prettiest bays are to the east at Villefranche (which attracts a young lively crowd; see pp. 299–300), Beaulieu (old sedate crowd; see p. 301) and St Jean-Cap-Ferrat (well-heeled laid-back crowd; see pp. 300–301).

NICE–BARCELONNETTE

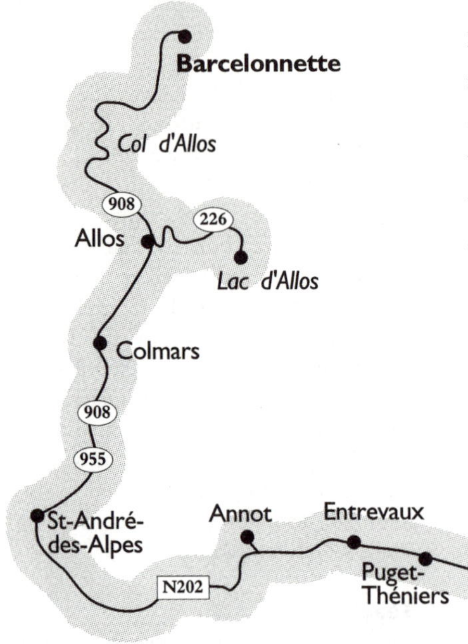

Heading due north out of Nice, this route immediately takes to the hills, with the option of going via the deep Gorges de la Vésubie before joining the main route west along the Var Valley, which is punctuated by quaint old villages and towns. From St-André-les-Alpes onwards, it twists up the Verdon Valley, the surrounding scenery becoming more and more Alpine.

MAIN ROUTE: 182 KM

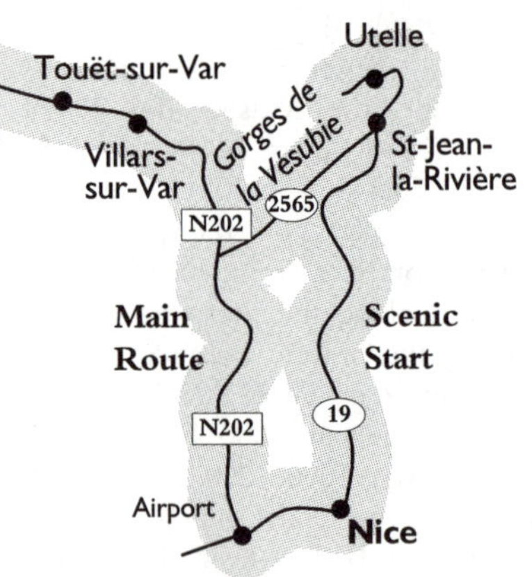

ROUTE

MAIN ROUTE

Head out of Nice towards Nice Airport. Opposite the airport, take the N202 north. Follow it through **Villars-sur-Var**, **Touët-sur-Var**, **Puget-Théniers**, **Entrevaux** and **Annot**. At **St-André-les-Alpes**, turn right onto the D955, which follows the Verdon River to **Colmars** and **Allos**, before turning into the D908 for the last stretch over the **Col d'Allos** into **Barcelonnette**. Distance 182 km; allow 3–4 hours.

SCENIC START

As an alternative to the initial drive up the wide, flat Var valley, you can begin with a visit to the Gorges de la

Colour section:
(i) The old centre of Nice (p. 281); Lac d'Allos in the Alpes de Haute-Provence (p. 292).
(ii) A classic Mediterranean view from Eze (p. 301).
(iii) Port Grimaud (p. 338); Bormes-les-Mimosas (p. 339).
(iv) St Tropez (p. 340) – the fashionable Café Le Gorille and the beach; Market scene in Toulon (p. 333)

Vésubie. From *pl. Masséna* in the centre of Nice, drive inland up *av. Félix Faure* and under the motorway onto the D19. Follow it up the **Gorges de la Vésubie** to **St-Jean-la-Rivière,** where the narrow D32 hairpins up through **Utelle** to the **Madonne d'Utelle** viewpoint. Returning to St-Jean-la-Rivière, take the D2565 south down the other side of the gorge to join the N202. Turn right to join the main route. Extra distance 27 km; extra time about 2 hrs.

GORGES DE LA VÉSUBIE

The optional scenic start to the route climbs into the mountains through **Levens** to overlook the Vésubie River in its deep gorge far below. At the next village, **Duranus**, a viewpoint enables drivers to make the most of the dizzying view. It also bears two plaques commemorating the *Saut des Français*, Republican soldiers who were hurled over the cliff edge by Nice guerrillas in 1793. The road continues upwards to **St-Jean-la-Rivière** (285 m), where the D32 leads tortuously up to the little fortified village of **Utelle** (800 m) and the **Madonne d'Utelle** sanctuary (1174 m) for a splendid panorama over the Alpes Maritimes. On the way back down the gorge, the road hugs the steep cliffs above the milky green river, often threading beneath overhanging rocks.

VILLARS-SUR-VAR

Tourist Office: *Hôtel de Ville; tel: 04 93 05 70 04.* Open Mon–Fri 1000–1200.

Two km up a steep twisting lane through vineyards, off the main N202, this quaint old village has the distinction of its own *Appellation Controlée* wine, Côtes de Provence. The first vineyards were planted in the Middle Ages. On 24 June visitors can join the annual St Jean procession along mountain tracks to the **Chapel of St Jean du Désert** for a festive picnic.

TOUËT-SUR-VAR

Tourist Office: *Hôtel de Ville; tel: 04 93 05 75 57.* Open Mon–Sat 0900–1130.

This small medieval village clings tenaciously to a sheer cliff like a fortress. Narrow alleyways and steep steps lead between terraces of quaint old houses whose balconies brim with flowers. The **Église de St Martin**, restored in 1986, straddles a waterfall on huge stone pillars. The newer, less interesting part of the town is down around the main road and railway station (unstaffed) on the **Train des Pignes** line (see p. 127). For four days in the middle of Aug each year, a local festival, **Lou Festin**, takes over the village.

PUGET-THÉNIERS

Tourist Office: *Maison du Pays; tel: 04 93 05 05 05,* on the N202 next to the station. Open daily 1000–1200, 1400–1900.

Accommodation and Food

There's little to choose between the two typically French small-town hotels on the main square, *pl. Conil* – **L'Univers**; *tel: 04 93 05 00 43* (cheap) and **Laugier**; *tel: 04 93 05 01 00* (cheap). Both have very acceptable restaurants where you can eat outside under the trees. **Campsite: Lou Gourdan**; *tel: 04 93 05 10 53* (caravans) by the **River Var**, with a big swimming pool.

Sightseeing

This thriving little town beside the Var and Roudole Rivers lies at the foot of a steep rocky ridge. Served by the Train des Pignes, it has plenty to offer tourists, including a swimming pool with 45 m slide, tennis, fishing and canoeing. Activities including canoeing, canyoning and hikes are organised by **Azur Nature**; *tel: 04 93 05 05 88*, a leisure centre with a small lake by the Var.

Seven hundred years ago, the Knights Templar moved in. Many of the houses in the narrow old streets date back to that time and bear the insignia of the knights. One street, *r. Gisclette*, still contains the rings used to thread the chains which barred it each night. The local people are very proud of **La Liberté Enchaîneé**, a striking bronze statue of a naked woman by Aristide Maillol, which commands pride of place in the main square. It was dedicated to the memory of Auguste Blanqui, a local *agitateur*, born in 1805, who spent 40 years behind bars for campaigning for the rights of workers. In 1911 the clergy were scandalised when the statue was first put near the church, so it was hastily moved. It was hidden for safety in the local abattoir and, during World War II, in Nice, but the locals insisted on having it back after the liberation in 1945.

ENTREVAUX

Tourist Office: *Tour du Pontlevis; tel: 04 93 05 46 73.* Open July–Aug Mon–Sat 0930–1230, 1400–1900, Sun 1000–1200, 1400–1800; Sept–June daily 1000–1200, 1400–1700. The office is in the **Porte Royale** at the drawbridge into **Ville Fort**. It organises various guided tours of the town and its citadel. **Station**: *tel: 04 93 05 41 38.*

The **citadel,** 135 m above this little town, is the most dramatic sight in the whole region. It is reached by a sloping path, sometimes steps, which zig-zags up the steep rocky hillside. A 10-franc coin gets you through the turnstile at the bottom (any hour). The climb – 20 mins up, 15 down – is well worth the effort, as you are rewarded by a magnificent view over the town and along the Var Valley, coupled with sheer admiration for those who built it. Though it is mostly ruined, several rooms and their roofs remain and some restoration work is now being carried out.

The town was a place of strategic importance for centuries – a fort in Roman times, then a border post between the kingdom of France and the Duchy of Savoy in the Middle Ages. It was fortified in 1690 under the guiding hand of Louis XIV's illustrious engineer, Vauban. You enter the old part, **Ville Fort**, over a drawbridge across the River Var between two of the towers. Altogether 17 of them are still intact and even the cathedral is built into the ramparts.

The Luciani family's **Musée de la Moto**; *tel: 04 93 79 12 70* (open July–Aug daily 0900–1200, 1400–1900; Sept–June by arrangement; free) has 68 motorcycles and scooters from 1901 to 1968.

ANNOT

Tourist Office: *pl de la Mairie; tel: 04 92 83 23 03.* Open Jul–Aug Tues–Sat 1000–1200, 1500–1700; Sept–June, daily 0900–1200, 1500–1800 (closed Sun afternoon). **Station**: *tel: 04 92 93 20 26.*

Accommodation

The central **Beauséjour**, *pl. du Revely; tel: 04 92 83 21 08* (cheap) is a family-run hotel-restaurant with 19 rooms. **Campsite: La Ribière**, *rte de Fugeret; tel: 04 92 83 21 44* (caravans; open Feb–Nov).

Sightseeing

At the end of the 14th century this little market town stood on the borders of Provence, Piedmont and the County of Nice. In the 18th century, nut oil distilleries, lavender processing and tile manufacture brought wealth and prosperity. Then the demise of nut oil brought decline until the advent of tourism. The mild climate makes it a popular summer resort, offering pursuits like walking, tennis, golf and horse-riding.

Set in the Vaïre Valley at an altitude of 705 m and surrounded by mountains, the town combines Alpine ambience with Provençal charm. The old centre, just off the main road, has a Romanesque **church** and squares shaded by plane trees. Many of the tall buildings along the narrow tortuous streets and vaulted passageways still have 17th-century carved stonework. *R. Craponne* leads to the *pl. des Platanes* next to a bridge over the Vaïre which dates back to Roman times.

The town is famous for the **Grès d'Annot**, large sandstone boulders which are scattered around the town, some having been incorporated into the houses. Many of the rocky outcrops around have been moulded by erosion into weird shapes, making for some spectacular walks. The caves of the **Chambre du Roi** are particularly remarkable and served as a retreat in times of invasion.

Highlight of the year is the Whitsun festival of **St Fortunat**, commemorating the end of the Napoleonic Wars. Grenadiers dressed in red and white uniforms march through the town.

ST ANDRÉ-LES-ALPES

Tourist Office: *r. Principale; tel: 04 92 89 02 39.* Open mid June–Sept Mon–Sat 0830–1230, 1430–1900; Oct–mid June Mon–Sat 0900–1200, 1330–1730, closed Wed pm. Organises free guided walks and mountain bike tours in the hills during July and Aug. Walking and cycling route leaflets available.

The **Chalet-Hôtel Le Clair Logis (***LF***)**, *rte de Digne; tel: 04 92 89 04 05; fax: 04 92 89 19 36* (cheap) is well-positioned about 500 m from the centre, with 12 rooms and a restaurant. **Campsite: Les Iscles**; *tel: 04 92 89 02 29*, is a municipal campsite by the lake with 200 spaces.

Situated between mountain ridges near the end of Lac de Castillon in the broad valley of the swift Verdon River, this small resort makes the most of its setting. The world paragliding championships have been held here, as the ridges of **Mont Chalvet** (1616 m) to the west provide perfect jumping-off points and the prevailing winds can usually be relied on to waft the fliers gently into the valley. **Alpes de Haute Provence Aéroglisse**, *tel: 04 92 89 11 30*, runs paragliding courses and flights. On the way fliers can enjoy superb views of the turquoise **Lac de Castillon** and green mountainsides patched with *robines* – stretches of crumbly grey clay which are a characteristic feature of the area. The lake is in fact a reservoir created by damming the Verdon with the 90 m wide **Barrage de Castillon**, 10 km south. The shallower part near the village is popular for watersports.

COLMARS

Tourist Office: *pl. Girieud; tel: 04 92 83 41 92.* Open July–Aug daily 0800–1200, 1400–1900; Sept–June Tues–Sun 0830–1200, 1400–1700 (closed Thur, Sun pm). The tourist office organises an impressive programme of activities during summer, including walking, riding, synchronised swimming and inter-village sports days. *Ski de fond* takes over in winter.

Le Chamois, *tel: 04 92 83 43 29; fax: 92 83 45 54* (cheap) is a chalet-style hotel with traditional food and large garden and playground. A **gîte d'étape** (hostel), *tel: 04 92 83 41 92*, occupies the medieval hospital/town-hall/barracks. **Campsite: Le Bois Joly**; *tel: 04 92 83 40 40* is a small site near the village (caravans; open May–Aug).

This is the most striking village in the

upper Verdon Valley. Enclosed by fortified walls, it is also guarded by two forts. Built in 1527, when it was on the frontier of Savoy and Provence, the fortifications were strengthened by the military architect Vauban after the Duke of Savoy declared war on France in 1690. The **Fort de Savoie** surveys the scene from rocks to the north where the Romans had previously built the temple to Mars – *Collis Martis* – which gave the village its name. You can walk its ramparts and see inside during exhibitions (June–Sept 1400–1830).

In the village itself, tiny squares with flower-decked fountains punctuate the network of narrow streets.The shuttered stone buildings include the 17th-century **Église de St Martin**.

ALLOS

Tourist Office: *04260 Allos; tel: 04 92 83 02 81.* Open July–Aug Mon–Sat 0830–1900, Sun 0900–1200, 1500–1830; Sept–June Mon–Sat 0830–1200, 1400–1830, Sun 0900–1200, 1500–1800.

There are numerous apartments geared particularly for the influx of skiiers in winter. **HI: La Foux**; *tel: 04 92 83 81 08.*

In summer the resort (1425 m) makes the most of its position surrounded by mountains at the top of the Verdon valley with the **Mercantour National Park** (see p. 254) to the east and north. Outdoor activities like paragliding, mountaineering, kayaking and mountain-biking are organised as well as guided walking and riding. There is also a small lake, **Lac des Sagnes**, for watersports.

In winter, Allos combines with **Le Seignus** (linked by cable-car) and **la Foux d'Allos** (7 km up the valley) to form the **Val d'Allos** ski area. The modern chalet-style apartment blocks designed for skiers look out of place on the hillsides when not surrounded by snow.

LAC D'ALLOS

From **Allos**, the D226 zig-zags upwards for 13 km with views of the conical **Mont Pelat** (3051 m), the highest peak in the Provençal Alps. As you enter the Mercantour National Park, the landscape becomes truly Alpine, with rowans, pines and lichen-covered rocks. After passing the spectacular **Chadoulin Waterfall**, the road ends 1km before the blue mirror-like **Lac d'Allos**, cradled in the mountains at a height of 2229m. A track continues down to a little chapel, **Notre-Dame-des-Monts**, and refuge/restaurant (open Jul–Aug) at the water's edge. Carved out by a huge glacier 20,000 years ago, the lake is bordered by a jagged ridge, the *Tours du Lac*. Local tourist offices organise themed walks Sun–Fri July–Sept.

COL D'ALLOS

From **Allos** the road twists and turns up the green valley past **La Foux** and over the bleak 2240 m high pass of **Col d'Allos**, to continue through the mountains beside banks of wild flowers, waterfalls and, even in summer, patches of snow. There are beautiful views towards the peaks of **Grand Cheval de Bois** (2839m) and **Le Cimet** (3020m). The route then drops down through woods to the small ski resort of **Les Agneliers** and continues up and down the hillsides with dramatic views over the **Gorges du Bachelard** far below. Shortly before Barcelonnette, a scenic side-road climbs to **Pra Loup**, a ski resort built in the 1960s.

BARCELONNETTE

See p. 118.

NICE–GRASSE

Leaving the busy suburbs of Nice, the scenic route turns away from the coast to climb into the hills. Past Tourettes-sur-Loup, a lower road heads up one side of the wooded Gorges du Loup to join a higher one which twists back along the other side to the hillside village of Gourdon, with ever-widening views over the spectacular Loup Valley, far below.

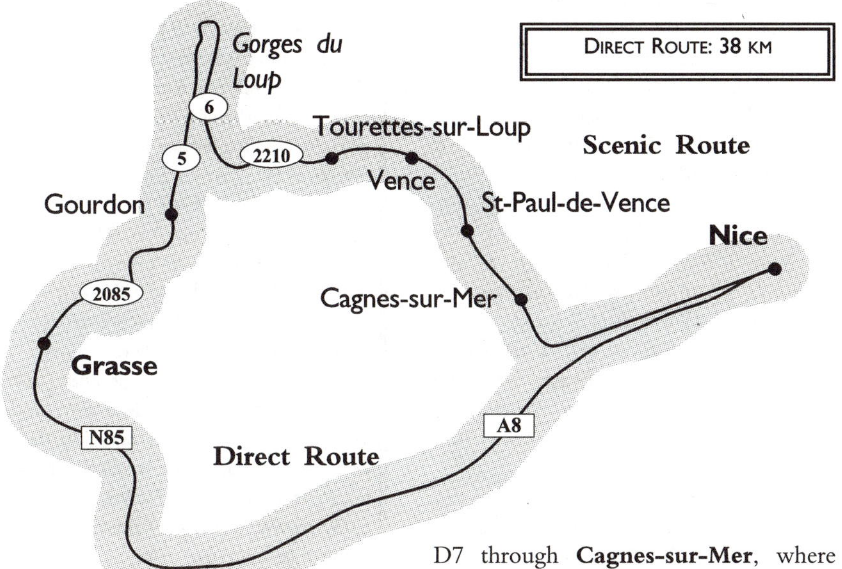

DIRECT ROUTE: 38 KM

ROUTES

DIRECT ROUTE

Take the A8 from **Nice Airport** for 22km to the junction with the N85, just south of Mougins. This leads straight to **Grasse**, 16km further on. The whole journey takes just under 1 hr.

SCENIC ROUTE

Leave **Nice** by heading west along the *Promenade des Anglais* and past the airport on the N98, turning right onto the D7 through **Cagnes-sur-Mer**, where there are lovely views as the road climbs through **St Paul-de-Vence** to **Vence**. From there, the D2210 leads towards the **Gorges du Loup**, passing medieval villages perched precariously above the valley. Take the D6 up the east side, then the D3 back down the west side through **Gourdon** to link up with the D2085 into **Grasse**. Total distance is about 65km and journey time about 2 hrs.

CAGNES-SUR-MER

Tourist Office: *6 blvd Mar Juin; tel: 04 93 20 61 64.* Open June–Sept, Mon–Sat 0900–1245, 1500–1900; Oct–July, Mon–Sat 0830–1215, 1400–1800. Also at

Cros de Cagnes (on the seafront), *20 av. des Oliviers; tel: 04 93 07 67 08*. Open June–Sept, Mon–Fri 0900–1800, Sat 0900–1300, Sun 1000–1300.

Accommodation and Food

Most of the hotels and apartments are near the sea in **Cros de Cagnes** or around the station. For accommodation near the beach, try the **Hôtel de la Serre**, *22 blvd de la Plage, 06800 Cagnes; tel: 04 93 20 10 54; fax: 04 93 22 45 61* (cheap), which has a shady terrace (hotel closed Nov). **Le Cagnard** (*RC*), *r. sous Barri; tel: 04 93 20 73 21; fax: 04 93 22 06 39* (expensive) is a grand establishment in a 14th-century building on the ramparts, in the old town, Haut de Cagnes. This is also the best area to eat, both for its hilltop setting and the quality of restaurants like **Restaurant des Peintres**, *71 Montée de la Bourgade; tel: 04 93 20 83 08* (expensive). **Campsites**: Many sites including **Panoramer**, *Chemin des Gros Buaux, Val Fleuri, tel: 04 93 31 16 15* (caravans).

Sightseeing

The town divides into three very different parts – **Haut de Cagnes**, a medieval citadel with ramparts, steep streets, covered passageways and arcades; **Cagnes-Ville**, a busy modern town centre with most of the shops, and the resort of **Cros**, by the sea, next to the famous **Côte d'Azur race course**; *tel: 04 93 22 51 00*. Renoir spent the last 12 years of his life at the Maison Les Collettes, an isolated house in an olive grove overlooking the sea. Today it is the **Musée et Domaine Renoir**, *chemin les Collettes; tel: 04 93 20 61 07* (open Wed–Mon, 1000–1200, 1400–1700; FFr.20), where the rooms have been kept as he used them 80 years ago. Eleven of his paintings and a bronze, *Venus Victrix*, are also on show.

Olives

The cultivation of olives was introduced to Provence by the Greeks in around 606 BC, and became a productive peasant crop in the centuries which followed. A young tree starts to bear fruit in its fifth or sixth year, reaching its full yield after 25 to 30 years. Harvesting begins in November, lasting in some areas through to January. Although previously this was very much a family affair, with everyone lending a hand, nowadays mechanical harvesters (which grab the tree trunks and shake them until the olives fall down) are increasingly used. A mature tree produces around 30 kilos of olives, yielding up to 5 or 6 litres of oil. The first pressing of the olives produces the best oil, sold as *vierge extra* (extra virgin), with the residue being pressed again to produce fine or extra fine. Although many olive groves in the region have been lost (a hard frost in 1956 destroyed thousands of trees), Provence, especially the Bouches-du-Rhône area, is still the main producer of olive oil in France, with over 5,000 growers processing their crop through co-operative mills.

In Haut de Cagnes, the 14th-century **Château Grimaldi**, *pl. Grimaldi; tel: 04 93 20 85 57* (open daily 1000–1200) houses three different museums, on the history of the olive tree, modern art and portraits of the singer Marie Laurencin.

ST-PAUL-DE-VENCE

Tourist Office: *2 r. Grande; tel: 04 93 32 86 95*. Open daily 1000–1800 (1900 mid June–mid Sept).

Parking: there is plenty of space available – at a price – including the underground, multi-storey St Claire.

Accommodation and Food

There are just two small hotels (both *RC*) in the village itself, including the prestigious **Saint Paul**, *86 r. Grande; tel: 04 93 32 65 25; fax: 04 93 32 52 94,* (expensive) and a number of good restaurants.

To pay less, look along *rte de la Colle* outside the old walls. **Camping**: **Caravaning Saint Paul** (4-star), *chemin du Malvan; tel: 04 93 32 93 71* (open Easter–Oct). An entertaining place to eat is **La Colombe d'Or** (expensive); *pl. des Ormaux; tel: 04 93 32 80 02*, if only to see its paintings by Picasso and Matisse and the murals on the terrace by Léger.

Sightseeing

St Paul is one of the most picturesque hilltop villages near the coast. Its winding cobbled alleys and small 16th-century houses are surrounded by ramparts – a reminder that it was once a frontier village on the border of Savoy. During the 1920s, painters, poets and writers arrived and stayed in force. Today the narrow streets are still lined with galleries and studios, while tourists also pass through in considerable numbers. A walk around the ramparts provides good views beyond the red rooftops and cypress trees towards Nice. Those who pause for a drink at the **Café de la Place** can watch *pétanque* being played on a large *piste* shaded by plane trees.

One of Europe's most interesting modern art museums is nearby. The **Fondation Maeght**, *rte Passe-Prest; tel: 04 93 32 81 63* (open July–Sept 1000–1900; Oct–June 1000–1230, 1430–1800; FFr.25) was built by the Maeght family who were friends of Matisse. The garden is a quirky sculpture park, designed by Miró.

VENCE

Tourist Office: *pl. du Grand-Jardin; tel: 04 93 58 06 38*. Open July–Sept, Mon–Sat 0900–1900, Sun 1030–1230; Oct–June, Mon–Sat 0900–1200, 1400–1800.

Accommodation and Food

La Victoire, *pl. du Grand-Jardin; tel: 04 93 58 61 30; fax: 04 93 58 74 68* (cheap) is a well-situated small hotel on the edge of the Old Town, overlooking gardens which once belonged to the *seigneurs* of Vence. The most interesting restaurants are to be found in the narrow streets of the Old Town.

The **Auberge des Seigneurs**, *pl. du Frêne, tel: 04 93 58 04 24* (moderate), by the entrance, serves local fare in a medieval setting decorated with paintings donated by impecunious but hungry local artists. A few mins walk away, **La Rosarie**, *av. H. Giraud; tel: 04 93 58 02 20; fax: 04 93 58 99 31* (expensive), is a small hotel decorated in traditional style. **Camping**:

Pétanque

First played in the 12th century, boules is a fundamental part of French life. In every town and village you will find a group of men, young and old, clustered on a dusty ground under the shade of the plane trees, all concentration fixed on a group of shiny balls. The idea, as in British grass court bowling, is to get as close to the peg as possible. In the south, a slightly different, and more leisurely version is played. In boules, the player takes a run up before throwing. Pétanque was invented in June 1910, when Jules Le Noir, who had one leg and was incapable of running, created a variation in which players stand behind a line and throw from a stationary position. The name is an abbreviation of *pé tanco* in Provençal, or *pied tanqué* in French (literally 'immoveable foot').

Domaine de la Bergerie, *rte de la Sine, tel: 04 93 58 09 36* (caravans).

Sightseeing

Despite being surrounded by holiday villas, Vence seems far removed from the glitzy coast. The lively **Old Town**, with its small shops and restaurants, clusters round the 12th-century **Cathedral** which stands on the site of a Roman temple to Mars. A 1500-year-old sarcophagus serves as its altar. A Roman forum once stood on the *pl. du Peyra*, but the town's main claim to fame is the **Chapelle du Rosaire**, *av. H. Matisse; tel: 04 93 58 03 26* (open Tues, Thur 1000–1130, 1430–1730). This was built and decorated by Matisse in 1949–51 to thank the nuns who nursed him through an illness. With blue and yellow stained-glass windows and simply-drawn Biblical scenes on white walls, he considered it to be his finest work, though the drawings led to great controversy at the time.

TOURETTES-SUR-LOUP

Tourist Office: *2 rte de Vence; tel: 04 93 24 18 93.* Open July–Aug, Mon–Sat 0900–1230, 1500–1830; June, Sept, Mon–Sat 0900–1230, 1430–1730.

Accommodation and Food

For a scenic place to stay nearby, try the **Auberge des Gorges du Loup**, *06490 Le Pont du Loup; tel: 04 93 59 38 01; fax: 04 93 59 39 71* (cheap).

Sightseeing

This is another delightful medieval village whose outer row of houses, built on the steep rocky ridge overlooking the deep Loup Valley, once served as fortifications. From the car park on the main square, you walk through two ancient gateways into the smart old streets which lead to the 18th-century château. Contemporary art exhibitions are held here, reflecting the fact that many painters, as well as weavers, potters and jewellers have studios in the village. Many display their work in galleries and craft shops, particularly in the *Grand'Rue.*

Fields of violets, cultivated for perfume and candied sweets, surround the village. The *Fête des Violettes* takes place in Mar, with a parade of floats decorated with violets and mimosa. **La Confiserie des Gorges du Loup**, *Le Pont du Loup; tel: 04 93 59 32 91,* is a small factory which makes crystallised fruit and chocolates (free guided tours, Mon–Fri 0900–1200, 1400–1800).

GOURDON AND THE GORGES DU LOUP

Tourist Office: *La Mairie, pl. Victoria; tel: 04 93 42 54 83.* Open daily 1400–1800.

The road up to Gourdon along the deep Gorges du Loup – the 'Road to Heaven' – is spectacular as it winds up through oak forests, leaving the river far below. On the way it passes two waterfalls, **Cascade de Cournes** (40m high) and **Cascades des Demoiselles**, and the great **Saut du Loup** cave.

Perched high on sheer 300m rocks above the river, Gourdon first served as a fortress to guard the valley in Roman times. Its 9th-century **castle**, now a museum, was the stronghold of the Counts of Provence until 1235. Rebuilt in 1610, it now houses the **Museé Historique,** which includes one of Marie-Antoinette's writing desks, and the **Museé d' Art Naïf** which features paintings from 1925 to 1970; *tel: 04 93 09 68 02.* Open June–Sept 1100–1300, 1400–1800, Oct–May (except Wed) 1400–1800; FFr.20. There are spectacular views from the castle's terraced gardens which were laid out by André Le Nôtre, the famous landscape gardener, in the 17th century. Cars have to be left in the large car park beside the sloping road up to the village's medieval gateway. *Pl. Victoria* provides splendid views over the Côte d'Azur stretching from the Esterel hills to the mouth of the Var at Nice.

GRASSE

Tourist Office: *cours HCresp; tel: 04 93 36 03 56.* Open July–mid Sept, Mon–Sat 0900–1900, Sun 0900–1230, 1330–1800; mid Sept–June, Mon–Sat 0900–1230, 1330–1800.

Getting Around

Grasse is a busy town but is easily covered on foot. Cars can be left at meters or in one of the car parks which are mainly on the northern side. Though cars are permitted in the old town area, the streets are very narrow. The tourist office hires out headsets (FFr.20 per day) with a commentary (English version available) about the walking trail, marked with 'Gs' on the pavement, which leads round points of interest, especially in the old town. Themed tours including *Create your own perfume* and *Flowers and gardens* are organised during the summer.

Accommodation and Food

The town has a good choice of hotels, most cheap–moderate. Chains include *Ib* and *LF*. **Pension Michele**, *6 r. du Palais de Justice; tel: 04 93 36 06 37* (cheap) is a small hotel handily-placed for the town centre. **Hôtel de la Bellaudière**, *78 rte de Nice; tel: 04 93 36 02 57; fax: 04 93 36 40 03* (cheap), has 17 rooms and a terrace restaurant with pretty views, 3km west of the town centre.

For a quieter location, head north into the hills to **Le Relais Impérial**, *rte Napoléon, St Vallier-de-Thiery*, 12 km along the N85; *tel: 04 93 42 60 07; fax: 04 93 42 66 21* (cheap).

You can always eat well in Grasse, notably at **La Bastide de St Antoine**, *av. H. Dunan; tel: 04 93 09 16 48* (expensive), recently opened by the leading French chef, Jacques Chibois. At boulangeries, try a *fougassette*, a brioche loaf flavoured with orange blossom.

Events

Say it with flowers. There is a **Rose Festival** with concerts and exhibitions in May and a **Jasmine Festival** with procession and fireworks in Aug.

Sightseeing

Set in a horseshoe of hills overlooking the distant sea, Grasse is the centre of the world's perfume industry, employing nearly 3000 people and training all the famous 'noses' who create those heady smells. Mimosa, jasmine, lavender and roses flourish on the sunny hills which rise to the town from the coast, though the 30 perfume factories now mostly use imported flowers and chemical essences. As main roads sweep traffic around the edge, it's easy to miss the heart of the old town, an area of narrow streets filled with shops and restaurants.

The **Musée Internationale de la Parfumerie**, *8 pl. du Cours; tel: 04 93 36 80 20* (open June–Sept daily 1000–1900; Oct, mid Dec–May, Wed–Sun 1000–1200, 1400–1700; guided tours July–Aug Mon–Fri, 1600 (Wed, Sat in English); FFr.30, depicts the history of perfume and its production. Its exhibits include a collection of antique to modern bottles and a rooftop greenhouse of fragrant plants with a 'Guess the Smell' display. Perfume factories offering free guided tours and factory-price sales include **Galimard**, *73 rte de*

Perfume

For 400 years, Grasse has been the centre of the world's perfume industry, ever since the French royal family invited Signor Tombarelli, a celebrated Italian perfumer, to settle there. At the time, there was a craze for perfumed leather (to mask its strong natural smell), particularly for use in gloves, as worn by the French Queen, Cathérine de Medici. In Grasse, hide-tanning was already a flourishing trade. The local people also made perfumed creams, particularly from jasmine, which had been brought from China and thrived in the area's rich red soil. Soon Grasse was famous for its 'smelling skins'.

The main bases for good perfume are jasmine, roses, mimosa and orange blossom – the essential ingredient of eau de Cologne – which all flourish on the sunny slopes of the Riviera. During the 18th–19th centuries, the perfume business expanded considerably as new techniques were developed for extracting the essential oils from the flowers, including distillation and maceration in hot fat. More and more factories opened in the area and names like Fragonard, Galimard and Molinard became synonymous with the world's finest fragrances. Today, Grasse's 30 factories have an annual turnover of FFr.3000 million, though most of the essences are now imported.

Jasmine is one of the most expensive to obtain. An expert picker can gather 4kg of flowers in a morning – about 30,000 blooms – but nearly 10 million, weighing around a ton, are needed to make just 1 kg of essence. Not surprisingly, only the top perfume houses now use it in any quantity. The fragrances are created by mixing floral oils with ingredients like sandalwood, camphor and ginger. This is a skill in which Grasse's master perfumers – known as 'noses' – lead the world. They work like alchemists, surrounded by thousands of little bottles, blending and smelling many different essences. Most are trained chemists but first and foremost, a 'nose' has to be an artist.

Cannes; tel: 04 93 09 20 00; **Molinard**, *60 blvd V.Hugo; tel: 04 93 36 44 65;* and **Fragonard,** at two locations – in the town centre at *20 blvd Fragonard; tel: 04 93 77 94 30* and *La Fabrique des Fleurs, Les Quatres Chemins, rte de Cannes; tel: 04 93 77 94 30.* All are open daily 0900–1830 (closed 1230–1400 Nov–Apr).

The old town centre looks almost Italian with high buildings, intimate squares and arcades. The austere 12th-century **Cathédrale de Notre-Dame du Puy** (open daily 0830–1100, 1430–1800) houses paintings by Rubens and also the *Washing of the Feet* by the 18th-century artist Jean-Honoré Fragonard who was born in the town. His birthplace, **Villa-Musée Fragonard**, *23 blvd Fragonard; tel: 04 93 40 32 64* (open June–Sept, 1000–1300, 1400–1900; Oct–May 1000–1200, 1400–1700; FFr.20) has a beautiful garden. The house itself contains *trompe-l'oeil* murals attributed to his son, Alexandre, a prodigy who painted them at the age of 13. Magnificent replicas of four paintings which he offered to Louis XV's favourite, the Comtesse du Barry, representing the steps of amorous conquest: *the rendezvous, pursuit, letters* and *the lover crowned,* are on display.

Thirty ship models are on display in the vaulted rooms of the **Musée de la Marine**, *Hôtel Pontevès, 2 blvd du Jeu de Ballon; tel: 04 93 07 10 71* (open June–Sept, daily 1000–1900; Oct–May Mon–Sat 1000–1200, 1400–1800.

NICE–MENTON

The Corniche between Nice and Menton on the Italian border is one of the most beautiful coastlines in the world, as the tail-end of the Alps plunges into the Mediterranean. Avenues of palm trees decorate the promenades of a succession of small resorts; millionaires' palaces hide away amongst the maritime pines; and medieval villages perched on rocks high above peep down to the sparkling sea.

DIRECT ROUTE: 29 KM

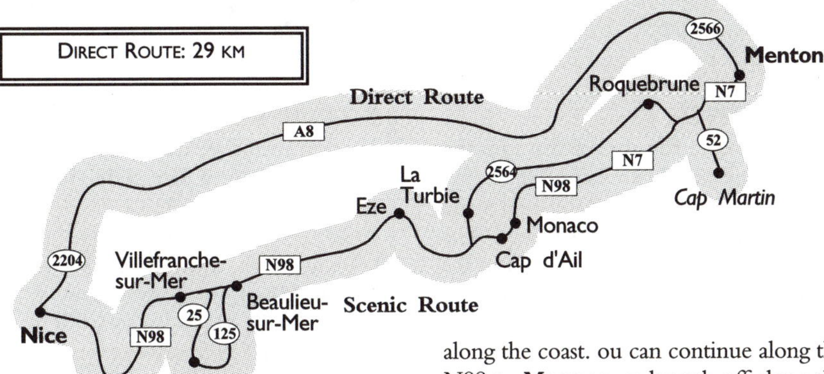

ROUTES

DIRECT ROUTE

Drive inland from **Nice** on the D2204 which runs north-east past *pl. Masséna* to join the A8 motorway. After skirting **Monaco**, turn off onto the D2566 to **Menton**. The journey takes about 30–45 mins depending on traffic, which can be heavy.

SCENIC ROUTE

Continue east along the **Nice** seafront beyond the *promenade des Anglais* on the N98 and follow it round the coast to **Villefranche-sur-Mer**. Turn there for the side track to the **Cap Ferrat** headland. From **Villefranche**, continue on the N98 through **Beaulieu-sur-Mer** along the coast. ou can continue along the N98 to **Monaco** or branch off along the D2564 to **La Turbie** and then to **Roquebrune**, from where you can join the N7 to continue the route. If you go through Monaco, on the far side the N98 takes you straight onto the N7 which goes to **Menton**.

The N98 seaside road is known as the **Basse Corniche**. The N7 is the **Moyenne Corniche** and, giving the best coastal views of all, is the **Grande Corniche**, the D2564. The A8 motorway is higher still! Distance via the Basse Corniche is 43 km; allow about 1–½ hrs, depending on traffic.

VILLEFRANCHE-SUR-MER

Tourist Office: *Jardin F. Binon, 06230 Villefranche*, near the *Basse Corniche; tel: 04 93 01 73 68*. Open July–Sept daily 0830–2000; Oct–June Mon–Sat 0845–1200, 1400–1900.

Accommodation and Food

The majority of tourist accommodation is in villas and apartments but there are also around 20 hotels, including the **Welcome**, *quai Courbet; tel: 04 93 76 76 93; fax: 04 93 01 88 81* (moderate), which is right in the centre on the main quay. The narrow seafront promenade, *quai Amiral Courbet*, by the tiny central harbour is the best place to find a terrace restaurant overlooking the bay. Try **La Mère Germaine**, *tel: 04 93 01 71 39* (moderate) which is renowned for its fish.

Sightseeing

Boasting one of the deepest bays on the Mediterranean, Villefranche often has large cruise ships moored off-shore and even the occasional aircraft-carrier. The long sandy beach is one of the best in the area. Beside it, the *promenade des Mariniers* sweeps round the wide scenic bay. Near the small Port de la Santé harbour, the Italianesque **waterfront**, a row of colourful buildings with terrace restaurants, overlooks the sea. In 1957 artist **Jean Cocteau** decorated the beautiful little **Chapelle Saint Pierre**, *quai Courbet, tel: 04 93 76 90 70* (open Tues–Sun 0930–1200, 1400–1800; FFr.12) with striking modern frescos of Biblical scenes on a fishing theme. Once used for storing fishing nets, it is dedicated to the town's fishermen.

A maze of old narrow streets climbs up the hill into the medieval fortified town. One of them, *r. Obscure*, actually runs through a tunnel under the buildings. On the west side of the bay, a promenade circles a cliff below the Citadelle to **Port de la Darse**, a larger harbour with boatyards and a small marina. The **Citadelle**, *tel: 04 93 76 61 00* (open June–Sept 1000–1200, 1500–1900; Oct–May 1000–1200, 1400–1700; closed Sun am and Tues; free), built in 1557 by the Duke of Savoy, houses three small museums including **Musée Volti** which is devoted to the modern artist Volti's striking bronze sculptures of women. The others display modern paintings and ceramic figures.

Side Track from Villefranche

St Jean-Cap-Ferrat

Tourist Office: *59 av. D. Séméria; tel: 04 93 76 08 90.* Open July–Aug Mon–Fri 0830–1200, 1330–1730.

Accommodation

To rub shoulders with the rich and famous, try **Hôtel Royal Riviera**, *3 av. J. Monnet; tel: 04 93 01 20 20; fax: 04 93 01 23 07* (expensive), one of the Leading Hotels of the World group, or **Grand Hôtel du Cap Ferrat**, *blvd Gén. de Gaulle; tel: 04 93 76 50 50; fax: 04 93 76 04 52* (expensive), which has its own funicular railway to take guests down to its terrace restaurant and Olympic-size pool. *Hf* and *RC* are also represented.

Sightseeing

On the peninsula jutting out to sea east of Villefranche, this exclusive resort is like a private estate, spreading itself discreetly amongst the woods which cover the headland. Dotted amongst the lush vegetation above its pretty coves, high fences and tall gates festooned with security cameras guard some of the world's most expensive homes, the hideaways of royalty and rock-stars. Long shining limousines occasionally glide in or out, but darkened windows ensure that the anonymity of the occupants remains unsullied. The tiny harbour is lined with restaurants, tranquil even in high season, and surprisingly inexpensive, no doubt because the glitterati prefer to eat at home, undisturbed by stares from other diners or the intrusions of the paparazzi. Somerset Maugham lived here in the 1920s.

A clifftop footpath leads around the edge, through pine woods, providing extensive views back along the coast over *Villefranche* to the west and *Beaulieu* to the east. On the hump of the hill is one of the Riviera's most exotic villas, **Musée Ephrussi de Rothschild,** *tel: 04 93 01 33 09* (open mid Feb–Nov 1000–1800 (1900 July–Aug); Nov–mid Feb Sat–Sun 1000–1800; FFr.34). It was created, with absolutely no expense spared, between 1905 and 1912 by **Béatrice de Rothschild**, daughter of the head of the Rothschild bank and wife of another wealthy banker. Her lavishly-decorated and sumptuously-furnished *Belle Époque* salons display the *objets d'art* she liked to collect. Outside, seven exotic themed gardens with terraces, paths, pools and fountains enjoy splendid views over the bay.

BEAULIEU-SUR-MER

Tourist Office: *pl. Clémenceau,* (outside the station); *tel: 04 93 01 02 21.* Open Mon–Fri 0900–1230, 1430–1900; Sat 0900–1230, 1500–1900; Sun 0900–1230.

Accommodation and Food

Amongst a handful of hotels, the **Riviera**, *6 r. P. Doumer; tel: 04 93 01 04 92, fax: 04 93 01 19 31* (cheap) is a modest establishment with a shady courtyard, 150m from the sea. *Bvld Mar. Leclerc* is a good bet for restaurants and *salons de thé*. Chain hotels include *RC* and *Hf*.

Sightseeing

It was Napoleon who christened Beaulieu ('beautiful place') and few would disagree. The little town spreads up a hillside around a pretty bay, **Baie des Fourmis**, with views across to the wooded Cap Ferrat headland. Grand villas, palm trees and avenues of flowering oleanders conspire to give it a graceful air, much favoured by European royalty at the turn of the century. The mild climate also attracts retirees, giving it a relaxed, if not comatose feel. **Villa Kerylos**, *tel: 04 93 01 01 44* (open July–Aug 1000–1900; Sept–Oct and Dec–June 1030–1230, 1400–1800; FFr.30) is an exact replica of the house of a wealthy Athenian, c.5th–1st centuries BC. It was built by a rich archaeologist at the turn of the century complete with marbles, ivories, bronzes, mosaics and the Mediterranean lapping at its doorstep.

EZE

Tourist Office: *pl. du Gén. de Gaulle tel: 04 93 41 26 00.* Open daily 0900–1800. **Branch**: kiosk on lower coast road (RN 98) near **Eze Bord de Mer** train station; *tel: 04 93 01 52 00.* Open June–Sept Mon–Sat 0900–1300, 1415–1700.

The **Moyenne Corniche** (N7) leads into **Eze Village**, perched on the hillside, or you can take the higher **Grande Corniche** (D2564), built by Napoleon, then turn off and wind down into the village. The **Basse Corniche** (N98) runs along the bottom of the hill through **Eze Bord de Mer**, the separate part of the village just above the sea.

Accommodation

Chain hotels include *RC*. **Campsite**: **Romarins**, *Grande Corniche; tel: 04 93 01 81 64* (caravans).

Sightseeing

Perched on a 427m rock high above the Mediterranean, the medieval eagle's nest of Eze commands spectacular views. From the busy modern part of the little town, steep tortuous steps climb up to the medieval village itself. Along its narrow streets, an array of boutiques, galleries and souvenir shops lurk in the tiny ground floors of old buildings. The only one to survive intact from the Middle Ages is the **Chapelle des Penitents Blancs** which is decorated with enamel panels – you peep into it through a grille. Another landmark is the 18th-century **parish church**, which has a baroque nave. A medieval festival, **Eze Atmosphere d'Autrefois**, with costumed re-enactments is staged in the old village on the last weekend of July (FFr.20).

Crowning all is the **Jardin Exotique**, *tel: 04 93 41 10 30* (open July–Aug 0830–2000; Sept–June 0900–1200, 1400–1900; FFr.12), created in 1949 by Jean Gastaud, an agricultural engineer, on the site of a 14th-century castle. Its maze-like network of sloping paths and steps takes you past shrubs and fiercely-spiked South American cacti. The view from the top is the best on the Riviera. On clear days you can see as far as **Corsica** to the south and **St Tropez,** 100km to the west.

At sea level, **Eze Bord de Mer** nestles beside the Mediterranean, surrounded by lush vegetation. Some of the inhabitants are descendants of a group of Russian refugees who settled there after fleeing the 1917 revolution. **Le Cap Estel**, *le Bord de Mer; tel: 04 93 01 50 44; fax: 04 93 01 55 20* (expensive), is a mansion built by a Russian prince, now serving as a luxury hotel.

For walks, a network of wooded paths make their way up the hillside from the sea at **Eze Bord de Mer** and **St Laurent d'Eze**, 2km to the east. The route winding up to Eze Village is known as the *Chemin de Nietzsche* as it was a favourite of the famous 19th-century German philosopher, Friedrich Nietzsche – allow 1hr 30 mins for the climb.

CAP D'AIL

Tourist Office: *106 av. du 3 Septembre; tel: 04 93 78 02 33*. Open Mon–Fri 0915–1200, 1430–1900, Sat–Sun 0915–1645 (closed Sun, Sept–June).

Sightseeing

Heading east on the **Basse Corniche** (N98), **Cap d'Ail** (*Peninsula of Garlic*) is the last of the Riviera's little resorts before this glamorous coastline is punctuated by Monaco. It is a popular beach stop with excellent swimming, albeit off a pebble beach. Cap d'Ail also boasts one of the coast's best youth hostels, with a splendid view of the Mediterranean: **Relais International de la Jeunesse**, *Villa Thalassa, av. R. Gramaglia; tel: 04 93 78 18 58*. Open May–Sept. The maximum stay is three nights, since most people want to stay a lifetime.

MONACO

See p.261.

LA TURBIE

Tourist Information: *Mairie; tel: 04 93 41 10 10.*

The **Grande Corniche** (D2564) above the coast leads through the hills behind Monaco to the quiet hill village of La Turbie (480m), a popular haven for Monégasques, many of whom have homes there. Indeed the narrow streets of elegant 13th-century houses beyond its two medieval gateways are sometimes so deserted, as well as perfectly picturesque, that they could easily be a film set waiting for cameras to roll. Geraniums trail from window-boxes and giant flowerpots, bougainvillaea scents the air and the occasional cat preens in a shady courtyard. Not even a single shop to buy a postcard. One assumes that the occupants have found far more effective ways of making money.

At the top of the village, in *pl. T. de Banville*, stands one of the most extraordinary sights on the Riviera, the **Trophée d'Auguste** (*Trophy of the Alps*), *tel: 04 93 41 10 11* (open Apr–June 0900–1800; July–Sept 0900–1900; Oct–Mar 0930–1700), a 35m high white stone monument built as a memorial to the power of Rome 2000 years ago. It stands on the Roman **Via Julia** which ran from Genoa to Cimiez (the northern part of Nice) at the point where Italy met Gaul and was inscribed with the names of the 44 Ligurian tribes conquered by the Roman legions. Having fallen partly into ruin over the centuries, the monument was rebuilt in 1930 (10m lower than its original height). In the grounds are a model of the original monument, a small exhibition, engravings and a video presentation.

From the terrace below, the view down to Monaco is breathtaking. In the foreground, smart villas and their glistening blue pools, surrounded by trees, cover almost every inch of the hillsides. Monaco itself is laid out almost like a model with the Musée Océanographique and Casino silhouetted against the blue sea. Definitely a place for binoculars!

ROQUEBRUNE

Tourist Office: *20 av. P. Doumer tel: 04 93 35 62 87*. Open daily 0930–1230, 1500–1900 (closed Sun, Sept–Jun). Branch: *promenade R. Schumanm, tel: 04 93 41 61 28*. Open July–Aug 1000–1230, 1515–1900.

ACCOMMODATION

Hôtel-Restaurant Les Deux Frères, *06190 Roquebrune-Village Cap-Martin, tel: 04 93 28 99 00, fax: 04 93 28 99 10* (moderate), has an excellent position near Roquebrune castle with a panoramic terrace overlooking Cap Martin and the sea Chain hotels include *Hf*..

SIGHTSEEING

Although joined together administratively, Roquebrune, a hilltop village with steep alleys and medieval buildings, and **Cap Martin**, a seaside resort far below on a headland, are two very different places. Having been ruled by a succession of major European powers, they finally opted, with Menton, to become French rather than Italian in 1860.

Roquebrune clusters around its ancient **castle** (open Sat–Thurs 0800–1200, 1400–1700 (until 1900 July–Aug); FFr.12). Dating from 970, it was much fortified in the 15th century by the Grimaldis of Monaco and still has its dungeon and square keep. On the terrace below, a striking bronze statue of a nude girl reaching out to the sky, by Arnold Chromy, commemorates the 50th anniversary of the end of World War II.

SIDE TRACK FROM ROQUEBRUNE

After joining the N7, whether approaching from Roquebrune or from Monaco, turn right onto the D52 for Cap Martin.

CAP MARTIN

The secluded villas in lush gardens on the leafy penisula of **Cap Martin** have been favourite hideway for many celebrities. Coco Chanel and the architect Le Corbusier both had homes built there and Winston Churchill was a regular visitor. To foster the resort's artistic tradition, leading writers take part in a literary festival every Oct.

MENTON

Tourist Office: *Palais de l'Europe, av. Boyer; tel: 04 93 57 57 00.* Open July–mid Sept Mon–Sat 0830–1830, Sun 1000–1200; Sept–July Mon–Sat 0830–1230, 1330–1800. **Branch**: *Bus Station, esplanade du Careï; tel: 04 93 28 43 27* (summer only). **Post Office**, *cours Georges V; tel: 04 93 28 64 84*, has *poste restante*, currency exchange. Open 0800–1830 (1800 Thurs), Sat 0800–1200.

Menton is very walkable, with the main town and sights concentrated at the eastern end of the long pebbly bay, near the Italian border. To visit the hinterland with its dramatic hilltop villages, take one of the buses which run regularly from the *esplanade du Careï* bus station.

Accommodation and Food

Sadly Menton's hotels are a disappointment. Once a resort for Europe's monied classes, reaching its peak in 1882 when it played host to Queen Victoria and her entourage, the town has slipped into relative slumber. Now many of its once palatial hotels have been carved up into retirement apartments. The grand entrances where troupes of staff greeted each arriving guest are barely recognisable and the great ballrooms, drawing rooms and dining-rooms divided into humble hutches. Current holiday accommodation is nothing special, but includes a high proportion of self-catering apartments which are popular with families. For lower budget hotels, try around the station, especially *r. Albert 1er*. The family-run **Hôtel de Londres**, *15 av. Carrot,; tel: 04 93 35 74 62, fax: 04 93 41 77 78* (moderate) has a restaurant which attracts many local people (moderate). Closed mid Oct–mid Dec. **HI**: *plateau St Michel, rte des Ciappes de Castellar; tel: 04 93 35 93 14.* Open Feb–Nov. **Campsites**: **Camping Municipal du Plateau St Michel**, *rte des Ciappes de Castellar; tel: 04 93 35 81 23*, is next to the youth hostel and has a superb sea view. Chain hotels include *IH*, *Hf*, *LI* and*Mo*.

Menton is synonymous with lemons. Indeed the town's most popular fruit is practically its only claim to gastronomic fame. Lemonade is a speciality, as are marzipan sweets in the shape of the hallowed citrus.

For dining, Italian-influenced places are best, in the old town around *r. St Michel*. Cafés and bars also line the sea front. For picnickers, the market in *pl. aux Herbes* (opposite the *Hôtel de Ville*) is one of the best on the Riviera, especially lively at weekends. Look out for Italian sausage and cheese. The surrounding hill villages have small family-run restaurants specialising in local country cuisine.

Events

The 2-week **Lemon Festival** in Feb is the highlight of the year, with a programme of associated cultural events including classical music and theatre. Elaborate sculptures covered in lemons and oranges decorate the town, based on a different theme each year. Parades of floats decorated with thousands of oranges and lemons are followed by lavish firework displays. Seats for the main events cost between FFr.50 and FFr.150.

Sightseeing

This is the warmest place in France (average temperature 17°C in Jan) – hence both the famous lemon groves and high proportion of retired people. The pace of life is slow, but this border town is attractive, retaining a strong Italian influence, and boasts one of the Riviera's best markets. The waterfront houses are Italianate in style and *salamis, fresh pasta* and *biscotti* are

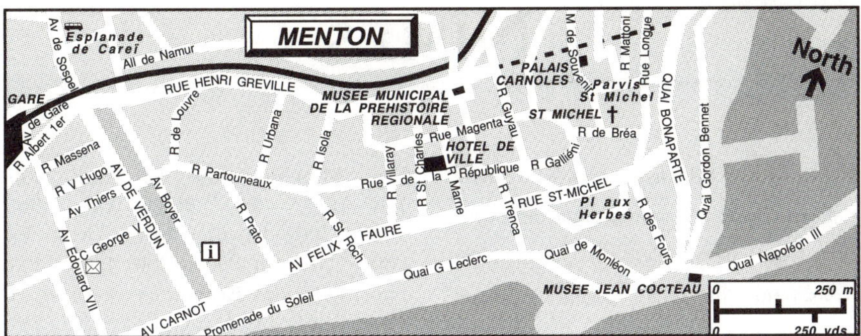

all well to the fore in the markets and shops.

Begin by heading along the sea wall around the small port, where there are fine views back to the pastel façades of the old town. Wander up the steps from the port to the *Parvis St Michel* and its view down over the sea. The town's narrow streets and some of the houses were constructed by the Grimaldis of Monaco in the 15th century. The **Église St Michel**, built in 1640, is impressive, with a fine 16th-century altarpiece and wooden statue of St Michael.

To the west, the **Palais Carnolès**, *av. de la Madone*; *tel: 04 93 35 49 71* (open Wed–Mon 1000–1200, 1500–1900 (1800 Sept–Jun); FFr.10) once belonged to a Prince of Monaco and now houses an interesting art collection featuring Impressionist and modern paintings.

In the town centre, the **Hôtel de Ville,** off *r. de la République*; *tel: 04 92 10 50 29* (open Mon–Fri 0830–1230, 1330–1700; FFr.5) contains a *Salle des Mariages* lavishly decorated by Jean Cocteau. There is also a colourful **Musée Jean Cocteau**, *bastion du Vieux-Port, quai Napoléon III; tel: 04 93 57 72 30* (open Wed–Mon 1000–1200, 1500–1800; free) at the east end of the beach, containing mosaics, pastels and pottery by the artist who took inspiration from the 'loves of the fishermen of Menton'. The **Musée Municipale de Préhistoire Régionale**, *r. Lorédan-Larchey; tel: 04 93 35 84 64* (open Wed–Mon 1000–1200, 1400–1800; free) exhibits various remains of humans who lived here 80,000 years ago; the skeleton of Menton Man, found in nearby caves, who was born 30,000 years ago; and dioramas of cave life.

Out of Town

A steep twisting 7km drive – or beautiful but strenuous walk – inland leads up to **Sainte Agnès** (754m). Allow 3hrs up and 2 hrs down if you decide to go on foot. Perched around the ruins of a 12th-century **castle**, this is the highest coastal village in Europe. The view stretches down over Menton and the coast as well as inland to Castillon, Mount Gros and Mount Agel.

The village is also an excellent place to eat, boasting several good-value establishments serving gargantuan meals. **Fort Sainte Agnès**, *tel: 04 93 35 84 58* (open 1500–1830; FFr.20), a 1930s blockhouse partly built into the hillside, formed the southern end of the Maginot Line, the chain of defensive fortifications built by the French in the 1930s, south from Luxembourg.

NÎMES

Nîmes, with 132,000 inhabitants, is the largest and least obviously charming of the three delta cities, but nevertheless has magnificent Roman sites and some delightful medieval streets. In the 6th century BC, nomadic Celts founded a settlement near a gushing spring, associated with the water god, Nemausus, who gave his name to the town. Over the centuries, it became an opulent city at the crossroads of two major Roman routes.

Nîmes has been badly battered over the years, by everyone from the Visigoths to the Moors, and as a Protestant stronghold, during the Wars of Religion. It also managed to make its fortune in textiles during the Middle Ages and again, recently, from an influx of high-tech industry. To help revitalise the city, former mayor Jean Bousquet sponsored a bold building programme, resulting in many magnificent modern structures such as the Carrée d'Art , Martial Raysse's sculptures in the Place d'Assas, Jean-Michel Wilmotte's redevelopment of Les Halles, the Musée des Beaux Arts and the Hôtel de Ville, and Jean Nouvel's ambitious residential complex, Nemausus, to the south of the city centre.

Tourist Information

Tourist Office: *6 r. Auguste, 3000 Nîmes; tel: 04 66 67 29 11.* Open Easter–end Sept, Mon–Fri 0800–1900 (until 2000, July–Aug), Sat 0900–1900, Sun 1000–1700; 1st Oct–Easter, Mon–Fri 0800–1900, Sat 0900–1200, 1400–1700, Sun 1000–1200. **Branch**: *in the station; tel: 04 66 84 18 13.* Open 0930–1230, 1430–1830 daily.

Arriving and Departing

Airport

Nîmes, Arles and the Camargue share a small airport near St-Gilles, 10 km south of the city off the Nîmes–Arles autoroute; *tel: 04 66 70 49 49*

By Car

There are excellent road connections with Montpellier and Avignon. Clear signs lead you to the périphérique, then leave you going round the one-way system in never-ending circles. To foil this merry-go-round, you may need to venture down tiny alleys barely able to take a car. There are well-positioned 24-hr underground car parks in *blvd Gambetta* and *esplanade C de Gaulle* while several others open 0700–2200 Mon–Sat. Take your possessions with you as there have been thefts here.

By Bus

Bus Station: *r. St Félicité* (behind the rail station); *tel: 04 66 29 52 00.* Regular bus services run to Uzès, Pont du Gard and the Camargue.

By Train

Station: **Gare de Nîmes**, *blvd Sergent Triaire; tel: 04 66 23 50 50*; for reserva-

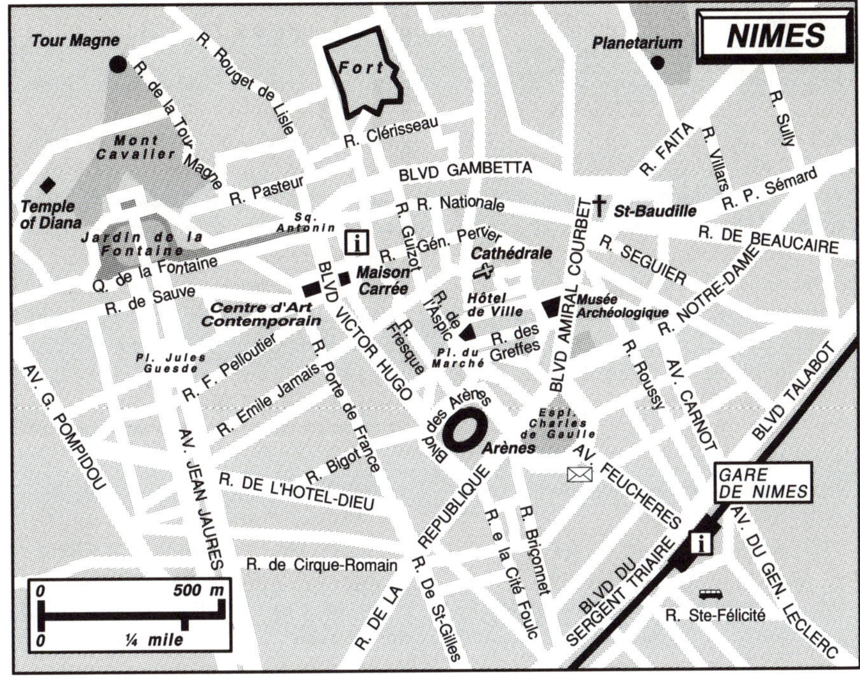

tions, *tel: 04 66 78 79 79*. Information 0800–1800, Sat 0900–1215, 1400–1800. Five mins walk south-east of the centre along *blvd V Hugo, esplanade C de Gaulle* and *av. Feuchères*.

Getting Around

The Tourist Office provides excellent free town plans and a map for disabled visitors. The city walls have long gone, but their passing is marked by a circle of broad boulevards. With few exceptions, the sights are all within easy walking distance inside this perimeter. There are regular **buses**; the most useful is the *Huit en Ville* which circles the boulevards and the station every 7 mins. **Walking tours** of the old town leave the Tourist Office (daily, July–Sept at 1000; FFr.25). From May to Oct, a **Tourist Train** leaves for a guided tour of the town, every 45mins between 1000 and 1930 daily, from the Esplanade opposite the old Palais de Justice, *tel: 09 75 45 56* (FFr.25; children under 12 free). **Taxis**: *tel: 04 66 29 40 11*; the company also offers a 40 min guided tour for FFr.150. **Bicycle hire**: at the station left luggage counter, *tel: 04 66 29 72 41.*

Staying in Nîmes

Accommodation

In summer months the city can get crowded and Nîmes hosts conferences all year round. Booking is always advisable and essential during the major ferias (bull-fighting festivals) which attract more party-goers than Munich's beer festival.

Hotel chains include *Ba, BW, Ch, Cn, Ct, Ib, IH, Mc, Ne, Nv* and *RS*. For a taste of the good life, try the grand 4-star **Hôtel Impérator Concorde**, *quai de la Fontaine;*

tel: 04 66 21 90 30; fax: 04 66 67 70 25 (expensive) a favourite of the top toreadors, which also has an excellent haute cuisine restaurant, **L'Enclos de la Fontaine** (expensive; open 1215–1400, 1915–2200) and charming neo-classical gardens. Inexpensive accommodation is best found along *blvd des Arènes*, or around *blvd Amiral Courbet*. The **New Hotel de la Baume**, *21 r. Nationale; tel: 04 66 76 28 42; fax: 04 66 76 28 45* (cheap), is a carefully restored 17th-century mansion in the heart of the city. The **Plazza**, *10 r. Roussy; tel: 04 66 76 16 20; fax: 04 66 67 65 99* and **L'Empire**, *1 blvd Saintenac; tel: 04 66 67 25 81; fax: 04 66 67 85 29* (cheap) are both less exciting but still comfortable and well-run.

HI: *chemin de la cigale; tel: 04 66 23 25 04*, 3km from the station (bus no. 2: Stade). **Campsite**: *Domaine de la Bastide, rte de Générac; tel: 04 66 38 09 21*, 5km to the south (bus no. 4: Générac).

Eating and Drinking

Traditionally Nîmes has been considered a culinary backwater, and it can be difficult to find a good full meal – locals seem to prefer pizza or salad. However, there are local specialities, which should be sampled. *Brandade de Mor*, a salted cod paste mixed with olive oil, and *tapenade,* an appetiser of ground olives, anchovies and herbs, both date back to Roman times. *Pelardon*, a mild goat's cheese from the surrounding hills, is amongst the best in France, while sweeter tooths will appreciate the *Croquants Villarets*, small almond biscuits. Thirty restaurants specialising in Nîmois cuisine have banded together as *Les Agapes à la Nîmoise*; their brochure, with addresses and telephone numbers, is available from the tourist office.

Blvds V Hugo and *Amiral Courbet* have a number of large, brash brasseries. The maze of little side roads between the Arena and Maison Carrée has some delightful cafés and crêperies, such as **Ô-Délices**, *2 pl. aux Herbes; tel: 04 66 36 11 16* (moderate), next to the cathedral. **Le Paradis du Couvent**, *21 r. du Grand Couvent; tel: 04 66 76 26 30* (cheap) is an informal family-run restaurant patronised by locals, with excellent food and a warm welcome. Other good restaurants include **Le Caramel Mou**, *r. Jean Reboul; tel: 04 66 21 27 08* (moderate); **Le Chapon Fin**, *3 pl. du Château Fadaise; tel: 04 66 67 34 73* (expensive; closed Sun); and the **San Francisco Steakhouse**, *33 r. Roussy; tel: 04 66 21 00 80* (moderate) which serves American food, French-style, with added specialities such as ostrich and bison.

Legendary Blues

During the Middles Ages, Nîmois textile merchants invented a canvas cloth which they dyed blue with indigo. Popular amongst Genoese sailors, because of its durability, the cloth was discovered by an American entrepreneur, who took the Genoese trousers to California, adding metal rivets for added toughness. In time the cloth 'de Nîmes' became known as denim; the Genoese trousers as jeans; the name of the businessman was Levi Strauss.

Communications

Post Office: *blvd de Bruxelles,* near *pl. de la Libération, tel: 04 66 76 67 06.* Open 0830–1800.

Money

Several major banks, including Banque Chaix and Crédit Lyonnais, have branches on *blvd V Hugo*. **Société Générale**, *7 blvd Amiral Courbet; tel: 04 66 76 50 00.*

Entertainment

Nîmes is proud of its cultural heritage, and opera, dance, theatre and live music are all plentiful. There is a free fortnightly listings magazine, *Nîmescope*, available from the tourist office and a 24-hr information line gives details of current events, *tel: 04 66 36 27 27*. For tickets and information, try **Fnac**, *La Coupole des Halles, blvd Gambetta; tel: 04 66 36 33 33*. **Été de Nîmes** is an annual summer-long programme of music, dance and theatre. July sees the annual **Jazz Festival**. **Ferias** (Spanish-style bullfighting festivals), take place throughout the summer, but the biggest are in Feb (Mardi Gras), May (Whitsun) and Sept (*Vendange,* grape harvest); information from the tourist office, reservations: **Regie des Arènes**, *r. Alexandre Ducros; tel: 04 66 67 28 02.*

Shopping

For mainstream shopping, head for **Les Halles**, a huge modern mall redeveloped on the site of the old market. The lanes in the area around the cathedral have some fine upmarket boutiques. The **Centre Anglais**, *8 r. Dorée; tel: 04 66 21 17 04*, has an excellent collection of English-language books. Every Thurs evening (1700–2200) in July–Aug, the centre of Nîmes is taken over by a huge arts and crafts market.

Sightseeing

Museums in Nîmes are synchronised: opening times year round are 1100–1800, closed Mon; admission FFr.22. Better value, if you plan to do them all, is a three-day **Forfait** pass (FFr.60), covering the Musée Archéologique, Musée du Vieux Nîmes, Musée des Beaux Arts, the Carré d'Art and the Planétarium. It does not cover the Arena – which is, inevitably, the must-see-at-any-cost attraction. The **Passeport de Nîmes** is a 1-year pass, including absolutely everything and discounts for some events, costing FFr.100 (take a photo and ID).

The 1st century AD **Arènes**, *blvd des Arènes* (open May–Sept 0900–1830; Oct–Apr 0900–1200, 1400–1700, guided tours only; FFr.22) is one of the best preserved Roman amphitheatres in the world. Designed to host spectacles from gladiators to animal combat (such as bear-baiting and bullfights) and mock naval battles (when flooded), it could seat over 23,000 spectators on 34 terraces, reached by a maze of five ring galleries and stairways. From the 7th century onwards, it was converted into a fort and was besieged several times before Languedoc eventually became part of France in 1226. Its walls continued to house a thriving village until 1786–1809, when ardent classics scholars forcibly removed its inhabitants, to return it to its former glory. These days, it is back to its original purpose, housing grandstand events from bullfights to rock concerts. A modern cover has been devised to create an indoor stadium seating 7000 in winter.

The **Maison Carrée**, *r. Nationale; tel: 04 66 36 26 76* (open May–Sept 0900–1900, Oct–Apr 1000–1200, 1430–1800; free) is an outstandingly well-preserved Roman temple, in the centre of the old Forum, at the exact crossroads of two great Roman roads, leading west to Spain and north to Germany and Britain. Dedicated to the Imperial cult, it was built in the late 1st century BC to honour Caius and Lucius Caesar, the grandsons and adopted sons of the emperor Augustus. Since then, it has been a monastery, stable, church and archive. Now fully restored, it houses a small museum about the temple and Roman Nîmes.

Next door, like a well-glazed sugar lump, the **Carrée d'Art**, *r. Nationale; tel:*

04 66 76 35 70, designed by British architect Sir Norman Foster, houses Nîmes' Mecca of modern art, the futuristic **Centre d'Art Contemporain** (open 1100–1800 winter; 1100–2000 summer; closed Mon; admission FFr.20). Nearby, the **Cathédrale de St Castor**, *pl. aux Herbes; tel: 04 66 67 27 72*, celebrated its 900th birthday in 1996, although most of the present building dates from 1646. The interior is less compelling than the façade, which is festooned with delightful Romanesque sculpture. Next door, in the former Archbishop's palace, is the **Musée du Vieux Nîmes**, *pl. aux Herbes; tel: 04 66 36 00 64* (open daily 1000–1800), with permanent and temporary exhibitions of Nîmois lifestyle and tradition, the best of the city's generally disappointing museums.

The **Musée Archéologique** (archaeology), *13 bis av. Amiral Courbet; tel: 04 66 67 25 57* (FFr.22), in a wing of a 17th-century Jesuit College, has a few interesting displays on Roman Nîmes and important, but appallingly displayed, collections of inscriptions and glass. Children will enjoy the local **Planétarium**, *av. du Mont Duplan; tel: 04 66 67 60 94* (Wed and Sat, 1500 and 1630).

South of the old city, the **Musée des Beaux-Arts**, *r. Cité Foulc; tel: 04 66 67 38 21*, has a fine collection, with works by masters including Rubens, Boucher, Watteau and Rodin.

To the north-west, the **Jardin de la Fontaine** (Fountain Garden), off *av. J Jaurès* (open access, free), is the site of the still gushing spring, dedicated to the water god Nemausus, which led to the foundation of the city. In the 18th century, the city's textile merchants asked for the sludgy pond to be cleared out. The astonished engineer discovered an extensive temple complex and the town went on to create France's first public garden, with a magnificent array of neo-classical walkways, stairs and statues. To one side is a 2nd-century **Temple of Diana**, used for a while as a Benedictine convent. On the slopes of Mont Cavalier, above the park, the **Tour Magne** (open May–Sept 0900–1900, Oct–Apr 1000–1230, 1330–1800; FFr.12) is the oldest surviving Roman monument in France (15BC), a bizarre 34-m tower, built on top of pre-Roman ramparts, whose original purpose is unknown. Steps lead to the top for fine views.

Other smaller Roman remains scattered throughout the town include the **Castellum**, off *r. Gautier*, a huge cistern used for holding the water brought in to the town by aqueduct (over the Pont du Gard, see pp. 115–116) and the **Porte d'Auguste**, *blvd Amiral Courbet*, one of the original city gates with a replica bronze statue of Augustus Caesar standing by.

Crocodiles and Palm Trees

Roman Nîmes wisely backed the right side when it sent a legion to assist Octavius (the later emperor Augustus) against Mark Antony and Cleopatra at the epic battle of Actium in 31 BC. To celebrate the victory, the town struck a coin showing the Nile crocodile chained to a palm tree, surmounted by a victor's laurel wreath. In 1535, the French king François I turned this into the city's coat of arms.

Connection from Nîmes

To reach **Montpellier** and join the route to Perpignan (p. 276) or Le Puy (p. 272), take the A9 or N113 south-west; 54 km.

Orange

Orange was once an important Roman colony, a heritage reflected in its two major monuments. The pedestrianised town centre is also a pleasant place to linger, with cafés, shops and restaurants spread around a series of quiet, shady squares.

Tourist Information

Main Tourist Office: *cours A.Briand, tel: 04 90 34 70 88*. Open Apr–Sept Mon–Sat 0900–1900, Sun 1000–1800; Oct–Mar Mon–Sat 0900–1700. **Branch:** opposite the Théâtre Antique, *pl. Frères Mounet (tel as above)*. Open Apr–Sept daily 1000–1800. Exchange; ticket sales for events; but no accommodation bookings.

Arriving and Departing

By Road

Orange is 2km from Junction 21 of the A7 (up the Rhône Valley); the parallel N7 leads straight into the centre of town. **Parking**: the large car park at the *Arc de Triomphe* is free, otherwise there are nearly always places to be found in the *cours A. Briand* (meters).

By Train

Station: *av. F. Mistral; tel: 04 90 11 88 64* (information open 0800–1200, 1400–1700). For the town centre, head along *av. F. Mistral* or *r. de la République;* after *pl. de la République*, turn into *r. St Martin*.

By Bus

Bus Station: Gare Routière, *cours Pourtoules* (opposite the post office); *tel: 04 90 34 15 59*. Buses run to Carpentras, Vaison-la-Romaine, Avignon, Serignan-du-Comtat.

Getting Around

The town centre is compact and everything is within easy walking distance, except for the Colline St Eutrope, which involves a steep, 15-min walk: if you don't feel like tackling this, take the **petit train** from outside the Tourist Office, *pl. Fréres Mounet*, which goes up the hill as part of a 50-min commentated tour of the town (daily regular departures 0900–1900 Apr–Sept; FFr.25). There is also a hop-on, hop-off **shuttle bus** service around five major points of interest, departing from the car park on the east side of the Arc de Triomphe (FFr.30 including entrance to museum and théâtre). **Taxis**: *pl. de la Gare, tel: 04 90 34 57 42*.

Staying in Orange

Accommodation

Orange has a good selection of hotels across all price ranges. Chains include *Ib, Ct, Mc*. The characterful **Hôtel Arène** *(**IH**), pl. des Langes; tel: 04 90 34 10 95; fax: 04 90 34 91 62* (moderate) has a long-standing reputation as Orange's finest hostelry, run by Gérard and Danielle Coutel. It has 30 rooms and stands in a quiet location overlooking a small square. The **Louvre et Terminus** (*LF*), *89 av. F. Mistral; tel: 04 90 34 10 08; fax: 04 90 34 68 71* (moderate) is another good hotel, with a welcoming ambience and traditional charm. It also has a pool and garden.

Also popular is the **Hôtel Glacier** (*LF*), *46 cours A. Briand; tel: 04 90 34 02 01; fax: 04 90 51 13 80* (cheap–moderate), which is a stone's throw from the theatre and has 28 well-equipped, comfortable rooms tastefully decorated with Provençal fabrics. In the lower price range, the **Fréau**, *3 r. de l'Ancien-Collège, tel: 04 90 34 06 26* (cheap) is very popular but has just 10 rooms (booking advisable). Out of town there are a couple of elegant hotels such as the **Hostellerie du Vieux Château** (*LF*), *rte de Ste-Cecile, Serignan-du-Comtat; tel: 04 90 70 05 58; fax: 04 90 70 05 62* (moderate–expensive), which has just 7 rooms, a pool, and its own restaurant.

Campsite: **Le Jonquier**, *r. A. Carrel; tel: 04 90 34 19 83; fax: 04 90 34 86 54,* (1.5 km from the centre; caravans) which has a pool, tennis, and riding.

Eating and Drinking

Orange has a number of good restaurants, including the long-established **Le Parvis**, *3 cours Pourtoules, tel: 04 90 34 82 00* (moderate/expensive) where chef Michel Bérengier makes imaginative use of fresh local ingredients and also has a well-stocked cellar; good value. **La Roseliére**, *4 r. de Renoyer, tel: 04 90 34 50 42* (cheap/moderate) exudes atmosphere but some items on the menus can be disappointing. An excellent restaurant for seafood is the **Atrium**, *5 impasse du Parlement, tel: 04 90 34 34 17* (moderate) which has a lovely shaded terrace and features bouillabaisse, char-grilled fish and shellfish of all kinds. For traditional Provençal food, try **L'Aïgo-Boulido**, *20 pl. Sylvain; tel: 04 90 34 18 19*, or **Le Gaulois**, *5 pl. Sylan; tel: 04 90 34 32 51* (both cheap–moderate). A good place for a quick lunch is **Le 2000**, *3 pl. aux Herbes; tel: 04 90 34 10 48* (cheap) which has a wide selection of salads as well as good value *plats du jour.* Another option for lunch is to walk up the Colline St Eutrope to **Le Pigraillet**, *tel: 04 90 34 44 25* (cheap) where you can take a plunge to cool off before enjoying well-presented grills and salads beneath the shade of pine trees beside their pool. There are numerous pizzerias, one of the best of which is the **Pizzeria la Grotte**, *montée des Princes, tel: 04 90 34 70 98* (cheap).

Communications

Main post office: *blvd E. Daladier; tel: 04 90 11 11 00.* Open Mon–Fri 0830–1830 (closed Tues 1200–1330), Sat 0830–1200.

Money

There are several banks with exchange facilities on *r. de la République.*

Events

The **Théâtre Antique**, capable of seating 10,000 spectators, is still put to good use for events and performances of all kinds. During Roman times it was used for staging drama, comedies and even lottery competitions; during the Middle Ages mystery plays were performed here. In the 16th century houses were built in the theatre; these were cleared away in 1856 and the theatre reopened on 21 August 1869 for a choral and operatic festival which continues today as **les Chorégies**. This takes place in July; for bookings, contact: **Les Chorégies d'Orange**, *pl. Sylvan; tel: 04 90 34 24 24.* The theatre also holds a series of performances under the umbrella of **Les Nuits d'Été**, which may include everything from children's opera to magic shows and jazz, soul and funk concerts; details from **Service Culturel**, *Mairie; tel: 04 90 51 42 12.*

Shopping

The pedestrianised town centre around *pl.*

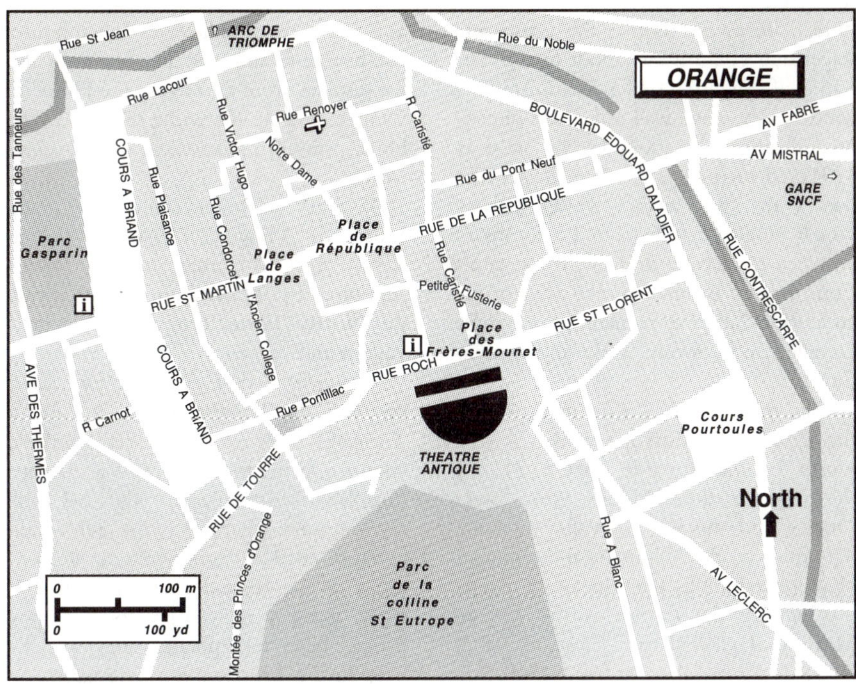

aux Herbes, pl. Clémencau, pl. République and *r. de la République* has a good selection of shops, including outlets for souvenirs, clothes, and books as well as food shops. Classic Provençal fabrics can be found at **Souleïado**, *1 r. de Mazeau; tel: 04 90 34 99 66;* and traditional santons at **Orange Souvenirs**, *9 r. Segond Weber; tel: 04 90 34 44 97*. On the ground floor of the **Maison de la Principauté**, *15 r. de la République, tel: 04 90 34 44 44*, the **Maison des Vins à Orange** features tastings and sales of wines from 17 vineyards in the Orange area. Pottery, crafts, and other local produce are also on sale here.

Sightseeing

Orange's star attraction is undoubtedly the remarkable **Théâtre Antique**, *pl. des Frères Mounet* (open daily 0900–1830 Apr–1st week in Oct, shorter hours outside this season; FFr.30 including the museum and guided tours (inc. English-language) which depart from the kiosk several times daily in July-Aug). Considered to be one of the best-preserved theatres of the Roman era, it is the only one to have retained its stage wall, which is over 100m long and rears up 37m above the ground. Built during the reign of Augustus, in 27–25 BC, it has a semi-circular auditorium (or *cavea)* which held over 9000 citizens, ranked according to nobility (inscriptions such as EQ G III, *Equites Gradus III*, or 'third row for knights' are still visible on the tiers of seating). The stage wall itself, though impressive, is but a shadow of its former self, and has retained only two marble columns out of the three tiers of over 80 columns with which it was once decorated. It also featured marble friezes, a stage curtain, and hidden doorways so that the actors and stagehands could move about freely. The statue of Augustus which dominates the centre of the stage wall today was discovered during excavations of the stage in 1931 and reconstructed. The theatre also had a massive canvas awning *(velum)*, which could be rolled out by means of winched capstans to protect the spectators from the sun or rain. To the west of the auditorium are the remains of a temple complex and a forum, baths and gymnasium.

The theatre nestles with its back into the **Colline St Eutrope**, and it is well worth the walk (or ride – see p. 311) to the top for the fabulous views over Orange and the Rhône Valley beyond. The ruins on the hilltop are the remnants of a fortress built by the princes of Orange.

Opposite the theatre is the **Musée Municipal**, *pl. des Fréres Mounet; tel: 04 90 51 18 24* (open Mon–Sat 0900–1900, Sun 1000–1800, Apr–1st week Oct; daily but shorter hours outside this season; FFr.30 including theatre). Housed in a 17th-century mansion, this features Roman statuary and mosaics and engravings of the theatre as it was in the Middle Ages, when houses had been built inside it. The first floor also has displays from the days of the House of Orange, and an interesting section on the block-printing of *indiennes*, or Provençal fabrics.

Within the town centre the grand **Hôtel de Ville**, *pl. Clemenceau*, has an attractive 17th-century façade, whilst adjoining it is the **Ancienne Cathédrale de Notre-Dame**, featuring a Romaneque portal.

Orange's second greatest monument, the **Arc de Triomphe**, *av. de l'Arc de Triomphe*, once stood at the northern entrance to the town on the Via Agrippa (the latterday equivalent, the N7, still swirls around either side of the arch). Built in about 20BC to commemorate the victories of the Second Gallic Legion, this triple archway is well-preserved despite having been incorporated into a castle keep in the 17th century. The panels on the attic (upper storey) depict in graphic detail the Roman legions' battles with the Gauls, whilst symbols of Roman maritime supremacy (galleys, anchors, oars) are also evident.

The Mistral

Provence has many different winds (Alphonse Daudet claimed to have identified 30 from his mill at Fontvieille) but the most famous is the Mistral (from *mistrau*, 'the master' in Provençal). Originating in the north/north-west, the Mistral builds up when there is high pressure over the mountains and is channelled down the Rhône Valley to the Mediterranean, sweeping across mid-Provence before dissipating itself on the Alpes-Maritimes. This dry, cold wind blows away everything in its wake, drying out the soil (farmers used to call it *mange-fange*, 'the mud-eater'), but leaving beautifully crisp, clear blue skies behind it. The Mistral has a reputation for enervating people and putting locals in a bad mood; it certainly sets windows and doors banging and roof tiles flying. Folk wisdom has it that the Mistral blows in cycles of three days (a Mistral blowing for nine days is not unknown), although if it starts up by night, it may blow itself out in a couple of hours. Other predominant winds include the *Marin*, a south-east wind which brings fog and rain; the *Labech*, a south-west wind which brings rainstorms; the dry, sand-laden *Sirocco*, which blows sweltering heat over the Mediterranean from the Sahara, and the *Tramontane*, which affects the Languedoc-Roussillon area.

ORANGE–SISTERON

This routetakes in charming town of Vaison-la-Romaine, notable for its extensive Roman ruins. From Vaison the route leads north-east, following the scenic valley of the Ouvèze into the mountains.

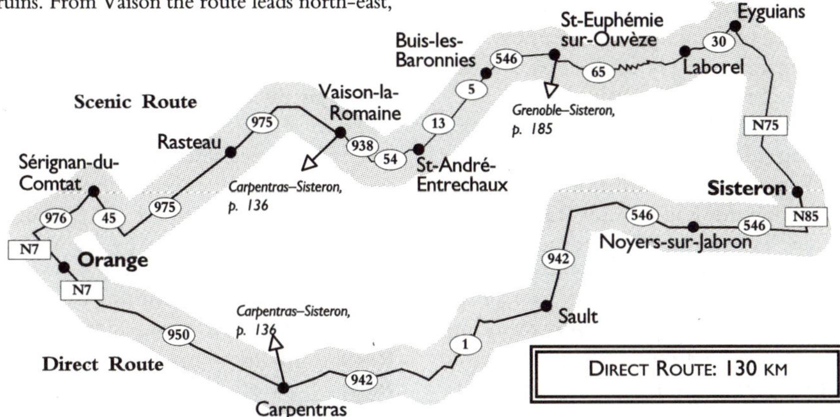

ROUTES

DIRECT ROUTE

Leave Orange heading south on the N7, then take the D950 to Carpentras, the D945 and the D1 to Sault. From Sault, continue along the D942, which becomes the D542 through Barret de Lioure. Branch right 6 km past Barret onto the D546, which becomes the D946, through Noyers-sur-Jabron, before turning left onto the N85 into Sisteron. Distance: 130 km; allow 3 hrs.

SCENIC ROUTE

Leave Orange heading north on the N7. Turn right onto the D976 1.5km after the Arc de Triomphe, for **Sérignan-du-Comtat**. Turn right in the village square onto the D45, then go left on the D975 through Camaret-sur-Aigues to **Rasteau**. Continue along the D975 to **Vaison-la-Romaine**. Leave Vaison by the D938 southbound, turning left onto the D54 and then left again, in St André Entrechaux, onto the D13. This becomes the D5, crosses the Ouvèze and continues into **Buis-les-Baronnies**. Follow the D546 through to **Ste-Euphémie-sur-Ouvèze**, where you join Grenoble–Sisteron route: for the remaining details, see p. 185. Distance: 67 km; allow 1½–2 days (including a day spent in Vaison).

ORANGE TO VAISON-LA-ROMAINE

The principal reason for visiting **Sérignan-du-Comtat** is to see the house and gardens which belonged to Jean-Henri Fabre (1823-1915), one of the most eminent entomologists of his period. The **Harmas de J-H Fabre**, on the D976 at the entrance to the village; *tel: 04 90 70 00 44* (open Wed–Mon 0900–1130, 1400–1800; FFr.15) contains the botanical garden planted by Fabre, with thousands of species of flowers and herbs in unkempt profusion (*harmas* is Provençal for a plot of untended land), complete with Fabre's home-made insect traps. Within the house itself there are displays of Fabre's prodigious published output as well as letters from Darwin and Mistral, hundreds of watercolours of fungi, his herbarium (containing some 325,000 specimens), and editions of his *Souvenirs Entomologiques*.

Leaving Sérignan the road traverses a plateau of vineyards, against the scenic backdrop of the Dentelles de Montmirail . The vineyards lead towards **Rasteau**, one of the leading producers in the Côtes du Rhône *appellation*, and just to the left of the main road outside the village itself you can sample and buy at the **Cave de Rasteau**, *tel: 04 90 10 90 10* (open daily 0800–1200, 1400–1830).

VAISON-LA-ROMAINE

Tourist Office: Maison du Tourisme et des Vins, *pl. du Chanoine Sautel; tel: 04 90 36 02 11.* Open daily 0900–1200, 1400–1745 (until 1845 July–Aug).

Accommodation and Food

Vaison's best-known hotel is the charming **Hostellerie Le Beffroi** (*CS*), *r. de l'Évêche; tel: 04 90 36 04 71; fax: 04 90 36 24 78* (moderate-expensive). Perched on the edge of the old town overlooking the river, it has and elegant restaurant and 22 rooms in a 16th-century setting, with modern furnishings and comforts. **Le Burrhus**, *2 pl. Montfort; tel: 04 90 36 00 11; fax: 04 90 36 39 05* (cheap-moderate) is right in the town centre and also very good, with individually furnished rooms. A good budget choice in the centre is the **Hôtel le Théâtre Romain**, *cours Taulignan; tel: 04 90 28 71 98; fax: 04 90 36 20 71 (*cheap), with plain but adequate rooms.

Campsites: Camping-Club International Le Carpe Diem, *rte de St-Marcelin* (1 km south of the town centre); *tel: 04 90 36 02 02; fax: 04 90 36 36 90* (caravans; open mid-Mar–mid-Nov) is one of numerous campsites in the vicinity (the tourist office can supply a list).

Vaison has a vast profusion of cafés, brasseries and restaurants; amongst those which can be recommended is the **Auberge de la Barvatelle**, *12 pl. Sus-Auze; tel: 04 90 36 02 16* (cheap-moderate), which specialises in the cuisine of south-west France. Near the Roman bridge, **Le Bateleur**, *1 pl. Théodore-Aubanel; tel: 04 90 36 28 04* (cheap) is a cosy little restaurant with just one menu but with a wide choice of Provençal specialities and desserts. In the old town, the **Restaurant de Vieux Vaison**, *8 pl. du Poids; tel: 04 90 36 19 45* (cheap) serves excellent pizzas as well as traditional dishes and has a terrace with a superb view across the river and Vaison. Vaison has an excellent **market**, which overflows from *pl. de Montfort* into the surrounding streets every Tuesday.

Sightseeing

Guided tours in English, duration 1½ hrs, take place each Fri at 1030 (July–Aug) and 1100 (Apr–June, Sept), departing from the Maison de Tourisme. The price is included in the Tous Monuments ticket (FFr.35) which covers the Quartier de la Villasse, Quartier de Puymin (including the Musée Archéologique), and the cloister of the Cathédrale Notre-Dame de Nazareth (all open daily June–Sept 0930–1230, 1400–1900; closing earlier outside the summer).

The first settlement at Vaison was a Celtic stronghold on top of the small hill to the west of the river. With the Roman conquest, a new town – Vasio Vocontiorum – developed on the fertile plains of the river's east bank. The settlement soon prospered, eventually gaining a population of around 10,000. It went into decline in the 3rd century. During the 12th century, Count Raymond of Toulouse built a castle on the site of the ruined Celtic fortress, and the population gradually drifted back into the old town for greater protection. But the *haute ville* was abandoned once more in the 19th century when the modern town was built over the ruins of the Roman city. Because of this, many major Roman buildings have not yet been unearthed. What remains still presents a vivid picture of life in one of the most important garrisons in Provence.

The visible Roman ruins are spread over a 15-hectare site on either side of the *av. Gén. de Gaulle* in the lower town. In the **Quartier de la Villasse**, to the west, a paved street, lined with what were once shops fronted by a colonnaded walkway, leads down to the baths next to the river Ouvèze. On the other side, an entranceway leads to one of the town's grand villas, the **Maison au Buste d'Argent**, so-called because a silver bust of its wealthy owner was found in the ruins. Behind this are a series of gardens and another vast villa, the **Maison au Dauphin**, which had its own set of private baths, fountains and formal gardens.

In the **Quartier de Puymin**, to the east, you immediately enter the remains of a huge villa, the **Maison des Mesii**, next door to which is a lovely colonnade, part of the public gardens, known as the **Portique du Poupée**. This part of the site abtts the hill, with the Roman theatre built into its northern slope. Seating up to 6,000 spectators, it is still in use for concerts and performances. Near the theatre is the **Musée Archéologique**, which contains a series of white marble statues, the silver patrician's bust from the Quartier de la Villasse, and other artefacts.

Beyond the Quartier de la Villase is the **Ancienne Cathédrale de Notre Dame de Nazareth**, a lovely Romanesque church dating from the 11th and 12th centuries. Alongside is the cloister (FFr.7 on a separate ticket) which has some finely-carved pillars supporting the arcades.

On the other side of the Ouvèze, reached via a high-arched, single span Roman bridge, the **Haute Ville** is a charming area whose maze of narrow streets and alleyways leads up to a ruined château, from where there are good views of the town and Mt Ventoux beyond.

VAISON TO STE-EUPHEMIE-SUR-OUVÈZE

Tourist Office: Buis-les-Baronnies: *pl. des Quinconces; tel: 04 785 28 04 59*. Open daily 0930–1200, 1500–1800; closed Sun pm.

Leaving Vaison, the road crosses a small plain before passing through **St André Entrechaux** and breasting a rise, with a lovely view of the vallley ahead and the Montagne de Bluye to the right. On the valley floor it follows the north bank of the Ouvèze, passing by the remarkable **Chapel of Notre-Dame de Consolations** perched high on a rocky promontory above the small village of Pierrelongue. Surrounded by steep escarpments, **Buis-les-Baronnies** is the main town in the district. The mild, dry climate of the surrounding countryside produces fruits, almonds, olives and aromatic plants in abundance. In the town where you can sample and buy essential oils, soaps, herbal products, and other regional goods. The weekly market (*pl. du Marché*) is on Tues. The **Place du Marché** itself is very attractive, with shops lining the back of a 15th-century arcade.

PERPIGNAN

Once capital of French Catalonia and now of Roussillon, Perpignan has an attractive Franco-Spanish ambience. Dancers in traditional costume take to the streets on high days and holidays to perform the traditional *Sardane* in the traffic-free old quarter. The avenues around them are lined with plane trees and palms, particularly beside the little River Basse just before it runs into the broader Têt. Basking in southern sunshine, the town buzzes with activity, and the Mediterranean's long sandy beaches are only 3 km away.

TOURIST INFORMATION

Tourist Office: *Palais des Congrès, pl. A. Lanoux; tel: 04 68 66 30 30.* Open June–Sept Mon–Fri 0900–1900 (Sat until 1800, Sun closed 1300–1500); Oct–May Mon–Sat 0830–1200, 1400–1830. Bureau de change. **Branch:** outside the Hôtel de Ville, *pl. de la Loge*. Open Mon–Sat same hours mid June–mid Sept. **Pyrenees-Roussillon regional information office:** *7 quai de Lattre de Tassigny; tel: 04 68 34 29 94/95*. Open 0900–1900.

ARRIVING AND DEPARTING

Aéroport Perpignan-Rivesaltes, *av. M. Bellonte; tel: 04 68 52 60 70*, 7 km northeast of the town centre. Shuttle bus to SNCF station connects with flights, 15-min journey, fare FFr.27. **Rail Station:** *av. Gén. de Gaulle; tel: 04 36 35 35 35.* **Gare Routière** (bus station): *av. du Gén. Leclerc; tel: 04 68 35 29 02.*

GETTING AROUND

Parking: The old centre is pedestrian-only and parking on the streets around it is meter-only, so head for a car park. *Pl. du Pont d'En Vestit* and *pl. de la République* are the most convenient for sightseeing. The sights and main shopping area are easily manageable on foot.

Bus: The local **CTP** bus network links the city centre efficiently with the suburbs and Canet Plage beaches, 30 mins away. Information: *Kiosque, pl. Péritel; tel: 04 68 61 01 13* (open Mon–Fri 0730–1230 and 1330–1930); day pass FFr. 25; single tickets, bought on board, FFr.6.50; carnet of 10 FFr. 50. **Taxis**: *tel: 04 68 34 59 49.* Guided walking tours around the old quarter start at 1500 outside the main tourist office (June–Sept; in French only).

STAYING IN PERPIGNAN

Accommodation

There is a good choice of hotels of all prices. Chain hotels include *Cl, F1, Ib, LF, Mc* and *Pr. Av. Gén de Gaulle*, leading up to the railway station is particularly well endowed with one and two-star hotels, including **Le Méditerranée**, *62 bis av. Gén de Gaulle; tel: 04 68 34 87 48; fax: 04 68 51 12 24* (cheap) and the **Hôtel Poste et Perdrix** (*LF*), *6 r. Fabriques Nabot; tel: 04 68 34 42 53; fax: 04 68 34 58 20* (cheap). Moving upmarket a little, the **Mercure** (*Mc*), *5 bis Cours Palmarole, tel: 04 68 35 67 66, fax: 04 68 35 58 13* (moderate) is well placed beside the old quarter and has its own car park. The top hotel, **La Villa**, *109 av. V. Dalbiez; tel: 04 68 56 67 67; fax: 04 68 56 54 05* (expen-

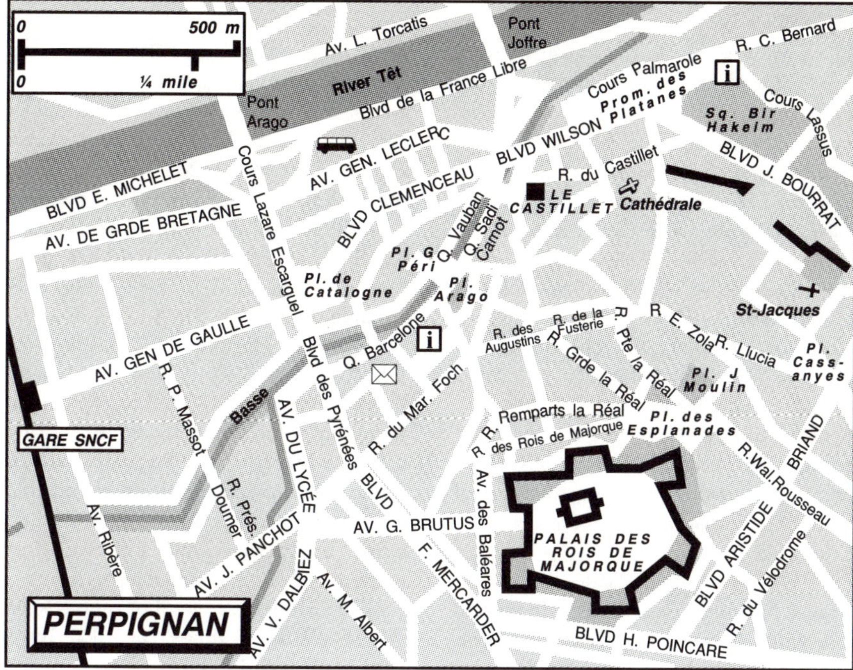

sive), occupies large grounds on the outskirts.

HI: Parc de la Pépinière, *av. de Grande-Bretagne; tel: 04 68 34 63 32.* **Campsite: La Garrigole**, *1 r. M.Lévy; tel: 04 68 66 30 22* (bus no.2 from rail station; stop: La Garrigole; a 5-min journey).

Eating and Drinking

One of the town's great pleasures is to eat outdoors along the avenues and narrow streets of the old quarter, sampling a wide choice of French and Catalan specialities. The most popular spot is *pl. F. Arago*, a square lined with magnolia trees. Small restaurants also lurk up narrow alleys, such as **Opéra Bouffe**, *impasse de la Division; tel: 04 68 34 83 83* (cheap) . *R. Fabriques Nadal* is almost given over to small restaurants, like **Casa Sansa** at *no 2; tel: 04 68 34 21 84*, where gypsy music serenades diners late into the night.

Communications

Post Office: *quai de Barcelone; tel: 04 68 34 40 65.* Poste restante. Open Mon–Sat 0800–1900 (until 1200 Sat).

Entertainment and Events

Discos, piano and jazz bars, American theme bars, brasseries and pubs are scattered throughout the old quarter.

Easter: **Festival of sacred music** during Holy Week and Spanish-style **Procession de la Sanch** on Good Friday, when sacred relics and a crucifix are carried to the cathedral by the red and black robed Brotherhood of the Holy Blood. June: the **Midsummer Festival of St Jean** is celebrated in grand style with folk music, fireworks, medieval market and dancing the *Sardane.* Fires are lit on the 2784 m high Mt Canigou (40 km inland) and torches from its villages are paraded into the town.

Shopping

The narrow streets in the old quarter are crowded with specialist shops. Look out for jewellery in the local red stone, *grenat*, and traditional Soleïado fabrics. For high quality pottery, glass, household items, head for **Maison Quinta**, *3 r. Grande des Fabriques*, or **du Côté de l'Orangerie**, *2 r. de la Révolution Française*. The main department store is **Nouvelles Galeries** on the corner of *blvd Clémenceau*. The residents love **markets**, like the daily one at *pl. de la République*. Shops in *r. Paratilla* specialise in dried fruits and Catalan spices. A flea market is held every Sun morning outside the Palais des Expositions and a bric-a-brac market on the second Sat of each month at *promenade des Platanes*.

Sightseeing

Almost Spanish in atmosphere, Perpignan is wealthy, ancient and overrun by visitors in summer. The town is best explored on foot by wandering the narrow streets of the old quarter with its 14th- and 15th-century buildings and shady squares, strolling the banks of the Basse and Têt, particularly along the *promenade des Platanes*. At the entrance to the old quarter, the **Loge de Mer**, built in 1397 as the headquarters of the town's sea trade, is an impressive Gothic building with fine Renaissance carved ceilings, now housing a restaurant. Next to it, the **Hôtel de Ville** is typical of the local Roussillon architecture with a facade built of river pebbles – often used because of the scarcity of stone in the area – and wide wrought-iron gates. *La Méditerranée*, a bronze nude by Maillol, stands on its patio. The **Cathédrale de St Jean**, *pl de Gambetta* (open daily 0730–1200, 1500–1900) is a grand Gothic building, also with facades in pebbles and red-brick. Its bell is encased in an intricate wrought-iron cage and inside there are gilded altarpieces. Next door, the large **Campo Santo cemetery**, *r. Amiral Ribeil* (closed Tues) is completely surrounded by cloisters, one of only two of its kind in Europe. **Casa Pairal**, *pl. de Verdun; tel: 04 68 35 42 05* (open Wed–Mon 0900– 1800; FFr.25) is a Roussillon folk museum, housed in **Le Castillet**, a 15th-century red-brick gatehouse with a pink dome – the only remaining part of the town's fortified walls. **Musée Rigaud**, *16 r. de l'Ange; tel: 04 68 35 43 40* (open Wed–Mon 0900–1200, 1400–1800; FFr.25), in an imposing 17th-century mansion, displays paintings by Hyacinthe Rigaud, who was born in the town in 1659 and became the court painter to Louis XIV and XV; also works by Picasso, Dufy and Maillol (a native of nearby Banyuls-sur-Mer).

The **Citadelle**, *r. des Archers; tel: 04 68 34 48 29* (open June–Sept 1000–1800; Oct–May 0900–1700; FFr.20) stands a few quiet streets away from the old quarter on a hill, Puig del Rey. This massive fortress incorporates the grand **Palais des Rois de Majorque** (the palace of the kings of Majorca). It was built in 1276 when the town, then part of the kingdom of Majorca, became its mainland capital city. Flights of steps zig-zag up to the gardens surrounding it. The Kings of Aragon once kept lions in the moat while the lions' food – goats – grazed on the lawns. From the roof of the entrance tower, **Tour de l'Hommage**, there are splendid views over the town to the snow-capped Massif du Canigou, an ancient symbol of Catalan unity. Two stairways on either side of the palace courtyard lead to grand rooms, including a reception hall and three chapels. The courtyard itself is often used for concerts.

Beyond the airport, off the D117, 450,000-year-old bones were discovered in a cave near the village of **Tautavel** in 1948, the oldest find in Europe. In its excellent museum, **Musée de Tautavel**, *tel: 04 68 29 07 76* (open Jul–Aug 0900–2100; Sept–June 1000–1800 (closed 1230–1400 Oct–Mar); FFr 35), the excavations and a life-size reconstruction of the cave bring prehistory to life.

Side Tracks from Perpignan

PETIT TRAIN JAUNE

From **Villefranche-de-Conflent**, 45 km inland along the N116, bright yellow metre-gauge electric trains with open carriages climb to the 1200 m Cerdagne plateau near the Spanish border, rattling for 63 km around hillsides, through deep gorges, over viaducts, in and out of tunnels and past terraced vineyards and tiny red-roofed villages. The line was constructed in 1910–11 to connect the remote villages in the foothills of the Pyrenees, but is now mainly used by tourists. Trains stop at 7 stations – and 13 more by request – on their way to **Latour-de-Carol**. Timetable and information at **Villefranche-Vernet-les-Bains station**; *tel: 04 68 96 09 18.*

PERPIGNAN TO THE SPANISH BORDER

The A9 autoroute speeds you straight across the flat Plaine du Roussillon and through the Chaîne des Albères hills to the Spanish border at le Perthus. Or the more interesting, but often busier, N114 leads to the Côte Vermeille, where it climbs around hillsides above the sea, dipping into the attractive little ports of Collioure, Port-Vendres and Banyuls-sur-Mer, on its way to the way to Cerbère.

COLLIOURE

Tourist Office: *pl de la Mairie; tel: 04 68 82 15 47.* Open July–Sept 0900–2000; Oct–Jun Mon–Sat 0900–1200, 1400–1800.

Accommodation and Food

Les Templiers, *quai de l'Amirauté; tel: 04 68 98 31 10, fax: 04 68 98 01 24* (cheap), overlooking the harbour and Château Royal, is famous for its paintings, which cover almost every inch of wall. Many are by famous artists who were friends of the Pous family who run it. The restaurant is noted for both its view and its fish. In a calmer position, a 10-min stroll up a hill behind the harbour, is the small modern **Hôtel Madeloc**, *r. R. Rolland; tel: 04 68 82 07 56; fax: 04 68 82 55 09* (moderate).

Sightseeing

Nestling by the sea at the foot of the first hills after miles of flat coastline, this charming little port has been a magnet for artists since Matisse settled here in 1905. His disciples, dubbed the Fauves (deer) for their wild use of colour, soon followed. Narrow cobbled streets, unspoilt despite being crowded with galleries, souvenir shops and people, lead back from its much-painted harbour where **Église Notre-Dame-des-Anges** stands guard; its tower was once a lighthouse. Alongside the quay, colourful fishing boats tie up to deposit their glittering heaps of anchovies. The **Château Royal**; *tel: 04 68 82 06 43* (open July–Sept 1000–1715; Oct–June 0900–1615; FFr.20) built by the Knights Templar in the 13th century and reinforced by Vauban in 1679, juts into the centre of the harbour. A popular sandy beach lies on its west side.

ST ÉTIENNE

This vast conurbation (with nearly 500,000 inhabitants) has been a key industrial centre since the 19th century, based on its extensive coal deposits and manufacturing expertise; the decline of the mines in recent decades has prompted a re-orientation towards hi-tech industries. One of its most attractive features today is a flourishing cultural scene, with a year-round programme of music, dance, opera, drama, and art exhibitions.

TOURIST INFORMATION

Tourist Office: *3, pl. Roannelle; tel: 04 77 25 12 14.* Open daily Mon–Sat 0900–1230, 1330–1900; Sun 1000–1300. It has a good range of information, leaflets and brochures and handles accommodation bookings. Guided tours of the town (four different itineraries) from mid June–Sept (FFr.30; hours and days variable). A booklet of tickets, valid for all the museums, the planetarium, and an audio guide to the town, is available for FFr.75.

ARRIVING AND DEPARTING

Airport

The **Aéroport Andrézieux-Bouthéon**; *tel: 04 77 36 56 10*, is located 14km to the north-west of the town, off the A72.

By Car

The city is at the junction of the A72 and A47 autoroutes; signposting out of the city is good. It is 59km from Lyon and 529km from Paris. **Parking**: On-street parking in the city centre is not always easy (particularly in the evenings), but there are several underground car parks, on the *pl. Hôtel de Ville*, *pl. A. Moine*, and opposite the Palais de Justice.

By Train

Main Station: **Gare Châteaucreux**, *pl. Stalingard*, a short taxi ride from the town centre. The city is 3hrs from Paris by TGV.

GETTING AROUND

The city centre is fairly compact and most of the major sights are within reasonable walking distance. The Musée d'Art Moderne is easily reached on the **tramway** that runs for 6km along *Grande Rue*, which forms the north-south axis of the city. There are **taxi** ranks at the *pl. Hôtel de Ville*, *pl. du Peuple*, and *Gare de Châteaucreux*. **Radio-taxis**: *tel: 04 77 25 42 42.*

STAYING IN ST ÉTIENNE

Accommodation

As a major centre for business and conferences, St Étienne has a wide range of hotels, many of them with convention facilities. Hotel chains include *Et, F1, Ib, IH, Mc, MO, Nv, RC.*

The **Hôtel Mercure-Altéa Parc de l'Europe** (*Mc*), *r. de Wuppertal; tel: 04 77 42 81 81; fax: 04 77 42 81 89* (moderate–expensive) is just south of the centre and the most luxurious hotel in town. A few mins from the city centre on a hilltop facing the golf course, the **Albatross**, *67 r. St Simon; tel: 04 77 41 41 00; fax: 04 77*

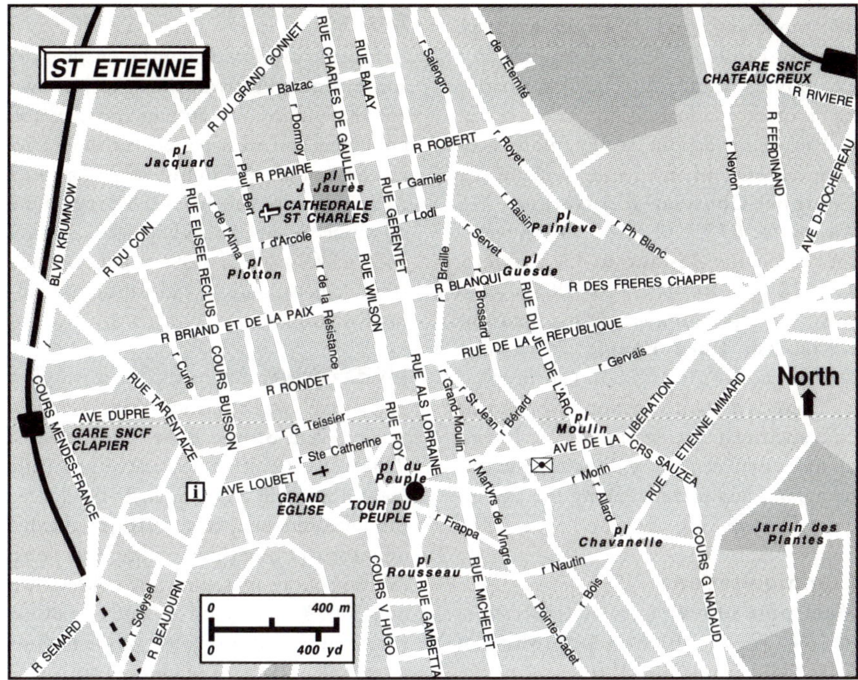

38 28 16 (moderate) is an excellent choice, with comfortable, fully equipped rooms, a quiet location, and the city's only hotel swimming pool.

Other three-star hotels (moderate) include the **Midi**, *19 blvd Pasteur; tel: 04 77 57 32 55; fax: 04 77 59 11 43*, and the centrally located, grand old **Terminus du Forez**, *31 av. D. Rochereau; tel: 04 77 32 48 47; fax: 04 77 34 03 30.* Good two-star options (cheap) include the 14-room **Le Baladin**, *12 r. de la Ville; tel: 04 77 37 17 97; fax: 04 77 41 70 34*, in a pedestrian street, and the **Le Cheval Noir**, *11 r. F. Gillet; tel: 04 77 33 41 72; fax: 04 77 37 79 19.*

HI: **Les Echandes**, *'Le Pertuiset', 42240 Unieux; tel: 04 77 35 72 94,* 17km from town centre. **Campsite**: **Camping Municipal**, *16 Allée Chantegrillet; tel: 04 77 33 18 62.*

Eating and Drinking

St Étienne is well served with restaurants, as might be expected in a city which is within the gastronomic orbit of Lyon. Those specialising in Lyonnaise cuisine include the **Le Glasgow**, *3 pl. Hôtel de Ville; tel: 04 77 32 33 57* (cheap–moderate), the **Corne D'Aurochs**, *18 r. M. Servet; tel: 04 77 33 34 31* (moderate), and **Le Boivin**, *8 pl. Boivin; tel: 04 77 41 90 96* (cheap).

Amongst the city's top-rated establishments are the **Clos de Lilas**, *28 r. Virgile; tel: 04 77 25 28 13*, and **André Barcet**, *19 bis r. V. Hugo; tel: 04 77 32 43 63* (both expensive). **La Ribandière** in the Mercure-Altéa Hotel; *tel: 04 77 42 81 81* (expensive), is also highly recommended. More reasonably priced options include the intimate **Restaurant à la Bouche Pleine**, *8 pl. Chavanelle; tel: 04 77 33 92*

47 (moderate), and **L'Amédée**, *3 pl. Grenette; tel: 04 77 32 63 22* (moderate–expensive), which has an imaginative menu of exceptional quality.

Recommendations at the more economical end of the scale include **Le Tournoël-Consulat d'Auvergne**, *3 r. Cugnot; tel: 04 77 32 32 62*, for Auvergnat cuisine; the **Restaurant La Verrière**, *13 r. Blanqui; tel: 04 77 32 48 12*, good value for tasty, simple dishes; and the **Restaurant Chez Benoît**, *76 r. Roler-Salengro; tel: 04 77 21 53 50* (all cheap).

There is a good selection of brasseries, cafés and restaurants around the *pl. J.Jaurès* in the town centre, with several ethnic restaurants and pizzerias along the adjoining *r. Dormoy*.

Communications

Main post office: *8, av. de la Libération; tel: 04 77 43 40 46* Open Mon–Fri 0800–1800, Sat 0800–1215.

Money

All of the major banks (most of which have change facilities) have branches in the city centre, many of them either on the central stretch of *r. du Président Wilson* or within one block to the south.

Entertainment

St Etiénne has six cinemas, a bowling alley, and 11 discotheques. The **Comédie de St Étienne**, *av. E. Loubet; tel: 04 77 32 79 26,* is a highly respected theatre. Theatre, music and dance are also staged at the **Novel Espace Culturel**, *9, r. Cottier; tel: 04 77 74 41 81*; the **Théâtre des Beaux Arts**, *19, r. H. Gonnard; tel: 04 77 32 55 21*; the **Palais des Spectacles**, *blvd J. Janin; tel: 04 77 42 88 42*; and the **Théâtre de Poche**, *34, r. de la Mulatière; tel: 04 77 38 09 77;* which specialises in vaudeville and children's shows.

Events

St Étienne's most noteworthy event is the annual **Book Festival**, which attracts over 200,000 visitors, 400 authors and over 100 publishers and takes place over three days in Oct; contact the tourist office for exact dates. The city also has a full programme of music events (including jazz, classical and rock festivals) as well as regular antique fairs, a cinema festival, and artistic and cultural expositions.

Sightseeing

St Étienne's star attraction is undoubtedly the excellent **Musée d'Art Moderne**, *la Terrase, tel: 04 77 79 52 52* (open daily 1000–1800; FFr.26). The light-filled interior (encompassing over 4000sqm of exhibition space) belies the sombre, functional exterior of this museum. The collection is now one of the most extensive outside Paris and a rich storehouse of contemporary work. The birth of modern art is well represented but the museum's greatest strength is in its post-World War II collections, with a particularly strong American section.

St Étienne's industrial past is evoked in the **Musée de la Mine**, *3, blvd Franchet d'Esperey, tel: 04 77 33 50 05* (open Mon 1400–1745, Tues–Fri 1000–1745, Sat–Sun 1000–1945; FFr.35). Occupying an old mine shaft leading into the city's western hills, it features dioramas of miners in action through the ages.

There is also the **Musée de Vieux St Étienne**, *13 bis r. Gambetta; tel: 04 77 25 74 32* (open Mon–Sat 1430–1800; FFr.10), which traces the history of the city and includes such curiosities as France's oldest railway ticket, and a **Planetarium**, *Espace Fauriel; tel: 04 77 25 54 92* (several sessions daily (usually in the afternoon); FFr.35).

ST ÉTIENNE–AUBENAS

On the eastern-most edge of the Massif Central, the Haut Vivarais is riven with deep, narrow gorges, through which you climb to reach spectacular viewpoints across the Massif itself and eastwards to the Alps. On either side of the Plateau du Haut Vivarais, dense forests of pine and chestnut envelop the road, with scattered villages (and two large towns) providing interesting stops en route. Allow 3–4 hrs (direct route); 2 days (scenic route).

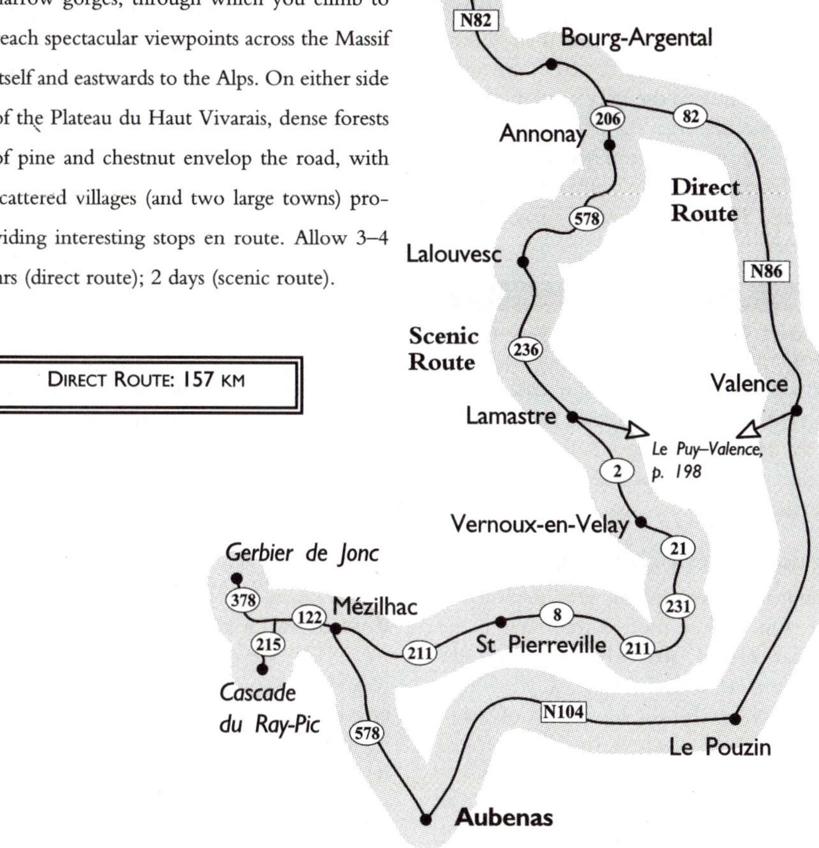

DIRECT ROUTE: 157 KM

ROUTES

DIRECT ROUTE

→ There is no parallel fast route, but the most direct journey is to by-pass Annonay on the N82, then take the D82 to connect with the N86 running south down the Rhône Valley. The road by-passes Valence, providing a connection to the Le Puy–Valence route (p. 198) – also possible at Lamastre on the Scenic Route. At Le Pouzin turn right onto the N104, following it through Privas to Aubenas.

Scenic Route

From St Étienne take the N82 to Bourg-Argental, branching off onto the D206 to reach **Annonay**. From here, follow the D578 and then the D578a to **Lalouvesc**, and then take the D532 and the D236 via the **Col de Buisson** into **Lamastre**. From Lamastre, take the D2 to **Vernoux-en-Vivarais** and then follow the D231 to reach the D120. Turn right and then left onto the D211 and the D8 to **St Pierreville**, then the D211 again to the Col des Quatre Vios and **Mézilhac**. From Mézilhac the D578 descends into **Val-les-Bains**. The D104 then leads into Aubenas.

ANNONAY

Tourist Office: *pl. des Cordeliers; tel: 04 75 33 24 51.* Open July–Aug Mon–Sat 0830–1230, 1415–1900, Sun 1030–1230; Sept–May Tues–Sun 0830–1200, 1415–1830. Hotel bookings. Guided visits of Vieille Annonay July–Aug Wed, Sat 1000 (FFr.10).

The Montgolfiers

The Mongolfier brothers, Joseph and Étienne, were descendants of one of the oldest paper-making families in France and achieved celebrity in the dying days of the *Ancien Régime* by succeeding in flying the world's first hot-air balloon. Using a burning mixture of damp straw beneath a spherical envelope, the first attempts took place in the grounds of the family papermill at Vidalon. On 4 June 1783 the first official flight took place, on the *pl. des Cordeliers* in Annonay, lasting about 10 minutes. Summoned by Louis XVI, Étienne directed another flight at Versailles on 19 September, with a cock, duck and sheep suspended in a cage beneath the balloon. It was left to Pilatre de Rozier, with his passenger the Marquis d'Arlandes, to make the first manned flight on board a *'montgolfière'* on 21 November that year.

Accommodation and Food

Annonay has surprisingly few hotels for its size. One of the most comfortable is the central **Hôtel du Midi**, *17, pl. des Cordeliers; tel: 04 75 33 23 77; fax: 75 33 02 43* (cheap), in the lower part of town, which has 40 spacious rooms decorated with motifs featuring the omni-present Montgolfiers. **Le Provençal**, *Champ de Mars; tel: 04 75 67 09 39* (cheap), is a smaller, family-run establishment with a great deal of provincial charm. The restaurant is also good value, and popular. Seven km outside Annonay the **Hôtel d'Ay**, *St Clair; tel: 04 75 67 07 38; fax: 04 75 67 07 38* (moderate–expensive) is comfortable and mainly geared to business clients.

Annonay's top restaurant is **Marc et Christine**, *29, av. M. Seguin; tel: 04 75 33 46 97* (moderate), where the menus are presided over by chef de cuisine, Marc Juillat. Also fairly sophisticated is the **Restaurant La Halle**, *10, pl. Grenette; tel: 04 75 32 04 62* (moderate–expensive). Housed in an old vaulted cellar, **Restaurant La Toupine**, *4 bis, r. Réduzière; tel: 04 75 67 59 38* (cheap), has a good reputation for honest cooking.

Sightseeing

Annonay's most famous association is with the Montgolfier brothers, who are commemorated with various street names, statues, a memorial *(av. M. Seguin)* and the recreation of their historic flight on the 1st Sun in June each year. Archive material on the Montgolfiers is also featured in the **Musée Vivarois César Filhoe**, *15 rue J-P. Béchetoille*; (open July–Aug daily 1400–

1800; Sept–June Wed, Sat, Sun 1400–1800; FFr.12). Alongside various folklore exhibits (including a typical Vivarois kitchen) are a superb 16th-century wooden crucifix, a 17th-century *pietà*, and numerous Moustiers faïences. There is also a room devoted to transport: one of the Montgolfiers' descendants, Marc Seguin (1786–1875), was responsible for the development of a boiler for steam engines.

The old quarter of Annonay, much of it recently restored, features several fortified gateways and picturesque houses from the 16th–18th centuries.

Outside Annonay (3km to the north-west) is the **Musée des Papeteries Canson et Montgolfier**, *Vidalon; tel: 04 75 69 88 00* (open July–Aug daily 1415–1800; Sept–June Wed, Sun 1430–1800), which is housed in the Montgolfiers' birthplace and features a paper-making museum with a traditional workshop.

LALOUVESC

Tourist Information: *rue St. Regis; tel: 04 75 67 84 20*, open July–Aug Mon–Sat 0900–1200, 1420–1800; hours variable rest of the year.

Accommodation And Food

Lalouvesc has two good hotels with remarkable views. The **Relais du Monarque**, *tel: 04 75 67 80 44*, is an old 17th-century post inn with 20 rooms while the **Beau Site**, *tel: 04 75 67 82 14*, has 33 rooms. Both are cheap–moderate and have restaurants.

Sightseeing

Perched in a hammock between two wooded hills at an altitude of 1050m, Lalouvesc is perhaps most notable for its extraordinary position. With a steep drop on its eastern side, it faces a panorama which extends far across the Rhône Valley to Mont Blanc and the Alps. There is an **orientation table** in front of the 19th-century **Basilique St Régis**. The church is named after a Jesuit missionary, François Régis, who died in Lalouvesc in 1640 and was canonised in 1737. Behind the church is a small **chapel**, containing a diorama of his dying moments.

LALOUVESC TO LAMASTRE

From Lalouvesc the road hugs the contours of the Montagne de Besset (1191 m at the summit) with glimpses through the wooded hillside of Mont Mézenc and the hilltop villages of Molière and Lafarre ahead. At the **Col de Buisson** (920m) the panorama extends across to Mont Mézenc and the Gerbier de Jonc to the west, with the vallée du Doux to the south. Beyond the village of Pailharès to the east, Mont Blanc can be seen on a clear day. At the crossroads there is a small **miniature Ardèche village** (open daily 1000–1200, 1400–1900; donation). From the Col de Buisson the road snakes down through a gorge to **Lamastre**.

LAMASTRE

Tourist Office: *pl. Montgolfier; tel: 04 75 06 48 99*, open Mon–Sat 1000–1230, 1400–1700. A wide range of brochures is available.

Accommodation and Food

At the meeting of seven roads (and the confluence of four rivers), Lamastre is a busy town with a wide choice of hotels. Top amongst them is the 3-star **Hôtel du Midi Barrattero Perrier**, *pl. Seignobos; tel: 04 75 06 41 50; fax: 04 75 06 49 75* (moderate), a 12-room establishment with an excellent restaurant (expensive). In the town centre are the **Grand Hôtel du Commerce** (*LF*), *10 pl. Rampon, tel: 04 75 06 41 53; fax: 04 75 06 33 48* (cheap), with a lovely ivy-covered façade, behind which lurks a charming hotel with really spacious, old-fashioned rooms and the **Hôtel des Negociants** (*LF*), *14 pl. Rambon; tel: 75 06 41 34; fax: 04 75 06 32 58* (cheap). Both have restaurants with outside terraces. In the old town **Chez Germaine**, *31 rue du Macheville, tel: 04 75 06 41 26* (cheap) has a good reputation for local dishes and a terrace with sweeping views (opening hours erratic, so call before making the steep climb up the steps to the old town).

From Lamastre, the D2 ascends the flanks of the Serre de la Roue (949 m) before reaching **Vernoux-en-Vivarias**, a typical Haut Vivarais village dominated by its 19th-century church. Descending from the plateau, the road twists and turns through the scenic gorges carved by the Dunière and then, on the other side of the main road, ascends again to St Pierreville, traversing one of the prettiest sections of the route through the dense chestnut forests which blanket the valley.

ST PIERREVILLE

The village's principal assets are two museums, each with its own personality, each focussed on different aspects of the Ardèche economy. The first is the **Maison du Châtaignier**, *tel: 75 66 64 33* (open July–Aug daily 1000–1200, 1500–1900; Apr–June, Sept–Nov, Wed, Sat, Sun and public holidays 1400–1800; guided tours 1000, 1500, and 1700; FFr.30) in the centre of the village. This excellent little eco-museum has displays on three floors describing every aspect of St Pierreville's *châtaigneraie* (chestnut forests), which cover around 300 hectares of the surrounding hillsides (see p. 153 for more on Ardèches chestnuts). Curiosities include the spiked boots used to collect the chestnuts from their deep leaf litter. The museum also sells chestnut products and produces a leaflet, *Balade au pays de la Châtaigne*, which details outlying farms and restaurants specialising in *produits du terroir* (local produce).

The other attraction is the **Musée Vivant de la Laine et du Mouton** (Museum of Wool and Sheep); *tel: 04 75 66 61 97* (guided visits only, July–Aug daily 1030, 1400, 1500, 1600, 1700; Sept–June Wed, Sun and public holidays 1500; FFr.30). The 1hr 30 mins tour encompasses everything from the evolution of sheep to the role of shepherds and the development of looms; there's also a large shop, with a wide range of good quality (but fairly pricey) woollen items.

The village has just one hotel-restaurant, the hospitable **Hôtel des Voyageurs**; *tel: 04 75 66 60 08; fax: 04 75 66 62 24* (cheap–moderate) which has been in the hands of the same family since 1895; specialities are game and fish.

MÉZILHAC

The village of Mézilhac lies just beneath a small summit marking the division of the Eyrieux and Ardèche basins. At the crossroads to the west of the village are a couple of café-restaurants geared to passing tourists, whilst on the summit itself (follow signs for the *table d'orientation*, a 5-min walk from the road) there are stunning views to the north-west (across to the Gerbier de Jonc), the north-east (the Cirque de Boutières and the chestnut forests of St Pierreville) and to the south.

SIDE TRACK FROM MÉZILHAC

At the Mézilhac crossroads, take the D122 right, then, just past the Suc de Montivernoux, turn left onto the D215 to reach the **Cascade du Ray-Pic**. Park in the car park and follow the path

(45 mins return) up to the waterfall, which forms a dramatic cascade as it tumbles down from the Bourges ravine, between two volcanic overhangs. Return down the D215 and turn left at the D122, taking the next right (D378) to the **Gerbier de Jonc**. The 1550m peak sits atop the demarcation line between the Rhône and Loire basins, and from the summit (45 mins return) there is a fabulous view across the Massif Central, with the Alps visible to the east on a clear day. At the foot of the peak's south-west slope several trickles of water emerging from the ground mark the source of the Loire. Return via the D122 to Mézilhac.

VAL-LES-BAINS

Tourist Office: *116 bis, rue J.Jaurès; tel: 04 75 37 49 27*. Open July–Aug Mon–Sat 0830–1200, 1400–1900, Sun 0900–1200, 1430–1900; Sept–June, Mon–Sat 0830–1200, 1400–1800. Rail and coach bookings.

Accommodation and Food

As a long-established spa town Val-les-Bains has a wide range of good-quality hotels and restaurants. Top of the range is the deluxe **Grand Hôtel des Bains**, *Montée de l'Hôtel des Bains; tel: 04 75 37 42 13; fax: 04 75 37 67 02* , set in 3 hectares of private parklands with its own thermal source. Across the river from the main *établissment thermal* is the **Grand Hôtel de Lyon**, *11 av. P.Ribeyre; tel: 04 75 37 43 70; fax: 04 75 37 59 11*, which has its own pool – as does the **Hôtel du Vivarais**, *av C.Expilly; tel: 04 75 94 65 85; fax: 04 75 37 65 47*, which is directly opposite the baths. All these are moderate–expensive and have smart restaurants. Two-star hotels (with cheap–moderate rooms) include the **Hôtel de l'Europe**, *86 r. J. Jaurès; tel: 04 75 37 43 94; fax: 04 75 94 66 62*; the **St Jean**, *112 bis r. J.Jaurès; tel: 75 37 42 50; fax: 04 75 37 47 33*, and the **St Jacques**, *8 r. A. Clément; tel: 04 75 37 46 02; fax: 04 75 37 47 33*. All of the campsites mentioned under Aubenas (see p.xxx) are near Val-les-Bains.

Of the restaurants outside the hotels the best is probably the **Runel**, *r.J.Jaurès; tel: 04 75 37 48 57*, at the top end of the town. There are also several *salons de thé*, a *crêperie*, and pizzeria.

Events

There is an annual **Spring Carnival** (weekend after Easter) and a midsummer **Games Festival** (3rd weekend in July), with dozens of different games ranging from darts to chess, backgammon, French regional games, and games from as far afield as Africa and the Far East. **Market** days are Thur and Sun.

Sightseeing

Squeezed into a narrow valley at the mouth of the river Volane where it disgorges into the Ardèche, Val-les-Bains is some 2km long but no more than 300m wide. It is an attractive town, with its old spa hotels and parks along the river banks, developed on a site with around 145 natural springs, whose carbonated, sodium-rich waters have been exploited since the mid 19th century. French visitors come here mostly for their *cures thermales* (particularly for diabetes), and as well as the main *Établissment Thermal* there is also a casino, mineral water bottling plant, and a range of sporting facilities. For visitors the main interest is the **Source Intermittente** (intermittent spring) in the *parc du Casino* which is primed to erupt at 6-hourly intervals (0530, 1130, 1730 and 2330 in summer; 0430, 1030, 1630, 2230 in winter).

ST ÉTIENNE–LE PUY

This route meanders alongside the picturesque Gorges de la Loire, with numerous ruined fortresses and ancient villages perched strategically above the river.

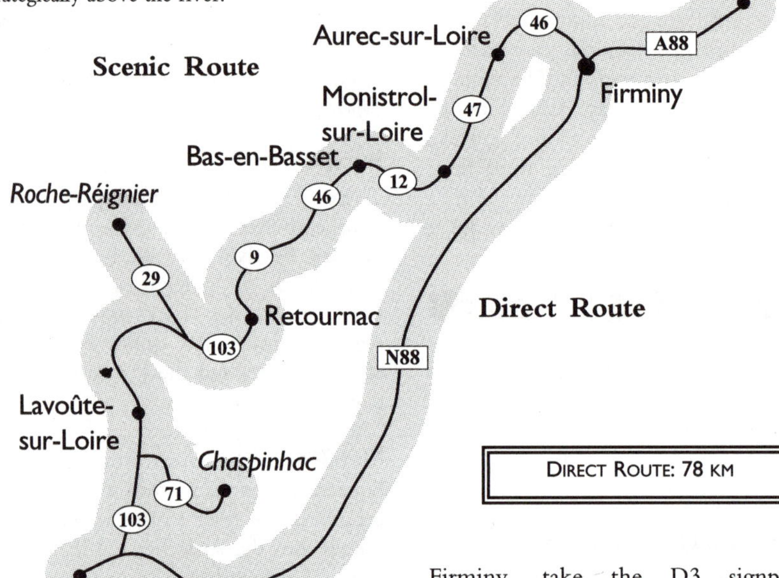

DIRECT ROUTE: 78 KM

ROUTES

DIRECT ROUTE

Leave St Étienne by the autoroute A88 south and follow it through to Firminy, where it becomes the N88. Follow this all the way down to Le Puy. Allow 1½–2 hrs.

SCENIC ROUTE

Leave St Étienne by the autoroute A88 south to **Firminy**. Leaving Firminy, take the D3 signposted Pertuisset, after which take the D108 to St Paul-en-Cornillon and then the D46 to **Aurec**. From Aurec take the D47 to **Monistrol-sur-Loire**, then follow the D12 across the Loire to **Bas-en-Basset**, turning left across the bridge on the D42 to Beauzac. Take the D46 and the D9 left to **Retournac**. From Retournac, follow the D103 and turn right on the D29 to **Roche-en-Réigner**, then return to the D103 following it through Vorey to **Lavoûte-sur-Loire**. Past here, the D103 leads through the Gorges de Peyredyre, after which take the D71 to **Chaspinhac**, and then the D103 again into Le Puy. Allow 1 day.

FIRMINY

Tourist Office: *Mairie de Firminy, pl. du Breuil; tel: 04 77 40 50 62.*

Accommodation and Food

Both the 2-star **Firm'Hôtel**, *37 r. J. Jaurès, tel: 04 77 56 08 99* (cheap); and the unclassified **Hôtel de l'Europe**, *3 r. V. Hugo, tel: 04 77 56 01 26;* (cheap) are centrally located. Firminy's best restaurant is the **Restaurant des Cordes**, *17 r. des Cordes; tel: 04 77 61 93 78* (moderate–expensive), and the town has numerous pizzerias, brasseries and bars around the *pl. du Marché* and *pl. du Breuil.*

Sightseeing

Still effectively part of the conurbation of St Étienne, Firminy is a manufacturing and marketing town with one main distinguishing feature – it possesses several unusual buildings designed by the celebrated Swiss architect Charles Edouard Jeanneret (1887–1965), better known as Le Corbusier. This is the largest cluster of his work found in one place in France, and indeed they were also his last creations. His **Unité d'Habitation**, *r. de la Font du Loup*, is the largest of four originally built (see also p. 235). The principle based town planning on a series of identical modular units whose proportions were calculated according to those of the human body. The concept was considered radical at the time, but influenced urban development throughout the world, so that these earliest works now seem to be little more than mundane concrete tower blocks.

Perhaps the most interesting building is the **Espace Le Corbusier**, *r. de St Just-Malmont; tel: 04 77 56 07 07,* a cantilevered structure overlooking his **stadium** and unfinished **Église St Pierre**. The Espace Le Corbusier now houses a youth and culture centre and operates **guided tours** (daily 1500 July–Aug, 2hrs 30 mins, FFr.30; other months by appointment).

AUREC-SUR-LOIRE

Tourist Office: *av. du Pont; tel: 04 77 35 42 65*, open Mon–Sat 0830–1200 and 1330–1800, Sun 0830–1200.

On the east bank of a loop in the Loire, this village is a popular base for watersports as well as hiking, riding, mountain-biking and other outdoor activities in the surrounding hills. The elegant **Château Fustier** is in the middle of the old village just off the main road: built in the 15th century it is currently undergoing restoration but the small **gardens**, with massive Cedars of Lebanon and other ancient trees, are open to the public.

MONISTROL-SUR-LOIRE

Tourist Office: *12 av. de la Libération; tel: 04 71 66 03 14*, open Mon–Sat 0930–1200 and 1430–1830, Sun 1000–1200.

This small town has a particularly mild climate which attracted the bishops of Puy-en-Velay who made it their second

The Loire

The longest river in France, at nearly 1000 km, the Loire almost cuts the country in two. It rises on 1551m Gerbier de Jonc, about 25km south-west of Le Puy, before wriggling north-west, over the edge of the Massif Central, in a series of dramatic gorges. Near Bourges, in Berry, it abruptly changes direction and character, to flow sluggishly across the plains, through the classic Loire Valley country of forests, sandbanks and romantic châteaux. Having dropped 1400m and collected water from one-fifth of France, it is 3km wide by the time it reaches the sea at St Nazaire, on the Atlantic coast.

residence and built the **Château Épiscopal** in the 15th century. Now a retirement home, the château is flanked by massive round towers (a later addition), and approached via the *allées du Château*, bordered by stately lime trees, from the *pl. Nèron*. Take the path around to the right of the château, where there is a viewpoint across the Loire valley, Bas-en-Basset, and the St Bonnet plateau to the west. Behind the main *r. du Commerce* the narrow streets of the *vieille ville* have many characterful old houses with overhanging eaves.

BAS-EN-BASSET

Tourist Office: *25 blvd.de la Sablière; tel: 04 71 66 95 44*, open Mon–Sat 1000–1230 and 1430–1800, Sun 0830–1230.

A growing industrial town, Bas-en-Basset's main attraction is the **Château de Rochebrun**, reached via a track 300m above the *pl. des Marronniers* (45 mins rtn on foot). A triple wall around the rocky promontory encloses the remains of this medieval castle (built between the 11th and 13th centuries), with the largest structure still intact being a round tower. From the castle ruins there are good views back across the town and the Loire Valley.

RETOURNAC

Tourist Office: *pl. Boncompain; tel: 04 71 65 20 50*, open daily 0915–1300 and 1430–1800 (summer), Mon–Sat 0915–1200 and 1400–1700, Sun 0930–1230 (winter).

Another popular watersports base on the banks of the river, **Retournac** is most notable for its unusual **church** with colourful brickwork and massive bell-tower. The interior houses a 16th-century Italian Madonna and Child. The town has two hotels, the 1-star **L'Univers**, *tel: 04 71 59 40 06*; (cheap) and the unclassified **Le Verre Luisant**, *tel: 04 71 59 42 97*, (cheap) as well as a **municipal campsite** on the riverbank at **Les Rives**, *tel: 04 71 59 42 97*, open May–Sept (caravans). Bars and restaurants include **La Taverne**, *tel: 04 71 65 21 24* (moderate) which specialises in fish; **Le Brasero**, *tel: 04 71 59 40 57* (cheap) and the **Auberge Le Gerbizon**, *tel: 04 71 59 20 68* (cheap).

Continue on the D103, turning right 2 km before Vorey onto the D29.

SIDE TRACK TO ROCHE-EN-RÉGNIER

This small hillside village high above the valley is dominated by an ancient defensive tower, from where there is a superb **panorama** of the Monts Velay, Monts du Forez and the sucs d'Yssingeaux. Return to the D103, and follow it southwards through Vorey, to Lavoûte-sur-Loire.

LAVOÛTE-SUR-LOIRE

Here you will find a Romanesque **church** with a remarkable 13th-century sculpted Christ. Follow signs in the village to the **Château de Lavoûte-Polignac**, *tel: 04 71 08 50 02* (open Easter, May, June, Oct daily 1430–1700, guided tours daily Aug and Sept 1000, 1230, 1400, 1800, June, July, Oct 1400 and 1800 only). Overlooking a loop in the Loire, this restored 13th-century château features numerous rooms furnished in period style with interesting paintings and tapestries.

SIDE TRACK TO CHASPINHAC

The D103 follows the **Gorges de Peyredeyre** to Peyredeyre, where the picturesque D71 on the left leads up to **Chaspinhac**. This small hamlet has a pretty Romanesque **church** built from red volcanic rock, from where there are views back down across the valley.

TOULON

France's second largest port and home to France's Mediterranean fleet, Toulon is a lively town with an impressive natural harbour. It has interesting museums, an excellent market, and many seafood restaurants.

TOURIST INFORMATION

Tourist Office: *pl. Raimu; tel: 04 94 18 53 00.* Open Mon–Sat 0900–1800, Sun 1000–1200. Hotel and restaurant reservations, events tickets.

ARRIVING AND DEPARTING

By Car

Approaching the town centre along Autoroute A50 from either direction you are pitched straight into roadworks and diversions connected with the building of a new road tunnel beneath the town: these works are likely to continue for the forseeable future, since the tunnel is already years behind schedule and suffering from engineering problems (such as, in 1996, the collapse of the tunnel roof 100m underground). When (or if) the tunnel is ever completed it will considerably relieve congestion, since at present traffic from the autoroute simply comes to a grinding halt in the town centre. **Parking**: There are several large underground car parks in the town centre, the most convenient being in *pl. de la Liberté* and *pl. des Armes.*

By Train

Station: **Gare SNCF**, *pl. Albert I; tel: 04 36 35 35 35;* reservations: *04 94 91 50 50.* North of the centre.

GETTING AROUND

The town centre is compact, and most sights can be reached on foot. Exceptions include Mt Faron and trips around the bay (see Sightseeing). **Taxis**: Gare SNCF, *pl. de la Liberté*; Gare Maritime, *pl. Monsenergue*; and other central points. **Radio taxis** (24 hrs), *tel: 04 94 93 51 51.* **Ferries**: Regular departures to Corsica and Sardinia: SNCM, *tel: 04 94 16 66 66*; shuttle service across the bay to La Seyne/St Mandrier, RMTT; *tel: 04 94 03 87 03.*

STAYING IN TOULON

Accommodation

Toulon has a reasonable selection of hotels; those in the town centre tend to be cheaper. Chain hotels include *Ca, Ct, Hd,* and *F1.* Within the centre some of the better hotels include the **Holiday Inn Grand Court** (*Hd*), *1 av. Rageot de la Touche; tel: 04 94 92 00 21; fax: 04 94 62 08 15* (moderate), which has 81 rooms, and **Le Grand Hôtel**, *4 pl. de la Liberté; tel: 04 94 22 59 50; fax: 04 94 22 10 29* (moderate), near the station. In the eastern surburbs along the coast, **Les Bastidières**, *2371 av. de la Résistance, Le Cap Brun; tel: 04 94 36 14 73; fax: 04 94 42 49 75* (moderate–expensive) is a characterful hotel in its own park, with a pool; while **La Corniche**, *17 Littoral F. Mistral, Le Mourillon; tel: 04 41 35 12; fax: 04 94 42 24 58* (moderate–expensive) has a view of the sea. Budget choices near the centre include the **Hôtel Europe**, *7 r. de Chabannes; tel: 04 94 92 37 44; fax: 04 94 62 37 40* (cheap), which has clean, simple rooms; the **Molière**, *12 r. Molière; tel: 04*

94 92 78 35; fax: 04 94 62 85 82 (cheap), with attractive rooms at a very reasonable price; and the **Grand Hôtel de Dauphiné**, *10 r. Berthelot; tel: 04 94 92 20 28; fax: 04 94 61 16 69* (cheap), in the pedestrian zone.

HI: Foyer de la Jeunesse, *12 pl. d'Armes; tel: 04 94 22 62 00; fax: 04 94 22 62 10.* Centrally located. **Campsite: Camping Les Mimosas**, *av. Marcel Paul, La Seyne, tel: 04 94 94 73 15* (caravans; open all year).

Eating and Drinking

Toulon has a large number of unpretentious restaurants, particularly good value for seafood. Along the port on *quai Stalingrad* restaurants, with outside terraces, offering fixed-price seafood menus, whilst in the central pedestrianised area around *pl. Victor Hugo* and *pl. Dr Aubin* there are a number of smart brasseries, fast food restaurants, and cafés. The town centre also has a good selection of ethnic restaurants, crêperies and the like. Some of the more pleasant restaurants (with sea views) are in the smart suburb of Le Mourillon, with a wide selection along the *Littoral F. Mistral*; these include **Bambou-Plage**, *11 plages de Mourillon; tel: 04 94 42 13 74* (moderate), with *moules* in every kind of sauce; the **Bistrot de la Corniche**, *17 Littoral F. Mistral; tel: 04 94 41 35 12* (moderate), with Provençal specialities and plateaux de fruits de mer; and **Le Marguerite**, *plage de Mourillon; tel: 04 94 03 19 13* (cheap), good value for grilled fish.

Communications

Post Office: *r. P. Ferrero; tel: 04 94 24 61 00.* Open Mon–Fri 0800–1900, Sat 0930–1200.

Money

Banks are located along *av. Gén. Leclerc* and *blvd de Strasbourg*, and there are change bureaux in the old town as well as on the port.

Entertainment

Toulon has half-a-dozen cinemas and numerous discos. Rock concerts, ice spectaculars and the like take place in the biggest concert hall in the South of France, the **Salle Zénith-Oméga**, *blvd Comm. Nicolas; tel: 04 94 22 66 66.* The **Grand Opéra Théâtre**, *blvd Strasbourg; tel: 04 94 92 70 78*, hosts opera and plays. Exhibitions, concerts and other events are listed in the free bi-monthly magazine, *Le Toulonnais.*

Events

Fête de la St-Pierre et Pêcheurs, with traditional Provençal maritime 'jousting' (June); **Festival du Musique** (June–July); **Jazz à Toulon**, France's only free jazz festival (July), the **Festivale de Danse** (July); **International Organ Festival** (Oct); and **Maritime and Underwater Film Festival** (Nov).

Shopping

The redevelopment and gentrification of Toulon's previously insalubrious red light district (adjoining the western end of the port) has created a new pedestrian area, linked to the main district around *pl. Victor Hugo*, with many chic boutiques and specialised shops springing up over the whole area. Otherwise the main shopping street is *blvd de Strasbourg*, where there are record and clothes shops as well as the department store **Galeries Lafayette**, *11 blvd de Strasbourg; tel: 04 94 22 39 71.* There are good food shops and an excellent **market** (daily except Mon) on *cours Lafayette.*

Sightseeing

Toulon has been a naval base since 1481

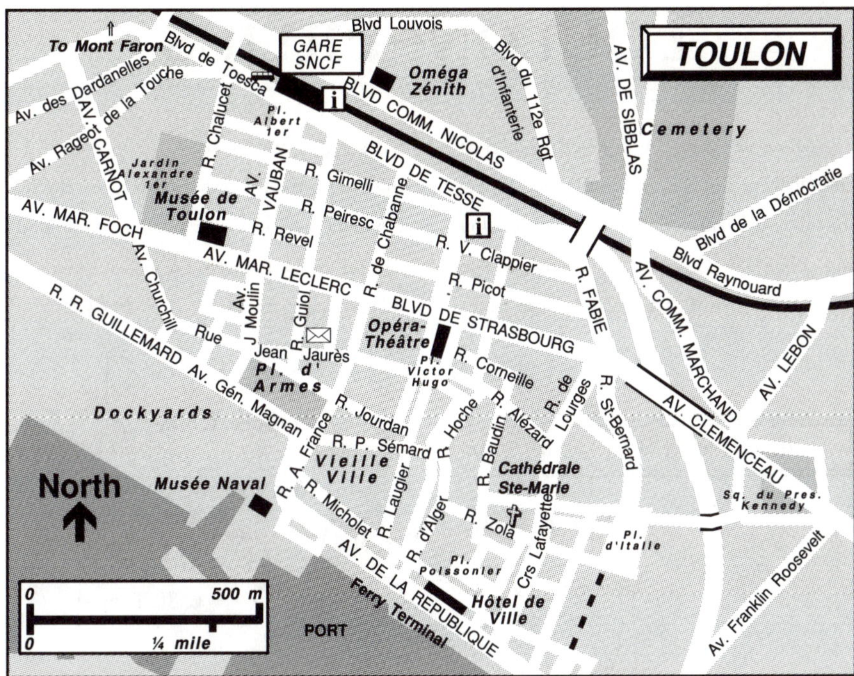

and is justifiably proud of its maritime heritage. A **Harbour Tour**, complete with a lively commentary on the ships of the Mediterranean fleet, from *quai Stalingrad* and *quai de la Sinse* (around FFr.45, with frequent departures throughout the day), is recommended. The port's maritime heritage is well documented in the **Musée de la Marine**, *pl. Monsenergue; tel: 04 94 02 02 01* (open daily 0930–1200, 1500–1900; FFr.25). Housed in what was once the gateway to the 17th-century arsenal, it has ships' figureheads and huge model galleons, plus carvings by Pierre Puget. The the balcony of the modern **Hôtel de Ville**, *quai Stalingrad*, is supported by two of the best-known works by Puget, his *Atlantes* and *Tiredness and Strength*, carved in 1657. Napoleon's historic role in defending Toulon from an Anglo-Spanish fleet in 1793 is commemorated alongside other events in the **Musée de Vieux Toulon**, *69 cours Lafayette; tel: 04 94 92 29 23* (open Mon– Sat 1400–1900; free).

Apart from a tour of the bay, the other main outdoor attraction is a trip up **Mont Faron** (584 m) which dominates Toulon. You can drive up yourself (via the rte du Faron), but it is a hair-raising 9 km and it's easier to drive (or take bus 40) to the **Téléphérique**, *blvd Amiral Vence* (open Tue–Sun 0900–1900; FFr.35). This whisks you up to the top in 10 mins, offering fabulous views of the coastline, Toulon and its harbour. At the top is the **Musée Memorial du Debarquement**, *Tour Beaumont; tel: 04 94 88 08 09* (open daily 0930–1130, 1430–1745; FFr25), commemorating the Allied landings in Provence in 1944. Plans had been smuggled out by the Resistance and four days after the first landings, French troops attacked the Toulon defences; the town was liberated on the 26th August.

TOULON–FRÉJUS

The Massif des Maures is one of the last great unspoiled areas of the South of France. There are three alternative routes between Toulon and Fréjus-St-Raphaèl, all of which go through the massif. The inland route penetrates right into its heart, while the coastal route skirts the fringes where it meets the sea. Beyond the Maures is France's most star-studded resort, St Tropez, and several other seaside ports and towns.

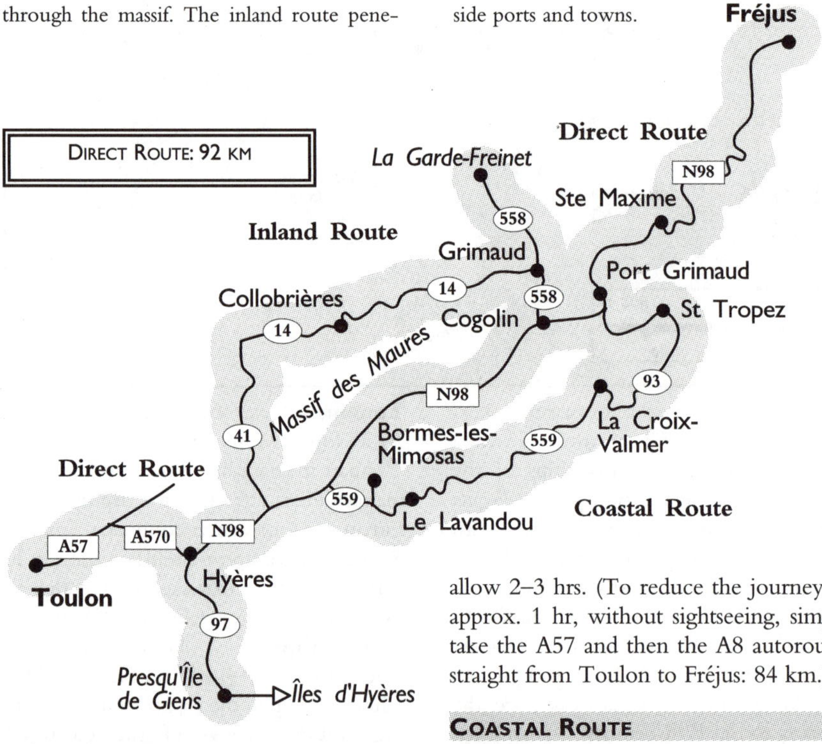

DIRECT ROUTE: 92 KM

ROUTES

DIRECT ROUTE

Leave Toulon on autoroute A57, branching off right onto the A570 to Hyères. Follow the N98 from Hyères through to the Golfe de St Tropez, and **Port Grimaud**, then along the coast to **Ste Maxime** and Fréjus. Distance: 92 km; allow 2–3 hrs. (To reduce the journey to approx. 1 hr, without sightseeing, simply take the A57 and then the A8 autoroutes straight from Toulon to Fréjus: 84 km.)

COASTAL ROUTE

Follow the Direct Route until 16 km past Hyères, then turn right onto the D559. After 3 km, turn left up to **Bormes-les-Mimosas**. Retrace your path to the D559 and turn left to continue to **Le Lavandou** and along the coast to La Croix-Valmer; there turn right onto the D93 and follow it through to **St Tropez**. Leave St Tropez on the D98A to rejoin the Direct Route at Port Grimaud.

Distance: 125 km; allow 1–2 days with sightseeing.

Inland Route

Take the Direct Route and 19.5 km after Hyères turn left onto the D41. At the junction with the D14 turn right to **Collobrières**. From there, take the D39, then the D14 through to **Grimaud**. From there go south on the D558 to rejoin the Direct Route at **Cogolin**. Distance: 109.5 km; allow 1–2 days with sightseeing.

HYÈRES

Tourist Office: *15 r. L. Gautier; tel: 04 94 65 41 42.* Open mid June–mid Sept daily 0800–2000; mid Sept–mid June Mon–Fri 0830–1800, Sat 0900–1200, 1400–1730. SNCF information and ticket counter.

Hyères is a major horticultural centre, mainly growing fruit and flowers but also palm trees: this trade started in the 1860s and reached its peak in the 1920s, when over a million palm trees were being exported annually. Today only three nurseries remain (growing 100,000 palms annually) but numerous palm trees line the boulevards of the town centre, laid out in the 19th century. This was once known as Hyères-les-Palmiers, a name now used for the whole urban district. Behind the town centre is the old quarter, whilst down on the coast there are several sandy beaches and three marinas (Port St Pierre, Port des Salettes and Port Miramar).

The old quarter, **Vieux Hyères**, is reached from *pl. Clémenceau* via a 13th-century gateway, the **Porte Massillon**, from where the streets lead up to *pl. Massillon* (site of the daily market). At the top of the square is the 13th-century **Tour des Templiers**, the last remnant of a Knights Templar lodge, whilst to the west are the **Collégiale St-Paul**, *pl. St-Paul*, and on the hill above, a vast, ruinous 13th-century **château**, from where there are excellent views across the town and the **Presqu'île de Giens,** a small island with a resort village, connected to the mainland by two narrow spits of sand.

Side-Track from Hyères

ÎLES D'HYÈRES

The nearest departure point for these islands is the **Gare Maritime de la Tour Fondue**, *Presqu'île de Giens; tel: 04 94 58 21 81*, with frequent departures to Porquerolles (crossing time: 20 mins), Port-Cros (1 hr) and the Île du Levant (90 mins). There are also ferries from Le Lavandou, the Port d'Hyères, Toulon and Cavalaire.

Spreading out eastwards from the Presqu'île de Giens, across the Rade d'Hyères, the islands have also been known for many centuries as the Îles d'Or (the Golden Islands) due to the glint of the mica shale rocks in their south-facing cliffs. A haven for sailors in ancient times, they were later inhabited by the monks of Lérins and then repeatedly attacked by pirates until fortifications were built in the 16th century. They continued to play a strategic role up until World War II, when American marines disabled German gun batteries on two of the islands prior to the Allied landings in Provence. The French military still have bases here. The great attraction of all three islands is the wild, untamed scenery, with numerous bike or walking trails meandering through landscapes scented by pine trees, eucalyptus and maquis scrub, often leading to excellent beaches.

The nearest, largest and most highly developed of the islands is **Porquerolles** (7.5 km long and 3 km across, covering 1257 hectares). Its port, also called Porquerolles, has cafés, restaurants and a couple of hotels. From the port, one of the most popular walks (90 mins return) or cycle rides crosses the island to the lighthouse on the south coast. Good beaches accessible on foot include the Plage d'Argent (1 km) and the Plage Notre Dame (2 km).

The second largest island, **Port-Cros**, is the most hilly and untamed of the three, with unique flora and fauna which led to its protection since 1963 as France's smallest national park. There is a 10 km walking circuit round the coast, as well as numerous other tracks criss-crossing the dense vegetation. The small port has a handful of restaurants and one hotel.

Much of the third island, the **Île du Levant,** is a military camp, but there is also a small section devoted to naturism, centred on the village of Héliopolis.

HYÈRES TO FRÉJUS

The busy town of **Cogolin** lies some 40 km on from Hyères.

Tourist Office: *pl. de la République; tel: 04 94 54 63 17.* Open July–Aug Mon–Sat 0900–1900, Sun 0900–1230, Sept–June 0900–1200, 1430–1830, Sat 0900–1200).

Cogolin is a major centre for the manufacture of handmade carpets, bottle corks and briar pipes: an astonishing variety of smokers' pipes are displayed in **Pipes Roux,** *74 av. G. Clémenceau; tel: 04 94 54 61 99* (open Apr–Oct 1000–1230, 1500–1900), and you can also see them being made in the workshops at **Fabrique des Pipes Courrieu**, *58 av. G. Clémceau; tel: 04 94 54 63 82* (open Mon–Sat 0800–1200, 1400–1900; shop also open Sun). The most famous carpet workshop is **Le Manufacture de Tapis**, *blvd L. Blanc;* (open Mon–Fri 0900–1200, 1400–1800; Fri until 1900), founded by Jean Lauer in 1928. Cogolin also has an attractive old quarter with a 14th-century **Tour de l'Horloge**, medieval doorways, and two chapels. A brochure detailing a walking tour of the old town is available from the Tourist Office.

Another 5 km brings you to the Golfe de St Tropez and the fantasyland of **Port Grimaud**, designed and built by architect François Sperry in the 1960s (and still being expanded), which now encompasses 8 km of canals with 2500 canal-side houses (painted in harmonious pastel colours), most with yachts or speedboats tied up at their moorings. Inevitably dubbed the 'Venice of Provence', it is amusing to see once (as a million visitors a year will testify), but the prices in restaurants and cafés will probably put you off a repeat visit. Most of it is off-limits to cars, so you can either wander at will over the cute bridges between 'islands' or you can take a waterborne tour with **Coches d'Eau**, *1 pl. du Marché; tel: 04 94 56 21 13.* There are good views of the whole ensemble from the tower of the **Église St-François-d'Assise**, *pl. de l'Église.*

From Port Grimaud the coast road follows around the bay into **Ste Maxime**.

Tourist Office: *promenade Simon Lorière, Ste-Maxime; tel: 04 94 96 19 24.* Open summer Mon–Sat 0900–2000, Sun 1000–1200, 1600–1900; winter Mon–Sat 0900–1200, 1400–1830.

This smart resort, facing St Tropez across the bay, has a large sandy beach in front of its palm tree-lined promenade (with numerous other beaches nearby), a small port and plenty of watersports. The town was once protected by the monks of Lérins, who built the **Tour Carrée des Dames,** *pl. d'Aliziers*, in the 16th century: this now houses the **Musée de la Tour**

Carrée (open Wed–Mon Apr–Oct 1000–1200, 1500–1800; Nov–May 1500–1800; FFr.15) which has exhibits on the maritime history of the town, Provençal costumes, and art exhibitions. St Maxime has a casino, nightclubs and discos, and innumerable hotels and restaurants.

BORMES-LES-MIMOSAS

Tourist Office: *pl. Gambetta; tel: 04 94 71 15 17.* Open July–Aug daily 0900–1230, 1500–1900; Sept–June Mon–Sat 0900–1200, 1400–1800. Guided visits Tues, Thurs, Sat July–Aug 1800; June-Sept 1700; Oct-May Sat 1500 (FFr.30).

Accommodation and Food

Bormes has several good restaurants and hotels. Amongst them **Le Grand**, *167 rte du Baguier; tel: 04 94 71 23 72; fax: 04 94 71 51 20* (moderate) has an air of faded grandeur, while **Le Bellevue** (*LF*), *14 pl. Gambetta; tel: 04 94 71 15 15* (cheap) is a small, family-run hotel; both have splendid views. **La Terrasse**, *19 pl. Gambetta; tel: 04 94 71 15 22* (cheap) is good value, with an excllent restaurant serving tasty regional specialities. Another restaurant worth seeking out is **Le Jardin des Perlefleurs**, *100 chemin de l'Orangerie; tel: 04 94 64 99 23* (expensive), where chef Guy Gedda presents an inventive gastronomic menu.

Sightseeing

Bormes is the first stop along our Coastal Route. Founded in the 12th century by a fishing community fleeing coastal raids, the *vieux village* of Bormes-les-Mimosas is 8 km inland but still has a port (La Favière, with a marina and sandy beach). The original seaside hamlet of **Cabasson** is overlooked by the 11th-century **Fort de Brégançon**, the summer residence of the French President.

The mimosas were brought back by troops of Napoleon III's army returning from Mexico in 1867. 'Les Mimosas' was added to the village's name in 1968. It is these abundant flowers – along with oleanders, eucalyptus, bougainvillea and many other scented plants – overflowing from every windowbox and garden in the steep cobbled streets which makes the village so popular with visitors. A marked walkway (ask for a leaflet from the Tourist Office) leads through the old streets past points of interest such as the ruins of the 13th-century **château**, the neo-Romanesque **Église de St Trophime**, and down the 83 steep steps of the *r. Rompi-Cuou* ('bottom-breaker' in Provençal). There is also a **Musée d'Art et d'Histoire**, *103 r. Carnot* (open Tues, Thur–Sat 1000–1200, 1600–1800, Sun 1000–1200; FFr.10) which features local history and paintings.

LE LAVANDOU

Tourist Office: *quai G.Péri; tel: 04 94 71 00 61.* Open Mon–Sat 0900–1215, 1430–1900, Sun 1000–1200.

Accommodation and Food

Recommended hotels include the **Auberge de la Calanque**, *62 av. du Gén. de Gaulle; tel: 04 94 71 05 96; fax: 04 94 71 20 12* (expensive), on the seafront; **L'Oustaou**, *20 av. du Gén. de Gaulle; tel: 04 94 71 12 18; fax: 04 94 15 08 75* (cheap), also on the seafront but with pleasant rooms at budget prices; and **L'Escapade,** *1 chemin du Vannier; tel: 04 94 71 11 52; fax: 04 94 71 22 14* (cheap–moderate) which is in a quiet back street and has tasteful, well-appointed rooms. The resort has some good seafood restaurants, amongst them **La Ramade**, *16 r. Patron Ravello; tel: 04 94 15 24 97* (cheap–moderate), which offers several good value menus featuring *marmite du pêcheur*, *daurade* and *bouillabaisse*.

Sightseeing

Until the beginning of World War II, Le Lavandou was the most important fishing port on the Var coastline, but now pleasure boats and luxury yachts crowd out the harbour. It's a popular resort (particularly with a younger crowd, since prices are not quite as sky-high as they are further along the Riviera), packed out with restaurants, nightclubs, discos and bars. The prime attraction is the good sandy beaches, of which there are around a dozen or more within the 12 km-long **Baie du Lavandou**, including the 2 km beach in front of the promenade at the resort. Other attractions include numerous watesports and trips to the nearby Îles d'Hyères (see p. 337), with frequent departures on hydrojets of the **Compagnie de Transports Maritimes Vedettes Îles d'Or**, *15 quai G.Péri; tel: 04 94 71 01 02*.

LE LAVANDOU TO ST TROPEZ

Tourist Office: *pl. de l'Ormeau, Ramatuelle; tel: 04 94 79 26 04*. Open Mon–Fri 0900–1230, 1430–1900.

From Le Lavandou the coastal road passes through several small resorts with good beaches (amongst them Aiguebelle, Cavalière, and Pramousquier), many of them backed up by the densely-wooded hillsides of the Maures. Beyond Rayol the road climbs up, with good views back across the bay as far as Cap Bénat, and then descends into the **Baie de Cavalaire**. After **La Croix-Valmer**, the D93 snakes around the hillsides of the Presqu'île de St Tropez with views out to sea (particularly at the **Col de Collebasse**). A left turn (1 km) leads to **Ramatuelle**, a lovely little market town built into the hillside with many narrow alleys overhung with arches. From here, the road descends to the **Baie de Pampelonne**, with St Tropez's famous beaches hidden away down tracks through the vegetation on the right side of the road.

ST TROPEZ

Tourist Office: *Gare Routière; tel: 04 94 97 45 21*. Open daily June–Aug 1000–2100 (to 1800/1900 rest of year). **Branch: Bureau d'Accueil**, *quai J.Jaurès* (tel as above). Open daily June–Aug 0930–1330, 1530–2030; rest of year as above.

Accommodation and Food

As might be expected, St Tropez has a huge range of deluxe hotels, many of them spread out behind the town and across the neighbouring Presqu'île de St Tropez. Within the town, one of the most elegant is **La Ponche**, *3 r. des Remparts; tel: 04 94 97 02 53; fax: 04 94 97 78 61* (expensive), a cluster of fishermen's cottages which have been turned into a discreet and chic hotel. Another excellent hotel is **Le Byblos**, *av. P.Signac; tel: 04 56 68 00; fax: 04 94 56 68 01* (expensive) which has 102 superb rooms. One of the few 'budget' choices within town is **La Romana**, *chemin des Conquettes; tel: 04 94 97 15 50; fax: 04 94 97 73 49* (moderate) which is set in a delightful little garden.

On the Presqu'île there are numerous exclusive properties, including the **Château de la Mesardiere**, *rte du Tahiti; tel: 04 94 56 76 00; fax: 04 94 56 76 01* (expensive), set high in the hills, and the superbly appointed **Soulieas**, *plage de Gigaro; tel: 04 94 79 61 91; fax: 94 54 36 23* (expensive), overlooking the Baie de Cavalaire to the east, with a gourmet restaurant.

Restaurants also tend to be on the expensive side: amongst those which offer reasonably-priced menus are **Le Baron**, *23 r. de l'Aïoli; tel: 04 97 71 72* (moderate), with a good value lunchtime menu; **Les Graniers**, *plage des Graniers; tel: 04 94 97 38 50* (cheap-moderate) which provided consistently good quality fish; and **Le Bar à Vin**, *13 r. des Feniers; tel: 04 94 97 46 10* (moderate) which specialises in *côte d'agneau* and *calamar à la Provençale.*

Sightseeing

One of the most famous resorts on the Riviera, St Tropez has been putting up with the eccentricities of celebrities and artists for over a century. Guy de Maupassant visited on his yacht in the 1880s, followed a decade later by the Impressionist painter Paul Signac, who persuaded Matisse, Dufy, Bonnard and others to follow. Between the wars it was the turn of writers (amongst them Colette and Anaïs Nin), but St Tropez's rise to international fame began with Roger Vadim's film *Et Dieu Créa La Femme* (And God Created Woman), starring the then unknown Brigitte Bardot. The bandwagon of celebrity fun has rolled on almost non-stop since then, with movie stars, models, and the glitterati frequently spotted on the beaches in the Baie de Pamplelonne to the east – such as Tahiti Plage, Bora Bora, Pago Pago and others – during the summer months. During the evening, the best places for star-spotting are the hugely expensive cafés (such as Le Gorille and Café Sénquier) on *quai J. Jaurès* on the port, facing the dozens of glamorous yachts tied stern-up at the quay.

Aspiring artists (and peddlers of tourist tat) still line the quaysides to paint the attractive, pastel-coloured houses which surround the port, but for a glimpse of the real thing head for the **Musée de l'Annonciade**, *pl. G. Grammont* (open daily June–Sept 1000–1200, 1500–1900; Oct, Dec–May Wed–Mon 1000–1200, 1400–1800; FFr.30). Housed in a former 16th-century chapel, this brilliant exhibition contains numerous Post-Impressionist works from the late 19th and early 20th centuries, including paintings by Signac, Bonnard, Matisse, and most of the artists who worked here.

On the same side of the port is **La Maison des Papillons**, *9 r. Étienne Berny;* (open Wed–Mon Apr–Sept 1000–1200, 1500-1900; Oct–Mar 1500–1800; FFr.15) which contains over 4500 specimens of butterflies, including a complete collection of French natives.

Behind the port is the attractive **old town**, with streets leading up past several medieval towers, the town hall and the 17th-century **Église de Notre-Dame de l'Assomption** to the **Citadelle**, from where there are good views of the tiled roofs of the town, with the Baie de St Tropez beyond. Within the Citadelle is the **Musée Naval** (open Wed–Mon mid June–Oct 1000–1800; Dec–mid June 1000–1700; closed Nov; FFr.30). The collection includes items relating to the maritime history of St Tropez, a superb reconstruction of a Greek galley and Spanish cannons.

MASSIF DES MAURES

Tourist Offices: Collobrières: *Mairie; tel: 04 94 48 08 00* (open Tues-Sat 1000–1200 and 1400–1800); **Grimaud:** *blvd des Aliziers; tel: 04 94 43 26 98*, (open summer Mon–Sat 0930–1230, 1500–1930, Sun 1000–1300; rest of year Mon–Sat 0900–1230, 1430–1830).

Stretching some 60 km along the coast between Hyéres and St-Raphaël and back some 30 km to the Argens River valley, the Massif des Maures is thickly forested with sweet chestnuts, oaks, pines and cork trees. Although some areas are now scrubland (due to forest fires), most of the forest is carpeted with an impenetratable undergrowth of myrrh and briar which gave rise to its Provençal name, *maouro* ('gloomy' or 'dark'). Mainly uninhabited (apart from a handful of villages and isolated farmhouses in valleys where vines are grown), the interior of the Massif is a magnificent wilderness traversed by often steep and winding roads, which offer lovely views.

Turning onto the D41, the road winds through dense chestnut and cork oak forest – the shaved trunks of the cork oaks either side of the road give the first indication of one of the region's main economic activities, the production of bottle corks. There are glimpses eastwards to the coast and inland to the valleys all the way up to the **Col de Babou** (415 m), where the view extends out to the Giens peninsula and the Îles d'Hyères. Soon after, you reach **Collobrières**, an attractive village with a hump-backed bridge over the Réal Collobrières which runs alongside the picturesque houses. Just the other side of the bridge, the **Confiserie Azuréenne** (open 0900–1300, 1400–1900) sells products made from the town's famous marrons glacés and other goodies; there are also several stalls (often outside producers' garages) which sell attractive souvenirs made from cork, and chestnuts. An excellent restaurant, **La Petite Fontaine**, *1 pl. de la République; tel: 04 94 48 00 12* (cheap) serves delicious meals accompanied by Collobrières' own rosé wines.

From Collobrières the road traverses the heartland of the massif to arrive at **Grimaud**. This photogenic hill village is named after the Grimaldi family (see p. 265) who owned it from the 10th century onwards; from their ruined château (open access) at the top of the village there are superb views of the Massif des Maures to the west and the coast to the south.

Sidetrack from Grimaud

LA GARDE-FREINET

Tourist Office: *1 pl. Neuve; tel: 04 94 43 67 41.* Open July–Aug Mon–Sat 0930–1230, 1500–1900; rest of year Mon–Sat 0930–1230, 1430–1830).

This pleasant village, 15 km north and less pretentious and touristy than Grimaud, straddles a pass across the Massif between the Golfe de St Tropez and the Argens valley. Thanks to its strategic position it was occupied for over a century by the Saracens, who taught the locals how to use the bark of the cork oak (bottle corks are still made here, as they are in Collobrières).

Above the village to the north-west are the remains of the Saracen stronghold, **Fort Freinet** (open access, 40 mins return on foot), which has magnificent views across the Argens Valley inland and across to the Baie de St Tropez.

The village has a handful of hotels and restaurants, as well as some interesting craft shops (wood sculpture, pottery, jewellery etc). On the village outskirts to the south (D558 towards Le Luc) is the rather unusual **Musée International de la Colombophile**, *Le Mourron Rouge; tel: 04 94 43 65 32* (open July–Aug 1000–1200, 1500–1800, closed Tues, Sun am; rest of year 1000–1200, 1500–1800, closed Tues, Sun; FFr.15) which is dedicated to the history of racing pigeons and dovecotes.

Curiously, there is also a restaurant in the village specialising in pigeon dishes, **La Colombe Joyeuse** ('the joyful dovecote'), *12 pl. Vieille; tel 04 94 43 65 24* (cheap). Perhaps those that escape the museum end up here?

LANGUAGE

Although some English is spoken in most tourist locations – hotels, tourist offices, etc. – in the main towns, this will not necessarily be the case in smaller places. Wherever you are, however, not only is it more courteous to at least attempt to speak some French, but you will undoubtedly find that the effort is appreciated, and may even elicit a reply in perfect English!

The following is a very brief list of some useful words and phrases, with approximate pronunciation guides. For drivers' vocabulary, see p. 34.

The *Thomas Cook European Travel Phrasebook* (£4.95/$7.95) lists more than 300 travel phrases in French (and in 11 other European languages).

GENERAL

Hello/Goodbye Bonjour/Au revoir *Bawngzhoor/Ohrervwahr*

Good evening/Goodnight Bonsoir/ Bonne nuit *Bawngswahr/Bon nwee*

Yes/No Oui/Non *Wee/Nawng*

Please S'il vous plaît *Seel voo play*

Thank you (very much) Merci (beaucoup). *Mehrsee (bohkoo).*

I'm sorry, I don't understand Pardon, je ne comprends pas *Pahrdawng, zher ner kawngprawng pah.*

Do you speak English? Vous parlez anglais? *Voo pahrlay ahnglay?*

Can you please write it down? Pouvez-vous l'écrire, s'il vous plaît? *Poovehvoo laycreer seelvooplay?*

AT THE TOURIST OFFICE

Do you have a map of the town/ area? Avez-vous une carte de la ville/ région? *Ahveh-voo ewn cart der lah veel/rehzhawng?*

Can I reserve accommodation here? Puis-je réserver un logement ici? *Peweezh rehzehrveh ang lozhmahng eessee?*

Do you have a list of accommodation? Vous avez une liste d'hôtels? *Vooz ahveh ewn leesst dohtehl?*

ACCOMMODATION

I have a reservation in the name of . . . J'ai fait une réservation au nom de . . . *Zheh feh ewn rehsehrvahssyawng o nawng der . . .*

I wrote to/faxed/telephoned you last month/last week. Je vous ai écrit/faxé/ téléphoné le mois dernier/la semaine dernière. *Zher voozeh ehkree/faxeh/tehlehfoneh ler mwah dehrnyeh/lah sermayn dehrnyair.*

Do you have any rooms free? Vous avez des chambres disponibles? *Voozahveh deh shahngbr deesspohneebl?*

I would like to reserve a single/double room with/without bath/ shower. Je voudrais réserver une chambre pour une personne/pour deux personnes avec/sans salle de bain/douche. *Zher voodray rehsehrveh ewn shahngbr poor ewn pehrson/poor dur pehrson avek/sawns sal der banne/doosh.*

I would like bed and breakfast/(room and) half board/(room and) full board. Je voudrais le petit-déjeuner/la demi-pension/la pension complète. *Zher voodray ler pewtee-dehjewneh/lah dermee-pahngsyawng/lah pahngsyawng kawngplait.*

How much is it per night? Quel est le prix pour une nuit? *Khel eh ler pree poor ewn nuwy?*

Is breakfast included? Est-ce que le petit-déjeuner est compris? *Ehsker ler pertee dehjerneh eh kawngpree?*

May I see the room? Puis-je voir la chambre? *Pweezh vwahr lah shahngbr?*

I would like to take the room. Je prends la chambre. *Zher prahng lah shangbr.*

I would like to stay for . . . nights. Je voudrais rester . . . nuits. *Zhe voodray resteh . . . newyh.*

At what time/where is breakfast served? A quelle heure/où servez-vous le petit-déjeuner? *Ah khel ur/ooh serveh-voo ler perteedehjerneh?*

Do you accept travellers' cheques/ Eurocheques/credit cards? Vous acceptez les chèques de voyage/les Eurochèques/les cartes de crédit? *Voos aksepteh leh sheck der vwoyazh/laze eurosheck/leh kart der krehdee?*

May I have the bill please? Pouvez-vous me donner la note, s'il vous plaît? *Poovehvoo mer doneh lah nott seelvooplay?*

Eating and Drinking

I would like a cup of/two cups of/another coffee/tea. Je voudrais une tasse de/deux tasses de/encore une tasse de café/thé. *Zher voodray ewn tahss der/der tahss der/oncaw ewn tahss der kafeh/teh.*

I would like a bottle/glass/two glasses of mineral water/red wine/ white wine, please. Je voudrais une bouteille/un verre/deux verres d'eau minérale/de vin rouge/de vin blanc, s'il vous plaît. *Zhe voodray ewn bootayy/ang vair/der vair doa mynehral/der vang roozh/der vang blahng, sylvooplay.*

Do you have any matches/cigarettes/cigars? Avez-vous des allumettes/ des cigarettes/ des cigares? *Ahveh-voo dehz ahlewmaitt/deh cigaraytt/deh sigar?*

I would like a table for two. Je voudrais une table pour deux personnes. *Zher voodray ewn tabl poor der pehrson.*

Do you have a non-smoking area? Vous avez une zone non-fumeurs? *Voozahvah ewn zohn nong fewmur?*

Do you have any vegetarian dishes, please? Avez-vous des plats végétariens, s'il vous plaît? *Ahvehvoo der plah vehge-htahryang, sylvooplay?*

Could I have it well-cooked/ medium/rare please? Je le voudrais bien cuit/à point/saignant. *Zher ler voodray beeang kwee/ah pwahng/saynyang.*

May I have some/some more bread/ water/coffee/tea? Puis-je avoir du pain/encore du pain/de l'eau/du café/du thé? *Pweezh ahvoar dew pang/ahngkor dew pang/der lo/dew kafeh/dew teh?*

May I have the bill, please? L'addition, s'il vous plaît! *Laddyssyawng, sylvooplay!*

Where is the toilet (restroom), please? Où sont les toilettes, s'il vous plaît? *Oo sawng leh twahlaitt, sylvooplay?*

Asking the Way

Excuse me, can you help me please? Excusez-moi, vous pouvez m'aider s'il vous plaît? *Ekskewzaymwah, voo poovay mahyday seelvooplay?*

I am looking for the . . . . Je cherche . . . . *Zher shaersh . . . .*

. . . the hotel/the tourist information office/the castle/the cathedral/the old town/the city centre. . . . l'hôtel/ l'office de tourisme/le château/la cathédrale/la vieille ville/le centre ville. *. . . lohtel/lohfeece de tooreezm/ler shatoh/la kahtehdrahl/lah veeay veel/ler sahngtr veel.*

How far is it to . . . from here? . . . c'est loin d'ici? *. . . say looahng deesee?*

Thank you for your help. Merci pour vottre aide. *Mehrsee poor votrayd.*

Shopping

How much does it/this cost? Quel est le prix? *Kehl eh ler pree?*

I would like that one/a (half-)kilo of . . . , please. Je voudrais cela/un (demi-) kilo de . . . , s'il vous plaît. *Zher voodray ser-lah/ang (dermee)keelo der . . ., seel voo play.*

Driving Distances and Times

These distances between main centres generally follow autoroutes and Routes Nationales, not necessarily the shortest routes. Timings are approximate, do not allow for breaks and assume good driving conditions.

	km	miles	hours
Aix-en-Provence to . . .			
Clermont-Ferrand	379	237	4¾
Grenoble	279	174	3½
Lyon	281	176	3½
Marseille	31	19	½
Nice	176	110	2¼
Paris	759	474	9½
Perpignan	305	190	3¾
St Étienne	327	204	4
Clermont-Ferrand to . . .			
Aix-en-Provence	474	296	6
Grenoble	297	186	3¾
Lyon	172	108	2¼
Marseille	410	256	5
Nice	640	400	8
Paris	425	266	5¼
Perpignan	450	281	5½
St Étienne	147	92	1¾
Grenoble to . . .			
Aix-en-Provence	279	174	3½
Clermont-Ferrand	300	188	3¾
Lyon	105	66	1¼
Marseille	310	194	3¾
Nice	332	208	4¼
Paris	573	358	7¼
Perpignan	450	281	5½
St Étienne	158	99	2
Lyon to . . .			
Aix-en-Provence	281	176	3½
Clermont-Ferrand	172	108	2¼
Grenoble	105	66	1¼
Marseille	313	196	4
Nice	472	295	6

	km	miles	hours
Lyon to . . .			
Paris	462	289	5¾
Perpignan	450	281	5¾
St Étienne	60	38	¾
Marseille to . . .			
Aix-en-Provence	31	19	½
Clermont-Ferrand	410	256	5¼
Grenoble	310	194	3¾
Lyon	312	195	4
Nice	188	118	2½
Paris	772	483	9¾
Perpignan	320	200	4
St Étienne	340	213	4¼
Nice to . . .			
Aix-en-Provence	176	110	2¼
Clermont-Ferrand	640	400	8
Grenoble	332	208	4¼
Lyon	472	295	6
Marseille	188	118	2¼
Paris	932	583	11¾
Perpignan	480	300	6
St Étienne	490	306	6¼
Perpignan to . . .			
Aix-en-Provence	305	190	3¾
Clermont-Ferrand	450	281	5¾
Grenoble	440	275	5½
Lyon	450	281	5¾
Marseille	320	200	4
Nice	480	300	6
Paris	864	540	10¾
St Étienne	470	294	5¾
St Étienne to . . .			
Aix-en-Provence	327	204	4
Clermont-Ferrand	147	92	1¾
Grenoble	158	99	2
Lyon	60	38	¾
Marseille	340	213	4¼
Nice	490	306	6¼
Paris	520	325	6½
Perpignan	470	294	5¾

Hotel Codes
and Central Booking Numbers

The following abbreviations have been used throughout the book to show which chains are represented in a particular town or city. Most chains have a centralised worldwide-reservations system in every country where they have hotels. Most telephone calls are either completely free (usually incorporating *800*) or charged at the rate for a local call (e.g. 0345 in the UK). (Aus=Australia, Can=Canada, Ire= Ireland, NZ=New Zealand, SA =South Africa, UK=United Kingdom, USA=United States of America.)

Accor
This encompasses Ibis, Mercure, Novotel and Sofitel, with central reser vation nos that cover them all
Aus *(1 800) 642 244*
Can/USA *(800) 221 4542*
UK *(0171) 724 1000*

Ba **Balladins**
France *(1) 64 46 49 00*
UK *(0171) 287 3171*

BB **B&B**
contact individual hotels

BW **Best Western**
Aus *(1 800) 222 422*
Can/USA *(800) 528 1234*
Ire *(1 800) 709 101*
NZ *(09) 520 5418*
SA *(011) 339 4865*
UK *(0800) 393130*

Ca **Campanile**
France *(1) 64 62 46 46*
UK *(0181) 569 6969*

CI **Comfort Inn**
Aus *(008) 090 600*
Can *(800) 221 2222*
France *(05) 908536*
Ire *(1 800) 500 600*
NZ *(0800) 808 228*
UK *(0800) 444444*
USA *(800) 228 5150*

Cn **Concorde**
Can *(800) 888 4747*
UK *(0800) 181591*
USA *(800) 888 4747*

Co **Confort**
France *(1) 43 36 17 00*

Ct **Climat de France**
Can *(514) 845 1236*
France *(05) 11 22 11*
UK *(0171) 287 3181*
USA *(800) 332 5332*

Dm **Demeure**
France *(1) 48 97 96 97*

Ex **Excelsior**
UK *(0345) 40 40 40*

FI **Formule I**
contact individual hotels

GT **Golden Tulip**
Aus *(008) 221 176*
Can/USA *(800) 344 1212*
Ire *(01) 872 3300*
NZ *(0800) 656 666*
SA *(011) 331 2672*
UK *(0800) 951 000*

Hd **Holiday Inn**
Aus *(800) 221 066*
Can/USA *(800) 465 4329*
Ire *(1 800) 553 155*
NZ *(0800) 442 222*
SA *(011) 482 3500*
UK *(0800) 897121*

HI **Hostelling International**
France *(1) 44 89 87 27*
UK *(0171) 248 6547*

Hn **Hilton**
Aus *(1 800) 222 255*
Can/USA *(800) 445 8667*
NZ *(0800) 448 002*
SA *(011) 880 3108*
UK *(0345) 581595*

Hy **Hyatt**
Aus *(1 800) 131 234*
Can/USA *(800) 233 1234*
Ire *(1 800) 535 500*
NZ *(0800) 441 234*
SA *(011) 773 9888*
UK *(0345) 581 666*

Ib **Ibis**
France *(1) 60 77 27 27*

IH **Inter Hotel**
France *(1) 42 06 46 46*
UK *(0171) 287 3231*

LF **Logis de France**
France *(1) 45 84 83 84*

Mc **Mercure**
Can/USA *(800) MERCURE*
France *(1) 60 77 22 33*
UK *(0181) 741 3100*

Md **Méridien**
Aus *(008) 331 330*
Can/USA *(800) 543 4300*
NZ *(0800) 445 577*
UK *(0171) 439 1244*

NH **Nuit d'Hôtel**
contact individual hotels

Nv **Novotel**
Can/USA *(800) NOVOTEL*
France *(1) 60 77 51 51*
UK *(0181) 748 3433*

PC **Première Classe**
contact individual hotels

Pu **Pullman Hotels**
see Ibis

QI **Quality Inn**
USA *(0800) 228 5151*
see also Comfort Inn

RC **Relais & Chateaux**
Aus *(02) 957 4511*
France *(1) 45 72 90 00*
UK *(0171) 287 0987*
USA *(212) 856 0115*

Rm **Ramada**
Aus *(1 800) 222 431*
Can *(800) 854 7854*
Ire *(1 800) 252 627*
NZ *(0800) 441 111*
UK *(0800) 181737*
USA *(800) 854 7854*

RS **Relais du Silence**
France *(1) 44 49 90 00*
UK *(1) 44 49 90 00*

Sf **Sofitel**
Can *(800) SOFITEL*
UK *(0181) 741 9699*
USA *(800) SOFITEL*

TH **TimHôtel**
France *(1) 44 15 81 15*

CONVERSION TABLES

DISTANCES (approx. conversions)

1 kilometre (km) = 1000 metres (m) 1 metre = 100 centimetres (cm)

Metric	*Imperial/US*	*Metric*	*Imperial/US*	*Metric*	*Imperial/US*
1 cm	3/8ths in.	10 m	33 ft (11 yd)	3 km	2 miles
50 cm	20 in.	20 m	66 ft (22 yd)	4 km	2½ miles
1 m	3 ft 3 in.	50 m	164 ft (54 yd)	5 km	3 miles
2 m	6 ft 6 in.	100 m	330 ft (110 yd)	10 km	6 miles
3 m	10 ft	200 m	660 ft (220 yd)	20 km	12½ miles
4 m	13 ft	250 m	820 ft (275 yd)	25 km	15½ miles
5 m	16 ft 6 in.	300 m	984 ft (330 yd)	30 km	18½ miles
6 m	19 ft 6 in.	500 m	1640 ft (550 yd)	40 km	25 miles
7 m	23 ft	750 m	½ mile	50 km	31 miles
8 m	26 ft	1 km	5/8ths mile	75 km	46 miles
9 m	29 ft (10 yd)	2 km	1½ miles	100 km	62 miles

24-HOUR CLOCK

(examples)

0000 = Midnight	1200 = Noon	1800 = 6 p.m.
0600 = 6 a.m.	1300 = 1 p.m.	2000 = 8 p.m.
0715 = 7.15 a.m.	1415 = 2.15 p.m.	2110 = 9.10 p.m.
0930 = 9.30 a.m.	1645 = 4.45 p.m.	2345 = 11.45 p.m.

TEMPERATURE

Conversion Formula: °C × 9 ÷ 5 + 32 = °F

°C	°F	°C	°F	°C	°F	°C	°F
-20	-4	-5	23	10	50	25	77
-15	5	0	32	15	59	30	86
-10	14	5	41	20	68	35	95

WEIGHT

1kg = 1000g 100 g = 3½ oz

Kg	Pounds	Kg	Pounds	Kg	Pounds
1	2¼	5	11	25	55
2	4½	10	22	50	110
3	6½	15	33	75	165
4	9	20	45	100	220

FLUID MEASURES

1 litre(l) = 0.88 Imperial quarts = 1.06 US quarts

Litres	Imp.gal.	US gal.	Litres	Imp.gal.	US gal.
5	1.1	1.3	30	6.6	7.8
10	2.2	2.6	35	7.7	9.1
15	3.3	3.9	40	8.8	10.4
20	4.4	5.2	45	9.9	11.7
25	5.5	6.5	50	11.0	13.0

MEN'S CLOTHES

UK	Europe	US
36	46	36
38	48	38
40	50	40
42	52	42
44	54	44
46	56	46

MENS' SHOES

UK	Europe	US
6	40	7
7	41	8
8	42	9
9	43	10
10	44	11
11	45	12

MEN'S SHIRTS

UK	Europe	US
14	36	14
15	38	15
15½	39	15½
16	41	16
16½	42	16½
17	43	17

LADIES' SHOES

UK	Europe	US
3	36	4½
4	37	5½
5	38	6½
6	39	7½
7	40	8½
8	41	9½

LADIES' CLOTHES

UK	France	Italy	Rest of Europe	US
10	36	38	34	8
12	38	40	36	10
14	40	42	38	12
16	42	44	40	14
18	44	46	42	16
20	46	48	44	18

INDEX

References are to page numbers. **Bold** numbers refer to the planning maps at the end of the book; e.g. **3:B4** means square B4, map page 3.

A

Abbeys:
- Grande Chartreuse 223
- Hautecombe 222
- Montmajour 104
- Sénanque 145
- Silvacane 71–72
- St-Michel-de-Frigolet 105
- St-Roman 106
- Thoronet 77

Abîme du Branabiau 250
Accidents 32–33
Accommodation 15–16
Agay 179, **4:C7**
Agde 277–278, **1:B6**
Aigues-Mortes 90–91, **1:B8**
Airports 35–36
Aix-en-Provence 60–65, **4:C3**
Aix-les-Bains 221–222, **3:C9**
Alba-la-Romaine 197
Alès 273, **1:A8**
Allos 292
Alpilles 101
Ambert 169, **2:B8**
Anduze 152
Aniane 252
Annonay 326, **2:D7**
Annot 290–291
Ansouis 71
Antibes 134–135, **4:C8**
Apt 112–113, **4:B3**
Architecture 51–52
Ardèche chestnuts 153
Arlempdes 195
Arles 80–85, **1:B10**
Arpaillargues 117
Art and artists 49–51, 57
Aubagne 244, **4C:3**
Aubenas 196, **2:C4**
Aurec-sur-Loire 331
Auzon 165, **2:A7**
Avignon 92–97, **1:A10**

B

Bagnols-les-Bains 154, **2:B4**
Bagnols-sur-Cèze 109
Baie de Cavalaire 340
Baie de Pampelonne 340
Baie des Anges 286, 287
Baie des Fourmis 301
Baie du Lavandou 340
Balazuc 111
Bandol 246
Barbegal 104
Barbentane 104–105
Barcelonnette 118–119, **4:A7**
Barjac 110, **2:C3**
Barre-des-Cèvennes 153
Barrême 126, **4:B6**
Bas-en-Basset 332, **2:C7**
Beaucaire 106, **1:B10**
Beaulieu-sur-Mer 301, **4:C9**
Beaumes-de-Venise 137, **4:A2**
Belley 220
Bés river valley 172
Besse 161
Béziers 278–279,**1:B5**
Bicycles 18
Billom 167
Biot 135
Blanche valley 172
Blesle 165
Bollène 217, **1:A10**
Bonnieux 72, **4:B3**
Bories 145
Bormes-les-Mimosas 339
Boucieu-le-Roi 200
Bouillabaisse 233
Breakdowns 32–33
Breil-sur-Roya 255, **4:B9**
Brignoles 76, **4:C5**
Brioude 165, **2:A7**
Buis-les-Baronnies 317, **4:A3**
Bullfighting 84, 91
Buses 24

C

Cabannes Vieilles 257
Cagnes-sur-Mer 293–294, **4:C8**
Calanques 245
Camargue 87–89
Camping 16–17
Canal du Midi 277
Cannes 121–124, **4:C7**
Canoeing 248
Cap d'Agde 277–278
Cap d'Ail 302
Cap Martin 303
Car hire 28–29
Caravanning 16–17
Carcassonne 280, **1:B2**
Carnival 285
Carpentras 141–143, **4:A2**
Carry-le-Rouet 240
Casamaures 184
Cascade de Cournes 296
Cascade du Ray-Pic 328
Cassis 244–245, **4:C3**
Castellane 126, **4:B7**
Castillon-du-Gard 116
Cavaillon 73–74, **4:B2**
Cévennes 149–154
Cézanne 61, 63
Chambéry 220–221, **3:C8**
Channel Tunnel 38
Chartreuse (liqueur) 223
Chartreuse-de-St Croix 227
Chaspinhac 332
Châteauneuf-du-Pape 217–218
Châteaurenard 99, **1:B10**
Châteaux:
- Avignon 88
- Castenet 154
- Chavaniac-Lafayette 166
- Crussol 213
- Domeyrat 166
- If 234
- Lavoûte-Polignac 332
- Montauban, 104
- Murol 162
- Roquedols 250
- Rousson 274

Chazelles-sur-Lyon 226
Chemin de Fer de la Mure 129
Chorges 173, **3:C4**
Cime de la Bonette 259
Cirque de Navacelles 251
Cirque du Salso Moreno 259
Clauzel Dam 200
Clermont-Ferrand 155–162, **2:A9**
Clues de Barles 172–173
Cogolin 338
Col d'Allos 292
Col de la Cayolle 260
Col de Luens 126
Col de Murs 143
Col de Turini 256–257
Collioure 321, **1:D4**
Collobrières 342, **4:D5**
Colmars 291–292, **4:B7**
Concoules 154
Corbières Mountains 280
Corniches 299–302
Corps 128–129, **3:C5**
Côte Bleue 240
Crémieu 220
Crêt d'Œillon 227
Currency 19
Customs 19–20

D

Daudet, Alphonse 27, 53, 104
Defile de Donzère 216
Denim 308
Die 187, **3:B5**
Digne-les-Bains 171–172, **4:B6**
Disabled travellers 20
Discounts 20
Domaine de Charance 128
Domaine de Villaret 274
Dore Valley 168–169
Draguignan 79, **4:C6**
Driving 28–34
Durance Valley 114

E

Electricity 21
Embassies 26–27
Ensuès-La Redonne 240
Entrecasteaux 77
Entrevaux 290
Estaque 240

Étang de Vaccarès 89
Eurostar 38
Eze 301–302

F

Faïence 68
Feria 84
Ferries 36–37
Firminy 331, **2:C7**
Flamingos 89
Florac 275, **2:B3**
Fontaine de Vaucluse 146–147
Fontvieille 104
Food 21, 47–49
Forcalquier 113–114
Forêt de Venasque 143
Fos-sur-Mer 242
Fragonard, Jean-Honoré 298
Fréjus 174–177, **4:C7**
Fuel 34

G

Ganagobie, Prieuré de 114
Gap 128, **3:C4**
Genolhac 154, **2:C3**
Geology 41–42
Gerbier de Jonc 329
Gergovia 164
Giens 337
Gignac 252, **1:B6**
Gigondas 137
Glanum 101
Golfe-Juan 131–132, **4:C8**
Gordes 144–146, **4:B2**
Gorges:
  Allier 166
  Ardèche 110–111
  Bachelard 260, 292
  Bourne 186
  Doux 200
  Guiers Mort 223
  Hérault 252
  Jonte 249–250
  Loup 296–297
  Méouge 140
  Mondane 200
  Nesque 139
  Peyredeyre 332
  Tarn 248
  Vésubie 289
  Vis 251
Gourdon 296–297
Grand Cañon de Verdon 69
Grasse 297–298, **4:C7**
Graveson 99
Grenoble 181–184, **3:B6**
Gréoux-les-Bains 67–68
Grimaldi family 265, 342
Grimaud 342
Grottes:
  Choranche 187
  Clamouse 252
  Cocalière 274
  Dargilan 249
  Demoiselle 251–252
  Lauriers 251
  Thouzon 148
  Trabuc 152
Guignol 206
Guillaumes 260

H

Health 21–22
History 43–46
Holidays 24
Hyères 337, **4:D5**

I

Îles d'Hyères 337–338
Îles de Lérins 124, 132, 133
Îles du Levant 338
Îlot du Fangassier 89
Insurance 22
Isle-sur-la-Sorgue 147–148, **3:A1**
Isles de Stel 90
Isola 258, **4:B8**
Ispagnac 248
Issoire 164, **2:A8**
Itineraries 55–59

J

Jausiers 259
Juan-les-Pins 133

L

La Bollène-Vésubie 257
La Brigue 256
La Chaise-Dieu 169, **2:B7**
La Chapelle-en-Vercors 187
La Ciotat 246, **4:D3**
La Couronne 240
La Croix-Valmer 340
la Fayette, Marquis de 166
La Garde-Freinet 342, **4:C6**
La Grand-Combe 275, **1:A7**
La Grande-Motte 91, **1:B8**
La Mure 129, **3:C5**
La Napoule-Plage 180
La Palud-sur-Verdon 69
La Roque-sur-Cèze 110
La Tour d'Aigues 71
La Turbie 302–303
La Voulte-sur-Rhône 214
Lakes:
  Allos 292
  Bourget 222
  Castillon 291
  Sautet 129
  Serre-Ponçon 119–120, 173
Lacoste 72
Laffrey 129–130
Lalouvesc 327, **2:D6**
Lamastre 327–328, **2:D6**
Langeac 166, **2:A6**
Language 22, 34, 52–53, 343–344
Lanuéjols 154
Laragne-Montéglin 188, **4:A5**
Laroque 251
Lattes 91
Lavaudieu 165
Lavender 140
Lavoûte-sur-Loire 332, **2:A6**
Le Bleymard 154
Le Chambon-sur-Lignon 199, **2:C6**
Le Claps 188
Le Corbusier 331
Le Lavandou 339–340, **4:D6**
Le Maz de la Barque 154
Le Monastier-sur-Gazeille 195, **2:B6**
Le Mont-Dore 160–161, **2:A8**
Le Panier 235–236
Le Pont-de-Montvert 154, **2:B3**
Le Pra 259
Le Puy-en-Velay 189–193, **2:B6**
Le Sambuc 89
Le Shuttle 37–38
Le Thor 148
Le Val 76–77
Le Vigan 251
Les Demoiselles Coiffées 120
Les Échelles 223
Les Lecques 246
Les Saintes-Maries-de-la-Mer 89–90. **1:B9**
Les-Baux-de-Provence 101–103
Loire river 331
Lourmarin 72
Lubéron 73
Luc-en-Diois 188, **3:B4**
Lumière brothers 205
Lurs 114
Lyon 201–208, **2:D9**

M

Maillane 99–100
Malaucène 138, **4:A2**
Maps 22–23
Marseille 228–236, **4:C3**
Martigues 241–242, **4:C2**
Massif de l'Esterel 179–180
Massif de la Chartreuse 222
Massif des Maures 341–342
Matisse, Paul 286, 295
Maussanne-les-Alpilles 103–104, **1:B10**
Mayle, Peter 27, 73
Mazet-St-Voy 199
Mende 275, **2:A4**
Ménerbes 73
Menton 304–305, **4:B9**
Meyrueis 249, **1:A5**
Mézilhac 328, **2:C5**
Mialet 152
Mistral, Frédéric 97, 100
Mistral, the 314
Monaco 261–266, **4:B9**
Monistrol-sur-Loire 331–332, **2:C7**
Mont Aigoual 250, **1:A6**
Mont Blanc 223
Mont Chalvet 291
Mont de la Saoupe 245
Mont Faron 335
Mont Lozère 154
Mont Pelat 292
Mont Ventoux 138
Mont Vinaigre 179
Montbrun-les-Bains 140
Montdardier 251
Monte-Carlo 261–266, **4:B9**
Montélimar 214–215, **2:D4**
Montferrand 159
Montgolfier brothers 326
Montpellier 267–271, **1:B7**
Montpeyroux 164, **2:A8**
Monts de Forez 169
Motorail 40
Mougins 124

Moustiers-Ste-Marie 68–69, **4:B6**

N

Napoleon 130
Narbonne 279, **1:C4**
Nice 281–287, **4:C8**
Nîmes 306–310, **1:B9**
Nostradamus 239
Notre-Dame de Salagone 113

O

Olives 294
Olliergues 169
Opening hours 23
Oppède-le-Vieux 73
Oppidum St Blaise 242
Orange 311–314, **1:A10**

P

Pagnol, Marcel 27, 54, 244
Palavas-les-Flôts 91, **1:B7**
Parking 33–34
Parks and nature reserves:
Cévennes 149–154
Ecrins 120
Haute-Provence 173
Les Isles 274
Pilat 227
Pont de Gau 88
Volcans 160
Passports and visas 23
Pays des Cathares 280
Perfume 298
Pernes-les-Fontaines 148, **4:B2**
Perpignan 318–321, **1:D4**
Pétanque 295
Petit Train Jaune 321
Pic de l'Ours 180
Pilgrims' route 193
Plage de Piémançon 89
Plain de Crau 239
Plateau de Corion 197
Police 32
Pont d'Arc 111
Pont du Gard 115–116
Pont Julien 113
Pont-de-Dore 168
Pont-en-Royans 186, **3:B6**
Popes 96
Porquerolles 337–338
Port Grimaud 338
Port-Cros 338
Post offices 23–24
Pra Loup 292
Prades 249
Prat Peyrot 250
Presqu'île de Giens 337
Public holidays 24
Public transport 24
Puget-Théniers 289–290, **4:B8**
Puy de Dôme 160
Puy de Sancy 161

R

Rail 38
Ramatuelle 340
Rasteau 316
Retournac 332, **2:C7**
Rhône wines 217
Riez 68, **4:B5**
Riquet, Paul 277, 279
Road signs 30, 31
Roads 29, 38–40
Roche-en-Régnier 332
Rocher du Cire 139
Rocher St Josephe 193
Roquebrune 303
Roquemaure 109
Roussillon (Vaucluse) 143–144
Roya Valley 254–255
Royat 160, **2:A9**
Ruoms 111, **2:C4**

S

Sablet 137
St Agrève 200, **2:C6**
St André Entrechaux 317
St André-les-Alpes 291, **4:B7**
St Anthème 169, **2:B8**
St Croix-en-Jarez 226–227
St Étienne 322–324, **2:C7**
St Étienne-de-Tinée 258–259, **4:A8**
St Gilles 87, **1:B9**
St Guilhem-le-Désert 252
St Hippolyte-du-Fort 153–154
St Hugues de Chartreuse 223
St Jean-Cap-Ferrat 300–301
St Jean-du-Gard 152
St Julien-Chapteuil 198, **2:C6**
St Laurent d'Eze 302
St Laurent-de-Trève 153
St Laurent-des-Arbres 109, **3:C7**
St Martin-d'Ardèche 110
St Martin-d'Entraunes 260
St Martin-en-Haut 225
St Martin-la-Plaine 226
St Martin-Vésubie 257–258
St Maximin-la-Ste-Baume 75–76, **4:C4**
St Même Waterfalls 223
St Mitre-les-Remparts 242
St Nectaire 161–162
St Paul-de-Vence 294–295
St Paul-Trois-Châteaux 216, **2:D3**
St Pierre-de-Chartreuse 223
St Pierreville 328
St Raphaël 174–177, **4:C7**
St Rémy-de-Provence 100–101, **1:B10**
St Roman-en-Gal 211–212
St Saturnin 164
St Tropez 340–341, **4:D6**
St Vincent-Les Forts 172–173
Ste Agnès 305
Ste Énimie 249, **2:A3**
Ste Maxime 338–339
Salernes 77–78
Salin-de-Giraud 89
Salon-de-Provence 238–239, **4:B2**
Sanary 246
Sanctuary de la Salette 129
Santons 76
Saorge 255
Sault 139–140, **4:A3**
Savines-le-Lac 120
Security 25
Séguret 137
Self-catering 16
Sérignan-du-Comtat 315
Sète 277, **1:B6**
Sisteron 126–127, **4:A5**
Sospel 254, **4:B9**
Soyons 213
Speed limits 31–32
Stendhal 184
Sucs 199
Syene-les-Alpes 172

T

Tain l'Hermitage 212, **2:D6**
Tarascon 105–106, **1:B10**
Tautavel 321
Taxis 24
Telephones 25–26
Tende 256, **4:B10**
Thiers 168, **2:B9**
Thueyts 195, **2:C5**
Tinée Valley 259
Tolls 29–30
Touët-sur-Var 289
Toulon 333–335, **4:D4**
Tourettes-sur-Loup 296
Tourtour 78
Train des Pignes 127
Trains 24

U

Utelle 289
Uzès 116–117

V

Vaison-la-Romaine 316–317, **4:A2**
Val d'Allos 292
Val-les-Bains 329
Valdeblore 258
Valence 212–213, **2:D5**
Vallauris 132–133
Valleé de Merveilles 256–257
Vallon-Pont d'Arc 111, **2:C3**
Van Gogh, Vincent 27, 50, 85, 100, 101
Vauvenargues 66–67
Venasque 143
Vence 295–296, **4:C8**
Vercingetorix 159, 164
Vernoux-en-Vivarais 328, **2:D5**
Vichy 162, **2:B10**
Vienne 210–211, **2:D8**
Villages perchés 144
Villard-de-Lans 186
Villars-sur-Var 289
Villecroze 78
Villefort 154, **2:B4**
Villefranche-sur-Mer 299–30, **4:C9**
Villeneuve-lès-Avignon 108–109
Viviers 215–216, **2:D4**
Vizille 130, **3:C6**
Vogüé 111
Voiron 223, **3:B7**

W

Wine 21, 47–49

Y

Youth hostels 17
Yzeron 225

Reader Survey

If you enjoyed using this book, or even if you didn't, please help us improve future editions by taking part in our reader survey. Every returned form will be acknowledged, and to show our appreciation we will give you £1 off your next purchase of a Thomas Cook guidebook. Just take a few minutes to complete and return this form to us.

When did you buy this book? ______________________

Where did you buy it? (Please give town/city and if possible name of retailer)

When did you/do you intend to travel in the South of France?

For how long (approx.)? ______________________
How many people in your party? ______________________

Which cities, national parks and other locations did you/do you intend mainly to visit?

Did you/will you:

- ☐ Make all your travel arrangements independently?
- ☐ Travel on a fly-drive package?

Please give brief details: ______________________

Did you/do you intend to use this book:

- ☐ For planning your trip?
- ☐ During the trip itself?
- ☐ Both?

Did you/do you intend also to purchase any of the following travel publications for your trip?

Thomas Cook Travellers: *Provence*
A road map/atlas (please specify) ______________________
Other guidebooks (please specify) ______________________

Have you used any other Thomas Cook guidebooks in the past? If so, which?

Please rate the following features of On the Road around the South of France for their value to you (Circle VU for 'very useful', U for 'useful', NU for 'little or no use'):

The 'Travel Essentials'section on pp. 15–27	VU	U	NU
The 'Driving in Fance' section on pp. 28–34	VU	U	NU
The 'Touring Itineraries' on pp. 55–59	VU	U	NU
The recommended driving routes throughout the book	VU	U	NU
Information on towns and cities, National Parks, etc	VU	U	NU
The maps of towns and cities, parks, etc	VU	U	NU
The colour planning maps	VU	U	NU

Please use this space to tell us about any features that in your opinion could be changed, improved, or added in future editions of the book, or any other comments you would like to make concerning the book:

____

____

____

____

____

____

____

____

____

____

Your age category: ☐ 21-30 ☐ 31-40 ☐ 41–50 ☐ over 50

Your name: Mr/Mrs/Miss/Ms
(First name or initials) _______________________
(Last name) _______________________

Your full address: (Please include postal or zip code)

____

____

____

____

____

Your daytime telephone number: _______________________

Please detach this page and send it to: The Project Editor, On the Road around the South of France, Thomas Cook Publishing, PO Box 227, Thorpe Wood, Peterborough PE3 6PU, United Kingdom.

We will be pleased to send you details of how to claim your discount upon receipt of this questionnaire.

KEY
to colour maps
A9 Autoroutes (toll roads)
A81 Autoroutes (motorways)
N164 Main Roads
15 Minor Roads
0 10 km
0 5 miles
© Thomas Cook Ltd 1997
North
Gaillac
Albi
Carmaux
St Sernin
St Afrique
Millau
Peyreleau
Nant
la Cavalerie
le Caylar
Mont Aigoual
Levigan
Ganges
St Jean
Anduze
Alès
Combe
Vézénobres
Lédignan
Lussan
Bagnols
Uzès
Orange
Bédarrides
Sorgues
Avignon
Remoulins
Châteaurenard
Nîmes
Beaucaire
Tarascon
St Rémy
Maussane
Bellegarde
Arles
Istres
Port-de-Bouc
Port St Louis
Camargue
les Stes-Maries-de-la-Mer
St Gilles
Vauvert
Aigues-Mortes
le Grau-du-Roi
la Grande-Motte
Lunel
Gallargues
Sommières
Castries
Quissac
Gardon
Vidourle
Rhône
St Martin-de-Londres
Montpellier
Palavas
Fabrègues
Frontignan
Sète
Mèze
Gignac
Hérault
Lodève
Clermont
Pézenas
Roujan
Agde
Béziers
Bédarieux
Cessenon
Orb
Capestang
Valras Plage
Narbonne Plage
Gruissan
Narbonne
Lézignan
Sigean
Port-la-Nouvelle
Port-Leucate
Port-Barcarès
Salses
Rivesaltes
Perpignan
Canet-Plage
Saint Cyprien
Elne
Argeles
Collioure
Cerbère
Port Bou
Côte Vermeille
le Boulou
le Perthus
la Jonquera
Spain
Thuir
Millas
Prades
Villefranche
Mont-Louis
Vernet
Amélie
Prats-de-Mollo
Pyrenées
Tech
Têt
Agly
Tuchan
Saint Paul
Axat
Quillan
Lavelanet
Mouthoumet
Lagrasse
Limoux
Mirepoix
Capendu
Carcassonne
Caunes-Minervois
Aude
Castelnaudary
Saissac
Revel
Mazamet
Castres
Brassac
St Pons
La Salvetat
Lacaune
Murat
Fayet
Réalmont
Graulhet
A
B
C
D
1
2
3
4
5
6
7
8
9
10

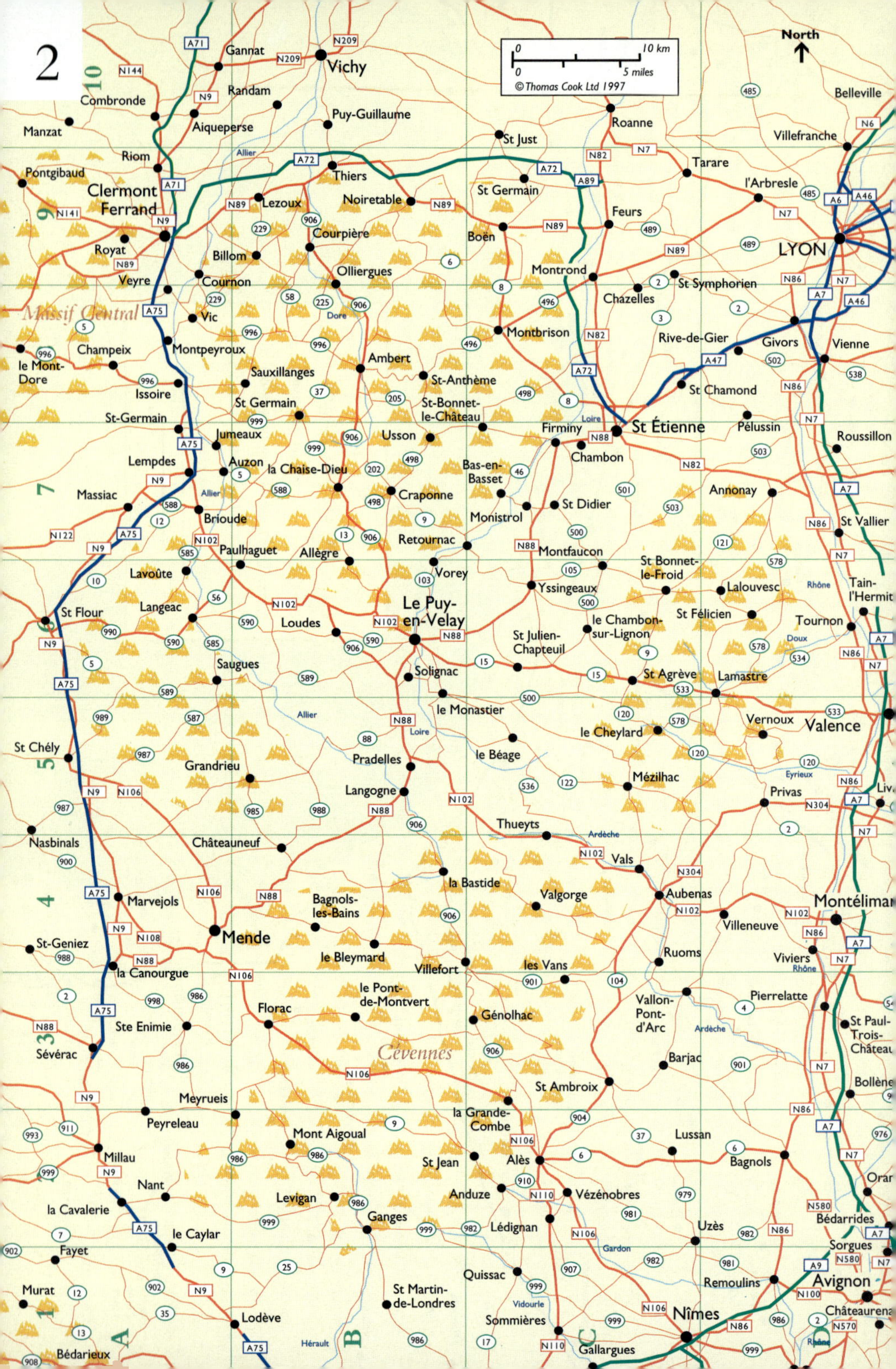
2
North
0 10 km
0 5 miles
© Thomas Cook Ltd 1997
Vichy
Gannat
Randam
Combronde
Manzat
Aiqueperse
Puy-Guillaume
Riom
Thiers
Pontgibaud
Clermont Ferrand
Lezoux
Noiretable
Courpière
Royat
Billom
Veyre
Cournon
Olliergues
Massif Central
Vic
Champeix
Montpeyroux
le Mont-Dore
Sauxillanges
Issoire
Ambert
St Germain
St-Germain
St-Anthème
St-Bonnet-le-Château
Usson
Jumeaux
Auzon
la Chaise-Dieu
Lempdes
Massiac
Brioude
Craponne
Bas-en-Basset
Paulhaguet
Allègre
Retournac
Lavoûte
Vorey
Le Puy-en-Velay
Langeac
Loudes
St Flour
Saugues
Solignac
le Monastier
Pradelles
St Chély
Grandrieu
Langogne
Nasbinals
Châteauneuf
la Bastide
Marvejols
Mende
Bagnols-les-Bains
le Bleymard
St-Geniez
la Canourgue
Villefort
le Pont-de-Montvert
Florac
Génolhac
Ste Enimie
Sévérac
Cévennes
Meyrueis
Peyreleau
Mont Aigoual
la Grande-Combe
Millau
St Jean
Alès
Nant
Levigan
Anduze
la Cavalerie
Ganges
Védénobres
Lédignan
le Caylar
Fayet
Quissac
Murat
St Martin-de-Londres
Lodève
Sommières
Bédarieux
Hérault
Vidourle
Gallargues
Nîmes
St Just
Roanne
St Germain
Boën
Feurs
Montrond
Montbrison
Chazelles
St Symphorien
Tarare
l'Arbresle
Belleville
Villefranche
LYON
Rive-de-Gier
Givors
Vienne
St Chamond
Firminy
St Étienne
Chambon
Pélussin
Roussillon
Monistrol
St Didier
Annonay
Montfaucon
St Vallier
Yssingeaux
St Bonnet-le-Froid
Lalouvesc
Tain-l'Hermitage
St Julien-Chapteuil
le Chambon-sur-Lignon
St Félicien
Tournon
St Agrève
Lamastre
Vernoux
Valence
le Cheylard
le Béage
Mézilhac
Privas
Thueyts
Vals
Aubenas
Valgorge
Montélimar
Villeneuve
les Vans
Ruoms
Viviers
Vallon-Pont-d'Arc
Pierrelatte
St Paul-Trois-Châteaux
Barjac
St Ambroix
Bollène
Lussan
Bagnols
Orange
Uzès
Bédarrides
Sorgues
Remoulins
Avignon
Châteaurenard
Allier
Loire
Dore
Ardèche
Eyrieux
Doux
Rhône
Gardon
A B C D
1 2 3 4 5 6 7 8 9 10

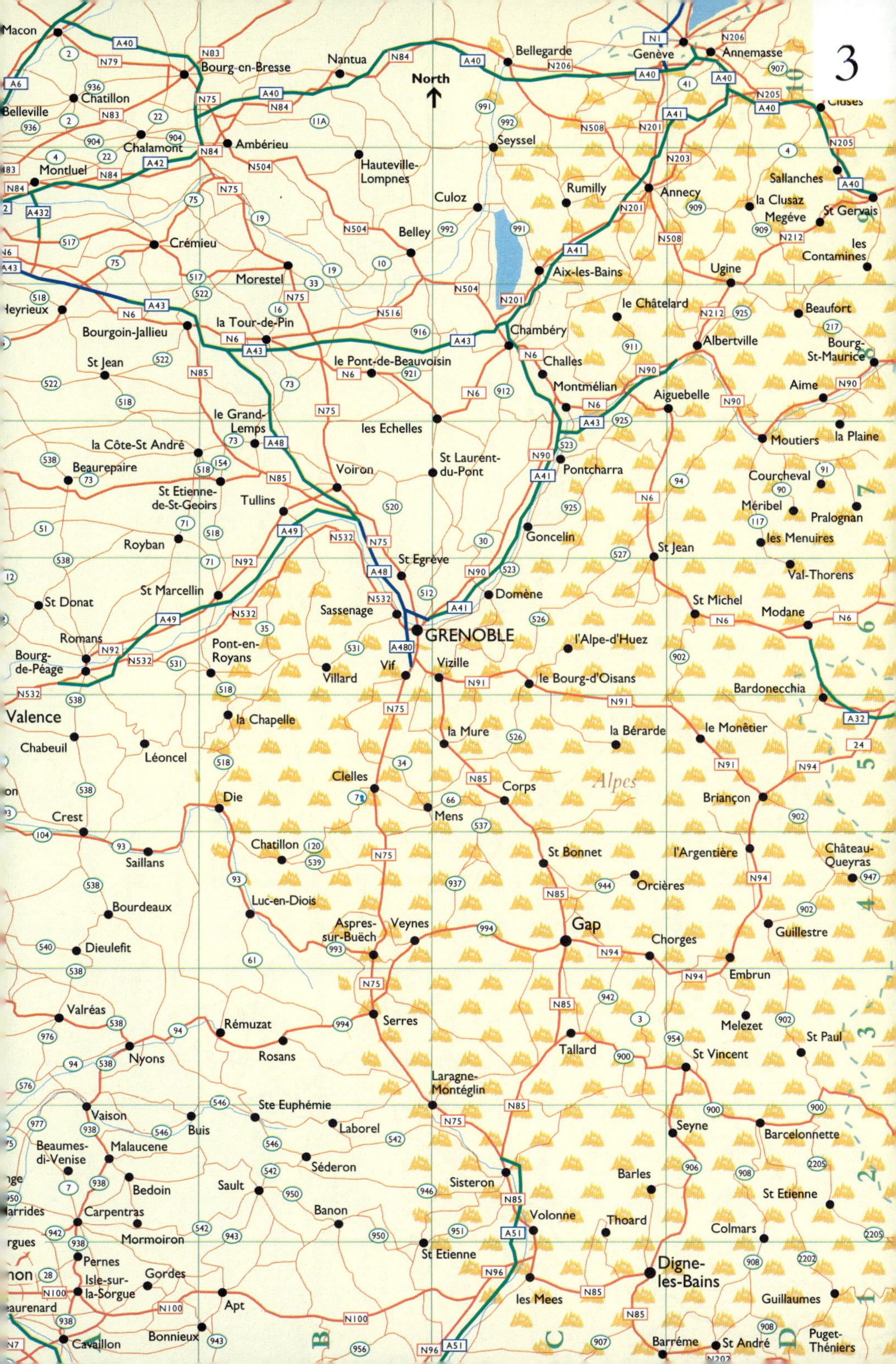
North
Macon
Bourg-en-Bresse
Nantua
Bellegarde
Genève
Annemasse
Chatillon
Belleville
Chalamont
Ambérieu
Hauteville-Lompnes
Seyssel
Montluel
Culoz
Rumilly
Annecy
Sallanches
la Clusaz
Megéve
St Gervais
Cluses
les Contamines
Crémieu
Belley
Morestel
Aix-les-Bains
Ugine
Heyrieux
Bourgoin-Jallieu
la Tour-du-Pin
le Châtelard
Beaufort
Chambéry
Albertville
Bourg-St-Maurice
St Jean
le Pont-de-Beauvoisin
Challes
Montmélian
Aiguebelle
Aime
le Grand-Lemps
les Echelles
la Plaine
Moutiers
la Côte-St André
Beaurepaire
Voiron
St Laurent-du-Pont
Pontcharra
Courcheval
St Etienne-de-St-Geoirs
Tullins
Méribel
Pralognan
les Menuires
Royban
Goncelin
St Jean
St Egrève
Val-Thorens
St Marcellin
St Donat
Domène
St Michel
Modane
Sassenage
GRENOBLE
Romans
Pont-en-Royans
l'Alpe-d'Huez
Bourg-de-Péage
Villard
Vif
Vizille
le Bourg-d'Oisans
Bardonecchia
Valence
la Chapelle
la Mure
la Bérarde
le Monêtier
Chabeuil
Léoncel
Clelles
Corps
Alpes
Die
Mens
Briançon
Crest
Saillans
Chatillon
St Bonnet
l'Argentière
Château-Queyras
Orcières
Bourdeaux
Luc-en-Diois
Aspres-sur-Buëch
Veynes
Gap
Guillestre
Chorges
Dieulefit
Embrun
Valréas
Rémuzat
Serres
Melezet
Rosans
Tallard
St Paul
Nyons
St Vincent
Laragne-Montéglin
Ste Euphémie
Vaison
Buis
Laborel
Seyne
Barcelonnette
Beaumes-di-Venise
Malaucene
Séderon
Sisteron
Barles
Bedoin
Sault
St Etienne
Carpentras
Banon
Volonne
Thoard
Colmars
Mormoiron
St Etienne
Pernes
Digne-les-Bains
Gordes
Isle-sur-la-Sorgue
les Mees
Guillaumes
Apt
Bonnieux
Cavaillon
Barrême
St André
Puget-Théniers

4
Avignon
Marseille
Aix-en-Provence
Toulon
Cannes
Nice
Digne-les-Bains
Orange
Carpentras
Cavaillon
Apt
Manosque
Sisteron
Castellane
Draguignan
Fréjus
St Raphaël
St Tropez
Hyères
Antibes
Grasse
Menton
Monaco/Monte Carlo
Ventimiglia
San Remo
Bordighera
Cuneo
Barcelonnette
Aubagne
la Ciotat
Cassis
Bandol
la Seyne
Brignoles
St Maximin
Salon
Martigues
Istres
Miramas
Arles
Tarascon
St Rémy
Vaison
Nyons
Valréas
Bollène
Sorgues
Isle-sur-la-Sorgue
Gordes
Pertuis
Riez
Moustiers
Vence
Cagnes
Villefranche
Beaulieu
Golfe-Juan
Agay
le Lavandou
Giens
ILES D'HYERES
North
© Thomas Cook Ltd 1997
10 km
5 miles